"This fine work was widely praised by Dutch readers when it first appeared in the Netherlands, going through several printings. Now all of us English speakers can see what the enthusiasm was all about. The subtitle correctly presents the book as an 'introduction,' but it is more than that. For me it has served—and will continue to serve—as a much-needed refresher course in how to bring new vitality to the exploration and twenty-first-century updating of the best of the theology that we have received from the past!"

— RICHARD J. MOUW
Fuller Theological Seminary

"Despite the impact of Dutch Reformed theology in the English-speaking world, few contemporary sources are translated. With this new dogmatics, we may be considerably caught up. Yet this volume is not in the least provincial. Deeply informed by biblical studies as well as the history of doctrine, the authors engage a wide range of conversation partners. As insiders, legatees, and contributors to continental theological developments, they offer a crucial perspective for ecumenical conversation."

— MICHAEL S. HORTON
Westminster Seminary California

"It is essential that Christians know what they believe and why they believe what they profess. This is one of the best and most helpful one-volume summaries of Christian thought published in the last several decades. Valuable for Christians everywhere in the world, regardless of their cultural and linguistic heritage, van der Kooi and van den Brink's *Christian Dogmatics* is accessible, clear, inspiring, informative, and very readable. This work should be in every pastor's library. It would also make an excellent resource for a church study group."

— CHARLES VAN ENGEN
Latin American Ministries, Inc.
School of Intercultural Studies,
Fuller Theological Seminary

"To the surprise of a variety of its critics, the oft-maligned discipline of dogmatic theology is showing signs of renewed health of which this volume is one. Now non-Dutch readers can see for themselves why this *Christian Dogmatics* became such a best-seller in its native land. It provides a cogent, fresh, confident statement of the Christian faith that honestly engages the tough challenges our modern world throws at it. In addition, this work is a *pedagogic* success: each chapter begins with a clear statement of aims, provides measurable goals, and makes meaningful connections to contemporary issues and questions. This is a great text for students of Christian theology that is also accessible to all who want to deepen their understanding of the faith."

— JOHN BOLT
Calvin Theological Seminary

Christian Dogmatics

AN INTRODUCTION

Cornelis van der Kooi and Gijsbert van den Brink

Translated by Reinder Bruinsma with James D. Bratt

WILLIAM B. EERDMANS PUBLISHING COMPANY
GRAND RAPIDS, MICHIGAN

Wm. B. Eerdmans Publishing Co.
2140 Oak Industrial Drive NE, Grand Rapids, Michigan 49505
www.eerdmans.com

Originally published in Dutch as *Christelijke dogmatiek: Een inleiding*,
© 2012 Uitgeverij Boekencentrum, Zoetermeer, Netherlands
English translation published 2017
Printed in the United States of America

ISBN   978-0-8028-7265-4

23 22 21 20 19 18 17   1 2 3 4 5 6 7

Library of Congress Cataloging-in-Publication Data

Names: Brink, Gijsbert van den, 1963- author.
Title: Christian dogmatics : an introduction / Gijsbert van den Brink and
    Cornelis van der Kooi ; translated by Reinder Bruinsma with James D. Bratt.
Other titles: Christelijke dogmatiek. English
Description: Grand Rapids : Eerdmans Publishing Co., 2017. | Includes bibliographical
    references and index.
Identifiers: LCCN 2016053088 | ISBN 9780802872654 (hardcover : alk. paper)
Subjects: LCSH: Theology, Doctrinal. | Reformed Church—Doctrines.
Classification: LCC BT75.3 .B7513 2017 | DDC 230/.42—dc23
    LC record available at https://lccn.loc.gov/2016053088

Contents

Preface to the English Edition

We are greatly indebted to Reinder Bruinsma, who is an experienced translator of Dutch theological literature into English, for providing a very reliable and smooth translation of this voluminous work in a relatively short time. Our American colleague Jim Bratt (Calvin College, Grand Rapids, MI), has carefully checked the flow of the English, pointed out possible sources of misunderstanding for an Anglo-Saxon audience, and proposed quite a few improvements, in both style and content. We are greatly in his debt. We also thank our former student-assistant Ruben van den Belt for providing us with references to English versions of sources we originally quoted in Dutch or German.

Since we realized that it would not make much sense to quote sources that are available only in Dutch, we substantially reduced the number of references to Dutch sources. Yet, we intentionally did not go to great lengths to remove every trace of the Dutch context within which this volume originally took shape. Especially in the case of twentieth-century Dutch theologians who have been (and in many cases still are) very influential in the Netherlands and beyond (e.g., in South Africa), and because of the scope, originality, creativity, and quality of their theological work, we decided to leave instructive references to their work unaltered, even though for now it may be available only in Dutch. Here we are thinking especially of the work of twentieth-century theologians like K. H. Miskotte, O. Noordmans, and A. A. van Ruler. It is good for an international audience to see that Dutch theology did not stop with Kuyper and Bavinck, however important the work of these two earlier giants was and still is. Finally, we decided to refer to German sources in English translation, where one was available, but we did not hesitate to quote German sources when there was no Anglophone alternative.

CORNELIS VAN DER KOOI &
GIJSBERT VAN DEN BRINK
Amsterdam, January 2016

Preface to the Original Edition

We decided to title this book *Christian Dogmatics*. For a number of reasons such a title may evoke questions or even be seen as a provocation. Who in their right mind would consider publishing a book with this title? Dogmatics is surrounded with so many negative associations that the word alone creates an immediate barrier. Moreover, the adjective "Christian" can be quite pretentious. (Do we think we can write for the entire Christian tradition?) We therefore begin with a few remarks telling why we refer to this book on dogmatics as Christian. It is true enough that we cannot possibly write for the whole Christian tradition, or even do limited justice to Christianity in all its diversity. And we admit at the outset that we write from within the context of the Reformed faith tradition. This work, however, is not intended as a dogmatics for Reformed Christians only. Dogmatics must always keep the entire faith community in mind. What Karl Barth wrote about confessions of faith (GA 3:610) applies in a derived sense to this book: we are dealing with insights that arose in specific circumstances, within a specific tradition-historical constellation, but that need to be submitted to the judgment of the entire (world) church, and not just to a part of it.

Likewise, the term "dogmatics" deserves a few comments. Why did we choose this word, rather than some synonym that would sound somewhat milder? The choice is meant to be evocative rather than provocative. In this dogmatics we do not think of "dogma" as teachings that have been imposed in an authoritarian way; rather, dogma is simply what the Christian church wants to continue to emphasize: the momentous news of God's intervention in Jesus Christ. The church has found things that it does not want to surrender, which it regards as the basis for an unbelievable perspective in life. It is precisely this meaning, with all that it entails, that the word "dogma" conveys. If this is provocative with regard to secularism—which of course has also affected us—then we are just where we want to be: "where the rubber hits the road."

This book is part of a long tradition. From the very first, Christian believers have attempted to describe, as clearly as they could, the content of the Christian faith—to defend it and to connect it with the general knowledge that was at their disposal. We believe it is worthwhile to continue this tradition. Not without reason, we nowadays see a lot of suspicion with regard to a focus on cohesion, completeness, or attempts to be systematic. We have lost the self-evident confidence of former generations, which presumed to possess an extensive knowledge of God. We must recognize our humanness, with all its limitations. However, this recognition does not change the content of what we have received in the sources of the Christian faith. Especially in a time in which the Christian faith tradition is under immense pressure, it is essential to keep it alive. In this book we are eager to show that we are dealing with a living tradition. We thus refer not only to classic studies but, throughout the book, to recent studies about the themes that we discuss.

A few remarks about the limitations of this book are in order. As the subtitle indicates, this volume is meant as an introduction. Dogmatics is a domain with various specializations—subdisciplines in which topics may be further refined and inspire further discussions. We often avoid such discussions, because they will be understood only at a later stage, against the backdrop of the major outlines that we will draw. We realize that these major outlines could and should be further qualified—but not in this work. As is the case in any other craft, not everything can be learned in one lesson. It helped us to ask ourselves not what all *could* be said but what we think a beginning theology student *should*, as a start, know and understand. We have done our best to stimulate the critical faculties of the reader. A decent dogmatics does not just tell people how things are but tries to show why certain choices are made and what internal problems must be addressed. Unavoidably, we must speak about problems. Where there are no problems, dogmatic reflection becomes superfluous. However, it can demand great intellectual effort, as well as provide much spiritual joy, to think as adequately as possible about such problems. At times it will suddenly give us the sense that, because of it, we have come to know God better.

In almost every section throughout the text, we present some paragraphs in smaller type. The material in these paragraphs provides information beyond what is covered in the regular-sized text, going deeper on a particular point or providing a broader discussion. Readers may wish to read all of them or might choose to pass over certain ones if they go beyond the reader's level of interest.

Who are the readers we want to reach? From what we just said, it is clear that we first of all have students in mind, with the intellectual equipment and skills that the present generation is expected to possess. We hope that they will get a feel for the nature, the importance, and the attractiveness of this area of study. Students in theology and in religious studies must acquire knowledge about many subjects, together with the appropriate skills. We insist that acquiring a more than average insight into the content of Christian faith must be part of this process, considering its indelible stamp on Western culture and society during the past two millennia.

At the same time, we hope that others besides theology students will profit from this book. It has been written in an accessible way (Latin and Greek, for instance, is always translated, and there is a minimal use of German), which will help students in other disciplines to learn some important things from it. We are also thinking of pastors who want to refresh their knowledge, of academics in other branches of scholarship, and of journalists who may not themselves share in the Christian faith but are nevertheless expected to write about it in a professional manner. On this last point, we often notice serious defects. At this moment in time, when our cultures largely consider Christianity a relic of the past, much terrible nonsense is said and written about what Christians allegedly believe. Critics of the faith are often content with simplistic ideas of what they think is Christian. They would do well to consult, from time to time, a contemporary book on dogmatics so that they can modify their ideas to reflect more closely what Christians actually believe. And then—last but not least—this book is for all those who are interested in theology, who themselves may have questions about their faith and want to know more about current discussions. In fact, questions about faith are common to us all.

In content, this book might perhaps best be labeled "loyally orthodox." That is, we seek to connect with the teaching tradition of past centuries but simultaneously try to be open to those who claim to have a better understanding of certain issues. As a result, we will often criticize the tradition, but always with a sense of loyalty—always conscious that we have the privilege of being receivers. Not without reason, the word "recipient" will return time and again in this book.

Another limiting remark: we will focus mainly on the *Western* tradition. Although we occasionally will take a glance at Eastern Orthodoxy, we realize that we cannot touch on everything that happens in the world church. We are also very aware that many interesting and important things happen outside the traditional regions of Western theological reflection (Europe, the United States, and other Anglo-Saxon areas). However, rather than pretending that we can give an overview that includes everything, we also limit ourselves in this regard. This self-restriction may rightly be regarded as a weakness, but it also might be seen as a form of contextual theology: we focus on the Western world because it is essential to support the church in *this* part of the world, on the basis of the plausibility structures that are current in the West.

In this specific context everything is changing, and the faith communities move together with these changing structures. This observation leads us to a remark about the necessary broadening of the task of dogmatics. Dogmatics is a contemporary form of giving an account of our faith. Therefore, it not only deals with concepts but is connected by many different threads with religious practices and living faith communities. The Christian community not only thinks but also sings, praises, hopes, prays, and obeys; it tries to shape people's lives and also poses questions. The primary task, when giving a contemporary account of the faith, is to phrase meaningful questions and propose plausible answers. Dogmatics will always do so in a dialogue with the tradition, with the church, and with a view of our own times. As a result, dogmatics changes and will continue to do so. We therefore hope to have future opportunities to provide updates. Anyone with advice may find us through the publisher or the Internet.

Then, just a few words on how this book may be used. This book is a complete unit, from beginning to end, which means that the sequence of topics is of great importance. Each chapter, however, has been written as a complete discussion of its topic, which allows readers to profitably study any single chapter. Inevitably, this approach has resulted in a certain amount of overlap.

Each chapter starts with a short section with the heading "Making Connections." These sections may of course be skipped. They are meant to be didactic introductions that appeal to the reader's own creativity. In this introductory section we try to establish a link between the topic of the chapter and what is happening in our present-day society and contemporary culture. This effort will hopefully make it clear that dogmatics is far from an abstract business but is connected by a thousand and one threads to everyday life. We find traces of dogmatic questions and themes in many diverse cultural expressions—in the so-called higher culture, as well as in the so-called lower culture. Discovering these threads helps us to see how certain dogmatic themes are still relevant today, and how these themes may relate to what can be said about these cultural themes from a Christian angle. Moreover, it helps us not only to concentrate on acquiring knowledge and deeper insight but also to develop something that we like to call *hermeneutical competence*, a wonderful phrase that refers to understanding things in such a way that we can, using all our creativity, see connections—a skill that theologians certainly need to master in their work (for example, in preparing sermons). Each chapter ends with a list of published works that will be of special use, for instance if one wants to go deeper into the material when writing a paper or a thesis. None of these lists is exhaustive. At the end of the book is a bibliography listing items that have more general reference to our topic. Throughout the text we refer to this broader list by mentioning the last name of the author, followed by an abbreviation of the title of the work (e.g., Barth, CD). Other text references mention an author's name plus year of publication (e.g., Berkhof 1985); such citations refer to the bibliography at the end of each chapter.

In addition, a few comments now on other editorial decisions. First, in the use of various Bible versions, we have been intentionally inconsistent, even though we have mostly used the Revised Standard Version. In some cases we have modified existing translations. Second, a remark about the use of the male pronoun for God is also relevant. God is not a male person but supersedes any sexual differentiation. To help remember this point, we sometimes repeat "God" where one would expect the personal pronoun. Finally, where possible, we also speak of Father, Son, and Holy Spirit, in an effort to remain as close as possible to the concreteness of these names.

Finally, we express our appreciation to those who have read part of the text and have provided us with comments and with additional material, and who have encouraged us in various ways. We mention, in particular, Eddy van der Borght, Henk Jan Damstra, Willem-Henri den Hartog, Gerard den Hertog, Barend Kamphuis, Margriet van der Kooi, Bram Kunz, Jan van der Linden, Eveline van Staalduine-Sulman, Henk Vreekamp, the staff of the section Dogmatics and Ecumenism of the Theological Faculty of the Vrije Universiteit in Amsterdam, and all who reacted to our blog, which we regularly published during the last months of the writing process. We are very grateful to Arend Smilde and Tini van Selm for their meticulous stylistic and linguistic corrections of the text. And great thanks to the publisher, Nico de Waal, who stimulated us, enabling smooth progress during the entire process.

C. van der Kooi
G. van der Brink

1 Dogmatics as Disciplined Thinking about God

Definitions and Aims

AIM

In this chapter you may expect a number of things. Specifically, we intend to:

- define what Christian theology is all about and where it differs from religious studies (1.1)
- explain the target audience for theology (1.2)
- dispel possible fears about the adjective "systematic" in "systematic theology" (1.3)
- explain the relationship between systematic theology and dogmatics (1.4)
- show how (un)systematic dogmatics is (1.5)
- indicate how dogmatics is related to other disciplines (1.6)
- provide a survey of the major tasks of dogmatics (1.7)
- present a typology of concrete forms of contemporary theology (1.8)
- argue that theology is, ultimately, not a scholarly discipline but a mode of existence (1.9).

This chapter will not deal with the question of the content of faith, why people believe, or what is unique to the Christian faith. We will address these questions later in the book, beginning with chapter 2.

MAKING CONNECTIONS

1. Take two minutes to write down a list of the associations that emerge in your mind when you hear words like "dogmatics" and "doctrinal." Then note whether those associations are neutral, positive, or negative. What happens when you repeat this exercise with the term "systematic theology"?

2. People of faith might have their suspicions about theology and theologians. What might these be? And what do *you* think — what kind of help do *you* expect from theology?

1.1. Theology as Reflecting about Faith

We might define theology, in a preliminary way, as "reflecting about God." Admittedly, theologians also think about a range of other things—for instance, about humanity, about evil, about the world and its future. But in theology our thinking about such themes happens in the context of faith in God. It then deals with the consequences of this faith for the issues that confront every human being. "Thinking about faith" in this broad sense provides a description of theology that will suffice for the moment.

This book is specifically about *Christian* theology. That is, Christian theology is reflection on the Christian faith. It presupposes that there is something like "the" Christian faith. This immediately raises a question, for many people nowadays argue that Christianity is so pluralistic that one cannot lump all forms of it together. Looking at what Christians believe and have believed, they are impressed by the enormous pluralism they see—and rightly so. This observation leads them to the conclusion that it is impossible to formulate a definitive core of what it means to be a Christian. It appears that, looking at Christian faith in different cultures, times, and contexts, it is impossible to detect a single common denominator. If so, there is not something like "the" Christian faith but only a large number of quite diverging forms and interpretations of what Christians believe. Others, however, think that the search for Christian theology is precisely the attempt to discover what may, within this great variety, justifiably claim the Christian label. They see this as the fascinating question that lies at the basis of everything: what statements and practices of faith are truly Christian? And which ones are, in the terms we use today, sub-Christian instead?

At this stage we do not yet have to answer the question of whether we can point to something like "the essence of Christianity." For now, then, we formulate our definition without a definite article, leaving a number of options open: Christian theology is thinking about Christian faith.

In 1973, when H. Berkhof had to choose a title for his book on dogmatics, he consciously decided to omit the definite article. He opted for *Christelijk geloof* (Christian faith). In so doing, Berkhof referred to the great nineteenth-century German theologian Friedrich Schleiermacher, who called his survey of Christian dogmatics *Der christliche Glaube* (1821-22)—*with* the definite article. Later, Adolf von Harnack underlined a similar essentialism in his book *Das Wesen des Christentum* (The essence of Christianity, 1900). However, the discussions that followed Harnack's book showed, at the very least, the difficulty of pinpointing the essence of Christianity or of the Christian faith. Nonetheless, theologians continue to search, perhaps not so much for the essence of Christianity as for what might be labeled genuinely Christian on the basis of its sources. John Webster is a good example of a contemporary dogmatician who is passionately engaged in this quest (see his brief theological autobiography in Marks 2002, 129-36).

It is important to understand the word "reflecting" in our definition in a literal way. Faith precedes, and thinking follows. It could be said that theologians pursue faith by thinking about it. This statement presupposes that they themselves are believers. Or in any case, they must be ready, willing, and able to try to step into the shoes of believers. This exact attitude is probably rare, for normally we see a theologian as someone who speaks from the inside, from the basis of faith. Thus, theology more typically is reflecting on the faith in which the theologian himself or herself participates. To use a term that has become common: one can do theology only from a "participatory perspective."

We do not mean that only believers can be involved in the study of faith. Whether one does or does not believe, one can study questions and themes regarding faith in a nontheological manner. The same also applies to any non-Christian faith. In that case one opts for the so-called exterior, or nonparticipatory, perspective. That is, the observer looks at a particular religion—it may even be one's own religion—from the outside and poses questions such as, how did we get the Bible? What do Buddhists believe about nirvana? How do Shiite and Sunni Muslims differ? Obviously, such questions may be answered without oneself being a believer. The discipline that studies this type of questions is usually referred to as religious studies. The plural here indicates that it is an umbrella term that covers various subdisciplines: religious psychology, the history of religion (or more specifically: the history of Judaism, Islam, etc.), sociology of religion, philosophy of religion, biblical studies, and so forth.

The difference between theology and religious studies is such that often the two fields are not offered at the same institution, or in any case, not as part of the same department. Educational institutions that deal with religion tend to make a definite choice between the participatory and nonparticipatory perspectives—or if they combine the two, to study them in separate programs. Theology from a particular faith perspective is usually offered at theological institutions that have been established for that purpose. Religious studies may form an independent program at a university, but nowadays it is usually placed with the humanities. A third option may be that an institution offers the opportunity for theological reflection from more than one faith perspective. This usually happens at a divinity school or department of theology, where a serious attempt is made to allow for as constructive a theological dialogue as possible between the various forms of theology without reducing or ignoring the often immense differences between them.

The authors of this book work at an institution that belongs to this third category. Though this type of educational institution is rare in the Netherlands, we consider its approach quite productive for the academic study of religious questions and themes, and very instructive for our students. On the one hand, no one is expected to leave one's faith (or its absence) at the door when entering the university or to put it on a back burner. That requirement would create a very artificial situation in which believers will feel shortchanged. On the other hand, this approach precludes students from focusing only on their own tradition, unaware of what happens outside of it. One of the competencies that may be expected from theologians, as well as from religious scholars, is to constructively deal with the major differences between faith traditions in our Western culture.

It should be noted that, in the past, the picture differed somewhat further, with an educational model that, with some adaptations, still exists. Theological faculties in various Dutch universities took a religious-studies approach to the Christian faith in particular. The student took courses in, for instance, the history of the religion of Israel, New Testament exegesis, or church history of the twentieth century. These subjects were ideally taught in an impartial manner, that is, from a nonparticipatory perspective. At the same time, they provided an excellent basis for the so-called ecclesiastical courses, which were facilitated by various faith communities. In this domain such courses as dogmatics, theological ethics, and practical theology were offered—that is, disciplines that presuppose a faith perspective. In this *duplex ordo* (dual arrangement) the participatory and nonparticipatory perspectives are carefully linked, but without any fusion.

It is important not to overemphasize the differences between theology and religious studies, however real they may be. They need each other. Theology needs to be informed by the wealth of data, theories, and methods that are found in the field of religious studies. We will see how theology has its own mandate and methods, but without the input from the subdisciplines of religious studies, it runs the risk of becoming "fuzzy," out of touch with empirical reality. Practical circumstances demand this approach too, since a large percentage of the students who choose to study the phenomenon of religion do so because of existential personal questions. As a matter of principle, however, the object of their study requires something like theological reflection as well. To give an example: We can never do full justice to the Gospel of John by a thorough study of its text-critical, exegetical, religion-historical, and theological background, without considering the main aim of the author or redactor of the book, namely, that we as readers will believe that Jesus is the Messiah, the Son of God (John 20:31). It would certainly be artificial to avoid all discussion about whether the claim of the gospel writer is justified. In practice, where one tries to follow this approach, we often see that, in a hidden way, all kinds of theological judgments play a role. Or we see an attempt to talk about the meaning, the interrelatedness, and the aim of the branches of religious studies in a nondenominational (or even interreligious) theology. The question of truth is, however, not that easily disposed of.

1.2. The Three Audiences of Theology

Much more fruitful than the endless discussion about theology versus religious studies is the approach that takes its point of departure from the question of who in fact constitutes the audience for our theological work. Well, first of all, theology is useful for every believer. All believers do well to reflect on the nature, the content, and the scope of their faith, which most of them realize. Martin Luther (1483-1546) said, "All of us are theologians; that is to say: every Christian is a theologian" (WA 41:11). But we may also state that, from a professional angle, both theology and religious studies must target three user groups (or "fora," or "publics"): academia, the faith community, and society. Each of these three groups includes people who are, albeit in various ways, deeply interested in religious matters. The *academic world* wants to see a critical-scholarly approach to the questions that concern religions. Here a temporary inner distance from one's own religious views will often be useful. *Faith communities* attach much value to an approach that does not avoid the hot issues but also wants to address the question of truth. Here it is useful not to bracket one's own faith but rather to stake out one's convictions. Finally, our *society* will benefit if representatives of various religious traditions are not so ignorant that they deal with each other by way of reflex, as strangers, and in a hostile manner. It is impossible to appreciate what you know little or nothing about, and we can effectively prevent the dangerous mechanisms of excluding and demonizing only if leaders and members of the various religions (and other worldviews) are not led by caricatures but are well informed about what characterizes those who believe differently.

Theological seminaries, institutions for religious studies, and theology departments may be expected to place different accents, but they have a responsibility toward all three of these audiences. University theologians and seminaries will primarily target their own faith community, but in doing so they should take great care not to ignore the scholarly criteria that academia and society impose on university-level education. Experts in religious studies, however, must not assume that faith is merely an object of detached academic study. They should realize that for many people it is a flesh-and-blood reality that puts its stamp on all aspects of life. Moreover, in their relationship with society, theology departments must never overlook academic standards. But they should also move beyond a mentality of simply providing the answers that their supporters are looking for.

Whatever their type of educational institution, students should be able to give a reasoned account of their faith—and look at things from different perspectives. On the one hand, they must be capable of adequately expressing what they themselves believe and why; on the other, because they have acquired the necessary scholarly distance, they must be able to put themselves in the shoes of people with different religious convictions and worldviews, enabling them to interact with integrity with those who have a belief system other than their own.

In accordance with what has just been said, the emphasis in this book is on the perspective from within; we want to think about religious matters from within the Christian faith tradition. We will do so, however, with the critical approach of every academic context, that is to say, with arguments that separate sense from nonsense, choosing between the pros and cons of various convictions and presentations of faith. Whether one may call the kind of theology we introduce here *scientific* in the broad sense (here note the German term *Wissenschaft*) is largely a matter of definition. In particular, the jury is out on the question whether theological statements are open to independent verification (see Leonhardt 2001, 70-75). But even when this statement is denied, we have sufficient parallels with scientific methodology to justify calling theology a scientific—or in any case a properly academic—discipline (see Brink 2009, 96-98, 193-209).

David Tracy (1981) speaks of the three "fora" of theology, and we are indebted to David Ford (1999) for the way he developed this idea in terms of the "three publics of theology."

1.3. Systematic Theology

Above we defined theology as "reflecting about faith in God." Such a definition is rather rudimentary. We may define theology a little more precisely as the attempt of thinking believers to clarify the nature and content of their faith. Etymologically, theology has to do with a *logos* about *theos*. The Greek word *logos* has been extremely important in the Christian tradition, and we will regularly encounter it in what follows. Briefly put, it means an intellectually responsible discourse, a rational explanation. We are dealing with theology when such an explanatory discourse has God as its object. To underline the rational and ordered character of theology, we often refer to *systematic* theology.

We may well ask ourselves whether that expression does not suffer from an internal contradiction. Is it possible to speak in a rational, systematically ordered way about things that far surpass our human understanding? For if there is one thing that we can say about God, it is that "God" represents the mystery under, behind, and above all the visible reality that surrounds us. His reality cannot be charted systematically in the same manner in which we would describe the operation of molecules and atoms. Do we not at the very most catch only some glimpses of the divine secret behind our reality? And besides, even if God is more than such a glimpse for us, we cannot simply locate that experience in a system. On the contrary, such an experience will often question some of our convictions and relativize them. It is said that Thomas Aquinas (1224-74), one of the greatest thinkers of all times, after a mystical experience in December 1273, declared that he considered all his theological writing as "a bushel of straw." After this experience he never

7

again touched systematic theology, and his daunting *Summa theologiae* remained unfinished.

It does not take a Bible scholar to discover from reading the Bible that the faith of Jews and Christians is indeed less a matter of rational reflection and more one of experiences, visions, and emotions, calling and obedience, bewilderment and amazement, sin and grace, trust and worship. If so, why does faith need that rational, systematic reflection? We should not too readily dismiss this question. By approaching the mysteries of faith in a systematic manner, we may even destroy our faith with our arguments. Rational thinking about faith may even be a way to keep God at a distance and to evade the appeal that God directs to us. The Danish philosopher Søren Kierkegaard (1813-55) ridiculed theology professors who behave like a kind of merchant in theological concepts, while, in spite of all their learning, they have hardly understood what the Christian faith, what concrete discipleship of Christ, means. And the British author C. S. Lewis (1898-1963) said that there will be theologians at the bottom of hell who were more interested in their ideas about God than in God himself. Do not these prospects make all detached, rational, and systematic discourse about God rather risky?

Indeed, we face a risk that theologians, in particular, must be aware of. However, this does not imply that we should therefore give up all systematic theology or harbor a constant suspicion toward it. It does mean that we must constantly consider two things.

1. Good theology has its source in faith. In this connection we do not speak of having "faith" as having certain cognitive convictions about God (e.g., that God exists), but as living in a relationship with God, rooted in the appeal of the gospel of Jesus Christ to conversion and dedication. As we will see later in this book, Jesus of Nazareth challenged people to put God and God's kingdom first in their lives. Responding to that appeal means from then on living *coram Deo* (in the presence of God). Just as a pilot who approaches an airport follows the instructions of the air traffic controller in the tower, Christians will adjust their lives to the signals God has given them in Jesus Christ. They do so, trusting that their lives will thus reach their destination. Their faith impacts their way of life, their priorities, and the things they hold to be true. In this connection theology has a serving, mediating, and, at times, critical role. When Christian theology is detached from this context of the believer's life of faith, it can easily become a noncommittal and external kind of brainteaser. Understandably, its focus on the abstract will mostly create aversion. The history of theology has plenty of examples of system-building that, in

retrospect, do not cease to amaze us, for they became completely detached from the concrete life of faith. For this reason, through the ages, theologians have recognized their task in a motto that we first encounter with Augustine of Hippo (354-430), one that was later expanded, in particular, by Anselm of Canterbury (1033-1109): *fides quaerens intellectum* (faith seeking understanding). To this day many theologians have been inspired in their work by this motto. Faith is their point of departure and their source of inspiration. This faith, however, is in search of understanding. It seeks to grasp what is involved and to act accordingly. This perspective leads to an ongoing quest toward an ever-deeper understanding and an ever-more-adequate active response. Theological reflection aims—nothing more and nothing less—to provide useful assistance in this search. It is a form of loving God with our mind. Theology as reflecting on the faith thus always presupposes a restrained passion for God and God's kingdom that is part and parcel of the life of faith of the believer.

Nowadays we may be more alert than previously to ensure that faith and theology remain connected; a yearning for abstract speculations must be avoided. Remarkably enough, this change is partly due to philosophical influences. Witness the influential thinking of Ludwig Wittgenstein (1889-1951), who maintained that faith is a mode of life rather than (primarily) a system of truth claims. We might also point to Emmanuel Levinas (1906-95), who powerfully argued that the litmus test of all religion is found in ethics—in how we react to the appeal of others toward us. We do not need to accept all of the ideas of these philosophers and their followers if we want to do justice to some of their valuable insights.

For a rather recent dogmatic proposal inspired by the motif of *fides quaerens intellectum*, see Migliore, FSU.

2. When in our theology we use words such as "rational" and "systematic" in connection with thinking about faith, we do nothing that is in fact alien to the notion of faith—as long as we understand these words in the right way. Often they refer to a cold, detached, and businesslike approach, which does not sit well with the warmth and passion associated with faith. But we may also give them a different connotation, which is needed to clarify what theology is all about.

Suppose you read an Agatha Christie thriller. Gradually, you suspect more and more that one of the persons in the plot could be responsible for the gruesome death of the sympathetic victim in chapter 1. Numerous indications point in that direction, and eventually you are quite sure about your suspicions. But then suddenly something happens in the next-to-last chapter. The person you suspected of having committed the murder appears to have had nothing to do with the crime and has in fact acted in good faith. The last chapter makes clear what really happened: someone who throughout the book seemed totally innocent was in fact the cowardly perpetrator of the crime.

What happened as you read this thriller? Either consciously or subconsciously, you were constantly trying to determine how the various events described fit together. What is the significance of this or that seemingly unimportant event? Does this strange, rather flippant statement have any significance? Is it possible that someone who proceeds so slyly and with so much violence as Mr. X is, after all, trustworthy and stands in the clear? There are many incidents that fit into the overall picture and that reinforce the cohesion that you have established as you kept reading. However, in a good thriller, at a certain point things take—in a somewhat credible manner—a totally unexpected turn that forces you to revise your expectations in order to understand what is really going on.

When we call theology a systematic activity, we mean exactly the following: just like the reader of a thriller, the theologian tries to determine how the things of God, humanity, and the world fit together—how these things make sense. In actual fact, all of us think this way all the time; it is part of what it means to be a human being. Spontaneously, all the time, we are looking for links and relationships, and we draw conclusions from everything we experience. We do so by thinking properly. We would find it quite difficult to do otherwise for any length of time. The specific characteristic of systematic theologians is that they do so (1) by conscious reflection and (2) from the perspective of faith in God. The first aspect they share with other "-ologists"; the second, with other believers. Together with all who believe, they insist that our existence and the world in which we live find their ultimate meaning in God. While most believers consciously reflect from time to time on the contours of this meaning—with the realization that human thought always has its limitations—theologians try to do so in as ordered a manner as possible. For instance, they try, as systematically as possible, to think though the dilemma of how God can be almighty and unlimited in love and yet allow so much evil and suffering in the world. Sometimes they feel they have found an answer, but often they must reconsider their solution when faced with experiences in everyday reality. In this way theology is always rooted in our own time and circumstances.

In summary, the rational exercise of systematic theology is certainly not unnatural or only a matter of dry theory. It does require the ability to look at facts from an objectivizing distance. It is also true that this effort may go very wrong, as we see in the scholastic-intellectualistic character of some works on dogmatics. But judging from the best representatives of this discipline—and such a standard ought to be the basis for our judgment of this branch of theology—systematic theology is as natural as making sense of life, and just as fascinating as thinking about the plot of a good thriller. Our faith will therefore not be obscured by our systematic thinking but will be clarified by it—which is the aim of systematic theology.

Berkhof gives a beautiful commentary on how systematic reflection on God and God's salvation may be integrated with faith and love for God (1985, 13–15). The comparison with reading a book with a plot is further explored by Higton (CD, 6–27). The word "systematic" is also employed in other disciplines to refer to a subdiscipline (systematic botany, systematic pedagogy, systematic philosophy), but there the adjective seems to be somewhat less current than in theology. In theology, systematic theology is often regarded as a separate discipline, next to other disciplines, in particular biblical theology and historical theology (or history of theology).

1.4. Dogmatics

How does the process of systematic-theological thought relate to the discipline of dogmatics? There appears to be some confusion regarding this point, which has to do with the term "dogmatics" having a significant image problem. In our daily speech it often has a negative connotation, being associated with inflexibility and abstraction. The same applies even more so to words like "dogmatist" or "dogmatic." A dogmatist is usually seen as a rather inflexible person with a limited view of things; his or her attitude is often labeled dogmatic. The underlying term "dogma" (i.e., doctrine) also suffers from an inflation of meaning. In our postmodern era dogmas are not much appreciated. Most people regard a dogma as something you cannot understand but must simply believe because the church (or some other institution) tells you so and is not willing to reconsider its traditional position.

    In fact, the church has only a few dogmas in the sense of officially formulated statements regarding our faith that are meant to be considered infallible. In the early church the christological and the Trinitarian dogmas were developed concerning the nature and person of Jesus Christ and the Trinity. Later, the Roman Catholic Church on its own promulgated a number of dogmas (in 1215 the doctrine of transubstantiation; in the sixteenth century the dogmas about Scripture and tradition, grace and free will, the sacraments and the sacrifice of the Mass; in the nineteenth century about the so-called immaculate conception of Mary [1854] and the infallibility of the pope [1870]; in 1950 about the ascension of Mary). However, dogmatics deals with far more than these dogmas: it tries to describe all major elements of the Christian faith in a coherent manner. In general, "dogmatics" focuses on the major content (or, to use a classical term, the "teachings") of our faith. (Some books on dogmatics do not even mention the dogma of the ascension of Mary.) The term "dogmatics" may therefore be somewhat confusing, since dogmatics deals only in a limited way with dogmas.

Because of these issues some people prefer to use the term "systematic theology" instead. But apart from this phrase failing to excite most people, it has a problem of its own. Systematic theology is more than just dogmatics. At the very least, theological ethics should also be included, which is thinking about the right kind of action (or, more broadly, the good life) from the perspective of faith. In addition, another branch of systematic-theological reflection has recently attained an independent status, namely (theological) hermeneutics. This subdiscipline gives central place not so much to correct doctrine or to the good life but to the question of an adequate transferal of meaning. It deals with questions such as, How, in our Western context, which has been subject to much change, can we understand and translate the message of the Christian faith in such a way that it will retain its power to convince? How might the answer be different in, say, the context of South Korea? To what extent were authoritative doctrinal texts impacted by the social, political, and cultural circumstances in which they originated, with all the individual and corporate interests that played a role in this process? Against this background, what may be said about their abiding meaning and relevance for today? Must we, for instance, still say that Jesus is "one in essence" with the Father, or might we today express what was at stake in the distant past in another, perhaps better, way?

There is no doubt that in practice dogmatics, ethics, and hermeneutics constantly need and presuppose each other. There is much to be said for keeping them together. Prominent Christian theologians—like Augustine, Aquinas, John Calvin (1509-64), and Karl Barth (1886-1968)—have consistently incorporated hermeneutics and ethics in their surveys of dogmatics. This inclusion has helped to clarify, for example, the point that dogmatics has real consequences for human activities, and that these concrete actions could not remain un-Christianized but had to be thought through and corrected from a gospel perspective. Likewise, hermeneutics cannot be simply detached from dogmatics, for what is the use of having truths that no longer appear to be relevant? And vice versa: What do we do with all kinds of insights that may appeal to us and are relevant but may not be true?

Therefore, dogmatics, ethics, and hermeneutics cannot be separated from each other. Together they determine the playing field of systematic theology. This conclusion, however, also implies that dogmatics is not the only phenomenon that may claim the epithet "systematic theology." The two terms are not simply interchangeable. In this book we have therefore chosen to avoid the dilemma by freely using the much-maligned term "dogmatics." This has become the classic label for the field into which this book will induct the reader. And we have the impression that, in spite of the problems referred to, most people have a correct intuitive sense of what is at stake with regard to dogmatics. As we proceed, we will keep dogmatics and hermeneutics close together. The process of giving hermeneutics an independent status has not yet progressed to the point that we can already treat it that way. The situation with regard to ethics is different. For decades, ethics has been a more or less distinctive discipline that demands its own approach and expertise. Yet, however regrettable it may be in the light of all these points, we will have to move on without taking time to further discuss ethics per se. With our apologies to ethicists, we will use the term "theology" somewhat loosely for this composite of dogmatics with hermeneutics.

In the previous paragraphs we spoke about *theological* ethics and *theological* hermeneutics because there are also philosophical variants of these two disciplines. With regard to "dogmatics," as early as a century ago A. Kuyper (1898, 166-70) made a vigorous plea for this label. Some argue for replacing it with "systematic theology." Indeed, in the Anglo-Saxon context systematic theology is usually considered identical with dogmatics. But as we already indicated, we will stick with the more precise term "dogmatics" and will consider it an honorable name. We hope that it will soon be clear from this book that dogmatics is not tied to a rigid traditionalism or an uncritical faith, but that, in fact, in dogmatics all questions may be posed and be the object of reflection. Barth (CD I/1:1) defined dogmatics as "the scholarly self-examination of the Christian church with regard to the content of its characteristic discourse about God"; furthermore, "as a theological discipline dogmatics is the scientific self-examination of the Christian Church with respect to the content of its distinctive talk about God." Under the heading "No Fear of Dogmas!" Sauter (2003, 21-27) provides a valuable discussion of the various shades of meaning and misunderstandings that surround terms such as "dogma" and "dogmatics." For contemporary introductions to Christian-theological ethics, see O'Donovan 1986 and Verhey 2002, and for recent surveys of theological hermeneutics, Jensen 2007 and Thiselton 2009. A useful reader containing twenty classical texts from modern theological hermeneutics is Sarisky 2015.

1.5. The (Non-)Methodical Character of Dogmatics

Remarkably enough, dogmatics has no firmly established method. This deficiency has always made its status rather ambiguous. How can we adequately measure its results if we cannot provide a more or less objective description of how theology must be practiced? Indeed, no unambiguous criteria can be given. A dogmatic concept gains its power to convict by the degree to which it provides insight into complex problems. However, what some persons may perceive as convincing may not be regarded so by others. This observation is true, however, not just for theology but also for history and the other humanities. In these fields the role of human creativity happens to be more extensive than in the "harder" sciences, and creativity flourishes best when there are only a few rules that tell us how to proceed. Remarkably enough, we see how, in actual practice, an intersubjective consensus develops to a major degree about the difference between good and not so good theology. Friend and foe, for instance, agree that Karl Barth was one of the greatest theologians of the twentieth century. This judgment is based on more than just his enormous productivity (not all practitioners of this field who have written profusely are prominent theologians, although many important theologians have left us a large oeuvre). It has to do with quality. Anyone with any expertise in this area who studies Barth's theology will sense that, whether or not one finds his arguments convincing, positions are here taken on the basis of a vast knowledge about things in theology and culture that really matter. And those positions are subsequently worked out and defended in numerous detailed analyses.

To repeat: such evaluations do not arise on the basis of a more or less generally accepted method, for, as we mentioned above, such a method does not exist. On the one hand, we can speak of a more hermeneutical approach to dogmatics, and on the other hand, of a more analytic approach. The former approach takes its point of departure from certain authoritative texts and statements in order to discover their core meaning. These may be biblical statements ("God is love"), confessional formulas (the church is "catholic"), classical doctrinal conclusions (the works of the Trinity present themselves as indivisible), or complete books (Calvin's *Institutes*). The authority of such texts and statements is presupposed; in classical books we move straightaway within a given tradition that is considered meaningful. However, this move does not end all discussion but rather is its beginning. For it is essential to properly *interpret* those texts, statements, and their connecting links. This correct approach must also be distinguished from interpretations that are incorrect (i.e., wrong, irrelevant, and without value). In the end we must formulate their essence in our own words.

The analytic approach is less interpretive and more argumentative. It seeks first of all to carefully define and correlate important concepts. For example: how do we define "all-powerful," and what do we mean when we apply this term to God? In this approach in particular, it is important that dogmatic statements are consistent (not contradictory) and coherent (all elements fitting together); and it must be shown how all kinds of possible objections may be answered. It often happens that the various options are so arranged that we move from the very problematic proposal of author A to the slightly less problematic proposition of theologian B, and finally arrive ourselves at the most satisfactory conclusion. So, whereas the hermeneutical approach gives full emphasis to the issue of meaning, the analytic approach wants to ensure that the question of truth is not lost sight of.

For further elaboration of this difference between the hermeneutical and the analytic approaches, see Sauter and Stock 1976, 21-30. For an attempt to give both the hermeneutical and the analytic criteria a place in systematic theology, see Brümmer 2006, 453-70. Notice, however, that Brümmer himself gives far more weight to the analytic aspect, which illustrates how difficult it is to integrate the two approaches, although it should be mentioned that, in his later works, Brümmer does try to do justice to the hermeneutical aspect. In any case, it is inadvisable to play one aspect off against the other (as "personally involved" versus "cold," "biased" versus "proper thinking"). Theologians with a hermeneutical predilection should learn to explicitly deal with the issue of truth, while analytic theologians may learn from their hermeneutical colleagues to first of all thoroughly acquaint themselves with the tradition. The most creative theologians succeed in moving from more hermeneutical to more analytic considerations, ensuring that both aspects fit together. The work of Wolfhart Pannenberg serves as a magnificent example of this balance.

In addition, there have always been very influential "irregular" theologians who were not very methodical. Their work tends to be more aphoristic, more meditative, and—in the true sense of the word—more "pious" in nature. In the English-speaking world we might think of P. T. Forsyth (1848-1921). In the Dutch context we may point to O. Noordmans (1871-1956) and W. Barnard (1920-2010) as good examples of this category.

1.6. Dogmatics and Some Related Disciplines

It is probably more fruitful to take a look at how dogmatics relates to other disciplines than to focus too long on the question of method. In general, one might say that dogmatics has a creative and constructive relationship with three other disciplines: biblical theology, the history of theology, and contemporary philosophy. The dogmatician must have an adequate training in those fields. However, a person can hope to be an expert in only one of these domains if he or she is involved with it full time. Therefore, the dogmatician must be content with a general familiarity with the other fields. At most, one can become a specialist in only one of these areas, usually the area that one has specialized in from the beginning. If one wants to become an all-around theologian, in most cases it is best to specialize in one of the constituent areas rather than in dogmatics itself. We will now take a closer look at how dogmatics intersects with each of these domains.

In doing so, we touch upon the so-called theological encyclopedia, that is, the systematic relationship between the areas that together form theology. We would—following the gist of an influential book by Friedrich Schleiermacher—make a plea to consider areas like biblical scholarship and church history as full-fledged theological disciplines. Schleiermacher compared theology with a tree. He saw the roots as faith (true piety), the trunk as the study of the Bible and of church history, the branches of systematic theology as forms of relating our faith to the present, and the foliage as the place where the tree flows into practical theology (see Schleiermacher 1990). By way of analogy, we would also regard these areas not as independent entities that aim to increase our knowledge but as related disciplines each inspired by the search of faith. Each, in its own distinct way, contributes to our insight into the relationship of dependency between God and humanity, or, to state it in a less typically Schleiermacherian way, to the reflection and clarification of what the Christian faith is about.

Christian faith is, first of all, nourished by the Bible. Like other Christians, the dogmatician regularly interacts with the Bible. The dogmatician knows that the Bible is somehow normative for what may be called Christian faith. Not in a simplistic way (with an equal "vote" for each individual Bible text), but normative nonetheless. For we are faced with a testimony that through the ages has been accepted as authoritative, because the church has realized that in the Bible we listen to the first witnesses of God's revelation. We notice, time and again, that also more liberal Christians, who do not want to make high claims about the authority of the Bible, nonetheless like to refer to it. The Bible seems to have a certain authority, irrespective of what theoretical arguments are given. For that reason the Bible will play a crucial role in any presentation of Christian dogmatics. As a professional theologian, the dogmatician will have to explain how he or she uses the Bible when dealing with the findings of biblical scholarship. It does not suffice to simply listen to the sound of certain individual texts as definitive "proof" for a certain point.

This method of the so-called *dicta probantia* (proof texts) has often been dominant in Christian dogmatics, in particular in its more scholastic phases. Even in the dogmatic works of someone like Herman Bavinck (1854–1921; see Bavinck, RD), long strings of Bible texts are given that are supposed to provide biblical proof for a certain idea—with minimal attention, however, to the specific color, context, and weight of each of these texts. In this methodology the Bible becomes a repository of isolated statements that all have a certain doctrinal content, but it fails to do justice to the differences in literary genre, to the unique intent of various narrative units, and to the specific biblical-theological patterns of (parts or collections of) Bible books. It stands to reason that, as a result, the appeal to Scripture in this type of dogmatics has become discredited. But there are other ways to proceed. For the use of Scripture in contemporary dogmatics, see Sauter 2003, 211–27; see also chapter 13.

One must be able to grasp the tendencies, developments, and discoveries in the areas of exegesis, the history of the religion of Israel up to the Hellenistic period, and biblical theology. Often one will have to rely on general surveys, but that step in itself will help to avoid the impetuous running after certain temporary fashions. Yet, it requires a great deal of knowledge and intuition to determine what is of abiding significance and to avoid arbitrary approaches. Nowadays, dogmatic scholars will especially have to form an opinion about the enormous plurality and internal contradictions that biblical scholars identify in the Bible. Where exactly is the unity, or at least the common theme, in this huge diversity?

Moreover, it is clear that, after the closure of the canon, the study of its content and significance has always continued. The Bible has passed through a long process of tradition and interpretation and was not dropped in its original form into our world of faith. We find this notion in so-called fundamentalist circles rather frequently, but it is naive. More moderate evangelical Christians often tend to go in that direction too, but they are more willing to be corrected when they realize that they are not the first people to read the Bible. There is a centuries-long tradition of theological reflection on the message of the Bible. The German theologian Gerhard Ebeling (1912–2001) maintained that the history of the church is, in fact, the history of the interpretation of the Holy Scriptures. This wording is certainly pushing the point too far, but dogmaticians cannot do otherwise than to position themselves somewhere in the history of Bible interpretation. For that reason they must pay due attention to the history of the church and of theology. Dogmaticians do not know everything and must therefore be in constant dialogue with those who have preceded us in the study and interpretation of the Christian faith.

This requirement seems to be even more important in theology than, for instance, in the natural sciences. The voices from the past still play a major role in the reflection on how to adequately express our faith. The statement of G. K. Chesterton applies to theology as well as to the humanities more broadly: "Tradition is democracy extended through time." We can now only smile when we think of the scientific ideas of Aristotle (384–322 BCE), but his philosophical ideas must still be taken very seriously, not just for historical value but because of their enormous influence. Even today they offer valuable insights, although other philosophers operate within other frameworks. The same is true also of such theological giants as Augustine, Luther, and Calvin. It is difficult to imagine that there will ever be a moment when we can simply say, Well, they belong to the past! In dogmatics this is true of many lesser-known authors as well. Many solutions we propose for problems in dogmatics have already been discovered in the past. So have many erroneous responses!

Often a distinction is made, on the one hand, between dogmatics and, on the other, biblical studies, church history, philosophy of religion, and so forth. It is suggested that dogmatics operates on the basis of a prejudice of faith, while the other disciplines are considered to be neutral. As we stated earlier (when discussing the views of Schleiermacher), this contrast is incorrect. Biblical studies, church history, and other disciplines do require a great deal of hard work. But the same also applies to dogmatics. The backgrounds and consequences of various options must be carefully scrutinized and tested as to where they lead. This operation, however, does not complete the work in any of these domains. If the Bible is a collection of religious texts, assembled because of the common elements in their message, nothing is more in harmony with biblical studies than to ask further questions about the nature of this biblical "canon." If the history of the church and of theology (just as other forms of history) may be studied only from a particular perspective, why could this perspective not be one that is informed by faith? In any case, one will have to select and arrange the data by the use of some criteria as to what is important and what is not. It is impossible to tell everything. The perspective for the study of historical theology is usually also to some extent determined by the convictions one already holds—by the dogmatics (or antidogmatics) that one cherishes in the back of one's mind.

Therefore, we must not suggest that biblical scholars and historians are mere handymen—the "woodcutters and water carriers" (see Deut 29:11) of dogmatics, whose task is restricted to transporting the material for those who do the "real work." Rather, there is a constant interaction between disciplines of equal status that continue to influence each other. Dogmatics must listen attentively to biblical studies and historical theology, while ideally these two must also be treated as distinct theological disciplines, that is, on the premise that ultimately both deal with God and how he relates to humanity and the world. For this reason, we also speak of biblical and historical *theology*, underscoring that the Bible and history must not be studied in any neutral fashion but from a theological angle.

As important as the past may therefore be for the dogmatician, he or she must never be a prisoner of the past. Unlike the historian of religion, the dogmatician should not reduce his or her work to *description*, to simply reporting the positions of other people. Dogmatics is confronted with the challenge of telling us what, in today's context, is the core of our faith—and to do so in an intelligible and authoritative manner. For this reason dogmatics, in the third place, must enter into dialogue with contemporary philosophy and consider the developments that have taken place in that field. Through the ages we see an interaction between the dominant forms of philosophy and theological ideas—in particular, in one direction: from philosophy to theology. If we remain unaware of this pattern, we may, also today, be caught in the trap of thinking that we are giving a "pure" interpretation of the biblical message, even while we are pouring it into the prevailing thought forms of this day and age, thereby perhaps seriously mutilating it. History provides us with many examples of this error.

In the German-language areas, in particular, dogmatics has tended to be strongly tied to the philosophy of religion, that is, the philosophical approach to religion in general. Note, for example, the journal *Neue Zeitschrift für systematische theologie und religionsphilosophie* (New journal for systematic theology and philosophy of religion). One might say that what the dogmatician does from a participatory perspective, the philosopher of religion does from a nonparticipatory perspective. The relationship between them, however, is not always totally harmonious. The differences in approach are, for instance, much more substantial in forms of theology that are inspired by Karl Barth than in liberal streams. See Leiner 2008, §§73-88, for a discussion of the similarities and differences.

Still, dogmatics will want to use the kind of language that is broadly accessible, and not only to those who are part of its own faith tradition. Dogmatics has been referred to as the counterpart of mission in the domain of thought. This comparison also suggests that there must be a thorough knowledge of, and interaction with, contemporary philosophical trends. At times the dogmatician may adopt certain methods, as, for instance, in the domains of logic, theory construction, and concept analysis. At times there may be an overlap between certain philosophical and Christian ideas (for an early example, see Acts 17:28). It may be that dogmatic ideas can be translated into contemporary philosophical concepts. One should, however, ensure that such a translation happens consciously and with the required expertise! If not, translation can easily become treason.

The dogmatician thus tries to connect the biblical data, the theological views of the past, and contemporary thought and to express them in new propositions that formulate the truth and express the faith. Since the whole process depends on creativity in providing clarification, it should be clear that there is no one single method in dogmatics. The only thing that may be said is that dogmatics must connect with these three disciplines—biblical studies, historical theology, and philosophy—in a way that solves problems and brings clarification.

For a striking description of dogmatics as "the analogy of missions in the domain of thought," see Weber, FD 1:64. McGrath (1990, 79-81) rightly points to the great importance of "doctrine" for faith itself. If we may define faith as trust and commitment, together with obedience, it is crucial that we know in whom we believe. "It is this vital need to know *about* God which underlies the importance of Christian doctrine. Doctrine is concerned with defending and explaining the utter trustworthiness, integrity and truthfulness of God, as we know him in Scripture and through Jesus Christ" (81).

We want to give a final indication of the lines between various disciplines. Dogmatics is also closely linked to apologetics, by which we traditionally mean the defense of the Christian faith against all sorts of criticisms to which it is subjected. This definition has given apologetics a rather defensive connotation—as if the Christian faith is characterized by defensiveness, because it supposedly presents a less-than-solid worldview. In addition, apologists may, at times, be subconsciously inclined to adopt the patterns of thought of those they want to combat. As a result, they may in fact jeopardize the uniqueness of the Christian faith they want to defend.

For this reason, Karl Barth, for example, long held back from any significant involvement with apologetics. He felt there was a major risk that the Christian faith would become caricatured if one were to adopt the models of thought of one's critics. (He saw how it had happened, for instance, to Rudolf Bultmann, whom he considered a kindred spirit.) Barth maintained that it is impossible to reason slowly but surely toward Jesus Christ by using a foreign model of thought, that one who does not begin with Christ will never find him in the end. For this reason, we must, when we want to give an account of our Christian faith to a broad public, simply be very direct and put our cards on the table. In his own dogmatics Barth faithfully followed this procedure by constructing his theology in a totally Christocentric way. We must add, however, that Barth eventually became more appreciative of the apologetic project, more aware of how dogmatics and apologetics do not necessarily exclude each other.

There is ample evidence that the Christian community continues to need a voice with an apologetic orientation. As society becomes increasingly secular, and as the Christian faith is increasingly subjected to a wide range of criticisms, there is a heightened sense that Christians need to know how they can best respond with good arguments when they receive all kinds of reproaches. Rather than elevating apologetics into a separate discipline, however, we think it better to integrate it into dogmatics. This gives it a place in a positive, comprehensive elucidation of the content of the Christian faith, rather than in a discourse with inevitably defensive undertones. Moreover, because of a constant orientation toward the sources of the faith, apologetics will shift less easily to very dissimilar philosophical models. And finally, in its turn, dogmatics will be protected against fuzziness when it has to seriously assume its responsibility of giving an account of the Christian faith to secular and religious forms of criticism. In short, good dogmatics will, certainly in our culture, have an apologetic nature.

When dogmatics fails in performing this task, it will, to its shame, see how non-theologians or "ordinary" pastors and their publications assume greater significance with regard to the apologetic orientation of the church than professional theologians. In this connection, we may be grateful for the work of apologists like G. K. Chesterton and C. S. Lewis, as well as, more recently, Tim Keller, the leader of the Redeemer Presbyterian Church in New York City.

1.7. The Tasks of Dogmatics

At the end of the previous section we made a comment about one of the tasks of dogmatics that we must expand a little further. What precisely are the tasks of dogmatics? What is the use of dogmatics?

The first thing that must be said is that dogmatics has no use whatsoever—at least not with regard to anything that goes beyond its specific aims. In principle, the dogmatician, just like any other scholar, is interested only in the quest for truth and nothing but the truth. These are, of course, big words. But they do, in any case, underscore that the search for truth does not stop where faith begins. On the contrary, faith allows for many questions that can often be shoved under the carpet, regardless of whether such a dismissal proceeds from the view that, from a scientific perspective (and therefore, in every way), nothing can be said that will make any sense. Faith may even give rise to questions that cannot be posed outside of a faith context, as, for instance, why God permits evil. Below is a short list of extremely important questions for which there are no strictly scientific answers. These are questions every human person who wants to understand life will, sooner or later, be asking. Apart from dogmatics, perhaps only in the domain of philosophy does something like systematic reflection take place regarding these issues:

> Does our human discourse about God refer to a God who really exists, and if so, how might we know him?

Does the universe in which we live have any purpose, or does it
  result from mere chance?
Does the life of an individual human being have any meaning? And
  does history have meaning, and does it move toward a goal? If
  so, what is it?
Is human action 100 percent determined by nature plus nurture, or
  is it characterized by a certain degree of freedom?
Why do we experience so much suffering and evil in our world?
Are the Jews a people like all other people, or do they differ more
  from other peoples than these groups differ from each other?
Was Jesus of Nazareth an ordinary human being, or was he more
  than that?
Is guilt ineradicable, or can it be annulled?
Can believers, as they claim, experience God's Spirit, or do they
  merely fool themselves?
What kind of book is the Bible really?
What is the sense of trying to do what is good?
Is death the end of everything?
Do chaos, suffering, and evil have the last word in the history of
  the world?

These are the kind of questions dogmatics tries to clarify through
its reflection from a perspective of faith—often in more or less this order. Dogmaticians are eager to deal with these questions, and no one
can deny these are very important questions on which much depends.
Therefore, they want to do everything possible to find answers. Somewhat more modestly, a dogmatician wants to discover how far he or she
can get in finding answers to these and similar questions in the light of
faith. Dogmatics is not for people who already know everything but for
curious people with many questions—and who do not too quickly succumb to the relativistic notion that everything is simply a matter of one's
taste, as if it is clear in advance that there are no better and worse answers
to these questions.

Along these lines, the first task of dogmatics can be described as
clarifying human existence in the light of faith, thus providing orientation
to people who want to know what the faith implies for their view of life.
Apart from this (1) clarifying and orienting task, however, dogmatics has
a few other functions. The most important ones are (2) its *regulative* and
(3) its *innovative* roles. A few words now about each of these.

As already stated, dogmatics does not take place in a vacuum.

Therefore not every answer to the questions in the above list can be simply exchanged for some other answer. In the past the Christian faith community has found some things and made a number of discoveries it does not want to lose. These findings have been recorded in texts and decisions that have acquired more authority than the ideas of random theologians, namely, in dogmas and confessions of faith. On the basis of this heritage there are things that must, at a minimum, be said if one wants to speak in a Christian way (e.g., that God is the Creator of heaven and earth); other things may not be said (e.g., that Jesus was nothing more than a prophet), and still other things are *just* outside of what we may say (e.g., that God is responsible for evil). In this way dogmatics regulates our discourse about God. It determines, we might say, which "grammatical" rules apply in our use of Christian language. In this regard dogmatics has (2) a *regulative*, or *normative*, character. It must always remind the faith community of its past and its reservoir of crucial experiences, of convictions that can withstand criticism, that have found their definitive form, and that determine what may be called Christian discourse.

The regulative function of dogmatics received major impetus through a fundamental book by George Lindbeck (1984). Lindbeck sharply distinguishes this regulative role from two other concepts: a "propositional" and an "experiential" understanding of Christian teachings. The former (doctrines as immediate truth claims) is characteristic of conservative theology; the latter (doctrines as the result of religious experience), of liberal-modern forms of theology. The postliberal theology promoted by Lindbeck would thus be characterized by a regulative (or in Lindbeck's terms, a cultural-linguistic) approach to doctrine. In reality, however, what we find is more a matter of *both-and* than of *either-or*. Dogmas and doctrines may claim to represent truth (albeit quite hesitantly), to express faith experiences, and to provide rules for a purely Christian discourse.

We do not mean to imply that the dogmatician will only look back, for in addition to this normative task, dogmatics also has (3) an *innovative* task. Here it looks particularly to the present and the future. Christian theology does not consist of a continuous recycling of old material; it connects this old material with the experiences and challenges of the present. This process also includes interdisciplinary cooperation with, for example, the empirical sciences, the humanities, and so forth. Theology must engage in such dialogues if it is to remain relevant for people in today's world, with all that this goal involves. But it enjoys doing so, since it gives great satisfaction to express the faith in such a way that others who believe differently or not at all may join the discussion. In doing so, it helps an upcoming generation of believers to find their way and to make sense of things. The circle can be drawn even wider, since dogmatics may show contemporaries—whether or not they are believers—how the faith makes a difference, and how in the end it relates to *their* questions and problems.

This attempt to express the relevance of faith does not imply that it will have to be watered down. Karl Barth, for instance, revived the doctrine of God by a renewed reflection from the center of the Christian faith, namely, the person and work of Jesus Christ. In so doing he found a powerful response to the widespread tendency to make God serve our own ideological (and often nationalistic) purposes, by projecting our own ideas and desires on God. Today too there are theologians who advance new propositions for an adequate conceptualization of the faith in the light of our times. This effort is exciting, even though such propositions may backfire or have a limited validity. Thus, in the past decades quite a few theologians have worked on elaborating the concept of the so-called social Trinity (see further, chap. 3). Yet, so far it is unclear whether the Christian community will see this innovative approach as a positive element for its pilgrimage through time.

Whatever the case, in all these different ways dogmatics provides orientation and meaning. It tries to put the content of Christian faith into words, which is, as we saw, not a matter of purely intellectual conviction or of building speculative castles in the sky; it is to answer questions and problems that meet us in real life. On this basis dogmatics wants to articulate, teach, and strengthen a specifically Christian view of, and interaction with, the things of life.

Here we follow a long tradition (with people such as Augustine, Petrus Ramus, Johannes Cocceius, Wilhelmus Amesius, and many others) of considering dogmatics as a practical, wisdom-oriented discipline. We find an elaboration of what such an approach may entail, for instance, in Charles Wood, *The Question of Providence* (2008). In his proposal for a Christian doctrine of divine providence, Wood responds to the question "How may we understand what happens in the world in relationship to God?" For him, this is far from a speculative question, for how God relates to reality has everything to do with the question how we should relate to it. See below in 6.7.

Above, we intentionally used the words "questions and problems" several times. We are always conscious of our questions, but we may have problems without realizing it. Dogmatics not only wants to deliver answers to the questions people ask (which is what Paul Tillich seemed inclined to think it wanted) but also wants to sharpen our eye for the real problems, perhaps for the questions that God has for us. See Kooi (2008) for analysis of the tasks of dogmatics as given above.

1.8. Forms of Contemporary Theology: A Typology

In the previous sections we saw that good theology and dogmatics must always include interaction between the old and the new, the past and the present. Being firmly rooted in tradition, systematic theologians will direct their applications and innovative proposals to their own time and context. That is, a theology that wishes to have an impact on the Western world must take cognizance of the major shifts and cultural changes that have occurred in past centuries—the shift from premodern thought to the modernity of the Enlightenment, and from this modernity to today's postmodernity; the shift from a society with different religious factions to the present global village, in which everything is connected worldwide with everything else, and in which adherents of divergent cultures and religions meet. And finally, we have the transition of a predominantly Euro-American Christianity to a postcolonial Christianity that is mostly found in, and supported by, communities in the Southern Hemisphere.

Even those who agree with this agenda will not easily agree on which form of theology is most adequate to it. Christians have always had different opinions on the matter, and unfortunately, but understandably, it does not appear that this situation is about to change. We have already noted a certain tension between the various tasks of dogmatics—in particular, between its past-oriented expectations and its innovative, future-oriented assignment. We can always shift the weights on the axis from the past to the future. Conservative theologians will usually place much emphasis on the abiding significance of the doctrinal decisions of the church in the past. Those decisions have proven their value and cannot be set aside without serious consequences. They will watch carefully that innovative proposals not be at odds with these accepted statements. Liberal theologians, in contrast, will place more stress on the present and emphasize that a Christianity will not survive that does not keep up with the times but wants to stick to hopelessly antiquated ideas. This approach implies the necessity of following contemporary models of thought. In addition, we have, third, "critical" theologians, who look toward neither the past nor the present but let the future determine the shape of theology. An orientation toward the past or the present, they fear, will easily lead to an uncritical and narrow-minded theology, without much flavor, that will quickly put Christians to sleep. It is crucial for theology to think from a perspective of the future of the kingdom that God has promised, and to act accordingly. This orientation will result in a critical theology that is at right angles with the status quo of injustice and inequality.

Theologies of, for example, John Calvin and Karl Barth may (admittedly in different ways) serve as examples of the conservative approach; Friedrich Schleiermacher (1768-1834) is usually regarded as the father of liberal theology. The icon of critical theology has become Jürgen Moltmann (b. 1926)—in particular, the liberation theology that he inspired.

Following is a rather rough sketch of five dominant forms of theology. A somewhat more refined classification of five types of doing theology is provided by the German-American theologian Hans Frei (1922-88).

1. *Theology as a philosophical discipline.* Here theology resembles religious philosophy. Contemporary philosophy determines fully what content our discourse about God may have. Only Christian concepts that agree with current philosophical discourse are deemed acceptable. Frei mentions the American theologian Gordon D. Kaufman (1925-2011) as an example of one who favors this type of theology. The title of Kaufman's book *God the Problem* (1972) clearly indicates what kind of theology this is. Kaufman's theology is totally saturated by the idea of Kant (1724-1804) that, in the final analysis, we cannot say one sensible word about the "real" things that lie behind the phenomena we perceive with our senses. We thus can speak about God only in very general terms. There are also contemporary thinkers in Europe who speak about God (and we could therefore say, strictly speaking, are theo-logians) while allowing their views to be completely determined by their philosophical inclinations—for instance, in the French phenomenological tradition.

2. *Theology as a search for the most common denominator between faith and culture.* In this second form of theology the Christian tradition remains a source for our knowledge of faith, but we can discover its meaning and determine its value only in the light of current philosophical trends. In other words, an exterior model of thought is utilized to define what must be seen as the heart of the biblical message. The best-known representative of this type of theology is undoubtedly Rudolf Bultmann (1884-1976). He ingeniously used the philosophy of Martin Heidegger (1889-1976) to indicate what, in his opinion, is the core of the Christian

faith. What the Bible refers to as "the law," we should, according to Bultmann, see as what Heidegger deemed "inauthentic existence." The gospel will lead us to what Heidegger applauded as "authentic existence," in which we lose our anxiety and no longer hide in ourselves. Everything that cannot be brought under these categories must be filtered away as time-conditioned (note Bultmann's famous demythologizing of the New Testament).

3. *Theology as correlation between faith and culture.* In this case Christianity and culture are co-equal sources that continuously interact. Christian theology and other worldviews may learn much from each other in an open dialogue. In this process these other worldviews (and also other disciplines, such as the natural and social sciences) will not prescribe what Christians must or "still can" believe but will clarify the essence of the Christian faith. The most important difference from type 2 is that no particular school of thought (such as existentialism) is regarded as the absolute norm; rather, various discourses have their input, depending on what they can contribute in different areas. No single worldview needs to be totally accepted, as there is an attempt to learn from many different angles. The maestro of this correlation-theology was the German-American theologian Paul Tillich (1886–1965), mentioned above, who as a Christian theologian was in constant search for dialogue with other philosophies, worldviews, scholarly disciplines (psychology, in particular), and the arts. Tillich regarded Christian doctrines primarily as symbols that were intended to answer the deepest human existential questions. The statement "God is our Creator" is, for instance, a powerful and encouraging symbol when we are confronted with powers that threaten our lives, and "kingdom of God" stands for the conviction that history is not meaningless.

4. *Theology as an apologetic discipline.* Here the emphasis shifts to the faith tradition, with the Bible as theology's most important source. However, the Christian message must constantly be clarified anew and defended with the help of generally accessible knowledge and concepts. Again in type 4 we find an intensive dialogue with other disciplines and worldviews, but in this case the dialogue proceeds under another banner, namely, the attempt to explain the Christian truth and make it acceptable. The person who is undoubtedly the most skilled in this form of doing theology is Wolfhart Pannenberg (1928–2014). In his extensive oeuvre Pannenberg carries on his dialogue with the natural sciences, history, many branches of philosophy (anthropology, philosophy of science, metaphysics), and other religions—all with the primary goal of showing

that the Christian view of reality offers a better understanding of how the world operates than any other approach.

5. *Theology as Christian self-description.* In this fifth type, the message of the Bible—or, more precisely, God's revelation in Jesus Christ—is everything. The Christian faith must not let itself be influenced by other powers or sources of revelation. It is not culture that stands in judgment over the gospel or determines what continues to be relevant, but it is the gospel that judges and criticizes culture. Preferably, the apologetic dialogue with culture must be avoided, since this interaction can only lead to a watering down of the revelation in Jesus Christ. Translation usually leads to betrayal, which applies to the translation of the Christian message into whatever contemporary concepts we choose. Karl Barth was the theologian who, with his enormous intellectual power, put this type of theology on the map and developed it.

For this typology, see Frei 1992, 28-55; for a slightly different version, see Ford 1999, 20-30. In the previous sections of this chapter we have used some of the same examples as Frei and Ford, as well as some others. In our book readers may expect a form of theology that generally moves between types 4 and 5. But the other types will be treated fairly, even though we feel that quite a few objections may be put forward against the theological methods these types promote. For a brief description of the life and work of the contemporary theologians mentioned above (and many others), see Ford and Muers 2005, and Musser and Price 1996. Acquainting oneself with such surveys would, by the way, provide an excellent introduction to the study of Christian theology. In addition, we would like to point to Grenz and Olson 1996, which is an instructive, passionate, and accessible book about the use of systematic theology.

1.9. Theology as Mode of Existence

So far we have described theology and dogmatics primarily as a particular discipline—one of the many that one might study at an academic level. But many who are involved with it feel that theology is more than this. Theology carries with it a unique mode of existence. Barth and his followers referred to this as a *theologische Existenz* (theological mode of existence).

This theological mode of existence involves more than acquiring a substantial amount of knowledge, more than doing theology as creatively as possible. It concerns the cultivation of a certain underlying passion.

This passion is, first, a passion for God and his kingdom. As the word indicates, a true theologian speaks about God. But his or her passion also concerns the people of God and the world of God. This dimension will perhaps not radiate from every page the theologian writes. It is a *cultivated* passion; that is, it lies in the background and will typically surface in a restrained manner. This limitation relates to the ability to maintain distance, which is part of the theological mode of existence. That is to say, as a theologian, one is able to look at the faith that is lived by people from a *distance*. It is possible to formulate abstractions and speak about them in intelligible language. Dogmaticians perhaps speak more about pneumatology than about the Holy Spirit, and more about eschatology than about heaven. This preference may be risky, but things will go wrong only when they speak exclusively in a detached kind of language. To a certain extent they must speak in terms of "-ologies" if they want to maintain an overview of the various parts (loci) that together form the content of the Christian faith, and to quickly see how, in a particular array, these elements may fit together. A sentence like "Barth suffers from pneumatological anemia" is typical theological jargon (apart from the question as to whether or not it is true).

As can happen in other areas of scholarship, such concepts help to create a jargon that is understood by representatives of different denominations and worldviews, enabling them to carry on a meaningful communication. Where believers without theological training will often listen to the views of others without understanding them and with great distaste, a common terminology enables theologians to learn about each other's views in a fruitful—but often critical—dialogue. In other words, part of the theological mode of existence is the ability to change one's perspective and, through a common theological language, to empathize with the faith-worlds of other groups of believers.

At the same time, it also belongs to life-as-theologian that one will always return to the "simple faith" and not get lost in a critical attitude, whatever one's ability to talk about faith in abstract terms and to retain a critical distance. It is crucial to know when you must be critical, but also when you must leave your critical attitude behind, in order to believe as a child in what Paul Ricoeur (1913-2005) has called a "second naïveté."

References

Berkhof, Hendrikus. 1985. *Introduction to the Study of Dogmatics*. Translated by John J. Vriend. Grand Rapids: Eerdmans.

Brink, Gijsbert van den. 2009. *Philosophy of Science for Theologians: An Introduction*. Frankfurt: Lang.

Brümmer, Vincent. 2006. *Brümmer on Meaning and the Christian Faith: Collected Writings of Vincent Brümmer*. Aldershot: Ashgate.

Ford, David F. 1999. *Theology: A Very Short Introduction*. Oxford: Oxford University Press.

Ford, David F., and Rachel Muers, eds. 2005. *The Modern Theologians: An Introduction to Christian Theology since 1918*. 3rd rev. ed. Oxford: Blackwell.

Frei, Hans W. 1992. *Types of Christian Theology*. New Haven: Yale University Press.

Grenz, Stanley J., and Roger E. Olson. 1996. *Who Needs Theology? An Invitation to the Study of God*. Downers Grove, IL: InterVarsity Press.

Jensen, Alexander S. 2007. *Theological Hermeneutics*. London: SCM.

Kaufman, Gordon D. 1972. *God the Problem*. Cambridge, MA: Harvard University Press.

Kooi, Cornelis van der. 2008. *Goed gereedschap maakt het verschil: Over de plaats en functie van de christelijke dogmatiek*. Amsterdam: Vrije Universiteit.

Kuyper, Abraham. 1898. *Encyclopedia of Sacred Theology: Its Principles*. Translated by J. Hendrik de Vries. New York: Scribner's Sons.

Leiner, Martin. 2008. *Methodischer Leitfaden Systematische Theologie und Religionsphilosophie*. Göttingen: Vandenhoeck & Ruprecht.

Leonhardt, Rochus. 2001. *Grundinformation Dogmatik: Ein Lehr- und Arbeitsbuch für das Studium der Theologie*. Göttingen: Vandenhoeck & Ruprecht.

Lindbeck, George A. 1984. *The Nature of Doctrine: Religion and Theology in a Postliberal Age*. Philadelphia: Westminster.

Marks, Darren C., ed. 2002. *Shaping a Theological Mind: Theological Context and Methodology*. Aldershot: Ashgate.

McGrath, Alister E. 1990. *Understanding Doctrine: Its Relevance and Purpose for Today*. London: Hodder & Stoughton.

Musser, Donald W., and Joseph L. Price, eds. 1996. *A New Handbook of Christian Theologians*. Nashville: Abingdon.

O'Donovan, Oliver. 1986. *Resurrection and Moral Order: An Outline for Evangelical Ethics*. Leicester: Inter-Varsity Press.

Sarisky, Darren, ed. 2015. *Theology, History, and Biblical Interpretation: Modern Readings*. London: Bloomsbury.

Sauter, Gerhard. 2003. *Gateways to Dogmatics: Reasoning Theologically for the Life of the Church*. Grand Rapids: Eerdmans.

Sauter, Gerhard, and Alex Stock. 1976. *Arbeitsweisen systematischer Theologie: Eine Anleitung*. Munich: Kaiser.

Schleiermacher, Friedrich D. E. 1990. *Brief Outline of Theology as a Field of Study*.

Translated by Terrence N. Tice. Lewiston, NY: Edward Mellen Press. Orig. German pub., 1811/1830.

Thiselton, Anthony C. 2009. *Hermeneutics: An Introduction*. Grand Rapids: Eerdmans.

Tracy, David. 1981. *The Analogical Imagination: Christian Theology and the Culture of Pluralism*. New York: Crossroad.

Verhey, Allen. 2002. *Remembering Jesus: Christian Community, Scripture, and the Moral Life*. Grand Rapids: Eerdmans.

Wood, Charles M. 2008. *The Question of Providence*. Louisville: Westminster John Knox.

2 Is There a God?

Prolegomena

AIM

This chapter is a continuation of the first chapter, in which we described the place and nature of dogmatics. By way of a more extended introduction, we now want to pose the question as to what we are dealing with when we speak of Christian faith. What is it, and why would a person want to cultivate such a faith? For there is no conclusive evidence for the existence of God. Or is there? What are the causes or grounds on which Christian faith rests? To what kind of experiences, data, or origins does Christian dogmatics point when it wants to give an account of this faith? In very general terms we might answer: Christian faith points to revelation as its basis. In chapter 5 we will further discuss this concept. At this point we want to stress that revelation does not fall from the sky as a *Fremdkörper* (a foreign body). It may, at least to a certain extent, be approached through phenomena of this world: our thinking, our experience, and our religious impulse. In this chapter we seek to discover where and in which domains we find cause to speak about God. In Christian dogmatics the chapter that deals with this kind of introductory questions has traditionally been called prolegomena. Prolegomena are a sort of introduction to the actual content of dogmatics, explaining its main principles or foundations. The Roman Catholic tradition speaks of "fundamental theology" in this connection.

After reading this chapter, you will, it is hoped, be able to say something meaningful about:

- the pros and cons of internal and external prolegomena (2.1)
- why our reason is unable to prove God's existence in a general, convincing way (2.2)
- the question of whether we can find traces of God in this world (2.3)

- the role that the human experience of life might play with regard to gaining access to faith and to discovering reasons for faith (2.4)
- why it is not self-evident to understand Christian faith from the phenomenon of religion (2.5)
- the way in which church tradition and the faith community guide us in matters of faith (2.6)
- the role of the Bible and of the person of Jesus in the prolegomena (2.7).

MAKING CONNECTIONS

1. Take two minutes to write down what you feel is one (or *the*) good reason to believe in God. Or, if you do not believe in God, what is your reason for not believing in him?
2. Now do the opposite. Put yourself in the shoes of someone who, unlike yourself, does not (or does) believe, and note what you think might be his or her most important reason for not believing (or for believing).
3. Read Peter De Vries's novel *The Blood of the Lamb* (Boston: Little, Brown, 1961), chap. 16, where Dan Wanderhope, the desperate father of a deathly ill young girl, throws a cake into the face of the statue of Christ. And then, "Very slowly, very deliberately, with infinite patience, the icing was wiped from the eyes and flung away. I could see it fall in clumps to the porch steps. Then the cheeks were wiped down with the same sense of grave and gentle ritual, with all the kind sobriety of one whose voice could be heard saying, 'Suffer the little children to come unto me . . . for of such is the kingdom of heaven.' Then the scene dissolved itself in a mist in which my legs could no longer support their weight, and I sank down to the steps. I sat on its worn stones, to rest a moment before going on. Thus Wanderhope was found at that place which . . . was said to be the only alternative to the muzzle of a pistol: the foot of the Cross" (237–38). What do you think of these alternatives? To what extent is religious belief based on existential experiences rather than intellectual reasons?

2.1. From the Outside to the Inside:
Some Dotted Lines toward Faith

Why would we agree with the way in which God is confessed in the Christian church? The answer to this question is far from self-evident and un-equivocal. In this chapter we discuss a few reasons or grounds that are often given in this connection. We will say something about the proofs for God's existence, about nature, about human affections or emotions, and in general, about the phenomenon of religion. We do not want to suggest, however, that after reading this chapter someone will have sufficient reasons to believe. If that were the case, this chapter would have to be regarded as a form of apologetics. Or it might be referred to with a concept that is current in Roman Catholic theology: *fundamental theology*. Traditionally, in fundamental theology a floor is laid, so to speak, on which actual theological themes (the loci) may be built. But whether such a floor is solid enough remains to be seen. There is considerable skepticism on this point in Protestant theology, so we speak somewhat more modestly about prolegomena. Etymologically speaking, this word means "the things said beforehand." These prolegomena satisfy the feeling that, in speaking of the Christian faith, we cannot come to the point straightaway. Before we can speak of God, creation, sin, and redemption, some things must be said by way of introduction. What, in fact, is faith? Why would we believe? Where does believing intersect with general human experiences? And what is dogmatics? Is it a science or not? What is its goal? We discussed these last points in the previous chapter. Here we explore the nature of Christian faith and the fields that allow us to understand it, or at least approach it.

Confusion abounds about the status of prolegomena. Are the prolegomena part of dogmatics, or are we still in some preliminary, neutral area? In the Middle Ages people referred to the *praeambula fidei*, literally "the portals of the faith." It was the area where the proofs for God's existence were dealt with. Philosophy was the domain where both believers and unbelievers could agree on a number of elementary topics. At first, Protestantism showed little enthusiasm for prolegomena. Luther, Melanchthon (1497–1560), and Calvin saw dogmatics as an appropriate survey of the main subjects that needed to be addressed in a Bible-based discussion of the faith: the law, the Apostles' Creed, the Lord's Prayer, and the sacraments. Not until the second generation of Reformers came on the scene was there a renewed sense that a discussion of introductory matters was needed. In the era of rationalism (ca. 1650–1750) the prolegomena were regarded as a general, philosophical discourse about God that sometimes was given more weight than dogmatics itself. We can say that, on this line of thought, prolegomena remain external to actual faith. It is a search for experiences and convictions that people share with all human beings, a way of seeking access to the Christian faith. We continue to encounter this approach in the first edition of Schleiermacher's *Christian Faith*, which deals with some concepts that are borrowed from philosophy, before the author gets into actual dogmatics. Schleiermacher later clarifies that he had not intended his borrowing from philosophy as a way of laying a floor under his theology but sought to assign a place to Christian faith within the parameters of intellectual life in general.

The ambivalence found with Schleiermacher has remained to this day. Under the antispeculative sentiment that arose in the second half of the nineteenth century, the prolegomena have increasingly been seen as topics that are, in fact, an integral part of the faith. This perspective makes the prolegomena internal. With Bavinck we find, as part of the prolegomena, an extensive chapter about the foundational principles of dogmatics that he clearly develops within the contours of the tradition of philosophical realism (RD 1:207-35). Karl Barth maintained that an approach from the outside is, as a matter of principle, impossible. He defines prolegomena as matters that must be said, not in advance, but *first*—and as far as he is concerned, this saying has to do with the Word of God (CD I/1:26-44). Dogmatics presupposes that God has already spoken. We can immediately put all our cards on the table and do not have to construct a convoluted argument as a basis for faith, which never succeeds. Berkhof begins, just like Schleiermacher, with the phenomenon of religion and then proceeds to define the Christian faith as a particular species of a revealed religion (CF 1-25). That is, we must make two "jumps": from religion or spirituality in general to the group of revealed religions (Judaism, Christianity, and Islam), and then from this group to Christian faith itself.

Since the Second Vatican Council, Roman Catholic fundamental theology "has shifted away from the attempt to set forth a rationalistic defense of that church" and discusses the very same issues that are dealt with in Protestant prolegomena (Becker 2015, 373; see also O'Collins 2011). By maintaining the concept of fundamental *theology*, however, it is not suggested that these reflections are offered from a pretheological, neutral vantage point. For this reason, Protestant theologians have recently started to adopt this term instead of the colder word "prolegomena" (e.g., Becker 2015).

Since the beginning of the present century the attempt to make the Christian faith intelligible and accessible by proceeding from the phenomenon of religion has once more become very popular. Christianity, however, is often regarded as a religion that has outlived itself. Institutional Christianity has been marginalized, and other forms of faith, spirituality, religiosity, and rituals have to a large extent taken its place (see Taylor 2007). Under the influence of our modern times the religious impulse in our culture has undergone a transformation toward a much more individualized form, detached from established institutions like denominations, media organizations, or political parties. Religion has not disappeared, and the old premise that the modern times would bring the disappearance of the spiritual and religion now has few supporters. The interest in rituals, in collective forms for seeking meaning, is manifest in Western society. As a result, the religious impulse undergoes an important metamorphosis in our post-Christian society. In addition, the increased visibility of Islam in the Western world (not its emergence: Islam has been there for a long time) also contributes to people, more than before, regarding Christian faith as just one religion among many.

We doubt that religion as a human phenomenon in itself offers much of a suitable basis for explaining the Christian faith. Today, many people dislike institutional religion because, among other things, of the social pressure or even the violent extremism it appears to foster. It cannot be denied that, from a phenomenological angle, Christian faith may be one religion among many. It does not follow, however, that, from a theological perspective, when we deal with the question of how to understand the Christian faith, the route via religion is to be preferred over, for instance, an approach that positions faith in the category of moral or aesthetic experience or in the framework of historical events. The experience of beauty may put people on a track toward God; so also may a deep conviction about good and evil as absolute values. Becoming acquainted with the history of Israel, the life of Jesus, and the rapid increase of the number of his followers may also do the same, as might an intense search for contact with the transcendent as is practiced in many religions. Christian faith touches on all these aspects of reality.

None of these approaches, however, is clearly to be preferred above any other. From a theological viewpoint, we must bring God into the picture if we want knowledge of God. Consider what Jesus said to his disciple Peter after Peter's confession that Jesus is the Messiah: "Blessed are you, Simon Bar-Jona! For flesh and blood has not revealed this to you, but my Father who is in heaven" (Matt 16:17). That is, no single thing in our reality has the privilege of revealing God, but anything may be used by God in his revelation. It is God who makes God known. Or in a more commonly used phrase: God reveals himself through his Spirit. The real ground of our faith is therefore God in his revelation. If God were not to show himself, if he would not turn toward us in actions, events, and words, we would not know him.

For that reason our point of departure in this book is not from the outside but from the inside. We are thus not claiming to be neutral observers or referees who, from the outside, attempt to weigh the various claims made by our faith. As we remarked in the previous chapter, this introduction to Christian dogmatics is written on the basis of personal involvement.

To remain neutral when dealing with faith and religion is very difficult, if not impossible. Faith and religion have an immediate appeal to the human person. Our personal involvement or distance inevitably makes itself felt. But to be involved does not automatically imply that one is biased or takes shortcuts with regard to the truth. A good musician is usually a lover of music, and a good plasterer will appreciate skillful restorations. A love for one's profession does not make one blind but discerning (*ubi amor, ibi oculus*, "where love is, there is insight"). Likewise, involvement in faith and professionalism may go together and even stimulate each other.

We conclude: the only ground for faith in God is God himself—nothing and no one else. It would suffice for Christian dogmatics to offer this reference to God as the sole ground of our faith. We would then have no need for the rest of this chapter and might move right on to chapters 3 and 4, which deal with the topic of God. We have chosen differently, not primarily out of principle, but rather for pragmatic, cultural, and pastoral motives. Many people find it disappointing when the question Why believe? is answered only by pointing to divine revelation. Does not every religion claim to be a revealed religion? And do not these claims to some extent all contradict each other? Many people are thus looking for something else—to a kind of proof that the Christian faith is true. Some make it a precondition if they are to regard Christian faith as a serious option. The British mathematician and philosopher Bertrand Russell (1872-1970) is said to have prepared an answer for a possible meeting with God after his death if God asked why Russell did not believe: "Not enough evidence, God, not enough evidence!" But is there really too little evidence for our faith? Has God failed miserably? Should he make a better effort to convince us that he exists—that is, if he is eager that we believe?

For an answer to this question, we will look at some of the domains where such evidence might be found. In doing so, we will proceed from wider domains of reality to smaller domains. We will begin with the spheres of reality that many people share and will end with some areas where we mainly find believers (or those who want to become believers). We will further pursue the link between faith and intellect and pay special attention to whether or not faith can be proven rationally (2.2). To what extent is the human intellect a domain from which faith might emerge, or that might induce us to become a believer? We proceed point by point to pose this question with regard to the world (2.3), to the existential experience of being human (2.4), to the religious impulse (2.5), the Christian tradition and the faith community (2.6), and the Bible and Jesus himself (2.7). To what extent are these domains windows that allow us to catch a glimpse of God?

First, a preliminary remark. In our search for the sources or grounds of faith, it is useful to distinguish between the reasons individuals or groups of people may have for faith and the grounds that Christian dogmatics proposes. For there is a difference.

Based on a distinction derived from the theory of science, we might say that dogmatics focuses primarily not on the *context of discovery* but on the *context of justification*. This distinction was developed by Hans Reichenbach (*Experience and Prediction* [Chicago: University of Chicago Press, 1938], chap. 2), who argued that there often is a major difference between the circumstances that lead scholars to a certain discovery and the final arguments that provide the scientific foundation for this discovery. Similarly, there is a difference between the place where people find faith and the foundational grounds for that faith. In this chapter we will deal primarily with the first aspect, while the second aspect will be discussed in chapter 5.

The self-image of the contemporary believer differs considerably from what it used to be half a century ago. A person now considers himself or herself to be an individual who must make an authentic choice and who wants to be responsible for that choice. We will leave aside the question whether this view is feasible in actual practice or whether it goes back instead to the modern myth of the autonomous self. There are reasons to support either position. Because of the inner sense of responsibility it has become less easy to appeal to institutions such as the church, tradition, denominations, or the Bible. Instead, the question of why one should believe is experienced as one that we each need to respond to at an individual level. At the same time, the urge toward authenticity results at this point in overload, for most Christians are only vaguely aware of the grounds of their faith. They simply regard themselves as people who believe, and this position is not simply evidence of a failure to assume responsibility. We therefore should not attach too much importance to our exercise in this chapter; the Christian faith does not totally depend on the prolegomena. Nonetheless, we will pay some attention to them for they may be of help to people like the father of the mentally disturbed boy of the Gospels. Confronted with the question of whether he believed in Jesus's power to heal his son, the father exclaimed, "I believe; help my unbelief" (Mark 9:24). In our postmodern (but not postreligious) world, there are many who, at least from time to time, recognize themselves in this paradoxical cry.

The prominent Canadian philosopher Charles Taylor (2007) points out how, compared to the past, belief and unbelief have changed character in one essential aspect. Those who nowadays believe often find it easy to understand those who don't, and they might even experience themselves as unbelievers. The opposite is also true: those who are not officially religious often regard faith as a real option and have some idea as to what it might mean to become religious oneself. This change in attitude has to do with globalization and the influence of the media and has become more overt than in the past. This cultural shift is one reason for us to pay more attention in the prolegomena than has been customary in recent dogmatics to the approach that does not begin with the certainty of faith but does tend toward this position. Still, also with regards to the content of dogmatics, the common doubts and objections against faith must be taken seriously. Recent publications that do so in an intelligent and accessible manner (e.g., Keller 2008; but one might also think of the continuing interest in the books of C. S. Lewis) receive ample attention, and rightly so.

2.2. Why There Is No Absolute Proof for God's Existence

It seems desirable to have an absolute and convincing proof for the truth, or at least the relevance, of the Christian faith so that everyone can see that it is about something real. Many would probably be quite satisfied if there were such proof for the concept to which the Christian faith is often conveniently reduced: belief in God's existence. There is, however, no such convincing evidence. We may draw this conclusion from the fact that the Christian faith is not a generally accepted conviction. At the same time, we should wonder whether we must actually long for such evidence. In fact, there are at least eight reasons why we should not be amazed about or lament the absence of such a "hard," generally convincing, proof.

1. There is no form of religious belief that can be proven in a way that will convince most people, so it should not surprise us that the same applies also to the Christian faith. The belief system of an atheist is, in fact, even more difficult to prove, since it concerns a statement (i.e., "God does not exist") about something that supposedly does not exist. Non-existence statements are notorious for being far more difficult to verify than existence statements. It takes the discovery of only two rhinoceroses to verify the statement that rhinoceroses exist. However, to verify the statement "Rhinoceroses do not exist," one must search every square mile of the earth, and even then it is possible that the rhinos may, in the meantime, have moved from one place to another. Strictly speaking, an atheist who wants to prove his or her position must question all persons who claim to have met God and test their experiences. If there is only one person whose claims are true, the atheist has no support for the nonexistence of God.

Whether someone's claim is justified can never be settled scientifically because of the character of Christian faith as transcendental (i.e., as superseding empirical reality). Christian faith shares this fundamental characteristic with all religions, for the word "religion" concerns, by common definition, (collective) forms of involvement with a transcendent reality. Even if we believe that this transcendent reality leaves many traces on this earth, we can at best hope to see these earthly traces rather than to discover their transcendent source—which will therefore always remain a topic of debate. It is as Jesus has Abraham say in the story of the rich man and the destitute Lazarus: "If they do not hear Moses and the prophets, neither will they be convinced if someone should rise from the dead" (Luke 16:31). In other words, whatever miraculous signs God may give to prove his existence, it always remains possible to deny their divine source, if only by regarding them as anomalies for which no explanation has as yet been found.

In this connection Berkhof (CF 52-54) speaks of the earthly, indirect nature, even (paradoxically enough) about the hiddenness, of revelation. "Even if God, for example, would reveal himself in a mysterious voice, a blinding flash, or an experience of rapturous ecstasy, these would still be phenomena that are part of our earthly reality. They are thus thinkable apart from an encounter with God, and in themselves do not prove anything" (53). Thus we may say that revelation is fundamentally unprovable. This conclusion is related, on the one hand, to our creaturely limitations (no one can "see" God, John 1:18), which will fall away only at the eschaton ("his servants shall worship him; they shall see his face," Rev 22:3-4) and, on the other hand, to the freedom in which we are created: God does not force himself upon us as a brute fact; rather, he touches our shoulder or takes our hand. For that reason we must emphasize that earthiness is the earthiness of revelation. God does present himself; it is just that we need the so-called eyes of faith to recognize him.

2. There is, however, something else. The Christian faith teaches us that we are sinful beings. Chapter 8 will show that sin is primarily a theological category: sin implies that we try to keep God away from us, since we think that God disturbs us and robs us of our freedom. It is thus not strange that we do not let ourselves be easily convinced of God's existence, intuitively preferring to explain away the things that point in this direction. It is part of our sinfulness that we do not want to find God. For that reason we prefer to push signals of him away or to distort them, rather than to take them seriously. In Reformed theology, in particular, many have, on the basis of Paul's Letter to the Romans, developed a sharp eye for the often subtle and ingenious manners in which people change God into something else—and change something else into their god. This view has been developed also in the Roman Catholic tradition, in particular by those inspired by Augustine.

According to a famous statement of Calvin, the human heart is a constant factory of idols (*Inst.* 1.11.8). Through idolatry—the identification of God with a part of created reality—we succeed in keeping God under control and in manipulating him for our own purposes (the biblical example par excellence is found in 1 Sam 4). Fed by this tradition, with its critical attitude toward every ideological perversion of our faith, Karl Barth was able at the beginning of the twentieth century to unmask and confront such processes as the identification of God with the cause of German nationalism. It also led him to a very critical stance toward the tradition of the proofs for God's existence, since the God for whom we think we can find proof is usually no more than an extension of our own thoughts and desires. The true God is totally different, and we can get to know him only in his revelation.

In the Roman Catholic tradition we might point to the Jansenist thinker Blaise Pascal (1623-62), who in his *Pensées* (Thoughts) regularly carries on a dialogue with people who are searching for arguments to prove their faith (and, remarkably enough, appears to share in this search himself). With reference to the Christian doctrine of sin, Pascal suggests that we have no reason whatsoever to expect that we might have a clear view of God or might acquire it in a simple way. Those who dismiss faith because they feel that God himself could have done a little more to give them clarity paradoxically confirm the point the Christian church has made through the ages, namely, that as human beings we have, to a large degree, lost our sense for God; our antenna is no longer attuned to the signals that God emits. This disconnect results in a lot of static on the line. However, God allows himself to be found by those who persist in their determined search for him (see Pascal 1995, esp. frag. 194).

3. In general, proofs play only a minor role in our lives. The things we believe only when offered proof (e.g., that $36 \times 35 = 1{,}260$—most people need a calculator to verify this fact) are most often not very exciting. In fact, most things that are really important—as, for instance, the love we have for someone—can, strictly speaking, not be proven, which does not bother us in the least. A man who keeps worrying until the day of his death whether his wife truly loves him, since he has no objective proof, we would judge to be sorry and quite irrational. The certainty associated with love is immediate and not derived like, for instance, a conclusion that is deduced from premises. The same is true also for the certainty that characterizes faith, since, like love, faith is rooted in a personal relationship—in this case, with God.

The Latin term for this immediate certainty is *certitudo*; it is reported that on his deathbed the Heidelberg Reformer Caspar Olevian (1536–87), when asked whether he was sure of his future with God, replied with a single word: *certissimus* (very sure). This type of existential certainty stands in contrast to *securitas*, the irrefutable certainty of a mathematical argument that is absolutely certain but does not require any commitment. So-called irregular thinkers like Martin Luther, Blaise Pascal, Søren Kierkegaard, H. F. Kohlbrugge (1803–75), and Karl Barth in his early years stress the immediate, nonreasoned character of the certainty of faith. Blaise Pascal has left us the famous statement "The heart has its reasons which reason itself does not know" (*Pensées*, no. 680; Pascal 1995, 158). By "reason," Pascal refers to mathematical arguments, and by "heart," to the intuitive, existential certainty that belongs to the realm of faith. "It is the heart that feels God, not reason: that's what faith is. God is felt by the heart, not by reason" (*Pensées*, no. 680). Remarkably enough, this faith did not keep Pascal from also offering a rational defense of the Christian faith in this apologetic book. However, his memory of an ecstatic nighttime experience of God's presence was decisive. We know of this experience from his *Mémorial* (1654), which was found in the lining of his coat after his death (Pascal 1995, 178–81).

4. Viewed from an epistemological perspective, there is no objection against believing without having absolute proof for the content of one's faith. We have hardly any idea about the grounds or origins of our most elementary convictions—and there is nothing wrong with that. Consider, for example, the moral conviction that we may not kill another person. We do not have to explore this conviction before accepting it as valid. The same is true of faith in God. In the era of modernity it has often been suggested that there cannot be faith without proof. In this regard John Locke (1632–1704) may be considered a prototype. He believed that our religious convictions are justified only if they can be based on other generally accepted convictions; that is, if we want to proceed in a rational manner, the strength of our faith ought always to be proportional to the evidence that we might put forward. With regard to the Christian faith, this requirement would mean that, before claiming justification to believe in God, it must be proven before a general public that God exists. However, this requirement of an absolute foundation is epistemologically flawed, if only because it is impossible to provide an underlying foundation for everything we believe.

During the last decades analytic philosophy has been very interested in this sort of "evidentialism," as aptly defined by William K. Clifford: "It is wrong, always, everywhere, and for anyone, to believe anything upon insufficient evidence" (1877, quoted in Clark 2000, 158). Closely tied to this idea is so-called classic foundationalism, which claims a narrow basis for epistemological claims that do not need further proof because they are immediately evident (something that is not deemed to apply to epistemological claims of a religious nature). Both currents of thought have landed in heavy water in recent discussion, since their claims were too soft. In particular, Reformed epistemologists such as Alvin Plantinga, Nicholas Wolterstorff, and William Alston have shown that we are, in principle, justified to believe in God without proof. They drew their inspiration from Calvin (thus we speak of *Reformed* epistemology), who argued that it is completely natural to believe in God, even if we cannot present any evidence (*Inst.* 1.3). Plantinga and others point out that there are many things we believe in everyday life without any evidence (e.g., that our senses do not deceive us, that Australia exists, that we had breakfast yesterday, that committing a murder is wrong) and that there is no reason to think that we should make an exception for religious beliefs. See the studies of Plantinga, Wolterstorff, and Alston in Plantinga and Wolterstorff 1983, and further, Plantinga 2015; Clark 2000, 191–97, provides a brief survey. The influence of Locke on the long hegemony of evidentialism and foundationalism is well analyzed in Wolterstorff 1996.

5. Do these considerations make faith something purely subjective, fully dependent on whether we happen to have met God in a way as we might have met our spouse? No, for even though we have no objective proof for God's existence, we can point to numerous relevant factors. Believers may, for instance, refer to events or circumstances that resulted in an inner conviction that God exists and argue that what was true for me, may also be true for others. They may point to other people they know who have deeply impressed them with their faith, or to instances of answers to some of their prayers, or to the simple trust in God of the faith community to which they belong, or to the way in which they were, at a critical moment, reminded of certain Bible texts or of something that was important for them. Such considerations that emerge from particular experiences are often more powerful than philosophical arguments. The philosopher William Alston (1921–2009) tells us, for instance, that his return to the Christian faith (from which he had earlier distanced himself) was not inspired "by abstract reasoning but by experience—the experience of the love of God and the presence of the Spirit, as I found this in the community of the believers. I did not reason myself back to faith" (quoted in Morris 1994, 27–28).

Some of these experiences and considerations may have a meaning that far exceeds our private situation. For that reason they may be given the form of an *argument* that may also be convincing to others. The so-called classic proofs for God's existence may be understood in this way. These are not proofs in the strict sense of the word, nor have Christians proposed them as a basis for their faith. But they are considerations that, to the extent they are true, have a universal significance; they were therefore advanced in hopes that the penny would also drop for others. This mentality led to the arguments of the early Christian apologists in the second century, to the ontological argument of Anselm (eleventh century), and to the so-called five ways of Aquinas (thirteenth century) to deduce God's existence from creation (STh I.2.3). Today most of these considerations and arguments have lost their force. Other arguments continue to be suggested in old and new forms, and some new arguments have been added, such as, in the 1970s, the newly discovered "anthropic principle," that is, the incredible "fine tuning" of the universe to support intelligent life.

The role of this type of argument is not *demonstrative* (strictly speaking, nothing is demonstrated or proven) so much as *provocative*; such arguments have an appeal, they evoke something, they call for an awareness of a reality that comprises and rises beyond our own reality. They show that faith is not weird and does not necessarily require a *sacrificium intellectus* (sacrificing of our intellect). Therefore they appeal to us; they ask us not to close ourselves from this transcendent reality a priori but instead to search for God. Of course, not all arguments appeal with equal force, and some work better in some periods and for some persons than for others. The "big three" among the arguments for the existence of God will always have a broad appeal:

1. the *cosmological argument*, which suggests that every effect must have a cause and that this causal chain must have a beginning somewhere (which renders meaningless the oft-repeated question, Who made God? for "God" is precisely the word for that which has not been made but is at the beginning of everything);
2. the *teleological argument*, which, after every sense of purpose had been removed from biology, rediscovered just such purpose in cosmology (in particular, in the anthropic principle); and
3. the *ontological argument*, which suggests that there must be an ultimate being, an argument that still has many competent supporters.

In addition, one might think of various other arguments—primarily, the *moral argument*, which, with Kant, argues from an objective moral standard to its guarantor. None of these is fully convincing, which does not mean that they belong on the trash heap of history.

All these arguments are tied to a particular context and depend on the individual person; they work only for those who accept their premises, which varies not just in different cultural situations but also for each person. They are much more instrumental than foundational, for they take as their point of departure what a person already believes and then try to show that the existence of God follows. For that reason some arguments will have more appeal for some people, and in some eras, than others. They thus have a relative importance, which does not negate all their value.

An argument that we find personally quite appealing is the following:

Premise 1: Jesus of Nazareth believed that God's kingdom would come and called everyone to repentance.
Premise 2: Jesus of Nazareth was not mistaken when he brought this message.

Here we have a kind of proof for God's existence, but it has validity only for someone who is prepared to believe P2 (and, of course, P1, which is hardly debatable). When someone does not believe P2, we can try to put considerations on the table that plead for P2 (as will someone who doubts the correctness of this argumentation). But this process cannot be endless. There comes a moment when we must say with Luther, "Here I stand. I cannot do otherwise." In short, arguments are certainly useful, but there is a point when it is apparent that faith precedes evidence and does not flow from it.

Today it is generally agreed that medieval thinkers like Anselm and Aquinas intended their proofs of God's existence to be, not so much a rational road to faith, but a means to connect, from a perspective of faith, God with our thinking (Anselm) or our world (Aquinas). Only later, after the emergence of the Enlightenment (from Descartes onward), did these proofs acquire a foundational role with regard to faith; faith now became fully founded on them and more and more colored by them. A good survey of the classic proofs in contemporary analytic philosophy of religion is found in, for example, Davis 1997. Spitzer (2010), among others, shows that this tradition is not fully past, as is also clear from the many studies of Richard Swinburne. He suggests that the various arguments have cumulative force, that is, each of them has only a limited significance, but they reinforce each other and together make it more probable that God exists than that he does not (see, in particular, Swinburne 2004). A contemporary version of the cosmological argument led a prominent atheistic philosopher to abandon atheism in the final phase of his life, to start believing in (a) God and to accept the possibility of revelation; see Flew and Varghese 2007. Very instructive with regard to the person-related and instrumental character of the proofs is Mavrodes 1970, 22–35. At an earlier stage Ian Ramsey (1957, esp. 61–80) underlined this deeply personal character of arguments for God by arguing that, for example, the causal and teleological arguments, like other instances of religious language, are evocative rather than demonstrative: they are aimed at evoking a "disclosure" of God. Sudduth (2009) shows that even the Reformed tradition did not reject the arguments for God's existence, provided that they were based on our faith and not regarded as its absolute foundation. As early as Calvin, we find the thought that faith has its only source in the Word of God, but that arguments may nonetheless have a supportive role.

6. Apart from the fact that, viewed objectively (i.e., without presupposing the truth of the Christian faith), we may point to some arguments that plead for its intellectual credibility, we may also uncover major prob-

47

lems in alternative worldviews. Some feel this approach is even more important. Alvin Plantinga (b. 1932), for instance, is of the opinion that Christian faith does not need to be proven but that it is meaningful to critically evaluate the main competitors. For that reason Plantinga has focused on an analysis of the problems that are connected with the most widespread competitors of the Christian faith, namely, forms of naturalism. This kind of critical analysis is especially important in situations where the competing worldview has gradually become the standard view in a society, that is, the worldview that is regarded as the norm (e.g., in the media), needing no further justification. This is now the case in major parts of the Western world (esp. in the academic world) with regard to naturalism. For those who see themselves as vacillating between a religious and a secular faith, it can be helpful to put to the test—with critical and astute observations—the widespread idea that a secular worldview such as naturalism is self-evident.

Naturalism is, roughly speaking, the worldview that assumes there are only natural causes for all that happens in the cosmos, which means that there is no God or any other supernatural power. For a recent version of Plantinga's criticism, see Plantinga 2011, 307–50. From a much more cultural-historical and cultural-sociological perspective, Charles Taylor (2007) also discusses in *A Secular Age* the credentials of the Christian faith in relationship with its main competitors, in particular, naturalism (which he refers to as antihumanism) and humanism. Of special interest with Taylor is that, contrary to Plantinga, he takes seriously the conditions of modernity (e.g., the desire for autonomy and authenticity) but, at the same time, concludes that the worldview thus engendered cannot be separated from the realm of the transcendent, that is, from faith in God.

Those who opt for this route must in all honesty also face the arguments that are brought against the Christian faith. Some of them are quite formal and sound rather artificial and will convince very few. Others, however, have a broad appeal with respect to widely shared experiences and prove more powerful. Undoubtedly, the strongest of these arguments centers on the problem of evil, which we will discuss later in this book (in particular in chap. 8, about sin).

A frontal attack on the reasonableness of religious faith is found in the writings of Herman Philipse (2012). Philipse's criticism of religion is ingenious, but also rather technical and artificial, and it will, as a result, probably convince very few people. Principally, Philipse enters the discussion only within the framework of what he calls *rational theology* or *natural theology*, that is to say, "on the basis of premises that non-believers will be able to endorse, or without appealing to the alleged authority of a revelation" (14). However, Philipse presupposes a fundamentalist concept of revelation that ignores the common understanding of revelation as involving experiences of God and faith that take a hold on those who have them. These experiences are transformational and lead, not just to the acceptance of a certain number of propositions, but rather to a totally different approach to things, a different way of facing life. In the discussion about the (un) reasonableness of faith, believers cannot simply put those experiences in brackets, just as secular people cannot do so with experiences that lead them to reject faith. The interpretation of texts and the weighing of arguments are never done neutrally and objectively but always from a particular perspective (or paradigm, to use a term from the theory of science). Such a worldview perspective is not set in concrete, but at the same time one cannot be simply detached from it; it will always have to be taken it into account. Since Philipse is not prepared to carry on the discussion in this manner, his arguments remain shallow and often (e.g., when he deals with the resurrection of Christ, 170–82) repetitive. Those who read Philipse's debate with Richard Swinburne (his most important theistic partner in this dialogue) with some background in church history will frequently be reminded of the duel between Celsus and Origen in the second and third century. Admittedly, this discussion must constantly be taken up by Christians in order to prevent, in the famous words of Schleiermacher (1981, from his second letter to his disciple Lücke, 1829), the knot of history from being so unraveled that Christianity is associated with barbarism and science with unbelief. However, one should not have too many positive expectations from such a debate, since the decision whether to believe in God can never take place on a purely theoretical level.

We think that Philipse is more influential when he appeals to the sentiment broadly shared in Western society that, in the final analysis, science and faith cannot be combined. However, this view is under much attack in the current science-and-religion debate, especially from a historical point of view (e.g., Harrison 2015) and appears untenable on further analysis (note the arguments in Plantinga 2011, esp. 65–125). It should be stated, however, that Philipse's atheism is less problematic for faith than so-called agnosticism (Houtepen 2002) or so-called apatheism, that is, the posture of religious indifferentism. The broad indifference with respect to religious questions that has spread over Europe in a way unprecedented in history can be blamed only on a superficial approach to life. Atheism may well be preferred, for although it does not share in the answer given by faith, it does take the question about the existence of God (or, the Absolute) to be essential and inevitable (see Berkhof, CF 9).

49

7. Suppose that God's existence might be proven in a way that would convince most people. In such a situation, one could no longer claim that proof for God's existence is lacking. There would no longer be any reason to ask God for more clarity. But would more people choose to believe as a result? That would remain to be seen. In the religious sense of the word, faith is not only, not even primarily, giving assent to certain truth claims (e.g., the claim that God exists), but first and foremost an attitude toward life—an existential turning toward God that gives our existence a fundamental and abiding orientation toward him. If God were to give an overwhelming proof for his existence (if this were possible, considering the remarks we made above), this situation would result only in a faith that is forced upon us by the facts. It would be the kind of faith that James ascribes to the demons (James 2:19), who believe in God (i.e., they are convinced that he exists) but have certainly not entered into a positive relationship with him. Faith that follows from such "hard evidence" differs crucially from faith in the real sense of the word: a trusting commitment to God that is accompanied by a sense of wonder, respect, and love. This true faith represents much more than a rational conviction. It allows us to be touched in an existential way that cultivates our desire to live for God.

Rational arguments may often be manipulated in a certain direction, which leads to the question of whether our hesitation or refusal to believe in God may often not be primarily motivated by an unwillingness to enter into a faith commitment—in biblical parlance, by the choice of the human heart (Prov 23:26).

In post-Reformation scholastic theology we find in this connection some interesting refinements of the concept of faith. The most important distinction is between "historical" faith (*fides historica*) and "saving" faith (*fides salvifica*). The former is the conviction of certain truths about God, the latter is the kind of faith that brings us into a right relationship with God. In this view historical faith is not without value, but *fides salvifica*, which cannot be enforced by any kind of proof (see Luke 16:31, to which we already referred), is essential. See Heppe, RD 20.32.

8. Finally, it remains very much a question whether the God whose existence we want to establish with the classic proofs may be identified with the God of Israel, whom the followers of Jesus began to worship, in the spirit of their Lord, as "our Father." In the most favorable case, the proofs for God's existence focus on one particular aspect of God: his transcendence. The God who is the conclusion of the ontological, cosmological, and teleological arguments is the highest Being, which, as

first cause of everything and in harmony with its providential character, leads to their purpose. But these arguments tell us nothing about Jesus Christ or about such matters as the incarnation, the atonement, and the Trinity—despite the New Testament presenting the true identity of God only in the person and the work of Jesus: "No one has ever seen God; the only Son, who is in the bosom of the Father, he has made him known" (John 1:18).

Of course, one could say that being able to discover a part of God's identity through a good use of our intellect is a positive thing in itself, modest as it may be. The problem is that this part that can be proven may easily receive greater weight than the unexpected things that hold central place in the New Testament, such as God's becoming human in Christ to provide salvation, the Spirit's wanting to convince us of this truth, and so forth. This exact problem appeared in the seventeenth and eighteenth centuries, when the Christian faith was increasingly founded on the proofs of his existence: God became more and more the far-away Being who somewhere pushes the buttons. It was precisely this God that became increasingly the object of severe philosophical criticism in European culture. This criticism began rather modestly with Kant, who believed that we, as limited human beings, greatly overestimate our epistemological capabilities when we think we can prove the existence of a transcendent God. It became more vicious and more widespread with the great masters of suspicion: Ludwig Feuerbach (1804-72), Karl Marx (1818-83), Friedrich Nietzsche (1844-1900), and Sigmund Freud (1856-1939). And it led in the twentieth century to a massive secularization. One might ask whether the venom of the critics of religion (apart from Nietzsche, whose criticism was all-encompassing) was, in fact, directed against the God of the Bible, for his actions are characterized by a loving compassion for human beings. The criticism of religion was primarily intent on dealing with the "God of the philosophers," who could supposedly be proven, a Supreme Being who rigidly and impassively controls everything from the top of the pyramid. It could well be that the theologians who in the modern era based their faith on their intellect, that is, on the proofs for God's existence, rather than simply on the Bible, thereby introduced a Trojan horse into the citadel of faith. For in so doing, the Christian faith—though far different in nature from philosophical theism—was placed in the firing line of the criticism aimed at the latter.

On the Protestant side, this line of thought was further elaborated by Eberhard Jüngel (b. 1934); see especially his magnum opus, Jüngel 1983, in which he presents the Christian faith (as faith in the Crucified One) as a third way between (philosophical) theism and atheism. In the Catholic tradition a similar analysis is given by Michael Buckley (1987, another classic). For developments in the seventeenth century, see especially the instructive and accessible study of Placher (1996, esp. 164-78, "The Marginalization of the Trinity"). Earlier, the influential Dutch theologian K. H. Miskotte (VW 8:10-49) pointed to the dialectical relationship between religion and atheism/nihilism. If, on the basis of widespread religious ideas, one starts theologically by applying various all-words to God, rather than beginning with the special revelation of the Name, one prepares the way for atheism. A God who as an all-seeing eye looks down upon us and who, being almighty (seen as an unqualified power with respect to good and evil), makes us experience all kinds of things, will sooner or later evoke resistance and disgust. But atheism proves to be so empty and barren that the vacuum will soon be filled again by the old gods in new garments. The pendular movement can be stopped only by a theological emphasis on divine revelation. Note that the "proof for God" that we prefer (see above, point 5) is based on the story of the Bible and is not prior to it.

For all these reasons it is inadvisable to try to lay a foundation for Christian theology along some line of evidence that methodologically precedes the content of our faith. Christian theology itself, however, will look for good reasons that may elicit faith in fields where it may be given a place and made intelligible. This effort is in line with the ideal we mentioned in chapter 1: *fides quaerens intellectum*. Faith itself seeks understanding and insight. It does not regard it an honor to be identified as the ultimate form of unreasonableness and impossibility, as some like to suggest, appealing to a statement of Tertullian (ca. 160-ca. 220): *credo quia absurdum* (I believe because it is absurd)—a statement that is an erratic blind alley in Tertullian's work rather than a main characteristic of his theology).

The rest of this chapter must therefore be read in the light of *fides quaerens intellectum*. We refer to a number of aspects of reality, or domains besides reason, where our faith may break through and by which it may be formed. There are many such domains, which indicates that the Christian faith by no means hangs on one thin thread. It may rather be compared to a broom, which rests on a bundle of bristles. The broom gets its strength from a collection of fibers that may not all be visible separately. Most of them we hardly notice, yet they give support to the broom. It will continue to function, even if some of the bristles are worn or have fallen out. The faith of most people is similar. It exists, but they cannot precisely list all the factors on which it rests. At times believers can tell us something about what has become important for them, but often they cannot. Faith belongs to the "slow" things in human existence; we are not conscious of many of them, just as an iceberg is mostly below the water level. Nonetheless, people can often tell us something. They believe because they may have had an experience of God or have lived through a series of events that have put a stamp on their life story. Others point to the great mystics; others again, to the church and its rituals, its buildings, or its hymns. Augustine tells us that the sermons of Ambrose of Milan (ca. 333–97) made a deep impression on him, and even today sermons are often the means that put people on the track of faith. For some, the faith and life of a colleague have been decisive. One's family setting or work environment may be the domain where faith is nourished. Others point to nature or to the Bible as the places where their wonderment emerged and where God made himself known. For most people, faith rests on a combination of such grounds. These grounds, and the domains where they are found, are diverse and dissimilar.

In the remainder of this chapter our strategy is to increasingly narrow down these domains of reality from those that are very broad to those that relate more explicitly and specifically to the Christian faith. Later on in the book we will return to several of these domains and expand our remarks. For instance, here we touch on the role of the cosmos. We discuss in more detail the theological significance of that domain in chapter 6, on creation; the importance of the faith community is further explored in chapter 14, on the church.

2.3. The World as a Trace of God

We start with a broad domain of reality that for centuries was pointed to as the domain where God in some way may be found, namely, the creation. The reason is rather obvious. If God is the Creator of heaven and earth, we would expect the world to reflect its Maker in certain ways, to bear his stamp. We begin with a well-known (and for some, a notorious) example from the Belgic Confession of Faith. Article 2 starts as follows:

> We know God by two means: First, by the creation, preservation, and government of the universe, since that universe is before our eyes like a beautiful book in which all creatures, great and small, are as letters to make us ponder the invisible things of God: God's eternal power

and divinity, as the apostle Paul says in Rom 1:20. All these things are enough to convict humans and leave them without excuse. (OF 26–27).

This article states explicitly that God makes his power and divine nature known in the creation. This statement contrasts sharply with the everyday experience and conviction of many people today. In Western culture faith in God is not something that is automatically called forth by the earthly reality that surrounds us. In historical perspective, however, we find that this situation is quite recent. Until the middle of the nineteenth century, faith in God as the supreme power was broadly anchored in Western culture. Natural knowledge of God was an awareness that was generally shared, and faith in God was perceived as a matter of looking around with open eyes and drawing the appropriate conclusions. Those who opened their eyes inevitably concluded that there is a Creator who is the causal agent, the goal, and the architect of the edifice of humanity and the world. It was supposed that an awareness of God was innate (as the Stoics thought—for instance, Cicero). This idea was further developed in various ways. Thus Thomas Aquinas concluded in his *quinque viae* (five ways) that there had to be some ultimate authority. He deduced this position from the existence of movement, causality, contingency, degrees of goodness and beauty, and purpose, concluding that we call this authority God.

When we formulate this idea a little more precisely, we must say that tradition usually distinguished two moments in the natural knowledge of God (*theologia naturalis*): the *cognitio insita* (the innate knowledge of God, also referred to by Calvin as the *sensus divinitatis*, the sense of the divine) and the *cognitio acquisita* (the acquired knowledge of God). We are born with the former; the latter arises when we look around at creation and thereby acquire a direct, unequivocal impression of God's power and majesty. The two forms of natural knowledge of God are not separate from, but impact, each other: the slumbering innate knowledge of God—probably a vague awareness more than explicit knowledge—is triggered and reinforced when one experiences the world as God's creation.

In Scholasticism the *cognitio acquisita* received a very pronounced elaboration in the form of the a posteriori (i.e., derived from experience) proofs for God's existence. But both forms of natural knowledge of God are, in principle, detached from human reason; one does not need to have a certain IQ to grasp convoluted arguments to feel an instant admiration and respect for the creation when one sees the rugged mountain ranges—and thereby also to become convinced of God's existence. In that sense the domain of the world definitely differs from that of reason. For this and related points, see Heppe, RD 4.5; Bavinck, RD 4:126–32; Muller, PRRD 1:167–77; and especially Pannenberg, ST 1:76, 107–19.

As we saw, Immanuel Kant demolished the self-evident nature of the classic proofs for God. It should be noted, however, that he did have great respect for the teleological argument and no less for the moral argument. Kant saw the goal-orientedness of reality and our indubitable moral awareness as powerful arguments for the existence of God as the goal and the provider of meaning for life, on the one hand, and, on the other, for God as the giver of the moral law. It is perhaps impossible to have theoretical or scientific knowledge of God in the same way that we acquire knowledge about the things that exist in time and space, but the idea (or, in Kant's terminology, the postulate) of God is indispensable for humanity and true civilization. Nonetheless we must localize God, especially, within the "realm of freedom" (i.e., the human spirit) and not in an extension of the "realm of nature."

Other developments, such as the rise of Darwinian evolutionary theory, with its idea of the endless struggle for survival in nature, also led to loss in our contemporary culture of the almost self-evident way in which the Belgic Confession connects God with the world. A naturalistic climate has increasingly become dominant in the scientific world, which now typically rejects any grounds or reasons other than those that can be verified and, preferably, are open to repetition.

Liberal theology after 1850 reacted to the new cultural situation by making a rigorous separation between the natural sciences and the humanities. This step led to a practical and theoretical dualism: God is not a thing among other things but is of a completely different order. The natural sciences do not have the instruments to trace God. In contrast, the humanities and theology focus on humans as beings with spirit and freedom. Faith, the arts, and morality demand some other kind of reasonableness that does not fit with the measuring, weighing, and counting of the scientific approach. It is part of the nature of faith that we sense ourselves to be the object of a touch, a drawing near, an event that escapes our grasp. These notions were developed in the nineteenth century under the influence of Friedrich Schleiermacher and Wilhelm Dilthey (1833–1911) and were further refined in the twentieth century when God was detached not only from nature but also from the human spirit. God does not coincide with human spiritual life, as the pre–World War I theo-

IS THERE A GOD?

logians thought, but was quite distinct from it. God presents himself in an event (*Geschehen, Geschichte*), but such presentation does not bring him into our grasp, and therefore we are unable to manipulate him. Karl Barth, in particular, pointed to this latter aspect—manipulating God for our own ideological goals—as such a great danger that he resolutely abandoned natural theology, the tradition that believed it could draw at least a dotted line toward the reality of God.

Accepting this practical and theological dualism as its point of departure, Christian theology in modern times has taken the view that faith in God cannot be forced upon us on the basis of empirical reality. A good example of one holding this view is Eberhard Jüngel, who speaks about the "nonnecessity" of God. By this word he does not mean that faith in God is unimportant. On the contrary, God is and remains "the mystery of the world." God's nonnecessity points to a surplus. Inside the circle of the light of faith, things receive a significance and a brightness that is not on the outside. People do not become believers on the basis of arguments of necessity. Believing in God is something totally different than needing him to close the gaps in our empirical knowledge. The latter would imply the presupposition that we can find a route from our reality toward God, or climb a ladder that would reach God. The uniqueness of faith, however, is precisely the surprise of God's coming from the other side. Faith recognizes God's revelation as a gift that presents itself to us in freedom. Faith, therefore, is not primarily a rational exercise but an experience of being known, of being found and being spoken to.

The uniqueness of faith as a gift and a surprise is found in a broad range of thinkers. In his GMW, Jüngel has worked out this phenomenology of faith in an impressive way. Faith goes beyond the contrast between chance and necessity. It positions itself as a contingent givenness, evoked by God's presenting himself in the history of Jesus. We find similar thoughts with such Dutch theologians as Miskotte and Noordmans. Referring to the Old Testament, Miskotte suggests (VW 8:151-55) that God's revelation occurs "groundless in our midst," that is, revelation is contingent and comes to us by surprise: "Where does YHWH suddenly come from?" (153). There was no ground, no cause in the world, from which we could argue our way toward him. He suddenly announced himself in the midst of history. Noordmans stated that faith is a "distinct element" in life. That is, God cannot be deduced from something else; he is no extension of our rational faculties but positions himself in freedom (VW 2:238-39). The notion of a donation or gift also plays a crucial role in the work of contemporary philosophers who proclaim "the end of metaphysics," in particular of those who operate in the phenomenological tradition of E. Husserl, M. Heidegger, and others and who subsequently made the so-called theological turn, such as J. Caputo and especially J.-L. Marion. About them, see, for example, Henriksen 2009. It thus seems that we here find an important interface between contemporary theology and philosophy.

The recognition of the nonnecessity of God does certainly not imply God's nonexistence. The proposition of God's nonnecessity aims primarily to emphasize that the terminology of causality and necessity evokes associations that could easily lead us astray, namely, that God is "good for something" and must therefore be noticed as we think and look around us. Moreover, this terminology falls short of the personal terms that the Bible employs when speaking of God. In our culture we cannot without impunity pretend to speak of God in the deepest sense when we speak of him in general ontological language, calling him, for example, the Transcendent or the Absolute. When Jesus teaches his disciples to address God as "our Father," we understand that this personal language far exceeds the notion of causality (*causa*). The word "Father" does not deny the causal relationship between God and humanity, but it focuses, rather, on the protective and caring nature of his fatherhood.

It is a matter of debate whether the notion of causality (that God is the necessary beginning of the world) is still useful in contemporary theology in view of its scientific connotation. Jüngel responds negatively to this question, arguing that the concept of *causa* is so far removed from the meaning that the Christian faith attaches to God's fatherhood and his love that Christian theology would be advised not to use it any longer. By way of contrast, however, Pannenberg in his entire apologetic theology tries to secure a place for this notion (see his ST 1:63–118). Recall what we discussed earlier in this chapter about the new appreciation for the teleological argument, discovered in the anthropic principle, or the fine-tuning of the universe. Something similar is true of the cosmological argument that there must be a first cause (Rutten 2012). We conclude that causal considerations do have their use in the prolegomena, but at most can be regarded only as auxiliary; they may evoke faith but cannot serve as its foundation. Those who put the full weight of faith and theology on these arguments will easily overplay their hand (i.e., from a scientific perspective it is not necessary to see God as the cause of the world) and will also obscure the personal character of the God of Israel, the Father of Jesus Christ.

Even though faith cannot be extracted from the reality that surrounds us, we should not think of faith as simply arbitrary. Faith is no irrational jump into the deep. When we look at the world from the angle of faith, we inevitably find traces of God and feel that we can make more sense of it all than can those who look at reality from another perspective.

For this reason, apologists even in the second century saw traces of Jesus Christ, the Logos, in the world; they spoke in this connection of the *logos spermatikos*, literally, the scattered word. They maintained that, despite all forms of error and distorted knowledge of God, the eternal Word, which according to John 1 was with God from eternity, was present everywhere in reality as a seed. In other words, God's wisdom, goodness, and greatness can be found in the order, structure, and trustworthiness of this reality, even though these attributes may have been distorted by thinkers and poets. The great Christian thinkers, each in their own way, tried to maintain the positive link between Creator and creation. To state it differently, they recognized that this reality, in spite of sin and evil, bears the stamp of God's goodness. That is also the gist of article 2 of the Belgic Confession, which was quoted above. God not only is the origin of the reality that surrounds us but also has left his traces in it.

In the early church this idea was especially articulated through the concept of the Logos as the connecting link between God and the world. For Augustine the creation is an expression of God's thoughts; traces of it may be found even in the Trinity. We find this intrinsically Platonic mode of thinking also with Aquinas. In late medieval theology (from Dun Scotus onward) the relationship between creation and God's will became more dominant. God's choice for this ordering from among a multitude of possibilities ensures that the reality was a result of his will and thus was given in freedom. The order and structure of reality thus remained a mirror of God's will and design. The Enlightenment with its concept of natural religion only further accentuated this approach.

Only in twentieth-century theology did the idea that creation points directly to the Creator come under heavy attack. In his *Römerbrief* Karl Barth dismissed the idea of a direct line between God and the origin of this world. Also Dutch theologians such as K. H. Miskotte (1894-1976), O. Noordmans and, more recently, A. van de Beek (b. 1946) are very critical of attempts to look for traces of God in the empirical reality around us. They feel that this reality has been so deeply spoiled by evil that there may at best remain only a dotted line. Barth proposed early on that the cross is the only place where it becomes visible that this world is God's world (Barth, ER 159-61, 221; R2 218-21, 386). This theme was also touched upon by Dietrich Bonhoeffer (1906–45) in his famous prison letters ("God consents to be pushed out of the world and onto the cross; God is weak and powerless in the world and in precisely this way, and only so, he is at our side and helps us," letter dated July 16, 1944; WDB 8:479) and was further worked out by Jürgen Moltmann in a "theology of the cross." Nowadays, similar thoughts are voiced by thinkers in the area of faith and science (e.g., Southgate 2008, 48–52, 56–59, 75–77). The cross is the place where we discover that this world belongs to God. For it is the place, not just where God judges all our deeds, but also where he shares in the suffering of this world and takes it upon himself. In this line of thinking there is thus no direct relationship between this world and God; there is only a broken link that runs through judgment and cross. Paradoxically, however, precisely in its suffering and evil the world still points to the Christian faith—and even to its very heart, namely, the cross of Christ!

In contrast, we find an increasing number of more philosophically inclined thinkers who plead for greater continuity in our understanding of the relationship between God and the world. Thus Paul Tillich defined God as the ground of being and even as being itself (ST 1:235), the foundation that grounds this world and all its questions. A recent, very pronounced elaboration of this view of continuity is found in the thesis that certain phenomena in the world unmistakably testify of intelligent design (ID). Supporters of this view argue that a look at nature should convince us that nature depends on an intelligent designer. This view led to intense discussion in the period 2005–10. Its opponents feared that this idea would once again make faith in God dependent on compelling rational proof, and some supporters of ID indeed felt the need for this level of proof. However, as we pointed out in 2.2 (para. 5), "proofs" are inevitably relative to the individual person and have a character that is instrumental rather than inescapable. Just as in the domain of reason, it is impossible to discover the ground for Christian faith in the world. Yet, it is possible to draw some dotted, "cross-shaped" lines that suggest to us that the world is not a quirk of fate but belongs to God.

2.4. The Complex Domain of Experience

Another important source or domain that is linked to Christian faith and that allows us to allot faith its place is that of human experience and the explanation of such experience. In general, one might say that the answer to the question of why one should believe Christian theology lies in the experience that human beings have had in their history, both individually and corporately as a community. However, the concept of experience is rather complex, as it can refer to different things. We need to be more precise as to what kind of experience, and whose experience, we are speaking of. We may have past or present experiences in mind. They may concern our own life history (such as dreams, as many Christians who have converted from Islam relate) or experiences of a miraculous escape. However, they may also transcend the personal realm, such as experiences with rituals, architecture, the arts, and music. For these areas often offer access to a reality that is experienced as higher than that which can be measured and weighed. Finally, to make things even more complicated, our experiences never stand in isolation but are embedded in interpretation. The theologian Edward Schillebeeckx (1914–2009) stated that experience is always *interpreted* experience. Long-existing experiences are the mold that explain and shape new experiences, and both mutually influence each other.

We notice this relation in the Bible, as was stated by the Old Testament scholar Gerhard von Rad (1901–71) and many of those who were inspired by him. For example, when the New Testament testifies that Jesus rose from the dead, it uses an existing concept. Isaiah and Ezekiel spoke of the resurrection of the dead as the eschatological (end time) act of God. Jesus meeting his disciples as the Living One was an astounding event, but it could somehow be interpreted and given its place in accordance with this Old Testament concept. Of course, the New Testament gives a new interpretation to this expectation: namely, it does not apply to the entire nation, but to the Living One. Experience is thus always accompanied by some explanation, with interpretation on the basis of earlier concepts. However, these earlier concepts are adapted and reinterpreted in the process.

Emphasis on the all-encompassing role of interpretation can give rise to the suggestion that experiences of the divine are merely constructions of the human spirit on the basis of preexisting concepts. Even God himself then becomes a construction of the human spirit and the imagination. This constructivism has been rather popular of late (e.g., in the later work of H. M. Kuitert), but the argument is strongly reductionist and ultimately self-defeating. For consistency would demand that we regard our own constructivism as itself a construction of the human spirit, but the recognition of the need for human interpretation can, without any problem, be tied to the recognition that what we receive in our experience has substance because it has to do with real events. Von Rad saw real events as the ground of a flow of history in which the meaning of those events was continuously proclaimed and was, through new acts of God, constantly re-interpreted in a range of new traditions. New experiences thus lead to a new understanding and adaptation of old concepts. An extreme example is the census by David. In one instance (2 Sam 24:1), God himself is the instigator, but a later reinterpretation attributes that role to Satan (1 Chr 21:1). Often the shift is less dramatic, such as in the case of the resurrection: the encounters with the living Lord after Jesus's death on the cross lead to a reinterpretation of the concept of resurrection. For a short survey, see Schillebeeckx 2014, 9–16, and for the various layers of the concept of experience, see Berkhof, CF 55–60.

Since the last few decades of the twentieth century, the appeal to re-ligious experience as the ground of theology has reemerged. Experience is contrasted with logical reasoning, with an authoritarian proclamation of the Word, and with a dogmatic tradition. We speak of a theology of experience when the concept of experience becomes the fundamental category of theology.

Friedrich Schleiermacher is the great example in modern times of a theologian of experience. He argued that systematic theology finds its object in human re-ligious experience. The religious experience of the present becomes the ground of faith and the object of theology. According to Schleiermacher, systematic the-ology is in fact derived from human piety. However, Schleiermacher did not see this relation as a purely individual matter. He regarded the Christian community as the place where people are connected in many different ways and are together guided by God's Spirit (*Gemeingeist*). This community functions as a bridge over time by which we, in the present, are in touch with the perfect divine conscious-ness of Jesus. Concepts like sin, grace, and sanctification are in fact experiences that have been poured into words and thoughts. The merit of this approach is that Schleiermacher permits every believer to participate with his or her own experi-ences. God is not just a concept, a valuable thought or moral conviction, but may be found in the immediate life experience of each human being. In our primary link with the universe we are already connected with the mystery of the divine.

In the nineteenth century Schleiermacher's proposal found widespread support and is currently regaining popularity. God is not simply a concept or something at a great distance but is the ground with which we are connected. We might call this immanentism. The risk of this theology is quite apparent. When God is to be sought in our own experience, he may easily become identified with it, with our experience, collective or individual, being presented as the voice of God. The lack of clarity regarding a norm or critical criterion is the weak point of this approach.

In Schleiermacher's track we may today point to another domain of the human spirit besides that of theoretical reasoning. In a time when God is no longer sought in the order of things, in causality, the domain of emotions is the place where we experience God as the secret of the world. Affection, indignation, anger, nostalgia, delight, disgust, or anxiety—these are affections or emotions with which we react to what we experience. They may be just a different road to our reality, as a mystery that we can never fully fathom, but they nonetheless make us into what we are. When we are overcome by an experience of beauty or vulnerability, we are, as it were, touched by something we cannot arrange for ourselves. It is gifted to us. Desire, trust, resistance, bewilderment, and astonishment may be discovered as contemporary approaches to God (see Houtepen 2002). These experiences do not stand on their own but may, through faith, be understood as signals that point beyond themselves.

Or do we, with that reference to God, jump to an imaginary world, one that is only the product of our fantasy? This objection to the projection theory can never be fully answered rationally. But in contrast with that theory, faith in God positions itself as a unique kind of experience, one that we do not so much construct but one that overpowers us. That there is more, that we might speak rather of an experience of perceiving meaning rather than of giving meaning, is a faith interpretation that sees how things fall into place.

Consider two examples on this point:

1. In an almost forgotten but beautiful apologetic piece, H. Berkhof (1979) related how he once shared four basic existential experiences with his atheistic colleague R. F. Beerling: awe for the mystery of life, dismay about the horrors of our reality, a sense of duty to act in ways that show how things can be different and better, and hope that such acts will prove not to be meaningless. Berkhof remarked that, in his own life, there was, almost unnoticeably, a fifth existential aspect: that of *faith*, the trust that the deepest intentions of this life will at last be realized. Berkhof linked this faith to the salvific event that we find in the Bible. This fifth aspect does not annul the first four existential experiences but relativizes them and inspires him to allow himself in the present to be led by God's final intentions. "I feel that I grow toward my destiny" (243). Berkhof then en passant asked whether Beerling had any idea what this fifth existential experience might be. For, in a way, he had already gone four-fifths down the road of faith.

2. Once upon a time there were twins, two boys, who had just been conceived and were growing in the dark of the womb. They developed and became

conscious of each other and of their environment. They laughed and said: "How marvelous that we were conceived! How great that we are alive!"

Together they began their discovery of the world in which they lived. When they discovered their umbilical cord, they were happy: "Look, our mother loves us so much that she shares her life with us!"

Weeks turned to months. The boys saw how they were changing dramatically. "What does this mean?" one of them asked.

"If this continues, it must mean that there will be an end to our stay in this world," the other said.

"But I do not want to leave," the first one said, "I want to stay here forever."

"We have no choice," the second one replied. "Maybe there is life after birth."

"But how can there then be life? It would mean that we would have to cut the umbilical cord, and how could we live without this connection with our mother? We do see evidence that others have been here before us but not that anyone has ever returned to tell us there is life after birth. This must be the end!" This first twin became increasingly desperate and distraught. "If conception ends in birth, what, then, is the purpose of the womb? It is meaningless. Maybe there is no mother after all."

"But there must be a mother," the other objected, "for how else did we get here? How else did we stay alive?"

"But have you ever seen our mother?" the first one retorted. "Maybe she exists only in our imagination. Maybe we just constructed her in our thoughts because we liked the feeling it gives us."

And so their final days in the womb were full of anxiety and desperation. But at last came the day of birth. When the boys, not without difficulty, had left their world, they opened their eyes and cried out of pure joy. What they saw went far beyond their wildest expectations. (For Henri Nouwen's telling of this popular story, see Nouwen 1994, 19-20.)

We believe that the importance of this kind of fundamental, existential question for apologetics and for the discourse of faith is often greatly underestimated. Far more than all kinds of rational considerations, they make people sense what Christian faith is about and that it must be a real option. They not only appeal to our intellect but touch the deeper layers of our being. And the spark may just catch on. When hit by an arrow from the other shore, we are aware that we are seen, that we are the object of concern, are judged, loved, and placed in a perspective of hope. Yet, not even in such experiences may we search for the ground of faith; they do not prove anything and do not eliminate faith as being accompanied by a turning in the direction of God (i.e., conversion). But they do give us some touches, some invitations, that may be the start of a new way of approaching life. Those who are open to these taps on our shoulder (see 1 Kgs 19:5) will find how they place all earlier experiences in another light—the light of faith.

Once again we conclude that the truth of faith cannot be proven, but that the experience of faith can be described and is not meaningless. It may be the basis on which we can invite others to have their own experiences. The shift in subject is characteristic for the structure of the faith experience. (That is, I am not the one who determines, but I am being determined and am seen.) In this receptivity, however, we are not passive but quite active. Still, these formal statements are an abstraction of what is received in faith; its substance has to do with salvation and grace. Roman Catholic theology tends to define the experience of the divine as a fundamental ground, as some kind of hidden foundation, while Protestant theology prefers to describe it as an external movement toward humanity.

2.5. Christian Faith and the Phenomenon of Religion

Does the Christian faith point to religion? In the first part of this chapter we stated that it is not self-evident that the phenomenon of religion leads to Christian theology. It does not mean we should totally ignore religion in general or the relationship between Christianity and the other religions, however, for religion is part of human experience. Therefore we shall make a few remarks in this section about the relationship between Christianity and religion in general. In 5.6 below we will deal more specifically with the relationship between Christianity and the other main religions.

By far the largest part of humanity lives with a religious awareness and considers itself to be believers, that is, as being connected with a transcendent reality. In that light it should be unbelief (i.e., the non-religious worldview), not belief, that ought to called to account for its position. Globally, a relatively small minority claims to be nonreligious. Nonetheless, this widespread religiosity does not allow us to assume an immediate bridge to the Christian faith. Religion per se does not provide self-evident access to understanding what the Christian faith is about and what constitutes its content. In fact, the Christian has a rather torn and difficult relationship with religion as a general human phenomenon. Of course, the Christian faith is one religion among many and must be studied as such. But when we ask for the grounds of Christian faith, it soon appears that it occupies a unique position. When we describe religion in brief as involvement with an all-encompassing and all-determining reality, a fundamental question immediately arises. *Where* does this all-encompassing and all-determining reality manifest itself, and what is the nature of our involvement with it? In nature religions the determining reality coincides with the world itself; nature is seen as divine and omnipresent. The problem with the so-called revealed religions (Judaism, Christianity, and Islam) is that revelation no longer coincides with the world but with the messages of prophets as mediators of revelation. And thus categories like commandment and covenant play a role. Moreover, Judaism and Christianity occupy an even more particular position, since they refer to the election of Israel or, in the case of Christianity, to the person of Jesus Christ and his ministry. This particularity differs from the normal pattern in the world of religion.

In the context of the revealed religions just mentioned, the world loses its automatic divine status. A general religious experience is now judged by something external. This desacralization has had enormous consequences in the Western world. The world lost its divine character; it was "emptied." It became accessible to experimental and, later, scientific research that would prove to be a great blessing. At the same time, it opened a vacuum that would be occupied by new powers and entities claiming to be decisive or authoritative. Think of modern science as a determining power, or of ideologies that claim to offer an all-encompassing explanation and interpretation of life: liberalism, capitalism, Marxism, national socialism, the idea of progress, consumerism, and other isms. We might also add Nietzsche's nihilism. He followed the logic of the secularization of the world and concluded that henceforth we would have to look after ourselves. Instead of seeing ourselves as small and dependent on God, or instead of embracing a lofty ideal of what it means to be human (Plato), we must heroically take our fate into our own hands; we must be strong and courageous and accept life in its full vitality. Such is the birth of the *Übermensch*. K. H. Miskotte has described nihilism and the loss of a religious view of life as two phenomena that are dialectically connected; again and again the one evokes the other, and old gods continue to return in new garments.

Miskotte differentiates between three basic phenomenological types: pagans, who regard nature as divine; Jews, who, through a revelation of the Name, have been called to obedience to God and whose relationship with nature has forever been broken; and Christians, who know of the Name and of atonement but who always face the risk of falling back into paganism.

H.-M. Barth (D) offers an example of a Christian dogmatics that develops a consistent comparison with other religions. For an approach from the angle of comparative theology, see Keith Ward's (1994-2000) tetralogy on God and revelation, God and creation, God and human nature, and God and community.

The process of desacralization poses an enormous challenge for Christian theology. It makes it impossible to point to a world that is divine in nature; instead, it must point to a revelation in the past (the gift of the covenant and the law, the prophets, the mission of Jesus Christ, the gift of the Spirit) that is historical in nature and represented in the present through the ministry of the church. This arrangement implies a drastic reduction of the grounds to which Christian theology can refer. The truth of the gospel cannot at all times and all places be called forth and made available by mystical experience, esoteric induction, or practice. Such attempts will almost inevitably lead to malformation and confusion.

In short, we do not deny that human religious awareness may be a road toward the Christian faith. It may help us in our sincere search for God. But we remember Calvin's observation that the religious urge, the *sensus divinitatis*, may come to the front much more often in explicit or subtle perversions of the way in which God has made himself known. In a culture that manifests a widespread interest in the cohesiveness of life (holism, spirituality, esoteric movements), Christian faith is confronted with many difficulties, just as the imageless faith in YHWH faced major challenges in Israel. Both have, at first glance, less to point to. Nature religions and the esoteric live from what is always at hand; in contrast, the Judeo-Christian tradition points to what is not at hand. It invites us to learn from what is invisible. It posits an intrinsic relationship with a specific tradition, with a faith community that meets together around sacred scriptures; and as far as Christianity is concerned, it implies an extraordinary coming of God into the world. Only through the power of the Spirit does the believer become involved with these movements in his or her inner being. Let us, then, explore these three aspects to see what guiding capacity these three categories that come from the outside might nonetheless have.

2.6. Tradition and Community

Christian theology always directs us to a very important domain—a source that may be referred to by the term "tradition" (Lat. *traditio*, Gk. *paradosis*). Think of the Roman Catholic Church or the Eastern Orthodox churches. In these churches experience certainly plays a determining role, in the form of the experiences of former generations that have been handed on. We are not the first but stand on the shoulders of our ancestors. Etymologically, "tradition" means "handing over." It may refer to the *process* of handing over (*actus tradendi*) but also to the *content* of what has been handed over (*traditum*). In Western Protestant theology the word "tradition" is rather unpopular. It smells of encrusted lava, of a burden one is glad to be rid of. The Reformation contributed to this suspicion. The Word of God was to be the source of faith, and the church, with its traditions, rituals, and customs, had to be evaluated according to that criterion. Reformation meant restoring the church to what it was when it originated in the first centuries. Frequently the Reformation and Rome were contrasted as Bible against tradition. The Protestants claimed they were appealing solely to the Bible as the Word of God, while the Roman Catholic Church was said to place the Bible and the apostolic tradition on an equal footing. But is this picture correct? In recent decades there is a growing awareness that Protestants are likewise nourished by a tradition. It is increasingly recognized that faith has its bedding and roots in such a tradition. And on the other side, we notice that many Roman Catholics have accepted the priority of the Bible.

Still the thought that the believer stands on the ground of tradition remains firmly established in the Roman Catholic Church and in the churches of the East (the Eastern Orthodox and Oriental Orthodox churches). Here tradition functions as one of the foundations of faith. It is based on the idea of an uninterrupted line from the first witnesses, the apostles, via their successors and disciples, to the bishops and patriarchs, and finally to the present bishop of Rome. Through this chain the truth is supposed to have been handed on as a treasure. This historical connection is referred to as the apostolic succession. In Protestantism this handing over is not automatically linked to the church and its offices, for they may be in error. The apostolic succession takes place where people remain faithful to the word of the apostles—in other words, to the gospel, or more broadly, to the Bible. This remains an important correction. Yet, the average Protestant has come to see that we always read the Bible standing on the shoulders of those who have gone before and have gained a certain authority with us. Protestant theology increasingly recognizes that in our faith we depend strongly on concrete communities where people experience faith and where the Bible story is told and interpreted. Rarely do people discover faith outside the embedding of a concrete faith community. Faith is not simply a very individual choice, but it can emerge when it becomes evident what the faith means for others. When these others come from the past, we speak of tradition; when they are in the present, we point to a (faith) community. The community of believers may consist of the family, but it is not restricted to that, nor does it depend on large numbers. Rather, fire ignites fire. The church, the local community of faith, in whatever institutional or "liquid" or virtual form, is a place or environment where faith thrives, and which provides it with guidance.

In this connection we may refer to article 5 of the Belgic Confession, which deals with the authority of the Holy Scriptures: "We receive all these books, and these only, as holy and canonical, for the regulating, founding, and establishing of our faith. And we believe without a doubt all things contained in them, not so much because the church receives and approves them as such, but above all because the Holy Spirit testifies in our hearts that they are from God, and also because they prove themselves to be from God. For the blind themselves are able to see that the things predicted in them do happen." Three grounds are mentioned in this statement: the testimony of the church, that of the Spirit, and the internal evidence of the Bible. These three are interconnected. The confession does not indicate how they are connected, but it does emphasize that all three play a role.

Tradition and community also pertain to our thinking about God and how our reality relates to him—that is, to theology. For through the ages, theology has guided tradition and contributed to its shape, while a faith community without any theological reflection is unthinkable. Theology is also intended to keep the road of human thought and life open toward God. Like the other domains we have discussed, theology cannot be regarded as the ground of our faith, for faith is in fact the ground of theology; but theology can help rediscover an access to faith. When we struggle with doubt (and this word applies especially to pastors or others who are interested in theology), we would do well to read the classic theologians. If we open ourselves to the way in which great thinkers like Augustine, Luther, H. F. Kohlbrugge, Barth, or Pannenberg (to mention just a few) try to make sense of things in the light of the Christian faith, we will find that, almost imperceptibly, we begin to go with (or at times against) them. At the very least, such a study of the tradition that has shaped us helps us to understand who we are, and sometimes it helps us to see better who God is and what it means to have faith.

See, for example, Williams 2005 about the importance of studying the tradition—from an Anglican point of view, which is somewhere between the Protestant undervaluation and the Roman Catholic overestimation of it.

2.7. The Bible and the Life of Jesus as Access Roads to Faith

Tradition and community are always connected with the Bible. For this reason, we take the next step from the periphery toward the center of faith by adding the Bible as one more road that leads to faith. In the final analysis we still have not arrived with the Bible as the ground of faith, as is evident in the word "revelation." We might say that God's revelation is behind and under the Bible. But in neither the Roman Catholic nor the Protestant tradition do revelation and Bible coincide. Still, with the Bible we get close to the heart of the matter.

In chapter 13 we will take a closer look at the theological position of the Bible. There we will, so to speak, look at the Bible from above, as the Word that comes from God. In the prolegomena we cannot yet use such far-reaching terms, for we are still searching for the access roads to faith and do not yet presume it. Nonetheless, the Bible must be mentioned in this context, for the simple reason that the Bible is a domain that stimulates faith in a special way. This perspective also applies when we do not yet regard the Bible as the canon or source of God's revelation but merely as a kind of archive of religious experiences of people who lived in the past. Whatever status we may attribute to the Bible, it is without any doubt a unique archive of experience. For example, we may read the book of Deuteronomy as a collection of Israel's experiences with God and of Israel's later reflections on these experiences.

Of course, Israel may have been mistaken in its interpretation of these experiences, just as the authors of the New Testament may have made errors in their reports of the impressions Jesus made on them. When we read the Bible, we cannot exclude this possibility beforehand. But neither can we without further consideration reject the invitation, or even the appeal, that is found in the words of the Bible. It often seems as if the Bible writers ask us loud and clear, Does it not appear that God has manifested himself in these and other events in the world of our experience? Would you, reader, not also be able to see and experience things in this way? We would, as readers of the Bible, lose all credibility if we would not even be interested in such claims and not be willing, in some way, to consider them. It would be strange if we, like some religious scholars, would like to know everything about Isaiah or Paul and about all sorts of religious-historical elements behind their writings—but not about their claims that they encountered God.

This focus on *God* as the proper subject of the biblical texts is an important characteristic of a recent movement in biblical hermeneutics, the so-called theological interpretation of Scripture. See 13.5 for more information below.

Such an avoidance is even stranger when we consider that the Bible writers explicitly state that they want to hand on their faith. The Gospels, for instance, have at times been referred to as literature with a bias (Berkhof, CF 273): they want not just to describe events but to convey a message and appeal to their readers. And therefore they tell about these events from a kerygmatic perspective.

A clear example is found in the Gospel of John. The book presents itself as a product of the experiences of early Christians with Jesus as the Son of God (John 20:30-31). The author of the gospel leaves us in no doubt as to what he intends: to let the next generation share in what the first circle of disciples experienced, and thereby to let them participate in the experience of the love of God. The events reported in the text are not selected simply to inform us; they also are intended to appeal to us and ask us to become involved. They were written down "that you may believe that Jesus is the Christ, the Son of God, and that believing you may have life in his name." No doubt because of the Bible's character as appeal, missionary organizations prioritize the distribution of Bibles, even in situations where there is hardly any help in reading and interpreting the Bible—simply trusting that reading itself will be a blessing.

People do not need to have a clear idea of exactly what the Bible is before they start reading it. Even without high expectations, people may suddenly experience its transforming power. They do so because the Bible is not just a system of truth claims but, in the final analysis, a word or address. We are spoken to as human beings; we receive a name as we are summoned as Jew or unbeliever to become a child of God's promise. Christian faith is basically recognizing this appeal and letting it be true. It means receiving with open arms this Word that comes to us, knowing intuitively that, to use the words of H. Berkhof (1914-95), it is in fact God whom we encounter. In this experience we know that we are put in the light, judged, invited, and transformed. When God approaches us in his speaking—or, to put it in classic Reformed terms: when God's Spirit connects with the Word—we can no longer see ourselves as isolated and alone; we are placed in a situation where God addresses us and where we are close to him.

This is the fundamental experience of faith that we hear about in the story of the Ethiopian ambassador in Acts 8. In fact, it happened to him just when he had become interested in reading a biblical manuscript. Very specifically, in his case, it appears to be the person of Jesus that aroused his interest. This focus was not by sheer accident, for in whatever way one may think about the relationship between the Old and the New Testaments, and in whatever way one may want to underline the unique place and importance of the Old Testament, the story of Jesus Christ remains somehow the climax of the Bible, whereby many pieces of the puzzle fall into place. If, without any preparation, the Bible seems able to serve as a book that leads to faith, this quality must certainly also be true of the person of Jesus. Even when we have not come to the point where we regard Jesus as the Son of God or the Second Person of the triune Being, he can impress us, touch us, and put us on a totally different track of thinking and living—as he often did during his life.

For that reason we must, finally, in thinking about the roads that can lead to the Christian faith, also speak of the person and ministry of Jesus. It might seem that, in so doing, we arrive at the center of the circle of faith, but not so. For just as in the case of the Bible, we may also speak of Jesus from the outside—in fact, that is where all speaking of Jesus, every Christology, has its beginning. Even for the disciples Jesus was, in the first instance, an ordinary rabbi whom they happened to have met. However, their experiences with Jesus became decisive for themselves and, after them, for the Christian church. This reorientation occurred and occurs in widely different ways. Some find that they are especially attracted by his message, others by his self-sacrificing love, others again by the power with which he, according to reports, rose from the dead. (In chap. 10 we shall explore these three angles in more detail in connection with the doctrine of the offices, in which Jesus's ministry is pictured, respectively, as that of a prophet, a priest, and a king.)

In any case, in the end Jesus himself always makes the difference. When we consider the roads that lead to faith, Christianity always points in a special way to Jesus, in whom God and his salvation come to us. His life and person are the ultimate point of reference for Christian theology. They point to Jesus as the definitive intermediary between God and humanity. For this reason, the church prays in Jesus's name and calls him Mediator. The significance of this attribution becomes very clear in Jesus's prayer practice. Jesus's prayers embody the unique communion between Jesus and his Father. Repeatedly, we read about this relationship in the Gospels. However, in the well-known prayer that begins with the words "Our Father," Jesus invites his followers to share in that communion (see John 17). In this way he wanted, already prior to his death, to connect people with God. And after he makes a space for us with God, he creates space for God in us by his Spirit. When the church follows Jesus and in obedience to him prays the Lord's Prayer, it enters this space of intimate communion between Jesus and the Father that the Spirit has created. This move brings us, as we ask the question "Why believe?" in touch with what the church would later refer to as the Trinity. The road that offers access to faith is ultimately, more than anything else, the new communion that, at the Father's initiative, the Son has opened to us in the power of the Spirit.

Since this communion is a gift that comes to human beings by way of surprise and not as the result of ever-ongoing reasoning, we will in the next chapter further explore the ontological ground under this very special experience. We will discuss what it means when God lets himself be known as the Tri-une. Then we will deal with the doctrine of God. Subsequently we will, in a following round, return to the revelation event in which God makes himself known and which is the real ground of our faith.

References

Becker, Matthew L. 2015. *Fundamental Theology: A Protestant Perspective*. London: Bloomsbury.

Berkhof, Hendrikus. 1979. "Salto vitale." In *Niet te geloven* [Unbelievable], edited by R. F. Beerling et al., 233–45. Deventer: Van Lighum Slaterus.

Buckley, Michael J. 1987. *At the Origins of Modern Atheism*. New Haven: Yale University Press.

Clark, Kelly James, ed. 2000. *Readings in the Philosophy of Religion*. Peterborough, ON: Broadview Press.

Davis, Stephen T. 1997. *God, Reason, and Theistic Proofs*. Edinburgh: Edinburgh University Press.

Flew, Anthony, and Abraham Varghese. 2007. *There Is a God*. New York: HarperOne.

Harrison, Peter. 2015. *The Territories of Science and Religion*. Chicago: University of Chicago Press.

Henriksen, Jan-Olav. 2009. *Gift, Desire, and Recognition: Christology and Postmodern Philosophy*. Grand Rapids: Eerdmans.

Houtepen, Anton. 2002. *God—an Open Question: Theological Perspectives in an Age of Agnosticism*. London: Continuum.

Keller, Tim. 2008. *The Reason for God: Belief in an Age of Skepticism*. New York: Dutton.

Mavrodes, George I. 1970. *Belief in God: A Study in the Epistemology of Religion*. New York: Random House.

Morris, Thomas V., ed. 1994. *God and the Philosophers: The Reconciliation of Faith and Reason*. Oxford: Oxford University Press.

Nouwen, Henri. 1994. *Our Greatest Gift: Meditations on Dying and Caring*. New York: HarperCollins.

O'Collins, Gerald. 2011. *Rethinking Fundamental Theology*. Oxford: Oxford University Press.

Pascal, Blaise. 1995. *Pensées and Other Writings*. Translated by Honor Levi. Oxford: Oxford University Press.

Philipse, Herman. 2012. *God in the Age of Science? A Critique of Religious Reason*. Oxford: Oxford University Press.

Placher, William C. 1996. *The Domestication of Transcendence: How Modern Thinking about God Went Wrong*. Louisville, KY: Westminster John Knox.

Plantinga, Alvin. 2011. *Where the Conflict Really Lies: Science, Religion, and Naturalism*. Oxford: Oxford University Press.

———. 2015. *Knowledge and Christian Belief*. Grand Rapids: Eerdmans.

Plantinga, Alvin, and Nicholas Wolterstorff, eds. 1983. *Faith and Rationality: Reason and Belief in God*. Notre Dame: University of Notre Dame Press.

Ramsey, Ian T. 1957. *Religious Language: An Empirical Placing of Theological Phrases*. London: SCM.

Rutten, G. J. E. 2012. *A Critical Assessment of Contemporary Cosmological Arguments: Towards a Renewed Case for Theism*. Amsterdam: Vrije Universiteit.

Schillebeeckx, Edward. 2014. *Interim Report on the Books "Jesus" and "Christ."* Translated by John Bowden and Ted Schoof. Collected Works 8. London: Bloomsbury. Orig. pub., 1978.

Schleiermacher, Friedrich D. E. 1981. *On the "Glaubenslehre": Two Letters to Dr. Lücke*. Translated by James Duke and Francis Fiorenze. Chico, CA: American Academy of Religion.

Southgate, Christopher. 2008. *The Groaning of Creation: God, Evolution, and the Problem of Evil*. Louisville: Westminster John Knox.

Spitzer, Robert. 2010. *New Proofs for the Existence of God: Contributions of Contemporary Physics and Philosophy*. Grand Rapids: Eerdmans.

Sudduth, Michael. 2009. *The Reformed Objection to Natural Theology*. Farnham: Ashgate.

Swinburne, Richard. 2004. *The Existence of God*. 2nd ed. Oxford: Clarendon.

Taylor, Charles. 2007. *A Secular Age*. Cambridge, MA: Harvard University Press, Belknap Press.

Ward, Keith. 1994–2000. *Tetralogy in Comparative Theology*. 4 vols. Oxford: Clarendon.

Williams, Rowan. 2005. *Why Study the Past? The Quest for the Historical Church*. Grand Rapids: Eerdmans.

Wolterstorff, Nicholas. 1996. *John Locke and the Ethics of Belief*. Cambridge: Cambridge University Press.

3 God as Three in One

The Doctrine of the Trinity

icon of the Old Testament Trinity by the Russian icon painter Andrey Rublev. What makes this icon so special? Can you tell which of the three figures represents the Father, which the Son, and which the Holy Spirit? What kind of spirituality does the icon reflect?

3.1. The Trinity as the Gateway to the Doctrine of God

After having discussed the question of the existence of God in the previous chapter, we now deal with who and what God is according to the Christian faith. We will not be following the customary route, however. Usually, a book on dogmatics begins—under the heading "The Doctrine of God"—with a discussion of the being of God and his various attributes. These treatments can be quite detailed and verbose. Then, at the end we tend to find an often much shorter discussion of God's triune nature. At that point it is shown that God is not only infinite, compassionate, omnipotent, and immutable but also triune—that is to say, that Jesus Christ and the Holy Spirit are somehow also part of God. This approach can easily lead to the conclusion that the various attributes seem to belong to a God who is detached from Jesus Christ and from the salvation history that finds its focus in him. Frequently, philosophical categories that are current in the culture of the author are enlisted to clarify the concept of God. The unspoken assumption is that accepting large parts of the Christian doctrine of God does not presuppose any connection with Jesus Christ.

Both in medieval and in later Protestant Scholasticism the doctrine of the Trinity was usually developed along a fixed route directed by three questions: (1) whether God exists, (2) who and what God is, and (3) how God is. Under the first heading (*an Deus sit*) the question of God's existence was discussed, along with supporting arguments. The second question (*quid* or *quis Deus sit*) usually introduced a comprehensive treatment of God's being and divine attributes. The third question (*qualis Deus sit*) was answered through the doctrine of the Trinity. For examples and variants of this structure, see Muller, PRRD 3:153–59. Muller correctly points that this threefold approach is based on classical rhetoric. However, his attempt to refute the criticism of Barth and his followers on this score misses the crucial point they wanted to emphasize, namely, that this approach inadvertently isolates the doctrine of the Trinity from the doctrine of God as a whole, thus causing the doctrine of God to rest on a "general" basis.

To mention some rather arbitrary examples: in this approach the meaning of attributes like God's immutability and absolute power is often derived not directly from the Bible but from current ideas of what immutability and absolute power need to entail. Immutability might imply, for instance, that God has no feelings (since feelings can always change), while omnipotence might mean that God, in determining and executing his will, is not subject to any restrictions, since he is simply able to do anything. If some relevant Bible texts are brought in to support these notions, they are usually interpreted within an already-established frame of reference. The spectacles of interpretation are provided. In other words, this approach assumes that everybody can imagine what properties ought to be attributed to God and what these attributes more or less encompass, with the Bible being needed, at most, for retrospective illustration. The Christian teaching that God is triune, however, is much more difficult to explain without the Bible. For that reason it was usually deemed advisable to leave this notion until the end, as a kind of supplement, after the "more important" pieces had been dealt with.

In this connection the *perfect-being* method that Anselm developed in his *Proslogion* has become well known: when we say "God," we refer to "that than which nothing greater can be thought" (Lat. *id quo nihil maius cogitari possit*, sometimes abbreviated IQM). That is basically the meaning the word "God" has acquired in our daily usage. Anselm concluded from this definition not only that God must exist (following a complicated line of reasoning that has become known as the ontological proof) but also what attributes he has. God has all the attributes that contribute to someone's greatness, and in their maximum quantity. But we can ask concerning each of these attributes whether it is good to have it. And if so, does it mean that God has that quality to a maximal degree? For example, Anselm believes it is better to have power than to be powerless; therefore, a divine being must be all-powerful. We do not need the Bible in order to know that God must be omnipotent or what that word implies. Similarly, Anselm attributes to God a maximum of knowledge, impassibility (for suffering is not good!), compassion, justice, benevolence, and eternity (*Proslogion*, chaps. 6-11). The doctrine of the Trinity comes in at a later stage (chap. 23)—and in a much shorter form—as the concept of God that has been found to coincide with "all that we believe [from the Bible] about the divine being."

It certainly makes sense for the doctrine of God to emphasize that God fundamentally differs from creation and from us human beings because he does not suffer from all sorts of limitations that we face, and because he possesses many positive attributes in a perfect way, while we have none of these. God is not another name for something in ourselves or for some part of creation that we are attracted to—as with farmers in ancient cultures, for instance, who deified fertility. God is far above anything creaturely, as is expressed in article 1 of the Belgic Confession. There it is confessed that God "is eternal, incomprehensible, invisible, immutable, infinite, almighty, perfectly wise, just, good, and the overflowing fountain of all good." It is easy to criticize such abstract language. However, we must recognize that, in accordance with a long tradition (which, in fact, began already in Greek philosophy), the authors were distancing themselves from too simplistic and too human a picture of God. As the pre-Socratic thinker Xenophanes (ca. 570–475 BCE) jibed, if cows were to have a god, it would most certainly look like a cow.

So there is a lot of good to be said about the way in which traditional dogmatics has underscored God's *transcendence*, that is, God's radical otherness when compared with everything else. Nonetheless, this emphasis was somewhat inappropriate, since it was clear from the very start that we were speaking of the God of Israel and the Father of Jesus Christ, the concrete God who made himself visible in a series of acts and events that Christians began to refer to as salvation history. Theology's traditional image of God may all too easily merge with images of non-Christian origin, such as the ultimate Being from Platonic philosophy, the unmoved Mover of Aristotle, or the all-determining highest Being from later Enlightenment thought. In the nineteenth century this idea of a God who stands alone, unmoved, and omnipotent at the top of the pyramid came under heavy attack from the emerging criticism of religion exemplified by Feuerbach, Freud, and Marx. Ominously, it turned out to be almost impossible to distinguish this image from the God of the Bible. Precisely for that reason Christian theology learned, especially because of the efforts of Karl Barth, to base the doctrine of God much more resolutely on theology's core business: the very special way in which God revealed himself in Israel and was identified with Jesus Christ and the Spirit of Pentecost.

We join this recent turn in asserting that the doctrine of God, with the related treatment of the divine attributes, must be approached from the basis of the doctrine of the divine Trinity. Then there can be no misunderstanding that, speaking from a Christian perspective, God can be thought of only as the Trinity; the Christian church confesses no other God than the Father of Jesus Christ in communion with the Holy Spirit. In that sense the doctrine of the Trinity may be regarded as the Christianized version of the doctrine of God. The church does not worship an anonymous Supreme Being but the God who has made a name for himself in Israel and has gotten a face in Jesus Christ. The divine attributes will also have to be viewed and studied from this perspective, for they do not concern—as has often been suggested—a "universal" divine being, but the triune God. This perspective implies that, right from the start, these attributes must be colored and interpreted by God's sovereign turn toward us human beings in the history of Israel, Jesus Christ, and the Spirit.

There are numerous examples in history of studies that first deal at length with the attributes before getting to the doctrine of the Trinity, but the paradigmatic cases are Thomas Aquinas (STh I.2–26 and 27–43) and Schleiermacher (CF, paras. 170–72; yet he judiciously suggests that the doctrine of the Trinity needs to be constructed anew from the oldest sources). The sharp criticism of Karl Rahner (e.g., in Feiner and Löhrer, MS 2:317–97) on how the theological tradition has split apart the tractates *De Deo trino* and *De Deo uno* ("On the triune God" and "On the one God") has become famous. But even Berkhof stays with this tradition. Being disappointed with its classical form, he even decided toward the end of his life not to incorporate the doctrine of the Trinity in his doctrine of God at all but to deal with it at the end of his treatment of the doctrine of Christ (CF, paras. 19–23 and 38).

In Calvin's *Institutes* the attributes receive little attention, and the doctrine of the Trinity much more. Calvin wanted to stay close to the Bible and practical faith and feared the "idle speculations" that would arise if we isolate various elements of the doctrine of God and make them stand alone. His dictum was, "Hence it is obvious, that in seeking God, the most direct path and fittest method is, not to attempt with presumptuous curiosity to pry into his essence, which is rather to be adored than minutely discussed, but to contemplate him in his works, by which he draws near, becomes familiar, and in a manner communicates himself to us" (*Inst.* 1.5.9). In his own doctrine of God, therefore, Calvin focused to a large extent on the doctrine of the Trinity, which over time he accepted as fully biblical (1.13; see also Letham 2004, 253, 265, 267–68). In the twentieth century many followed Barth's example by prioritizing the doctrine of the Trinity over a discussion of the divine attributes (e.g., Genderen and Velema, CRD 143–64 and 164–92; see also 135), but few did so as consistently as Wolfhart Pannenberg (ST 1, chap. 6, as sequel to and colored by chap. 5) and Robert Jenson (ST 1, esp. chaps. 4–9 and 13). See above, chapter 2, for the consequences of mixing the Christian doctrine of God with philosophical ideas about God, which became the target of the prominent critics of religion in the nineteenth century.

Most Christians today spend little time thinking about the doctrine of God's triune nature. Orthodox Christians believe that God is triune, but they usually find it quite difficult to explain what this concept means and what makes it important. We find frequent mention of the theme in hymns and the liturgy, but in the daily life of the believer, faith in the Trinity hardly plays any role. More liberally oriented Christians typically have little use for the doctrine of the Trinity, as they deem it to be irrational. For non-Christians the doctrine of the Trinity remains very objectionable. Jews as well as Muslims regard it as a serious heresy because they feel it resembles a mild form of polytheism. Western agnostics have some appreciation for faith in God, but this stops at the point where God is thought to consist, in some mysterious way, of three entities. The association with multiple personality disorder becomes rather obvious, and the concept of a Trinity thus becomes a good reason not to pursue Christianity any further.

Against this background it is remarkable to note that the doctrine of the Trinity has made an important comeback among Christian theologians, beginning in the last decades of the twentieth century. Worldwide, an ever-increasing number of theologians from a wide range of denominations have discovered the doctrine's ecumenical significance, seeing that it involves a faith tradition shared by the universal church and thus serves as a distinguishing characteristic of the largest religion in the world (Kärkkäinen 2007, xv). At least as important was the realization that the doctrine of the Trinity does not stand in isolation but is interrelated in various ways with other aspects of the Christian faith. Some have even suggested that it is the organizing center of all Christian theology. Neglecting the doctrine of the Trinity, they feel, causes all sorts of problems for systematic and practical theology. Others do not go as far as wanting to develop a complete "Trinitarian theology," but most no longer think that the doctrine of the Trinity was a later theological invention developed under the influence of the Hellenistic environment of the early church. Despite the Greek concepts that were used to develop it, the doctrine of the Trinity is, in the final analysis, not a product of foreign soil but one that clearly has biblical roots. This particular claim will be the topic of our next section.

The "renaissance" of the Trinity in contemporary systematic theology has unleashed a flood of new literature. Kärkkäinen 2007 offers an insightful survey of a number of important twentieth-century treatments with viewpoints not just from the West but also including Latin American, Asian, and African perspectives. For the backgrounds and forms of the current renaissance, see also Schwöbel 1995, 1-30, and Grenz 2004.

3.2. Proto-Trinitarian Patterns in the Bible

When we try to do justice to the Bible as a whole, we will discover something like a doctrine of the Trinity. It is not there fully developed or in a final form—the church needed several centuries before it was able to adequately formulate the doctrine of the Trinity—but its origin, roots, main principles, or whatever term you want to use, are apparent from the Bible. Those who want to do without the doctrine of the Trinity will inevitably need to find an alternative concept, for instance, the idea that God is not only one but also singular (a deeply rooted idea in Greek philosophy), or the thought that there are several gods (an option that survived for a considerable time in Marcionism). However, the more subtle alternatives to orthodox Trinitarianism had a longer life: the concept that God is one person in three forms, and the idea that God the Father is a little more divine than the Son and the Holy Spirit.

The first theory is known as modalism (Father, Son, and Spirit are merely *modi*, i.e., manifestations of God, who is in essence one) or Sabellianism (after Sabellius, third-century leader of the modalists in Rome). It is a form of monarchianism: the idea that there can be only a singular God who alone (*monos*) is the origin (*archē*) of everything. The theory that God the Father is a little more divine than the Son and the Spirit, or, unlike the other two, is the only really divine being, is referred to as subordinationism.

It became clear, however, that all these alternatives fail to do justice to the complexity of the New Testament's statements about God; they even fail to do justice to the Old Testament, where we already find evidence of distinct identities in God. They are therefore suboptimal, so to speak, as they do not adequately succeed in taking all the relevant data into account when offering an explanation.

Let us start with a look at the Old Testament. As an example we may take the history of the Akedah, the "binding" of Isaac in Gen 22. First, we meet God himself, who addresses Abraham and tells him to sacrifice his son (v. 1-2). When, subsequently, Abraham is on Mount Moriah and is at the point of killing his son, the Angel of the Lord addresses him in the same way as God did—by calling his name—but tells him not to proceed

(vv. 11-12). After Abraham has sacrificed a ram rather than his son and has given the place a name, the Angel of the Lord calls a second time, "from heaven" (vv. 15-18). Then we read that he said, "By myself I have sworn, says the LORD, because you have done this, and have not withheld your son, your only son, I will indeed bless you" (vv. 16-17). Thus we see that the Angel of the Lord appears as someone who differs from God but at the same time is identical with God. Remarkably enough, the Angel of the Lord is not some kind of intermediary but speaks, just like God himself, "from heaven." It appears at first that each has his own distinct message: God tells Abraham to kill his son, while the Angel forbids him to do so. Is God the bringer of bad news and the Angel the messenger of good news? The story reaches a climax, however, in verses 16 and 17, when God and the Angel appear to be one and the same. God totally identifies himself with his Angel, and Abraham does not need to fear that God will ask yet something more from him.

Similar patterns of distinctiveness-and-identity in God are found in other ancient Old Testament stories, such as the return of Hagar from the desert (Gen 16), Jacob's conversation with Leah and Rachel about the incident near Bethel (Gen 31), the calling of Moses (Exod 3), the birth of Samson (Judg 13), and especially the visit of YHWH to Abraham in the form of three men (Gen 18), the story that was pictured around 1410 by the Russian painter Andrey Rublev in the world-renowned icon that we already mentioned. Exodus 23 is also very intriguing: "Behold, I send an angel before you, to guard you on the way and to bring you to the place which I have prepared. Give heed to him and hearken to his voice, do not rebel against him, for he will not pardon your transgression; for my name is in him. But if you hearken attentively to his voice and do all that I say, then I will be an enemy to your enemies and an adversary to your adversaries" (vv. 20-22). Here, once again, we see a startling change (which is more than a stylistic discontinuity) in which God shows himself to be distinct from the Angel before he fully identifies himself with him: "if you hearken attentively to his voice and do all that I say." Furthermore, the text unequivocally states the basis for this explicit identification: "for my name is in him." This is an extremely interesting expression, especially when we compare it with the New Testament to see how God gives his name to Jesus (Phil 2:9, 11).

For further discussions on these topics, see Schwöbel 2009, 30-37, and Oeming 2002.

Note that we can find similar indications in the Old Testament when the

Spirit of God (*ruach YHWH*) is mentioned. Often acts of God are attributed to this Spirit, and in these cases we also learn that, on the one hand, God's Spirit has his own identity (his own "color" and character, so to speak) distinct from God but, on the other hand, may be totally identified with God himself.

In short, a close reading of numerous passages in the Old Testament takes us a long way toward understanding what happened when the insight emerged in the early church that formed the basis for the doctrine of the Trinity. From a New Testament perspective this "proto-Trinitarian foundational pattern" (Schwöbel) becomes even more concrete. We discover in the Gospels how Jesus addresses God as his Father and in his preaching calls upon the people to turn toward the Father. From the beginning of his public ministry Jesus pointed the people toward God. According to Mark's brief statement, Jesus's mission was to proclaim the good news about God (1:14). This good news has everything to do with the kingdom or the kingship of God: "The time is fulfilled, and the kingdom of God is at hand" (1:15). Numerous parables focus on the way this kingdom of God operates. It is abundantly clear that this kingdom is not of this world, because it does not focus on power and elevated positions but on compassion for lost people. The parables show that God's kingdom is characterized by grace, love, and pardon and condemns all who reject these qualities. Jesus's entire ministry was thus totally theocentric. He was totally absorbed by the all-surpassing significance of God and of life under a just and peaceful rule. We notice that, even when someone cried out that Jesus was not just anybody and declared, "You are the Messiah, the Son of God," Jesus asked the people to remain quiet about this comment (Mark 3:11-12; 8:30). At times he even forbade people to speak about his miracles (Mark 1:44; 5:43; 7:36; 8:26). And when someone addressed him as "Good Teacher," it almost seems as if Jesus was startled and wanted to correct this person straightaway: "Why do you call me good? No one is good but God alone" (Mark 10:18). John reports him as saying, "I do not seek my own glory" (John 8:50), "but I honor my Father" (John 8:49). In short, everything Jesus said and did was aimed at making us give God his rightful place. This is very obvious in the first three requests of the Lord's Prayer (Matt 6:9-10).

How does God himself react to this approach of Jesus? As the gospel story proceeds, the answer becomes gradually clearer: by doing the exact opposite, that is, by placing Jesus in the spotlight and by referring to him as his beloved Son par excellence. Only twice in the Gospels does God himself speak directly, and in both cases it is to identify himself with

Jesus and to place him in the center. First, at the baptism in the Jordan (Matt 3:17; Mark 1:11; Luke 3:22), and later at Jesus's transfiguration (Matt 17:5; Mark 9:7; Luke 9:35; note also the summary account in John 12:28). And when things finally reach their climax and Jesus does what he said he would do and fully complies with the will of the Father, even going as far as the cross, it is the Father who raises him from the dead. Today, New Testament scholars refer to this as an act of *rehabilitation*. By doing so, the Father shows in an unsurpassable manner that this man was right in what he said about him. If from now on someone wants to know the Father, he must go to Jesus; he must consider his message, his acts, his death and resurrection. From now on we must recognize that he who has seen Jesus has seen the Father (John 14:9). Even more than in the other gospels, we find in the Fourth Gospel the deepest and most complete reflections on these links, and we see how the kingdom of God (i.e., eternal life) is tied directly to faith in Jesus (John 3:16). For this reason, Jesus—from Easter on, as Rudolf Bultmann put it—changed from being the proclaimer into being the one proclaimed. From the resurrection on, the Father has glorified the Son (see John 17:5) by giving him a name that is above every other name (Phil 2:9). This name can be only the divine name. Furthermore, he has given Jesus a mandate and full power in heaven and on earth (Matt 28:18) and has taken him into his heavenly glory (Luke 24:51; Eph 1:20; 4:10). There he has put all things under his feet (1 Cor 15:27; Eph 1:22). From that moment on, the Father puts the Son in the spotlight. Just as the Son had always pointed to the Father, so the Father now constantly points to the Son. Everything in the New Testament is now about Jesus. Nobody is asked to remain silent anymore about his being the Messiah. On the contrary, now the entire house of Israel, says Peter, may know that God made him Lord (*kyrios*—the Greek rendering of the divine name, YHWH) and Messiah (Acts 2:36). In the proclamation of the good news about God, as the disciples now took over the preaching from Jesus, the core is the key position that Jesus now occupies. For just as consistently as the Son had distinguished himself from and had pointed the people to the Father, the Father now distinguishes himself from and points to the Son: "No one knows the Father except the Son and any one to whom the Son chooses to reveal him" (Matt 11:27).

But how can the Father put Jesus in the spotlight when Jesus is no longer in our midst? And how can the Son make the Father known without being physically present on earth? There is a universal consensus in the New Testament that these things happen through the Spirit. Often the Spirit is referred to as the Holy Spirit, to underline that he (or she—*pneuma*, the Greek word, is grammatically neuter) is in all aspects on God's side. This Spirit, by whom Jesus himself had been conceived, inspired, and equipped for his task (Matt 1:18–20; 3:16; 12:28; Mark 1:10; Luke 1:35; 3:22; 4:14, 18–19; John 1:32–33; 3:34; see also chap. 10 below), is now sent into the world to ensure that everywhere the Son, through the Father, will hold center stage. The sending of the Spirit is attributed both to the Father (John 14:16, 26) and to the Son (John 16:7). In that sense it might even be stated in retrospect that Jesus was baptized with the Holy Spirit (Matt 3:11) so that his followers would receive this Spirit (Luke 11:13; John 7:39). The Spirit will "give life" (John 6:63) and will teach Jesus's followers how they can speak of the significance of Jesus, even under the most difficult circumstances (Luke 12:12; Matt 10:20; Mark 13:11).

By way of conclusion, we may thus say that the Spirit continues Jesus's mission on earth. He brings people in touch with the forgiving love of God by bringing them in contact with Jesus (John 16:14a), and he urges them to continue the proclamation of the kingdom. Those who receive the Spirit will, as a result, also glorify the Father and the Son. So the church has taught from the very beginning. There are no indications that, even in the earliest phase of Christianity, there was ever a time when Jesus was not worshiped and glorified. The theory, popularized in a somewhat attenuated form in the late twentieth century by H. M. Kuitert (b. 1924), that people gradually attributed to Jesus ever more elaborate metaphysical compliments until at last he was identified with God, is today almost universally rejected as contrary to all we know about the earliest days of the Christian church. From the beginning there was general agreement that "no one can say 'Jesus is Lord' except by the Holy Spirit" (1 Cor 12:3b). People realized that the Spirit had inspired them to give Jesus the title of *kyrios*, which in the Old Testament is a prerogative of God. Apparently, the Spirit does not play the Father and the Son off against each other; rather, he brings them together. For that reason the New Testament can interchangeably refer to the Spirit as the Spirit of the Father and the Spirit of the Son.

After this tour through the Gospels, let's pause for a moment. How far have we come? What have we found? Have we proven that there is a biblical basis for the doctrine of the Trinity? No. The doctrine of the Trinity is the result of a later elaboration of these data. However, the New Testament does clearly show this pattern of mutual involvement of Father, Son, and Spirit in the drama of salvation history.

Pannenberg (ST 1:337–47) appositely summarized the biblical-theological lines that we traced above by drawing on the idea of "mutual self-distinction." He does not see the texts in which Jesus pictures himself as "lower" than the Father (e.g., Mark 10:18; John 14:28) as evidence for the nondivinity of Jesus (as liberals usually do), nor as applying only to Jesus's human nature (as conservatives do). Rather, they signal that Jesus, precisely because of his desire *not* to be like God (as Adam wanted; Gen 3:5–6), is the true Son of God. Indeed, we might say that "Jesus shows himself to be the Son of God precisely in his self-distinction from God" (ST 1:310). In this way Father, Son, and Spirit are focused on bringing back humanity to God in mutual respect for each other and in unrelenting love. For recent defenses of the old liberal theory of Jesus's gradual identification with God, see Kuitert 1999, 178–81, and Ehrman 2014. For criticisms of this idea, see the studies of Bauckham, Hurtado, and Roukema that will be mentioned in chapter 10.

The New Testament also shows us that, as an extension of this mutual involvement of Father, Son, and Spirit, it became customary in the so-called economy of salvation to mention these three, or two of the three, in a single verse or two. Examples of the twofold ("binitary") terminology are found in the introductions of all the epistles in the Pauline corpus, for example, in Rom 1:7, 1 Cor 1:3, 2 Cor 1:2, Phil 1:2, Gal 1:3, 2 Thess 1:1–2, and 1 Tim 1:1–2. We find Trinitarian formulas in Matt 28:19 (the baptismal formula), 2 Cor 13:13 (the New Testament blessing), Gal 4:6, Eph 5:18–20, 1 Pet 1:1–2, and Jude 20–21. This list is still not solid evidence that Father, Son, and Spirit share in the same divine nature (i.e., that all three are God). But it does indicate that in this manner they constitute the focus of the Christian worship of God.

However, it remains important to stress the priorities in our argument. Those who want to find the biblical roots for the doctrine of the Trinity should beware of pointing to a few isolated texts. We should always refer instead to the foundational proto-Trinitarian patterns of God's saving acts, which can be found, as outlined above, in both the Old and the New Testaments. In the tradition of the doctrine of the Trinity, the fundamental question is not how God is constituted; the focus is first of all on the consistently emphasized cooperation of Father, Son, and Spirit in the project of allowing guilty human beings to participate in God's kingdom, and thereby in eternal life. Here we are at the core of the event that the Gospels and the Epistles want us to thoroughly understand. For this reason, we have dealt with this matter so extensively; we hope the reader will be open to this focus.

3.3. From an Economic to an Ontological Trinity

It is possible, of course, to maintain that, of the three persons who play a role in the New Testament drama of salvation history, only the Father is truly God. Jesus and the Spirit may then just be instruments that take part in what God does. They might represent, as it were, three different aspects of God's involvement with us: Jesus is the prophet par excellence, who proclaims God's message, and the Spirit is another word for what God does in human beings. To put it in theological language: God and the Spirit might be merely factors in the economy of salvation. Or in more popular idiom, in the plan of salvation God acts as the Father of the Son and the Sender of the Spirit; they are of the same spirit in the execution of this plan. But, so runs the idea, even though the plan executed is a scheme initiated by God, God is much more than a plan of salvation. In his real essence he hides behind Jesus and the Spirit and has unexpected depths. When we are face to face with Jesus, so the theory runs, we do not by definition stand face to face with God. Jesus is *the* (or at least *a*) way to God, which is also true of the Spirit. When, by following that road or these roads, you have reached God, you can leave Jesus and the Spirit behind. They are like scaffolding that can be removed when the building is ready. And so, eventually, we are left with a singular God.

This line of reasoning has been explicitly rejected by the church in the doctrine of the Trinity. The reason is that it would attribute to salvation history, as it is presented in the Bible, a secondary, subordinate position. It would mean that the gospel of the crucified and risen Lord and of the sending of the life-giving Spirit is not the actual event in which we learn to know God. Rather, it becomes a stepping-stone toward a possibly different God who hides behind the economy of salvation. But this approach, the church says, fails to treat the message of salvation with sufficient seriousness. In the Bible, God makes himself known not only in Jesus Christ and in the Spirit but also as the God who identifies himself unreservedly with Jesus Christ and the Spirit. No higher, deeper knowledge of God is possible than this knowledge. In that case, we must take another and decisive step. We must say that there is no other God than this God. In turning toward us human beings, to which the gospel bears witness, God has unconditionally defined himself as the God who is fully one with the Son and the Spirit. Only in this way do we take in full seriousness that whoever has seen Jesus has seen the Father (John 14:9), and that it is the Spirit who searches the depths of God as the only one who can know God and can share that knowledge with us (1 Cor 2:10–14). This knowledge, given by the Spirit, is not an abstract, theoretical knowledge, not a vague mystical knowledge; it is a knowledge based on a concrete involvement in the salvation-historical acts of God in Jesus Christ.

For this reason, the early church was not content to stay with the view of the so-called economic Trinity, which suggests that Father, Son, and Spirit cooperate only for a limited time. The church has understood that it can do justice to the *kērygma* (the Greek word for the message, i.e., the core message of the Bible) only by taking the final step. If this is the way in which God reveals himself to us, this must also be the way in which he truly exists. For we would relativize God's revelation in Christ and in the Spirit if we were to surmise that behind this "front" there is a totally different God, an unknown Mr. X, a hidden God—the *Deus absconditus* of whom Luther was so afraid. It would imply that we are back where we started, still unable to say anything sensible about God. But the gospel wants to impress upon us that this God, who gave his name to Jesus and to the Spirit, is the only true God and that we may come to know him as he is through Christ and the Spirit. The doctrine of the Trinity, in other words, protects the core of the biblical message. God is light, and in him there is no darkness whatsoever (1 John 1:5). These words are true only, in the famous words of Karl Rahner, if the economic Trinity is the immanent Trinity, and vice versa.

See Rahner 2004, 88, also TI, vol. 4. Much has been argued about the correct interpretation of this "rule of Rahner," but basically, Rahner by this insistence wanted to preempt all kinds of speculation about God's Trinitarian being that remains detached from the history of salvation; rather, we know nothing about God and about God's triune being apart from salvation history. The common reference to the economic versus the immanent Trinity can cause misunderstandings. It does not mean that there are two trinities, but that we can view the triune nature of God from two perspectives: from the perspective of God's turning toward us, and from the perspective of God's essential being. The main idea is that the latter aspect in the epistemological process is determined by the former. It does not mean that God is not bigger than what we learn through revelation about him, but it does imply that he is not essentially different. In his revelation we see into God's heart.

The philosophically loaded term "immanent" may lead to an incorrect concept of a God who is locked into himself. Some therefore prefer to speak instead of an economic and an ontological Trinity. There is much to be said for this wording, but "immanent Trinity" has become so generally accepted that we can hardly avoid it.

Thus, if God's being conforms to his threefold revelation rather than being very different from it, then God must also be threefold. Consequently, Jesus and the Spirit belong essentially and eternally with God. They share in the divine essence, since God's name is in them (note Exod 23:21).

An intriguing, oft-discussed question in this connection is whether God's Trinitarian identity was fully complete from the very beginning, or whether it has been enriched by what has happened in the course of history. If God *becomes* "our Father" as the result of the work of Christ and the Spirit, something must also happen to himself—something that is essential for who he is. Here we experience the tension between, on the one hand, taking totally seriously the dynamic and dramatic terms the Bible uses when speaking about God's interaction with us and, on the other hand, classic metaphysics with its emphasis on God's immutability, self-sufficiency, and perfection. How do these elements relate to each other? According to some, it is God's perfect life in itself (Webster 2006, 2008) or his unchangeable self-sufficiency (Swain 2013, 29) that carries the economy of salvation of which the gospel bears witness; God gives us his fatherly goodness, which he has in and of himself. Others, however, wonder whether we should "reason back" in this manner, behind the gospel. Does this approach not make, as it were, God's goodness into something God himself has little influence on, since he simply finds himself as such—just as we humans also simply experience ourselves with the character we happen to have? But the gospel dos not speak this way about God. It speaks of the concrete, central act in which God turns to us, in Jesus Christ. In line with this thought, some, like Bruce McCormack (2000), suggest that this act of God's self-definition in Jesus Christ—his decision to be, in him, a God of grace, *precedes* logically (not chronologically) his triune being and constitutes that being. In this light, our entire salvation depends, not on how God happens to be constituted, but on his free choice in which he loves us in Christ—to which the Gospels bear witness. That choice makes God the God he is. Others, like Robert Jenson (ST), reason more eschatologically than protologically, claiming that, in his interaction with his people, God gradually shows who he is. In this view, God's trajectory of his revelation in Christ and in the Spirit is decisive, and ultimately determines his identity.

We do not argue here for one or the other of these positions in this complex matter. But we want to sensitize our readers to its importance: the choice we make and the point of departure we take determine to a large extent our doctrine of God and thus impact all our theological thinking. For more on this discussion, which is focused mainly on the correct interpretation of Barth's doctrine of God, see Dempsey 2011; and for our own approach to these matters above, see chapters 4 and 9, and below, the small print at the end of section 15.9.

3.4. The Development of the Doctrine in the Early Church

The development of the doctrine of the Trinity in the early church has been chronicled in many scholarly studies and textbooks. We will not attempt to summarize these accounts here, but we must have a clear idea of some of the major steps in that development to gain a good understanding of the main points of the doctrine. This section will provide a very succinct overview of those steps and then will lead on to another crucial phase in the history of the doctrine: its role in the Great Schism between the Eastern and the Western church, in 1054.

With regard to the early church, the studies of Ritter (1965), Kelly (1977), and Hanson (1988) have gained the status of classics. Recent publications such as Markschies (2000) and Ayres (2004) are also important. Some of these studies deal with the first three centuries, while others focus on the crucial fourth century.

The earliest Christians did not yet have an adequate way to express the things that we discussed in the previous section. A great number of images and expressions were used to try to come to grips with the plurality in God; the language used was fluid and produced a number of widely differing triadic expressions. Theophilus of Antioch (d. ca. 185) and Irenaeus of Lyons (d. ca. 202) felt they should differentiate between "God, the Word, and Wisdom," but for Theophilus the Word was identical with the Spirit, while Irenaeus identified the Word with Christ and the Spirit with Wisdom. With the passing of time, both concepts were understood christologically: Jesus is both the Word (John 1) and Wisdom (Prov 8:23-24). Some terms and expressions that were used to describe the relationships between Father, Son, and Spirit gradually found more recognition and assent than others. Often these words indicated subordination: the Son and certainly the Spirit (if the Spirit was mentioned at all) were a step lower than the Father.

The thinking of Origen (ca. 185-ca. 254), for instance, was both remarkable and influential. He argued that there never was a time when the Logos (the Word, Christ) did not exist. Enlarging upon texts like Ps 2:7 and Isa 53:8 ("who shall declare his generation?" KJV), Origen followed Irenaeus in referring to the "eternal generation" of the Son (something human beings will never understand, since, in our way of thinking, generating something must happen at a moment in time), a concept they took to mean that the Father and the Son share in the same nature. Both are uncreated, but only the Father was "ungenerated," while the Son was eternally generated by the Father. As the sun is one with its rays and its warmth, so the Father, Son, and Spirit are one—but of course the sun remains the source for the rays as well as for the warmth, and not vice versa. For Origen this understanding meant that the Father has the highest place in the Godhead. The Father alone is *autotheos*, God from himself; Christ, in contrast, is *deuteros theos*, a second God (*Contra Celsum* 5.39). The Spirit (about whom Origen has much less to say) is also eternal and uncreated but subordinate to the Father and the Son. Later Arius (ca. 250–336) would take up this line of thought, but in order to avoid tritheism, he made a far-reaching decision, saying that only the Father is truly and fully God.

As time went by, the problem of how to reconcile unity and plurality in God became more acute; however, more uniformity developed in the terminology that was used. With Tertullian in the West, Latin concepts like *trinitas*, *persona*, and *substantia* gained dominance. In fact, Tertullian proposed the remarkably orthodox formula that God is a trinity of one "substance" and three "persons." Those three persons are inseparable, but contrary to what the modalists thought, they could be separated on an ontological level. Thus, the threeness in God that is revealed in salvation history may be reconciled with God's oneness. This language provided an important boost toward solving the problem. Meanwhile, in the Greek-speaking East, concepts like *hypostasis* and *ousia* became common, but for a considerable time it remained unclear how exactly these related to each other and to their Latin equivalents. Ultimately, after a long search and extensive debate at the Council of Constantinople (381), the lines were drawn by stating that God is *one being in three persons*—in Greek, one *ousia* in three *hypostaseis*. In this way an attempt was made to do justice to the unity of God and to take seriously the threeness that is found in the New Testament. Against the gnostics, the unity of Creator and Redeemer was affirmed (for there is only one God); against the modalists, the real distinctiveness of Father, Son, and Spirit; and against the subordinationists, the full equality of the three. How was this formulation achieved?

The Council of Nicaea (325) agreed that Jesus was "of the same being" (Gk. *homo-ousios*) with the Father. These were not words used in the Bible but were intended mainly to refute Arius and his followers, who considered Jesus as God's "first creature." Even though there were Bible texts (such as Col 1:15 and Rev 3:14) that at first glance seemed to support the Arian view, the church understood that, by following this track, Jesus

91

would become a kind of demigod, somewhere between God and humanity, while God himself remained unknown. For by this logic Jesus could not be God's supreme revelation, as God would be much higher than Jesus. This approach fit well with the contemporary Greek-Hellenistic worldview but not with the basic pattern of the New Testament. Paradoxically, by using the Greek term *homo-ousios*, concepts from the Greek environment were enlisted to prevent Jesus from being encapsulated in that same environment. For since he was "of the same essence with the Father," Jesus could not be seen as one of many intermediary beings or as a being that happened to be elevated. He was radically at the side of God.

It is important to understand that this decision was far from purely theoretical. Both sides knew that the issue also involved soteriology. According to the view of the Arians (about Arius himself, we know very little), Jesus could help us because he modeled how we could turn toward God; because he was a creature like us, we should be able to live as he lived. Arius's opponent Athanasius, however, argued that a creature cannot bring us back into communion with God; only God can truly save lost human beings. Therefore, Jesus must be fully God (Gk. *holos theos*). Some considerations about liturgy and the practice of faith also played a role. If Jesus is not fully God, reasoned Athanasius, it would not make sense to baptize in his name or to call upon him in prayer (*Contra Arianos* 2.41–42). In this connection Athanasius applied the rule that the laws that regulate our prayer also determine our faith (*lex orandi lex credendi*, the rule for our prayers is also the rule for our faith).

With the decision of Nicaea the doctrine of the Trinity was, as it were, partly finished. It emerged first of all from the urge to do justice to the fundamental experiences of the earliest Christians that in Jesus Christ and his life on earth we are dealing with God in the fullest sense. In 381 a similar decision was reached about the Holy Spirit, and as a result the doctrine of the Trinity received its final form. The Council of Nicaea did not put an end to the debate, however, and would only later, in retrospect, be regarded as an important milestone.

Initially, it remained unclear what the relatively new and controversial term *homo-ousios* exactly meant. It was clear that Arius and his followers could not agree with such expressions as "true God from true God" and "begotten, not made" (Nicene Creed). It was also clear that God could not be detached from the man Jesus of Nazareth and from everything he did and experienced. But the full meaning of "of the same essence" would crystallize only after Nicaea by a process of ongoing discussion, confusion, and disunity. What did it mean that Jesus and the

Father are of the same essence, and thus one and the same person? This wording might once again imply a type of modalism in which the two differed only in their manifestations but were at bottom identical. Or did the *homo-ousios* mean that Christ and the Father both belong to the same "kind," similar to the way two human beings belong to the species *Homo sapiens*? But in that case we would once again be confronted with two gods. Or maybe even with three, for, according to the baptismal formula (Matt 28:19), would not the Holy Spirit, just like Jesus, be at God's side rather than being just a creature?

None of these options was very satisfying, and most participants in the debate preferred to dissociate themselves from the confession of Nicaea with its awkward *homo-ousios*. They developed "semi-Arian" alternatives that once again put Jesus a little lower than the Father. It was mainly because of the tenacity of Athanasius (ca. 296–373), who, as a young deacon, had participated at the Council of Nicaea, that a return to the subordinationist view—and thereby to a belated capitulation to a Greek philosophical concept of God—was prevented. And it was due to the creativity of the so-called Cappadocian church fathers—Basil of Caesarea (ca. 329–379), Gregory of Nyssa (ca. 335–ca. 395), and Gregory of Nazianzus (ca. 329–89)—that an alternative emerged that distinguished the three persons without making one of them subordinate to the others. The Cappadocians proposed to make a clear distinction between the terms *ousia* and *hypostasis*, two core concepts that, at the time, were often used interchangeably. They conceived of a formula in which Father, Son, and Spirit are one divine being (*ousia*) but in three persons (*hypostaseis*).

This approach was adopted by the Council of Constantinople and became the shortest formula of what would be known as the Trinitarian dogma. This unique solution is usually referred to as the Cappadocian settlement, the Cappadocian solution for the confusion in terminology and concepts that had arisen after Nicaea. The strength of this solution, of course, depends on the exact meaning of *hypostaseis*. Usually it is taken to describe some form of independent existence, but the best translation of the term remains a matter of controversy. In any case, it implied much more than that the one God could put on three masks, an association that (in spite of Tertullian's efforts) continued to accompany the Latin equivalent, the term *persona*, which had been borrowed from the theater. For the Cappadocians, *hypostasis* pointed to something that could be counted and to which one might attribute certain characteristics. But the Cappadocians thought specifically of this "something" as having a personal identity, as is attributed to Father, Son, and Holy Spirit in the biblical stories. Robert Jenson therefore suggested translating *hypostasis* as "identity" (1982, 105–11; ST 1:106), which may be a good idea. We believe that the traditional translation ("person") is still defensible, so long as we realize that we are not referring to persons in the modern, post-Cartesian sense of independent individuals, but to persons who cannot be detached from each other because they are mutually interdependent as far as their identity is concerned. For that reason we have put the word "person" in quotation marks, although we will not continue to do so hereafter in any consistent manner.

Jenson also satisfactorily explains that we may continue to refer to the entire Trinity as one person—as God—without implying that we must thereby recognize four divine persons (ST 1:119–23).

Father, Son, and Holy Spirit therefore all derive their own uniqueness or identity from their mutual relations. The guiding thought had already been judiciously formulated by Athanasius: the Father is Father only because of the Son, as a human father derives his fatherhood from the fact that he has a son. The Cappadocian Fathers further clarified this foundational thought: the unique relationship with the Son—and by the same logic, the equally unique relationship with the Spirit—is precisely what distinguishes the Father as Father; the same applies mutatis mutandis for the Son and the Spirit. In this way, Gregory of Nyssa says that Father, Son, and Spirit are indeed three distinct divine persons, just as Peter, Paul, and Barnabas were three distinct human persons (*Contra Eunomium* 1.227).

The question might be posed as to why, between 325 and 381, the view arose to describe the Spirit too as being of one essence ("consubstantial") with the Father and the Son. Was that not a little too much of a good thing? Was a binitarian concept that safeguarded Jesus's divinity not complicated enough? It was precisely in the fourth-century controversy with those who doubted the divinity of the Spirit that it became clear that the Trinitarian concept was not to be relinquished. It was not based just on some Bible texts that linked the Spirit to God; it had much more to do with the pneumatological insight developing in the early church that we human beings do not have the Spirit at our disposal and that we cannot manipulate the Spirit. A spirit that does not issue from God would automatically be on the side of the creatures and open to such manipulation. Nor would such a spirit be able to genuinely connect us with God. We would be left out on our own. Only because the Spirit is radically on God's side is he able, through the Son, to incorporate us into communion with the Father. However, this work can happen only if the Spirit belongs fully, as a distinct person, to the divine essence.

This soteriological insight played a major role in the labors of Athanasius and the Cappadocians and would eventually lead to the confession that the Spirit "is Lord and gives life" and must "be worshiped and glorified together with the Father and the Son" (the Niceno-Constantinopolitan Creed of 381, an expansion of the Nicene Creed; hereafter we will refer to both forms simply as the Nicene Creed).

Understandably, the Cappadocians had to vigorously defend their views—particularly the "social metaphors" they employed—against suspicions of tritheism, the worship of three gods. Were they in fact confessing one God? In response, they further articulated the character of the unity of the three divine persons. First, they consciously limited the uniqueness of Father, Son, and Spirit to their relationships of origin. In many other ways Father, Son, and Spirit do not differ from each other as might three persons chosen at random, but only in the manner in which they are related to each other and are generated by each other. We have seen that in this connection the term "generation" (Gk. *gennēsis*) was used to describe the relationship between the Father and the Son; for the relationship between the Father and the Spirit, Gregory of Nazianzus coined the term "issued" (Gk. *ekporeusis*, after John 15:26). In the West theologians preferred to speak of the two processions (Lat. *processiones*) of the Son and the Spirit from the Father, while reserving for the Father the term "spiration" (Lat. *spiratio*; Kasper 1984, 278-79). Apart from the so-called hypostatic attributes—properties that belong only to one person and in a certain sense constitute that person—the three are completely equal and share in one and the same divine essence.

Many, including the great historian of doctrine Adolf von Harnack (HoD 2:306-9), think that the Cappadocians also wanted to emphasize the unity of God by stating that the Father alone is the "source of goodness"; if so, the Son and the Spirit would not only "proceed" from the Father but also derive their divinity from the divine essence that the Father alone has in himself. In this way the unity of God was situated in the constitutive role of the Father. This position opens the danger, however, that a subtle form of subordinationism would creep back in. Before you know it, the Father may once again become the highest principle in the Godhead. Recent research suggests that (probably for this very reason) the Cappadocians were hesitant to describe the Father as the source of the Godhead. Instead, this seems to be a later development in Eastern Orthodoxy (see Meesters 2012).

The most elegant way in which the Cappadocians argued against the suspicion of tritheism was by means of the theory of "perichoresis," or mutual indwelling. Admittedly, this term appeared only with John of Damascus around 745 (in *On the Orthodox Faith* 1.8), but the concept already had the full attention of Athanasius and of the Cappadocians. It intends to say that Father, Son, and Spirit mutually "dwell" in each other. The thought behind this concept was originally even more flexible and dynamic. It points to a continuous mutual penetration and surrounding (Gk. *perichōreō*) of Father, Son, and Spirit; they totally submerge in one another. Where the Father is, we also find the Son and the Spirit; they each fill the others in every way. This is a beautiful way of saying that uniqueness and unity do not necessarily diminish each other. The biblical background for the theory of perichoresis is evident. In John's Gospel, in particular, we regularly read that Christ and the Father are one (John 10:30), that the Son is in the Father and the Father in the Son (John 14:10; 17:21). We are strongly urged to believe this truth (John 14:11). Moreover, this unity is presented as a model for the unity of believers with Christ (John 17:12) and their unity among themselves (v. 21). The Trinity in some way resembles an open circle. People who have become estranged from God are invited to allow themselves to be brought back into communion with the Father in the Spirit through the Son.

In the West, especially since Augustine, God's unity has received much more emphasis than his threeness. Possibly under the influence of Neoplatonism, Augustine was sure that, before anything else, God must be singular (*simplex*); in line with Greek Neoplatonic thought a *complex* being had to be imperfect. Augustine recognized that there nevertheless had to be three "persons" in God, but in one place he moans that he does not understand what this means (*De Trinitate* 7.4). The suggestion of the Cappadocians that, from a Christian angle, personal *community* rather than *substance* is the foundational ontological category (i.e., the "highest being") seems to have bypassed him. The enormous influence of Augustine on theological development in the West consequently meant that, for many centuries, God's threeness (and thereby the plurality, the sociality in the community) was hardly emphasized. Recent scholarship has cautioned, however, against too strong a criticism of Augustine, for his *De Trinitate* is far too rich and multifaceted to be evaluated only in black-and-white terms. Attention to the way in which Father, Son, and Spirit relate to each other and to humanity in salvation history is certainly not absent from that text. But so far as the main ideas were concerned, Augustine placed the accent elsewhere, which would be determinative for subsequent major parts of Western Christianity. For instance, he developed psychological analogies in his search for the "traces" of the Trinity

(Lat. *vestigia Trinitatis*). Although he himself would be the first person to relativize the value of this type of analogy, Augustine was nevertheless of the opinion that the combination of oneness and threeness in God may be compared with, for example, the combination of memory, knowledge, and will in the human psyche. This analogy began a long tradition of looking for clever parallels to the Trinity that usually mystify rather than clarify, since they have been completely detached from the economy of salvation, which gave rise to the doctrine of the Trinity in the first place. Moreover, almost all these analogies prioritized the unity of God and gave second place to God's threeness. The Reformation would later do away with this type of analogy as senseless and unbiblical speculation; Calvin was not at all interested in such theories (*Inst.* 1.13.18).

However, the Reformation did not break with another expression that had become almost unassailable since Augustine, namely, the famous rule that the *opera trinitatis ad extra indivisa sunt*: the exterior acts of the triune God (i.e., those that are oriented to the creation) are indivisible. Such works must be attributed in equal measure to the Father, the Son, and the Spirit. Only the interior works (*ad intra*), which are between the persons of the Trinity, are divided. Only in this realm is it true that what the Father does differs from what the Son does; and the same is true for the relationship of the Spirit to the other two. Robert Jenson (b. 1930) states correctly that there is no problem with this rule in itself, as long as we recognize that Father, Son, and Spirit are not involved in the exterior works in exactly the same way either (ST 1:110–14). The New Testament itself uses various pronouns that point to distinctive elements in the acts of Father, Son, and Spirit. Following this line of thinking, the Cappadocians liked to say that the works that are directed toward creatures originate with the Father, are realized by the Son, and are perfected by the Spirit (Gregory of Nyssa, *To Ablabius: That There Are Not Three Gods*, 125). The indivisibility of the works thereby becomes the result of Father, Son, and Spirit perfectly complementing each other in their acts through their perichoretic mutuality. This understanding reflects exactly the picture of the economy of salvation that we find in the New Testament. But in the West this view could no longer be stressed after Augustine, since the *indivisa* rule suppressed all difference (e.g., very clearly with the later Anselm; see Oberdorfer 2003, 285). Yet, nobody was really happy with this result, and on the basis of the faith as it was lived—especially in monastic spirituality—people explored the limits of possible alternative understandings. Hugh of St. Victor (d. 1141), for instance, developed the so-called doctrine of appropriations. Early forms of this doctrine can be detected in Augustine and Hilary of Poitiers (ca. 315-67), but Hugh felt the urge to develop these thoughts further. He meditated on what each of the persons of the Trinity had contributed to his salvation, and he praised Father, Son, and Spirit in separate prayers. Here he met a wall, however, since tradition taught that the exterior works of God are indivisible. Yet, he felt that we could mentally attribute ("appropriate") different works specifically to one person of the Trinity, since this person was involved with a particular work in a particular way. To be sure, in so doing one should never forget that such appropriations are not fully justifiable, since, strictly speaking, the external activities of God are indivisible. Still (to cite the best-known appropriations), we may say that the Father is involved in a special way with the work of creation, while the Son is specifically involved in the work of salvation, and the Spirit in that of sanctification. Thomas Aquinas adopted this theory (STh I.39.8), and we also find it in Protestantism (e.g., Heidelberg Catechism, Q/A 24). However, one should not stretch this separation too far. When Abelard suggested that these appropriated attributes could be allocated *exclusively* to the respective persons of the Trinity, he was condemned by the Council of Sens (1141) and by Pope Innocent II (1130-43).

Not condemned was the attempt of Richard of St. Victor (a disciple of Hugh) to approach the doctrine of the Trinity, not in the Augustinian way of starting from the unity of God, but rather from threeness. From the Johannine statement that God is love, Richard concluded that there must be three persons in God, for true love cannot be directed to itself but must be directed to the other. Love can be perfect only if it does not get stuck in an exclusive contact between two loving partners, but only if you want someone else to be just as much the object of the love of the other as you are yourself. Therefore, Richard concluded, the perfect love of God cannot exist without a community of three persons. This line of reasoning was quite speculative and raised questions. (Why not four persons? Is a monogamous marriage based on an egoistic kind of lie?) But it did take into account biblical stories about God's loving attitude toward humanity. Moreover, in this way Richard was one of the few who preferred a "social" over a psychological doctrine of the Trinity. On the two Victorines, Hugh and Richard, see the brief study in Olson and Hall 2002, 57-60, and in somewhat more detail on Richard (and more critical with regard to contemporary interpretations), Bok 1996.

We should appreciate the appropriations theory, since it offered some space for the uniqueness of the work of each Trinitarian person. At the same time, it was in some sense a stopgap. It would not have been needed, had theologians realized that it can never be the intention of the *opera* rule to deny all distinctiveness in the Trinitarian activities.

In the meantime, the most beautiful and biblically authentic way to combine the oneness and the threeness in God (to the extent that we are able to do so) remains the doctrine of perichoresis. Whether it is *adequate* to express the oneness of God remains a question, for, as we saw, it finds its point of departure in the threeness in God. For this reason, the quest for a more ontological anchoring of the divine unity has always continued through the centuries, albeit with ambivalent results. Maybe we have to conclude that the mystery of the doctrine of the Trinity is not primarily how the one God can exist in three persons, but how the three Trinitarian persons can be conceived of as an ontological unity without ending in modalism.

3.5. Does the Spirit Also Proceed from the Son?

The degree to which a gradual estrangement developed between the West and the East with regard to the doctrine of the Trinity manifested itself in a painful way in the Great Schism of 1054. In that year the church of the West, centered at Rome, and that of the East, led from Constantinople, excommunicated each other. Several other issues played a role, but the immediate reason was the Western church's unilateral addition to the Nicene Creed of the word *filioque*, "and from the Son." This practice had begun in Spain a few centuries earlier, probably not intentionally but as the result of a lack of reliable translations of the Greek creed. Its aim seems to have been to exclude any form of Arianism and to recognize that, when it comes to the "procession" and the sending of the Spirit, the Spirit is in no way inferior to the Father. In the background we find once again the theology of Augustine, who considered the Holy Spirit as the bond of love that connected Father and Son. Thus the Holy Spirit moves between the Father and the Son and, in that sense, proceeds from both.

But Augustine had another and even stronger argument for his thinking. Just as the New Testament refers to the Spirit as the Spirit of the Father (e.g., Matt 10:20), it also refers to the Spirit as the Spirit of the Son (Gal 4:6) or of Christ (Phil 1:19; Rom 8:9). Therefore the sending of the Spirit may be attributed to both (cf. John 14:26 with 15:26 and 20:22). Augustine adds that the Son does *principaliter* (first and especially) proceed from the Father. So, the Father is the first source, although subsequently the Spirit also proceeds from the Son. But words like "first" and "subsequent" should not be taken literally, since there is no earlier or later in God's eternity. From a temporal perspective the procession from the Father and the Son is therefore equally original. And so, before too long, it was said without any further qualification that the Spirit proceeded from both Father and Son. To Eastern ears, however, this wording had a very strange sound. We have seen how carefully the Church of the East, ever since the Cappadocians, had dealt with the hypostatic attributes: only with regard to these did the three divine persons differ from each other. But to confess that the Spirit proceeds from the Father as well as from the Son is to shortchange the uniqueness of the three persons, even if good, anti-Arian arguments are used. For it means that the Father and the Son are, without any differentiation, equated so far as their relationship to the Spirit is concerned. This arrangement is a threat, in particular, to the uniqueness of the Father and gives the Spirit a very subordinate place. For the Spirit is the only one who lacks an attribute that both the Father and the Son possess. Especially in the East the church had had to deal with the Pneumatomachi ("opponents of the Spirit"), which was all the more reason to give the Spirit his full weight. Thus, with the *filioque* the West acted like a bull in the china shop of the meticulously formulated Eastern concept of the Trinity.

It was to be expected, therefore, that this point would lead to a conflict between East and West. It even led some people in the East—in the footsteps of the ninth-century Patriarch Photius—to teach a *monopatrism* by way of reaction, which asserted that the Spirit proceeds only from the Father, with no role whatsoever for the Son (for the nuances, see Letham 2004, 205). In this way Photius even pushed aside the Greek church fathers who had definitely maintained a role for the Son in the procession of the Spirit, albeit of a different nature than that of the Father. The Greek fathers based their views on the New Testament, where we find a relationship between the Son and the Spirit that is distinct from that between the Father and the Son. This distinction becomes quite clear in the story of Jesus's baptism in the Jordan, for instance, when not only is the voice of the Father heard, but the Spirit also descends in the form of a dove (Luke 3:21–22). This difference permitted Cyril of Alexandria (ca. 376–444) to state that the Spirit "rests in the Son" or "radiates through the Son." After Photius, the Eastern church usually applied the biblical data only to the Spirit's mission in history and not to his eternal procession. Those data spoke exclusively, as it were, to the economic and not to the ontological Trinity.

The impact of the *filioque* controversy has often been exaggerated. Eastern theologians (even in the twentieth century, as with Vladimir Lossky [1974]) could point to the *filioque* as the source of almost all problems that the Western church has experienced. It was argued that the pope was put in Christ's place and thus was placed above the Spirit, meaning that the pope was also supposedly in charge of the gifts of the Spirit as they functioned in local churches. The *filioque* was also said to have served as a means of justifying traditional authoritarian ecclesial structures. These charges may contain a kernel of truth, but such structures have not been unknown in the Eastern church. Furthermore, Protestantism rejected the pope but maintained the *filioque*. Western theologians who conclude from the rejection of the *filioque* that the East gives insufficient attention to Christ and soteriology are also mistaken, as is clear, for instance, from the great popularity in the East of the so-called Jesus prayer: "Lord Jesus Christ, Son of God, have mercy on me, a sinner."

It would be wrong to draw any quick conclusions about these claims, as the complex historical reality points us in a different direction. Yet, there is no doubt that we are here faced with different approaches to the Trinity. The tendency of the Western church to be flexible with regard to the hypostatic attributes, for example, is related to its predisposition toward modalism—as if, after all, the distinctiveness of the three persons is not so important. For its part, the tendency of the Eastern church to limit the procession of the Spirit through the Son (John 16:7; 20:22) to the history of salvation has led to a structural difference we noted above between the economic and the ontological Trinity, and thereby eventually—especially since Gregory Palamas in the fourteenth century—to a dichotomy between the "energies," or attributes, of God that can be experienced and his unknowable eternal essence. As a result, Eastern theology became *apophatic* (from Gk. *apophēmi*, "deny"), meaning that God's essence is unknowable and unspeakable, so that we can speak meaningfully about God only in negations. Ultimately, we do not know who God is and must be content with our experiences of God's temporal manifestations. This dichotomy gave Eastern spirituality its mystical and often quietistic (i.e., resigned) inclinations. Faith often became rather detached from practical life.

Through the centuries the search has continued for solutions to the problems that arose over the *filioque*. In fact, the positions of the two sides have become very close to each other. For example, the Uniate churches (Eastern churches that have accepted the authority of Rome), since the middle of the eighteenth century, have been allowed to use the original creed without the *filioque*. Here the two versions of the text are seen as complementary. The official Roman Catholic view now attributes the dispute to a misunderstanding. The word for "proceed" is said to have a different meaning in Greek than in Latin; thus there are two different creeds—one original, the "great creed," and a later regional creed—that do not contradict but complement each other. The first is said to express the relations in origin among the divine persons, while the second, with the *filioque*, seeks to underline the consubstantiality between the Father and the Son. This idea was suggested by Walter Kasper (1984, 215–21) and has subsequently (in 1995) become official under his influence. This interpretation seems rather artificial, however, for it is strange that no one previously understood that there were two creeds. It appears instead to be inspired by the Roman Catholic desire to retain the *filioque*. No wonder that the reactions from the Eastern Orthodox side were quite negative, in spite of their appreciation for the attempt to find a way out of the stalemate.

For criticism regarding the Roman Catholic attitude, see Oberdorfer 2003, 287–88. In 1875 the Old Catholic Church returned to the original text of the creed. In 1978 the Lambeth Conference advised the churches under its umbrella no longer to use the word *filioque* in the liturgy. However, the United Lutheran Church of Germany, as recently as in 2008, recommended that its associated churches continue to use the *filioque*. In the confessional documents of the United Protestant Church in the Netherlands (PKN), the recent discussion is reflected in the decision to place the words "and from the Son" in square brackets, so as to indicate that this was a later addition; the same is done by the Reformed Church in America (RCA) and the Christian Rerformed Church (CRC) in America (see OF 15). Still, there has been little reflection on this issue in Reformed circles—but see Torrance 1994, 110–43; Letham 2004, chapter 10.

We believe the solution must be found in the recognition that the West cannot change a common creed unilaterally and without discussion. Moreover, it should not seek to retain the word *filioque* at all costs. Likewise, the Eastern church should be unequivocal in rejecting monopatrism, for if the Spirit proceeds from the Son in time, this must also apply to eternity. If God were to totally differ in himself from his historical revelation, we would still, in spite of his revelation, not know with whom we are dealing, and our salvation would be unsure. The East might also be a little more generous in recognizing that adding the word *filioque* does not have to be heretical so far as content is concerned. What counts is that the term be explained as pertaining to the singular procession of the Spirit from the Father through the Son. The word *filioque* was never intended to say that the Spirit proceeds from the Father and from the Son as from two different sources (such a "double procession" would undermine the unity of God). Rather, it intended to convey the idea that the Spirit proceeded in a flowing movement from the Father and the Son, as from one source. In this the Father has the primary function, as we have heard Augustine say, so that the term *filioque* may also be interpreted as "via the Son" or "through the Son," which is in harmony with what the Greek fathers liked to say.

If the West were just to scrap the *filioque*, it would be pretending that nothing has happened through the ages and that the clock could simply be turned back. Such an attitude would reflect a serious disregard for history. As far as the East is concerned, it is likewise impossible to regard the *filioque* merely as underlining the consubstantiality of the Father and the Son and thus to interpret it in a nonliteral way. This approach would continue to bring misunderstanding. It would be much better to replace the term with *per filiumque*; according to this term (with biblical roots), the Spirit proceeds from the Father "through the Son." This wording not only does justice to the primacy of the Father and the distinction between the Father and the Son, but it also stresses that the Son himself is the first *receiver* of the Spirit. Through the Son, who received the Spirit from his Father, the Spirit goes into the world, distributing and applying salvation in Christ. In this way justice would also be done to the New Testament's Spirit-Christology, which sees Jesus par excellence as the one anointed with the divine Spirit (see also chap. 10). That is, the Spirit not only follows Jesus but also precedes him in his procession from the Father! This relation applies to time (see Luke 1:35), as well as to eternity. Moreover, various other connections in the New Testament between Father, Son, and Spirit may be inferred. Pannenberg, in particular, has correctly pointed out that the Bible focuses on the relationships not just in the origin of the three persons but in other respects as well (ST 1:299). We do not agree with Pannenberg and his disciple Oberdorfer (2001), who seem to think that all of these details must be included in the creed, however, so long as the creed does not restrict the space for the many different relationships that the New Testament suggests.

The essential element in all these relationships is that the Holy Spirit is the Spirit of the Father and belongs on God's side as a matter of principle. We, with our human spirit, are not associated with this Spirit and cannot direct it. The Spirit blows however he chooses to (John 3:8). This fact gives meaning to the so-called epiclesis prayer, the prayer that the Spirit be present as we read the Bible in worship. But no less essential is holding simultaneously that the Spirit of the Father is also the Spirit of the Son. This wording implies that the Spirit does not pervade the entire creation as a kind of divine aura but wants to be concretely operative where testimony about Jesus is heard.

3.6. The Doctrine of the Trinity and Islamic Monotheism

So far we have seen how the doctrine of the Trinity furnishes the necessary framework for understanding the story of Jesus as the story of God. Nonetheless, over the centuries the doctrine of the Trinity has been the occasion for a misconception, namely, that in reality the Christian church worships three gods. This misunderstanding continues to exist in Islam in particular, even though some Muslims today recognize that this view is indeed a misunderstanding. The fact remains that, for most Muslims, the Christian doctrine of the Trinity is a major stumbling block. It raises the question whether an effective dialogue with Muslims is possible on this topic.

When we look at the Qur'an, it seems that the concept of Trinity is prima facie denied. In surah (chap.) 4:171 we read, "People of the book, do not go beyond the boundaries of your religion. Only speak the truth about God. . . . Believe in God and in his apostles, and do not say 'three.' God will not pardon idolatry. Anyone who worships other gods besides God has strayed very far." And in 5:73 it is said, "The unbelievers are those who say, 'God is one of three.' There is only one God. If they do not stop saying this, all of them who do not believe will be severely punished." In 5:116 we even find an imaginary discussion that God will have with Jesus on the last day: "Jesus, Son of Mary, did you ever tell humanity, 'Worship me and my mother as gods besides God?'" To this Jesus of course replies that he never said any such thing. Muslims refer to such verses frequently when they argue against the doctrine of the Trinity. From a historical perspective, however, we must seriously doubt that these statements are attacking the Christian doctrine of the Trinity. For Christians do not worship other beings besides God; that would amount to the purest idolatry also from a Christian point of view. Moreover, Mary is not part of the Trinity, as surah 5:116 suggests.

These warnings must therefore relate to the polytheistic religions or the syncretistic deformations of the Christian faith that were current in the period before Muhammad and were abundantly present in the area around Mecca. Even before Muhammad came on the scene, the Kaaba in Mecca already was a holy place dedicated to the worship of various local gods by a range of desert tribes. We know the names of some of these gods. Surah 53:19-20 mentions that the pagans of Mecca believed that three of these—Al-Lāt, Al-Uzzā, and Manāt—were daughters of Allah. We cannot, however, exclude the possibility that tritheistic misunderstandings of the Christian faith were also present. In any case, Muhammad saw it as his task to call a halt to such coarse ideas and gave Islam its austerely monotheistic flavor (see George 2006, 112-13). What the Qur'an rejects, however, is not so much the Christian doctrine of the Trinity but a pagan belief in many gods. Christians do not object to this stance. On the contrary, they totally agree, for just like Muslims, they confess that there is only one God. The Old and the New Testaments battle just as fiercely against the polytheism of the surrounding culture as does Islam.

This confession of God's unity has its roots in the so-called Shema, the ancient creed of Judaism that we find in Deut 6:4: "Hear, O Israel: The LORD our God is one LORD." Jesus himself quotes these words in citing Deut 6:4-5 as the first of all commandments (Mark 12:29), and we also find it in Paul (1 Cor 8:4, 6). Christians show no tendency to downplay this statement or to de-emphasize the oneness of God because of their faith in the Trinity. Christians would be able to fully agree with the first part of the Shahadah, the Islamic confession of faith: "There is no God but God." (These words may well go back to Deut 6:4.) The Christian faith therefore takes nothing away from the *tawhid*, the fundamental unity of God, which is so essential for Muslims (see Volf 2011, chap. 7). The question remains, however, as to how this unity is to be understood. At this point the roads diverge, and we should not try to hide this fact. Not without reason we see Christianity and Islam as two distinct religions, not as variants of the same religion.

This conclusion does not mean that Allah must by definition be another God than the God of the Bible. It seems to us that the question of whether or not Christians and Muslims worship the same God is mainly semantic. It all depends on what conditions one requires for accepting two entities as identical. The morning star and the evening star, originally viewed as distinct, were found to be identical. But what about the famous ship of Theseus in Plato's *Phaedo* (58a)? Was it still the same ship after all its planks had been replaced with planks of a different kind of wood? Philosophers continue to intensely debate these types of questions, without coming to a clear consensus. In fact, whether we see Allah as identical with the God of the Bible or as a different god is not a decisive point. Christian dogmatics does not suggest one position or the other for, in the first case, it will always have to be added that Muslims and Christians know God in very different ways, while in the second case it will have to be affirmed that there certainly are similarities between Allah and the God of the Bible. There is no doubt that the Arabic word for Allah was already in use for addressing God before Islam emerged, and Arabic Christians continue to use this term in their worship of the God of the Bible. For a recent argument that Christians and Muslims worship the same God, see Volf 2011; the contrary view, for which equally good arguments can be made, is defended, for example, by John Piper; see http://www.desiringgod.org/articles/a-common-word-between-us.

Christians worship not only the God whom they, following Jesus's example, call their Father, but also the same Jesus, in the communion of the Holy Spirit. This is possible only if they both belong to the Godhead, for God does not give his glory to anyone else (Isa 42:8; 48:11). It would indeed be blasphemy (Arab. *shirk*) to equate someone who is not God with God, but it is something totally different to believe there is a richness of life in the one divine reality.

God cannot be compared with a self-sufficient individual who stands lonely at the top of the pyramid; from a Christian perspective that would be a very poor interpretation of God's oneness. "The eternally rich God" exists in a wealth of mutual relationships. And not just since creation. God did not need us to relieve any loneliness or to experience love. For God is love (1 John 4:8, 16). From all eternity the divine reality is constituted in a perichoretic movement of giving and receiving, in which Father, Son, and Holy Spirit lovingly embrace each other. This giving love is also shared with humanity and became flesh and blood in the man Jesus of Nazareth. His life of disinterested self-giving, even to the cross, was not a tragic accident but the ultimate revelation of God's one essential being. In this way the doctrine of the Trinity fills and enriches monotheism—a concept that, when separated from this Trinitarian explanation, would remain too bleak and inflexible to serve us well in our dogmatics. Far from threatening or destroying God's unity, the doctrine of the Trinity provides an enriching depth to this fundamental article of faith. In our dialogue with Muslims we can only try to convincingly share our belief that this inner richness of God's being—the plurality in God—does not destroy but rather articulates God's oneness.

3.7. The Practical Significance of the Doctrine of the Trinity

In this final section we pursue further the question of the practical significance of the doctrine of the Trinity. It is commonly complained that the Trinity is a purely abstract dogma that has nothing to do with the actual faith of "ordinary" Christians. It is true that, just as other Christian doctrines, the doctrine of the Trinity has a regulative intent. That is, in itself it is not an object of faith and proclamation, but it "regulates" what is and is not meaningful in what we say and believe about God. We might say that the doctrine belongs to the type of routine care that is not applied every day but that cannot be neglected if we want to maintain a healthy life of faith. In that sense the doctrine of the Trinity certainly has a practical significance, even though it might not be apparent at first sight.

This practical significance becomes clear only when we explore the ways in which it provides boundaries for Christian faith with regard to the various options in today's spiritual marketplace. These ways are sixfold. All six are ancient but still alive today as real, meaningful options. But all of them fail to do justice to the close connection between Father, Son, and Spirit in the salvation event as described in the gospel. The doctrine of the Trinity is intended to guard this priceless and unique gospel story, in which God lets himself be known through Christ and the Spirit. In describing the six ways to apply the Trinitarian grammar of the Christian faith, we closely follow Higton, CD 86.

> *No Son without Father.* Christians cannot be content with simply presenting Jesus as a historical figure who taught us many important truths and gave us a good moral example. Those who want to do justice to the New Testament cannot possibly see him only as a prophet or a teacher of wisdom, for his sole intention was to bring us into contact with the person he considered always and everywhere to be most important, namely, his God and Father. Therefore, one cannot be a follower of Jesus without turning around and being directed toward God. Anyone who thinks differently about the Jesus of the New Testament does not speak of the beloved Son of God.
>
> *No Father without the Son.* The Christian faith maintains that we can never come so close to God that the person and work of Jesus lose their true importance. Cross and resurrection are never a way station (as the Corinthians and other Christians who were influenced by Gnosticism might have thought) that we can leave

behind in a moment of mystical ecstasy and unmediated knowledge of God. Jesus is the road toward God, but not in the manner of a man on a journey who forgets his route as soon as he has reached his destination. On the contrary, Christians "can never find a place in the heart of the Father where there is no presence of the crucified and risen one: there is no leaving Jesus behind on the way to God" (Higton, CD 86). Those who are of another opinion speak about a god other than the "God and Father of our Lord Jesus Christ," whom the New Testament proclaims.

No Son without the Spirit. Christians believe it is impossible to have a relationship with Christ that has not been prepared and mediated by the Spirit. Without the Spirit, Jesus will remain locked up in the past as an admittedly important but nevertheless rather mysterious historical figure—or as immensely far away in heaven. Only the Spirit makes the supreme importance of Jesus clear to us and bridges the "ugly broad ditch" (the *garstige breite Graben* mentioned by Lessing) between the past, with its chaotic mass of historical events, and the present. And it is the Spirit who brings Jesus down from heaven to the human heart, by persuading that heart that it loves nothing more in heaven or on earth than this Jesus (Belgic Confession, art. 26). Without the Spirit, Jesus remains at a distance and does not become the living Jesus who comes to meet us in the New Testament.

No Spirit without the Son. Thus, a Christian is filled with the Spirit, but that Spirit never takes us to such exalted heights that the cross on which Jesus died no longer has a message for us. A spiritual person will never find himself or herself so far off in heavenly spheres that the self-giving and the sacrifice of Jesus will no longer determine who we are and what we do. For the Spirit gives joy and comfort *through* the cross and the resurrection of Christ. He does not produce a feel-good faith in which everything revolves around our self-affirmation and positive thinking. Any form of spirituality in which I detect myself, or myself in God, without any reference to Jesus is therefore sub-Christian. It may make us spiritual people, but it does not mean we have become Christians. All those who believe they can bypass Jesus in a spiritual way talk about another *spiritus* than the Spirit of the Father and the Son.

No Father without the Spirit. Without the Spirit we can never believe in God in a Christian way. The Christian faith is not about a faraway, distant God who long ago put the world in place like an intelligent watchmaker and then never gave it another thought. It is possible to have a rational kind of faith in such a deistic God, but we can hardly pray to such a God. Believing Christianly means that, through the Spirit of Christ, we have been brought into a relationship with the Father. In this context the Bible uses surprising terms like "being born again" or "being made alive" through the Spirit. To be in God is therefore a passionate experience; we could even say it involves being divinely inspired. We can know this communion with the Father only if we have been introduced to it by the Spirit—unless there is another Father than the one who, according to the New Testament, sent his Spirit.

No Spirit without the Father. Finally, the Spirit never detaches us from the concrete plans and intentions of God regarding our specific earthly reality. Through Christ he brings us back to the heart of the Father. He will never allow us to forget God's kingdom and its righteousness. No, he lets us "groan" with the creation until that kingdom becomes fully realized (Rom 8:26). It was the same Spirit who inspired Jesus in his proclamation of that kingdom in the first place. The Spirit does not allow Christians to withdraw into an atmosphere of religious self-help but equips them for a life of gratitude and service. To think differently means that one speaks of another Spirit than the Spirit of the kingdom of the Father.

In this way the doctrine of the Trinity sets the boundaries for the arena where Christian faith can flourish. It should thus be clear that it does indeed make a difference how we think about God. For God is the one we respect more than anyone or anything else. For that reason our view of God also impacts, consciously or subconsciously, the way we regard other things. Jürgen Moltmann (1993) in particular has demonstrated that the doctrine of the Trinity has an impact even in a social or political sense. If we see God as a communion of equal persons who are mutually connected in love, we will look at sociopolitical issues differently from someone who worships only an omnipotent individual at the top. In the former case we will look for communion and connectedness also in our human society and derive our identity from equal relationships with others. In the latter case we will easily slip into thinking about societal relationships in hierarchical terms, under authorities that legitimize their behavior by claiming that they somehow reflect God, to whom everybody must submit.

We readily admit that simplistic correlations (such as that a Trinitarian view of God leads to democracy and equality, while monistic ideas about God lead to dictatorship and tyranny), are easily refuted when we look at historical-empirical reality. The kings of the Old Testament, for instance, had to deal with prophets sent by God and could therefore not easily develop into a dictator, even though they had never yet heard of the Trinity. But there is no doubt that the doctrine of the Trinity does make a difference in how we think about God. We will therefore continue this theme in the next chapter, where this doctrine will provide the lens through which we look at the biblical names and attributes of God.

For recent discussions of the legitimacy of a "social" or (better) "relational" doctrine of the Trinity as distinct from the "psychological" or "classical" view, see Sexton 2014 and Brink 2014. A defense of the (classical?) view that the doctrine of the Trinity expresses the mystery of God and should not be put to other theological uses is Holmes 2012. Though it is generally acknowledged that it is too simplistic to oppose both views as Eastern versus Western or Greek versus Latin (a thesis that has, rightly or not, been traced to Théodore de Régnon [1892-98]), the debate as to which version Christians should prefer is far from settled.

References

Augustine. 1993. *On the Holy Trinity, Doctrinal Treatises, Moral Treatises*. NPNF[1], vol. 3. Grand Rapids: Eerdmans. Orig. pub., 1887.

Ayres, Lewis. 2004. *Nicaea and Its Legacy: An Approach to Fourth-Century Trinitarian Theology*. Oxford: Oxford University Press.

Bok, Nico den. 1996. *Communicating the Most High: A Systematic Study of Person and Trinity in the Theology of Richard of St. Victor (d. 1173)*. Paris: Brepols.

Brink, Gijsbert van den. 2014. "Social Trinitarianism: A Discussion of Some Recent Theological Criticisms." *International Journal of Systematic Theology* 62:331-50.

Dempsey, Michael T., ed. 2011. *Trinity and Election in Contemporary Theology*. Grand Rapids: Eerdmans.

Ehrman, Bart. 2014. *How Jesus Became God: The Exaltation of a Jewish Preacher from Galilee*. New York: HarperOne.

George, Timothy, ed. 2006. *God the Holy Trinity: Reflections on Christian Faith and Practice*. Grand Rapids: Baker Academic.

Grenz, Stanley J. 2004. *Rediscovering the Triune God: The Trinity in Contemporary Theology*. Minneapolis: Fortress.

Hanson, Richard P. C. 1988. *The Search for the Christian Doctrine of God: The Arian Controversy, 318-381.* Edinburgh: T&T Clark.

Holmes, Stephen R. 2012. *The Quest for the Trinity: The Doctrine of God in Scripture, History, and Modernity.* Downers Grove, IL: IVP Academic.

Jenson, Robert W. 1982. *The Triune Identity: God according to the Gospel.* Philadelphia: Fortress.

Kärkkäinen, Veli-Matti. 2007. *The Trinity: Global Perspectives.* Louisville: Westminster John Knox.

Kasper, Walter. 1984. *The God of Jesus Christ.* New York: Crossroad.

Kelly, John N. D. 1977. *Early Christian Doctrines.* 5th ed. London: Black. Orig. pub., 1958.

Kuitert, H. Martinus. 1999. *Jesus: The Legacy of Christianity.* London: SCM.

Letham, Robert. 2004. *The Holy Trinity in Scripture, History, Theology, and Worship.* Phillipsburg, NJ: P&R Publishing.

Lossky, Vladimir. 1974. "The Procession of the Holy Spirit in Orthodox Trinitarian Doctrine." In *In the Image and Likeness of God,* 71-96. Crestwood, NY: St. Vladimir's Seminary Press. Orig. pub., 1948.

Markschies, Christoph. 2000. *Alta trinità beata.* Gesammelte Studien zur altkirchlichen Trinitätstheologie. Tübingen: J. C. B. Mohr.

McCormack, Bruce L. 2000. "Grace and Being." In *The Cambridge Companion to Karl Barth,* edited by John Webster, 92-110. Cambridge: Cambridge University Press.

Meesters, Albert C. 2012. "The Cappadocians and Their Trinitarian Conceptions of God." *Neue Zeitschrift für systematische theologie und religionsphilosophie* 54:396-413.

Moltmann, Jürgen. 1993. *The Trinity and the Kingdom.* Minneapolis: Fortress.

Oberdorfer, Bernd. 2001. *Filioque: Geschichte und Theologie eines ökumenischen Problems.* Göttingen: Vandenhoeck & Ruprecht.

———. 2003. "Brauchen wir das Filioque? Aspekte des Filioque-Problems in der heutigen Diskussion." *Kerygma und Dogma* 49:278-92.

Oeming, Manfred. 2002. "Vestigia trinitatis? Vorahnungen der Trinität im Alten Testament!" *Glaube und Lernen* 17:41-54.

Olson, Roger E., and Christopher A. Hall. 2002. *The Trinity.* Grand Rapids: Eerdmans.

Pontifical Council for Promoting Christian Unity. 1995. "The Greek and Latin Traditions regarding the Procession of the Holy Spirit." *L'Osservatore Romano: Weekly Edition in English,* September 20, pp. 3 and 6.

Rahner, Karl. 2004. "Remarks on the Dogmatic Treatise 'De Trinitate.'" In *Theological Investigations,* 4:77-102. Limerick, Ireland: Mary Immaculate College.

Régnon, Théodore de. 1892-98. *Études de théologie positive sur la Sainte Trinité.* 4 vols. Paris: Victor Retaux.

Ritter, Adolf M. 1965. *Das Konzil von Konstantinopel und sein Symbol: Studien zur*

Geschichte und Theologie des II. ökumenischen Konzils. Göttingen: Vandenhoeck & Ruprecht.

Schwöbel, Christoph, ed. 1995. *Trinitarian Theology Today.* Edinburgh: T&T Clark, 1–30.

———. 2009. "The Trinity between Athens and Jerusalem." *Journal of Reformed Theology* 3:22–41.

Sexton, Jason S., ed. 2014. *Two Views on the Doctrine of the Trinity.* Grand Rapids: Zondervan.

Swain, Scott R. 2013. *The God of the Gospel: Robert Jenson's Trinitarian Theology.* Downers Grove, IL: InterVarsity Press.

Torrance, Thomas F. 1994. *Trinitarian Perspectives: Toward Doctrinal Agreement.* Edinburgh: T&T Clark.

———. 1996. *The Christian Doctrine of God: One Being, Three Persons.* Edinburgh: T&T Clark.

Volf, Miroslav. 2011. *Allah: A Christian Response.* New York: HarperOne.

Webster, John. 2006. "God's Perfect Life." In *God's Life in Trinity*, edited by Miroslav Volf and Michael Welker, 143–52. Minneapolis: Fortress.

———. 2008. "Life in and of Himself: Reflections on God's Aseity." In *Engaging the Doctrine of God: Contemporary Protestant Perspectives*, edited by Bruce L. McCormack, 107–24. Grand Rapids: Baker Academic.

4 "Great Is Thy Faithfulness"

The Names, Attributes, and Essence of God

AIM

In chapter 2 we discussed the question of whether there is a God (in the Latin of the classic doctrine, *an Deus sit*). In chapter 3 we dealt with the doctrine of the Trinity, traditionally discussed in reply to "how God is" (*qualis Deus sit*). We are now left with the question that usually comes second, namely, who or what God is (*quis/quid Deus sit*). This rubric typically covers the so-called attributes, or properties, of God, sometimes preceded or followed by reflections on the divine being. We have decided to change the usual order because we feel that, from a Christian perspective, the doctrine of the Trinity is the heart of the doctrine of God. That is, we can adequately consider the being and properties of God only in light of the doctrine of the Trinity.

In the following pages we intend to:

- sensitize the reader to the special *relational* nature of our knowledge of God (4.1)
- provide a survey of some important names of God in the Old Testament (4.2)
- do the same regarding the names of God in the New Testament (4.3)
- explain how and why this proliferation of divine names led to a doctrine of God's properties (4.4)
- discuss the theory of Hellenization and thereby answer a key question about the influence of Greek philosophy on the Christian concept of God (4.5)
- explore whether it is possible to adequately express divine reality in human terms by means of analogy (4.6)
- demonstrate how latent problems in the doctrine of God can be avoided by approaching the divine attributes from a Trinitarian perspective, put-

ting God's condescension first and seeing the properties of God's transcendence as qualifying this turning toward humankind (4.7)

- discuss how, on the basis of God's properties, we can and must take one more step in our dogmatic formulations and speak of God's very being (4.8).

MAKING CONNECTIONS

1. Fewer and fewer people in Western Europe still believe in God, and in the American religious census, the number of people indicating "no religion" is rising. Why? Does it have to do with the development of science and technology? In any case, many people indicate that they still believe in some higher power, in "the divine," or at least in "something." Does that mean anything, or are these really other words for God? If possible, discuss these questions with a group.

2. Our concept of God is largely determined by the attributes or properties we ascribe to God, consciously or subconsciously. It makes a big difference whether we see God primarily as sovereign, transcendent, and holy, or as loving, pardoning, and close to us. What is your image of God, and why is it that image instead of something else? Is there something like a "biblical image" of God that may help us adjust and correct our ideas?

4.1. Knowing God as Relational Knowledge

"Our wisdom, insofar as it ought to be deemed true and solid wisdom, consists almost entirely of two parts: the knowledge of God and of ourselves. But as these are connected together by many ties, it is not easy to determine which of the two precedes and gives birth to the other." With these monumental words Calvin begins his *Institutes* (1.1.1). There is considerable debate about the historical tradition behind this statement, but whatever the case, according to Calvin we cannot speak about God in an objective manner. From the very start, we are personally involved in this matter. We cannot make any "existentially neutral" statements about God, as we might, for instance, about neutrino particles, numbers, or being in love. For God is not an entity like other entities, not a phenomenon that is open in principle to observation and analysis. Continuous rigorous research will not enable us to discover all kinds of interesting facts about

God. God transcends the level of everyday empirical sensation; knowledge of God is therefore of a different order than factual knowledge. This knowledge is by definition relational; that is to say, it is embedded in the relationship that God has initiated with us. Apart from this relationship, we know virtually nothing about God.

Calvin's favorite way of expressing this awareness is to say that our knowledge of God is embedded in piety (*pietas*), the reverential and trusting bond with God. This personal involvement is invoked by God's gracious turning toward humanity as Creator (*Inst.*, bk. 1) and Redeemer (*Inst.*, bk. 2). Calvin has scant interest in who God is apart from this condescension toward us. He tends to quickly dismiss such ideas as idle speculation; he wants to know who God is for us.

We think that this focus remains the most important point of departure for a doctrine of God. We must not expect to discover all kinds of interesting details from an aloof, detached position. We cannot form an independent opinion about God at a safe distance and then, on that basis, decide whether or not we will believe in him. In speaking of God, we inevitably speak of the one who wants to relate to us, who appeals to us, calls us, judges us, and yearns to show us his grace. It is within this relationship—in classic terms, within this covenant bond—that God allows himself to be known. The unique fact is therefore that we can come to know God only if we journey together with him along the path of faith. And it is impossible to plan or chart that journey beforehand. There are no guarantees as to what will happen along the way. We are like Abraham, who was for good reason called the father of all believers; he was called to leave his region of birth and to travel to a place unknown, knowing only that the God who had called him would show him the way (Gen 12:1, also Heb 11:8). Apparently, we will learn to know the God of Abraham only as we journey with him. And even then, we have no grip on him; we will not "grasp" him.

It is extremely important for the church today to retain this view of the non-objectifiable human knowledge of God. Many late-modern people are deeply religious (Albert Einstein is a good example) but have distanced themselves from the church out of the feeling that its God is too small, too easy to comprehend by a series of ecclesiastical formulas. Indeed, there is a real risk lest what the church has to say about God be reduced to a few ready-made doctrinal or spiritual points that can be easily swallowed by a traditional middle-class audience—the idea, for instance, that God is nice and friendly and that we can please him if we would just be a little nicer and friendlier too. Or that God will reward our piety by giving us success (the so-called health-and-wealth gospel). These shallow concepts reemerge from time to time but tend to be rather fleeting, for they are at such variance with the complex and unruly reality.

In this connection we may point to Ps 77:19, where we find a remarkable reflection on Israel's crossing of the Red Sea (or Reed Sea; Exod 14):

> Thy way was through the sea,
> thy path through the great waters;
> yet thy footprints were unseen.

The way of God is not objectifiable and cannot be defined through the "clear and distinct ideas" that René Descartes made mandatory for philosophy; all the more so for God's being. But we can still follow God along his way. Psalm 77 continues with the assurance that God led his people like a flock (v. 20), even though his footprints remained unseen. God prepares a way for the journey. Along the way he provides enough light to take the next step, but often no more than that (Ps 119:105). In Isa 43 we discover how God's saving presence is not apparent until the very moment when people cannot even take that one step and are threatened on all sides. It is precisely then that God, as Israel's Holy One, provides a route of escape:

> When you pass through the waters I will be with you;
> and through the rivers, they shall not overwhelm you;
> when you walk through fire you shall not be burned,
> and the flame shall not consume you.
> For I am the LORD your God,
> the Holy One of Israel, your Savior.

(Isa 43:2–3)

Remarkably enough, God does not promise a route around the fire or above the water. Three times we read that the route is *through* the difficulties. And so it apparently is. But three times as well the statement is accompanied by the word "not." Believers receive no preferential treatment so as to avoid life's disasters. They can rest assured, however, that in the midst of these God will not abandon them to destruction but will show his saving presence. This, apparently, is how Israel's God is; we cannot chart his actions beforehand.

The awareness that our ability to say anything substantial about God depends on God's coming to us is deeply anchored in the Jewish-Christian tradition. Nonetheless, it remains important to stress the point. As human beings, we are somehow inclined to shape God according to the limited scope and content of our own thinking. Inevitably this means that we reduce God to someone who is approximately like ourselves without our weak points, only magnified. Sigmund Freud had a point with his projection theory, although he was not the first person to propose it; Christian dogmatics had already discussed it. For, however much Christian dogmatics has been suspected of confining God to human concepts, it has always realized that such a view should not and cannot be allowed to stand. God transcends our thoughts and projections. Throughout all Christian reflection on the faith, we discover the motto *Deus semper maior* (God is always greater). Augustine long ago observed, "If you comprehend it, it is not God" (*si enim comprehendis, non est Deus*; Sermo 117.3.5; see Geest 2010).

As we have seen (in 3.1), Anselm describes God as *id quo nihil maius nihil cogitari possit*. This phrase must not be translated "the highest thinkable" (see *Proslogion*, chap. 15) but, in a more cumbersome manner, "that than which nothing greater can be thought." Thomas Aquinas said that God cannot be confined to a *genus*, to something that belongs to a particular category (*Deus non est in genere*; STh I.3.5), since God is not part of any broader category. Aquinas tried to break open the prevailing metaphysical concepts and distinctions of his time in such a way that our language would not be closed to the transcendental character of God, which goes beyond our thinking. However, later scholastic theology once again bred overly concrete images of God—for instance, God as a despot who was beyond the law (*ex lex*), or as being more than satisfied when we humans simply do our best (*facere quod in se est*). Calvin did not like such ideas. It worried him greatly that human nature is "a perpetual factory of idols" (*Inst.* 1.11.8), that we have a persistent tendency to domesticate God and make him serve our own purposes.

Reformed theology, in particular, with its well-developed doctrine of sin, has had a sharp eye out for such a distortion of faith into an ideology—a sin that ultimately defies the Old Testament prohibition of making idols (Exod 20:4). At the same time, the Reformed tradition closely tied all knowledge of God to biblical revelation as a description of the way God goes with us. As we follow this route, we certainly do not learn everything about God, but only "as much as is necessary for us" (Belgic Confession, art. 2). Knowledge of God is thus primarily relational knowledge, which we acquire along the path of faith. G. C. Berkouwer, an important theologian of the twentieth century and our inspiration on this point, expressed this connection as "a correlation between faith and revelation" (Berkouwer, SD 3:164). In dogmatics we are not dealing with objective propositions or theories about God, but with the things that are confessed about him, based on our faith experience of being addressed by God's revelation.

To take the way that God goes with us as our point of departure means, in Christian language, to begin with God's turning toward us as Father, Son, and Spirit. In the footsteps of Israel, Jesus Christ, and the early church, we come to know God as a God who, in his love, wants to safeguard us and the world. In this manner he comes to meet us, and in this manner we come to know him. Here, then, we find our starting point for speaking about God.

Even though God allows himself to be known along this route, it does not imply that, as we follow this track, we can understand him. For it is precisely in his condescension toward us that God shows how far he transcends our understanding in his highness and otherness. God's turning toward us in no way detracts from his transcendence—the two aspects presuppose each other. For that reason many classic texts and church confessions recognize the incomprehensibility (in the Latin of classic theology, the *incomprehensibilitas*) of God. It does not mean that we can never be sure about God's intentions, but rather, that our cerebral capacity is too limited and too underdeveloped to have a full understanding of God. In itself, that limitation is not so strange. It is much more astonishing, in fact, that we do understand so much of reality. Among the tens of thousands of kinds of living beings that populate the earth, *Homo sapiens sapiens* is the only one with the sort of brain that is adapted to such understanding. However, when it comes to divine reality, we human beings do not understand much more than chimpanzees understand about the laws of nature. We cannot comprehend (*comprehendere*) God's reality with our brain. Only in the relationship that he initiates with us, as we journey together with him, can we learn who and what God is. Martin Luther expressed this point as follows: only experience (*experientia*) makes a human being into a theologian (WA TR 1:16.13 [no. 46]). Some traditions within Dutch Reformed Protestantism and its American offshoots use the word *bevindelijk* (roughly, "experiential-pietistic") for this concept.

Partly nourished by postmodern philosophy, which is critical of all narrowly defined epistemological claims of modernity, contemporary theology is highly sensitive to this nonrational (or experiential or mystical) element of our knowledge of God. In this connection we often hear of apophatic theology, which holds that we really do not know much about who and what God is; whatever thoughts or statements we do have about him are inadequate and therefore must be denied. It is easier to say what God is *not* than to state what he is. In the Eastern Church this accent has always been important. Athanasius referred to God as incomprehensible being, and the Cappadocian Fathers stressed that God does not exist in the same manner as created things; therefore, we can ultimately not know him. Only the path of mystical experience allows us to get in touch with the divine, with what in the East became known as God's *energies*. This "negative theology" entered the West particularly through the mysterious Pseudo-Dionysius the Areopagite (this anonymous theologian reportedly lived around 500 but was identified in the Middle Ages with the Dionysius who was converted by Paul on the Areopagus, Acts 17:34). As a result, his words acquired an almost apostolic authority. Though the apophatic theology in the East was considered superior to the kataphatic (positive, propositional) theology in the West, the two approaches were mostly seen as correcting or balancing each other. In the West truly apophatic thinkers such as Meister Eckhart (ca. 1300) and Nicholas of Cusa (fifteenth century) remained exceptions. Thomas Aquinas described three roads that lead to knowledge of God (ST I.13.1–5). He maintained that we should not just negatively deny all earthly imperfections with regard to God (the *via negativa*) but should also, positively, ascribe the causes of all good things to God (the *via causalitatis*) and regard him as the one to whom all good properties belong in the highest degree (the *via eminentiae*). In this regard the contemporary apophatic trend in theology can at times hardly be distinguished from secular agnosticism, which shows the necessity of a correction from the angle of a confessing (kataphatic) theology. Nonetheless, the apophatic accent remains important as a reminder of the very specific, given and fragmentary character of the Christian knowledge of God.

Although our knowledge of God is relational, it does not imply that this knowledge is not real. God may be incomprehensible, but that does not make him unknowable. This is an important distinction. On the ever-varying track of God's involvement with us, we continue to deal with the same God. His actions fall into recognizable patterns, so that God has acquired a certain *reputation* from the ways in which he interacts with human beings. The experiences of biblical people with him were often surprisingly similar. In fact, these were frequently collective, such as the crossing of the Red Sea, and evolved into faith traditions. Some of the faith traditions were confirmed when they were incorporated into the canon of the Bible and thus acquired normative status.

In the Bible concrete names and properties attributed to God express, so to speak, the constant elements in his interactions with us. In the Lord's Prayer, for instance, God is addressed as Father, and Jesus's disciples are invited to use this form of address. It seems that this concept has the capacity to denote something that is true about God, something about God that can be known. And in the familiar text John 3:16 ("For God so loved the world . . ."), we are told that God loves and that his actions are motivated by love. This is a very concrete and far-reaching statement about who God is and about what defines his identity. In this way, all kinds of statements of faith that have their origin in the human relationship with God convey some content. It may well be that conveying such content is not their primary intention; the Lord's Prayer, for instance, intends first of all to praise God and make requests of him. Yet, in this praise and these requests, something concrete is said about God. This element of content—or in contemporary language, this truth claim—cannot be totally filtered away.

It has become quite common to encounter attempts to filter truth claims out of faith statements, done so on the supposition that statements of faith are merely expressions of experiences, demonstrations of trust, a moral commitment, a hopeful perspective on reality, and so forth. Certainly they do not constitute "is statements," that is, assertions about a really living God, let alone genuine knowledge of God. In theology this position is known as *nonrealism*. In the Anglo-Saxon world it became especially popular through the philosophy of Ludwig Wittgenstein and the theology of Don Cupitt (see Crowder 1997, but see also the response in Moore 2003). The features that nonrealists attribute to statements of faith (expression of trust, etc.) are certainly valid; it is correct to emphasize that faith statements are not detached propositions. The big problem is that faith statements cannot be reduced to the features so referred to without destroying their character in an essential way. A statement such as "The LORD is my light and my salvation" (Ps 27:1) is surely a statement of trust, but in addition it points to a particular situation, condition, or fact that is presupposed. It means more than simply, "I look at the future with confidence." Thus, statements of faith, whatever else they may be, are also factual statements about God and his relationship with us and with reality.

In short, in the doctrine of God we are not unfolding theoretical speculations but reflecting on the way in which God is spoken of, based on his relationship with humanity.

4.2. The Names of God—Old Testament

Paying attention to the names of God in the Old and New Testaments helps us trace some characteristics that are essential to the concept of God in the biblical writings. Especially we should note carefully the names given by the sixteenth-century Bible translators, who referred to the central name in the Old Testament as Lord—in today's theological literature usually rendered as YHWH. This stands for the so-called Tetragrammaton (i.e., four-letter word), which we find in the Hebrew Bible. We do not know how this preferred name for Israel's God was originally pronounced; in any case, it was not said as "Jehovah," as has often been thought, and possibly also not as "Yahweh." Quite early in Judaism the divine name was no longer pronounced at all for fear of violating the third commandment of the Decalogue (Exod 20:7). Wherever the Tetragrammaton was found in the Scriptures, "Adonai"—a common word that meant "lord"—was read instead. We may find this response to be rather exaggerated, but it shows great awe for the divine name. To leave the name unpronounced shows that people had no handle on God and could not manipulate him.

Nonetheless, God did reveal his name. By so doing he stepped out from hiddenness into the world as we experience it and allowed himself to be addressed. Otherwise no one could ever have known God. In the Old Testament God appears at various times and places to different people. We call such an appearance a *theophany*. Often it occurs at a crucial moment in someone's life. God makes himself present as an occasion of encouragement, adoration, or admonition. A theophany may occur in the form of a dream or a vision (Gen 28:12), in a special encounter (Gen 18; 32:24-32; Judg 13:3-7), or (often) in some unspecified way (Gen 12:1; 26:2, 24). In any case, Abraham experienced such a theophany several times, as did Isaac and Jacob. Frequently the event included everyone who was connected with the recipient in one way or another; they too were included in the encouragement or the admonition. It seems that God is keen to have encounters. He uses them to connect with people who are the focus of his attention. He is a God of relationships who looks for communion and communication; to use more traditional terms, he wants to make a covenant with people, an enduring mutual relationship (seen most clearly in Gen 17:1-2).

Moses received one of the most remarkable theophanies. According to the story in Exod 3, God appears to him in a burning bush that is not consumed in the fire. When Moses sees this bush and approaches to take a closer look at this strange spectacle, he learns that this is not what he is supposed to do. Instead God speaks out of the bush and tells him to take his shoes off, "for the place on which you are standing is holy ground" (Exod 3:5). God then makes himself known as "the God of your father, the God of Abraham, the God of Isaac, and the God of Jacob" (v. 6). It is clear that God has seen the misery of the Israelites, who have been oppressed in Egypt, and has come specifically to call Moses with the assignment to lead the people out of their precarious situation. It stands to reason that Moses has his doubts and wonders what he is to say when the Israelites ask who has sent him. Apparently, reference to the ancestors is not enough in this situation; there must be a name if the people are to call upon God and to appeal to him in their distress (Rad, TOT 1:181-82). Then the text continues as follows:

> God said to Moses, "I AM WHO I AM." And he said, "Say this to the people of Israel, 'I AM has sent me to you.'" God also said to Moses, "Say this to the people of Israel, 'The LORD, the God of your fathers, the God of Abraham, the God of Isaac, and the God of Jacob, has sent me to you': this is my name forever, and thus I am to be remembered throughout all generations." (Exod 3:14-15)

In response to Moses's question about the name of the God who was sending him, he hears the name YHWH. The peculiar thing is that YHWH can hardly be called a name at all. It is a word derived from the Hebrew verb "to be" or, more dynamically, "to live." It may be translated in different ways—for instance, as "I am who I am," but also in a future sense, as "I will be who I will be." The older translations often use capital and small caps to indicate the very special character of this name.

In accordance with the special character of the divine name, traditional dogmatics has ascribed the property of life (*vita*) to God. God is, first of all, the Living One. In actual fact we must say that only God lives in the true sense of the word and that our life is a derived and temporal existence that originates in "the fountain of life" (Ps 36:9; cf. Acts 17:28). In this connection Amandus Polanus remarks that in God *vita* and *vivere*—the noun (life) and the verb (to live)—coincide (Heppe, RD 5.10). This combination points to a dynamic quality, the same quality that strikes us in Exod 3. Those who with Aquinas (STh I.13.11) follow the Septuagint and render the divine name as "he who is" (*qui est*), and on that basis define God as the true being (*ipsum esse*), do not do full justice to this dynamism and make the image of God too static. It becomes quite clear from the context of Exod 3:14 that God promises

Moses his saving presence and involvement. Today many Old Testament scholars see shades of meanings other than "being" and "living" in the stem of this verb, but these also contain the same connotations of dynamism and involvement (e.g., Feldmeier and Spieckermann 2011, chaps. 1, 29).

In any case, YHWH expresses God's *freedom*. God is who he is; he does not allow himself to be manipulated or even to be defined. He remains who he is in how he relates to his people, for he wants to be there for them. Perhaps we should even say that this is the only way in which he *can* be there for them. If God would allow us to have him in our grip, he would eventually become nothing more than an extension of our own goals, with all the ambiguities this relationship implies. In any case, it is for good reason that Moses once again hears the other characterization of God: the God of Abraham, Isaac, and Jacob. This series of names points to God's faithfulness across the generations. The names of the patriarchs are a reminder of the history of God's involvement with people who often only listened to him halfheartedly, failed continuously, and went their own dubious ways before allowing themselves to be put back on track toward God's future. The God who kept looking for them and kept appealing to them will also not let their offspring down. Moses and the Israelites, in turn, must also deal with this God who does not let them get away with a nicely worded theological definition of who he is but speaks to them, launches an appeal, and commissions people with assignments for the implementation of his plans—all to reveal himself to them along this route. Never in his entire life would Moses get away from the God he met on that memorable day in the desert.

The passage in Exod 3 is an extremely fruitful text for understanding the doctrine of God. Through the ages it has constantly spurred theological reflection. The points referred to above have emerged time and again, though with varying emphases. The transcendence and elusiveness of God and the surprising way in which he comes to save his people bear a close connection, which is revealed in God's name. God wants to involve us and relate to us. For this latter aspect, see especially Higton CD, 32–36; under the heading "The God Who Addresses," Higton points out that God in his freedom more frequently makes himself heard than seen (34); indeed, in the Old Testament, seeing God is often surrounded by fear of the numinous (Exod 33:20; Judg 13:22).

In the theological tradition the close link between God's transcendence and his presence is a prominent theme, especially in Calvin. It received a central role in Barth, who described God as "der Liebende in der Freiheit" (the one who loves in freedom). Berkhof coined the dual conceptuality of transcendence and condescension in this connection, and B. Wentsel even derived the title of his compact dogmatics—"God Is Present"—from the revelation of the divine name in Exod 3. Exodus 3 clearly demonstrates that God's transcendence must not be interpreted as a detached loftiness; it emphasizes that the high and holy God is the one who comes and bends toward the world. For a comprehensive view of the theological meaning of Exod 3, see also Allen 2011.

The rest of the Old Testament includes numerous stories that further elaborate upon the identity of this unique God. The work of the prophets with their oracles was a constant reminder of the communion in which God wants to live with his people. The Old Testament regularly repeats the short formula "I am the LORD, your God." The revelation of the divine name is thus much more than an interesting fact that is worth knowing; it constitutes the covenant that God makes with his people.

This covenant comes under constant threat, mostly because Israel finds itself in a situation in which other gods court the favor of the people. Large parts of the Old Testament are focused on this fierce controversy. The big question is whether YHWH may rightfully claim to be a comprehensive name for God—in Hebrew, *Elohim*—or whether he may be identified with the natural, vegetative, and sexual powers of the fertility cults of Israel's neighbors. Archeological discoveries give an ever-clearer picture of how strong these cults were in the Israel at the time (see Becking et al. 2001). The intense struggle comes to a preliminary climax in the dramatic story of Elijah on Mount Carmel, which leads the people to confess: "The LORD, he is God; the LORD, he is God" (1 Kgs 18:39). This same confession is found in the credo of Deut 6:4, which we quoted earlier, the so-called Shema (Heb. *shema*, "hear!") Yisrael: "Hear, O Israel: The LORD our God is one LORD." He is the only God who deserves our worship and adoration. Thus we see a development toward *monolatry* (the worship of one God). Israel, however, never reached the stage of what we call *monotheism*, the recognition that there is only one God. In the New Testament, too, the worship of the God of Israel continued in a context in which many powers, forces, influences, and gods were still claiming to be worthy of worship. Seen from a biblical perspective, there is nothing new in the fact that Western Christians today experience their faith in a pluralistic religious environment.

The other Old Testament names for God fit in the brief survey presented above. The name YHWH Tsebaoth (Lord of the heavenly armies, Lord of hosts), for instance, emphasizes the unparalleled greatness of God. Loneliness does not accord with divine glory, and therefore God is presented as being surrounded by an army of heavenly beings. Other names are composites of El, the singular form of Elohim, such as El Shaddai (God the most powerful one, Gen 17:1; 28:3) and El Elyon (God the most high, Gen 14:18). But God may also be referred to as Baal (lord, owner; Hos 2:18), Adonai (commander, Gen 18:27), or Melek (king, Isa 6:5); meanwhile, as we already saw in chapter 3, hypostatic titles eventually emerged, such as "the Name" and "the Power." These names all underline God's transcendence, but they do not ignore the aspect of God's condescension toward humankind. Berkhof, for example, points out that the concept of *kabod* (honor, glory), which appears to express God's sovereignty in a very pregnant way, is also closely tied to God's presence in the temple and the salvation he brings to his people (e.g., Ps 29:2, cf. v. 11). In the Old Testament the names of God are closely linked to God's communication and communion with people (see Korpel and Moor 2011, a book that, notwithstanding its title, is mostly dedicated to God's speaking).

Another important feature for the doctrine of God is that the older names often have a more general, Canaanite background (the history of religion helps us to trace this aspect) and were subsequently applied to Israel's covenant God YHWH. He adopted various functions of the original deities but not without severe criticisms of their arbitrariness or inhuman practices (note Gen 22 as a criticism regarding child sacrifice). Who the God of Israel is must, in the end, become clear from his acts, and he wants his name to bear the stamp of those actions.

4.3. The Names of God—New Testament

The New Testament gives a central place to the experience of those who meet the God of Israel in the person, ministry, and events surrounding Jesus of Nazareth. In chapter 10 we will take a closer look at the connection between the doctrine of God and Christology, but for now we can state that, according to the New Testament, God may be known uniquely through Jesus Christ. In Acts 10:38 the experience of the first Christians is summarized by relating how God anointed Jesus with the Spirit, and how Jesus subsequently "went about doing good and healing all that were oppressed by the devil, for God was with him." The same can also be said of others, but the New Testament goes further. Jesus demonstrated in a definitive way who God is. For this reason, he is called a reflection of "the glory of God [note our discussion of *kabod* above] and . . . the very stamp of his nature" (Heb 1:3). The evangelist John also makes it a point to connect Jesus with God's *kabod*. God's glory becomes, as it were, flesh and blood in the walk and actions of this one: "And the Word became flesh and dwelt among us, full of grace and truth; we have beheld his glory, glory as of the only Son from the Father" (John 1:14). The Greek verb that is translated "dwelt" alludes to the tabernacle, to the *shekinah*. In Jesus, God lives among the people. And John then adds: "No one has ever seen God; the only Son, who is in the bosom of the Father, he has made him known [*exēgēsato*]" (John 1:18).

In this last statement John returns to the Old Testament motif that no human being is capable of actually seeing God (see 4.2 above). Yet, this hiddenness does not prevent God from entering the realm of human experience. In Jesus's ministry in particular, God explains himself, makes visible who he is—even, we could say, using the related English verb, that Jesus has *exegeted* God for us. As we will see in chapter 10, he did so by presenting himself as the one with a divine mandate and thereby regularly identified himself with God as he acted and spoke on his behalf. The relationship between Jesus and God is so strong and immediate that, on this basis, God acquires a new name and in the New Testament is referred to as the Father (Matt 11:25-27; John 5:19-44) or even "our Father" (Matt 6:9). Admittedly, we find this title also in the Old Testament, but only a few times (e.g., Isa 63:16; Mal 1:6). The high frequency and the independence that "*the* Father" acquires in the New Testament can be understood only in the context of Jesus's example and initiative.

Because of the close relationship between Jesus and God the Father, we find that, after the resurrection, the word "Lord" (Gk. *kyrios*) becomes the most common title for Jesus. A high point in the Gospel of John is Thomas's confession, when he addresses the risen Lord as "my Lord and my God" (John 20:28). This title is so remarkable because *kyrios* in the Septuagint—the Greek translation of the Old Testament writings—is the Greek translation of YHWH, the divine name in Exod 3. This is a highly important fact for the doctrine of God. God is not just the highest of all, who in his heavenly glory far exceeds human beings (even though this feature certainly remains present; e.g., see 1 Tim 6:16). God is also the one who in Jesus Christ mixes with the people and shares in the vulnerable conditions of their existence, which John refers to as the "flesh." The highness and holiness of God, his numinous quality, does not disappear, as we can notice in many New Testament passages about Jesus and his ministry (e.g., Luke 5:8). However, God's definitive turning toward us in Jesus predominates. Concretely, we can say that, in Jesus, God gets very much involved, in a personal and immediate way, with humanity's guilty estrangement from him and with the misery in which we have landed. The story of Jesus's death on the cross is therefore of crucial importance for the Christian doctrine of God. Paul writes in an astonishing paradox that "they crucified the Lord of glory" (1 Cor 2:8), that is, the YHWH of the *kabod*. We see here how the person of the crucified and risen Jesus Christ puts an abiding stamp on our concept of God.

This "abiding," however, remains somewhat controversial in the theological tradition. Van Ruler referred to the incarnation of Christ as an intermezzo, arguing that in the eschaton Jesus will, so to speak, disappear from the image of God. In the early church Marcellus of Ancyra (ca. 285-374) held a similar position: the role of Jesus and of the Spirit was limited to creation and redemption, and eventually only the Father would remain. For Marcellus as well as for Van Ruler, 1 Cor 15:28 was an important proof text. Marcellus's conclusions, however, were rejected at the First Council of Constantinople (381), which added words to that effect to the Nicene Creed (325): "whose reign shall have no end." Van Ruler likewise has received but little support for his view—and rightly so. Even in the book of Revelation Jesus continues to share in the worship of God, which is described as continuing for ever and ever (e.g., Rev 5:12-13).

This is all we will say for now about the New Testament names for God, since we will return to these interconnections more extensively in chapter 10, in the context of Christology. Here we conclude that the Christian doctrine of God finds its point of departure in the manner in which God presents himself in the Old Testament, and in the further and decisive clarification of that image of God in the New Testament in Jesus's ministry. Moreover, on the basis of the Old Testament we can distinguish two fundamental and closely related motifs in the human knowledge of God. On the one hand, we encounter a deep awareness of God's highness or transcendence. God is the Holy One, who is not to be identified with but far surpasses our world and its laws. On the other hand, there is a second, equally important motif: we encounter the God who turns toward us in appeal and judgment, but also in his quest for our salvation and the restoration of our communion with him. God's holiness and his condescension toward us become even more concrete in the New Testament testimony of the person of Jesus Christ. Both lines—that of God's holiness, as well as that of his turning toward us, are further extended. It would be wrong to see here a contrast between the Old and the New Testament. But it becomes clearer that God's love and grace toward people take first place and that his holiness is a qualification of it.

In the Johannine epistles that relationship is expressed in the lofty words "God is love" (1 John 4:8, 16). Ultimately, this is the most fundamental statement we can make about God.

4.4. From the Names to the Properties

In thinking and speaking about God, the church has never been satisfied with simply listing the biblical names and titles, as we did above. From the very start it has felt the need to provide a more comprehensive picture of who God is and in so doing has attempted to describe the various properties of God as adequately as possible. This effort did not always stem from a desire to speculate or go beyond biblical bounds; in fact, the Bible itself encouraged such elaborations. When in Exod 34 God once again appears to Moses, he presents himself by referring to a few of his "properties." Here also we are struck, just as in Exod 3, by the combination of God's turning toward us and his transcendence, love, and holiness:

> The LORD passed before him, and proclaimed, "The LORD, the LORD, a God merciful and gracious, slow to anger, and abounding in steadfast love and faithfulness, keeping steadfast love for thousands, forgiving iniquity and transgression and sin, but who will by no means clear the guilty, visiting the iniquity of the fathers upon the children and the children's children, to the third and the fourth generation." (Exod 34:6-7)

Later we find references to such series of attributes in the prayers of the people. In Num 8, for example, Moses appeals directly to God's forgiving nature as it was formulated by God himself in Exod 34. But even more frequently these summaries of divine properties occur in the worship of the faithful. The best known of these is probably the one involving the individual believer in Ps 103 (esp. beginning at v. 8), but in Ps 145 the words of Exod 34 recur as a doxology:

> Great is the LORD, and greatly to be praised,
> and his greatness is unsearchable.
> One generation shall laud thy works to another,
> and shall declare thy mighty acts.
> On the glorious splendor of thy majesty,
> and on thy wondrous works, I will meditate.
> Men shall proclaim the might of thy terrible acts,

and I will declare thy greatness.
They shall pour forth the fame of thy abundant goodness,
and shall sing aloud of thy righteousness.
The LORD is gracious and merciful,
slow to anger and abounding in steadfast love.
The LORD is good to all,
and his compassion is over all that he has made.
All thy works shall give thanks to thee, O LORD,
and all thy saints shall bless thee!

(Ps 145:3–10)

Here we notice three things. First, not only is an individual believer (as in Ps 103) singing about the attributes of God, but the believer in this psalm calls upon the entire faith community to join in worship of the Lord; it even appears that this praise is embedded in the collective prayer. Second, the emphasis in this doxology falls on the properties that involve God's turn toward us. The attributes of God's transcendence are certainly not ignored (v. 3: "Great is the LORD"), but these qualities are subordinated to the confession of God's mercy toward humanity. Third, there is a close tie between God's acts and his properties; they are mentioned as following each other. Apparently, in the practice of praising God there is a need to glorify him not just for what he does but, above all, for who he is. As we concentrate here on the doctrine of the divine properties, it is important not to lose sight of this doxological context.

The Greek from which we get the commonly used terms "orthodox" and "orthodoxy" shows us that, strictly speaking, they refer not to correct doctrine but to correct praise. In their origin they refer to the appropriate words and thought patterns for praising God and praying to him, whether by individual believers or in the assemblies of the Christian community. Dogmatics, especially the doctrine of God, is to be regarded as an aid in our worship. Correct doctrine is not a formal system of propositions to which we must give assent but is embedded in our worship. The core of the matter is that we worship the true God, not some kind of idol (honor to whom honor is due!), and that we worship the true God in the right way. The right kind of worship thus demands a right kind of doctrine, an "orthodox" discourse that does justice to the one who is worthy of our praise. It is because of this doxology that we must carefully define our doctrine of God.

In the meantime we may feel that in a passage like Ps 145 the properties of God are listed in a rather fragmentary and haphazard way, and with considerable overlap to boot (e.g., goodness and mercy). Only when the early church had to give an account of its faith in its Hellenistic environment did the need arise for a more systematic approach and further reflection. In fact, contemporary Judaism already led the way here, with the Jewish philosopher Philo (25 BCE–39 CE) playing an important role. Just as in the Septuagint, Philo rendered the divine name of Exod 3 in Greek as *ho ōn* (he who is), and the fathers of the early church adopted this phrase. In so doing, they went along with the concept of being that was current in the Hellenistic culture that surrounded them. Consequently, they translated their faith in God into categories that their contemporaries understood. The challenge that every contemporary doctrine of God faces is to determine the extent to which it is confirming the Italian expression *traduttore, traditore*—"translators are traitors." This charge has been fiercely asserted by those who have detected—and bemoaned—a so-called hellenization of Christianity in the early church, but such claims are nowadays evaluated with more nuance. In the next section we will deal with the question how to evaluate Greek philosophical influences on the development of the Christian doctrine of God.

The theory of the hellenization of Christianity was advanced in particular by the great historian of religion A. von Harnack (1851–1930), who saw this phenomenon, which emerged from the second century on, as both inevitable and regrettable. He believed that our challenge today is to return to the "simple gospel" as a way of life rather than as a system of doctrine. Later observers showed less sympathy for this process by which the early church made the Christian faith increasingly Greek; they regarded it as giving in to an alien seduction. On this view, Greek philosophy and the Jewish/Hebrew Bible were contrasted more or less as black and white, as for instance in the frequently reprinted study of the Norwegian theologian Thorleif Boman (1960). We also find clear language to this effect in Brunner (D 1:137–56). The change toward a more nuanced approach began with a significant essay by Pannenberg (1971, orig. 1959) and a study by Helmut Gollwitzer (1965). Biblical scholarship helped to show that simply contrasting Jewish and Greek thinking (as we find in someone like Ferdinand C. Baur, 1792–1860) does not do justice to the far more complex reality in Palestine around the beginning of the Christian era. The two traditions had reached a synthesis a few centuries earlier and had more or less melded together. But criticism regarding the Christian adoption of the Greek concept of God has never ceased completely and can still be found with Moltmann (spread over his entire oeuvre), Jenson (ST 1:9–11, 112–13, 131–33), and Gunton (2002). We must therefore continue to take it seriously.

4.5. Dealing with the Greek Heritage

What was so characteristic of "Greek" thinking about God? The term is used to refer to Plato (ca. 427–ca. 347 BCE), Aristotle, and other classical philosophers but also to the influence of their ideas on later philosophical schools, such as the Stoics and Middle- and Neoplatonism, which coincided with the development of early Christianity. However different their ideas may have been, all these schools shared some common characteristics. People were constantly in search of the ultimate ground or final cause of everything, leaving behind all kinds of current popular piety and mythology. Over against myth the philosophers placed the Logos, or reason. This Logos formed the most prominent link between our world and the divine reality in which it finds its cause for existence. The path to knowledge of divine reality is therefore a route of abstract reasoning backward from visible material reality to its divine starting point, called the *archē*.

When Plato speaks of God, he is thinking of an impersonal spirit that exists in ultimate transcendence "beyond all forms of being." Aristotle regards God as the highest possible form of being, from which everything that exists is derived. This being is in itself totally immovable, yet it moves all things and draws them as a magnet toward itself. The Stoics also saw immovability as an important divine property and so, by extension, as an important human ideal. This perspective considers that transcendent properties in particular characterize the divine—attributes that are absent from our human experience or, at best, that are difficult to find. God is spiritual and far removed from all matter. He is the totally other who exists in timeless eternity—who, in fact, is unknowable. The divine is the One (*to hen*), according to the Neoplatonic Plotinus (third century CE), which implies that in him there is no complexity whatsoever and no constituent parts. God is therefore not subject to change (for change points to complexity) or subject to emotions (for emotions are mood changes that have an exterior cause). This line of thinking gives us the short list of attributes that we find in various Christian confessions of faith: God is spiritual, eternal, one, unchangeable, immovable, and incomprehensible in his lofty transcendence. And beginning in the nineteenth century (after the Enlightenment opened up the tradition for critique), this position also leads us to all kinds of criticism from theologians, namely, that the Christian doctrine of God must be purified as quickly and radically as possible from this mixture with Greek concepts. Far from God being a kind of unmoved Mover, the Bible pictures him rather as the *most moved* Mover (Pinnock 2001).

But are things as simple as this? Here we discuss, in turn, three arguments—one historical, one doctrinal, and one biblical-theological—which together, although not negating this criticism, relativize it. First of all, we must recognize how the encounter between the early Christian church and its "Greek-thinking" environment was a historical inevitability. The simple fact that the New Testament was, like the Septuagint, written in Greek had far-reaching consequences. The question had to be posed constantly of how the concepts that were found therein related to contemporary language, whether everyday or intellectual-philosophical. In some cases a Greek concept intentionally received a new, specifically Christian connotation; in other cases a rather uncommon Greek concept was put to use (e.g., *agapē* for unselfish love). But always the original meaning continued to resonate, at least in the background. Moreover, the Greek language offered possibilities for an abstract, definitive way of expressing oneself that Hebrew, with its pictorial stories, did not have. (The idea of a difference between two linguistic worlds has a basis in fact.) In addition, there were also exterior pressures on the Christian community to think about how its view of God related to that of its environment. From the start, the novelty of the Christian faith led to distrust and persecution. In their attempt to disarm the ideological basis of these attacks, the apologists—the first Christian theologians, who lived in the second century—argued that the Christian faith was not at variance with the Logos and was therefore not irrational or unnatural but on the same intellectual level as contemporary philosophical-religious schools. For that reason the content of the biblical faith had to be expressed and interpreted with the aid of Greek terms and intellectual models.

Second, the universality of Israel's God gave an important dogmatic reason for this approach as well. According to the biblical discourse about God, God, while admittedly being primarily the God of Israel, is also the God of all peoples and the entire world. From the perspective of religious history, God may have started "on a small scale" as the tribal god of a nation of slaves, but he eventually emerges as "Lord of heaven and earth" (Matt 11:25). Even in the Old Testament this universality is fully recorded. In Abraham all nations on earth will be blessed (Gen 12:3). The earth and its fullness, the world and those who live therein, are God's (Ps 24:1). Melchizedek (Gen 14:18–20) and Balaam (Num 22–24) are in his service. He anoints Cyrus for the implementation of his plans (Isa 44:28; 45:1). He is God to "the ends of the earth!" Before him "every knee shall bow, every tongue shall swear" (Isa 45:22–23), and he will prepare a "feast of fat things" on his mountain for all peoples (Isa 25:6–12). Even the metropolis

Nineveh is within his reach (Jonah). The New Testament picture is very similar. God is also the God of the Roman centurion (Matt 8:5–13) and of the Syro-Phoenician woman (Matt 15:21–28). He did not ignore other peoples (Acts 14:16–17 [cf. 17:26–28]; Rom 1:20). Thus, when contemporaries of the early Christian church also speak about God—the one, universal God—Christians were obliged to take their ideas into account, without assuming that traces of God were totally absent from this Greek thought.

Third, biblical theology had cause to take a serious look at the Greeks' thinking about the divine, for both the Old and the New Testaments ascribe properties to God that, to say the least, are very similar to those of Greek philosophy. The Bible too refers to God's majesty, immortality, immutability, unity, eternality, and invisibility. We already saw in chapter 2 that, in this philosophical contemplation about God, the Christian faith saw an ally in its battle against the many forms of polytheistic religion then popular. This relevance applied in no less measure to the struggle against the dualistic ideas of a gnostic nature that were very influential in Bible times. The Christian faith maintains that one God is the creative cause of all that exists besides him, including the earthly material reality that gnostics saw as rooted in a divine antipower. On many points the early Christian thinkers felt at ease with the view of God in Greek philosophy. Yet, they did not just copy it without criticism, considering how much they were impacted by the gospel of Jesus Christ.

So, what went wrong in the Christian adoption of the Greek philosophical concept of God? We believe it happened at two points. We will discuss the first here and the second in the next section. The first issue is the major difficulty that Christians experienced in combining the properties of God's transcendence with the attributes that relate to his condescension toward us. The problem is not that, in slavish imitation of the leading intelligentsia, they simply started to ascribe various properties to God's transcendence, for they could do so from their own sources—from the Bible and the Jewish and Christian tradition. In those sources, however, God is at the same time a living, creative, and saving power who turns toward us humans, a power about whom we may speak in terms derived from personal relationships. The philosophers could regard these properties only as an impermissible (or at best inappropriate) anthropomorphism. Because the Christian theologians did not succeed in making an organic connection between the God who remains aloof and the God who turns toward us, the two ideas remained separate from each other. In a context where philosophy disdained anthropomorphic elements in human discourse about God, it soon led to foregrounding the property of transcendence in reflections on faith. In this atmosphere it seemed, for instance, more correct and more profound to state that God cannot change than to say that he is love. That God is love would, at most, be saying something about his revelation, while stating that he cannot change would say something about his being. This led to the development of an imbalance in the Christian view of God.

In the actual practice of faith, things were often different; in the hymns and prayers of the faith community, the astonishment about God's condescension toward sinful men and women retained a primary place. Liturgical practice and the Bible offered resistance. But it cannot be denied that the one-sided emphasis on God's transcendence did, over the centuries, leave its traces in Christian spirituality. We may think of the veneration of the saints, which in a certain way aimed to help bridge the gap that was seen between God and human beings.

Through the ages many have tried to synthesize the Greek-philosophical approach and the content of biblical faith, but these attempts were rarely successful, as the philosophy usually received priority (Augustine being a positive exception). The most impressive example is found in the theology of Thomas Aquinas (thirteenth century). However, twentieth-century research has shown that the biblical-theological dimension of Aquinas's doctrine of God was much more extensive and decisive than had long been assumed. Nonetheless, Aquinas saw the ideas of Aristotle in particular as a significant tool. Arabic scholars were instrumental in rediscovering Aristotle's work, and Aquinas and others gratefully employed it for the Christian doctrine of God. Aquinas starts with the general question about the being, properties, and acts of God, so that who God is (or is not) is in the first instance discussed with reference to the classic answers of Aristotle's metaphysics, while the section about God's interaction with the world uses more biblical language. However, when he deals with the specifically Christian concept of God in relation to the doctrine of the Trinity, Aquinas offers a speculative, philosophical interpretation of the immanent Trinity rather than foregrounding the biblical stories about the Father, the Son, and the Spirit. This is also true for many other representatives of medieval Scholasticism.

Among the Reformers, Calvin and especially Luther were very critical of the concepts and speculative character of the scholastic doctrine of the Trinity. But apparently this critique was soon forgotten. Numerous theologians of later Protestant orthodoxy (between the sixteenth and eighteenth centuries) adopted the pattern of medieval scholastic thought without much further ado, including its basis in a general, highly transcendent view of God in the *locus de Deo*. Their preferred description of God is that of an eternal and infinite spiritual being, adding only toward the end any reference to a number of properties regarding God's turn toward us. This pattern is also visible in the confessional documents of the era. The Westminster Shorter Catechism (1647), for instance, defines God as "a Spirit, infinite, eternal and unchangeable, in his being, wisdom, power, holiness, justice, goodness, and truth" (question 4), a statement that, as late as the mid-nineteenth century, Charles Hodge could praise as "probably the best definition of God ever penned by man" (ST 1:367). It should be noted, however, that this definition is given in reply to the question "What is God?" (not "Who is God?"), as is typical of post-Reformation orthodoxy.

4.6. From Creation to Creator? Analogy and Revelation

A second element also became problematic in Christian theological reception of Greek-philosophical thinking about the divine, namely, the assumption that it is possible to reason, also apropos of the Christian doctrine of God, from the reality that surrounds us back to God. We see the most explicit example of this principle at work in so-called *perfect-being theology*, represented supremely by Anselm of Canterbury (see, in particular, his *Proslogion*). Starting with God's perfection (*perfectio*), Anselm was able to unfold the doctrine of God without ever once consulting the Bible. Nor did he even need to look around at empirical reality; he simply asked himself whether a human property was to be regarded as negative or positive. If negative, such a property could not, of course, be attributed to God. If positive, it could be attributed to God to the maximal degree. This approach led him to a series of terms that began with "all" or "un-" or "omni-," which have characterized the doctrine of divine attributes ever since.

Perfect-being theology has seen a remarkable revival over the last few decades, particularly in the work of analytic philosophers of religion. It should be noted that with them the apophatic element that we find in Anselm is missing, but they seem confident that we can get a long way toward determining who and what God is simply by our reasoning. For a well-developed doctrine of the divine properties along those lines, see Morris 1991, and for a (somewhat nuanced) recent Dutch example, Bac 2010. Likewise, Brink and Sarot 1999 work in this tradition, even though they begin each chapter with a biblical orientation toward the property under discussion. The focal point of this type of philosophical theology is the search for consistency and coherence and for solutions to the logical problems that arise in this context. When discussing God's omnipotence, for instance, much attention is given to the question of whether God can make a stone that is so heavy that he cannot lift it. Even though such reflections may be very instructive, they can easily lead to speculations that have little to do with the essence of Christian discourse about God. In any case, something is wrong when it is deemed possible to develop a doctrine of God without taking into account the meaning of the Bible, revelation, faith, and even Jesus Christ.

The problem with this method is its uncritical use of notions and value judgments from one's own cultural and mental world. In Anselm's world, for instance, just as in the world of Greek philosophy, emotions were regarded as negative, and for that reason it was believed that no emotions should be ascribed to God. Of course, such thinkers knew that such ascription in fact occurs repeatedly in the Bible, especially in the Old Testament. They simply dismissed it as a manner of speaking that was used only to compensate for our limited understanding. Calvin likewise regarded biblical statements about God's remorse, anger, and sadness as a matter of accommodation (adaptation) to human weakness. But the question remains whether in this process the Christian writings are allowed to play a primary role, or whether some deep-rooted presuppositions of our own culture are at work, albeit in a camouflaged way.

We can determine which properties may be considered good and, accordingly, may be ascribed to God in the highest measure, and which imply limitation and must therefore be denied to God, *only by reading the Bible and especially by looking at the way in which Jesus Christ has demonstrated to us who God is*. Not all cultures consider values like mercy, compassion, and humility to be positive, while Christian theology has wanted to attribute each of these to God on the basis of what has been revealed in the Bible, in particular, in the history of Jesus Christ (see Holmes in Webster et al., OHST 58). We simply cannot develop a doctrine of divine properties without consulting the Bible.

This conclusion is also clear when we look at another method used to reason from created reality to God, namely, the *via causalitatis*, or path of causality. This method rests on the principle that causes in some way always have something in common with their consequences. This in itself is a rather shaky premise (sculptors do not have to look like their sculpture), which can be maintained only by assuming a degree of commonality, or analogy, between Creator and creature, a "commonality in being" (*analogia entis*). All created reality reflects in a preliminary and limited manner the way in which God exists. So far as human beings are concerned, this analogy could be based on the doctrine of the image of

God (see chap. 7). But it was argued that the *entire* creation in some way shared in God's being. Here reference is often made to participation ontology, a theory of being (ontology) holding that somehow every created entity shares (participates) in the essence of the Creator.

Thomas Aquinas, in particular, suggested this path; contrary to Anselm's proposal, it starts not so much from our thinking but from the essence of things. Aquinas may well be considered the master of the classic theory of analogy. He was very much aware that God is unique, different from us humans and other creatures. Therefore, we cannot one-for-one apply the terms that we use for interhuman relationships (goodness, justice, wisdom, etc.) to God with the same meaning. In other words, these terms are not used univocally, as the word "yellow" is in the two phrases "that bike is yellow" and "this car is yellow." But neither are the words we apply to God totally equivocal, with no overlap in meaning (as the word "bank" is in the sentences "the ship was stranded on the river bank" and "I will put my money in the bank"). The truth is somewhere in between, says Aquinas. We apply our terms to God in an *analogous* way. Such use is possible because there is indeed an analogy—that is to say, a partial commonality—between the Creator and the creation. For instance, God is perfectly good, and we can to some extent discover what this word might mean by looking at the people he made, who can be good in a finite and limited way.

Aquinas very clearly understood that God is the first referent of a concept like goodness (STh I.13.6). Only God is good in the absolute sense; when we call human beings or human actions good (or just or wise), it is always in a relative, derived, and imperfect sense. The criticism of Barth—the other master of the analogy model—did not pertain primarily to this point but rather to the fact that Aquinas, on the basis of his theory of the *analogia entis*, could reverse the direction of things. Ontologically speaking, primacy remained with God, but from a noetic perspective it seemed to be with humanity. For that reason Barth emphasized that the concept of analogy involves foremost an *analogia fidei*—an analogy that we cannot discover on our own on the basis of empirical reality, but in which we believe because of divine self-revelation that enables us to speak correctly about God. Barth argues that, in the Bible, God himself gives us the words that may be properly used when speaking of God. See CD II/1, §27.2, esp. 231–33. It is important to note that the doctrine of analogy does not necessarily point to a path along which we come to know God (nor was this Aquinas's concern), but it does point to a way of understanding our own language. In other words, the doctrine of analogy is not an epistemological theory, although in actual practice, the two elements got easily intertwined. For this reason, we must understand Barth's resistance to the concept of the *analogia entis* as an extension of his fight against natural theology, and why he regarded this theory (which he called "the invention of Antichrist"!) to be the only decisive reason why he could not become a Roman Catholic (CD I/1:xiii). For a thorough discussion of the history of the concept of analogy and its attendant philosophical and theological questions, see Jüngel, GMW, §§17-18, and also White 2010.

Over the centuries and up to the present, Aquinas's ideas of analogy have inspired many to take up their pens. Is the participation ontology that lies in the background of Aquinas's thinking not Greek (or specifically Neoplatonic) rather than Christian? But even if we try to detach the concept of analogy from this theology, problems remain. How can we specify what we mean when we say "God is good" when, in our earthly realm, we see only weak and imperfect examples of what is unchangeable, good, or just? Are we not back with a kind of *perfect-being theology*, a magnification and projecting onto God of everything that we ourselves would like to have more of? And in the end, does not every analogy (partial commonality) rest on univocity, that is, on the assumption that at least part of the meaning of a predicate must remain the same when we apply it to God—and that we must know which part this is? The latter point was argued by John Duns Scotus (ca. 1265-1308), who believed that our speaking about God must be univocal with our speaking of everyday matters. For Scotus this in no way meant that we can, so to speak, get a handle on God, for he drew a sharp distinction between the theory of meaning and ontology: God as "infinite being" is totally different from finite creatures. In the era of the Enlightenment, however, philosophical theology was developed without any reference to the Bible or any other special revelation.

Today we face the opposite situation. Trust in the possibility that we human beings would be able to know who and what God is has so far diminished that, even among Christian theologians, it has almost become a cliché to state that of course we can speak only metaphorically about God, in images and stories. We must do so, searching and trying to find our way, without being able to say exactly what basic meanings of our metaphors may apply to God. For metaphors are not just a pleasant adornment of our language ("they built a monster of a house"); when we speak of God, they are an irremovable characteristic. At this point we believe that everything depends on our trust in God's self-revelation through his historic acts as we read about them in the biblical witness.

Just as it is possible to say something about human persons on the basis of their acts, so we can speak of God—at least if it is true that God is not just the Transcendent One who exceeds our earthly reality but also the one who has decisively made himself known in Israel's history and in Jesus Christ. Because of divine self-revelation (and thus not because of a supposed ontological commonality between Creator and creation), it can become clear which common aspects of meaning in such words as "just" and "loving" may or may not be applied to God, or where we may find the analogy. In that self-revelation we often discover a major shift in the meanings that we commonly attribute to words. For instance, Jesus says that real greatness depends, not on the degree of power one can wield, but on the degree to which one is willing to serve others. Jesus himself is great in exactly this way (Luke 22:24-27).

In recent years the crucial role of Duns Scotus in this part of the history of the humanities in Europe has received much more attention; for example, see *Modern Theology* 21.4 (2005), a special issue that highlighted his historical and contemporary significance. Two years later this discussion prompted Pannenberg (2007) to republish his Habilitationsschrift (a second dissertation to qualify as a university professor in Germany), with which he had completed his studies in 1955, adding a short postscript of further clarifications (212-15). In 1999 McFague published an influential book in which she argued that all discourse about God is metaphorical. This view is also abundantly present in continental European theology. A convincing argument in defense of the proposition that it is possible to speak of God in literal terms (i.e., by using standard definitions given in dictionaries) is Muis 2011. From a philosophical angle something similar was proposed by Alston 1989 (39-63), while Brümmer, who extensively studied the role of metaphors and "models" in the doctrine of God, remarks, "It is therefore wrong to assume that all concepts relating to God are in this sense metaphorical" (1992, 55).

A definitive role in God-talk in general is further played by the profound hermeneutical studies of the French philosopher Paul Ricoeur, for instance his *La métaphore vive* (1975).

The answer to the question of what value our words have when they are applied to God (e.g., in the form of predicates of properties) can be given only on the basis of a constant orientation to the biblical writings. In these writings numerous chronicles, testimonies. and stories are found about how, for instance, God's goodness differs from human goodness, without making the concept of goodness meaningless when it is applied to God. Like perfect-being theology, analogy theory works only when it is not detached from its biblical background. This is the precondition for talking adequately of God's properties as reflections of God's acts.

4.7. The Trinity as the Organizing Principle for the Doctrine of God's Properties

When we ponder the combination of transcendence and condescension, as happened prototypically when God appeared to Moses in Exod 3, we can understand why in the dogmatic tradition God's properties are usually put into two categories. The attributes in the first category articulate God's transcendence, and those in the second, his presence. The names for the two categories have varied, as has the precise division between them. Sometimes theologians call them the positive and negative attributes of God; the first group is defined through use of the *via eminentiae*, and the second, through the *via negativa*. Others speak of absolute and relative attributes; the first category intends to say something about God in himself, the second, about God in his relational turning toward us and the world. In the post-Reformation era the division into incommunicable and communicable attributes became most common.

The choice of these words is, in itself, quite remarkable, since the term "incommunicable" suggests that God would be unable to share the properties in question with us, and the theology of the Reformers did lay much stress on the sovereignty and omnipotence of God. Stephen Holmes was correct to point out that it would be better to speak of the communicated and not-communicated divine attributes (in Webster et al., OHST, 59). He also rightly made clear that the different categorizations do not fully overlap. For instance, immortality is both a negative attribute of God and also a communicated property—at any rate, in traditional Reformed theology—since angels are also assumed to be immortal (59). In order to avoid such discussions, we prefer to speak of the attributes of divine transcendence and the attributes pertaining to God's condescension, or turning toward us.

The intention of this division into two groups no doubt agrees with a tension that Bible readers have noticed. On the one hand, God is and remains totally different from us humans, incomparable in his glory and power; but on the other, he has chosen to let some of his perfections be reflected in his creatures. Thus, human beings can demonstrate love but are not omnipresent. As we noted earlier, however, the two lists of properties have often been placed side by side without sufficient interconnection. This arrangement makes it appear as if there is a kind of conflict, or at least a degree of tension, in God's being, which could in turn lead to a latent dualistic faith experience. For if God is merciful and loving, he is "also" just and holy, and when one is confronted with God and one's life is weighed in his scales, one never knows which of the two will win out.

But in the Bible God's unity comes first. Even though at times the tension in God may rise to a high level (e.g., in Hos 11:7-9), it is part of his perfection that he does not have to negotiate between his various properties, as if they referred to entities outside of him. All God's attributes are, in fact, expressions of his single being. When we speak of God's faithfulness and justice, for instance, we notice how the First Epistle of John links these two without any hesitation. Referring to Jesus Christ, who has provided us with a picture of who God is, John says: "He is *faithful* and *just*, and will forgive our sins and cleanse us from all unrighteousness" (1 John 1:9).

If we find it difficult to see this linkage, it is because we are used to a Roman concept of justice, in which every person receives what is his or her due: the good get a reward, and the bad, a just punishment. Lady Justice has a set of scales and a sword in her hands for a reason; she must carefully weigh the deeds of every person and then settle on a just punishment. In the Bible the concept of justice derives from Hebrew *tsedaqah*, which has as its primary meaning that God remains faithful to his covenant and will not permit it to be destroyed by the evil that people do. In this light we can see how God, in his justice, would also look for the possibility of forgiveness so that his covenant would remain intact. This is the kind of justice shown in a concrete situation by Joseph when he decided to abandon Mary. By doing so, it would not be Mary but he himself whom everyone would detest, since he had refused to accept the responsibility for Mary's child (which everybody would assume was his). So Joseph planned to abandon her to protect her from the fate that would undoubtedly be hers as soon as her alleged adultery became public; he would remain faithful to her by taking this fate vicariously on himself. See Matt 1:19, where we read that Joseph secretly wanted to abandon Mary because he was "just."

In order to avoid such misconceptions, we believe that we need to conduct our thinking about the properties of God's transcendence and condescension from a central point of view. After everything we said in the previous chapter, it will come as no surprise that this must be the

Trinitarian point of view. The biblical testimony informs us that God reveals himself in turning toward us as Father, Son, and Spirit. That is, God is first and foremost the one who would have us know that he wants us to be saved, to find happiness and redemption. We need not fear that, when God turns to us in this way in the gospel, he might be harboring second thoughts as the most high, holy, and righteous God. The important thing is to learn to take God at his word, that is, as he makes himself known to us in his condescension.

According to the biblical testimony this turning of God toward us is found in the special acts by which God creates salvation in the midst of misery and hopelessness. These are particularly the acts that are commemorated and celebrated by the faith community during the Jewish and Christian feast days. To name just the latter: Christmas, Good Friday, and Easter, but also Pentecost—all with their Old Testament background— call to remembrance the specific times and phases of God's coming in Christ and the Spirit as the firm foundation on which our faith rests.

In this connection it is rather painful to note that, compared with many other Christians, ultra-Calvinists are more faithful and committed to celebrating the Christian feasts but at the same time find it more difficult to really believe that the forgiving love of God, which is the substance of those feasts, is also meant for them. The fear of this "other" God, the God of just punishments (which Luther called the *Deus absconditus*, the hidden God) is simply too great to overcome. God's love is taken seriously only when it is felt in one's own heart. But this paradigm shows a remarkable and ironic similarity with other groups of Christians (liberal, postmodern, and also evangelical) for whom the individual experience of faith is the operational norm. A. A. van Ruler's essay about ultra-Reformed and liberal, now in VW, vol. 4, still remains very instructive about such similarities (and differences) between the heresies of left and right.

In sum, if we are serious in our belief that God has made himself known through the Bible as the triune God in the economy of salvation, we will have to take this belief as our point of departure for thinking and talking about God's attributes. The who and what about God are preeminently demonstrated in his coming to us human beings throughout history.

We therefore put first the attributes that concern God's turning toward us, but not with the intent of thus denying or relativizing the properties of his transcendence. We regard the latter as elements that qualify the unique nature of God's condescension. In this way we can think much more coherently about God than if we were to leave the two series of properties disconnected, side by side. We believe that this is the biblical track as well, for in the Bible, God's holiness, anger, and revenge are not independent qualities separate from his grace and mercy; they appear only when God's turn toward us is rejected and his offer of love scorned. God's is not a weak kind of love that makes no choices, but a holy love that wants us to change and be renewed. God's anger is the flip side of this coin. It is the "top of the flame of his love," J. H. Gunning Jr. (1829–1905) tells us. "A God who is never angry would not be a God of love. In the Bible God's anger is nothing but the zeal, the jealousy of love" (Gunning, BidO 2:165).

Hosea 11 offers one of the most impressive and dramatic illustrations of this principle. There we see how the tension over the stubbornness of the people rises to its apex, even penetrating God's deepest being. The destruction of Israel appears inevitable. God considers reversing the exodus from Israel and thus altering the entire history of salvation (v. 5). Israel's attitude leaves no space whatsoever to continue the relationship of love and faithfulness (v. 7). But then the story takes a sudden turn. Rather than the expected, definitive confirmation of his judgment, we find that God cannot bring himself to take this step. We even read, "My heart recoils within me" (v. 8). God therefore decides not to execute his "fierce anger." He simply cannot do with the kingdom of the ten tribes (here referred to as Ephraim) as he did with Admah and Zeboiim (v. 8)— two cities near Sodom and Gomorrah that were destroyed together (Gen 19:29; Deut 29:23) and so thoroughly wiped off the map that even their names disappeared from collective memory. God wants to spare the Northern Kingdom this fate. The same love that caused his anger against Israel to wax so fierce eventually also prevented God from implementing his punishment. One might think that God gives his holiness a little less weight in this episode, but the opposite is true. Because God, the Holy One, is in Israel's midst, he will not flare up in anger anew:

> I will not execute my fierce anger,
> I will not again destroy Ephraim;
> for I am God and not man,
> the Holy One in your midst,
> and I will not come to destroy.

> (Hos 11:9)

"For I am God and not man." When faced with such perverse behavior as Israel demonstrated, human beings would give up, lose their temper, and take revenge, which is what we usually see. But God is different. Here his holiness means especially that he is different in this respect, that he acts much more consistently from love. The two properties do not stand separately beside each other but are intrinsically connected. God's holiness does not diminish his love but ensures that this love will have the final word in the covenant drama. In this way the attribute of God's transcendence qualifies the nature of his turning toward us. God's love is a holy, pure, consistent love, in which he himself assumes the failures of the people.

With regard to holiness as the radical otherness of God, see Mettinger 1988, 152; according to the book of Hosea, Israel does not escape God's judgment, but this fate is no longer the final end: by way of the judgment, a new beginning is possible. We thus see a dialectic (a powerful back-and-forth movement) between judgment and mercy, a dialectic that in the end is "dissolved" in mercy. We might say that, because of the continuity of the covenant, God turns against himself and is victorious over himself. From a Christian perspective we see here a prefiguration of the Trinitarian salvific event, where the Son is abandoned by the Father (Matt 27:46) and dies under God's wrath (Gal 3:13) but is reconnected with the Father by the Spirit through resurrection from death to life (Rom 1:4; 1 Tim 3:16; 1 Pet 3:18). In this way the conflict of sin and judgment in God is overcome. Note Jüngel's description of God as "the original unity of life and death for the sake of life" (GMW, x, 299, and elsewhere).

Hosea 11 may be regarded as a high point in the Old Testament revelation of God. Sodom and Gomorrah, Admah and Zeboiim were not spared but received their final punishment. Only later do we read about the experience of God's anger disappearing behind his compassion (Isa 54:8; Lam 3:32; Ps 30:6). Does this further testimony signify a development in God? Must God himself, in the conflict with his people, find a path toward salvation? The question should not be answered too quickly with a denial. Yet, such a development is, on the one hand, in harmony with God's most profound being, while, on the other hand, it nowhere leads to a superficial concept of love in which judgment and anger no longer have a place (see John 3:17; 18:36; Heb 12:29, and the many texts about judgment in Revelation). God's love-in-holiness always aims for our sanctification and will therefore not abandon us. Berkhof (CF 126–40) is right when he points out that both the Old Testament and the New Testament expect that for "those who permanently resist Yahweh there will be a judgment of wrath which will be a final word"; this wrath, however, does not involve something that was determined long beforehand but is "something that is forced upon God as the reverse side of his (spurned) love" (135).

Whatever we can say about God's omniscience (*omniscientia*), omnipresence (*omnipresentia*), omnipotence (*omnipotentia*), immutability (*immutabilitas*), infinity (*infinitas*), impassibility (*impassibilitas*), self-sufficiency (*aseitas*, better translated "existing in himself"), and unity (*simplicitas*) also has deep roots in the biblical witness. It should not be quickly dismissed merely as Greek. In the Bible, however, these properties do not stand on their own but qualify the nature of God's turning toward us. For instance, in Ps 139 God's omniscience and omnipresence give no cause for fear and distress but, on the contrary, offer comfort and a sense of protection to believers who find themselves in difficulty (v. 19b), wondering how far God's arm in fact reaches. The answer, amazingly, appears to be even so far as Sheol, the realm of the dead (v. 8). As we read the creed, we find that God's omnipotence is closely tied to his fatherhood: God is not just the Omnipotent but the almighty Father (*pater omnipotens*), who realizes his plans in his Son and through his Spirit (Apostles' Creed). God's immutability does not imply that he remains elevated in rigid impassibility, far above our earthly to-and-fro, refusing to be affected by anything. Rather, it means that he remains faithful, with unyielding tenacity, to his plans, promises, and intentions. For this reason, he can also change his tactics when it appears that to do so would help achieve these ends.

Thus we read the famous texts about God's remorse in the Old Testament (Gen 6:6; 1 Sam 15:11; 2 Sam 24:16; 1 Chr 21:15; Jer 18:7-10; Amos 7:3, 6; Jonah 3:10, etc.) In response to people changing—whether for good or for ill—God often adapts his plans. Such adaptations mean, not that he regrets earlier actions, but that he changes strategy in his attempts to reach the same goal. In this sense the very same chapter of the Bible can say that God regrets his choice of Saul as Israel's king (1 Sam 15:11, 35) but also that "God is not a man that he should repent" (1 Sam 15:29; see also other texts that refer to God's inability to change—Num 23:19; Mal 3:6; Jas 1:17). These comments, however, do not mean that we can massage away the sharp bends in God's interaction with us. What he has built, he breaks down; what he has planted, he plucks up (Jer 45:4). In the Old Testament, in particular, God follows an unpredictable course in which, in his exclusive choice for Israel, he may even give orders for what we would today call genocide (Deut 7:2; Josh 6:17, 21). Yet, in the Old Testament (esp. with the prophets) we find traces of God's decisive turning toward the benefit of all peoples, which will become the defining approach in the New Testament; from then on, God wants to be God only in the manner of the Son of Man, who unites Jews and gentiles (Eph 2:14). In the death of Jesus Christ, God's judgment and love converge in a way that is decisive, from which God will never step back (2 Cor 1:20). In the midst of all faults and turnings—always, however, leaving a "remnant" and thus always also ensuring continuity—God remains the God of unchanging faithfulness. An instructive source is Beek 1990.

God's infinity points to his infinite power and his infinite fullness as the overflowing source of all life and being (Allen, RT 56). God's impassibility and self-sufficiency (i.e., God's independence of sources outside of himself for his continued existence) indicate that God cannot be destroyed by all the evil on earth, despite all the trouble he suffers because of us. This evil is so baffling and reaches so deep that we should be glad that God can withstand it rather than, like us, waiting to see how it will all play out. God's simplicity, finally, means that God is characterized by oneness, so that his properties cannot be played off against each other and that he is utterly serious about his merciful turning toward us.

Starting in the 1960s, all emphasis was placed on the attributes of God's nearness to us (in one word, using a term of the later Barth, on God's *Menschlichkeit* (humanness), but now a cautious change has come about. In a new orientation toward the classic (Roman Catholic and Protestant) doctrine of God, prominent systematic theologians including Colin Gunton (1941-2003), Paul Molnar, and John Webster (b. 1955) have begun to highlight the necessary importance of the properties of God's transcendence. In interhuman relationships we see how we must first be ourselves before we can really be someone for others. Mutatis mutandis, this principle also applies to the doctrine of God. If God is truly to be there for us humans as the God who is close to us, he must first of all be the eternally rich God in himself. This point can be further explored by demanding attention for the independent significance of God's immanent triune nature (Gunton 2002, chap. 6; Molnar 2002) or by offering, in close connection with the doctrine of the Trinity, new articulations of the various properties of God's transcendence (Webster 2006; 2015, 13-28). In any case, we believe that the two sets of divine properties can be explored only in their mutual relationships—something that was initiated prior to Barth by I. A. Dorner (SCD, vol. 1), an important nineteenth-century theologian who strongly influenced Barth on this point.

This line of thought, we feel, also means that Christian dogmatics must be reticent in assimilating purely philosophical definitions of certain terms, which often are more than willing to offer their services in the construction of a doctrine of God. For instance, an undifferentiated view of God's omnipotence cannot be derived from the Bible, as if God could do everything in his power detached from everything else—his so-called *potentia absoluta* (see Brink and Sarot 1999, 139–59). Likewise, we must reject a view of God's immutability that fails to do justice to the flexibility that characterizes God's actions as they are reported in the Bible. In the following sections we will explore somewhat further the negative consequences that can result from absolutizing (i.e., detaching from the biblical context) another attribute in the doctrine of God: his *simplicitas*, or simplicity.

The tendency to play off the properties of God's transcendence over against those of his immanence is deeply rooted, also in some contemporary theologians. Moltmann (1993, 70), for instance, posits God's compassionate fatherhood over against his lordship, while John Frame (2002), by contrast, manages to produce more than 400 pages about God's lordship, sovereignty, and so forth before suggesting that Jesus's self-humiliating love might also indicate something about who God is (442). For a criticism of both moves, see Stephen Williams in McCormack 2008, 177–78, who justifiably asks, "Why not integrate talk of lordship, almightiness, love, fatherhood, servanthood, friendship, freedom and obedience instead of forcing antitheses?" Barth is without doubt the person who most impressively produced that integration; on the basis of his Christocentric sensitivity, he succeeds in keeping the various attributes together organically. He finds his point of departure in God as *der Liebende in der Freiheit* (the one who loves in freedom, CD II/1:257) and then proceeds to discuss these properties in matched pairs: "the perfections of God's love" (grace and holiness, compassion and justice, patience and wisdom) and the "perfections of God's freedom" (unity and omnipresence, endurance [Barth prefers this term over immutability] and omnipotence, eternity and glory). For a summary, see Kooi 2005, 348–63.

In our opinion it is impossible (as Frame proposed) to go back to a pre-Barthian nonchristological understanding of the doctrine of God. The Christian concept of God is not generally theistic in nature, with a specifically Christian appendix coming only at the end. From the very start it is determined and colored by the one who was "in the bosom of the Father" and has made him known (John 1:18). In John's eschatological vision we discover at the center of God's throne "a Lamb standing as though it had been slain"—a picture of the crucified and risen Christ (Rev 5:6). He is the image of God (Col 1:15), which will apparently determine our view of God in eternity. We should not try to think about God apart from him.

In distinction from Barth, however, Berkhof (CF, §§21–23) and LeRon Shults (2005, 205–93) do not want to pair up God's properties of transcendence with those of his turning toward us, since such combinations will always have something arbitrary about them, in spite of all the unexpected perspectives they might open to our view. Barth, for instance, connects God's omnipotence with his "endurance," while Berkhof ties it to God's defenselessness, and Shults, to God's love. But it is not clear why we should make precisely these connections. We prefer to explore all properties of God's transcendence as qualifications of his turning toward us. We lack space to detail this position with respect to all of God's properties, so we confine ourselves to the above remarks. For a thorough comparison between classic scholastic, contemporary philosophical-theological, and Barthian approaches to the doctrine of God, see Velde 2010; Holmes 2007 offers a comparison between Barth and two later approaches that were influenced by Barth. An in-depth analysis of Barth's use of post-Reformation scholastic sources appears in Reeling Brouwer 2015.

4.8. From God's Properties to God's Being

We must take one last step in this chapter by responding to the question of what we may now say of God's being. We may feel very reluctant to take this step. Do we not grossly overestimate ourselves if, as sinful humans, we think that we can say something about God's very being? Should we not be much more modest? The idea that we can craft some beautiful theories but that, when push comes to shove, we "of course" cannot know how God is in reality has a strong intuitive appeal. Kuitert (2011) has expressed this perspective in the proposition that theology is not about knowledge of God. He thinks we can have knowledge of how people have thought about God, how they have pictured God, and what properties they have attributed to him—but not knowledge of God himself. With this dour statement he voices a sentiment found among many in late modern European society: it remains a mystery who and what God is.

Many places in the New Testament make palpable the astonishment that the mystery of God has actually become publicly accessible because of Jesus Christ's appearance on earth. "Great indeed, we confess, is the mystery of our religion: He was manifested in the flesh" (1 Tim 3:16; see also Rom 16:25-26, Eph 1:9; 3:8-9; 2 Pet 1:16; 1 John 1:1-3; and see Luke 1:1-4). Christian theology understands itself as having been evoked by this shocking experience that God as he really is has made himself visible in Jesus. God is a public secret. That experience does away with all agnosticism and religious relativism, and those who want to live in the wake of this revelation (usually referred to as Christians) cannot agree with the general idea that all religions are in essence the same and that we remain ignorant about how things really are. For that reason we cannot regard the doctrine of God's attributes as a halo that people have constructed around God; we must treat it in all seriousness as a reflection of God's triune being. When we move beyond the divine properties to God himself, we do not enter a sublime emptiness or impenetrable fog, but we meet the triune God who has opened himself up for discourse through those attributes. In fact, precisely in an agnostic and atheistic context the doctrine of the properties must confidently occupy a legitimate space, for they point us to a place of sublime light.

In this connection the doctrine of the attributes framed by the German theologian Wolf Krötke (2001) is highly instructive. From the context of the fiercely secular and atheistic former East Germany (for Krötke's touching personal history, see his self-portrait in Henning and Lehmkühler, STGS 259-74), he suggests that we should henceforth speak of God's properties as *Gottes Klarheiten* (God's transparencies). God does not hold anything back in coming to us in salvation history, especially in Christ (Krötke is a disciple of Barth and Jüngel). Therefore, it would be wrong (with A. Ritschl, W. Herrmann, and others) to simply regard God's attributes as predicates of his actions. In a context in which God appears to be forgotten, it seems of great importance to view the properties as characteristics that inform us about who God in essence is and that enable us to speak in clear language about him. Thus God's properties are transparent and allow us to see God himself. Krötke connects this core quality with the notion of God's glory (Gk. *doxa*), which is so central in the New Testament and which he feels expresses exactly what is meant by this transparency and radiance. His doctrine of God's attributes may be seen as an elaboration of 1 John 1:5: "God is light and in him is no darkness at all."

In view of the great number of divine properties that we can distinguish, it is not so easy to give them all equal weight. As a result, we not only see a tendency to relativize these attributes with respect to God's being but also notice in the literature a second tendency: to regard one property as the most essential and then to somehow attach all the others to it. The property that is undoubtedly mentioned most often in this respect is God's love. This reason is not only because nowadays in many societies (and not only in the West) love is seen as the ultimate value. It is also because the New Testament appears to define God as love. We nowhere find direct identifications of God with other attributes (e.g., "God is power"; "God is immutable"; "God is infinite"), but we do find such identification of God with love in 1 John 4 (vv. 8, 16). In the nineteenth century Albrecht Ritschl (1822–89) attempted to make love the guiding principle of the doctrine of God. Even though we began to see this same process in the Enlightenment (when the fatherly love of God was often seen as the most important tenet of the Christian faith), there had not been a theologian who "to that extent wanted to exclude all other aspects, except love, from the concept of God as Ritschl" (Aulén 1927, 323). Something like wrath, for instance, was to have no place in our concept of God. A century later Jüngel made a similar suggestion, though with more nuance. He considers his main publication to be a consistent interpretation of 1 John 4:18 (GMW x). The other properties of God (e.g., his freedom) refer to aspects of his love and may be seen as second-order predicates.

Jüngel even argues that, in the expression "God is love," subject and predicate are to some extent interchangeable. God is love, but love is also God. This may not be true in an epistemological sense (we know God as love only through the revelation in Christ, even though the love between human beings is an important analogy) or from a logical perspective (God is prior to love, yet he is also its source), but it is true ontologically: God's being is not determined in the least by anything else but love. He completely coincides with it (see GMW 316–17 and throughout). But this approach gives texts from 1 John 4 undue theological and ontological weight. The context of that passage is in fact rather soteriological in nature: that God is love is deduced from the fact that God sent his only begotten Son into the world so that we might live through him (1 John 4:9). Therefore, "God is love" is no analytic judgment or anything self-evident, and it does not annul other experiences that we might have of God.

We believe that the tensions between dispositions for action and the underlying properties that the Bible ascribes to God need not be smoothed out in this manner. The nature and content of God's condescension are partly determined by the attributes of his transcendence. For that reason we prefer to let the various properties stand in their strained mutual relationships rather than to focus on one and subsume all the others under it. All God's properties are equally essential.

This point of view is difficult to maintain in actual practice. Apart from the two factors already mentioned (our reticence and the drive to rank the attributes), we, third, struggle against the dubious, centuries-long influence of a Greek-philosophical understanding of the simplicity of God (*simplicitas Dei*). This is the classic divine property that is most hotly discussed in contemporary dogmatics, with as many supporters as opponents engaged in the debate. In the scholastic formulation derived from Greek philosophy, God's being does not consist of different elements, for being composed of various elements is a sign of weakness and vulnerability; what consists of parts may fall to pieces. Since God is the most perfect being, any chance of that fate must be totally excluded. Therefore God is not a composite; there are no real distinctions in God. At most those distinctions—that is, the attributes of God—are just imaginary notions, useful aids for our limited human brain that should not be taken too seriously from a theological point of view. The scholastic Lutheran theologian J. A. Quenstedt (1617–88) commented, "If we want to speak about God in a proper and careful manner, we must say that God has no attributes" (*Theologia didactico-polemica* [1685], 1.8.3).

This line of thought leads to some extremely problematic consequences. First, there is the danger of declaring all Trinitarian distinctions inappropriate, for these must also be taken as imaginary (which may explain why in the West the doctrine of the Trinity has often become an afterthought). Second, if the attributes of God disappear behind the simplicity of his being, then they too become imaginary. This entails a contradiction in terms: it would mean that God's properties are not truly his but rather ours, with God himself thus becoming unknowable. Third, it should be noted that the only way to salvage attributes out of this impasse would be to make them all identical, which is exactly what happened in the scholastic tradition. Making all God's attributes identical made it possible to maintain that they all correspond with his being. Thus, God is wise, omnipotent, and just. But if so, God's wisdom must be the same as his omnipotence, his justice, and so forth, and it cannot make theological sense to separate the properties from one another. In the one God they fully coincide. Yet, we face this type of consequence only if we accept the premise that anything composite must be defective and imperfect. This strong monistic element was more or less surreptitiously transferred from Greek-Platonic thought to Christianity. We plead instead for a restrained elaboration of the doctrine of God's simplicity that builds strictly on the Bible. Such a commitment will take us to the view that God is "of one piece" and in that sense is totally trustworthy (see Matt 5:48, where the Aramaic background of "perfect" indeed points to something like "out of one piece"). For the rest, the doctrine of God's simplicity can well do without the philosophical baggage that has so often been put on it.

We should remain critical with regard to the Greek heritage in the Christian doctrine of God and to all the abstract speculation that goes with it. This does not imply, however, that we should hold the scholastic method as such responsible for the misconceptions around the *simplicitas* doctrine; we are critical only of some particular philosophical-theological content.

The criticism of the classic *simplicitas* doctrine was initiated by Plantinga 1980 (but note already Brunner, D 1:293) and was adopted by Wolterstorff (2010, 91–111). The *simplicitas* doctrine is not found in the Reformers (see McCormack 2008, 8–9), who generally felt little need for an elaborate doctrine of divine properties, since they gave more attention to God's relationship to us than to God in himself. However, the simplicity of God is confessed in such ecclesiastical documents as the Belgic Confession (art. 1; contra McCormack 2008, 8), although there it appears possible to base it on the biblical data. Stephen Holmes (2001) provides a clever but not totally convincing defense of the classic scholastic (and patristic) doctrine. We consider his frequent reference to the Shema (Deut 6:4) as a proof text for the *simplicitas* doctrine to be unjustified. This text does not deal with the *simplicitas* or plurality in God, but with God wanting to be the only one and does not tolerate other gods besides him (see Pannenberg, ST 1:444–45).

Just as in the case with *simplicitas*, so we must be cautious with regard to interpretations of any other property that has been influenced by Greek philosophy. God's *impassibilitas* (his inability to suffer), for instance, does not mean that God is invulnerable and cannot feel pain. In numerous instances the Bible, especially in the Old Testament, tells us that God indeed feels pain (e.g., see Talstra 2009). The doctrine of impassibility emphasizes, as we already mentioned, that God is not derailed by evil and misery. In that sense impassibility is a property that stresses God's transcendence, qualifying the nature of his condescension. When God in his love turns toward us and initiates a relationship with us, he remains in charge of history and in that sense stands above it. He does not become one of its many victims. When, nonetheless, he suffers from the evil that humans perpetrate (Gen 6:6) or experience (Isa 63:9a), it is because he has in his freedom decided to make himself vulnerable in this respect.

When it comes to the relationship between God's being and God's attributes, we agree with Berkhof (CF 119–21), who is right in posing the question of whether these two aspects are in principle related in God as they are in us, who have been created in his image. A philosophical disposition toward abstraction and an impersonal concept of God should not tempt us to make things more complicated than they are (perhaps we must here refer to Col 2:8). As human beings have but one character and, in that sense, demonstrate *simplicitas*, so it is with God. At the same time, this one character has numerous traits, or attributes. God even has an infinite richness with regard to properties. Yet, he is not everything; he is not sinful, not created, and knows of no limitations. Thus, God has certain attributes and not others. The attributes that God has form his being; in that sense God "is" his attributes. Each of them offers a certain perspective on what God is in the essence of his being. Berkhof illustrates this concept beautifully as a circle in which the various properties are sectors rather than segments; that is, they run from the outside toward the center. "However small the slice, it leads to the heart" (CF 114). And thus we confess "in each attribute . . . the fullness of God's being from a different perspective" (121).

Krötke (2001) makes exactly the same point when he casts God's properties as *Klarheiten* (transparencies) connected with God's glory. And Berkhof (CF 120-21) skillfully charts a path between the many pitfalls in this field. We quote at length a few of his statements: "We should not consider this relationship [between God's being and his properties] in such a way that those properties would change God's *simplex* being into something composite . . . , and we may not think of those attributes as a separate world of energies and substances besides God's being, as a kind of appendix from which he himself may be considered as detached. On the other hand we should do away with this *plurality* in order to save the *simplicitas*. We are, therefore, not entitled to say that in the final analysis all properties refer in exactly like manner to the *simplex* being of God. The richness of plurality would then become a phantom. Neither are we to say that this plurality of properties only exists to satisfy our subjective intellectual endeavors. It is therefore not a statement about God's being, but rather about our limited understanding thereof" (CF 120-21). In view of these striking characterizations, we must, once again, express our regret that Berkhof did not consider God's being as triune and therefore has not—in any case not consciously—allowed it to be colored by God's acts toward us in Christ and the Spirit.

Thus, we can conclude that many concrete things may be said about God. In many places the Bible does so without hesitation, and such statements are to be taken seriously. It should not escape us, however, that the Bible says these things particularly in the context of praise. Apparently, when we list God's properties, our concern should not be to get some kind of intellectual grip on God; even if we think we can say something about God's being in dogmatics, this is not because we ourselves are able to discover so much about God. On the contrary, in hymns and liturgy individual believers and especially the faith community return to God what they received from him and who he is therein is demonstrated for us:

> Bless the LORD, O my soul;
> and all that is within me, bless his holy name! . . .
> The LORD is merciful and gracious,
> slow to anger and abounding in steadfast love.
> He will not always chide,
> nor will he keep his anger for ever.

(Ps 103:1, 8-9)

Words like these give voice to what happened when people at a certain moment in their lives encountered God. This is how they met him. And from what God did for them they conclude spontaneously who and what, apparently, God is. This then they return to him, for "it is good to give thanks to the LORD" (Ps 92:1). Just as it is good when we magnify people around us by expressing what we appreciate in them, it is even more appropriate to let God know in song and prayer how he has surprised us.

References

Allen, R. Michael. 2011. "Exodus 3." In *Theological Commentary: Evangelical Perspectives*, edited by R. Michael Allen, 25–40. London: Bloomsbury.

Alston, William P. 1989. *Divine Nature and Human Language*. Ithaca, NY: Cornell University Press.

Aulén, Gustav. 1927. *Den kristna gudsbilden genom seklerna och i nutiden*. [The Christian image of God in past and present]. Stockholm: Svenska Kyrkans Diakonistyrelses Bokförlag.

Bac, J. Martin. 2010. *Perfect Will Theology: Divine Agency in Reformed Scholasticism*. Leiden: Brill.

Becking, Bob, et al. 2001. *Only One God? Monotheism in Israel and the Veneration of the Goddess Ashera*. Sheffield: Sheffield Academic Press.

Beek, Abraham van de. 1990. *Why? On Suffering, Guilt, and God*. Grand Rapids: Eerdmans.

Boman, Thorleif. 1960. *Hebrew Thought Compared with Greek*. Translated by J. M. Moreau. London: SCM.

Brink, Gijsbert van den, and Marcel Sarot, eds. 1999. *Understanding the Attributes of God*. Frankfurt: Lang.

Brümmer, Vincent. 1992. *Speaking of a Personal God: An Essay in Philosophical Theology*. Cambridge: Cambridge University Press.

Crowder, Colin, ed. 1997. *God and Reality: Essays on Christian Non-realism*. London: Mowbray.

Feldmeier, Reinhard, and Hermann Spieckermann. 2011. *God of the Living: A Biblical Theology*. Waco, TX: Baylor University Press.

Frame, John M. 2002. *The Doctrine of God: A Theology of Lordship*. Phillipsburg, NJ: P&R Publishing.

Geest, Paul van. 2010. *The Incomprehensibility of God: Augustine as a Negative Theologian*. Leuven: Peeters.

Gollwitzer, Helmut. 1965. *The Existence of God as Confessed by Faith*. Translated by James W. Leitch. Philadelphia: Westminster.

Gunton, Colin E. 2002. *Act and Being: Towards a Theology of the Divine Attributes*. London: SCM.

Holmes, Christopher R. J. 2007. *Revisiting the Doctrine of the Divine Attributes: In Dialogue with Karl Barth, Eberhard Jüngel, and Wolf Krötke*. Frankfurt: Peter Lang.

Holmes, Stephen. 2001. "Something Much Too Plain to Say: Towards a Defence of the Doctrine of Divine Simplicity." *Neue Zeitschrift für systematische theologie und religionsphilosophie* 43:137–54.

Kärkkäinen, Veli-Matti. 2004. *The Doctrine of God: A Global Introduction; A Biblical, Historical, and Contemporary Survey*. Grand Rapids: Baker Academic.

Kooi, Cornelis van der. 2005. *As in a Mirror: John Calvin and Karl Barth on Knowing God; A Diptych*. Leiden: Brill.

Korpel, Marjo, and Johannes de Moor. 2011. *The Silent God*. Leiden: Brill.

Krötke, Wolf. 2001. *Gottes Klarheiten: Eine Neuinterpretation der Lehre von Gottes "Eigenschaften."* Tübingen: Mohr Siebeck.

Kuitert, H. Martinus. 2011. *Alles behalve kennis: Afkicken van de godgeleerdheid en opnieuw beginnen* [Everything except knowledge: Kicking the habit of theology and starting anew]. Utrecht: Ten Have.

McCormack, Bruce L., ed. 2008. *Engaging the Doctrine of God: Contemporary Protestant Perspectives*. Edinburgh: Rutherford House.

McFague, Sallie. 1999. *Metaphorical Theology: Models of God in Religious Language*. Philadelphia: Fortress. Orig. pub., 1982.

Mettinger, Tryggve N. D. 1988. *In Search of God: The Meaning and Message of the Everlasting Names*. Philadelphia: Fortress. Repr., 2006.

Molnar, Paul D. 2002. *Divine Freedom and the Doctrine of the Immanent Trinity*. London: T&T Clark.

Moltmann, Jürgen. 1993. *The Trinity and the Kingdom*. Minneapolis: Fortress.

Moore, Andrew. 2003. *Realism and Christian Faith: God, Grammar, and Meaning*. Cambridge: Cambridge University Press.

Morris, Thomas V. 1991. *Our Idea of God: An Introduction to Philosophical Theology*. Notre Dame, IN: University of Notre Dame Press.

Muis, Jan. 2011. "Can Christian Talk about God Be Literal?" *Modern Theology* 27:582–607.

Pannenberg, Wolfhart. 1971. "The Appropriation of the Philosophical Concept of God as a Dogmatic Problem of Early Christian Theology" (1959). In *Basic Questions in Theology*, 2:119–83. London: SCM.

———. 2007. *Analogie und Offenbarung: Eine kritische Untersuchung zur Geschichte des Analogiebegriffs in der Lehre von der Gotteserkenntnis*. Göttingen: Vandenhoeck & Ruprecht.

Pinnock, Clark H. 2001. *Most Moved Mover: A Theology of God's Openness*. Carlisle: Paternoster.

Plantinga, Alvin. 1980. *Does God Have a Nature?* Milwaukee: Marquette University Press.

Reeling Brouwer, Rinse H. 2015. *Karl Barth and Post-Reformation Orthodoxy*. Farnham: Ashgate.

Shults, F. LeRon. 2005. *Reforming the Doctrine of God*. Grand Rapids: Eerdmans.

Talstra, Eep. 2009. "Exile and Pain: A Chapter from the Story of God's Emotions." In *Exile and Suffering*, edited by B. Becking and D. Human, 161–80. Leiden: Brill.

Velde, Dolf te. 2010. *Paths beyond Tracing Out: The Connection of Method and Content in the Doctrine of God, Examined in Reformed Orthodoxy, Karl Barth, and the Utrecht School*. Delft: Eburon.

Webster, John. 2006. "God's Perfect Life." In *God's Life in Trinity*, edited by Miroslav Volf and Michael Welker, 143–52. Minneapolis: Fortress.

———. 2015. *God without Measure: Working Papers in Christian Theology*. Vol. 1, *God and the Works of God*. London: T&T Clark.

White, Roger M. 2010. *Talking about God: The Concept of Analogy and the Problem of Religious Language*. Farnham: Ashgate.

Wolterstorff, Nicholas. 2010. *Inquiring about God*. Cambridge: Cambridge University Press.

5 Encountering God

The Doctrine of Revelation

This chapter will be successful if we achieve the following goals:
- clarify what revelation means as a fundamental theological category (5.1)
- determine the place of the doctrine of revelation in Christian dogmatics (5.2)
- show that revelation always occurs indirectly and therefore demands faith (5.3)
- provide a survey of the main forms or models of revelation that play a role in the Christian faith (5.4)
- show the sense and nonsense of the distinction between "general" and "special" revelation (5.5)
- initiate on this basis some reflection on a Christian view of other religions and dialogue with them (5.6).

MAKING CONNECTIONS
1. Think about when, and with what meanings, the words "revealed" and "revelation" are used. Which aspects seem to apply to the religious use of those terms, and which do not?
2. Did you ever sense that God was "revealing" himself to you? If so, try to explain to someone else (e.g., a fellow student, possibly a nonbeliever) what happened and see whether that person seems to understand what you are saying. If not, ask someone who thinks that he or she has been touched by God to explain to you why he or she is convinced that this was indeed a divine revelation.
3. Read some of the essays in Roy Anker, *Of Pilgrims and Fire: When God*

Shows Up at the Movies (2010), and then watch and discuss one of the movies discussed in this book (e.g., *Magnolia* or *Heaven*).

5.1. Revelation as Encountering God

Peter Roelofsma (b. 1962) did not receive a Christian education and never went to church as a child. He did, however, attend a Christian elementary school. In first grade he had a teacher who believed in God and, when telling Bible stories, dramatically told how God spoke with Abraham, Moses, Samuel, and Paul. The sincerity with which she told these stories made Peter feel that he too wanted to have such contact with God. But he had no idea *whether* something like that could still happen today or *how* it was possible. He prayed about it, but it did not seem to make much difference. From second grade on, his teachers were not so involved with God, and he learned little from them in this respect.

Peter became fascinated by the phenomenon of church. Perhaps he could meet God there! When he was twelve years old, his curiosity became too strong to resist. One Sunday morning, when his parents were still in bed (they always slept in quite late on Sundays), he sneaked out of the house in search of a church. He knew where to find a few in the center of Leeuwarden, where he lived at the time. The first church he saw happened to be open. He was welcomed in a friendly manner by two ladies at the entrance, but when they saw that he had come on his own, they sent him away. "You must come with your father and mother. Then you may come back." As he was walking home, he felt disappointed, but then he saw another church that was open. This time, no welcoming ladies—he could just step inside. "From this very moment," he wrote later, "I became part of a mystery that I would never get tired of." For four years he continued to go to church every Sunday morning at nine o'clock without his parents noticing and without anyone in the church asking him questions. When the pastor once spoke to him, Peter asked him whether he had ever met God. To his dismay the pastor said No and even denied that it was possible to meet God. "That only happened in the past, way back in Bible times." Then the pastor informed Peter's parents about Peter's regular church visits. Fortunately, they did not give Peter a hard time. But Peter's father told him he could meet God in *himself*—he did not need the church. His father had become interested in Eastern and New Age spirituality, which demand a high degree of self-control to escape the influences of karma and dharma on the road to a better life. So disciplined, a person might become worthy enough to meet God. However, this line of thought ran contrary to what Peter had learned about God. The God he was looking for was not only accessible to the few who succeeded in pulling themselves from the quicksand of their desires but to every human being on earth.

So Peter continued to attend church every now and then and to pray for an encounter with God. When he went to university, however, this desire receded into the background. After graduation he embarked on a scholarly career in the field of cognitive psychology. He earned an international award for the best dissertation in his discipline and, with it, the chance to present an invited address at a conference in Jerusalem. Roelofsma really looked forward to this event, for the top people in his field would be present. The night before his presentation, however, he had a vision of hell, where he saw himself in the midst of a screaming crowd. This did not fit with his worldview, for he did not believe in the existence of a hell. But the nightmare stayed with him, so after a successful presentation he began to read the Bible again and considered the implications of his dream. He participated in the scholarly game to produce as many publications as he could—but was that it? Why had he abandoned his search for God? Two years later, again during an academic conference (this time in England), he again felt the urge to wander into an open church on Sunday morning. It was a very lively affair, with one song after another. When the text of the song sounded a little outrageous, Peter refrained from joining in the singing. "Amazing grace" was not too bad, but he could not get the words "that saved a wretch like me" over his lips. Why "a wretch"? He wrote down what happened next:

> Suddenly, while the people were still singing, I saw a bright light that shone from above. It was overwhelmingly beautiful and, at the same time, frightening in its brightness. It made me bow my knees, and spontaneously I began to utter my remorse about all the things I had done in my life and had failed to do. . . . I could not hold back my tears. My life went by in a flash. For the first time I saw my life through God's eyes. I saw that I might be a success in the eyes of the world, but in his eyes things were different—indeed, a wretch. I prayed for God's forgiveness. Then I felt God's comforting presence, a loving authority, a source of unspeakable insight and wisdom, very near to me. This has never left me. Here I recognized Jesus Christ. Silently I cried during

the remainder of the service, making sure that nobody noticed it. (Roelofsma 2009, 76-77)

More than thirty years after Roelofsma first felt the desire to meet God, it finally happened. From that moment on, this experience put its stamp on his life. Roelofsma is still working as a cognitive psychologist, but during lunch breaks he often leads prayer meetings in the basement of the Vrije Universiteit Amsterdam.

It is worth telling the story of Roelofsma's faith pilgrimage in considerable detail because his experience is so remarkable. There are few people who experience an encounter with God in such a special way (and after such a long incubation period). Roelofsma had an unadulterated form of what happens to many others in a much more fragmented, less pronounced way. But his experiences may teach us a lot about what the Christian faith sees as *revelation*. We note seven characteristics:

1. The concept of revelation is a fundamental theological category. Faith depends on revelation, that is, on God's self-disclosure—a self-disclosure that takes the form of a personal encounter. For Roelofsma, this encounter fully answered the question of whether God indeed allows himself to be met.

2. Revelation occurs not only through the Bible but also in other ways: through dreams, visions, worship services, hymns, conversations, or being overwhelmed by a great light. The Bible itself says so. Recall the crucial opening verses of the Epistle to the Hebrews (1:1–2): "In many and various ways God spoke of old to our fathers by the prophets; but in these last days he has spoken to us by a Son." Even today people experience God disclosing himself, as the story of Roelofsma illustrates. (Or do all such experiences depend on a misconception?)

3. Still, from a Christian perspective, the Bible is the criterion of whether or not something may be regarded as a divine revelation. The Bible continuously played a decisive role at crucial moments in Roelofsma's pilgrimage. For him, everything originated with the biblical stories; he did not meddle in Eastern spirituality, for it did not accord with what he knew about God from the Bible (i.e., that every human being can reach God). Whenever he received a strange vision, it encouraged him to study the Bible anew.

Later in this book, in chapter 13, we will discuss the Bible in more depth, focusing in particular on the nature of its authority and its interpretation. Here we are concerned with the much wider category of revelation. In choosing this dual approach we follow the example of many theologians, including Calvin (*Inst.*, bk. 1), Bavinck (RD, vol. 1), Barth (CD I-II), Berkhof (CF), and Genderen and Velema (CRD). Exceptions to this rule include Ott (AG) and Wentsel (D, vols. 1-2).

4. Revelation does not confirm people in what they already know but disturbs, confuses, and irritates them—and yet does not let go. It breaks into a protected world from the outside; this world may even be academia. Revelation turns things on their head and unsettles firm ideas (such as "It is impossible to meet God"). Its shocking character is still somewhat present when the word is used in a secular, nonreligious context, for instance when a woman says that something was really "a revelation" for her. Revelatory experiences are always transformative: they make us into people who are different from what we were before.

5. But different in what way? The answer also becomes clear from the story about Roelofsma. Revelation not only expands our knowledge but leads to our experiencing an existential breakthrough to salvation and toward our destiny. In scholarly terms: revelation is not primarily an epistemological but a soteriological category (on "soteriology," see chap. 11). Revelation, therefore, does not first of all involve a number of supernatural truths but—to use the term that Roelofsma continuously employs—an encounter. Such an encounter is not a completely irrational event (as a scholar, Roelofsma would not have been able to deal with it), but it transcends our intellect and touches our total human existence, including our feelings, will, and conscience.

6. Revelation never occurs in a vacuum but in the midst of a forest of prior intuitions, events, desires, and, especially contradictions. In Roelofsma's case the contradiction arose not only from the multicolored world of religions (as when his father suggested Eastern spirituality as an option) but also from the world of the church (the friendly ladies who functioned as bouncers). Where God reveals himself he comes into view only along a road with lots of bends, turns, and disappointments. In dogmatics we refer in this connection to a dialectical (i.e., going back and forth) relationship between revelation and mystery (see Berkhof, CF 60-63). The person who receives revelation does not become arrogant but rather smaller

and more modest. "The more we come to know him, the less we are able to comprehend him with our intellect" (61).

7. Revelation is not a moment of extraordinary enlightenment, after which our daily routine resumes, but it leads to a new reality. In a fine study William Abraham (2006, 86) speaks of revelation as a threshold concept: it means passing over into a new home, a new mode of existence and experience. As long as you are outside, you can have only a vague idea of what you will find inside, but everything changes the moment you step over the threshold and enter a set of furnished rooms and corridors that make up the house.

In the rest of this chapter we explore further aspects of the doctrine of revelation and more.

5.2. The Doctrine of Revelation Must Know Its Place

Clearly, revelation is a fundamental category in Christian theology, for it concerns the source or sources from which we acquire our knowledge about God. We can say all sorts of things about God, but we also have to ask the simple question: how do we get such knowledge? How do we know? What causes people to believe all kinds of things, and how credible is it all? Discussing the doctrine of revelation confronts us with such questions, and so forcefully that it seems logical to begin our dogmatics right there; as a matter of fact, so it has often been done, for everything that might be truly said and believed about God finds its source in revelation.

We do not have to take the mystical route to understand that, in the end, true knowledge of God must come from God himself. Pannenberg wrote: "Gott kann nur erkannt werden, wenn er sich selbst zu erkennen gibt" (God can be known only if he gives himelf to be known; ST 1:189). On our own we can never bring God within the grasp of our knowledge as we can with ordinary things and (to some degree) other people. God, however, is by definition the one who far exceeds our empirically known reality. Our knowledge of God depends on God's own initiative in letting himself be known. But do not our reason and our experiences with creation constitute a source of knowledge of God? This idea has become extremely controversial in twentieth-century theology. The two world wars led to a thorough revisiting of the doctrine of revelation; it has been recognized that, where people search for knowledge of God in themselves or in their own environment, the result is often that God gets used for their own plans. To the extent that traces of the living God may be found in human reason, in our conscience, and in creation (see 5.5), it is due solely to God himself arranging for these traces—in other words, we owe it to revelation.

Nonetheless, we did not begin our book with a chapter on revelation. Very intentionally, we gave priority to chapters about the triune God. For this is what we find in the actual practice of faith: we first establish a contact with God, or at least with people who speak about him. In that way we form an opinion about what is meant by the term "God"—in any case, on the basis of what people around us say, but often by what we think as well. Only after some time does the question arise, how do we, in fact, know all this? How do I know whether it is true what people around me say about God? How much of this is actually true? (Some people precisely recall the time when this question first occurred to them. In the West the average age for that seems to have dipped rather quickly over the past few decades.)

In other words, when people believe in God, it is not because they first of all studied the epistemological foundations for their faith and then came to the correct conclusion by a logical process. We have faith long before we try to test its foundations; we first believe mostly on the testimony of people whom we have usually found to be credible. For instance, our (grand)parents, our pastor, or our teacher in the first grade. In combination with certain faith experiences and interpretations, this experience suffices for most people. They do not embark on a study of the trustworthiness of the sources of the revelation of their faith but live in accordance with the faith that has spontaneously presented itself through the faith community.

The American philosophers Alvin Plantinga and Nicholas Wolterstorff have convinced many that, from the perspective of epistemology (the philosophy of knowledge), there is nothing amiss with this manner of believing. When postmodernism arose, people typically turned away, with many others, from so-called classic foundationalism—that is, the widespread epistemological paradigm that, ever since the Enlightenment, held that we are entitled to speak of knowledge only when (1) something is undoubtedly true or (2) when something can be deduced in a logically correct way from propositions that are undoubtedly true. If a particular statement (or "proposition") cannot be classified under (1) or (2), we should not consider it to be true. This strict foundationalism has been found to be untenable, since every human being believes things that do not fall under these two conditions. Basic presuppositions, such as that our senses do not normally betray us, that life is not just a dream, and so forth, cannot be proven—and yet they lie at the basis of numerous other things we believe. In a similar way, Wolterstorff, Plantinga, and others argue that religious beliefs may be "properly basic," that is, may be a legitimate ground for other things we believe, even though we cannot deduce them from propositions that are undoubtedly true. See (among many later publications) Plantinga and Wolterstorff 1983 and, for a succinct summary, Plantinga 1997.

To summarize: in this book we follow the path of faith, which usually begins with expressing our faith and with testimonies that seem credible to us. Often there is a broad network of people and events that put us on the track of faith (see chap. 2). The process of coming to faith is not vertical—that is, from the foundation of revelation to the conclusion of faith—so much as it is horizontal; from a cloud of witnesses, faith in God streams more or less spontaneously toward us. Of course, the sources and the grounds to which those witnesses refer do play an important role, but not separately from these witnesses and this streaming.

The moment when we ask questions about the validity of their credentials dawns only when we discover that what these witnesses say is not shared by all other people. This not being shared by all others has become an experience increasingly true in Western culture with respect to the Christian faith. For that reason, during the last few centuries the doctrine of revelation has become increasingly important; at times it seemed to be the sole topic for dogmatics. In the eighteenth century it appeared that we could acquire knowledge about the most important things about God through human reason and creation—until Immanuel Kant demonstrated that our reason, because of its limitations via the use of our senses, cannot lead to sensible propositions about a transcendent God. Afterward, the leading Christian thinkers tried another approach, that of the divine Spirit who unfolds itself in the history of the world and so also in the human spirit (Hegel), or in our human awareness of absolute dependence (*schlechthinniges Abhängigkeitsgefühl*), which, as it were, connects our inner being with the realm of the divine (Schleiermacher). This approach resulted in a shift in the main themes of theology from topics concerning its contents to a strongly philosophical doctrine of revelation. We find that Barth, for instance, dedicates the first of his four-volume *Dogmatics* (CD I/1 and I/2) to the doctrine of revelation, even though he no longer develops its content on the basis of philosophical categories but on his views of the Word of God.

For a concise but very accurate survey of the way in which Western philosophy and theology have reflected on (un)knowability, see Gunton et al., PT 219–23 ("Can We Know Anything about God Anyway?").

From a Christian perspective, so much prior attention to the doctrine of revelation (i.e., to the epistemological sources of our faith) is neither normal nor healthy. It is totally impossible for most Christians today in Africa, Asia, or Latin America to relate to this approach. Neither is it in harmony with the Bible. For a considerable time Old and New Testament scholars have shown that the concept of revelation is only marginally present in the Bible. In this connection a book by F. G. Downing (b. 1935) with the title *Has Christianity a Revelation?* (1964) became well known. Downing argues that our greatest problem is not our ignorance, for which God must provide a solution by extending our knowledge through a series of revealed truths. The problem is rather our sinfulness, and the main subject of the Bible is how we may be saved from this situation by means of God's intervention. Therefore, the Bible focuses much more on who God is and what he does than on how we may get to know him.

Indeed, this latter question is but rarely asked in the Bible (e.g., in 1 Kgs 18). In fact, the Bible hardly has a special verb "to reveal" but refers to God's presenting himself to people in terms of appearing, speaking, opening people's ears, and making us see. Only in a few places do we find the verb *galah* for a divine revelation in the sense of a transfer of information (e.g., 1 Sam 3:7, 21; Amos 3:7; Dan 10:1). *Galah* did not, however, become a regularly used technical term for revelation (Jenni and Westermann, TLOT, vol. 1, s.v.). In the New Testament we find the verb *apokalyptō* (uncover, reveal) and its related noun *apokalypsis*, but remarkably enough, it is most often linked to the eschatological future: "as you wait for the revealing of our Lord Jesus Christ" (1 Cor 1:7) and "so that the genuineness of your faith . . . may redound to praise and glory and honor at the revelation of Jesus Christ" (1 Pet 1:7; see also v. 5, "ready to be revealed in the last time"). Characteristically, the last book of the Bible, which is so focused on the future, is called Revelation (Gk. *Apokalypsis*). In this case revelation is not primarily something that we can already have in the present but something that is part of the future. So at the very least we must say that the fullness of revelation still awaits us (Gunton 1995, 112).

People in the Bible do not ask, "How can I find a satisfactory theoretical basis for my faith?" but "What must I do to be saved?" In a dogmatics that wants to follow the biblical pattern, the first question is therefore not one of epistemology but of soteriology. As we will see, God reveals himself first and foremost in his saving acts. For this reason, we will ask in this book for the credentials of Christianity only after we have first given due attention to the God who reveals himself. The doctrine of revelation must know its proper place. The *content* of revelation is theologically more important than the *concept* of revelation.

However, this does not mean that we may, by way of reaction, marginalize the importance of the doctrine of revelation. Asking for the sources and basis for Christian statements of faith is certainly legitimate and merits due attention in a contemporary dogmatics. The Christian faith can amount to something only if it allows itself to be questioned. Critical questions must not be avoided with a naive appeal to the Bible. So, having seen in chapter 2 that there is a wide range of reasons to believe, and having discussed in chapters 3 and 4 who and how God is, we now ask: what, in fact, is the basis for our statements about our faith? What is the ground for Christian affirmations of faith? And how firm are the epistemological grounds for our faith? Here revelation emerges as the central concept. It is possible to know God, since God has revealed himself and has made himself known. Even if, according to the New Testament, revelation is something that in the first place pertains to the future, it does not mean that there is no link to events that take place or have taken place on earth. On the contrary, future revelation is all about unfolding the meaning and purpose of God's saving intervention as these found their crystallizing point in Jesus of Nazareth and have, since then, continued in the work of the Spirit. What happened before this, however, may from a Christian point of view be identified in and from Jesus Christ as revelation.

Colin Gunton (1995, 113) defines the relationship very properly: "What happened in Israel and in Jesus—anticipations of the end as they no doubt are—must nonetheless be construed as truly giving a form of knowledge in the here and now: the knowledge of faith. As, then, we treat it in theology, it is very much the realized aspects of revelation with which we are concerned." The term "knowledge of faith" is well-chosen. On the one hand, it underlines the aspect of knowledge in our faith, but on the other, it articulates the special character of this knowledge. Downing (1964) is right in affirming that the Bible is not primarily concerned with an intellectual pursuit in the everyday sense of the term, but rather with knowledge in the sense in which Calvin described faith as "a firm and sure knowledge of the divine favor towards us" (*Inst.* 33.2.7), that is, as saving knowledge. Calvin even begins his *Institutes* with the proposition that almost the entire subject matter of theology (which he regarded as wisdom, rather than a scholarly pursuit) consists of two sorts of knowledge: knowledge of God and knowledge of ourselves (*Inst.* 1.1.1). In the doctrine of revelation we deal with the question of how we can acquire this existential (but, for that reason, no less trustworthy) knowledge. See also, for the connection between knowledge and salvation in the Bible, McGrath, CT, 152.

We just stated that it is possible to know God, since God has revealed himself. This simple statement poses numerous questions. How did God make himself known? And to whom? And how can we be certain, since all religions make their own, very divergent truth claims? We study the first of these questions in 5.3 and 5.4, the second in 5.5, and the third in 5.6.

5.3. The Indirect Nature of Revelation

Many people think that a revelation from God is an extraordinary event that can be interpreted in only one way and therefore puts an end to all doubts concerning faith. At times young people pray, intensely and genuinely, for such a revelation when they find themselves at a crossroad in their lives: "Lord God, if you exist, please make yourself known in a way that leaves no doubt." When their lives go on without some special event, they conclude that apparently God does not exist and that their best option is to continue through life without faith.

The misconception here is to see revelation as an occurrence that makes every act of faith superfluous. Suppose that, in answer to such a prayer, some incontrovertible event takes place that supposedly proves God's existence. A relative who is seriously ill inexplicably recovers. Or God speaks directly in a dream. It remains quite possible to interpret such experiences without any reference to God. The British skeptic David Hume (1711–76) insightfully remarked that, from a phenomenological point of view, there is no difference between God speaking to you in a dream and your dreaming that God speaks to you. In other words, if God should speak to a person in a dream, it always remains possible to contend that the person simply dreamed something, so that this experience does not in any way prove that God has actually spoken. If God brings healing to a loved one, this can always be interpreted as an anomaly, an extraordinary event that cannot (yet) be scientifically explained but in the future undoubtedly will be.

In such instances we are confronted with a phenomenon we might label, following H. Berkhof, the *earthliness* of revelation; even more pointedly, we see the *mediating character*, the *indirect nature*, of every revelation. It is essential to take this feature into account, for it uncovers a common misunderstanding with respect to the doctrine of revelation. Apart from our being sinful human beings, we are created with many limitations; in our acquisition of knowledge we depend on earthly sensory perceptions. When God reveals himself to us, he can use only the world of our earthly experiences. Admittedly, these may be very extraordinary experiences (e.g., a thorny bush that catches fire but is not consumed by the flames), but these experiences are never without mediation and interpretation. They come to us in an experiential reality that is part of our world. Calvin has a sharp eye for these limitations, as we see in his so-called *doctrine of accommodation*. According to Calvin, revelation will not so much provide us with a picture of God as he is "in himself, but in relation to us" (*Inst.* 1.10.2). For instance, when it is suggested that God has hands, eyes, ears, and feet, we must understand that "God lisps with us as nurses are wont to do with little children" (*Inst.* 1.13.1). God comes down to our level and adapts to our world with its limitations; he "accommodates" in order to be understood by us.

However, as a result of the earthly, mediating character of revelation, revelatory experiences will always be multi-interpretable. They are, so to speak, signs "that will be spoken against" (Luke 2:34). They are always open to other interpretations, namely, as events that are simply part of our own world. We find this ambivalence awkward, since we often long for transparency. Some feel they can find this clarity in the Bible, for is this not the book in which God reveals himself in an ultimate way?! Yes, but that assertion also demands and presupposes faith. After all, the Bible is a collection of books written and assembled by a group of people; therefore, it remains possible to read it as such and nothing more, as a rather arbitrary collection of ancient Near Eastern religious writings. And even if we do consider the Bible to be God's Word, that belief says nothing about the way in which it is to be interpreted. To put it mildly, opinions on this subject differ significantly!

Does this mean that revelation is absolutely impossible? H. M. Kuitert seems to suggest something like this position with the famous statement (for which he will probably always be remembered) that all talk about "above" comes from "below," including the proposition that something comes from above. Whatever is said on earth about God is said by human beings; claims about revelation are always from people. Such statements were already true in Bible times; we find prophets or (other) biblical authors who claim that this or that is the word of God. So, we will have to take them on their word! Surely—but it is very well possible that we may indeed believe them on their word! Even though their experiences with God have been mediated, this subtracts nothing from the possibility that they stem from a direct address by God or from a divine intervention in the world. Here, then, is the offensive claim of the Christian faith (and of the other monotheistic religions): there is a God who, being outside of this world, makes himself known in this world and uses earthly phenomena to convey a transparent meaning.

Therefore Kuitert is right when he states that an appeal to revelation does not solve all questions regarding the origin of faith. Revelatory experiences may, if people so wish, always be interpreted in other ways than by connecting them to God; this comment is true even when they are as evident as they were for Peter Roelofsma. Even more, they *must* often be interpreted differently, as there are enormous numbers of revelatory claims—both within and outside official religions—that are mutually exclusive. None of these considerations proves, however, that Christian faith does not depend on revelation, and Kuitert (1976, 41–42; see also 142–43) is therefore wrong in claiming that such a conclusion follows. We prefer to join Kuitert's teacher, Berkouwer, in speaking of "a correlation between revelation and faith" (as we have seen in 4.1 above)—in other words, a mutual connectedness of these two as a result of which we cannot properly speak about God's revelation outside the personal involvement of faith (for this common thread in Berkouwer's theology, see Keulen 2010). When God reveals himself, it does not happen without normal ways of mediation (like a book, a voice, countless other means), but this mediation is intended to arouse faith in us and to transform us. A revelation succeeds only when this next step happens, and we may speak of success (G. Ryle) here in the sense of presupposing that something has truly "landed" with the receiver (see Gunton 1995, 113).

Together with the earthliness and indirectness of revelation, a third term is useful to mention, which we have already used in passing: *mystery*. It would seem that revelation is something that unveils and thus refers to something that is no longer hidden. True enough, but not the whole truth. For even in his revelation, God paradoxically remains the one who is hidden. We find this factor clearly in the proclamation of God's name to Moses (Exod 3:14, an extremely important Bible verse). The phrase "I am who I am" (or however else we want to translate the name; see above, chap. 4) points to God's sublime trustworthiness but also to his sovereign freedom. When God reveals himself, he does not open himself to manipulation, does not allow us to get him in our grip. God promises to be present, but in the way he chooses. To us this way is often hidden and impossible to follow. The reality is that God's thoughts are higher than ours (Isa 55:8). God's revelation does not remove all mystery and does not give a kind of panoramic view, a *God's-eye view*. On the contrary, even after God had revealed himself to Paul in Jesus Christ, he still had to write: "For now we see in a mirror dimly. . . . Now I know in part; then I shall understand fully, even as I have been fully understood" (1 Cor 13:12). Our knowledge of God will always remain limited. Even when God intervenes to save his people, he remains a hidden God (Isa 45:15). And even Moses, in spite of his sincere request, was not allowed to see God face to face but only from the back as God was passing by (Exod 33:12-23).

In our postmodern situation it is important not to overlook the mystery that accompanies God's revelation. Precisely at this point the Christian faith often comes under suspicion for making all-encompassing claims (just as other "grand narratives" do), thereby becoming potentially ideological and repressive. It must be admitted that some Christians do indeed create that impression. However, believers are not people who, because of some secret source of knowledge, possess the full truth and know everything better than others. There is no guarantee that they have better insight into the meaning of history than others. They have only experienced certain things that have made a deep impression, that have awakened the conviction in them that God is at work in this world and that this activity will ultimately be decisive for the world and for our future. Nevertheless, God will always far surpass us as far as knowledge is concerned. Over the centuries Christian thinkers have always recognized this imbalance: *Deus semper maior*—God is always greater—which they have said after Augustine (NPNF[1] 8:262). When a person has been touched by a divine revelation, he or she tends to be more rather than less impressed by the divine mystery that remains; the difference is that this mystery no longer diminishes a person's trust in God.

For revelation and mystery, see Migliore, FSU 22-26, McGrath, CT 152-53, and, as already mentioned, Berkhof, CF 60-63. Berkhof points out that revelation not only presupposes and unveils mystery but often assumes the shape of mystery. As Luther said, God reveals himself under the guise of the opposite—that is, not as compassionate but as indignantly punishing; not as present but as absent; not as powerful and high but as suffering and humiliated in the crucified Jesus. Indeed, Luther in particular reflected on this mystery that revelation takes. By revealing himself as a suffering servant, God demolishes our pride. A modern expression of this view is found in one of Dietrich Bonhoeffer's famous prison letters (July 16, 1944): "God consents to be pushed out of the world and onto the cross; God is weak and powerless in the world and in precisely this way, and only so, is at our side and helps us" (WDB 8:534).

When Christians believe that God has revealed himself, they are impressed simultaneously by God's abiding mystery and his majesty. God is never simply at our disposal. Getting to know God through his revelation should never make us into arrogant and pedantic people, but people who have been impressed by God, have come to believe in him, and want to take his wishes seriously.

5.4. Models of Revelation

So far we have answered the question of how God reveals himself by taking our cue from three keywords: indirectly, through earthly means, and mysteriously. It is now time to pursue further the *how* aspect by distinguishing between a number of different revelatory models. In each model a particular vehicle is singled out as the most important—or even the exclusive—way in which revelation occurs. In the end we can conclude that revelation may take seven concrete forms. It is not our intention to play these seven off against each other but to show that they each have their relative weight in a Christian doctrine of revelation. Here is the list of where God's revelation is thought to find its primary location:

1. in cognitive propositions that have been handed down in an authoritative way
2. in verbal communication
3. in personal presence
4. in historic events
5. in religious experiences
6. in human consciousness
7. in religious tradition.

Let us consider these options one by one.

The study that has become a classic on this subject is Dulles 1992. He recognizes from the above list models 1–2 and 4–6. Mavrodes (1988) uses a causation model (which we will not consider), a manifestation model (4–5) and a communication model. In his survey Hebblethwaite (PTCD 20-34) deals with models 1-2, 4, and 7. McGrath (CT 154-57) sticks with 1 and 3-5. Gunton's (1995) concise theology of revelation places most of these forms side by side, while rightly granting that a different weight must be ascribed to the "variety and multiplicity of the forms of revelation" (109). Finally, see W. J. Abraham on "the polymorphous nature of divine revelation" (2006, 58-61).

We do not pretend that ours is a complete list. We might, for example, have added that creation can be seen as a vehicle of revelation, a theme that will be treated separately later in this chapter.

1. *Cognitive propositions.* This phrase refers to the idea that revelation has been handed down to us in the form of certain propositions that cannot be doubted. The Roman Catholic tradition usually situates these revealed truths (*veritates*) in the Bible but also in the apostolic tradition; that is, a number of truths were revealed to the apostles and have ever since been handed down so that these belong to the unchangeable *depositum fidei* (deposit of faith) of the church. The Protestant tradition, by contrast, found the revealed propositions exclusively in the Bible. Contemporary theology is often negative about the idea that God's revelation is propositional in nature, namely, that it consists of separate doctrines that must be regarded as true. Indeed, the idea that the church is the guardian of a number of orally transmitted doctrines—that were never written down!—is, to say the least, rather problematic, as Roman Catholic theologians themselves agree nowadays. The same applies to the thought that the Bible is a kind of container of a range of distinct facts that are neatly ordered by the Protestant systematic theologian. For the Bible is much more than that—it is appeal, promise, study, history, admonition, and lots of other things, and we fail to do it justice if we reduce its message to a series of doctrinal statements.

We cannot deny, however, that the Bible does have a propositional element. Admittedly, when God allows himself to be known, that knowledge can never be reduced to propositions alone. But knowing someone always implies that we get to know certain things about him or her. We learn, for instance, that a person has a particular character or has done certain things. In that sense we might consider such propositions as "God is compassionate and just" or "Jesus died for our sins" to be parts of the content of our faith that have their roots in divine revelation—as revealed truths, if one wants to use that term. However, it remains extremely important to understand that such truths are not purely intellectual or cognitive in nature! Usually they have a very existential dimension. In the so-called creeds of Christianity (in particular, the Apostles' Creed) we find the essential propositions that Christians consider to be true on the basis of revelation. But even here these are not sterile truth claims but reflections on the good news of the gospel. To use the words of O. Noordmans, "The twelve articles of the Apostles' Creed are twelve promises" (H, 13).

A strong defense of a propositional view of revelation is found, for example, in Helm (1982, 36–42) and in Swinburne 1992, a book that from the start considers revelation to be a collection of revealed truths. Typical and still influential in some strands of American Protestantism is the approach of Hodge (ST 1:1ff.), who regards the individual truths in the Bible as the building blocks of theology, similar to the way physics operates with the data of nature. A more nuanced approach, such as that presented above, is found in Gunton (1995), who employs the term *credal propositionality*: "although credal statements are to be understood, for the most part, as doxological affirmations, that is in no way inconsistent with saying that they contain propositions, claims that things are such and such and so not their contradictories" (13). Strictly speaking, this type of credal proposition has not itself been revealed but is formulated in answer to revelation (14).

2. *Verbal communication.* A second model of revelation does not limit our attention to propositions but focuses on aspects of language in a broader sense. The clearest way to unpack the conviction that "God reveals himself" is to say that God *speaks*. Proponents of this model will immediately concede that this speaking must not be taken literally: when God speaks, he does not use vocal cords and in most cases does not cause vibrations in the air. Nonetheless, this model maintains that revelation is most adequately perceived as a complex of words spoken by God, or by calling it the Word of God.

Where may this Word of God be found? Karl Barth provided a profound answer to this question in his idea about the threefold form of the Word of God: this one Word of God comes to us in an incarnate, a written, and a proclaimed form. These three forms relate to each other as concentric circles and are closely connected. According to the Bible, the Word of God is, first of all, Jesus Christ. For good reasons he is referred to as the Logos (the Word), through which God reveals himself to us (John 1:1, 14, 18). He is the ultimate divine revelation. But in a broader sense, the Bible is also the Word of God, for it provides us with the only path of access to Jesus Christ. God also speaks to us through the Bible. And, third, the same applies to the church's proclamation in which the message of the Bible is explained and applied. The Bible cannot be understood without interpretation, and Barth thinks that the church provides the indispensable interpretative context for God's revelation as we find it in the biblical witness. However, according to Barth, the Bible and the church's proclamation are not automatically the Word of God. They *become the Word of God* whenever they are used to help us understand the meaning of the gospel. Only Jesus is the Word of God.

A similar approach to revelation as the speech of God mediated through the Bible is found in the American philosopher Nicholas Wolterstorff, although he is not keen on being linked to Barth. Like Barth, Wolterstorff does not believe that the Bible has been literally dictated; the Bible was written by human beings. But over the centuries God has taken their words and made these his own, like a president who makes the words of an ambassador his or her own and thereby gives these words authority. In that sense we can refer to the Bible as the Word of God, even though it was written by people, and God continues to speak to us through the human words of the biblical authors, which he has appropriated to himself.

We notice that those who defend a verbal-communication model regard the Bible in particular, or at least the message of salvation it conveys, as the central revelatory medium. They do not perceive the message of the Bible only, or even primarily, as a series of factual truths. The Word of God is first and foremost a word of judgment and grace (Barth), of promises and commandments (Wolterstorff). It therefore does not primarily appeal to our human intellect but makes our entire life the object of its criticism in the desire to make it free.

For Barth's view of the three forms of the Word of God, see CD I/1, §4; for Wolterstorff's model, see Wolterstorff 1995; and for a concise evaluation of Wolterstorff's views, see Hebblethwaite (PTCD, 21–24), who correctly underlines the parallels with Barth. For a similar opinion, see Vanhoozer, DD (e.g., 226–31). Thiemann 1985 also stands in this tradition of revelation as verbal communication; he stresses the importance of allowing ourselves to be drawn into the story of the Bible and to be addressed by the depth of its meaning, rather than trying to construct some pseudoscientific grounds for its revelatory claims (e.g., as Hodge does) or to make the Bible apologetically acceptable. For more on the Bible, see chapter 13.

3. *Personal presence.* The question arises whether everything can be said with words. Does not every one of our encounters far exceed what can be recorded in language? How could it be different when it comes to

meeting God? Some people therefore prefer to describe God's revelation as something like a meeting between persons. The best-known representatives of this encounter model are, no doubt, Barth and his colleague Emil Brunner (1889-1966). To them, when God reveals himself, he does not primarily provide information but demonstrates his presence. The revelation does not have to do mostly with ideas or truths about God, not even with commandments and promises, but with God himself. Brunner was in this respect heavily influenced by Ferdinand Ebner (1882-1931) and Martin Buber (1878-1965). In *Ich und Du* (1923) Buber contrasts the encounter between an "I" and an impersonal "it" with an encounter between an "I" and a personal "Thou." Revelation is an "I-Thou" relationship and, in that sense, is a *relational* event.

Truth is not found in a series of propositions about God but in an encounter with God. In his revelation—which, for Brunner also, is first and foremost in Jesus Christ—God shares himself with humanity. When we try to translate that event into a number of propositions or verbal statements about God, we reduce him from a "Thou" to an "it" and make him into an object. However, it is impossible to experience communion with an object, although such communion is precisely what God wants to achieve through his revelation. For Brunner, revelation is never merely a transfer of knowledge but the creation of a life-renewing communion.

The title of the study in which Brunner develops these thoughts speaks for itself: *Wahrheit als Begegnung* (Truth as encounter, 1938). The personal character of Brunner's view of revelation is very appealing. His reflections remind us of the way in which Peter Roelofsma experienced his encounter with God: as a genuine revelation that brought him into a lasting communion with God. But what if we do not meet God through such an experience? What if we do not have such a personal encounter, or what if we do not feel that (to use Barth's terminology) we are addressed by the Word of God? Does this mean that God has not revealed himself to us? Moreover, does not Brunner's model make revelation into something very subjective? These and other questions led some, after Barth and Brunner, to search for new approaches in the doctrine of revelation.

4. *Historic events.* Early in his career the German theologian Wolfhart Pannenberg, in particular, felt troubled by Barth's views on revelation. Together with some like-minded scholars from other theological disciplines, he tried hard to develop an alternative. His central idea is that we not look for the primary locus of revelation in words (which always depend on actually reaching us and being rightly interpreted by us) but rather much more

in concrete facts, namely in events that may be viewed as acts of God. We find such events particularly in the history of Israel and in the life, death, and resurrection of Jesus of Nazareth that is connected with this history.

At first Pannenberg was certain that the revelatory character of these events—and, especially of their climax, the resurrection of Jesus at Easter—could clearly be seen by anyone "who has eyes to see" (1979, 135). He means that anyone who is prepared to approach these events without prejudice and by the usual historiographical means can only conclude that in them God has been at work. This conclusion does not require special spectacles of faith. Knowledge of God is not reserved for those who had the privilege of some kind of mystical encounter or supernatural enlightenment, and who on that basis look at things through "eyes of faith." On the contrary: if we want to meet God, we need only to make good use of our natural eyes and we will see God at work in a publicly accessible universal history. The words that explain the historic acts of God and that proclaim their salvific significance are secondary and only follow actual events.

Pannenberg's fascinating new approach to the doctrine of revelation met with an enthusiastic reception but has also been fiercely criticized. In response, Pannenberg gradually modified his view somewhat. Without abandoning his central thesis, he came to interpret it in the sense that the events around the death of Jesus are not unequivocal but require a certain (faith) perspective to reach the conclusion of Easter. After all, some kind of a perspective that gives direction, a prophetic word from God, is necessary if one is to understand revelation. For Pannenberg, however, this is not an additional, external perspective but is the light that radiates from the salvation event itself (see 2 Cor 4:2-4). Yet, from the very start, Pannenberg posited an eschatological reservation. God's acts in salvation history are a preliminary anticipation of his ultimate future revelation. Not until the eschaton will "all flesh" clearly perceive that, and how, God was at work in history.

See Pannenberg (1969) for the early manifesto in which the most important contours of his theology are already visible. For a later, more nuanced discussion of the doctrine of revelation, see Pannenberg, ST 1, chapter 4 (esp. 249-54). Pannenberg's redefinition of revelation as history has been very influential. More or less in his footsteps, H. Berkhof, for instance, defines revelation as "a cumulative process of events and their interpretations" (CF 69). Berkhof's entire dogmatic structure has been stamped by this historic approach to revelation. However, there has also been much resistance to this close linkage of revelation and history—in the Netherlands, for instance, in the so-called Amsterdam School, including men like K. H. Miskotte and F. Breukelman, who remained firmly attached to Barth's view of revelation as a word event. For this criticism, see, for example, Bakker 2000.

5. *Religious experiences*. Often revelation and experience are contrasted as antipodes. If so, theology must begin either with divine revelation or with human experience. However, it is quite possible to locate God's revelation *in* human experience—for instance in the sort of religious experiences described in William James's classic study *The Varieties of Religious Experience* (1902). Generally speaking, these individual experiences are often mystical in nature. At certain high moments in our spiritual life we feel, as it were, lifted up and brought into a deep and peaceful union with God. Starkly in contrast with what someone like Pannenberg had in mind, mysticism locates the place where God allows himself to be known not outside ourselves in a more or less objective reality but inside the human subject. We also meet this view of revelation in what is called Pietism. One of its adherents, Angelus Silesius (1624-77), put it powerfully in a short verse: "Christ could be born a thousand times in Bethlehem—but all is in vain until he is born in me." These words do not deny the revelation that occurred in Bethlehem but significantly relativize it in view of the real work, God's revelation in the human heart, that is, in the soul. For only this very personal faith experience will ultimately give us the assurance of salvation.

It could be argued that this experiential model of revelation has become quite popular in our postmodern world. For good reason, the postmodern environment is often referred to as a culture of experience. Objective truth claims, including claims about revelation that supposedly have universal validity, do not have much credibility in such a culture. "Something is true only when I can feel it to be so" is a common assertion. Often such a comment connotes that something is true only if it makes me feel good. In this way spirituality and religiosity tend to acquire a rather noncommittal character; they focus on feelings of personal well-being and on an egocentric desire to be saved rather than on knowing God and living according to his will. There is hardly any real interest in what the truth about God really is; everyone must be happy with his or her own truth. In such a context the question arises whether we can still speak of (a revelation of) God at all. Do not our religious ideas just reflect a projection and extrapolation of our own experiences without any reference to any divine reality beyond us?

However real this critical question might be, this model none-theless does articulate an important aspect of revelation, namely, that revelation is complete (i.e., reaches its goal) only when it is experienced and recognized as such. In his revelation God does not continue to hover somewhere above our concrete human existence but comes down to our level, into the deepest layers of our inner life. And such coming, at times, is accompanied by emotions of joy, surprise, and delight as we experience God's presence in some intense manner.

For an attempt to break through the persistent contrast between revelation and experience by establishing a close link between the two, see Schwöbel 1992, 83–131.

6. *Human consciousness.* There is another route to take if we want to define revelation as experience and yet avoid the strictly individualistic approach of mysticism, Pietism, and postmodernism. Popular with liberal Christians, particularly since the nineteenth century, this model seeks the locus of revelation primarily in human consciousness. Basically, it asserts, we should abandon the notion that revelation is some kind of supernatural divine intervention, for it is difficult to imagine such interventions in an age when we look to science for explanations of reality. Thus we must learn to see the process by which we get to know God as a fully natural event.

Schleiermacher, the father of this model, maintained that, at the deepest level of their consciousness, human beings have a fundamental orientation toward God—a "taste and feeling for the Infinite," as he put it. At a basic and prereflective level, human consciousness is under the influence of the Infinite, of God. For this reason, God can be directly reached and experienced via human consciousness. In this way we get to know him, and on this basis alone can we formulate doctrinal propositions. The latter all follow the track of religious experience. Thus Schleiermacher does not think highly of doctrines that do not emerge from our experience (the Trinity, for instance). His approach has become very influential in both Protestant and Roman Catholic theology. We find an important version of it in Paul Tillich, who argued that our human consciousness at its deepest level is animated by an "ultimate concern," an ultimate involvement with the ground and meaning of our existence. Sometimes we may be miraculously seized by that "ground of our being" through an object, person, or event that becomes a religious symbol for us. Dogmatics focuses on the religious symbols that have come to operate in this manner with respect to God in the Christian tradition—in particular, of course, the person of Jesus. We find an important Roman Catholic variant in the theology of Karl Rahner (1904-84), who linked Schleiermacher's project with the Augustinian conviction that our human existence is directed toward God. Rahner's "transcendental method" is built on the idea that we humans are so constructed that we can experience a reality that transcends the things around us; behind the earthly things that we know and cherish lies the reality of God.

This model does not deny that it is God who makes himself known to us and that therefore we are totally dependent on his self-giving (for Schleiermacher, this was the most important motif). However, the discovery of the divine gift seems quite clearly to lie within a generally human reach. This makes it seem that we can arrive at trustworthy knowledge of God simply from the depths of our consciousness. The risk of this approach was sharply expressed by critics of religion like Ludwig Feuerbach: if all our thoughts about God emerge from human consciousness, are they not simply extrapolations of this consciousness rather than reflections of a God who stands above and outside ourselves? Does God in fact remain God on this approach—that is, the one who rises above our reality—or is he just an invention of a creative religious brain? Barth adds, is this God able to intrude into our world and judge us from the outside, as the Bible says he does? Can he still "bother" us?

For this chapter we considered using the title "Why Do You Come to Bother Us?," which reminds us of a question the Grand Inquisitor of Seville asks Christ in Dostoyevsky's novel *The Brothers Karamazov* (1880). Here we clearly touch on fundamental theological issues. For a concise but excellent survey of the various positions, see Ben Quash in Webster et al., OHST (328-40), who demonstrates how Barth's approach (revelation based on the Word that God speaks) emerged from a justified unease over this model. Nevertheless, we believe that this model contains an important element of truth, for God "is never far from each of us" (Acts 17:27). In chapter 7 we will see further that our being created "in the image of God" does indeed imply that we are directed toward God and have been constructed in such a way that we may know and serve God. For this reason, people who discover faith usually experience it as a process of coming home and reaching their true destiny as a human being. In that sense God's revelation does not destroy our humanness but, on the contrary, provides it with more space and fills it.

7. *Religious tradition.* In more recent proposals about the doctrine of revelation, we see a model emerging in which the ongoing Christian tradition is no longer regarded as merely a vehicle for the transfer of rev-

elation but as being itself part of the revelatory process. The premise here is that throughout history God reveals himself and his plans ever more clearly, with the result that we get to know him better and better. Since in his revelation God respects human freedom and uniqueness, we may detect some moral flaws in the Bible—for instance, with respect to the position of women, views of homosexuality, and the use of violence. As the history of interpretation progresses, however, it becomes clearer what God really wants; likewise, our understanding of what he wants. As a good teacher, God constantly raises the level of our insight and understanding. In this process he uses not only the ongoing tradition of biblical hermeneutics but also elements of our surrounding culture (e.g., human imagination as expressed in art).

Obviously, this model signals a remarkable innovation when compared to the classic idea that God's revelation ceased when the Christian canon was closed. With good reason it alerts us to the great importance of our continuing search for God's intentions against the background of what he has revealed thus far and in the light of contemporary cultural developments. Surely, in every period of history God can present new insights to us; did not Jesus himself promise that after his departure his Spirit would lead the church "in all truth" (John 16:13)? Does this not point to an ongoing process through the ages? Yes, indeed—but it is questionable whether this continuing process should be labeled as revelation rather than as the history of tradition or interpretation or something similar. Although we also recognize an element of truth in this seventh model, we feel that revelation and tradition are different categories and should continue to be viewed as such.

First, this model operates with far too optimistic a view of history. We may well ask whether our moral awareness is, in all respects, developing in a positive direction. The two world wars of the twentieth century lead us to suspect the contrary. And then we come, second, to the issue of the criteria that are to be used: how can we determine whether a particular new insight has indeed been given (i.e., revealed) by God or is purely a human opinion (for which, subsequently, all too often divine authority is claimed)? Our answer would be that such criteria may be found only in the authoritative witness of the Scriptures about the way in which the triune God has revealed himself as our Creator, Redeemer, and Restorer. God does not go back to what is prior to his definitive revelation in Jesus Christ (Heb 1:1). And only on the basis of the expectations and remembrances that relate to Christ and that have been accepted into the canon can we—led by the Spirit—determine which new insights may or may not contribute to a better understanding of God's character and intentions. After dealing with Christology and pneumatology, we will have a chapter (13) about the Bible and its interpretation, in which we will address this matter further.

The most powerful and fully developed plea for the idea of continuing revelation is found in two books that appeared in quick succession from the Anglican theologian David Brown (1999, 2000; at the end of the latter book he supplies a long list of criteria that, because of their significant number, would be hard to utilize). In the Netherlands H. Berkhof earlier expressed a plea to do away with the classic distinction between Scripture and Tradition (CF 84–108; he very intentionally writes "Scripture" and "Tradition" with capital letters), although he does maintain, with some reservations, the normative character of the Scriptures (104). We do not agree with him, but rather with Gunton (1995, 79–82, 113).

This survey of revelatory models is not complete, as we stated above at the beginning of this section. We could add a model that places the locus of revelation first and foremost in the praxis of faith, a thought that was further developed in liberation theology. Knowing God becomes especially apparent in doing the will of the Father (Matt 7:21); we therefore come to know God in a special way when the will of God is realized in acts of liberation. But this is no more (or less) than an aspect of truth that is part of a bigger picture. This bigger picture is best seen when we relate the various models to each other. Simply put, the core of the matter is that, from a Christian perspective, God has revealed himself in the life, death, and resurrection of Jesus Christ. The biblical witness of this Son of God (the Gospels), of the Father who prepares for his coming (the Old Testament), and of the Spirit who proceeds from him (the New Testament letters) remains constitutive and normative for what Christians regard as revelation.

5.5. General and Special Revelation—the Search for Universality

Does God reveal himself only in the history of Israel, in Jesus Christ, and in the ministry of the church? Or do we also find signals and traces of God elsewhere? In discussing the models of revelation, we concluded that we should relate them to each other and take the revelation in Christ as the normative criterion for discovering where else God might allow himself to be known. On the one hand, we must have an open eye for the scope and breadth of God's revelation, which might occur in unexpected places. On the other hand, we are dealing with a normative core, with decisive elements—a given revelation from which God, we believe, will not step back, and which the church therefore wants to safeguard in its liturgy, confession, and praxis. With regard to the scope and core of God's revelation, we are confronted with an issue that has traditionally been discussed under the heading "general and special revelation." The topic entails questions that, especially in Western theology of the twentieth century, became the subject of intense debate, climaxing in a fierce conflict that erupted in 1934 between K. Barth and E. Brunner. The issue at stake is much broader than that particular debate, however, being part and parcel of the structure of the Christian faith. We begin with a short introduction to the problem, offer some biblical background on the matter, and then present our own proposal.

The distinction between general and special revelation seeks to do justice to the fact that God not only made himself known in the history of Israel and of Jesus Christ but has also been active in other arenas. God allows himself to be met in everyday reality. Theology before Barth was quite generous in its recognition of general, or universal, revelation. Herman Bavinck wrote: "All that is and happens is, in a real sense, a work of God and to the devout a revelation of his attributes and perfections." That is, God reveals his power and majesty in nature and in history. Furthermore, "This general revelation has at all times been unanimously accepted and defended in Christian theology" (RD 1:307, 311). In recognizing this general revelation, theologians intended to say that knowledge of God is available not just for those who, on the authority of church and Bible, want to believe in God but that God has made evidence of his power, majesty, and goodness accessible to all. The existence of polytheistic religions, for instance, was seen as a fruit of this universal revelation of God (314-15). Nor are just nature and history relevant here, but also the inner life of human beings, where we find both a moral awareness and an indestructible sense of the divine.

Among the classic proof texts in the Bible for general revelation, reference is usually made to Pss 19 and 104, Rom 1:19-25 and 2:14-15, and Acts 17:22-31. In Rom 1, for instance, we read: "For what can be known about God is plain to them, because God has shown it to them. Ever since the creation of the world his invisible nature, namely, his eternal power and deity, has been clearly perceived in the things that have been made. So they are without excuse" (vv. 19-20). Apart from the question about the net effect of such a revelation, the claim expressed in these and other texts is quite clear. Admittedly, this passage finds its place in the context of the proclamation of the gospel, but we regard Barth's view— namely, that this passage concerns only the objective-judgment aspect of the gospel (1:16-17) and does not correspond to any subjective awareness of God on the part of the gentiles—to be artificial (CD II/1:119-20; see also I/2:304-5, as well as Demarest 1982, 124-26). Paul argues (1) that God has made himself known in a universal way in his works; (2) that the gentiles, at the very least, derive from this information a rudimentary awareness of God; (3) that they have no excuse when they suppress this awareness of God; and (4) that the gentiles therefore need Jesus Christ, just as the Jews do (3:22-24).

The claim of universality is not limited in the Bible to a handful of proof texts. Israel arrived at the conviction that God is not a local, place-bound deity but that he is the God of the entire earth. See, for example, Ps 24:1: "The earth is the LORD's and the fullness thereof, the world and those who dwell therein." The nations are urged to praise this God and recognize his acts (Pss 67:3-7; 68; 96-100). We especially note in the book of Genesis how the God of Israel is also known outside Israel as the Lord of heaven and earth. After God has connected himself in a special way with Abraham and his posterity (Gen 12; see below, chap. 9), we soon discover that God also enters the lives of people outside of this circle, as, for instance, the pharaoh (Gen 12:17-20) and Melchizedek (Gen 14:18-20). We think of the Wisdom literature: in some parts the book of Proverbs shows remarkable similarity with similar books from ancient Egypt; the book of Job in its entirety is situated outside Israel, and so forth. God's revelation in a series of acts in the history of Israel and in Jesus Christ apparently does not at all exclude the possibility that God also demonstrates his majesty and favor elsewhere. However, salvation history is the track where God established his covenant, so that he may thereby reach the entire earth. See further in chapter 9.

Meanwhile, we may well ask whether the term "general revelation" is still usable in the context of our contemporary culture. Originally, the word "general" (in distinction to "special") was meant to indicate only that, within revelation as such (*genus*), there is a part (*pars*) that is distinct—a special kind of revelation within the phenomenon of revelation as such. However, today people understand the adjective "general" more in terms of "ordinary," while "special" tends to connote "extraordinary" or "strange." Things can go wrong here, for revelation is never "ordinary." God is never present as a matter of course, but his revealing always bears the character of a gift, a surprise, a breaking-in, an invasion, or an offer. We must immediately add that these kinds of events, which from a Christian viewpoint are nothing less than experiences of God, are far more frequent that people realize. It may be better, therefore, to speak of the universality of God's revelation. This word, with its connotation of being worldwide, is also more in line with the pericope in Rom 1 (esp. v. 20) that we discussed in the technical paragraph above.

Christian theology recognized early on that God leaves his signals and traces everywhere in the world. Often this recognition had an apologetic purpose. Theologians wanted to demonstrate that what they had discovered in the particular, or special, revelation of God's kingdom through Christ actually fulfilled what the nations had been yearning for all along (see Rev 7:9-12). The apologists of the second century went back to the Johannine idea of the Logos, who had been with God from eternity but whose coming into the world "enlightens every man" (John 1:9). Because this "Word was sown" (Gk. *logos spermatikos*) in all people, Greek philosophers and poets (Socrates, the Stoics) were able to perceive silhouettes of the truth about God. Justin Martyr (second century), however, did not link this notion only to positive ideas. Although Christ made himself everywhere present as the eternal Logos, people completely distorted this idea; thus, "the world knew him not" (John 1:10). The supposition of a vague, partial but universal knowledge of God became a regular part of Christian theology. To illustrate this concept we refer once again to article 2 of the Belgic Confession, which we cited earlier (2.3) but for ease of reference wish to quote again:

> We know God by two means:
>
> First, by the creation, preservation, and government of the universe, since that universe is before our eyes like a beautiful book in which all creatures, great and small, are as letters to make us ponder the invisible things of God: God's eternal power and divinity, as the apostle Paul says in Romans 1:20. All these things are enough to convict humans and to leave them without excuse.
>
> Second, God makes himself known to us more clearly by his holy and divine Word, as much as we need in this life, for God's glory and for our salvation.

First, this article states outright that God allows himself to be known very broadly and that this knowledge is universally accessible; second, it tells us that we need the divine Word (i.e., the Bible) to get to know God in such a way that it will bring us salvation. That is, the revelation given by God in his Word is superior to the other and provides the normative context (whatever may be said about the first "book" is derived from the

Bible). In line with Paul, there was but little optimism about the effect of the universality of God's revelation, but it was certainly not denied that there is indeed a general, true knowledge of God (Brink 2011). We are reminded of the words of Paul that, "although they knew God they did not honor him as God or give thanks to him, but they became futile in their thinking and their senseless minds were darkened. Claiming to be wise, they became fools, and exchanged the glory of the immortal God for images resembling mortal man or birds or animals or reptiles" (Rom 1:21-23). With J. H. Bavinck (1895-1964) we may in this connection speak of a suppressing and exchanging motif (2013, 284-90).

The Reformation, in particular, strongly developed the thought that all knowledge of God is perverted by sin. This factor radicalized the soteriological character of God's revelation. It forced a break with medieval Catholic theology, which, by its structure of nature and supernature, seemed to suggest that knowledge of God is at the very least partly an epistemological issue.

When speaking here in a general sense of medieval theology, we must immediately add some qualifications. It has long been customary to attribute this sort of thinking in terms of a two-stage rocket of nature and supernature to Thomas Aquinas. A thorough study of Aquinas and his later interpreters, however, has shown that this strict separation in fact goes back to Cajetan (Thomas de Vio, 1468-1534). Although it has a certain resonance in the work of Aquinas, this two-story theology developed only when, in an intriguing process of change during late nominalism and the emerging Renaissance, nature increasingly acquired an independent status vis-à-vis the transcendent divine reality and was increasingly emphasized as an autonomous foundation of God's grace. Getting to know God thus becomes a problem, for the new model abandoned the theocentric worldview in which all things have their natural finality in God. A seminal study of the new picture of historic developments around this issue is the work of the Roman Catholic theologian Henri de Lubac (1896-1991); see, in particular, Lubac 1946, a study that brought him under suspicion of modernism and temporarily cost him his job, although he was subsequently rehabilitated.

The medieval person could arrive at a certain (and *certain*!) knowledge of God by looking at the world around him or her, the so-called natural knowledge of God. The proofs for God's existence (see chap. 2) built in a harmonious way on this natural knowledge and confirmed it. Even though people in the Middle Ages were less critical about the net result of this knowledge of God than would be the Reformation—which deemed it to be greatly suppressed and distorted by sin—the medievals still held that this natural knowledge of God was insufficient for salvation. From Scripture and Tradition the church had more specific knowledge of God and the salvation he offered (the Trinitarian concept, Jesus Christ, redemption from sin, and the sacraments). Through the sacraments human beings could share in this full salvation. In this way a two-stage structure developed that remained typical for large swaths of Roman Catholic spirituality. During Vatican I (1869-70) the idea of learning about God by looking at nature was still explicitly maintained against the tendency of the Enlightenment to declare knowledge of God through nature to be impossible. With an appeal to Rom 1:20, the council stated that "God, the origin and purpose of all things, may be known with certainty from the things that are created" (Denzinger, ES, §3004). Little attention remained for the a posteriori character of the proofs of God's existence (i.e., for the fact that they follow, and confirm, experiences of God).

In the twentieth century the recognition of a universally accessible, true knowledge of God met with increasing theological criticism. Beginning in 1932, Barth rejected it completely. When, with Bavinck, we state that everything that is and happens is the work of God, we run the major risk of identifying God with what exists and of distilling his will from what we see around us. In classic theology this "danger of identification" was always balanced by the special revelation in Christ, which implied a break with existing reality and emphasized the radical renewal of our sinful state. But if this special revelation was more easily detached—as happened on a large scale in Germany during the two world wars—things could quickly go wrong. There is no doubt that this question still marks a significant tension in Christian theology. Sometimes it seems as if the more attention is given to the universality of God's revelation, the less is given to the particularity of God's revelation in Jesus Christ. But the reverse is also true: excessive focus on the particularity may easily give the impression that God is imprisoned within the walls of the church.

The issue of general revelation became acute in the conflict between Barth and Brunner over natural theology. Already early in World War I Barth had become suspicious of theological appeals to existing reality and what it took as given. He found such assumptions at work in the way German theologians appealed to the religious feeling of the people, the general sense at the beginning of the war that God had united the German people in concord and perseverance against the brutality and annexation politics of the British—a sentiment that was referred to as *das Kriegserlebnis* (Kooi 1987, 63-68). Barth did not trust this appeal to lofty religious feelings, Western culture, modern civilization, and so forth. Knowledge of God is a knowledge of crisis, the cross, and the resurrection. At the end of the 1920s this suspicion was further reinforced when he noticed how theologians were appealing to modern consciousness, the state, and history. When the German Christians party began to regard Nazi hegemony as the actualization of God's will, Karl Barth knew for sure where to look for the root of the evil: in the openness toward modern culture, its sentiments and preferences, as a source for the knowledge of God. Or to use the term that had served for a considerable time already as a pejorative: natural theology. Accepting another source for knowledge of God (nature, religious consciousness, history, law, creation ordinances, people) in addition to Christ results, according to Barth, in a competitive relationship between these two sources in which the appeal to general revelation, in fact, relegates the appeal to special revelation to second place or even replaces it altogether. Barth did not respond halfheartedly. He broke with the age-old recipe of general revelation and put forward his main thesis that we deal only with one revelation, namely, God's revelation in Christ. For a good survey, including of the reactions from the Lutheran camp, see Fischer 1992, 76–96.

The difference between Barth and Brunner was quite subtle. Like Calvin, Brunner left only minimal space both for knowledge of God via creation and for the notion that we are at bottom oriented toward God. But Brunner could not, and did not wish to, fully deny such general revelation. This position drew heavy criticism from Barth, who had earlier shared the same opinion—criticism that was summarized in the extremely loaded title *Nein! Antwort an Emil Brunner* [No! Reply to Emil Brunner] (1934; see Brunner and Barth 2002). In retrospect we must conclude that, at the time, Barth was not fair in his judgment of Brunner, even when taking into account all that was at stake. Often it is suggested that Barth won this conflict, but Scottish theologians, both before and during the war, were more inclined to agree with Brunner's view (e.g., see Baillie 1939). For a very balanced and internationally influential evaluation of the discussion in Reformed circles, see Berkouwer 1955.

Barth's position was clearly formulated in the first proposition of the Barmen Declaration (1934), which originated under his guidance. This proposition, like the others in the document, has three parts: it begins with some Bible texts, followed by a positively worded thesis, and finally a rejection of what is thought to be at variance with both.

"I am the way, and the truth, and the life; no one comes to the Father, but by me" (John 14:6). "Truly, truly, I say to you, he who does not enter the sheepfold by the door but climbs in by another way, that man is a thief and a robber. . . . I am the door; if any one enters by me, he will be saved" (John 10:1, 9).

According to the testimony of the Scriptures, Jesus Christ is the one Word of God that we must hear and that we must trust and obey, in life as well as in death.

We reject the false teaching that the church should or could also accept, as a source of its proclamation, other events, powers, models and truths as God's revelation, in addition to this one Word of God. (Barth 1984, 2-3; cf. Cochrane 2003, 334)

It is abundantly clear that this confession breaks sharply with the two-source theory—or maybe better, the two-means theory—which in different ways dominated both the Roman Catholic and the Protestant traditions. We have already touched on the Roman Catholic tradition. The Lutherans referred to the two means of revelation as *law* (a concept that in actual practice almost completely coincided with natural revelation) and *gospel*, while the Reformed used the terms *general* and *special* revelation. Barth totally reversed this bifurcation. To have genuine knowledge of God, we must begin with the norm of all knowledge of God; from a Christian perspective such knowledge is exclusively the revelation in Christ (Sauter 2003, 44–57). General revelation or the law or nature does not provide access to God but is theologically of secondary importance. It is like the footprints of the fox on a path in the woods, which are recognized only by a trained hunter. In other words, only the Christian, whose eye has been honed by the Bible, will be able to recognize God's signals in nature and history.

Barth's Christocentric restructuring of revelation has long set the tone, and it still remains a beacon on the seashore. We do not derive the norm for Christian theology from our own culture, ethnic descent, or race, nor from what is politically current or the prevailing moral consensus. We find the source and norm for Christian theology only in the history of God's covenant with Israel and in Jesus Christ. There God established his salvation in a new community; there God acts on behalf of humankind amid the reality of sin and estrangement. Nonetheless, in the end Barth's rigorous solution could not satisfy, nor do we feel that it can serve as the final word. For recognizing the particularity of God's revelation does not exclude the possibility that his revelation also makes itself known in the midst of our everyday life. This life comprises more than superficial Western naturalism with its closed worldview wants to recognize. Pannenberg became the voice for this countermovement in the Protestant camp. He argued that, as human beings, we already live within the horizon of the search for knowledge of God. When reacting to questions about the meaning of life, people reach out for something that might give them meaning and that exceeds their finitude.

Pannenberg describes this perspective as "a nonthematic knowledge" of God that—however vague and ambiguous it may be—nonetheless presents itself as a living reality in our lives and cannot be suppressed (ST 1:112). It is like a ball that is pushed under water by modern, secularized consciousness, only to suddenly pop up with force, for example, in the form of new religious movements. Calvin referred in this connection to a *sensus divinitatis* or *semen religionis* (*Inst*. 1.3.1). As discussed in 2.3, Reformed theology has described this sense as a *cognitio* (or *notitia*) *insita* or *innata*: an innate knowledge of God, as distinct from a knowledge of God that is acquired from creation and that, as it were, activates this innate awareness: the *cognitio* (or *notitia*) *acquisita*. We believe that Berkouwer (1955, e.g., 150–51, 279–80) does insufficient justice to this point when he wants to speak of general revelation but argues that no natural knowledge of God whatsoever corresponds with it, so that knowledge of God through creation comes about only when it is viewed through the spectacles of the Bible.

Roman Catholic theology has always given more attention to the universality of God's revelation. Karl Rahner masterfully reinterpreted the Thomistic scheme of nature and supernature in the language of modern existential philosophy. We are transcendent beings; that is, we live within an infinite horizon that lures and commands us and never leaves us at peace. As human beings, we must discover something that we cannot give ourselves (Rahner, FCF 80–81). Rahner believes that this transcendent experience is, in fact, a self-disclosure of God, which receives its categorical expression in Christ and in the ministry of the church. Similar attention to the universality of God's self-revelation is found in the work of A. Houtepen (2002). In his Gifford Lectures, James Barr (1993) criticized Barth on the basis of biblical theology, particularly because, according to Barr, the notion of natural knowledge of God is found at various places in this theology. In the Anglican camp we see how Alister McGrath (who at this point was influenced by Barth via T. F. Torrance) has argued for the opposite view, by starting from a Christian-Trinitarian understanding. He attempts to demonstrate that complex natural reality may be just as well, or even better, understood on this approach than by employing secular paradigms. This natural theology (note the subtitle of McGrath 2008) does not arise from nature but is based on special revelation. It might therefore more aptly be called theology of nature.

We join the broad tradition of theologians like Calvin, Brunner, H. Bavinck, Berkouwer, Pannenberg, and Rahner who want to do justice to the universality of God's revelation. This universality is not necessarily based on motifs of creation theology but may also, and perhaps better, be understood from the cosmic breadth of God's work in Christ. For the firstborn from death is also the firstborn of creation (Col 1:15), and in the fullness of time everything in heaven and earth will be united in him (Eph 1:10). Precisely there it becomes evident that this world is God's world and that he does not abandon the work that his hand has begun. For this reason, "in principle there is nothing that does not touch on the contents of the Christian faith" (Berkhof, CF 4). Or to use the title of a book by Eberhard Jüngel, God is "the mystery of the world." Christian faith implies the limitless and incredible claim that all of reality finds its meaning and goal in God's love. But if so, then traces of this fact must be seen in that reality. God cannot be encountered solely in the domain of church and liturgy. If we meet him only there and not also in everyday life, we run the risk of actually living as agnostics and eventually will cross the bridge to atheism. For that reason it is important to point one another to, and remind one another of, the traces of God that may be found in everyday life. The Christian church should be the community of interpretation that takes this task as essential.

5.6. Christian Faith and Other Religions

The previous sections offer us a suitable launching pad for a discussion that has rapidly gained popularity in the twenty-first century: the relationship between Christianity and other religions. Clearly, we cannot speak of this issue in a neutral mode, as if we were placing our own status as believers or unbelievers in brackets in order to arrive at a more or less objective comparison and evaluation of the divergent claims put forth by different religions. Such an approach would be doomed to failure and will always turn out to be a magician's sleight of hand. Thus we pose the question of the relationship between the Christian faith and other religions as people who have been substantially shaped by what we have received as faith through the Christian tradition. So the question becomes, what can we say about other religions in the light of God's revelation that has claimed us in Christ and the Spirit? Especially, what can we say about the truth content and the salvation that may or may not be found in them? Is what happens in other faith traditions only unbelief and idolatry, or is there something more? This issue is certainly not merely academic. It is, in the first place, an existential question for many people, young and old, who may or may not have received a Christian upbringing and who must make a choice in the multireligious world that our society has become. But every possible answer presents itself nowadays in the context of violent political and religious conflicts around the world, of bloody attacks, frustration, anxiety, and terrorism. In Western society we are especially mindful in this connection of the relationship between Christianity and Islam and of the age-old history of anti-Semitism in a world that bears the stamp of Christianity. This context of violence and fear may not be decisive for the way we answer questions regarding truth and salvation, but we should not forget that every answer is given in this context and may in turn affect it. For that reason it is important not only what answer is given but also how it is given and in what spirit.

This section is about the basic question of the so-called *theologia religionum*, the theology of the religions: how do we, from a Christian-theological angle, understand what happens in the other religions? We treat this question in connection with the doctrine of revelation, since it stares us in the face when we speak of that topic. Having seen that God's (general) revelation, however fragmentary and incomplete it may be, basically has a universal operating range, the question naturally emerges as to how this revelation may also be found in other world religions.

In general, we believe that all religions somehow reflect the divine mystery that surrounds and challenges humankind. That is, no religion should be regarded in detachment from God's speaking and acting (Bavinck 2013, 236). That caution in itself should prompt us to show respect and pay close attention. We find that in Paul's speech on the Areopagus (Acts 17:22–31), the religion of the Greeks is not ridiculed; Paul states instead that their religious views could develop because of God's patience. He enters into a debate with his listeners, arguing that God intended that all people would "seek God, in the hope that they might feel after him and find him. Yet he is not far from each one of us" (Acts 17:27). In other words, Paul approaches them in a missionary spirit, with the greatest possible openness. However, he fails to get through to them when he comes to the point that he wants to emphasize: Christ and his resurrection. Through this one man God will finally judge the world, and for that reason the people of Athens—indeed, "all people"—would do well to convert to Christ without delay (v. 30). The Christian faith points to the place—to a people and to a human being—where God acts decisively. But this word proves to be a big stumbling block to the audience. Are not their existing religions and traditions good enough? English-language theologians speak of "the scandal of particularity" caused by the Christian faith because of its concentration on this sole Mediator between God and humanity (1 Tim 2:5).

What are the consequences of this view of revelation for the relationship between faith and other religions? To clarify this question, it seems best to refer to a well-known typology that has spread rapidly in the literature since being introduced by Alan Race (1983). It posits a threefold distinction between exclusivism, inclusivism, and pluralism. All three models impact the two distinct issues of truth and salvation. It is possible, therefore, to be an exclusivist with regard to one aspect but an inclusivist or pluralist with respect to the other. For the sake of clarity, however, we will keep the two aspects together in our survey below.

1. *Exclusivism* denotes the view that only our own religion is true. All other religions may be seen as expressions of rebellion against God. Or as Barth put it in a famous (or infamous) one-liner, *Religion ist Unglaube* (religion is unbelief; CD I/2:299). One must, however, not forget that Barth also includes Christianity under *Religion*. The difference is not, according to Barth, in Christianity but in God's revelation in Christ. Following this line of thought, many exclusivists (not Barth, however, who left the matter open) have argued that followers of other religions will not share in God's eternal redemption but will be lost. Salvation is possible only for those who believe in Christ: or in the words of the church father Cyprian (200–258), *Extra ecclesiam nulla salus* (There is no salvation outside the church; *De unitate ecclesiae*, 6).

2. *Inclusivism* means that the salvation confessed in one's own religion also takes in all sincere searchers for God elsewhere. Or to phrase it in the words of the Christian tradition: the grace of Christ is so rich that followers of other religions may also share in the eschatological salvation. When they truly do their utmost to seek God and to lead a good life, they may even be regarded as "anonymous Christians" (Rahner, TI 6:390–98). They may not know it themselves, but their manner of life demonstrates that they have, in fact, for some time already belonged to the Christian community. Moreover, in their religious tradition we can see various fragments of the truth that is more adequately confessed in the Christian religion, while Christians may often learn from the genuine piety that is seen among, say, Muslims or Hindus.

3. *Pluralism* represents the position that the truth claims and views of salvation of the various religions are all complementary aspects of the truth. They all entail partial (and rather arbitrary) expressions of an all-encompassing mystery. This position is often illustrated by the para-

ble of the blind people and the elephant. One grasps a leg and says that an elephant is massive and strong. Another touches the trunk and concludes that elephants are long and flexible. And so on. In this view all religions are both right and wrong. The most prominent proponent of pluralism is the British theologian and philosopher of religion John Hick (1922–2012; see, in particular, Hick 1989), who provided a philosophical undergirding for this position by enlisting Kant's distinction between noumenal and phenomenal reality. As human beings, we cannot know the noumenal reality of the *Ding an sich* (the object as such); we know only the world of phenomena but remain unable to say how these refer to ultimate reality. Pluralists further maintain that all believers in other religions will share in eternal life (however this concept may be expressed so as to apply to all religions). In any case, this destiny includes all those who concretely demonstrate their faith in a practice of love for others.

One might, of course, raise the question whether this threefold typology is exhaustive or whether other options might be available. From time to time various proposals pop up. One of the most persisting options is often referred to as relativism. In this view, often linked to the philosophy of LudwigWittgenstein, there is no all-encompassing concept of truth that allows us to compare the positions of the various religions in a coherent way. The definition of truth differs for each religion and is determined by the "language game" (or games) of the religion in question, as well as by the "form of life" in which this religion is embedded. For that reason the truth claims of the different religions cannot be evaluated on the basis of an all-comprising framework of understanding. We will not discuss this fourth option; for a further elaboration we refer to Maat 2009, especially 124–42.

On the surface, this threefold typology appears to be a clear and useful summary of the possible positions that Christian theology might take in the study of other religions. In recent years, however, it has been increasingly criticized. For one, the typology does not use neutral descriptions. Behind the terms chosen and the order in which they are presented (almost always moving from exclusivism via inclusivism to pluralism) lurks a hidden value judgment. The reader is almost imperceptibly pulled along by the suggestion that the typology moves toward a positive climax. The term "exclusivism" hints of a position that is arrogant, intolerant, and potentially dangerous. Those who support an exclusivist view of salvation may be tempted to define the other as an enemy or an apostate, thus facilitating the growth of a breeding ground for violence and terrorism. This result does not necessarily follow logically from what exclusivists actually believe (see Plantinga 1995). The question also remains whether the risk of such an attitude is greater than in other cases. It may be just as possible that an exclusivist, without being illogical, will treat followers of other religions very kindly and lovingly—as indeed many Christians do, so as to win them for Christ.

Inclusivism is most often regarded as understanding and kind, since everyone in search of God is seen as moving within the sphere of God's salvation. Yet, one can accuse this theory of imperialism. The uniqueness of other religions is greatly relativized on the basis of an allegedly higher or deeper insight into the full truth. People may claim to be Buddhists but in reality be Christians without being aware of it (a Buddhist might by the same token claim that Christians are anonymous Buddhists). It is extremely doubtful whether this view does justice to the real differences that undoubtedly exist between Christians and the Buddhists in question.

This last objection might apply even more strongly to pluralism. When Hick suggests that all religions are a manifestation of a higher, all-exceeding reality and that all religions have a part of the truth, he presupposes that he himself has an over-arching perspective. Thus pluralism is, in fact, no less exclusive than exclusivism, for here too we meet the thought that there is but one truth and that only the proponents of pluralism know it fully. Therefore, we must conclude that such terms as "exclusivism," "inclusivism" (which also excludes other standpoints), and "pluralism" are confusing and misleading.

We take our stand on the thought that continuously recurs in this book: Christian believers are first and foremost the recipients (i.e., the receivers) of salvation and not its producers. Like Paul in Acts 17, Christians can understand themselves only as men and women with whom God has already involved himself via Christ and the Spirit and for whom this involvement has become decisive. This event is the basis from which they look at the world around them and attempt to understand it. It means that lots of things will not be understood. We are, after all, only human. However, people who have come to know God in a decisive way in Jesus Christ and through the Spirit cannot ignore this knowledge. If Christ is indeed the Light of the world (John 8:12) and if the Spirit leads to the full truth (John 16:13), it follows that salvation and truth are found in and because of these two "hands of God." With Berkhof, we therefore affirm that God's revelation in Christ is normative for our understanding and our evaluation of alternative truth claims and alternative roads to salvation. Does this understanding make Christian revelation therefore exclusive? In the previous section we saw that in the Bible God makes himself known outside of the track of special revelation (i.e., the history of salvation), sometimes in a salvific way (e.g., in the cases of Melchizedek and Job). It is not our task to render a final judgment on the ultimate fate of those who live or have lived outside of the circle of the light of the gospel. The gospel tells us that judgment is solely Christ's prerogative and might, according to Matt 25:31-46, turn out to be surprisingly different from what we may think. As far as truth is concerned, we must conclude, in all simplicity, as has been argued repeatedly by H. M. Vroom (1945-2013), that religious convictions and intuitions may partly overlap (see Vroom 1996, 2006). Paul points to such an overlap (see Acts 17:28). We therefore cannot regard all religions as being identical or equal in value. We cannot separate views of creation, redemption, and the eschaton from a religion as a whole, as if these were separate parts; their content and meaning are always determined by other significant elements in that religion. We see, for instance, that the Jewish view of salvation differs structurally from that of Christianity (see chap. 9), and even more so from that of Islam. As we meet each other, we must depend on a critical dialogue in which the participants demonstrate a genuine desire to listen when the different background stories, sacred texts, and religious symbols are presented in their uniqueness. Such a dialogue can be meaningful only when there are important issues at stake and care is taken not to relativize beforehand what has been received in one's own faith tradition.

The question about what may be referred to as divine revelation is crucial in Christian dialogue with Judaism and Islam. Judaism, Christianity, and Islam all appeal to sources that are partly identical; all three may be counted as prophetic religions. But despite the similarities that may be recognized between them (e.g., in their high view of God and in their belief that creation is good and that human beings must be obedient), there is a difference in what is taken to be the peculiarity of God's revelation. Briefly put, Judaism believed in the election of Abraham and his posterity as God's people; Christianity adopted this idea of election but regards it as having been made concrete and fulfilled in Jesus Christ; at first sight Islam is the most universalistic religion, as it rejects the idea of the election of a particular person or people and takes Abraham merely to be a model believer who is an example for us—though, of course, the belief in Muhammad as *the* prophet is just as exclusive. But the search for a common core continues. A group of Islamic scholars points to this path in *A Common Word between Us and You* (2007) in reply to a notorious address in 2006 by Pope Benedict XVI in Regensburg, Germany. In this connection, note also the approach of Volf (2011), who emphasizes the need for peaceful coexistence in the public square. Earlier H. Küng and K. H. Kuschel offered a plea for an "Abrahamic ecumenism" for the sake of world peace. In both cases, however, we discern the tendency to erase the unique identities of both traditions (see Kooi 2012). For example, the role of the Qur'an in Islam, as the direct and unmediated revelation of God, differs crucially from that of the Bible in Christianity. The dialogue between these religions and our coexistence in the world is best served by a genuine interest in the other, in listening and sharing what one has personally discovered. The missionary drive and a willingness to engage in dialogue do not necessarily exclude each other.

A dogmatics that takes the encounter with the other prophetic religions (Judaism and Islam) as its consistent theme is H.-M. Barth, D; for a study that seeks to define the concept of revelation even more broadly by articulating a comparative study of religions, see Ward 1994.

We believe that a dialogue that is embedded in actual life is not meaningful just because of its public and political impact, but because the Christian faith itself provides an inner warrant for it. Christian dogmatics is a commentary on our life with God and our neighbor. In the awareness of the salvation that we have received, we may live our lives with this gift of salvation in Christ as our source, and in the expectation of his approach. On this basis we may recognize and appreciate all traces of God. The religious person, the agnostic, and the atheist, as well as the one who is interested in esoterics, is part of the world that, so the gospel tells us, God loves (John 3:16); as a result, it is also the object of God's coming toward us and of his appeal. However, this reality does not take away from the fact—as we saw with J. H. Bavinck—that there is much projection, repression, and distortion within other religions. All these things are present there, as they are in many expressions of a degenerated Christianity. For good reasons the Bible is very critical toward idols and the demonic aspects of pagan religiosity—the only proper attitude is to stay far away from them (Isa 44:9-20; Ps 115:4-8; 1 Cor 10:20). But Christian faith takes into account that, in the midst of all this, God may present himself in his freedom and love through the open relationships that followers of Christ enter into with those who believe differently. If we also take into account the hidden but never-ceasing work of the Spirit of God, who does not leave people alone and who can also reach people who are closed, then fear and the urge toward isolation are crushed and make place for openness and expectation.

It should also be noted that the encounter between religions happens only to a limited extent at the level of academic meetings and official dialogues. These efforts are certainly important as signals to leaders and communities, but the real dialogue takes place mostly where people in villages, cities, families, churches, or centers for asylum-seekers meet adherents of other religions in real-life situations. There, too, dogmatic reflection will prove meaningful. Hopefully, it will be possible to give a somewhat adequate answer to the question that Peter Roelofsma asked: whether it is possible to meet God.

References

Abraham, William J. 2006. *Crossing the Threshold of Divine Revelation*. Grand Rapids: Eerdmans.

Baillie, John. 1939. *Our Knowledge of God*. London: Oxford University Press.

Bakker, Nico T. 2000. *History as a Theological Issue*. Leiden: Deo.

Barr, James. 1993. *Biblical Faith and Natural Theology*. Oxford: Clarendon.

Barth, Karl. 1984. *Texte zur Barmer Theologischen Erklärung*. Edited by Martin Rohkrämer. Zürich: Theologischer Verlag.

Bavinck, J. H. 2013. "Religious Consciousness and Christian Faith." In *The J. H. Bavinck Reader*, edited by John Bolt, James D. Bratt, and Paul J. Visser, 145–302. Grand Rapids: Eerdmans.

Berkouwer, Gerrit C. 1955. *General Revelation*. Grand Rapids: Eerdmans.

Brink, Gijsbert van den. 2011. "A Most Elegant Book: The Natural World in Article 2 of the Belgic Confession." *Westminster Theological Journal* 73:273–92.

Brown, David. 1999. *Tradition and Imagination: Revelation and Change*. Oxford: Oxford University Press.

———. 2000. *Discipleship and Imagination: Christian Tradition and Truth*. Oxford: Oxford University Press.

Brunner, Emil, and Karl Barth. 2002. *Natural Theology: Comprising "Nature and Grace" by Emil Brunner and the Reply "No!" by Karl Barth*. Translated by Peter Fraenkel. Eugene, OR: Wipf & Stock.

Cochrane, Arthur C., ed. 2003. *Reformed Confessions of the Sixteenth Century*. Louisville, KY: Westminster John Knox.

Demarest, Bruce A. 1982. *General Revelation: Historical Views and Contemporary Issues*. Grand Rapids: Zondervan.

Downing, F. Gerald. 1964. *Has Christianity a Revelation?* London: SCM.

Dulles, Avery. 1992. *Models of Revelation*. 2nd ed. Maryknoll, NY: Orbis Books. Orig. pub., 1985.

Fischer, Hermann. 1992. *Systematische Theologie: Konzeptionen und Probleme im 20. Jahrhundert*. Stuttgart: Kohlhammer.

Gunton, Colin E. 1995. *A Brief Theology of Revelation*. Edinburgh: T&T Clark.

Helm, Paul. 1982. *The Divine Revelation: The Basic Issues*. London: Morgan & Scott. Repr., Vancouver, 2004.

Hick, John. 1989. *An Interpretation of Religion*. New Haven: Yale University Press.

Houtepen, Anton. 2002. *God—an Open Question: Theological Perspectives in an Age of Agnosticism*. London: Continuum.

Keulen, Dirk van. 2010. "G. C. Berkouwer's Principle of Correlation: An Attempt to Comprehend." *Journal of Reformed Theology* 4:97-111.

Kooi, Cornelis van der. 1987. *Anfängliche Theologie: Der Denkweg des jungen Karl Barth (1909 bis 1927)*. Munich: Kaiser.

———. 2012. "Towards an Abrahamic Ecumenism? The Search for the Universality of the Divine Mystery." *Acta Theologica* 32:240-53.

Kuitert, H. Martinus. 1976. *The Necessity of Faith; or, Without Faith You're as Good as Dead*. Grand Rapids: Eerdmans.

Lubac, Henri de. 1946. *Surnaturel: Études historiques*. Paris: Aubier.

Maat, Heleen. 2009. *Religious Diversity, Intelligibility, and Truth: An Inquiry into the Epistemological and Theological Aspects of Religious Pluralism*. Zoetermeer: Boekencentrum.

Mavrodes, George I. 1988. *Revelation in Religious Belief*. Philadelphia: Temple UniversityPress.

McGrath, Alister E. 2008. *The Open Secret: A New Vision for Natural Theology*. Oxford: Blackwell.

Pannenberg, Wolfhart. 1969 (orig. 1961). "Dogmatic Theses on the Concept of Revelation." In *Revelation as History*, edited by Wolfhart Pannenberg, 123-58. London: Sheed & Ward.

Plantinga, Alvin. 1995. "A Defense of Religious Exclusivism." In *The Rationality of Belief and the Plurality of Truth*, edited by T. D. Senor, 191-215. Ithaca, NY: Cornell University Press.

———. 1997. "Reformed Epistemology." In *A Companion to the Philosophy of Religion*, edited by Philip L. Quinn and Charles Taliaferro, 383-89. Oxford: Blackwell.

Plantinga, Alvin, and Nicholas Wolterstorff, eds. 1983. *Faith and Rationality: Reason and Belief in God*. Notre Dame: University of Notre Dame Press.

Race, Alan. 1983. *Christians and Religious Pluralism*. London: SCM.

Rahner, Karl. 2004. "Anonymous Christians." In *Theological Investigations*, 6:390-98. Limerick, Ireland: Mary Immaculate College.

Roelofsma, Peter. 2009. "De ontmoeting." In *Geleerd en gelovig: 22 wetenschappers over hun leven, werk en God*, edited by Cees Dekker, 66-87. Kampen: Ten Have.

Sauter, Gerhard. 2003. *Gateways to Dogmatics: Reasoning Theologically for the Life of the Church*. Grand Rapids: Eerdmans.

Schwöbel, Christoph. 1992. *God: Action and Revelation*. Kampen: Kok Pharos.

Swinburne, Richard. 1992. *Revelation: From Metaphor to Analogy*. Oxford: Clarendon.

Thiemann, Ronald F. 1985. *Revelation and Theology: The Gospel as Narrated Promise*. Notre Dame, IN: University of Notre Dame Press.

Volf, Miroslav. 2011. *Allah: A Christian Response*. New York: HarperOne.

Vroom, Hendrik M. 1996. *No Other Gods: Christian Belief in Dialogue with Buddhism, Hinduism, and Islam*. Grand Rapids: Eerdmans.

———. 2006. *A Spectrum of Worldviews: An Introduction to Philosophy of Religion in a Pluralistic World*. Amsterdam: Rodopi.

Ward, Keith. 1994. *Religion and Revelation: A Theology of Revelation in the World's Religions*. Oxford: Clarendon.

Wolterstorff, Nicholas. 1995. *Divine Discourse: Philosophical Reflections on the Claim That God Speaks*. Cambridge: Cambridge University Press.

6 Existence Given

The Doctrine of Creation

AIM

"I believe in God, the Father almighty, Creator of heaven and earth." This is the opening sentence of the Apostles' Creed – after the Bible, probably the best-known and most authoritative document in the Western church. Almost the first thing it says about God concerns his status as Creator. The Nicene (or Niceno-Constantinopolitan) Creed, which is popular with the Church of the East, opens with almost exactly the same words. In this chapter we will explore what this faith in God as Creator of heaven and earth entails. What does it mean that he is the Creator, and what does it mean that the world is created? How did Christians come to the point that they confessed God as the Creator, and how does God, since the creation, relate to the events of this world?

This chapter will have achieved its aim if, after having read it, you understand and can explain:

- what it means that the belief in creation has a Trinitarian dimension (6.1)
- what it says about creation that it results from a conscious act of will by God (6.2)
- the difference between the Christian doctrine of creation and dualistic and monistic cosmologies (6.3)
- how creation, salvation, and covenant relate to each other (6.4)
- why questions about how and when the world was created occupy only a modest place in the doctrine of creation (6.5)
- the ecological commitment to which the doctrine of creation leads (6.6)
- what is implied by the Christian faith in divine providence, and why creation and providence are often mentioned in one breath (6.7).

MAKING CONNECTIONS

1. Watch a film or DVD in which advanced technology is used to give a picture of life on our planet — for instance, *Deep Blue* (2003) or an episode from the BBC series *Planet Earth* (2006) or *Life* (2009). Jot down the thoughts that arise in your mind about the origin of all things.

2. Before you read this chapter, try to list the three themes or statements of belief that you think are the most important with respect to the Christian doctrine of creation. After reading the chapter, look again and consider whether you would still list the same things or make some changes.

6.1. The Creator Is the Triune God

We saw in chapter 3 how the doctrine of the Trinity is the fundamental basis for faith in God. Now, as we speak about God as the Creator, it is essential to retain this Trinitarian perspective. Traditionally, creation is especially attributed to the Father, as the Apostles' Creed indicates. However, such attributions (Lat. *appropriationes*) are never intended in an exclusive sense; the fact that creation is first of all the work of the Father does not exclude the involvement of the Son and of the Spirit, albeit in a different way (see Webster 2010).

The following quotation from the church father Irenaeus of Lyons makes it clear that this awareness is very deeply entrenched in the Christian tradition. Around 180 he wrote, "God will be glorified in his creative work by fashioning and modeling it after his own Son. For by the hands of the Father, that is to say, through the Son and the Holy Spirit, man . . . was made in the likeness of God" (*Against Heresies* 5.6.1). That is, Irenaeus tells us that humanity was not created directly by God the Father but rather through the mediation of the Son and the Spirit.

Using a metaphor that has become famous, he sees the Son and the Spirit as the "two hands" by which God created and by which he turns toward us. To reinforce this thought, Irenaeus refers to Gen 1:26. The remarkable plural form used in this passage ("Let us make man . . .") has from the very beginning led the church to think that the Father here speaks to the Son and to the Spirit, referencing the Trinity in veiled language. This idea has proven to be exegetically untenable, yet the way in which Irenaeus discerns a common involvement of Father, Son, and Spirit in creation does indeed have strong biblical warrant. In Gen 1 we read that creation resulted from God's speaking (i.e., through the word/ Word, v. 3), and in the prior verse we discover that the Spirit of God hovered over the waters. In view of the context of Gen 1 and also in view of what is said in other Old Testament passages about this Spirit (*ruach*) of YHWH, the intention is undoubtedly to stress that the Spirit engenders, inspires, and energizes life. "When you send forth your Spirit, they [the animals] are created; and you renew the face of the ground," says Ps 104:30. In Ezek 37 we find the same Spirit bringing dry bones back to life. On this basis the ancient ecclesial tradition without hesitation identified the Spirit with the Creator, as is echoed in the hymn *Veni, Creator Spiritus* (Come, Creator Spirit). In short, God creates through his word and through the Spirit. "By the word of the LORD the heavens were made, and all their host by the breath of his mouth" (Ps 33:6).

In the New Testament the Gospel of John in particular connects this creative speaking of God with Jesus Christ. The evangelist opens his work with a clear reference to Gen 1:1: "In the beginning was the Word, and the Word was with God, and the Word was God.... All things were made through him, and without him was not anything made that was made" (John 1:1, 3). In the following sentence John goes on to explain that, while on earth, the Word (Gk. *logos*) assumed physical form in Jesus Christ (John 1:14, 18). In the Pauline literature, for instance in the Letter to the Colossians, we learn about Christ that "in [*or* through] him all things were created" (1:16; cf. v. 17), while in the Letter to the Romans the Spirit is also closely linked with creation (8:23-26).

Moreover, it is important to understand that this Trinitarian character concerns not only the origin but also the continued existence of the world. The word "creation" has two aspects: it refers to the act of creation and to its result. The fact that the Son and the Spirit are, according to the Bible, involved in the creation work of the Father is therefore not just an interesting bit of information about that work but says something of how, from a Christian perspective, that work must still be viewed and something about how it continues to exist. Somehow the creation manifests traces of Christ and of the Spirit.

Christian theology shows a high degree of consensus on this point. (Brian Gerrish [CF 35-73], however, is an exception. Following a Schleiermacherian approach, he first discusses the doctrine of creation under the heading "theism as the presupposition of Christian faith" and then goes on to unfold the doctrine of redemption as exemplifying "the distinctive affirmations of the Christian faith," locating Christ and the Spirit only in the latter part of his dogmatics.) But the way in which the current mainline view is further developed is quite diverse. We give three examples.

1. K. Barth (CD III/1) approached the issue of creation mostly from a christological angle. The creation finds its meaning in Jesus Christ; his appearance was God's ultimate aim. We come to know God only through Christ, not through his creation as such. The creation is only the technical *Ermöglichung* (enablement, 97) of the covenant, that is, for the love relationship that God wants to establish with us in Christ. By taking this approach, Barth makes the statement from the Letter to the Colossians that all things have been created "in him" (1:16; see also Heb 1:2) the cornerstone of his doctrine of creation.

2. A. Beek (1996) also makes Christology his point of departure, but in a different way. He views the creation above all as a reality that has been marred by suffering and death, which he regards as an image of the suffering, crucified Christ. Christians should not be stunned by all the misery and distress in the world, for it bears the stamp of their Lord, who died on a cross. The goodness of creation—a notion that plays an important role in Gen 1—must, according to van de Beek, be understood as the goodness of the cross: just as God did not abandon his Son in the crisis of despair and forsakenness and death but raised him from the tomb, so he will not abandon his creation but will sustain it through all possible misery (177–84).

3. J. Moltmann (1993) sees creation particularly as the sign of the Holy Spirit, who lives in it. Moltmann does not deny God's transcendence but argues that, in view of our current secularization and the ecological crisis, we must especially emphasize God's immanence: creation is the dwelling place (Gk. *oikos*) where God lives through his Spirit. This emphasis is clear in the subtitle of Moltmann's book in the German original, *Ökologische Schöpfungslehre*, "an ecological doctrine of creation" (with "ecology" deriving from Greek words meaning "the science of the house"). Anyone who violates creation violates God's home, and implicitly God himself, for God's Spirit is present everywhere, in all creatures. Moltmann's ecology is at the same time pneumatological (12), for the creation bears the stamp of the indwelling Spirit. This awareness will ensure that Christians treat the creation with care and respect. See Bergmann 2005 for a similar approach (but drawing on Cappadocian theology).

We think that there are good grounds in biblical theology to allow Christian discourse about God to be colored by the victory that Christ gained in his death and resurrection. In the New Testament the cross is not presented as a form of tragic suffering but as a part of God's saving intention for his creation. He "in whom we have redemption, the forgiveness of sins," is the central focus of the creation, the one through whom God will reconcile with himself "all things [that] were created, in heaven and on earth" (Col 1:14, 16, 20). It does not mean that eventually all things and all people will be reconciled with God, but it does mean that there is a hope and a future for creation as such. In Christ, God does nor save people *from* the creation but *with* the creation. At the same time, there is reason to let Christian discourse about creation be colored by the "groaning" of the Spirit. For the Spirit has descended deeply in the creation, so deeply that he "groans" with us because of the overwhelming suffering to which creation has fallen victim. This suffering entails not only that of the enormous number of animals that are devoured each day or of humanity as a whole, but especially the despair of God's children. The Spirit shares in their tears and helps them in their weakness—that is, in their struggle to persevere in faith amid all their trouble (Rom 8:20, 25-26). At times such perseverance becomes too much. For this reason, the Spirit pleads that things may end (Rev 22:17), that our existence may be delivered from this deadly regime so that we may fully share in the glory that Christ has already received. The Spirit wants to bring everything into harmony with God's ultimate goal (Gunton 1998, 170).

We therefore see that the Christian doctrine of creation has a Trinitarian dimension. It is not just a general introduction, a summary of what all people except some diehards believe, and the basis on which more specifically Christian elements must be built. No, the doctrine of creation is itself in all respects Christian; it registers the conviction of those people who have come to know God in Jesus Christ and confess that he is the Creator of heaven and earth. For they know him as the God who loved the world to the extent that he was willing to give his Son to save it (John 3:16). The way in which we observe and experience the creation is therefore defined from the start by the "two hands" of God, which he has stretched out toward his creation: Christ and the Spirit. As soon as we forget this definition, the doctrine of creation will inevitably be secularized, and Christians will no longer regard reality in a way that differs fundamentally from the view of others (see Link 1991). But this understanding in no way takes away from the fact that, as said above, the work of creation is especially attributed to the Father (see also Heidelberg Catechism, Lord's Day 8).

6.2. Creation as an Act of Will and an Act of Goodness

Why is there something rather than nothing? This question—which is as old as human memory—has been answered by Jews and Christians in an astonishingly simple way: because God wanted "something." That I exist, that the world exists, that there is something like an immeasurable cosmos—it all depends on God's choice. Classic theology speaks in this connection of God's act of will to create, or the "creation decree." The cosmos would not have come about without this act of will by the triune God that finds its deepest ground in God the Father. What all did God create? In this respect we can hardly think too broadly. Hymns like Pss 24, 90, 104, and 148 sing about the vastness of God's creation, and chapters in Job (38–41) and Isaiah (40–44) impress us by their imagery of its greatness. The biblical expression par excellence for this vastness is "heaven and earth" (e.g., in Gen 1:1; Ps 124:8). This phrase designates what we today call the cosmos, the universe or—should there be more than one—the universes. To sum it up, we might say that everything that is not God has been created by God.

The chapters in Job just referred to teach us that the universe comprises more than we would, in our anthropocentrism, first be inclined to think. We do not even know whether God created life only on this earth. It is often suggested that the discovery of some extraterrestrial life would pose a major problem to the Christian faith. Not so. On the contrary, Christians have always believed in the existence of extraterrestrial life, namely, the angels. We mention angels here not because they must have a place somewhere in dogmatics but because their creation reminds us of at least two things. First, the frequent mention of angels in the Bible tells us that God created more intelligent life than only that on this earth. Even though we human beings are the object of God's special love and care, creation is not just about us down here. Second, the existence of angels reminds us that life is not restricted to having a physical body. In this chapter we do stress the goodness of our earthly-material existence in the face of all the suspicions about it down through the centuries. We also emphasize that we as human beings are through-and-through physical entities. But in his creation God is not restricted to matter. He also created angels, of whom we know little more than that they are "ministering spirits" (Heb 1:14).

Borrowing an expression from Col 1:16, the Nicene Creed states that God is the Creator of "all that is, seen and unseen" (OF 14). The reference seems to be to angels. The Belgic Confession explicitly mentions the creation of angels in its article 12. According to the Christian faith, created reality does not coincide with its visible aspects—there is more between heaven and earth. We must be reticent in speaking about this "more," however. The representations of the angelic world are pre-Israelite and have been conditioned by culture over the centuries (which is not to imply that they do not correspond with some reality). No doubt much in the theological tradition, and particularly in the arts, popular piety, and many forms of contemporary spirituality, goes far beyond the concrete and sober information of the Bible. The main biblical motif is that angels are in God's service; they do nothing out of their own initiative. Especially in the Old Testament, they are even identified with their divine Sender (note the figure of the *mal'ak* YHWH, the Angel of the Lord). Even when their Sender is not so clearly in view, they impress us by the holiness and majesty of YHWH (e.g., Isa 6), whom they represent. In the New Testament their name (Gk. *angeloi*, "emissaries, ambassadors") indicates that they are totally under God's command. There is no reason to think that every believer or every human being has his or her own guardian angel; the traditional proof texts for this thought, Matt 18:10 and Acts 12:15, are far from clear on this point. The imagery that we find at what we might call the fringe of the New Testament canon (Jude 6; 2 Pet 2:4), describing the fall of the angels, certainly gives food for thought but in itself carries too little weight to allow us to construct a well-defined metaphysical theory about the origin of evil on this basis. Besides, such a theory would actually only shift the problem of theodicy (for how could created angels choose evil?) and would leave us with as many questions as possible answers. Angels are not higher in the hierarchy of being than humans, who are created in God's image; Ps 8:6 gives that suggestion only in the Septuagint. But such thoughts do not erode the confidence that, from a Christian perspective, we have sufficient reason to affirm the existence of angels, even in great quantity (Matt 26:53) and variety (cherubs, seraphs, etc.). Note Genderen and Velema, CRD 276-82, but also the extensive comments by Barth (CD III/3:369-531), developed strictly in the context of God's acts in Christ. Although in our day and age many ideas about angels have more to do with New Age thought than with the Christian faith, we can welcome the greater openness nowadays for angels than was the case within the modern-empirical climate, when Occam's razor ("don't multiply [metaphysical] entities unnecessarily," i.e., explain unknown phenomena first in terms of known entities) often eliminated them entirely.

A number of extremely important insights follow from the basic Jewish-Christian conviction that God created all things through an act of will:

1. The creation is *contingent*. That is, it might not have been. Creation is not necessary, unlike, in the classic Christian tradition, the existence of God. (As Anselm argued, God, "than which nothing greater can be thought," must exist.) Therefore the creation is not "out of" God; it is not a divine emanation. Emanation, or "streaming forth," means that, just as a river must originate in a source and the sun rays come from the sun, so the creation naturally and automatically streams from its divine origin. The idea of emanation is characteristic of some Eastern religions and in important Greek-philosophical schools like Neoplatonism. In this approach there is no choice in the matter; there never was a time when the cosmos did not exist. The theory of "eternal creation," which we find in Aristotle, among others, teaches that the material world has always existed and always will. Therefore, it bears no structural difference from the divine but actually participates in the divine, even if on a lower level.

2. All that is created *depends on God*. Creation does not stand on its own two feet. This is true not only at its initial moment but for all moments that have followed. We live from minute to minute, from year to year, "on the breath of God's voice" (see Job 27:3; Heb 1:3). The doctrine of creation can therefore not be detached from the maintenance of creation (which, we will see below, is part of the doctrine of providence). Because God sustains with his hand this earth and all that is in it, it can continue to exist. If all that is created has its origin in God's act of will, its continuation equally depends on God's ongoing care.

3. God is eternal, but the creation is *temporal*. This insight is not the same as creation's being contingent. Something may be contingent without being temporal, namely, if God has willed it from eternity to eternity. But this is not true of creation. There was a time when we did not yet exist, and there will be a time when we will no longer be alive. Therein we differ from the Creator. This difference is true, even if we would like to say with Augustine (*De civ. Dei* 11.6) that God did not create everything *in* time but together *with* time, and that God therefore does not just live longer than we do but is completely outside every flow of time.

4. Created reality is not divine and therefore is not holy or sacred but *profane*. We do not have to suspect a spirit behind every tree or regard the trees themselves as enchanted. Animism is overcome in Jewish-Christian thinking. This position of course carries enormous ecological risks, for it may easily lead us to exploit the earth. However, we can explore, examine, or develop the earth without fear. However much we may be fascinated by the grandeur of mountain ranges and the endur-

ance of viruses, they do not need to instill in us a numinous fear, for they do not represent divine but created realities, just like us.

5. Thus, in summary, there is an *ontological* difference between Creator and creature; they have modes of existence that differ structurally. The Creator is eternal and has no source of life other than himself; we speak, in classical terms, of God's aseity (Lat. *a se*, "from himself"). All creatures, in contrast, however different they may be from each other, exist only because of God. Thus, from an ontological perspective, God and human beings are not in the same boat. Unlike us, God is not subject to time and coincidence, and he is not a victim of everything that may happen. This ontological difference is often defined by stating that God is *transcendent* (far above) with respect to his creation. God alone is divine and holy; the world is not divine and not sacred, but profane.

The various aspects of the Christian belief in creation mentioned so far help us understand why the phenomenon of natural science would emerge precisely in the Christian West. If the earth is contingent and not necessary, it will be *necessary* to study the earth if we want to find out more about it. Things are not determined by pre-given structures (as, for instance, in the Greek belief that the circular orbits of the planets are determined by the perfection of the form of the circle). The fact that the earth is profane and not sacred also makes it possible to conduct further research without committing some sort of sacrilege. That the earth is good (see below) gives added importance to further explorations that would lose value if the material world was only an evil imitation of reality. Without exaggerating the idea that the development of science is Christian, it is clear that the natural sciences developed only after the Christian doctrine of creation was no longer expressed in terms of concepts inherited from Greek philosophy. For a discussion with due attention to the nuances involved, see, for example, Gunton 1998, chapter 5, who also refers to important studies by R. Hooykaas (1972), T. F. Torrance (1981), and S. Jaki (1980).

6. Creation's origin in a divine act of will lets us deduce that the creation can present *itself* for what it is. It is no extension of God, no form of divine self-realization, but a genuine "over against." The creation does not originate from an unconscious reflex of God, as we might unconsciously scratch our arm when we feel an itch. When we say that God "willed" the creation, it means that he very intentionally chose to create; he could also have chosen not to do so. God did not need us to solve some problem confronting him. For instance, he did not create the world because he felt lonely, for as the Triune One, he had always been

"totally blessed in himself"—which means, perfectly happy. So why did he create us? The Christian answer is, because of his love. God wanted us to exist and to share with him the joy of existence.

For that reason God did not create us as a stray event but with a degree of independence, in an enduring mode of being. Created reality exists as what is not God, and that existence has been given by God (this point is aptly made, in particular, by Higton [CD 201]).

At this point we may give a short but pertinent illustration of the close tie between dogmatics and ethics. On the basis of what has been said, we can understand the Christian disapproval of suicide. From a pastoral perspective, of course, much more should be said about it, but ethically this disapproval has been standard throughout the Christian tradition. Other groups in society share this view, but from a secular perspective it is much more difficult to argue why suicide would be wrong. From a Christian angle there is an easy explanation: God wants us to exist, and as long as he keeps us alive, it is better to be than not to be. Likewise, Christian (or, in a broader sense, theistic) objections to abortion and euthanasia can be better understood in view of this basic conviction.

7. We can be even more precise by saying that creation is *intentional*. God has called it into being with a particular purpose. To repeat, the fact that God willed it means that there was no question of need or necessity on his part, nor does it imply that it was simply arbitrary. We do not just happen to be here, as a fickle matter of fate or as a by-product of a blind evolutionary process. We are not a sudden thought of God, a divine whim, but we were consciously intended by God with a clear goal in mind. This goal is not immediately realized. From its very inception there is a movement, even a tension, in creation: will Adam be obedient or will he not (Gen 2:17)? From the beginning, creation bears an eschatological orientation; it asks for a history by which it may achieve its purpose (see Gunton 1998, 12 and throughout; Fergusson in Webster et al., OHST 76). This goal is symbolized in Gen 1–2 by the Sabbath, the seventh day as a day of rest, in which God's work of creation culminates.

8. The two previous points indicate that creation is not something neutral, and certainly not something inherently evil, but rather something *good*. In Latin: not a *neutrum*, and certainly no *malum*, but a *bonum*. As an act of will, the creation is also an endowment, a gift. God favors the cosmos and humanity with their existence, just like that, free of charge. We cannot deny that all kinds of things have gone wrong in the creation, all of which does not negate its good beginning. Christians believe that

creation is no quirk, no arbitrary act by God, but a gift that reflects his be-ing, as a present usually reflects something about the giver. We discover not only God's power but also his goodness and love in his giving us and the cosmos our existence. The love that reflects God's being, as it binds Father, Son, and Spirit together, radiates toward the outside. The reverse is also true: the good gift of creation corresponds with God's being, even though it does not follow from it in a logical, inescapable way, since there is an act of will in between.

9. Finally, creation as a gift from God is neither a necessary ema-nation nor an arbitrary product, which ensures that it is *trustworthy*. In its order of structure and being, which follow the laws of nature, creation reflects the goodness and trustworthiness of God (see Gen 8:22). On the one hand, the laws of nature give such a measure of trustworthiness to existence that we feel we can rely on the things around us. We do not fear that things will suddenly behave differently today than they did yester-day, and usually our trust seems justified. On the other hand, the laws of nature do not so determine every aspect of life that all that occurs happens of necessity. Creation is neither a haunted house nor a bunker (Berkhof, CF 169). There is room for our human influence and, analo-gously, for divine intervention in the form of a miracle too. These are all points for further discussion. But such discussions are mostly about how exactly, and how heavily, the various aspects must be stressed.

To mention a few examples.

1. Few Christians will deny that the creation depends on God, but some point out that the creation records in Gen 1 and 2 also highlight other, no less important relationships: the mutual dependence between the creatures, and human depen-dence on the Creator, who involves the earth in his creative work (Gen 1:11-12) and permits the result of his work to depend in part on the human cooperation (Gen 2:5, 19-20). Such relationships must have a place in a Christian doctrine of creation (as argued by Welker [1999, 6-21]).

2. Few Christians will deny that creation is a good gift, but some prefer to reserve such terms as "grace" for the forgiveness of sins in Jesus Christ. Others go further and maintain that God not only has "emptied" himself in the incarnation of Christ but did so earlier in the act of creation, or that the creation is at the very least an act of divine self-restriction (as, for instance [but in our opinion not very convincingly], Moltmann 1993, 86-87).

3. Others find the relationship between the one-time calling of creation into being and its continued maintenance to be so important that they like to speak of *creatio continua*. Robert Jenson even states that God did not so much create

things but rather created a history, a story. He regards the disappearance of that insight to have been the great historical disaster that has hit the doctrine of creation (Jenson, ST 2:14). Others do not want to go that far and even like to avoid the term *creatio continua* (e.g., Genderen and Velema [CRD 258-59]), as they want to stay with the one-time act of creation "in the beginning"—something that Jenson too does not deny.

4. Then there are some who feel that the laws of nature are so all-determining for the entire interplay of things that little or no room is left for miracles (e.g., as God's answer to prayer). But others find it difficult to see God's hand at all in the inflexibility and trustworthiness of the laws of nature and therefore regard miracles as the "real" work in which God shows himself at work.

We will not pursue these discussions any further, but conclude by observing that this section has sketched out some of the most important contours of the Christian doctrine of creation on which there is a broad consensus.

6.3. Belief in Creation versus the Isms

What we have said so far probably does not sound too revolutionary for most readers because the concept of creation has deeply influenced Western culture—so deeply, in fact, that we hardly realize how remarkable the concept is. And even where our culture has abandoned the overt Jewish-Christian belief in creation, it continues to be subconsciously affected by its main features. It becomes very clear that this belief is far from self-evident when we compare it with some alternatives. Such existed already in the early centuries when Christianity was spreading; these alternatives have since gone underground, but without fully disappearing from our cultural history. Now that the Christian faith has lost much of its strength in the Western world, we see these alternatives gradually reappearing, although in new forms.

The Christian doctrine of creation developed in the first centuries of church history in a struggle against dualistic schools, particularly Gnosticism and the gnostic-influenced ideas of the Greek shipping merchant Marcion (ca. 85-160). The church rejected these theories as heretical because of a twofold teaching: for recognizing not one but two sources of being, good and evil, and then for linking the principle of evil to material reality. The latter impulse—to throw suspicion on material, earthly, and bodily reality—came from deep roots in the entire Greek-philosophical tradition from Parmenides (fifth century BCE) and Plato, and behind these sources also in Eastern religions like Hinduism and Buddhism. In his *Timaeus*, the peculiar work in which he offers a kind of cosmology built on ancient myths, Plato differentiates between three distinct realities: that of nonmaterial ideas, the divine demiurge (= craftsman, artisan), and indistinct, chaotic matter. The demiurge forms rather than creates, shaping this chaotic matter after the model of the eternal ideas. But owing to the obstinacy of matter, the work is not completely successful. For that reason our reality remains but a weak reflection of the world of ideas, a vague middle place between perfect ideal existence and formless nothingness.

In Marcionism as well as Gnosticism—a movement that has re-emerged today in esoteric forms of spirituality—we see a radical form of this type of thinking. The gnostics, some of whom saw themselves as Christians, cherished a collection of religious-philosophical ideas that betrayed a form of dualism, with spirit and matter, also heaven and earth, being linked respectively with good and evil. Plato's demiurge was identified with the Creator God of the Old Testament, a lower deity who had bungled his work. Fortunately, however, there was also the much more perfect God of the New Testament, the Father of Jesus Christ, who saves us from the perishable material world by giving us knowledge (*gnōsis*) of the higher spiritual reality. Thus, life is identified with spiritual knowledge, while evil is traced back to imperfect material reality.

Against the background of these popular trends, in its very first centuries, early Christianity developed the idea of *creatio ex nihilo*. Usually the term is translated "creation out of nothing," but "creation out of nothing*ness*" would be better, since it avoids the suggestion that this "nothing" might still be "something." Exegetical research (most famously in May 1994, but see the criticism of May's thesis in Craig 2004, 11–12) has suggested that we should be careful not to simply read this theory into Gen 1. Still, the theory can be found implicitly in the Bible (e.g., in the "in the beginning" of Gen 1:1; further Rom 4:17 and Heb 11:3). Ever since it was forcefully proposed by the church father Irenaeus in the second century in response to all kinds of gnostic thinkers, the idea of *creatio ex nihilo* rapidly gained popularity as the view of creation thought to optimally represent the Christian and also the Jewish faith. God did not just make or form the world from already existing material; he created it out of nothing. In this action he was totally independent, absolutely free and sovereign. We can hardly appreciate how new and unique this conviction was at the time. Outside of the Jewish-Christian tradition virtually everybody thought that "nothing comes from nothing," that all that exists has in principle always existed and always will. But the Christian church now proposed that all that exists, including material reality, owes its being to a creative act of the same God who came near to us in Jesus Christ to redeem us—to him, and to nothing or no one else.

This confession of a creation "out of nothing" was closely connected with a second controversial conviction, namely, the *goodness* of creation. Here the Genesis text did play a decisive role; six times it is repeated that God "saw that it was good," culminating in a seventh repetition, God saw "that it was very good" (Gen 1:31). This wording made abundantly clear how material reality must be regarded. Life on earth is not inherently evil but good; therefore we should not try to escape it but accept it as a gift from God. However fundamentally this differed from Greek-Hellenistic ideas, the two traditions nonetheless became mingled. Over the next centuries it was often forgotten that the doctrine of creation is a typically Christian view, God having created the entire cosmos through Christ; instead the idea emerged that the heavens of Gen 1:1 may perhaps be a higher reality closer to God than is the earth. Instead of being grounded in the incarnate reality of Jesus Christ, creation was linked to Platonic ideas. This dualistic approach, once introduced into the church, started a process of devaluating our earthly-bodily existence, which led, among other things, to a negative view of sexuality. This had not been so from the beginning, however.

Christian theology has undergone a major correction on this point in the twentieth century. Two Protestant theologians who, though differing significantly from each other, illustrate the change: the Dutch thinker A. A. van Ruler and the British systematic theologian Colin Gunton. Both have tried very hard to restore the unique, nondualistic, and life-affirming character of the Christian doctrine of creation to the spotlight. Van Ruler did so by pointing especially to the positive regard for "dust" in the Old Testament (VW, vol. 3); Gunton (1998), more influenced by Barth, did so by emphasizing the decisive role of Christ as the Mediator of creation portrayed in the New Testament and by pointing to the important contribution of Irenaeus in the development of the Christian doctrine of creation.

But is the fight against dualism still relevant today? Although its influences have always been around (and that despite heavy persecutions—e.g., against the Cathars in the south of France), dualism has not remained an important factor in stamping the culture of the Christian West except in the moderate form in which Christianity had embedded itself. Nonetheless, we can see a more pronounced trend of thinking in terms of two equally powerful basic principles of good and evil making headway today—for instance, in the science fiction films, computer games, and videos that crowd the multimedia world of the young. These products almost invariably depict a life-and-death struggle between good and evil powers, in which the outcome remains uncertain. An emotional life that is fed by a constant encounter with this sort of world is characterized above all by fear and *Verunsicherung* (uncertainty). Is ordinary life on earth worth living, or are we just the prey of evil powers? The confirmation of the goodness of existence that we have inherited continues to be an essential antidote to this basically pagan approach to life.

One might argue that the rejection of any sort of dualistic cosmology will necessarily lead to a *monistic* worldview. If God does not share the cosmos with a powerful anti-God, he apparently has everything to himself, and everything must be pervaded by his influence. Yet, Christianity also refused to take this road, though it certainly could have. For a long time the Old Testament attributed good and evil in equal measure to God (e.g., see Deut 32:39; Isa 45:5-7; Amos 3:6), even though it has been objected that one may hardly qualify punishing evil as a moral defect (see Lindström 1983). In any case, only later did a differentiation on this point develop (cf. 1 Chr 21:1 against the background of 2 Sam 24:1; see further under 8.8).

Greek thought also provided that option. In the influential revival of Platonism found in the religious philosophy of Plotinus, Platonic dualism was encircled by a more fundamental monism, so that even though the highest divine principle is separated by various intermediate entities from earthly reality, which is inhabited by evil, the two remain substantially connected. As we saw above, Neoplatonism teaches that the divine principle contains a fullness that serves as a source for the lower entities. Eventually, matter results from the emanation process. Though it is the lowest and least essential mode of existence, matter nevertheless is part of the divine mode of existence and not structurally separated from it. The light may be weaker than in its divine origin, but it still shines.

In its purest form, this monistic worldview coincides with *pantheism*, the belief that everything (Gk. *pan*) shares in the divine life, just as the divine coincides with everything. However, the Christian doctrine of creation differs as much from this view as it does from dualism. For, as we have already emphasized, the heartbeat of the tenet of creation is that God and the world are ontologically distinct. Therefore, the world is not divine, not even in the slightest degree. The cosmos does not spontaneously emerge from God, as a river flows from a source, but "stands trembling on the decision of God's benevolence" (Ruler, VW 4:546); it is simply the product of his personal intervention. In the meantime this mingling of Christian theology with the pantheistic side of Greek thought has left its own traces in Western culture. Mystically inclined thinkers as John Scotus Eriugena and Jacob Boehme, as well as modern philosophers like Spinoza and Schopenhauer, were pantheists.

It is characteristic for pantheistic monism that it is often accompanied by determinism: everything that happens, happens of necessity, guided by natural laws. There is a divine power in reality that propels things (e.g., for Schopenhauer, blind will). Contemporary forms of biological determinism fit this picture, like the idea (of Richard Dawkins and others) that the evolutionary process can be comprehensively described as a fight between genes that want to endlessly reproduce. Remarkably enough, in this context (parts of) nature are often referred to in personalizing terms. Our genes "want" all kinds of things; they are egoistic, engage in competition, and so forth. And even though evolution in this view is thought to proceed without any goal, it seems almost impossible to ban all traces of teleology from its language. Characteristics are attributed to nature that, in the Christian faith, belong only to God. Colin Gunton (1998, 38–40), from whom this section borrows some ideas, argues that ultimately we are confronted by two distinct ontologies that cannot be reconciled, two very different views of how reality is to be defined. Either the world is in the process of ever producing itself (in which case teleological language is inappropriate), or it is the work of a personal Creator.

This analysis strikes us as correct, even though we should take into account a third option in the form of what is called *panentheism*. This view holds that reality is found in God but that God does not coincide with it; rather, he exceeds it, stimulates it, and draws it in a certain direction. One metaphor often used in this connection describes the world as the body of God. In most cases we can move our body in many ways, so that, even though we continuously depend on it, we are more than our body. Nor did we make it ourselves. Similarly, God is not the almighty Creator but rather a powerful player who tries to pull the world away from chaos. This approach, in short, turns from the creation-out-of-nothing tradition back toward the idea of a gradual creation from chaos. This panentheism is developed particularly in the so-called process philosophy of Alfred North Whitehead (1861–1947), who derived his ideas from both Christianity and ancient philosophy. The idea enjoys broad popularity today—for instance, among those who study the relationship between religion and science (see Clayton and Peacocke 2004)—and claims congruence with the Christian faith by frequent appeal to Acts 17:28, where Paul says, quoting the pagan poet Aratus, "In him we live, and move, and have our being."

Panentheists often maintain that God's power is limited by various natural powers (just as we human beings often only have a limited power over our body), making an important concession thereby to dualism. This step allows them to free God from blame for the evil in creation. Another advantage, they feel, is to inspire greater and more ecologically responsible care for nature, although one may ask whether the Christian doctrine of creation does not offer enough motive in that respect (e.g., see Fergusson in Webster et al., OHST 83; also Fergusson 1998 and 2014, 100–103). Important objections to panentheism are (1) that it seems to make God a victim of suffering and pain, just as we are; (2) that our existence is not really willed and created by God; and (3) that it is doubtful whether God (in view of our being part of him!) can actually enter into a truly personal (covenant) relationship with us. For all such reasons we see panentheism as sub-Christian, as well as different from it. The question whether we are personal, acting beings is better explained from the perspective of a personal, acting Creator than from the angle of blind natural powers. For the metaphor of the world as God's body, see McFague 1993, an influential study.

We conclude that the Christian doctrine of creation is therefore both antidualistic and antimonistic in nature. But the major problem remains of explaining where evil comes from. Dualism may attribute it to a blind metaphysical power (e.g., eternal matter); panentheism in fact does the same. Monism can and must attribute evil to God so long as the reality of this evil is not denied. In the process God becomes rather Janus-faced; both good and evil proceed in equal measure from his nature, which is contrary to the testimony of the New Testament that in God "there is no darkness at all" (1 John 1:5).

The question of how the Christian faith views evil will be raised in various places in this book, for it is simply impossible to lock the issue into one box. In chapter 8 we will study the distinction between the limitations that are inherent in creation (e.g., the death of animals) and evil in the sense of everything that goes against God's will. On the basis of a belief in creation, we will state for now that this latter aspect, "real" evil, can be understood only as an extremely serious corruption of a good creation that is caused by humanity's misuse of the freedom we have been given. Evil is not a power in its own right or a power in God or outside

God. Rather, as Augustine so famously put it, evil is a privation—even a theft—from what is good (*privatio boni*). It can show its head only when something good has been made, just as we can speak of darkness only when there is light. Darkness is nothing but the absence of light. In like manner, evil is a parasite that, through human sin, attacks the goodness of God's creation and is detrimental to it. One might say that the responsibility for evil has hereby been apportioned: God as the Creator of humanity—that is, of an opposite with its own space to act—is responsible for the *possibility* of evil, whereas we are responsible for its *execution*.

We limit ourselves to this short comment here, since the problem of evil will be more extensively discussed in chapter 8 and elsewhere. For Augustine's profound view of evil as *privatio boni*, which Christianized an originally Neoplatonic approach, see his *Enchiridion* 11. However, our comments here are no denial of the fact that in actual practice Christianity has often shifted back and forth between dualism (the devil made me do it) and monism (ultimately all depends on God's will, as Calvin argued, for instance).

More important in Christian theology than questions about the origin of evil is the victory over evil. For the problem of evil is not going to be solved by profound thought on this subject or a precise picture of how we ever landed in this mess; redemption is the only solution (Pannenberg). Here again, the Trinitarian structure of the Christian belief in creation shows its deepest meaning. An essential element of the doctrine of creation is that the God who created the world is also the God who saves it with his "two hands"—Christ and the Spirit. We will see in a moment that the doctrine of creation can therefore not be isolated from the Christian message of salvation as a whole. Such a separation happens in extreme form in *deism*, which teaches that God at some time in the past initiated this world but then did not bother about it any more. Deism is the third interpretation of reality—in addition to dualism and pan(en)theism—that distinctly differs from the Christian belief in creation.

When dealing with the question of the origin of evil, some Jewish rabbis very imaginatively point out that the Tanak (and thus also the Christian Bible) for good reason begins with the letter bet (ב). This letter more or less has the form of a square that is open on its left side. But Hebrew is not read from left to right but from right to left. That is, the first letter of the Bible is open only in the direction of the text of the Holy Scriptures. The hint is quite clear: in the search for an answer to the question of evil, none is available prior to the text, or above it or behind it. The answer is solely to be found *in* the text, which tells about salvation from evil that God provides.

6.4. Creation, Covenant, and Salvation

In this section we elaborate on the statement made above to the effect that the doctrine of creation cannot be detached from the full Christian message of salvation. To do so requires us to get past the misunderstanding that the doctrine of creation is mostly linked only to the first chapters of Genesis. We need to examine the other contexts in which the Bible discusses creation so as to capture the full range of the biblical witness on the matter. Following Higton (CD 170-72) here, we begin with Ps 89 (NLT):

1 I will sing of the tender mercies of the LORD forever!
Young and old will hear of your faithfulness.
2 Your unfailing love will last forever.
Your faithfulness is as enduring as the heavens.
3 The LORD said, "I have made a solemn agreement with David, my
chosen servant.
I have sworn this oath to him:
4 'I will establish your descendants as kings forever;
they will sit on your throne from now until eternity.'" *Interlude*
5 All heaven will praise your miracles, LORD;
myriads of angels will praise you for your faithfulness. . . .
8 O LORD God Almighty! Where is there anyone as mighty as you,
LORD?
Faithfulness is your very character.
9 You are the one who rules the oceans.
When their waves rise in fearful storms, you subdue them.
10 You are the one who crushed the great sea monster.
You scattered your enemies with your mighty arm.
11 The heavens are yours, and the earth is yours;
everything in the world is yours—you created it all.
12 You created north and south.
Mount Tabor and Mount Hermon praise your name.
13 Powerful is your arm!
Strong is your hand! Your right hand is lifted high in glorious
strength.

¹⁴ Your throne is founded on two strong pillars—righteousness and
   justice.
   Unfailing love and truth walk before you as attendants.
¹⁵ Happy are those who hear the joyful call to worship,
   for they will walk in the light of your presence, LORD.
¹⁶ They rejoice all day long in your wonderful reputation.
   They exult in your righteousness.
¹⁷ You are their glorious strength.
   Our power is based on your favor.
¹⁸ Yes, our protection comes from the LORD,
   and he, the Holy One of Israel, has given us our king. . . .
³⁶ "His dynasty will go on forever; his throne is as secure as the sun,
³⁷ as eternal as the moon, my faithful witness in the sky!" *Interlude*
³⁸ But now you have rejected him.
   Why are you so angry with the one you chose as king?
³⁹ You have renounced your covenant with him,
   for you have thrown his crown in the dust.

In this hymn we find words about God's creative power, alongside words that sing of God's love for his people (vv. 15-17) and for the Davidic monarchy (vv. 3-4, 18-37). The stability of creation testifies to the trustworthiness of its Maker (vv. 2, 8, 11), and this same trustworthiness characterizes God's relationship with David and his posterity. Or does it? In the second half of the psalm (vv. 38-51) God hardly appears to be trustworthy. The covenant seems to be broken, and the dynasty of David is confronted with increasing misery. The king and the people have been deported into exile, and from a political perspective this situation seems to seal their fate. Apparently this was the situation in which this poem was created. But if so, we are not just hearing in those first verses a romantic description of the beauty of creation. Instead, we are pointedly *reminded* of God's faithfulness and power, as exhibited in creation, in order to keep our hope for God alive. In other words, the proclamation of God's creative power is not an isolated theme (a locus in dogmatics); its sole purpose is to strengthen our beleaguered faith by emphasizing that the powers of chaos and destruction that have assaulted the house of David will not have the final word. The poet resists such a scenario of doom. God's power is not restricted to the land of Palestine but comprises heaven and earth (v. 11), and in the same way that he remains faithful to his work of creation, he remains faithful to his people (vv. 15-18).

Faith in God's creative power and the hope for God's liberating intervention are closely linked in other Old Testament passages as well. A favorite passage of many readers in this connection is Deutero-Isaiah, which, besides the first chapters in Genesis, might present the most profound exposition of the Old Testament theology of creation. Most experts in exegesis also date this writing to the postexilic period. The subject once again is the fate of Israel and God's anointed Davidic king ("the servant of the Lord"); once again God's incomparable might is illustrated by referring to his work in creation, and once again this work of creation is enlisted with a view to encouraging the people about the future: Israel's God is the only true God, and he will not give up.

25 "To whom will you compare me?
   Who is my equal?" asks the Holy One.
26 Look up into the heavens. Who created all the stars?
   He brings them out one after another, calling each by its name.
   And he counts them to see that none are lost or have strayed away.
27 O Israel, how can you say the Lord does not see your troubles?
   How can you say God refuses to hear your case?
28 Have you never heard or understood?
   Don't you know that the Lord is the everlasting God,
   the Creator of all the earth?
   He never grows faint or weary.
   No one can measure the depths of his understanding.
29 He gives power to those who are tired and worn out;
   he offers strength to the weak.

(Isa 40:25–29 NLT)

The context of Deutero-Isaiah shows that this promise will be fulfilled in the approaching liberation from Babylonian exile. This is another example of the strong tie between statements about creation (vv. 26, 28) and texts about redemption (vv. 27, 29).

In fact, references to God's creative power are so strongly directed toward the future redemption that one school of thought has claimed the Old Testament belief in creation to be totally subservient to the belief in redemption. Nowhere, on this interpretation, is God's work of creation confessed in its own right; the belief that God created heaven and earth is only a derivative, a by-product of faith in God's redemptive acts. Furthermore, since belief in creation is not a central issue in the New Testament either but is always linked to salvation in Christ, it must be seen as a secondary matter in dogmatics. In sum, Exodus, the story of

God's liberating intervention, is of much more theological importance than Genesis. But this idea no longer finds much support. In and behind the Old Testament one clearly discovers more or less independent creation traditions that we have no reason to consider as secondary. Yet, in the biblical canon these traditions are closely tied to faith in God's salvific acts, and dogmatics must do justice to that close linkage.

The thought that, for Israel, belief in creation was merely an extrapolation from Israel's previous redemptive experiences with God (e.g., in the crossing of the Red Sea) was especially developed by the twentieth-century Old Testament scholar Gerhard von Rad (TOT, vol. 1). Around 1970, however, von Rad recognized that the Old Testament undoubtedly also contains creation texts (sometimes borrowed from its surroundings) that are not directed toward God's salvific acts—for instance, in Job and Prov 8. Von Rad's younger colleague Claus Westermann emphasized this aspect even more and spoke of the "two faces" of the Old Testament theology of creation. On the one hand, God is identified as the Creator of everything, while on the other, creation is specifically related to God's covenant with Israel (see Westermann 1994, 64–69, on the theological significance of the primeval story). For the broader issues, see also the comments by Berkhof in CF 157.

To clarify this relationship, let's take a moment to focus on a remarkable passage from Ps 89 (vv. 9–11), this time in the RSV:

> 9 Thou dost rule the raging of the sea;
> when its waves rise, thou stillest them.
> 10 Thou didst crush Rahab like a carcass,
> thou didst scatter thy enemies with thy mighty arm.
> 11 The heavens are thine, the earth also is thine;
> the world and all that is in it, thou hast founded them.

Who or what is the great sea monster Rahab in this text? When we study the context and look at parallel texts (Isa 51:9; Ps 74:14), we conclude that it refers to a kind of sea monster (see Isa 51:9) that was defeated by God during the creation of the world (v. 10). However strange this sequence may seem to us, this thought was widespread in the ancient Near East. In the creation myths of Israel's neighbors a lot of fighting goes on before things are finally settled in favor of the creation. The mythical opponents of the Godhead, who are keen to spread chaos and destruction, have their special power-base in the sea. And they are so dangerous that the reader of these stories has to worry that things might wind up totally wrong.

This scenario, very clearly, is not the case in the Old Testament. The struggle against the powers that bring chaos never leaves us in fear; the outcome is never in doubt. On the contrary, everywhere the sea is represented as a cosmic power (also in places where Rahab or Leviathan is not explicitly mentioned, as in Ps 93), the poem is sung from the perspective of a victory that YHWH won a long time ago. For that reason we find nowhere in the Old Testament a metaphysical dualism such as existed among Israel's neighbors. But we also find no mention that God, in his work of creation, ever had to put up a fight against the powers of chaos. As late as in Rev 21:1 we hear its echo when we are assured that—thank God!—the sea will no longer exist in the new world. We may speculate about the origin of the hostile powers of chaos, whether these are fallen angels or demons (the fall-of-the-angels hypothesis is defended in Lloyd 1997). But it may be best not to speculate and rather to allow that the prophets and the psalmists were simply making use of material from their pagan environment in their texts. They see the struggle against the primeval powers as a foreshadowing of the struggle for the redemption of God's people. This connection is very clear in Isa 51:

> Awake, awake, put on strength,
> O arm of the LORD;
> awake, as in days of old,
> the generations of long ago.
> Was it not thou that didst cut Rahab in pieces,
> that didst pierce the dragon?
> Was it not thou that didst dry up the sea,
> the waters of the great deep;
> that didst make the depths of the sea a way
> for the redeemed to pass over?
> And the ransomed of the LORD shall return,
> and come to Zion with singing;
> everlasting joy shall be upon their heads.
>
> (vv. 9–11a)

To sum up: creation is viewed as the first salvific act that God performed, an act of deliverance so special that it is on a par with the crossing of the Red Sea. When we read with this comparison in mind, we can sense the stupendous struggle of God against the sea powers of chaos.

When Gen 1:2 refers to the deep, or abyss, which was under the darkness, it uses the word *tehom*, which we find also in Isa 51:10 and which is similar to the name of the monster Tiamat that figures in the Akkadian epic Enuma Elish. Is it because he wants to fight the darkness that God's Spirit is seen hovering above the waters? Whatever the case, God's first creative act is to separate light from darkness. It seems quite easy, for God need only speak, and there is light (see Ps 33:6). But we still have a hint of the struggle that is hidden behind this phrase. With good reason the darkness is called "night," which in biblical language implies the idea of judgment.

The recording of such separations helps us understand why O. Noordmans concisely summarized his doctrine of creation in the motto "creating is separating" (H 64). We believe Noordmans goes too far when he apparently interprets the "is" as meaning "is equal to." As we have tried to show, creation also points to forming, bringing about, lovingly calling into existence what is not yet, and of favoring this newly existent item with a place. But creating *is* also a work of separating. From the start it is a forceful disentanglement of light and darkness, day and night, land and sea, so that humanity and the entire creation may live before God, able to enter into a relationship with him. Although creation and redemption do not totally overlap, they are closely linked. Already in his creative act God conquered the deep, dark powers that threaten our lives. He does the same again in the renewal of our existence in Jesus Christ (see 2 Cor 4:6 for this parallelism). Seen from the perspective of faith, our very creatureliness is a sign that God is serious about our life, our redemption, our salvation.

Even before these exegetical connections had been clarified, people who were intensely involved with the Bible intuited them. We find the meaning of the Christian belief in creation very beautifully expressed, for instance, in Lord's Day 9 of the Heidelberg Catechism, a passage that unfortunately has not become as well known as Lord's Day 10. In answer to the question of what is entailed by faith "in God the Father, the Almighty, the creator of heaven and earth," the catechism answers: "That the eternal Father of our Lord Jesus Christ . . . out of nothing created heaven and earth and everything in them, . . . because of Christ the Son. I trust God so much that I do not doubt he will provide whatever I need for body and soul." Here the factual information is hidden in a subordinate clause, and the main clause is used for confessing our unconditional security, in the face of all powers, in the God who has shown his grace toward us in Christ. Here too faith in God as Creator does not stand in isolation but is defined through the word "Father"—which is rightly linked to the sonship of Jesus—on the basis of faith in God as Redeemer. To put it more precisely: it is defined on the basis of the covenant that God wants to establish with us, a covenant that finds its ground and its fulfillment in the life and work of Jesus Christ.

Karl Barth further developed these ideas by formulating this link between creation and salvation in two key sentences (CD III/1:97, 231):

1. The creation is the external ground of the covenant.
2. The covenant is the internal ground of the creation.

These two theses structure Barth's entire doctrine of creation as he unfolds it in CD III/1. They imply that the intention of creation is to facilitate the history of God's covenant with humanity—a history, so Barth adds, that has its beginning, its center, and its culmination in Jesus Christ. This means for Barth (as it does for Karl Rahner) that Jesus Christ would have become incarnate even if the creation had not been perverted by sin (for a recent defense of this "supralapsarian Christology," see Driel 2008). That is a point for debate, however. One might just as well argue that Jesus Christ came only because sin entered creation, and came only to restore it. We opt for an in-between position. Better than saying either that the creation was from the very start focused on Jesus Christ or that it was a finished business right from the beginning, we choose to say that creation was directed toward the history that God wanted to enact with us human beings, a history in which we would flourish in his presence.

6.5. How and When Did God Create?

We now turn to questions about creation and evolution that trouble so many people. Let's begin by noting that these questions have not been introduced thus far, for there was no need to do so. The Christian doctrine of creation is much richer than merely providing an answer to the question of how and when the world was created. It entails much more than the matter of how we (Christians, but also secular Western people) experience the world and relate to it. And most of this richness is, from a worldwide perspective, far from self-evident. We think that it is important, therefore, not to underestimate, but to keep an eye open for, the enormous impact that the biblical belief in creation has on our thinking; we can easily lose sight of that broader influence when we proceed too quickly and one-sidedly to questions about creation and evolution.

Many theologians would even argue that these questions are completely irrelevant to the doctrine of creation. Rather, our relationship to God, to each other, and to our environment is the focal point of the Christian faith, which does not really depend on answers to the question of how the natural world has come into existence. On this argument, "creation" is a category that belongs to the domain of faith and meaning, while evolution is a totally different concept that belongs to the domain of science and explaining the world. Barth, for instance, tells us in a famous passage in the preface to the section on creation in his *Dogmatics* that he had long been wondering whether to deal with questions of faith and science at all, finally deciding that it would be a bad idea. In Barth's extensive CD III/1 we therefore find much that deals with the significance of what he refers to as the Hebrew legends in Genesis but little or nothing about the relationship between faith and science.

Nonetheless, we feel that a Christian dogmatics cannot simply ignore the question of the how and when of creation. Even though it will occupy a less important place than it does in many popular discussions, it is not completely detached from important theological issues—for instance, the nature of our image of God, the nature of the goodness of creation, and the nature of the authority and interpretation of the Bible as Holy Scripture. For that reason we will discuss this matter briefly, and will do so starting from the question of how the Jewish-Christian belief in creation relates to the so-called neo-Darwinian synthesis in evolutionary biology. Can these two get along, or does that attempt create insurmountable problems, as both conservative Christians and atheistic evolutionists argue?

If we want to make any progress on this front, we must first learn to ask the right questions. The appropriate question is not whether the Bible supports creation or evolution. It is clear that the Bible does not—at least not explicitly—present any evolutionary models.

On a more implicit level we might point to texts like Gen 1:11, 24 ("Let the earth bring forth . . ."), where the earth quite definitely is involved in God's creative acts. God does not create the world of plants and animals directly and without mediation, but by employing powers and possibilities that apparently are embedded in the earth. Interestingly enough, a comparable process does not apply to the creation of humanity, which is directly created by God (vv. 26-27; but cf. Gen 2:7).

It would be asking too much from the Bible to read evolution back into it. However, as the orthodox Reformed American theologian Benjamin B.

Warfield (1851–1921) perceived a century ago, creation and evolution are concepts that relate to different matters. Creation is about the origin of the world, while evolution (as the word indicates) pertains to its subsequent development. Creation happens from nothing, evolution involves a modification of something that already exists, and not its origin. In that sense evolution is by definition another type of phenomenon that is secondary to the original act of creation (Warfield 2000, 200–202; see also Warfield, W 10:380), something that is overlooked when the question is asked, Creation or evolution?

A more appropriate and important question asks how the Bible deals with contemporaneous worldviews, that is, with the overarching ideas of how the cosmos operates as that was understood in the day and age when the Bible was composed. The answer is that the Bible often incorporates these worldviews after having removed any religious interpretation they might have entailed. We find a clear example in Gen 1. It adopts the existing worldview (with a sky that separates the waters "below" from the waters "above"), not thereby to provide a scientific description of the cosmos but to give a theological proclamation of our dependence on God. To the extent that ideological connotations came along with that worldview, they are firmly rejected and detached from their context. Old Testament scholars almost unanimously believe that Gen 1 is intended as a polemic against the practices of solar and lunar worship that were current in Israel's environment (see Hasel 1974 for a classic essay in this connection). The presentation of the sun and the moon as lights in the sky that simply perform the tasks that God has assigned them is first and foremost an ironic and critical comment on these pagan practices. For is it not strange to give so much homage to created objects that can do nothing but perform what the Creator has commanded them to do?

It seems to us that the Bible itself thus models the way to approach questions about the relationship between the (Jewish-) Christian faith and evolutionary theory. There is no reason to reject this theory so long as it limits itself to a scientific picture of how the (biological) world operates. It becomes a very different matter when, whether consciously or unconsciously, the evolutionary approach is mingled with ideology and idolatry, which happens whenever it makes worldview statements that the natural sciences cannot possibly prove—for example, that life has no purpose, that humanity is a magnificent accident of nature, and that religion and morality are merely side effects of the struggle for existence. Note that our objection does not concern statements that cannot yet be proven but for which evidence may be found in the future. Rather, the sorts of statements we object to are not scientific at all; they deal with one's worldview and are ideological in nature. In them the evolutionary process is put forward as the absolute, ultimate explanation of almost everything—and thus usurps a place that, from a Christian perspective, is reserved for the Creator alone. In short, Christian theology must maintain a critical attitude toward *evolutionism*, as one of the isms (besides pantheism, dualism, deism, and more) that are foreign to Christianity. A choice on this matter cannot be avoided.

Does this mean that the integration of evolution as a purely scientific paradigm comes without any problems? Hardly. It is simply important that we see these problems as challenges. For what does it mean if we accept the view that, as human beings, we share a common ancestry with the apes—does this or does it not change our view of humanity in any way? What does it mean for the notion of a fall into sin if, at some point in the evolutionary development of the hominids, a moral awareness emerged (for this issue, see chap. 8)? What does it mean for our concept of God and of the goodness of creation if we grant that the earth has passed through hundreds of millions of years of struggle for life, including massive extinctions and suffering and death among the animals? What does it mean for our way of reading the Bible if it appears that the cosmos is billions of years older than had long been assumed from biblical accounts?

These are all significant questions, and we can easily go astray as we seek for answers. However, they are inescapable—even for those who are not convinced of the validity of evolutionary models that aspire to explain the development of life on earth. For even for these people, there remains the challenge of translating the gospel in such a way that it can relate to the lives of those who have no doubt whatsoever that evolution has occurred in many ways throughout history. Christians ought to face these challenges with a little more confidence than is often the case. After all, through the ages Christian theology has not resisted the worldviews that surrounded them—at least not indefinitely. Rather, it has tried to enlist these worldviews in the proclamation of its message. In the first centuries this engagement occurred with respect to the Greek way of thinking, even though theology sometimes granted it too much. Yet, gradually this worldview was opened up from within and Christianized. The same was true in the early modern period with respect to the Copernican worldview. We should not minimize the psychological stakes involved in this process. In the Copernican worldview the earth (and thus humanity too) was no

longer seen as the center of the universe. It is therefore perfectly understandable that theologians like Gisbertus Voetius (1589–1676) refused
to budge; besides, did not the Bible teach that the sun moves around the
earth, rather than the earth around the sun? Nonetheless, today no one
holds to what Voetius said. We have recognized that accepting the Copernican system does not result in the collapse of the Christian faith, or
even change the essence of its content. Similarly, Christians have to deal
with the theory of evolution, confident that, when it comes to questions
of origins, the "two books of God"—nature and the Bible—will ultimately
be consonant and not contradict each other. At the very least, we may say
that there is no reason to think that Christians have a calling to begin a
crusade against scientific worldviews, as long as their potential religious
implications are thoroughly screened.

It will be clear, based on what we said above, that we reject so-called creationism as a scientific attempt to prove a "young earth." We believe it is grounded
on an inadequate hermeneutic; it does not pay enough attention to the unique
character and theological intent of the biblical creation texts. (And often it hardly
considers other texts besides the first chapters of Genesis.)

The wealth of literature on the more general issue of creation and evolution further increased in 2009, the bicentennial of Darwin's birth. A twentieth-
century example of the integration of evolutionary theory with the Christian doctrines of creation and sin is found in Berkhof, CF 162–215. Another remarkable
attempt to do the same (Alexander 2014) is by a scientist who believes that "the
Bible is the inspired Word of God from cover to cover" (11). A bold but disputable theological proposal to explain the goodness of the creation in view of an
evolutionary world that is burdened with the reality of extinction, suffering, and
death is found in Southgate 2008. For sound and up-to-date biblical scholarship
on the meaning of Gen 2–3, see Walton 2015; a thoroughgoing analysis of the
relationship between scientific and biblical accounts of creation can be found
in Harris 2013.

6.6. Nonhuman Creation in Its Own Right

Besides angels, planets, galaxies, plants, and animals, God also created
human beings. In Gen 1 and 2, as well as elsewhere in the Bible, humanity
occupies a unique status amid all God's creatures, and for that reason
the doctrine of creation typically focuses there. In fact, humanity may
become almost the exclusive topic, not just because of Gen 1 but also

because of the many philosophical and theological issues that surround our mysterious selves. We have set aside a separate chapter on theological anthropology (chap. 7) to take up these matters.

But we want to avoid going there right away. We need to say more about God's enduring relationship with creation, that is, about God's providence. But first we must give special attention to the dazzling number of living creatures that God created besides human beings. This point has often been neglected in dogmatics on the (too easy) assumption that other creatures exist simply to serve humanity as the crown of God's creation. This assumption has undoubtedly led to a gross neglect or even ruthless exploitation of nature, especially since the scientific and industrial revolutions have provided us with so many more tools to subject the world to our wishes. The ecological problems that today rightly fill the agenda of world politics are closely connected to this abuse, regardless of the question of how serious a threat these problems pose.

For that reason we deal briefly here with the layers in the Bible and in the Christian theological tradition that tell of the importance of the nonhuman creation in its own right. We realize that even such an expression—just like the frequently used term "environment," which is always taken to be *our* environment—is still strongly anthropocentric in nature. Unfortunately, there is no unequivocal term to define all life on earth beyond humanity, a deficiency in language that already speaks volumes. But the doctrine of creation involves *all* creatures, not just humanity; it involves flora and fauna, stones and stars, comets and black holes. For now, we set aside further discussion of the nonliving creation, believing there is every reason for the doctrine of creation to pay attention to the enormous variety of species in our ecosystem as a whole. For this reason, we referred in "Making Connections" at the start of this chapter to some contemporary film documentaries that, using the most advanced technology, portray this rich diversity so impressively. Christians realize that this diversity may not be immediately obvious to all, but if we allow ourselves to be informed by the biblical text, we do catch a reflection of the endless variety in the Creator's creativity.

We want to especially emphasize three points in this connection. First, it is important that the diverse forms of life cannot be reduced to other forms of life. Here the Christian doctrine of creation offers an insight that is often overlooked or even denied in many naturalistic models of the understanding of reality. In our reflections on nature we must do full justice to its great pluriformity and not reduce it to only one or two forms of life and processes. This mistake occurs in the so-called *noth-*

ing-but approach: human beings are nothing but a further developed mammal or a magnificent accident; life is nothing but matter with a higher degree of organization; a thought is nothing but a combination of neurophysiological processes; the starry sky is nothing but a revolving nebula.

See Berkhof, CF 167–68, who rightly refers in this connection to the so-called philosophy of the cosmonomic idea (later usually referred to as Reformational philosophy), which was developed in the twentieth century by H. Dooyeweerd and D. T. Vollenhoven. Its concept of "modalities" distinguished a number (usually fifteen) of distinct aspects or modalities in creation that somehow all build on each other or refer back to each other, but nonetheless have their own integrity and therefore cannot be reduced to each other. Apart from the question whether the details in this system are fully convincing, we see this as a good and still meaningful attempt to describe the ever-ongoing variety of creation.

Second, we want to point out the independent relationship of the flora, fauna, and even lifeless matter to God, and vice versa, of God to them. This connection jumps out at us in the many psalms and prophetic passages where we are told that trees and mountains, hills and lakes, plants and animals praise God or are called upon to do so. God also establishes his covenant with the animals (Gen 9:10) and is active in feeding them (Ps 104:14, 21). God delivers them as he delivers human beings. The mountains and hills will erupt with joy when God liberates his people, and the trees in the field will clap their hands (Isa 55:12). Even the stones will shout "Hosanna" if people refuse to do so (Luke 19:40). Of course, this language is poetic and metaphorical, but admitting as much does not make it meaningless. At the very least it tells us that the earth is not only about humans but that there are other works of God's hands that are important. God knows that they exist and has a relationship with them. He created them even before he created us (Gen 1:12, 21). When we as human beings—even when our sufferings give us reason to do so—limit our thinking to ourselves, God reminds us that there is more to the world than just us (Job 38–41).

Since the beginning of this century there has been a growing interest in the theological status of animals. This development follows in part from interest in the matter among philosophers and in political circles (e.g., note animal-rights parties). Also, recent ethnological, primatological, and genetic research has opened our eyes to the significant relationship between humans and the other primates.

Many abilities traditionally regarded as uniquely human, such as rationality, the use of symbols, and language, have also been found in the higher primates, which from an evolutionary viewpoint seem to be close relatives of humans. These findings should not lead us to deny humanity's unique place in creation or to assume that there will also be an "animal heaven" or to propose that bearing the image of God may also apply to animals (for examples of these ideas, see a number of essays in Deane-Drummond and Clough 2009, a compilation that is instructive in this context). Neither is there any reason to speak of human beings as just another type of animal. However, it is important to ground God's image in humanity theologically rather than empirically (see further in chap. 7), and to emphasize the special relationship that animals have with God. This line of thought implies a crucial correction to major parts of the tradition (e.g., Calvin) but is fully justified in view of the biblical sources of that tradition. Important for the current revaluation of the theological status of animals has been the work of Andrew Linzey; see, for example, Linzey and Yamamoto 1998. For an exploration of ecologically sensitive resources (including resources that foster a respectful attitude toward animals) within the Reformed tradition, see Lane 2011.

Third, it is important to note the strong intertwining and mutual bond between all organisms. In any ecosystem everything depends on everything. As human beings, we do not stand over against nature but constitute an integral part of it. Whenever we think in terms of waging war against nature, winning automatically means losing, because sooner or later we will have to pay for our abuse. We are, in fact, more dependent on plants and animals than vice versa; they can do without humans without a problem (and have done so), but we need them. Inspired by the Bible, the Christian doctrine of creation puts a "hard return" between Creator and creatures, and we belong without a doubt to the category of creature. When Luther in his Small Catechism wonders about the meaning of the first article of the Apostles' Creed, he begins his answer as follows: "I believe that God has created me together with all other creatures" (see OF). There is the immediate awareness that we are in the same boat as all other creatures. When this awareness disappears, we may no longer experience ourselves as being one with creation and become careless in our treatment of nature, contributing to its destruction.

But is humanity not "the crown of creation"? We must recognize that this statement is not found in the Bible. In Gen 1–2 the Sabbath is the crown that God places on his creation (Moltmann 1993). However, Ps 8:5–8 does give warrant for this well-known expression and, we think, justifies its use. But we should straightaway recognize that this psalm starts with a strong awareness of human insignificance before the Creator, an awareness that has become ever more justified with the discovery of the unimaginable size and age of the universe. From this point of departure the second part of Ps 8 stresses what we call stewardship: God has in fact entrusted the enormous work of his hands to these tiny human beings! This responsibility causes the psalmist to express great amazement; he does not regard it as a matter of course, as many would later do. When stern words like "ruling" and "subjecting" are added (as in Gen 1:28, cited above), it absolutely does not imply permission to exploit the earth, destroy its resources, or engage in other forms of mismanagement. Rather, the words reflect the hard struggle for survival that had to be fought in the past—and that even today is fought by very many in the world. In our engagement with nature, life and death are very close; Jesus too may once have stepped on a bug. In all dogmatics, but especially in the doctrine of creation, we must avoid Docetism (the appeal to a world of mere appearances). The creation is not always romantic and touching, but more often rough and frightening. This reality affirms our calling to deal responsibly with nature as gardeners who may have to cut branches, but only to ensure that the garden will flourish.

A famous article by Lynn White (1967) cast full blame for the emerging ecological crisis on Christianity. White argues that Genesis teaches human dominance over creation, which led to the stunning exploitation of the earth that we currently see. But his conclusions have not withstood the test of time. Even though Christianity indeed had a desacralizing influence, it has become clear that the controversial texts in Genesis (esp. 1:28) have often been interpreted in the Christian tradition in terms of stewardship and not of dominance or the freedom to exploit. Ecology came under pressure only when, in the Enlightenment, nature was "disenchanted," and when science and technology were subsequently enlisted to make nature follow our command. In particular, when this action was accompanied by a materialism bent solely on economic gain (in Europe a worldview that gained prominence later than Christianity), things went radically wrong. However, it cannot be gainsaid that Christians have often allowed themselves to be carried along by such materialism or, more generally speaking, by an indifference toward creation that is at odds with their faith. Therefore, we should refrain from displaying an attitude of triumphalism, as if Christianity was, or is, always on the right side. For good reason Bouma-Prediger 2001 (67–86) writes about this tendency; McGrath 2002 is also informative but does not sufficiently highlight the dubious role Christians have often played in this history.

To conclude: on the one hand, the Christian doctrine of creation facilitated the abuse of the earth by no longer viewing it as sacred but as profane (see above); on the other hand, it often put the brakes on this abuse by defining the human task as one of stewardship. This brake was released the moment Europe began to secularize. Christians thus have ample reason to develop the doctrine of creation in a specifically ecological direction, as is happening, for instance, in so-called ecotheology, an area where (esp. since Moltmann 1993) a flood of literature has appeared. In doing so, we need not suggest, like some, that this earth is everything there is, for Christians do expect a new heaven and a new earth, as God has promised. But we need to exercise great care here. The eschatological expectation must not be abused, as sometimes happens, by mistreating the earth that has been entrusted to us. Here again we should keep the Trinitarian accent in mind; a creation that bears the traces of Christ and the Spirit deserves to be treated with care and respect. If God allowed himself in his Son to be so deeply drawn into this world in order to save it, and if he still pervades this earth in his Spirit in order to heal it, Christians cannot indifferently remain on the sideline when this same world is being destroyed, let alone be actively involved in the devastation.

6.7. Creation and Divine Providence

In dogmatics the treatment of creation is often followed by the doctrine of providence. What we have discussed to this point already indicates a close connection between the two. The Christian tradition confesses that not just the origin of the world but also its continued existence is an act of God; while recognizing that we are here dealing with two different deeds or activities of God, we have every reason not to isolate them from each other. The doctrine of providence, first of all, underscores that God remains actively involved with the reality he called into being; thus deism (referred to earlier), which teaches that God, after bringing created reality into existence, left it completely to itself, must be seen as sub-Christian. It cannot possibly do justice to the many biblical passages that testify to God's intense and lasting involvement with his world. In this section we examine further the nature of this involvement and the various forms it can take.

Of course we need to mention the arguments against the doctrine of providence. There is perhaps no part of Christian teaching that has dismayed so many people brought up in the church as the doctrine of providence. The criticism on this subject is loud, clear, and often very strong (esp. in the literature of the second half of the twentieth century). To begin with, the doctrine of providence is said not to take people seriously as active agents because it represses human freedom in favor of God's sovereignty. Worse still, the doctrine is said to make God responsible for all the evil in the world. Against this background it is not always easy to keep clear on what precisely the Christian tradition means by its doctrine of providence. Here we need to exercise some "retrieval theology," to use a term coined by John Webster (OHST 583-99). This theology seeks to explain issues by returning to the sources of the tradition; thus, "the task of a Christian theology of providence can only be undertaken by dipping in the sources that have been informed by the Gospel; it can only listen to prophets and apostles before it speaks—if not, it will have nothing to say" (John Webster, in Murphy and Ziegler 2009, 159).

As we listen to the testimony of prophets and apostles, we discover that God's providence has never been a self-evident aspect of faith. We can certainly say that the Enlightenment of the eighteenth century, the evolutionary theory of the nineteenth, and the world wars of the twentieth have not confronted the faith in divine providence with totally new problems. At most, we have become more deeply impressed than before by the seemingly purposeless and enormous extent of suffering and evil in the world. But the doctrine of providence originated, not in the denial of such suffering and evil, but in answer to it. So the question is not first and foremost whether the doctrine of providence will survive but whether we will survive; that is to say, whether we can hold on to the teaching of the Christian tradition that the world is at all times in God's hands. This teaching is a point of faith that comes under heavy attack, especially at moments when we are confronted with frustration, disappointment, and disasters. In this situation we might find a total lack of understanding, questions big as life, and even anger about God's rule. Such reactions are not necessarily unbiblical or unchristian. Yet, it is in the midst of such suffering that faith in God's unseen sovereignty can show its real value. "When my soul was embittered, when I was pricked in heart, I was stupid and ignorant, I was like a beast toward thee. Nevertheless I am continually with thee; thou dost hold my right hand" (Ps 73:21-23).

The word "providence," based on Latin *providentia*, entered the Christian vocabulary through the Vulgate, the Latin Bible translation that served the church in the West for many centuries. It is found in Gen 22:8, where Abraham replies to Isaac's rather obvious question with the veiled answer that "God will provide" (Vulgate *Deus providebit*) the lamb that will be sacrificed on Mount Moriah. It has often been remarked that this passage actually does not deal with God's providence, but we believe that it certainly does and that it offers a good example of what faith in God's providence is all about. In the first place, it is not a case of God foreseeing things before they happen but it refers to concrete evidence of God's care.

Providence does not so much concern itself with seeing things but with making things available, making provision. We may argue about this "pro" in the sense of "prior to," depending on whether we locate God's acts in time or in timeless eternity. But even in the latter case, we might still maintain that the act of God's care precedes the situation to which it is related, for in the Bible God's care and acting are also often described in terms of before and after (e.g., see Isa 65:24).

Second, the text refers to a very critical moment in Abraham's life, where the stakes are extremely high. Abraham does not know how to keep from becoming a child murderer. Precisely because he does not know, he puts his trust in God. However, Abraham has already come to know God in such a way that he relies on God, trusting that God will somehow be there for him. This response is what we call faith; according to later canonical testimonies Abraham is in fact a prime example of someone with faith (Rom 4; Heb 11:17-19). Providence is thus strongly related to this active surrender in faith, which—even in times of utter dismay, when there seems no way out, let alone a chance that we can tell God how to intervene—continues to hope for God's salvation and care.

If we want to grasp the essence of the doctrine of providence, we must start with what the tradition refers to as God's *providentia specialissima*—the "most special," loving care that God makes available to all who orient their lives toward him. We find a stirring New Testament description of this care in the Letter to the Romans: "What then shall we say to this? If God is for us, who is against us? He who did not spare his own Son but gave him up for us all, will he not also give us all things with him? . . . For I am persuaded that neither death, nor life, nor angels, nor principalities, nor things present, nor things to come, nor powers, nor height, nor depth, nor anything else in all creation, will be able to separate us from the love of God in Christ Jesus our Lord" (Rom 8:31-32, 38-39). These words are not to be interpreted as a kind of theory of history or some all-embracing explanation that enables us to connect everything that happens in the world to an act of God's will. It is 100 percent a personal conviction. At the same time, we must recognize the wider circles around this pregnant core of divine providence, for God is not our own private God. A Christian view rejects the possibility that God is concerned only with us or the group to which we belong but does not bother about the rest of humankind. For that reason Christians also believe that God has plans for people in general. This has traditionally been referred to as his special care, or *providentia specialis*. However, we can hold on to this belief only if we trust that God in one way or another also has his hand in everything that happens in the world, including such natural processes as sickness, natural disasters, death, and destruction, which are part of what happens and may strike anyone. This latter, most encompassing aspect of God's providence is called *providentia generalis*, or general providence.

The road we traveled in the previous paragraph is very important: from the special to the general. This direction cannot be simply reversed. We must start with the core of personal faith before concluding that (using an expression often attributed to Miskotte but derived by Miskotte [VW 4:214] from G. H. van Senden): "the core has a wide line of sight." It is therefore difficult to make the doctrine of providence plausible for people who place themselves outside of the circle of those who feel themselves to be addressed by God, and who in faith want to orient their lives toward God. It is only through their experiences with God that Abraham, Isaac, Jacob, Israel, and the church of Jesus Christ developed the trust that ultimately the whole world is in his hands. Apart from these faith-awakening experiences, little else can be said than that the world is an unimaginable mess and will probably always remain so.

The canon affirms God's continuing care and guidance for all creatures in many places. Some of the most remarkable examples are found in the Psalms (e.g., 33:5-22, where the factors we mentioned are closely interwoven) and in the Sermon on the Mount (e.g., God "makes his sun rise on the evil and on the good, and sends rain on the just and on the unjust," Matt 5:45). Each time the spotlight falls on God's care for those who realize that they depend on God, even when they are faced with dangers that threaten their existence, and when they lack faith: "But if God so clothes the grass of the field, which today is alive and tomorrow is thrown into the oven, will he not much more clothe you, O you of little faith?" (Matt 6:30). God's general providence with regard to all of reality, which follows the laws of nature, is most clearly found in Gen 9:8-17, though even there it is placed in the framework of the covenant that God established with the people for their salvation.

Here we take a different route from that of Berkhof (CF 215-24), who completely detaches God's special care for believers from general providence and concludes that the latter plays but a marginal role in the Bible (214). In fact, isolating the *providentia specialissima* is especially problematic.

When we look back at the development of the doctrine of providence in the Christian tradition, we must admit that this "framework of faith" has not always been kept front and center. Perhaps it was because faith in providence was widely shared in the Hellenistic world. Just as today many people with a barely articulated faith nonetheless are sure that nothing happens just "by accident," so too in ancient times. The Stoic thought that the universe is determined by rule (*logos*) and order, so that nothing happens accidentally, had wide support. This worldview gave the early Christians the impression that they shared this aspect of their faith with their neighbors. As a result, the doctrine of providence was never thoroughly Christianized, and these Stoic ideas were introduced into Christian teaching more or less without change (Wood 2008, 58–60). While the doctrine of God was Christianized—and God emphatically confessed as the Triune One—this did not happen with the doctrine of providence.

We see traces of this heritage into the seventeenth century, a heyday of optimistic theories about providence. In the sixteenth century, during the Reformation, we do find a more biblical dynamic and tension at hand on the subject. But the old philosophical influences were not completely filtered away; in fact, they were reinforced by new theological motifs that emerged in reaction to late medieval cooperative thinking, in which God and humans were assumed to cooperate on salvation. In their loathing for any doctrine of good works, Luther, Ulrich Zwingli (1484–1531), and Calvin were extremely outspoken about the all-comprising character of divine providence and of his "working alone." Luther entered into a polemic with Erasmus (ca. 1466–1536), writing *The Bondage of the Will* (1520); Zwingli dedicated a separate tract to the topic (*De providentia* [1530]), and Calvin dealt with it at length toward the end of his doctrine of God (*Inst.* 1.16–18). They opposed overly optimistic ideas about human free will and ascribed everything that happens to God's counsel. In this connection Zwingli used an unambiguously philosophical argument: an omnipotent highest being must have a hand in everything that happens; that "everything" includes sin, to which humans are more or less compelled (Lat. *cogi*). Calvin did not want to go that far but often pointed to our human inability to understand God's providential rule. Nonetheless, he did not want to differentiate between what God actively wills on the one hand and passively allows on the other. Calvin believed it would be a sign of weakness in God to permit something that he really does not want; therefore everything must be related to the admittedly hidden but always active will of God. Against the Stoics he argued that not fate but God rules; in practice, however, this distinction often seems not to make much difference.

We discover Calvin's influence, in particular, in the famous Lord's Day 10 of the Heidelberg Catechism, a text that became internationally known far beyond the circles where it had church authority. In his own comment on the Heidelberg, its author, Zacharias Ursinus, more than once quotes approvingly from the Stoic author Cicero. We certainly see Stoic influences at work when Lord's Day 10 defines God's providence as "the almighty and everywhere present power of God whereby, as it were by his hand, he upholds and governs heaven, earth, and all creatures," so that all things occur not "by chance." But when we read Lord's Day 10 in its context, especially after first reading Lord's Day 9, we clearly understand that the catechism wants to stress the unique God of the Bible, as it says very pointedly: the "Father of our Lord Jesus Christ is, for the sake of Christ his Son, my God and my Father." This very personal confession arises from the movement of the salvation that God, in Christ, has intended for us. It stands to reason, however, that when Lord's Day 10 is detached from its context—which can easily happen when it is the subject for a sermon—it elicits quite a few questions and resistance.

Lord's Day 10 became even better known when the Dutch author Maarten 't Hart made it the motto for his novel, published in English with the title *A Flight of Curlews* (1986). In this book 't Hart in many ways caricatures the Christian belief in providence, but it cannot be denied that Lord's Day 10 indeed seems to paint a picture of a God who "scatters cancer cells." Noordmans heavily criticized the wording of Lord's Day 10 for exuding too much of an unbiblical acquiescence (VW 2:160-70). But Miskotte, who lost his wife and daughter to food poisoning and thus knew what it was all about, defended Lord's Day 10. In fact, it often happens that people who have suffered a great personal loss find comfort in the knowledge that it did not happen to them without the involvement of the Father of Jesus Christ.

Thus, for a long time the doctrine of providence remained detached from any proper biblical context. Even Adolf Hitler could appeal to it during the Second World War when he declared that, by providence, Germany was entering the era of the Third Reich. This is a deplorable example of how belief in providence, when isolated from its biblical context, can become a brutal ideology that plays into the hands of dictators and repressors. For such reasons, when reflecting on our faith today, we must emphatically articulate God's providence in Trinitarian terms, from beginning to end. For all God's acts *ad extra*—that is, directed toward creation—take place "from the Father through the Son in the Spirit" (Gregory of Nyssa, *Ad Ablabium*; NPNF² 5:334). The common conviction that nothing happens accidentally, since everything is guided by a higher power, is not shared by all Christians and by many other spiritually inclined people. The doctrine of providence is no *articulus mixtus*, no "mixed" article that even non-Christians can to some extent understand and support. It has its own unique setting in the Christian faith—a setting of trust in the God whom we have learned to know in Jesus Christ and who, through his Spirit, shapes us to reflect his image. Only from this perspective can bold statements be made about the unlimited scope of God's care. These statements never convey neutral information but are statements of faith.

We can say the same thing about the various aspects of God's providence that traditional dogmatics has derived from the Bible. The best-known typology, which originated in Lutheran and Reformed post-Reformation theology, is that of conservation (*conservatio*), "going-with" (*concursus*), and governance (*gubernatio*). We deal briefly with these three elements, indicating how they presuppose the Trinitarian faith of the Christian faith community.

1. God's conservation may be interpreted quite literally. God holds his hand under this world, under our lives, and under everything that happens. He ensures that life goes on, all the time. This conservation is proof of God's faithfulness toward his creation. Usually, this conserving element of God's providence is mentioned first because it is closest to his work of creation. The conviction that God "does not forsake the work of his hands" (Ps 138:8) is deeply rooted in the Old Testament. It points in many different ways to God's continuous involvement in the world and the course of life. We may, for instance, think of the so-called nature or creation psalms (Pss 8, 19, 29, 104, 147–48) and of passages in Job and in (Deutero-)Isaiah.

The New Testament confirms and clarifies that God conserves the world in the coming of Jesus Christ (e.g., see 2 Cor 1:20). His ministry demonstrates that this is no easygoing process; on the contrary, a constant battle must be fought against the powers of death that threaten life. Jesus fought that battle by healing people who had already been written off by those around them and who had given up all hope themselves—lepers, psychiatric patients, and the chronically ill—and then by opening their lives to new opportunities (John 5:6-7). Jesus even fought for the conservation of true life by eventually giving up his own life. It is extremely important to take this christological aspect of conserving providence into account, because it demonstrates that, in the Bible, God's providence does not necessarily lead to passivity and acquiescence; it stimulates action. Because God in Christ is focused on the conservation of life, those who are in communion with him will learn to do the same, even in the most discouraging circumstances. This approach implies that, in the case of sickness, for example, we do not automatically just accept it as God's will but mount a faith-born resistance through a search for healing, even though there may come a point when the sick person will cease his or her resistance out of a faith-filled conviction that sickness and death are no longer the worst things that can happen to a Christian.

The Holy Spirit, as the one who "gives life" (Nicene Creed), is also closely involved in the conservation of the world. In this connection Reformed theology coined the expression "common grace" (*gratia communis*), which refers to the form of divine grace that makes it possible for the world to stay inhabitable, since people—despite all their limitations and sinfulness—nonetheless often want the best for each other. This grace is mediated by the Spirit in many different ways, just as is the "special grace" that enables people to live in a restored relationship with God: "The Spirit is sent not only to regenerate and indwell the saints but to enlighten and stir up the natural gifts of non-Christian artists, scientists, rulers and parents to contribute to the common good" (Horton, CF 365). This important thought is one with which everyone who observes life carefully can only agree: you do not need to be a Christian to contribute to society in a special, positive way. In fact, in history we find that non-Christians have often shown greater concern for humanizing society than have Christians.

Roman Catholic theology does not need a doctrine of general grace because it has a much more positive view of natural reality, rating it as just a little lower than the sphere of grace and the church. We first meet the notion of common grace in Calvin (*Inst.* 2.2.17; 2.3.3) to offset his austere view of sin. Calvin did not fully develop the idea into a separate doctrine, as happened later in the Dutch context in Kuyper's broad three-volume elaboration (1902-4). That, in turn, was attacked by K. Schilder (1977), who believed that the Bible is less positive about human society outside the church. Biblical warrant for this doctrine is often found in texts as Ps 145:9, Matt 5:45, Luke 6:35-36, and Acts 14:16-17. We would add Acts

28:2, where Paul and his companions point to the "unusual kindness" that was shown to them by the pagan people of Malta.

Yet, some serious objections might be raised against the teaching of general grace. It can lead to uncritical optimism regarding our culture, minimizing the consequences of evil in social structures, a fault Abraham Kuyper did not fully escape. It may also easily suggest a dichotomy in God's acts, as if God is inconsistent and operates with more and less pure forms of grace. But as long as we manage to avoid these misunderstandings, the prospect that God extends his goodness to people outside the Christian church can be very encouraging. It turns believers away from isolationism and dualistic apprehensions about society and leads them instead to cherish relationships and opportunities for cooperation with nonbelievers without always having to justify these with missionary intentions (Horton, CF 267). The experience of God's generous goodness and gifts may also protect us against a misplaced sense of superiority.

2. We have intentionally given the second aspect of God's providence the somewhat unusual label "going-with," or concurrence. This literal translation of *concursus* is less one-sided than the more frequently used word "cooperation," for this *concursus* affects not only our actions (*operationes*) but also our sufferings (*passiones*). The Bible speaks of God's *cooperation* and also of his *compassion*. God is with us also when we suffer, not in the sense of being a victim of events just as we are, but in the sense of being present and journeying with us through the land of pain. We catch a glimpse of this presence in the Old Testament (Isa 63:9), but it becomes especially clear in the Son, a high priest who can sympathize with us (Heb 4:15), and in the Spirit, who "groans" together with the suffering creation and, in particular, with the community of believers (Rom 8:23, 26). This is another feature of God's care that has not received adequate attention in the dogmatic tradition (for a good correction, see Migliore, FSU 133–34).

In the tradition, this "going-with" has been mostly linked to God's acts. This pairing is correct, for if it is true that in God we live and move and have our being (Acts 17:28), then God also has a part in all that we do. At the very least it means that God creates the conditions that enable us to act; without God's involvement we would not be able to do anything. This idea so naturally follows from the idea of conserving providence that not all sources mention the *concursus* separately. But those authors who do, want thereby to express something more: God may be active through human beings beyond simply enabling them to act. With Paul, Christians believe that, where salvation is concerned, God "is at work in you, both to will and to work" (Phil 2:13), without implying that we ourselves do not, and do not need to, work. This idea leaves us with two problems.

The first is the so-called problem of double agency. Can the same act have two different actors? However we answer this question, there is no doubt that God's activity plays out on a structurally different plane than ours. Ever since Thomas Aquinas, the tradition has tried to define this difference by using the concepts of *causa prima* (God is the "first cause") and *causae secundae* (human actors are the "second causes"). These terms remain useful if we realize that the one is not just an extension of the other. In an important study, American theologian Kathryn Tanner (1988) has shown how a correct view of God's transcendence is crucial at this point. Intuitively, we are inclined to think that the more God does, the less we do, and vice versa. Power has been called a zero-sum game, in which one party's gain is the other party's loss. But such a concept of God makes him too small, as if God has a "normal" human power, only infinitely greater. If we want to do justice to God's transcendence, we must be sure not to speak about the relationship between divine and human acts in terms of contrasts. Rather, we need to keep in mind two basic rules that emerge from the biblical witness:

1. God equips people and gives them space to act independently and effectively.
2. People are and remain absolutely dependent on God's all-encompassing and decisive action.

These two rules can align only if we see God's *concursus* not in terms of competition but in terms of equipping and stimulating. In Tanner's words: it is not about *tyranny* but about *empowerment*.

We come now to the second problem: how do we explain mutual responsibility when people use their freedom of action to do evil? If God cooperates with us in all we do, does it mean that God has a part in our sins? However far people have gone in ascribing all events to God, this question has always been answered in the negative. Yet, the answer can be quite paradoxical, for it is unclear how God's noncomplicity can be reconciled with his active involvement. We suggest that here too the Trinitarian approach leads us toward a sound solution. In Jesus we discover how and where God is actively at work (see John 5:17-19), and after his departure the Spirit continues this work on earth. In other words, we can speak about *cooperatio* only in a multilayered, differentiated way. God is minimally present in human sin, only in the sense that he creates the conditions that enable us to sin. God wanted people who would be able to sin but did not want the sin itself. But God is maximally present in the covenantal history with us human beings, as initiated by the Father, fulfilled by the Son, and completed by the Spirit.

The doctrine of providence, therefore, does not teach us that everything that happens is God's will; rather, it sharpens our eye so that we can more perceptively discern what happens in the world. Where is God at work? How can we understand theologically—that is, from God's perspective—what is going on? For an answer to this question we can rely only on the "two hands of God," Christ and the Spirit. We can confess the active involvement of God when what happens in the world conforms to the way of Jesus and where the fruits of the Spirit are really visible. There God works with heightened intensity, pervading human will and action. For that reason the Christian community regularly and attentively reads the biblical testimonies regarding the work of Father, Son, and Spirit so that our eyesight is sharpened and we learn how to look "Christianly" at what happens in the world and at how God is at work there (see Brümmer 1992, 125–27).

3. Finally now, the third aspect of divine providence: God's *gubernatio* (governance), or *directio* (leadership). Traditionally, this part of God's providence was conceptualized in rather static terms, as if God rules the world as a manager does a company, doing what needs to be done, minding the store. The Bible, however, speaks in much more dynamic—more precisely, in *eschatological*—terms about God's rule. The fact that God rules the world means, first and foremost, that he guides it in a particular direction, toward the final realization of his plans and promises. Therefore, history is geared toward the kingdom, for also in his rule the Father works via—and thus in the mode of—the Son and the Spirit. For the time being, God rules "from the wood of the cross" (Venantius Fortunatus, sixth century), that is, in spite of all kinds of misery, setbacks, and experiences of loss. History becomes ever more similar to Jesus's road to the cross, just as the apocalyptic portions of the New Testament teach. In addition, it should be noted that God works through his Spirit and not by (human) might or power (Zech 4:6). We should often pay more attention to small things than to powerful revolutions or major changes in society. Where people are touched by the s/Spirit of the gospel and on that basis experience a decisive renewal in their lives, there God is at work, guiding the world to its future destination. So, God's direction often proceeds via small

things and detours, another reason that God's providential rule is first and foremost a matter of faith and not something that can be gleaned from a newspaper. But it is precisely this faith that is certain that the outcome will not be a failure.

Brümmer (1992, 108–27) writes with good reason about our perception of God's acts from reading the Bible. We owe to Noordmans, among others, our stronger realization of the eschatological orientation to God's providence in general and the *gubernatio* in particular. Berkhof has suggested (most recently in CF 518–21) that history more and more resembles Jesus's road to the cross. He did not, however, proceed to a Trinitarian reformulation of the doctrine of providence, unlike Migliore and Wood, even though neither of them is quite consistent. Wood (2008) attributes conservation to the Father, concurrence to the Son, and the ruling to the Spirit, while Migliore (FSU 133–36) mostly connects the *conservatio* with the work of Jesus, the *concursus* with the Father, and the *gubernatio* with the Spirit. These correlations are rather arbitrary, however; we believe that all three aspects should be considered from a Trinitarian angle.

Much has been published by theologians since the last quarter of the twentieth century on the question of how we can understand the concept of divine action in view of the determining role of natural laws and empirical reality. Since 1988 the Vatican has, for instance, sponsored a series of conferences and publications over a number of years under the name "The Divine Action Project" (see Wildman 2004). Many scientists and philosophers appear to be skeptical about what is (pejoratively) referred to as "interventionism" (i.e., God's intervening in processes that are determined by the laws of nature). When events have a natural cause, it is difficult to conceptualize not only any miraculous aspect (*providentia extraordinaria*) but also the way God acts through the laws of nature (*providentia ordinaria*). Frequently reference is made to quantum mechanics, which seems, particularly in the so-called Copenhagen interpretation, to offer a new possibility for placing God's actions in a scientific frame. See for example, as *pars pro toto*, Shults et al. 2009, and for a powerful defense of interventionism, Plantinga 2011, 91–125.

References

Alexander, Denis. 2014. *Creation or Evolution: Do We Have to Choose?* 2nd ed. Oxford: Lion Hudson.

Beek, Abraham van de. 1996. *Schepping: De wereld als voorspel voor de eeuwigheid* [Creation: The world as the prelude to eternity]. Baarn: Callenbach.

Bergmann, Sigurd. 2005. *Creation Set Free: The Spirit as Liberator of Nature.* Grand Rapids: Eerdmans.

Bouma-Prediger, Steven. 2001. *For the Beauty of the Earth: A Christian Vision for Creation Care.* Grand Rapids: Eerdmans.

Brümmer, Vincent. 1992. *Speaking of a Personal God: An Essay in Philosophical Theology.* Cambridge: Cambridge University Press.

Clayton, Philip, and Arthur Peacocke, eds. 2004. *In Whom We Live and Move and Have Our Being: Panentheistic Reflections on God's Presence in a Scientific World.* Grand Rapids: Eerdmans.

Craig, William Lane. 2004. *Creation out of Nothing: A Biblical, Philosophical, and Scientific Exploration.* Leicester: Apollos.

Deane-Drummond, Celia, and David Clough, eds. 2009. *Creaturely Theology: On God, Humans, and Other Animals.* London: SCM.

Driel, Edwin C. van. 2008. *Incarnation Anyway: Arguments for Supralapsarian Christology.* Oxford: Oxford University Press.

Fergusson, David. 1998. *The Cosmos and the Creator: An Introduction to the Theology of Creation.* London: SPCK.

———. 2014. *Creation.* Grand Rapids: Eerdmans.

Gunton, Colin E. 1998. *The Triune Creator: A Historical and Systematic Study.* Edinburgh: Edinburgh University Press.

Harris, Mark. 2013. *The Nature of Creation: Examining the Bible and Science.* Durham: Acumen.

Hasel, Gerhard F. 1974. "The Polemic Nature of the Genesis Cosmology." *Evangelical Quarterly* 46:81–102.

Hooykaas, Reijer. 1972. *Religion and the Rise of Modern Science.* Edinburgh: Scottish Academic Press.

Jaki, Stanley. 1980. *Cosmos and Creator.* Edinburgh: Scottish Academic Press.

Kooi, Cornelis van der. 2000. "Die großen Taten Gottes: Bemerkungen zu einem unverzichtbaren theologischen Begriff." In *Post-Theism: Reframing the Judeo-Christian Tradition,* edited by H. A. Krop, A. L. Molendijk, and H. de Vries, 341–53. Leuven: Peeters.

Lane, Belden C. 2011. *Ravished by Beauty: The Surprising Legacy of Reformed Spirituality.* Oxford: Oxford University Press.

Lindström, Fredrik. 1983. *God and the Origin of Evil: A Contextual Analysis of Alleged Monastic Evidence in the Old Testament.* Translated by Frederick H. Cryer. Lund: Gleerup.

Link, Christian. 1991. *Schöpfung.* Handbuch systematischer Theologie 7. Gütersloh: Gütersloher Verlagshaus.

Linzey, Andrew, and Dorothy Yamamoto, eds. 1998. *Animals on the Agenda: Questions about Animals for Theology and Ethics.* London: SCM.

Lloyd, Michael. 1997. "The Cosmic Fall and the Free Will Defence." PhD diss., University of Oxford.

May, Gerhard. 1994. *Creatio ex Nihilo: The Doctrine of "Creation out of Nothing" in Early Christian Thought*. Translated by A. S. Worrall. Edinburgh: T&T Clark.

McFague, Sallie. 1993. *The Body of God: An Ecological Theology*. Minneapolis: Fortress.

McGrath, Alister E. 2002. *The Re-enchantment of Nature: The Denial of Religion and the Ecological Crisis*. London: Hodder & Stoughton.

Moltmann, Jürgen. 1993. *God in Creation: A New Theology of Creation and the Spirit of God*. Minneapolis: Fortress.

Murphy, Francesca Aran, and Philip G. Ziegler, eds. 2009. *The Providence of God: Deus habet consilium*. London: T&T Clark.

Plantinga, Alvin. 2011. *Where the Conflict Really Lies: Science, Religion, and Naturalism*. Oxford: Oxford University Press.

Schilder, Klaas. 1977. *Christ and Culture*. Winnipeg: Premier.

Shults, F. LeRon, Nancey C. Murphy, and Robert John Russell, eds. 2009. *Philosophy, Science, and Divine Action*. Leiden: Brill.

Southgate, Christopher. 2008. *The Groaning of Creation: God, Evolution, and the Problem of Evil*. Louisville: Westminster John Knox.

Tanner, Kathryn. 1988. *God and Creation in Christian Theology: Tyranny or Empowerment?* Oxford: Blackwell.

Torrance, Thomas F. 1981. *Divine and Contingent Order*. Oxford: Oxford University Press.

Walton, John H. 2015. *The Lost World of Adam and Eve*. Downers Grove, IL: InterVarsity Press.

Warfield, Benjamin B. 2000. *Evolution, Science, and Scripture: Selected Writings*. Edited by Mark A. Noll and David N. Livingstone. Grand Rapids: Baker Books.

Webster, John. 2010. "Trinity and Creation." *International Journal of Systematic Theology* 12:4–19.

Welker, Michael. 1999. *Creation and Reality*. Minneapolis: Fortress.

Westermann, Claus. 1994. *Genesis 1-11: A Continental Commentary*. Minneapolis: Fortress. German ed., 1974.

White, Lynn. 1967. "The Historical Roots of Our Ecologic Crisis." *Science* 155, no. 3767, pp. 1203–12.

Wildman, Wesley. 2004. "The Divine Action Project, 1988–2003." *Theology and Science* 2:31–75.

Wood, Charles M. 2008. *The Question of Providence*. Louisville: Westminster John Knox.

7 Human Beings and the Image of God

Theological Anthropology

AIM

This chapter goes into more detail on some issues we discussed in the previous chapter. We focus on one set of God's many creatures – human beings. We thereby enter the field of theological anthropology, which deals in particular with the question of what we can say theologically – that is, from the perspective of our relationship with God – about the human being as a creature. This field opens up a broad range of subjects, some of which we will have to pass by here. We think we have made a responsible selection of the most important and relevant issues to discuss.

This chapter will be fruitful if at the end you can:

- explain why the project of theological anthropology is not self-evident, but why it nonetheless has a legitimate place in Christian dogmatics (7.1)
- clarify the changing frameworks in which humanity has figured in dogmatics over the centuries (7.2)
- name and compare the various methods used in theological anthropology (7.3)
- explain the three main approaches to dealing with biblical information about humanity as bearing the "image of God," the *imago Dei*, and make a well-supported choice among them (7.4)
- express what the classic Christian manner of understanding humans as "body and soul" means in current discussions (7.5)
- give a reasoned answer to the question whether – and if so, in which sense – we are free (7.6)
- understand how essential our sexual differentiation is to being human (7.7)

- connect the question about the meaning of life with the so-called creation mandate (7.8).

MAKING CONNECTIONS

1. Imagine that you can eliminate all differences between people. What is left when you are done? What do people have in common, and what makes them unique compared to other creatures? Take five minutes to write down some preliminary thoughts in this vein about "the human being."
2. Are people free? Do they have a soul? Why, in fact, are we on earth? Try to answer these questions spontaneously, then ponder to what extent you owe these answers to the environment in which you grew up or to your own discoveries along the way.
3. In 1486 Pico della Mirandola published his now-famous lecture about the dignity of human beings (*Oratio de hominis dignitate*). This tract gives a sharp analysis of the spiritual climate that emerged in the Renaissance. Browse the Web to learn something of Pico's worldview and ask yourself what you think about it.

7.1. Anthropology as a Nonself-evident Locus in Dogmatics

It is not at all self-evident that something like a doctrine of humanity belongs in Christian dogmatics. There are at least three reasons for this view. First, human beings are not an object of Christian faith as are the Father, the Son, and the Holy Spirit. When we look at the early Christian confessions, there is no statement such as "I believe in man." In dogmatics—defined as reflection on the Christian faith—it is not immediately clear that human beings deserve a special place. In fact, O. Noordmans, an intriguing Dutch theologian, argued that they did not (H 47 = VW 2:241). Theology of course speaks about humanity, as well as about God, but typically about humanity in connection with God. Humanity "has no independent existence" and therefore "has no pretentions in dogmatics."

Second, we may wonder about how important a place humanity as such has in the Bible. Of course, every page of the Bible portrays very concrete people, but they display great diversity and variety. If there is anything that people in the Bible have in common, it is their need of redemption and reconciliation. A discussion about humanity as such might well be situated in other areas of dogmatics, for instance, in the doctrines of sin (harmartiology) or of salvation (soteriology). Still, we cannot help but see that—as today—people in the Bible differ so much from each other that it might not make sense to lump them all into one category. If they are categorized, the Old and the New Testaments always do so by a fundamental separation between Jews and gentiles. Even Christians were not seen as a *tertium genus* (a third kind; that distinction happened later), but as people who were completely rooted in either Judaism or paganism. Is not the concept of humanity, therefore, too abstract for us to say anything meaningful about it from a Christian angle?

Third, we must not ignore the lessons of history. When surveying the history of dogmatics, we are bound to meet many discussions about human nature: for instance, about how the soul enters the body (through procreation or a separate creation—i.e., *traducianism* versus *creationism*), about our psychic and intellectual abilities, how these interact, and so forth. All these theories are presented as typically Christian, but a closer look forces us to put many question marks in the margins.

Quite often ideas about human nature that were current in a particular cultural context (often under the influence of a certain philosophical school) were rather uncritically presented as Christian. Thomas Aquinas's anthropology, for example, was very elaborate, but much of it was borrowed from Aristotle rather than built on a careful study of the biblical text or on a Christian theological basis. When in the Reformation era Aristotle's influence radically diminished, a much more limited anthropology remained. However, we still find philosophical influences in the anthropology of someone like Calvin, albeit not of Aristotelian but of Platonic and Stoic origin.

For that reason Hendrikus Berkhof suggested that the realm of theological anthropology should be drastically reduced to just three insights that he considered to be central: (1) we are "respondable" beings, that is, called to respond, (2) we are rooted in love, and (3) we are truly free (CF 186–89). Today, however, these ideas are no longer uncontroversial. Many neuroscientists leave but little room for something like human freedom and tend to regard the notion as a bit of popular psychology, something that is universally accepted but has no basis in empirical reality and must therefore be deemed an illusion. Would it not be better if theologians finally closed their anthropology shop and left all thinking about human nature to the relevant scientific disciplines?

In the light of the above considerations, this is not such a strange question. Nonetheless, we choose not to follow its advice because there are weighty arguments against it. Admittedly, the church does not know anything like a "dogma of man." But in chapter 1 we saw that dogmatics does not restrict itself to reflecting on doctrines; we used a broader definition for dogmatics, namely, as making sense of things from the perspective of the Christian faith. Taking this definition as our starting point, there is good reason not to exclude Christian reflection on what it means to be a human being, all the more so when we realize that in the Christian faith the human being is very special and important. This is true not only in the Bible (e.g., see Ps 8) but also in the confessions of faith. While these documents do not make us into an object of Christian faith, we are told that Jesus Christ has descended from heaven and himself become human "for us and for our salvation" (OF 14). This is a very significant statement about human beings: we are important to God.

Second, in the Scriptures we are mostly pictured as people who are in need, as people who fail in many different ways and therefore need salvation, forgiveness, and reconciliation. So "humanity" might well belong under the heading of the doctrines of sin and salvation. But there is more to say, for the Bible also—or even primarily—presents humanity as a creation of God outside the context of sin. In particular, notice the first chapters of Genesis, texts that have always been of great importance for the Christian view of humanity, and we do well to read them very carefully. Later on we will discuss humanity as the object of God's redemption in the Son (chap. 11) and of God's renewal in the Spirit (chaps. 12 and 15). However, this is the place to reflect on what it means that, as human beings, we too are creatures of the Father.

But today can we not learn everything we need to know about human beings from (other) scholarly disciplines? That remains to be seen! Just as, in the past, not everything that claimed to be a Christian view of humanity was genuinely Christian, so today, not everything that is presented as a scientific view of humanity is genuinely scientific. Anyone who wants to chart the human phenomenon from the starting point of the empirical sciences can easily fall victim to tunnel vision and think that only things that can be empirically measured are relevant. Such scientism (taking science as the absolute truth) is not only unable to deal with many religious sentiments regarding humanity but also must reduce phenomena like love, morality, and ethical awareness to specific constellations of chemical reactions in the brain. But what it means to be human can in no way be adequately described in this manner. The empirical sciences can describe our various functions and behavioral traits but must remain silent when it comes to such real-life questions as those dealing with the identity, the future, and the meaning of life. Thus we need a broader perspective and feel strongly that a Christian anthropology can offer insights and ideas that have abiding significance for our understanding of the nature of humanity.

We do not mean to suggest that these ideas can be developed into a complete "Christian" view because, according to the New Testament, only the future that Christ will open up will reveal what we really are (1 John 3:2). Even so, we urgently need Christian insights and ideas about "being really human" if we want to critically analyze and unmask various secular views that direct human action. We believe we can no longer be satisfied with the three core ideas that Hendrikus Berkhof formulated in light of the long list of subjects that currently confront anthropology and that demand our reflection. In the following sections we will treat a number of these themes in theological perspective.

For a systematic justification of the special place and significance of theological anthropology in the context of cultural reflection on human nature, see Pannenberg (2004), who makes an attempt to illuminate and enrich, from a Christian-theological angle, what we know from philosophical and scientific sources. For the ideological-critical function, see Schoberth 2006, 26.

7.2. A Short Historical Survey

During the first centuries of church history human nature was not really a central theme in reflections on the Christian faith. That reflection, as we have seen, was mainly focused on the questions of who God is, who Christ is, and what the status is of the Holy Spirit. Humanity entered the picture only as a secondary factor—that is, as an object of God's concern. The most important thing that could be said about human beings had to do with their relationship as creatures with God. Humanity to the Fathers constituted a "metaphysical animal" that could find its ultimate destiny only in an orientation to the reality of God that precedes and supersedes us. Augustine summarized this common awareness in the opening section of his *Confessions*: "You have made us for yourself, O Lord, and our hearts are restless until they find their rest in you" (*Conf.* 1.1.1).

This theocentric character of the Christian faith experience survived the Middle Ages, for Calvin maintains that we cannot know ourselves without knowing God (*Inst.* 1.1.2). However, Calvin shows some ambivalence here, influenced as he is by the emerging climate of Renaissance humanism. In this connection it is interesting to place the opening passages of his *Institutes* and Augustine's *Confessions* side by side. Calvin says that there are many ties between knowledge of God and knowledge of ourselves, and that it is not easy to determine which comes first. We might consider whether theology starts with humanity and proceeds to God.

It is important that Calvin saw this movement as one of contrast. It is not our greatness that links us with God; on the contrary, "the miserable ruin into which the revolt of the first man has plunged us, compels us to turn our eyes heavenward. . . . We are accordingly urged by our own evil things to consider the good things of God" (*Inst.* 1.1.1). Only after he has made this need clear does Calvin take another route and decide to start his instruction in the Christian religion with our knowledge of God. He cannot be satisfied by using anthropology as his launching pad. Yet, Calvin's hesitation remains intriguing and remarkable, especially in the light of later developments in European culture.

When we take a look at the theology that later emerged under the influence of the Enlightenment, we see a radical break with the kind of thinking that starts from God and moves to humanity. From now on humanity becomes the point of departure. This change reflects "a turn to the subject," as it has been called in philosophy, starting with René Descartes (1596-1650) and developed much further by Immanuel Kant. Descartes found ultimate certainty in the famous *cogito* ("I think"); all other forms of knowledge must somehow be derived from this basis. This approach applies, not only to knowledge of our own existence (*cogito ergo sum*, "I think, therefore I am"), but also to knowledge of God's existence. Descartes thought it was quite possible to distill knowledge of God from knowledge about ourselves, and he made various proposals to this end. Immanuel Kant, however, in his comprehensive treatment of the character and limits of human nature, convinced many with his arguments that this approach is very problematic. Kant believed that our epistemological abilities are limited to what can be observed empirically, which does not include a transcendent God. Thus, proofs for God's existence that do not recognize this limitation are without value.

Still, the idea persisted that we will be able to say something that makes sense about God only by way of connection with our humanness. This approach reverses the order of Calvin, who starts with knowledge of

God. And so theologians after Kant began to anchor knowledge of God in the human subject, albeit in another domain than that of reason. Friedrich Schleiermacher must be credited with the most famous and influential attempt in this direction when he situated religion (the connection with God) in *eine eigene Provinz im Gemüt*, "a domain of its own within the human faculties." Schleiermacher was often taken, wrongly, to refer to human feeling(s) in this connection. The religious faculty, in his view, does not refer to our changing moods or sentiments but to a deeper, prereflective layer in our inner self that precedes even the separation between subject and object; there we sense ourselves to be part of the universe, connected to the divine, or "the Infinite," as Schleiermacher liked to say. Later, he expressed this basic idea more specifically in terms of the *schlechthinniges Abhängigkeitsgefühl*, "the awareness of absolute dependence," which we experience when looking at the universe (CF 1:12ff.). This awareness is common to all religions and lies at their deepest core. Dogmatic statements—especially, of course, those about God—must emerge from human experiences that are somehow related to this awareness of absolute dependence. Strictly speaking, therefore, they are not statements about God but about ourselves, about our own experiences and state of mind. And if they cannot be expressed along such lines (as Schleiermacher thinks is the case with the doctrine of the Trinity), their status becomes rather disputable. Anthropology has here become the determining factor, is even given primacy, in the church's reflection on faith.

The liberal theology of the nineteenth and twentieth centuries in various ways continued in the tracks of Schleiermacher. When speaking about God, it usually begins with humanity and human experience, but this experience can be understood and expressed in different ways. Bultmann's way, which is rooted in an existentialist climate, differs considerably from that of Schleiermacher. Karl Barth was the first to express the vital objection against this approach, namely, that when we *start* our faith reflection with humanity, we will *remain* with humanity. The atheistic philosopher Ludwig Feuerbach was right when he argued in this vein that theological statements are merely projections of statements we make about ourselves. They say nothing about God but everything about our own needs and ideas; thus theology is devoured by anthropology. This argument pushed Barth to develop a radical alternative to Schleiermacher's concept in an attempt to bring order to the issue. Taking his cue from Calvin, Barth argued that knowledge of God and of ourselves is possible only in the light of our knowledge of Jesus Christ. In him the true human and the true God are revealed. Theological statements and anthropological statements must equally be rooted in Christology, emerging from our understanding of who Jesus is.

After Barth, liberal theology encountered criticism from a totally different direction. (Or did Barth, as some have suggested, already anticipate this criticism and take it into account in his project?) Twentieth-century postmodern philosophy has come to doubt ever more strongly that there is, in fact, something like a static "human being." Already in the nineteenth century the emerging disciplines in the humanities helped make us aware of the enormous influence our cultural context exerts on the way we shape our life. Only by a careful study of all these contexts can we discover what is universal and essential in our humanness (and thus what is really part of our human nature) as opposed to what is culturally relative and accidental. These latter traits have recently appeared to be much more important than traditionally assumed. In the late twentieth century, after the so-called death of God, the death of man was also announced. The first had been proclaimed by Nietzsche, while the second must be credited to Michel Foucault (1926–84), who showed that "man" as a sovereign subject is a rather recent invention. When the pretenses of human knowledge are carefully dissected (or "deconstructed"), it becomes clear that these are, to a large extent, ideologically determined pretenses of power. That is, "man" is not an autonomous subject who stands at the beginning of our acquisition of knowledge but a construct in the service of institutional powers and interests (see Vanhoozer 1997, 162). These views are hammer blows to the framework of modernity. Human freedom, autonomy, rationality—they are all no more than phantoms. In reality we differ little from the animals.

Such a nihilistic view of humanity is found, not just in postmodern philosophy, but also with some neuroscientists and evolutionary biologists. They tend to regard every attempt to identify something uniquely human as a form of wishful thinking, particularly when it is linked with the idea of a unique human calling. However, one cannot escape the impression that such opinions do not primarily rest on scientific grounds but derive mainly from worldview considerations. We also often discern this cynical view in contemporary literature, film, and theater. On the one hand, theology will have to take these things seriously—and certainly the factual data that are offered by the various disciplines; on the other hand, it must also bring its own dimension to the debate, namely, the relationship between humanity and God. We should not neglect, finally, the enormous persisting but almost unnoticeable influence that Christian thinking about humanity still exerts.

We believe that a contemporary Christian theological anthropology should not be overly concerned by these variable cultural and philosophical constellations but should simply stay with the point of departure of Augustine, Calvin, and Barth: genuine—and we should probably add, in-depth—knowledge of humanity will be ours only from the light that the gospel sheds on our existence through God's actions in Christ and the Spirit, which show us that human life is not meaningless.

7.3. The Methodology of Theological Anthropology

Various approaches are possible for describing the characteristics of what it means to be human as they are illuminated from the perspective of the gospel. As a start, one might try to make a list of all the statements that can be found about the phenomenon of humanity in the various books of the Bible and see how they might add up. The risk here is not sufficiently taking into account the differences in literary genre among these books, and likewise, in ignoring the difference in importance among all these statements. (Those that are more or less made in passing should not get the same weight as basic insights.) For that reason many theologians choose instead to read the range of biblical data from the angle of a central point, which usually coincides with a certain locus in the body of dogmatics. Thus, in the twentieth century anthropology was approached from the perspectives of the doctrine of creation, the doctrine of the covenant, Christology, eschatology, the doctrine of justification, and the doctrine of the Trinity. We will give an example of each of these.

Karl Rahner, an important Roman Catholic theologian, proposed an anthropology that was rooted in nature, that is, in *the doctrine of creation*. Rahner fully accepted the Enlightenment's "shift to the subject" and the consequence that theology therefore has no option but to begin its task with a doctrine of humanity. Rahner believed that our orientation toward God is the fundamental characteristic of being human, here carrying an Augustinian thought over the watershed of modernity. He did not do so without giving some arguments, however. He pointed in particular to our *sense of the transcendent*; as human beings, we have learned not to be satisfied with what is but are geared toward that which transcends our existence. Unlike the animals, we are not fused with the reality that surrounds us but see an "unlimited openness for the limitless extent of all possible reality" (FCF 20). We believe that our existence has meaning, an orientation toward a goal beyond itself. Even before we are aware of it, our deepest urge is to reach for the absolute—that is to say, for God. Rahner opposes Feuerbach's contention that such an approach, by beginning with humanity, must inevitably remain stuck in anthropology. Theology and anthropology are not competitors and can move well together. Why can we not see this self-transcendence, which is so characteristic for our humanness, as something that is given to us? And also see that there is a subject that precedes us, that made us into the kind of being we are, and that will graciously provide a destiny for our existence? According to Rahner, Jesus Christ is the ultimate manifestation of these two realities: of our human openness toward God, but also of God's total openness toward us.

Hendrikus Berkhof's approach to anthropology opts for a basis in *the history of the covenant*. The Bible tells us that God wants an enduring personal relationship, a covenant, with humanity. This is the axis around which the Bible turns; the Bible is the record of the encounters that God initiates with us within the covenant framework, the history God writes with human beings. We must therefore pay close attention to these "revelatory encounters" if we want to discover how, from a Christian perspective, being human has a wider and more fundamental meaning than we are able to learn from the various scholarly disciplines. So, if humanity is built on this encounter with God, that very fact presupposes, first, that we are "responsible" beings—in other words, through and through rational beings. "From the standpoint of the Christian faith it is out of question to regard man as a self-contained being who later happens to enter into relationships with other beings" (CF 187). Second, this view presupposes that humanity is "built on love," because the Word by which God addresses us is full of the holy love that God himself is. We are the only beings that can "understand, enjoy, and respond to" this love (188). This orientation further presupposes, third, that we are in essence *free*, for love cannot exist without freedom. Berkhof argues that these three characteristics do not just apply to our encounter with God but are of fundamental importance for humanness as such.

Berkhof's approach of providing more content to theological anthropology by referring to the revelatory encounter that the Bible describes enables him to give more concrete attention than Rahner to the struggle that God must engage in to establish contact with us, and to safeguard that contact. As a result, in Berkhof's anthropology sin—our abuse of the freedom we have been given, by ignoring God's claim—gets a much more direct and sharper focus than in Rahner's proposal, which leaves us with rather harmonious and optimistic impressions. However, Berkhof deals rather blithely with important philosophical and theological matters that are of great significance for a Christian anthropology: what freedom, in fact, is; how the physical and mental aspects of humanness relate to each other; and how exactly we should understand our being in the image of God.

The *christological* approach is especially found in Karl Barth (CD III/2) and his followers. As we alluded to previously, Barth fears that attempts (such as that of Rahner) to ground theology in the human subject cannot ultimately do justice to either God or humanity. For that reason, we must not so much try to understand God on the basis of our ability for self-transcendence but, on the contrary, understand ourselves on the basis of God's ultimate act of self-communication—God's revelation in Jesus Christ. All around us we see only people who have fallen into sin and are marked by its effects. We therefore need a new revelation of God if we want to grasp what true humanness entails. That revelation has been given to us in the true man, Jesus Christ. With good reason the New Testament presents him as the image of God par excellence (2 Cor 3:18; Col 1:15). In him it becomes manifest that the true human being (*der wirkliche Mensch*) is the human being who lives in a relationship with others. For Jesus did not primarily live for his own sake but, out of his love for the Father, for and with others. He was sent for their salvation. The individual person per se, without these relationships with God and others, is not fully human. The *Grundform* (basic form) of being human is being together with other human beings (CD III/2, §45.2).

The *eschatological* method in anthropology is elaborated most clearly by Wolfhart Pannenberg (2004 and, already in essence, 1970). As did Rahner, Pannenberg wanted to align himself with contemporary secular insights about humanity, especially those of a philosophical nature. In this approach human openness (or "standing out," which is the etymological meaning of "existing") toward the world is often seen as the key to understanding what it really means to be human. Pannenberg too interprets this human self-transcendence as an openness that is ultimately directed toward the all-encompassing divine reality. But where Rahner appears to think of the openness primarily in vertical terms, Pannenberg supplies a strongly horizontal dynamic: reality is not yet complete, and only in the ultimate future (theologically speaking, in the eschaton) will it be possible to see it in its fullness. Being implicitly or explicitly aware of this timeline, we are future-oriented beings. So if we want to know what true humanness means, we should not look at its present, sinful, and deficient forms; too often our egocentrism perverts our proper exocentric orientation. Only from the perspective of our future destiny can the true nature of our humanness become clear: "It does not yet appear what we shall be" (1 John 3:2). But do we therefore remain in the dark about the true meaning of being human? Here Pannenberg listens to Barth: the destiny, and thus the essence, of what we humans are has already been made manifest in the appearance of Jesus Christ. Jesus's resurrection, in particular, is a prolepsis (i.e., anticipation) of the eschaton. In that sense Jesus is the eschatological man who, as the last Adam, sheds light on the true nature and meaning of the first Adam.

We find this same eschatological openness in the anthropology of Eberhard Jüngel. Following Luther closely (*Disputatio de homine*, WA 39/1:176), Jüngel provides a theological definition of humanity via *the doctrine of justification*. What and who we are is determined by the justification that we receive from God. Here Luther opposed an anthropology that went back to the Aristotelian-Thomistic view of human ability, according to which my humanness is determined by what I can do (willing, striving, knowing, etc.). Jüngel applies Luther's alternative to our time, when our identity seems to be defined by our economic value. Christian theology offers a fundamentally different view. Human identity is defined by the Word that tells us about the cross and resurrection of Christ. This approach makes human identity something external; it consists not at all in what we ourselves can produce but is found in Christ. In Christ's incarnation God identified with our death-doomed existence. This action defines us as beings who are allowed to live out of that Word, which comes to us and addresses us. Whatever else might be said about us, God does not freeze us in our past or in our biological limits; instead, he has destined us to be receivers of his love. This approach also clarifies what sin is—an attempt to escape from this role of recipient and to strive for self-realization. But by doing so, we thereby miss our destiny and ignore God as the precious secret of our existence. The most crucial thing that might be said about us from an ontological angle is that Christ has come to "bother" us, that he sat down beside the sinner and identified himself with the sinner. This action defines true humanness, for being truly human means refusing to be independent. It means welcoming the way that God addresses us with his Yes and living in harmony with this Yes (Jüngel 2014, 124-53; see also 1986, 127-38).

The *doctrine of the Trinity* is the most recent home provided for theological anthropology. This basis is closely linked to the rediscovery of the unique nature of the Eastern—more specifically, Cappadocian— doctrine of the Trinity (see above, chap. 3). For the first time in the history of thought, the Cappadocian church fathers gave absolute ontological priority to the concept of personhood. God is not a kind of eternal substance that somehow splits itself into three modes of being, but God is in essence *personal*. More specifically, God exists in three persons in an eternal, unbreakable mutual unity. This concept does not reflect the well-known individualistic view of the person that, with Boethius (ca. 480–ca. 524), became the dominant view in the West (a person is an individual substance of a rational kind); instead, it is an alternative view in which personhood is defined as being relational. Theologians like John Zizioulas (1985), Colin Gunton (e.g., CF 41–45), and Stanley Grenz (2001) have taken this the definition of what bearing the image of God means. Just like the divine persons, human beings are not individuals complete in themselves; rather, they are unique persons who find their identity in a relational being-in-communion with others. This approach helps us to see that true humanness is characterized by love and freedom (e.g., see Gunton, CF 44–45).

When we survey all these approaches, we notice that the results are less divergent than we might have suspected in view of the different methodologies. The christological and eschatological approaches, along with the Trinitarian, lead to giving relationality and being-in-communion a central place as the basic characteristics for anthropology. Nor are love and freedom essential marks of humanity only in a Trinitarian-structured anthropology; the same is true of Berkhof's covenantal-history approach, even though he opposes the Trinitarian angle. At the same time, all methods run the risk of pouring the biblical data about humanity into the mold of an a priori perspective. Does this still allow the Bible to speak for itself?

In what follows we do not prefer one method over the others but try to foster a continuous dialogue between the Bible and the voices of philosophy and science in discussing the various themes and dilemmas of theological anthropology. We take as our point of departure the central biblical notion of humanity as bearing the image of God. This expression is prominent in the first chapters of Genesis and continues to play an important role elsewhere in the Bible. What does this usage mean for theological anthropology (7.4)? That discussion will serve as a basis for our treatment of the so-called body-soul problem (7.5); from there we proceed to the question whether we are free and, if so, in what sense (7.6). Then we focus on the theological significance of our being sexual in the light of the way that this is highlighted in the first pages of Genesis (7.7). Finally, we reflect briefly on the issue of the meaning of human life—a matter that cannot be detached from our relationship to the created reality in which we have been given our place (7.8).

For extensive and up-to-date treatments of these topics (except for the theological significance of human sexuality), see Farris and Taliaferro 2015.

7.4. What Does It Mean That Human Beings Bear the Image of God?

The Jewish and Christian traditions are distinct among the ancient religions in believing that God and humanity are not somehow related. They posit, as we saw in the previous chapter, a structural, ontological difference between the Creator and all creatures. And humans belong, without any doubt, to the category of the creatures. They do not originate from God but from the earth (Gen 2:7; in that respect evolutionary theory does not suggest anything new). Nonetheless, they add that something connects God and humanity in a unique way: we have been created "after" (or possibly "in") the image of God. Admittedly, this image-of-God concept is not mentioned very frequently in the Bible—to be exact, ten times: three times in the Old Testament and seven times in the New—but in other places (e.g., Ps. 8; Eph 4:24) the idea lies implicitly under the text and influences the way in which humanity is spoken about.

It is important to remember that in the New Testament the image of God mostly has a christological connotation: Jesus Christ is the true image (Gk. *eikōn*) of God (2 Cor 4:4; see also Heb 1:3). Being without sin (Heb 4:15), he reflects God in the most perfect manner. Yet, this description of Jesus does not diminish the New Testament's view of every human being as a bearer of the divine image (1 Cor 11:7; Jas 3:9). The *imago Dei* concept bears not only a christological but certainly also an anthropological meaning. But what exactly is this anthropological meaning? We take as our point of departure the very first Bible text that refers to this concept—a text that, through the ages, has been extremely important for Jewish and Christian reflection on the nature of humanity.

> Then God said, "Let us make man in our image, after our likeness; and let them have dominion over the fish of the sea, and over the birds of the air, and over the cattle, and over all the earth, and over every creeping thing that creeps upon the earth." So God created man in his

own image, in the image of God he created him; male and female he created them. (Gen 1:26–27)

We begin with some points on which opinions do not differ, at least not to any major extent; then we indicate where the ways diverge (for the entire issue, see Cortez 2010, 16ff.). To start with: it is clear that an image reflects something and thus resembles this other object. If we are called the image of God, then we in some way resemble God, reflect God's reality. The additional term "likeness" may clarify this resembling a little further, but it does not add another, structurally significant element of meaning, as was regularly proposed in the past (e.g., by Irenaeus). Today exegetes all agree that there is no basis for suggesting any major difference between "image" and "likeness." It is clear that *all* people, both male and female, are bearers of the divine image; they are all in one category as reflectors of God. So where exactly do the issues arise with respect to this doctrine? The major differences lie between the structural, functional, and relational approaches to the *imago Dei*.

Traditionally, the image of God, as introduced in Genesis, was connected to a particular structural layer in human nature, a particular human ability. In fact, it was almost invariably seen as a spiritual ability that was thought to reside in the human soul. Some saw it in the human ability to choose our own direction, or the possibility of acting morally, but most often the image of God was linked especially to the human capacity for rational thought. Both in the early church and in medieval theology, reason was seen as that which uniquely separates us from the animals, which have no reason, and that connects us with God. Thomas Aquinas, for instance, saw in human reason a reflection of God's reason, that is, the Logos through which, according to John 1, God created the world (STh I.93.4). Seen from that angle, the image of God is located in the human capacity for thought. Today this idea is hardly defended by anyone, and for good reason.

First, there is the lack of exegetical support. Nothing in the Genesis passages or in the other "image of God" texts in the Bible connects the *imago Dei* with a particular human capacity. This whole approach makes it too tempting to start with what we see in our own cultural environment as our most characteristic element over against animals, and then to read it into the biblical text.

This error has occurred all too often. In fact, Berkhof complains that it is almost possible to write a cultural history of Europe by following the ways in which the *imago Dei* has been explained in dogmatics (CF 184–85). Invariably, theologians looked for what differentiates human beings from the animal kingdom. However, the Bible does not place much emphasis on the unique human capacity for bearing the image of God; even the heavens (Ps 19:1) and the entire creation (Rom 1:19) in certain ways reflect the work and being of God.

Second, many abilities that in the past were regarded as exclusively human (such as the ability to count or to grieve) also occur with some animals, even if these capacities are usually found in humans in exponentially greater measure. Thus, it becomes ever more difficult to select an ability that is exclusively human. Third, the question remains whether all people have this ability. Must we conclude that mentally handicapped people do not bear the image of God or have it to a lesser degree if this being in God's image is to be found in our rational capabilities? A publication of the World Council of Churches (2005, 23) is right in warning against the idea that only "perfect" people—people who are young, successful, and attractive—can fully reflect the image of God. Fourth, the structural approach to the image of God (which views the image of God as a particular structural layer in the human mind) implies a very individualistic concept; each human being is, as an individual, an image of God. This approach stands in tension with the emphasis of Gen 1 on humankind as a whole. Finally, on this approach the nonbodily aspects of our humanness are often put above bodily aspects, which is a priority that does not appear in Gen 1. There the entire human being is an image of God (see also Gen 5:1–3), not just our spirit, soul, or mind.

With good reason nowadays most theologians opt for another approach to the *imago Dei*. Two views, in particular, compete with each other: the so-called functional and relational views. Old Testament scholars point out that the concept of the image of God was well known in Israel's cultural environment (its *Umwelt*), although there it tended to be specifically tied to the king (Neumann-Gorsolke 2004). In neighboring nations the king, as the bearer of God's image, was called to rule society and to care as God's representative for the part of creation that was assigned to him. This responsibility, it is argued, would agree with a remarkable statement in Gen 1:26, namely, the command that humanity rule over the animals, which follows immediately after God decides to make humans after his image and likeness. This sequence, it is said, is not accidental; to be in the image of God is to be called to exercise a certain function—to care for the earth. In this approach the *imago Dei* does not primarily refer to what we are but rather to what we do, or should do: care for the earth.

The reference to the *Umwelt* raises the question of what weight we should give it. Often the Bible clearly breaks with the current way of thinking, which seems to be the case with regard to the ideology of kingship. It is far from accidental that the Bible never refers to the king as the principal bearer of God's image. This lofty designation belongs to each human being or, even more precisely, to humanity as a whole (Neumann-Gorsolke 2004, 314–15; see also Middleton 2005, 204–7)! Moreover, the functional approach, so far as biblical support is concerned, is mostly limited to Gen 1. Reading on from Gen 1 to Gen 2, we meet other uniquely human characteristics. For instance, in contrast with the animals, the human is lonely without a partner with whom to establish a meaningful relationship. When we move on to the New Testament, we discover still other aspects that may be tied to the image of God—especially pneumatological and moral aspects. The image of God receives ever stronger articulation where the Spirit brings people in conformity with the image of Christ, who is the true *imago Dei* (Rom 8:29; 1 Cor 15:49; 2 Cor 3:18; Eph 4:24; Col 3:10; for Christ as God's image, see 2 Cor 4:4; Col 1:15; Heb 1:3).

For a discussion of these texts, see Kelsey 2009, 936–1007; Kelsey (e.g., 956) rightly remarks that, where these New Testament texts attach the image of God to humanity, that image does not characterize a certain essence of the human being but a new identity in Christ, which is the source of the new life- orientation of the Christian faith community. Even so, we find Kelsey's distinction between the what question (What is our essential being?) and the who question (Who are we; what constitutes our identity?) to be somewhat artificial. In any case, it is extremely significant that the New Testament connects the essential aspects of our humanness with the new identity that believers in Christ receive through the Spirit. Therefore, we prefer to follow Grenz (2001) and Pannenberg (2004), who, with their view of the image of God as something yet to be realized, are further developing a famous statement of J. G. Herder: "We are not yet, but are daily trying to become, human beings" (Grenz 2001, 180). We think that texts like Eph 4:24 (about "the new nature, created after the likeness of God in true righteousness and holiness") and Col 3:10 must be interpreted in this soteriological-eschatological manner; they do not primarily point back to the original image of God but say something about God's purpose for those who have been saved in Christ. They connect humanity with the glorified Christ and thereby point to the future. We find ourselves unable to accept the exegesis of Heidelberg Catechism

Lord's Day 6, and wish to point out (contra Genderen and Velema, CRD 328-29, who do accept this exegesis) that salvation does add something to the image of God that was not originally part of it. By sharing in God's glory, the relationship with God becomes "fireproof." For this issue, also see Pannenberg, ST 2:210-15.

When we focus not only on Gen 1 but, as is customary in dogmatics, try to survey the entire biblical witness, we have every reason to take very seriously the relational approach to the *imago Dei*. We already encountered it in Karl Barth, and it has been accepted by many authors since then. Significant hints in this direction can already be found in Luther and Calvin, even though Calvin, in particular, usually still employs the language of the structural approach. The core of the relational view is the relationship that is initiated by God; God addresses us and expects to receive a response. We are the image of God in the sense that, being addressed by God, we will reflect this relationality and give it form in genuine interaction with our world. *In concreto* it is actually about God, who addresses us in his desire that we should live in a personal relationship with him for the sake of other people and of the animals (or even more broadly, for the sake of the entire creation). Supporters of the relational view underline, with Barth, that in Gen 1:27, immediately after the human's creation in the image of God, we read that God created the human male and female. This means, they say, that being in the image of God has everything to do with our fundamental interaction with the other, who is totally different from us but whom we cannot live without and with whom we live in a deep personal relationship.

Note that this description of what the *imago Dei* entails does not require a certain IQ or a measure of physical perfection in order to be a bearer of that image. There is no ideal of perfection that is placed on a pedestal, as if a successful, intelligent, and attractive person would optimally reflect the image of God. The only kind of perfection the gospel requires from us is the perfection of love (Matt 5:48). To the extent that people are able to enter into loving relationships with others, even though because of some handicap they might be mostly on the receiving end, they bear the image of God. In fact, by our lights this receptivity is primary and fundamental, for it fits with the fundamental dogmatic assumption that we are, according to the Christian faith, receivers and not producers of salvation. For further comments, see the document of the World Council of Churches (2005, 22-26) and Reinders 2008. See also the section on baptism in chapter 15. In baptism a particular human being is named and is connected with the Father, the Son, and the Spirit.

In what sense does this relational character reflect divine reality? Some authors argue that the use of the plural in Gen 1:26 is not accidental. Without immediately suggesting (as happened in the past) that this usage refers directly to the doctrine of the Trinity, it seems justified to interpret this plural form as some kind of plurality and relationality in God. God has never been lonely. This view can be maintained even under the interpretation of many biblical scholars, namely, that the first person plural in this verse here refers to the heavenly angelic court that surrounds God. When we then move along to the creation story of Gen 2, we note that the human is put in three relationships and that all three receive full attention: the relationship with God (vv. 8–17), with creation (vv. 15, 18–20), and with other people (vv. 21–25). The refrain of Gen 1 is "God saw that it was good." But only after the man and the woman have been given to each other does it appear that the one thing that was "not good" about creation (2:18) has been remedied. Subsequently, in Gen 3 the so-called fall of humanity is described in terms of a rupture in these same three relationships: the relationship with God (v. 8), with other people (vv. 7, 12, 16), and with creation (vv. 18–19). Later Bible stories will go to great length to explain the result of this rupture in relationships, which supports the idea that the image of God is found in this pure, threefold relationality.

This image of God, however, seems to have been so perverted by hostility and egoism as to raise the question of whether it will ultimately survive (e.g., see Jer 5:1). This question can be answered only in the New Testament by pointing to the true *eikōn* of God: Jesus Christ. He lives in true justice and holiness (Eph 4:24) in his relation with his Father and with all creatures. That is, he stands in those pure, unbroken relationships. While on earth, he was also continuously at work to create relationships with anyone who was open to such. He brings people together through his Spirit in a new community, the body of Christ, in which he does away with the former enmity between us and our God and between people, as he brings reconciliation (Eph 2:14–18). But from the very beginning Jesus Christ, as the antitype of Adam, is also deeply involved with creation (note Mark 1:13). Precisely as the image of the invisible God, he is the Firstborn of the entire creation, in whom everything was created (Col 1:15–16). In short, it seems to us that the relational approach to the image of God does most justice to the full biblical witness and to the sometimes dramatic dynamism in the description of our relationship to God, our fellow human beings, and creation.

Clearly, a Trinitarian approach to anthropology, as discussed in the previous section, provides an additional reason for supporting the relational view. However, we do not believe that the doctrine of the Trinity gives an argument for the relational approach to the image of God; rather, the reverse. When, according to the biblical evidence, our relationality reflects our being made in the image of God, it reinforces the idea that God is not solitary in himself but is a community of persons. For the connection between divine and human persons, see especially Schwöbel and Gunton 1991. We do not accept the frequent objection that the relational view is inadequately supported by the biblical text; apart from the reference to the man-woman relationship in Gen 1:27, this objection usually results from the idea that only detailed exegesis of small, separate units of Scripture can be taken seriously. This assumption fails to recognize the importance of, and even the justification for, considering relevant passages from across the entire canon and interpreting them in light of each other. The nature of the Christian faith demands that various texts should not be treated in isolation but should— while retaining their specific emphasis—be mutually connected in a search for a common design. One such common theme is the relational orientation of both God and humanity, a classic expression of which is the covenant. For further discussion, see 6.4. This relational orientation of human beings naturally presupposes certain structural and functional characteristics (see also Gen 5:3), but we do not see them as defining the image of God.

When we see the structural and functional characteristics of humanness as subordinate to our relational orientation as the true image of God, it leaves us with a number of questions that demand further reflection. First, we must wonder about the relationship between the physical and mental/spiritual aspects of our humanness. If we cannot locate the image of God in certain mental or spiritual capacities, what is the nature and status of these capabilities? More specifically, how do they relate to our body? (7.5). In addition, there is the question of whether we are able to freely enter into relationships, or whether our actions are fully determined by external or internal factors, by our education or our genes. Are we human beings really free in the relevant sense of the word? (7.6). A third question asks what we must say about our sexuality, since we legitimize our choice for the relational interpretation of the image of God on the basis (among other things) of the "male and female he created them" of Gen 1:27. What is the significance of being male or female within the total network of relationships in which we are involved? (7.7). Finally, we must ask how being bearers of the image of God determines the meaning of our human life in the totality of creation (7.8).

7.5. What Ever Happened to the Soul?

Christian theology not only has defined our status as image-bearers of God but also has considered our possession of a soul as an essential difference between humans and animals. We noted above that these two were often seen as one and the same: being in the image of God, it was said, consisted first and foremost in having an immortal soul. The idea of an independent soul that can exist independently from the body has had—and still retains—great significance for large groups of Christians. It is often taken to be the basis of human dignity, or even of the sanctity of human life. Moreover, our spiritual life, in the sense of a life in an intentional relationship with God, has been located in the soul as the deepest core of humanness. This core was thought to survive physical death. The human soul of the believer who has died is still often thought to go to heaven after death, where it will remain with God until the day of resurrection and then be reunited with the risen body.

For traditional interpretations of the nature of the soul, see Green 2004, 5–12. We should not underestimate how deeply these interpretations have become entrenched in the collective subconscious of Christendom over the ages. (One of the authors of this book still clearly remembers how, as a child, he saw the soul as a kind of invisibly small container, somewhere close to his heart.) However, the Protestant tradition has always—and we think, correctly—been somewhat reluctant to speak about the sanctity of life in this connection, since in the Bible the kind of sanctity in question is primarily attributed to God. But Protestants have usually agreed with Roman Catholics on the content of the term "human life," which, in contrast to animal life, is destined for eternity and therefore has something inviolable about it, which cannot be ignored with impunity.

The notion that humans consist of two substances, a body and a separate, nonphysical soul, has been referred to as substance dualism, namely, that there are two kinds of reality, a material and a nonmaterial, which each have a distinct origin. Nowadays this view has become quite controversial, and for good reason. Developments in biology, psychology, and the neurosciences all tend toward the conclusion that humans are much more of an organic unit of soul/spirit and body than has been traditionally thought. Time and again our so-called higher abilities turn out to have a physical substrate in bodily processes, particularly in our brain. To a large extent we must say that we *are* a body, rather than that we merely *have* a body. Science has shown us that concepts that portray the soul as an invisible and inviolable core of human existence lying beneath our physical functions (consciousness, thinking, feeling, etc.) are no longer tenable, for these functions are facilitated by physical and neurological processes in our brain.

For Christians these findings are not problematic per se. For almost simultaneously, biblical scholars have concluded that substance dualism has far less biblical support than had hitherto been thought. The idea of an immortal soul inhabiting a body has roots that are more Greek-philosophical than biblical. It should be noted that the contrast is not black and white, however. On the one hand, important Greek philosophical currents did not follow a dualistic mode (e.g., the Aristotelians and the Stoics). On the other hand, the entire Hellenistic culture was pervaded by dualistic imagery and opinions, and so it is only to be expected that we find these in the New Testament as well. One example occurs in Matt 10:28, where Jesus says, "And do not fear those who kill the body but cannot kill the soul; rather fear him who can destroy both soul and body in hell." We think it is difficult to deny that this wording shows a form of substance dualism. But does it mean that a dualistic understanding of our humanness is therefore biblical? At this point we must be careful. First, it is not too difficult to cite a number of biblical passages with a different view, not only from the more holistically inclined Old Testament, but also from the New Testament. Thus we read in 1 Tim 6:16 that only God possesses immortality, from which we might conclude that the author intends to say that we humans do not have an immortal soul that survives physical death.

But second, and more important, we should realize that such an appeal to separate Bible passages is problematic. When we try to determine what these Bible texts want to convey, we discover that their aim is not to defend a certain anthropological view. For instance, in 1 Tim 6 Paul wants to glorify God, not to make a statement about human nature. Something similar may be said about Jesus's words in Matt 10. Here Jesus wants to encourage his disciples, whose lives are endangered because of following him. They must not be discouraged when they are threatened with death, he says, for they can know that martyrdom will not mean a definite end to their lives. Their opponents cannot damage the deepest core of their existence. They should rather look to God, for God is in charge of matters of life and death. This message is communicated in Matt 10 in dualistic terms that would be universally understood in the contemporary Hellenistic culture.

It is important to use a careful hermeneutic when dealing with this issue, lest things be short-circuited. We see an example of this tendency in the work of the Chinese Christian Ni To-Sheng (1903-72)—better known in the Western world as Watchman Nee—who has been very influential in evangelical circles. In the only study that Nee (1968) allegedly wrote himself, he defends the dogmatic importance of a trichotomous anthropology on the basis of 1 Thess 5:23. Parallel to the triune God, he believes, human beings who are created in the image of God also consist of three elements: soul, spirit, and body. In this view the distinction between spirit and soul is crucial. However interesting these reflections may be, they cannot be accepted as a definition of *the* biblical anthropology. For in 1 Thess 5 Paul wants only to underscore that God's work of sanctification covers all aspects of our humanness, and he does so by using a trichotomous description that was current in Hellenistic culture (contra Shults 2003, 177, we do not feel that this latter aspect is to be denied).

The main thread that runs through the biblical approach to human nature is no doubt basically holistic (as in Berkouwer 1962). In most expressions and reflections the human being as seen as a finely meshed unit, in which such terms as *nephesh* (soul), *basar* (flesh), *ruach* (spirit), and *lev* (heart), and in the New Testament, *pneuma* (spirit), *psychē* (soul), *nous* (mind), *kardia* (heart), and *sōma* (body), each describe this unit from its own specific angle. *Basar*, for instance, often connotes the vulnerability and perishability of our existence; *nephesh* refers to humans as living beings with desires that are ultimately directed toward God as their source of life (Gen 2:7). *Lev* usually points to the "heart" of human existence, where we exercise our will and make decisions. There has been much discussion about Paul's anthropology, but it has not led to any different conclusion. Paul's understanding of human nature is more deeply marked by these Old Testament categories than by Greek-philosophical models. He does not, for instance, assign low value to the body (*sōma*).

At time, however, too little justice is done to the fact that Paul in some places does presuppose an anthropological duality (which differs from dualism)—for instance, when he contrasts the "outer" self with the "inner" self (2 Cor 4:16) and longs for the moment when he can leave his body and live with the Lord (2 Cor 5:8). Gundry 1976 provides a needed correction. For good surveys of Old and New Testament anthropology, see Wolff 1974 and Schnelle 1996, respectively, and for the subject as a whole, see also the essay of Joel Green in Brown et al. 1998b, 149-73.

It seems to us that this main thread in biblical anthropology—the concept of the human person as a psychosomatic unity—not only provides guidance to Christians but also supplies a clarifying framework for understanding many results of scientific research.

At the same time, we must face an important theological question: what implications does the "disappearance of the soul" have for the various functions and meanings that were traditionally attributed to the soul? Must we abandon these too, since all our acts can be reduced to brain functions that cease when we die? This is the message that atheistic "evangelists" such as Daniel Dennett (b. 1942) or, in the Netherlands, Dick Swaab (b. 1944) are eager to have us believe. They usually opt for what has been called a reductive physicalism; namely, we are entirely physical beings, and all our mental, moral, and religious experiences can be reduced to neurophysiological processes. Our spontaneous intuition that there must be something like a human spirit that makes decisions is merely a side effect (a so-called epiphenomenon) of these processes—very understandable and therefore widespread, but factually incorrect.

This physicalism is, in fact, the anthropological side of the worldview that used to be known as materialism and is now often referred to as naturalism (or more specifically, metaphysical naturalism, as distinguished from the merely methodological naturalism that is the common basis for scientific research). The controlling premise in these views is reductionist in nature: there is only matter. That is, there are only natural processes by which everything that needs explanation can be explained. Thus there is no God, and neither is there a human self or an "I." This metaphysical naturalism plays relatively well in the media, but it is generally recognized to be plagued by some major problems. The question remains whether it can do full justice to such phenomena as human consciousness and the human longing for transcendence (see Shults 2003, 182, 190), and even to the human ability to know. On this latter front it has often been argued that our ability to acquire knowledge can hardly be trustworthy if it has evolved in a purely naturalistic manner (see Beilby 2002 and Plantinga 2011, 307-50).

Reductive physicalism is certainly not the only option at hand besides classic substance dualism. There are at least two intermediate options: a moderate dualism and a nonreductive physicalism (see Murphy in Brown et al. 1998b, 24-25, and, for a more detailed survey, Cortez 2010, 69-92). Both have been developed in recent literature in many variations.

We think moderate dualism, as, for instance, defended by Cooper 2002 (see his essay in Farris and Taliaferro 2015, 27-42) and Turl 2010, has better credentials than often thought. Critics of dualism often attack the original Cartesian version without taking into account its more refined contemporary forms. Moderate dualism does recognize the existence of a fundamental ontological difference between spirit and matter but, in contrast to Descartes, does not totally exclude some form of relationship between the two. It is holistic and integrative in nature, in the sense that it stresses our unity as a totality in which body and spirit cooperate in mutual dependence for the sake of functioning well. The core of the human person is therefore not to be identified with a "soul" but with this totality. It remains possible that in death body and soul are separated from each other. Admittedly, we know of no mental life other than what is supported by a physical brain. But this does not mean that with God, who himself (whatever may be the precise meaning of John 4:24a) is to be regarded as a spiritual being, it would be impossible to support mental life in some other way, or even have it function without a physical substrate. It would be shortsighted to conclude that, if we do not know of any other form of life, it therefore cannot exist. However, most Christian dualists believe that only a restricted and preliminary form of existence remains after death, and that it was not without reason that Paul did not really want to be "unclothed" (2 Cor 5:4). The radical rupture that is caused by death must, from a Christian perspective, be taken seriously. But at the same time, the believer may be sure that his or her soul, as the center of consciousness and the bearer of psychical functions, will somehow continue to exist with God.

Most nonreductive physicalists (as in Brown et al. 1998a and Green 2004) tend to be skeptical about the value of any form of dualism, whether moderate or not. Their physicalism, however, is not monistic in nature as is reductive physicalism. There is only one "substance," and it has a material substrate, but the psychical aspects of our humanness are derived from and completely intertwined with this substance. We do not have something apart from our body that we might call a nonmaterial soul. Yet, humans are, in comparison with other species, physical organisms of unparalleled complexity. That complexity led to the emergence of "higher" capabilities, such as the ability to enter into personal relationships, the use of complex forms of language, consciousness of time, moral awareness, and spirituality. Some feel that this process has occurred through the new possibilities that resulted from *emergence*, that is, an increase in intensity and new configurations of separate "lower" abilities. However, the higher mental abilities are not unplanned side effects (i.e., epiphenomena) of, nor can they be simply reduced to, the physical processes from which they originated. The genie has escaped from the bottle, so to speak, and these factors are so real that neurophysiological processes may be, in a reverse direction, influenced by top-down causation. In this way of viewing things, I am more than the sum total of the behavior of the large number of cells and molecules in my brain; I am also, for instance, the one who is responsible for my actions. Likewise, morality and religion are more than useful projections in the evolutionary struggle for survival. The uniqueness of being human, in fact, is that we are profoundly conscious of ourselves, of others, of the world around us, and of God—those things that the Bible points to as the implications of our being in the image of God.

And when we die? Physicalists maintain that dying is really succumbing to death; nothing remains, not even a consciousness. For good reason the Bible refers to death as a radical judgment, an enemy that will be conquered only in the resurrection at the end of time (1 Cor 15:26). Yet, God is able to safeguard our identity in the interim, and the Bible supports and encourages us in believing that this protection will indeed happen. The continued existence of our personal identity through death is not because of an independent and indestructible soul that we carry along with us, however, but only because of the miracle of God's grace. When the Bible confirms the continuity and stability of our "self" through death, its certainty is only in the Spirit of Christ, who has been given to us as a guarantee (2 Cor 5:5). The Bible remains silent about how our personal identity is safeguarded through death. Does God somehow store our unique genetic information package until the day of resurrection? It makes little sense to speculate about such questions, for the dimension of time is also involved; if God is somehow "outside of time," might the same also be true for those who have died? If so, all talk about an interim loses its meaning. Seen in that light, it is not strange that Paul situates his "being with Christ" immediately after his death (Phil 1:23).

Both Roman Catholics and Protestants have traditionally believed that believers will enjoy a conscious relationship with God immediately after death. In the Roman Catholic tradition this teaching was officially confirmed by the Fifth Lateran Council (1513). For many Protestants this became the accepted view, especially after Calvin in 1542 turned against the thought of a so-called soul sleep (according to which the souls of believers have no consciousness until the day of the resurrection). This view is built, in particular, on Luke 23:43 and Phil 1:23. But the exegesis of these texts with regard to their eschatological implications is not without problems; in any case, neither of the two speaks of a human "soul."

However, they do support the concept—as does Job 19:27—of the retention of our human identity in death.

We do not have to make a final choice among the different varieties of nonreductive physicalism and moderate physicalism. Both theories allow us to maintain important functions that in the past were attributed to the soul, and both emphasize how precious we are in the eyes of God. Both theories also find support for many of their main insights in the way that the Bible speaks about human beings. But both also are vulnerable on a number of fronts. For the basics of Christian doctrine, however, it is sufficient here to show the framework within which Christian thought may move. Moreover, Christian thought has from the start been characterized by the required modesty with regard to our future mode of existence. John, for instance, writes, "It does not yet appear what we shall be" (1 John 3:2). Our faith must be satisfied with the knowledge that we will then be with Christ. In this connection, however, it is clear that contemporary physicalist reductionism cannot be reconciled with this hope, which belongs to the heart of the Christian faith.

The body-soul problem continues to baffle us. Although we have at our disposal more data than ever about the interaction between our brain and our mental experiences, opinions remain divided, and much remains unclear. We perhaps may never be able to fully comprehend the interaction between body and spirit. This would be like a computer that understands its own software—which is simply impossible. Such awareness of our own limitations, however, is deeply rooted in the Bible. It is precisely because we cannot grasp the secret of our humanness that we can continue to be endlessly amazed and wonder about the unbelievably beautiful and complex way in which we are made, for which we praise God (Ps 139:14).

We would like to add in this connection that, with the demise of substance dualism, the so-called capability theory, or faculty psychology, must also be regarded as obsolete. In many traditional dogmatics, from Augustine and Aquinas via Calvin (*Inst.* 1.15.7) to Voetius and other post-Reformation theologians, the human cognitive and volitional capabilities (mind and will) were seen as more or less independently operating faculties of the human soul. Much attention was given to their exact nature and mutual relationships. The most important question was usually, which faculty was to be considered primary? For Aquinas it was the intellect, while for Duns Scotus and others it was the will. Shults (2003, 180) rightly comments: "What were once called the faculties of the soul are now described as registers of the behavior of the whole person. Today personality as a whole is seen as the basis for understanding the parts." As a result, discussions about this issue are now largely obsolete. However, justice may be done to these traditional functions of the soul within a holistic framework. The transition to this new anthropological framework even set in motion a revaluation of the stepchild among the human faculties, our feelings and affections. Traditionally, these functions were counted among the lower capabilities and located at the level of our instincts, or at best in the animal soul (the part of our mental life that we share with animals). The humanities have more recently paid much more attention to the nature of our affects, emotions, and passions, since it has become clear that they are no less an authentic part of our personhood than rationality, and perhaps can hardly be distinguished from it. There is nothing wrong with this revaluation from a Christian perspective, considering the important role played by human, and even divine, emotions in the Bible.

7.6. Freedom

Closely related to the discussion about body and soul is the question of whether we are, as human beings, free in a significant way. One of the functions traditionally attributed to the human soul was as a "home" to our free will. Can we still maintain that we have a free will if we have no independent soul? Christian theology often deals with this question in the context of the doctrine of providence (as, recently, by Higton, CD), but the issue also presents itself as anthropological, apart from questions about the relationship between God's acts and ours. For that reason we will deal with this matter first. The question is: when I perform a particular act, can it be traced back to my conscious choice? Might I have chosen to act differently? Or does this freedom only seem to be so? Is my behavior fully determined by my genetic constitution and the outside influences that have an impact upon me?

Is everything controlled by nature and nurture, as it is increasingly argued by neuroscientists, who point to the way in which our brain functions? Experimental research by the American neurophysiologist Benjamin Libet (1916-2007) suggests that in many cases our brain already makes decisions before we are consciously aware of what is happening. Along the same line, brain researcher Victor Lamme (b. 1959) published a popular scientific book with the challenging title *Free Will Is a Fiction* (2010), even though he offers no proof for that claim in his book. He merely shows that our decision-making is to a great extent influenced by external stimuli, which means that the influence of our consciousness on our actions is not as significant as we are inclined to think. Lamme's book title fits with a contemporary trend that is usually referred to as *hard determinism*—the position that our behavior is so determined by causal factors that we can no longer speak of free choices. According to other scholars who are working in this field, including Libet himself but also the influential Portuguese neurologist Antonio Damasio (b. 1944), the available empirical data do not necessarily lead to that conclusion.

Looking at the *philosophical* discussion of the matter, we find that hard determinism has few supporters. An important argument against it is that it runs contrary to common sense, and philosophical theories that go against common sense always seem very problematic. For example, when I compose this sentence the way I do, it would seem that I have made a conscious decision to do so; I could have chosen to use other words, but the words I have typed seemed the best to me. Likewise for my coauthor: when he evaluates whether he agrees with what I have written or would like to see some changes, he will have some good reasons for what he does or does not want to say and will act accordingly. The fact that neuroscientists do not encounter the "I" in their research and are thus unable to locate it does not imply that it therefore does not exist. When we think no longer along Cartesian lines but holistically, it seems obvious that our I does not coincide with our consciousness but is more closely intertwined with our total psycho-physical existence—and with that ever-mysterious entity that continuously seems to slip away from us, which we refer to as the "person."

In any case, philosophy offers two other options that dominate the discussion, namely, *compatibilism* (also at times referred to as soft determinism) and *libertarianism*. Compatibilism argues that our actions may be causally determined but that they may nonetheless be considered to be free to the extent that they are inspired by our own wishes, motives, and intentions. They are not determined by external factors, as happens, for instance, when a man surrenders his money to a robber who threatens him with a gun; rather, they arise from internal factors, like my own wishes, motives, and intentions. In actual fact, I have no option but to be guided by my wishes, motives, and intentions—and in that sense I am determined. However, this is compatible with genuine freedom, since I am usually happy to be led by those wishes, motives, and intentions without anyone forcing me to. In contrast, libertarianism argues that all talk about such freedom is misguided, since we can be truly free only if we have genuine freedom to choose. It believes that the chain of physical causes and consequences is not closed, that there is true contingency and therefore true freedom in the way we act. I may perform action A, but I could, at the same moment, also have opted for action B, or I may not have acted at all.

A good survey of the debate, written by representatives of the various positions, is offered in Kane 2002 (for Libet's view, see 551-64). A short but clear presentation of the main arguments for and against compatibilism and libertarianism is found in Cortez 2010, 98-130. The arguments have become extremely complex, but it does not mean that a final solution is in sight. For concisely formulated but solid arguments against hard determinism, see Schoberth 2006, 142-43; for further literature, see Higton, CD 214.

When we turn from science and philosophy to Christian theology, we also find a diversity of opinion with regard to the question of whether human beings have true freedom of action. In the first centuries the Greek fathers rather unreservedly attributed free will to human beings. They focused on the Sermon on the Mount and the call to holy living. This position changed when Augustine moved away from his previous support of the idea of human free will. This was not due, as has often been thought, to his polemic with the British monk Pelagius; it resulted, rather, from his earlier reflections on the nature of grace. Augustine saw ever more clearly that grace must imply that, as humans, we owe our salvation fully to God. If we could choose to become Christians by opting to believe, it would mean we could earn our own salvation; in fact, God would be dependent on us, rather than the reverse. We do not find this approach in the Bible, however, because it goes against God's sovereignty. Therefore, Augustine concluded, the human will is not free, for it is bound by evil. When that bondage lifts and we arrive at our final destiny, it will be 100 percent free because, in his love, God sets us free and saves us.

The greatest minds in the history of theology—Luther, Calvin, Schleiermacher, Barth, but also Thomas Aquinas—agreed with Augustine. Our own will is not free to realize what is truly significant in life; we must fully depend on God's choice (about God's choosing, see 15.9). In his polemic with Erasmus on "the bondage of the will," Luther strongly emphasized the following point: we are like horses ridden by someone, either God or the devil. Just as with Augustine, Luther's view was rooted in his doctrine of grace. *Sola gratia* implies that we do not have free will when it comes to our eternal salvation, that grace is provided purely on the basis of divine compassion. Luther did not, however, deny every form of free choice in our daily life; on the contrary, he recognized that the free judgment of our will (the so-called *liberum arbitrium*) applies to matters that do not involve our relationship with God. In that sense this free judgment of the human will is part of our anthropological structure. Even though, because of the power of sin, we are no longer able to choose the good and have become slaves of the devil, our humanness still allows us to choose from various options in our everyday actions. Calvin does not deny this conclusion, although he felt it did not provide enough warrant for calling human beings free. He called this "so proud a title" for "so small a matter" (*Inst.* 2.2.7).

We must place this reluctance on the part of the Reformers in the context of the increased value the Renaissance attached to the phenomenon of the human being. In his *Oration on the Dignity of Man*, one of the most famous philosophical statements of the fifteenth century, the Italian philosopher Pico della Mirandola (1463-94) offered a startling formulation of this new view. Pico argued that God made us human beings in such a way that we ourselves can fully determine who we are. We are the only creatures who can be what we want to be, and the entire world lies open before us. We may strive for the higher things, for the purity of the angels, but we can also debase ourselves and behave like animals. This is true freedom, living the way one chooses to live. Even though Pico mixed this scintillating awareness of unlimited, but also dangerous, human freedom and autonomy with many strange esoteric elements, and even though we should not call his view optimistic (something later Kantians, who saw Pico as a precursor of Kant, have not sufficiently recognized), it does give a clear picture of the new intellectual climate of the Renaissance. It is precisely this climate of self-aggrandizement that the Reformers resisted because they saw it as the seed of a loose-from-God movement. As late as the mid-eighteenth century the American pastor-philosopher Jonathan Edwards followed Calvin in opposing the libertarian approach to the concept of freedom. In his book *The Freedom of the Will* (1754), Edwards defends compatibilism. As humans, we may freely choose what seems desirable to us, but what seems desirable to us depends on our inner disposition, which is part of how God created us. Human freedom therefore does not imply autonomy with respect to God.

Today the situation has changed, however. The greatest challenge to a Christian anthropology does not come primarily from liberal humanists who attribute unlimited freedom to human beings (that position has become rather outmoded, at least in science and philosophy), but from those who defend the kind of hard determinism we referred to above, which, with an appeal to science, *denies* all human freedom. Accordingly, some theologians of late have directed their guns particularly at the determinism that, to put it in everyday language, leaves us at the mercy of our genes. On the one hand, they take inspiration from Christian thinkers of the past who rejected the conceptual framework of philosophical determinism; on the other hand, they seek to demonstrate how an alternative to determinism is also possible today.

In the Reformed tradition we find examples of the first, historical approach with Asselt et al. 2010. This research group went back to some of their earlier publications on the concept of contingency as proposed by the profound medieval thinker Duns Scotus; Labooy 2002 offers a good example of the second, systematic approach. For a broad survey of the history of the Christian view of freedom, see Brinkman 2003.

By their support for libertarianism these contemporary theologians underline our responsibility for our own actions much more forcefully than any form of compatibilism would permit. This responsibility is not only in many ways presupposed and emphasized in the Bible, but it also facilitates current thinking about justice and morality. Whereas we hear from the hard determinists that our actions always have a neurobiological substrate, and from compatibilism that our actions are to great degree prompted by external forces (think, in our consumerist society, of the media, advertising, and fashion), we hear from the libertarianists that, in the midst of all these forces, there remains a degree of personal, responsible freedom that cannot be reasoned away in causal terms.

More needs to be said, however, for when—after hearing from science, philosophy, and theology—we go to the Bible, we find that the concept of freedom is more embedded in a soteriological than in an anthropological context. Freedom is not something we possess as creatures as a matter of course but *something to which God has freed us*. We take this point of view to be theologically decisive. In the Old Testament the liberating activity of God leads first of all to external societal freedom (in fact, the primordial experience of the delivery from Egypt is constitutive for Israel's faith in God); then gradually the accent shifts to inner personal freedom. "If the Son makes you free, you will be free indeed," the Johannine Jesus says to his Jewish discussion partners (John 8:36). This is such a foundational statement that its significance goes far beyond its immediate context. How can we relate this biblical view of freedom to the contemporary debates we referenced above? We would say, by thoroughly reconsidering where both the compatibilist and the libertarianist concepts of freedom lead us. If libertarianism is right, and I have the freedom to opt for action A or for action B without being determined by anyone, it remains totally unclear why I should choose to perform A rather than B. I could choose A, but I might just as well choose B and give equally good reasons for either choice. My eventual choice, therefore, is quite arbitrary. But if compatibilism is right, I may perform all kinds of voluntary acts while remaining a slave to my own inclinations, wishes, and passions. These do not always carry me where I want to go, let alone to my destination.

This disagreeable dilemma between arbitrariness and obstinacy shows us that we need a definition of the content of "genuine" freedom. To cite a famous distinction made by Isaiah Berlin (1958): freedom cannot be understood only in negative terms, as a state in which we are free from all sorts of powers and influences. It needs some positive content; it is also, and perhaps even primarily, the freedom to lead a good and authentic life. In this connection we may describe such a life as one in which we are not subject to addictive powers (including our own ego) or to misguided ideologies that enslave us, but in which we can be ourselves. In Christian terms, this is the kind of life "in the truth" to which God has set us free through Jesus Christ in the Spirit. This life is something that continues until we have, in the eschaton, reached the "glorious liberty of the children of God" (Rom 8:21). The Christian concept of freedom, thus, is above everything else Trinitarian and eschatological in nature; our freedom is not found behind us or in us but before us, because of the redemptive work of the triune God. When viewed from this angle, freedom constitutes an integral part of the *imago Dei*.

We saw earlier that the image of God in us must be understood relationally; it impacts our interhuman relationships and no less our relationship to God. Only when we live in an open relationship with God will we reach our destiny—which will happen definitively in the eschaton. Almost unanimously, the Christian tradition has expressed this thought of our innate search for a relationship with God in its teaching of the *desiderium naturale*, the "natural desire" for God that characterizes our humanness and makes us unique as compared with the animal kingdom. One does not need to be a believer to clearly see the point here. "In the heart of creation I have discovered an empty space, in which God, if he exists, would fit wonderfully well," wrote Dutch author Frans Kellendonk (1951–90; the quote is from an essay published in 1987). In fact, this quote became his most well-known sentence, though he added to it that unfortunately we cannot say that where our intellect ends faith begins. The unsurpassed classic formulation of the *desiderium naturale* comes from Augustine, in the opening paragraph of his famous *Confession* (1.1.1), which we quoted earlier:

> Man desires to praise thee, for he is a part of thy creation; he bears his mortality about with him and carries the evidence of his sin and the proof that thou dost resist the proud. Still he desires to praise thee, this man who is only a small part of thy creation. Thou hast prompted him, that he should delight to praise thee, for thou hast made us for thyself, and restless is our heart until it comes to rest in thee.

Restless is our heart until it comes to rest in God—this primordial experience runs like a red thread through the history of Roman Catholic as well as Protestant theology. True freedom is to serve God and live before him, because for this end we have been made. Fish do not become free when, because of a *liberum arbitrium*, they have the choice whether to live on the land or in the water. They have no life on the land, and thus they are free only when they are fish in the water.

The decisive point is not whether we have become Christians simply because we grew up in a Christian milieu or because we consciously made that choice. Who can fully discover the origin of personal faith anyhow? The same is true for other worldviews; one might, for instance, become an atheist from living in a certain cultural environment. Much more decisive is the question of whether it is true that only under an open heaven can we reach our destiny of true freedom. That this is indeed the case is the bold claim that Christian theology has placed on the table of culture over the centuries. For various examples and witnesses (among them Karl Barth, who was often said to deny the *desiderium naturale*), see Bok and Plaisier 2005. For the Trinitarian approach to the concept of freedom referred to above, we point to Higton, CD 195-201.

7.7. Sexuality

If being in the image of God must primarily be seen in terms of our relationality, this understanding, as discussed above, is closely tied to the context in which the image of God is presented in Gen 1:27. Immediately after the statement that God created us in his image, we are told that

God created us male and female. Thus it would seem that our gender is another fundamental defining aspect of our humanness. This conclusion fully accords with our present experience, in which sexuality plays a role in almost everything. Few things more profoundly preoccupy—also divide—people, churches, and societies than discussions about the experience of sexuality. These discussions almost always tend to be ethical in nature: they concern actions and what may be called good or not good in those actions. We will not deal with these matters concretely in this textbook on dogmatics, but as we saw in chapter 1, dogmatics and ethics are closely linked. For that reason in this section we pursue the meaning of our sexuality for theological anthropology. We will argue that discussions about the ethical dimensions of sexuality can be meaningful only if we give high priority to the question of the significance of God's having created us as sexual beings.

Many dogmaticians do not deal with this question. Gunton (CF 38–56), for instance, does have a chapter "Man and Woman," but despite the title he does not touch on the meaning of our sexual nature. We feel that a contemporary dogmatics should not skip this subject, if only because sexuality is indeed omnipresent in our open society, and because the way in which we deal with our sexuality is quite generally seen as one of the determining factors for our personal identity. This climate raises various questions and makes Christian theological reflection on the meaning and purpose of sexuality very relevant.

As a start, we must ask ourselves how essential our sexuality actually is for our humanness. We need to be realistic at this point. Sexuality is not everything, and those who are hardly, or not at all, involved in sexual activities can be excellent and complete human beings. Not surprisingly, on this matter the New Testament is quite relativizing in tone. In the light of the eschatological expectation that is raised by the parousia of Jesus Christ, people might consider relinquishing sexual bonds and relationships, as it might help them to be more oriented toward the coming kingdom (Matt 19:12; 1 Cor 7).

This line of thinking has exerted significant influence in the history of the church. It provides a warrant for voluntary or involuntary celibacy. But isolated from the Bible as a whole, this idea carries major risks. It can soon lead to the idea that sexuality, when considered more closely, belongs to the ambiguous terrain of evil and is not part of God's good creation. Even though that inference directly contradicts Genesis's words "male and female God created them," Gregory of Nyssa, for example, held that God created humans in this way in anticipation of the fall into sin (*De opificio hominis* [On the creation of man], 17; NPNF² 5:406-7). Because of the fall, the human race was doomed to die and would soon have become extinct had there been no provision for procreation. To prevent that consequence, God supposedly invented sexuality. Gregory and his supporters found an argument for their position in the gospel passage where the Sadducees question Jesus about the resurrection of the dead. Jesus replies that, in the resurrection, people will no longer marry but will be like the angels in heaven (Matt 22:30). This comment has been taken as proof that gender differences are intended only as a temporary emergency measure.

The text, however, does not say this. Jesus does not speak of our gender differences but only indicates that in the eschaton marriage will disappear. In this regard we will be like the angels because we will no longer marry. Apparently, marriage with all its legal ramifications is not essential for our human identity. From the first creation story, however, we see that our being male and female, however, *is* essential, for it connects our sexuality not with our sinful state but with our creaturely status. The idea that human sexuality must be regarded as a necessary evil cannot be distilled from the Genesis text. There our being male or female is presented as a matter of great importance for the way in which being in God's image was intended by God. Our sexuality is not a kind of secondary embellishment of what is at root asexual. An asexual human being is an abstraction. We do not have a genderless or bisexual core that relativizes our male or female state, but from the very first God created us as thoroughly physical, sexual beings: male and female God created us.

A Christian anthropology pleads for a recognition of sexuality as an essential part of our humanness. This recognition is tied to the positive view of our physical existence, which characterizes Christian teaching from beginning to end. For eschatology, this positive view meant that the early Christians began to articulate their faith in the resurrection of the body as they were challenged by a flood of Hellenistic worldviews that saw the body merely as an insignificant and temporary shell (see further chap. 16). In contrast to Neoplatonic-oriented common sense, Christians regarded the body not as belonging to the empire of evil but as part of God's good creation.

The recognition of our physical nature and sexuality as fundamental aspects of our humanness also is psychologically important, since the alternative often leads to repression. Those who repress their sexual nature are often later confronted with it in an uncontrolled and harmful manner.

Does this mean, then, that we are from our very beginning born as a man or a woman with all that difference entails? Are the typical biological, psychological, emotional, and social differences between men and women, as we see them around us, simply a matter of genetics? Yes, answer the so-called gender-essentialists. They argue that the physiological differences between men and women lead to essential differences at other levels. For instance, men are usually stronger, more aggressive, and more competitive, while women tend to be more empathetic and cooperative. As a popular book title puts it, "Men Are from Mars, Women Are from Venus." Men are more interested in achievements, women in relationships. Essentialists point to scientific research that suggests that many such differences between men and woman do not depend on cultural environment. Our views on gender—our ideas of what is typically male or female—are in that sense not arbitrary but depend on differences in the biological constitution of men and women. Who we are is closely related to the body in which we were born. Theologically, this view is often linked to the idea of God's *creation ordinances*, with "male and female he created us" thus implying that men and women have different tasks and roles in life, which it would be wrong to challenge.

Admittedly, there are intrinsic differences between men and women, and neither persons nor societies will function optimally when they are ignored. But more needs to be said because much of what we consider to be typically male or female is undoubtedly culturally determined.

When we remove all cultural sediments, we would probably find that there are equally significant differences within the genders as there are between them. Therefore, *social constructivists* emphasize in this debate the critical role our sociocultural context plays in developing gender images. Some of them want to differentiate between gender and sex, with "gender" meaning the culturally determined psychological roles of men and women, and "sex" designating universal biological gender characteristics. However, this differentiation is also controversial.

For instance, many "typically male" and "typically female" traits can be related to the structure and the size of a specific part of our brain, the corpus callosum, which differs for adult males and females. It is often overlooked that such biological differences may, over time, very well be related to the stimuli that result from cultural stereotypes about how a man or a woman is supposed to act; some research does indeed point in that direction. We know that our brains are flexible and are shaped by our experience, among other things. Also, some hormonal differences may be under- or overemphasized by our milieu. Then there are transsexuals, an often forgotten group in the Christian community. Their stories remind us that our gender is not as (or no more) univocally fixed as we have often tended to assume. In a way Simone de Beauvoir was undoubtedly correct when she suggested that women are not born as, but are made into, women—and the same applies to men. A good survey of this discussion is provided by Cortez 2010, 47-57.

At the same time, our sexuality (even if we take the phenomenon of transsexuality into account) unmistakably has a deeply rooted physiological substrate, which undercuts the credibility of social-constructivism in its extreme form.

Seen from a theological angle, we do not need to retract our statement that our sexuality has been decisive for our humanness from the very start, for "male and female God created us." In this light, our sexual identity is, in principle, a fact of nature. Yet, we should refrain from using it as a basis for sanctioning certain stereotypical role patterns, perhaps with an appeal to the divine creation order referred to above. Subconsciously, we run the risk of making all kinds of individual or collective ideals and preferences into absolute truths, as happened for long periods in the past when, with a dubious appeal to 1 Tim 2:15, married women were considered unsuitable for the labor market. We want to make this risk very clear, also as Reformed theologians, for ever since Calvin (*Inst.* 1.1.12), Reformed theology in particular has developed an acute sensitivity to the sin of idolatry, namely, creating certain fixed images and then regarding them as divine.

Having come thus far, it is important also to pose the question of what might be the purpose of our sexuality from a theological viewpoint—that is, when viewed on the basis of our relationship with God. Traditionally, this purpose has often been sought in the need to procreate, which certainly is an important aspect. Augustine and major segments of the church ever since (in particular, Roman Catholics) were able to point in this connection to Gen 1:28, where these newly created beings were immediately addressed as man and woman with the words: "Be fruitful and multiply, and fill the earth." Elsewhere in the Bible fertility is invariably presented as a sign of blessing, and infertility is seen as a curse, because life is ceasing rather than continuing. Nonetheless, it is not correct to regard procreation as the only purpose of our sexuality. If that were the case, a major part of humanity (including Jesus of Nazareth) would not be fully fledged humans. If our sexuality is essential for who we are and can find its purpose only in the sexual act of procreation, every person who is unable to have children would be an incomplete human being. That would be to give sexuality and procreation too much honor. The second creation story immediately adds to the first account that, apart from this aspect of procreation, man and woman belong together ("a helper fit for").

This line of thought prompted other, especially Protestant, theologians to look for the essence of our sexuality in our *relationality*—in our natural proclivity for mutual relationships. As already discussed, there is good reason to unfold the meaning of our being created in God's image in that direction; we have been made and called in such a way that we may reflect on a creaturely level the personal relationship between Father, Son, and Holy Spirit, and respond to the relationship God has initiated with us. There is an *analogia relationis* between God and us—not an analogy in essence (*analogia entis*) but a divinely initiated likeness in being directed toward the other. Yet, it remains problematic to follow Karl Barth (CD III/1:185–86; III/2:291–92; see also III/4, §54.1) by tying our human sexuality to this analogy, as if the *imago Dei* would be found simply in our sexual polarity. For there are many kinds of different relationships, and the image of God may just as well be reflected in nonsexual relationships of friendship and interpersonal involvement as in sexual relationships. Why, then, focus on our sexuality? Would something be lost if we did not have it? Even when (following Barth and McFadyen 1990, 31–32), we regard sexual relationships as paradigmatic in comparison with other kinds of relationships, this position does not make them essential. Those who view the gender difference in more general terms as a mutual relational interaction ignore its physical aspect. The Bible (e.g., in the Song of Songs) does not. So the question remains as to what might be the theological significance of the fact that we are physical-sexual beings.

Stanley Grenz (1950–2004), an American theologian, may help us in our reflections by his defining the meaning of human sexual differentiation in terms of *bonding*, that is, of connection and attachment. At the deepest level our sexuality has to do with our inborn desire to be attached to someone else, as we realize that in ourselves we are lonely and incomplete. The second creation story makes this desire clear in a sublime narrative (Gen 2:4–25). The created human appears to find fulfillment in nothing or no one else except in that other human being who is so similar and yet so different. It is, we believe, this deeply rooted need for a long-lasting completion of our own unfulfilled existence that forms the core of our sexuality. The primary and prototypical manner in which this basic desire for bonding and solidarity is expressed occurs in the lifelong bond of the heterosexual marriage, with sexual unity as its physical aspect. In theological-anthropological perspective this latter aspect finds its real place in such an enduring union. The sexual union destroys our isolation even more when it proves to be fertile and leads to new life (Gen 4). But those who have no children or have not married will also recognize this deep longing for being loved and giving love, for a relationship of mutual understanding, assistance, joy, and satisfaction. Those who have no sense of this longing do indeed miss out on a vital aspect of being human. In that sense sexuality is essential to our humanity.

See Grenz 2001, 276–303 (also for a discussion of the question how our sexuality, so defined, reflects something of God); see also the summary in Cortez 2010, 64–67. If the term "sex" is derived, via *sexus*, from the Latin *secare* (to cut), we must conclude that the above definition is close to the etymological background; as cut-off and divided beings we are incomplete, and we seek to end this situation in an enduring relationship with the other (Nelson and Longfellow 1993, xiv). We should not jump to the conclusion that such a "lofty" view is impossible nowadays because of the infinitely more "ordinary" approach of evolutionary biology. As typically portrayed, the latter tells us that human sexuality, like that of animals, is determined by aggression and dominance in the struggle to pass on our own genes. Females want the best genes for their progeny, while males are first of all interested in sex. This difference inevitably leads to a conflict of interests between the two genders, which results in endless misery. For a much more nuanced approach within evolutionary biology, in which sexuality is described (with empirical data) as an essentially cooperative enterprise toward a common goal, see the work of the evolutionary biologist Joan Roughgarden (2004).

These various thoughts imply that we will remain sexual beings until the eschaton. Marriage and its potential for procreation will then no longer exist; we already saw how the Christian tradition rejected that possibility from its inception. But the proclivity toward bonding, the desire for the completion of ourselves by finding our identity in the other, will find its final fulfillment in perfect communion with God and the new humanity. Such thinking explains why in the New Testament, wherever this eschatological future finds a foretaste in the individual and collective communion of faith in Christ, the emphasis on the man-woman relationship as the primary expression of our sexual desire fades away in light of this much more comprehensive perspective. Not without reason the

Roman Catholic doctrine of grace has made marriage one of the sacraments and thereby a foretaste of our eternal future.

We believe that the many concrete issues of sexual ethics must be approached with this *theological* view of the nature and purpose of human sexuality in mind. This perspective may not lead to unanimity (e.g., on the issue of same-sex marriages), but it may prevent hasty conclusions.

7.8. The Meaning of Life

We end this chapter with a short discussion about the question of the destiny of human life. What is the purpose of our life on earth? What is the meaning of our existence? These questions are as basic as they are broad. It would be easy to ignore them, for instance, by assuming that life has no intrinsic meaning, or by appealing to the common postmodern assumption that each person must discover that meaning for himself or herself. The Christian tradition, however, has neither avoided the question nor regarded it as unanswerable. The *Westminster Shorter Catechism* (1647) takes it to be the core of the Christian faith. We quote its famous opening passage (BC 175):

> *Question:* What is the chief end of man?
> *Answer*: Man's chief end is to glorify God, and to enjoy him forever.

That is, we are here on earth to glorify God and enjoy God in our lives. This answer naturally raises the next question, how may we may do this? At this point the misunderstanding may easily creep in that we glorify God particularly with "higher, spiritual" activities, such as through song, prayer, and donating money to the church and to mission organizations. In themselves these actions are indeed activities that can glorify God. Yet, they are not the first answer when we ask about the purpose of life. It is much better to listen first to the Bible stories about the creation of human beings. There we find explicit mention of the reason why we have been placed on this earth. We think, first of all, of the human *bonding* that we discussed in the previous section: natural relationships of love, loyalty, protection, and solidarity with our immediate environment. These in large measure determine what we live for, which is good.

But there is more to be said. In traditional dogmatics not only marriage but also work was seen as a God-given creation ordinance. This conclusion was based on the passages we read from Gen 1; immediately following "male and female he created them" comes "be fruitful and multiply, and fill the earth and subdue it; and have dominion over the fish of the sea and over the birds of the air and over every living thing that moves upon the earth" (v. 28). From early on, these lines have drawn much attention in the dogmatic reflection of the church. In just a few words they indicate that the newly created beings were charged with inhabiting the earth and making it inhabitable. The term "cultural mandate" has often been used in this context; it might also be expressed in such terms as "nature mandate," "creation charge," and "stewardship" to capture the commission we have here to deal with the creation in a responsible manner. Regardless of the terms we choose, we want to point to the key issue at stake.

The term "cultural mandate" was coined by K. Schilder (1890-1952), but the underlying idea is found earlier in A. Kuyper. The term has been adopted by, among others, American thinkers such as Francis Schaeffer (1912-84) and the Chinese church leader and theologian Kong Hee (b. 1964).

Broadly speaking, the issue of stewardship involves our work. Whether we are baker, software developer, artist, or worker in a protected setting for handicapped people, through our work we make a thousandfold contribution to the development of the hidden possibilities in creation. In large measure, this action gives meaning to the destiny of our life. By performing our daily tasks, we fulfill an important divine mandate and glorify God. We should note that the Bible does not introduce this mandate only after Gen 3, as if dealing with a result of sin. Work is not a collateral of sin but a part of creation—which may lead us to conclude that in the eschaton there will be not only song but also work! At the same time, we should not overemphasize this theme, for with good reason Gen 1 immediately goes on to speak of how God rested from his work, thus establishing a rhythm of work and rest that continues to be a blessing and remains for us a valuable directive (Exod 20:8). But at bottom it means that performing our daily work is definitely more than a necessary evil.

This awareness has remained stronger in Protestant theology and spirituality than in the Roman Catholic tradition. Faced with the high value that the latter placed on the celibacy of the clergy, Luther broadened the parameters: every vocation (as the word indicates) is a calling and is thus related to God. One kind of work is not higher than another, just as celibacy is not higher than married life. The important thing is to find our own task and place where we can develop and thus glorify God.

Even today, when the labor market has become far more flexible and diverse than in the past, we still do well to regard our work, and shape our task, as a meaningful contribution to the care and development of creation, in the service of humanity, and for the glory of God. Anthropology has confirmed that such an extrinsic orientation gives more satisfaction than earning a high salary or owning a prominent brand of whatever. The Canadian philosopher Charles Taylor (b. 1931) has helped us understand that the human self—also in our day and age—can develop fully only when it looks for the meaning of existence in social bonds, and when one's way of life is oriented toward "the higher things" that go beyond one's own individual existence. In addition, Taylor (himself a Roman Catholic) pleads (1989), in agreement with Luther and others, for a revaluation of ordinary life.

The cultural mandate can be especially linked to science, and there is something to be said for this connection. Certainly science has played a major role in the "subjecting" of the earth—unfortunately more than in protecting it—and has deep roots in the Judeo-Christian view of creation. With all their critical considerations (which are required regarding every way that science can be abused), Christians, in principle, have a positive attitude toward scientific research and its results.

It is important in this connection to be well aware of the specific relationship between the nonhuman creation and God. As we saw in the previous chapter, there are different answers to the question of how responsible Christianity might be for the ecological crisis, but the Bible is clear in many places that animals and plants, too, are intended to flourish to the glory of God. This teaching is certainly food for thought in our time and should stimulate us to give optimal care to our climate and environment.

So-called ecotheologians rightly reflect on how to avoid or resist any form of anthropocentrism in our Christian-anthropological reflection. We do not think that this caution requires us to apply the doctrine of the *imago Dei* to nonhuman organisms or to deny our human uniqueness. Nor is it viable to deny the mandate given at creation as the special calling and task that human beings have with regard to God's creation. However, we must define this calling, more pointedly than has been done in the past, with an awareness that we do not stand far above the world but that we are an integral part of all the processes that make it what it is. The idea that we have a privileged position as rulers over all of creation has caused much harm; we should no longer feed this notion but oppose it. The world is not our home where we can take it easy with our feet on the table; the intention is that the world will become God's home (Rev 21).

The thoughtful reflections of Conradie 2005 are important in this connection (regarding what has been said above, see in particular 9–16). In passing, he also provides valuable insights regarding the rapidly growing corpus of ecotheological literature. For a link between ecotheology and some classic Reformed ideas, see Conradie 2011.

The best way to understand our place in the totality of creation may well be to interiorize the spirituality of Ps 8. This psalm certainly emphasizes the special position of men and women in the midst of the other creatures; we have been entrusted with the care of the earth. But precisely because we are so conscious of the glory and majesty of the Creator, we will execute our tasks with utmost care. Whenever the psalmist sees God's handiwork—and today we see its unmatched complexity far more clearly and deeply—he is reminded of his own smallness, insignificance, and dependence:

> When I look at thy heavens, the work of thy fingers,
> the moon and the stars which thou hast established;
> what is man that thou art mindful of him,
> and the son of man that thou dost care for him?

(vv. 3–4)

The question mark at the end of this quotation expresses wonder and amazement. The aim of Christian theological reflection is not to reason that marvel away, but rather to keep and intensify it.

References

Asselt, Willem J. van, et al. 2010. *Reformed Thought on Freedom: The Concept of Free Choice in Early Modern Reformed Theology*. Grand Rapids: Baker Academic.

Beilby, James K., ed. 2002. *Naturalism Defeated? Essays on Plantinga's Evolutionary Argument against Naturalism*. Ithaca, NY: Cornell University Press.

Berkouwer, Gerrit C. 1962. *Man: The Image of God*. Grand Rapids: Eerdmans.

Berlin, Isaiah. 1958. *Two Concepts of Liberty*. Oxford: Clarendon.

Bok, Nico den, and Arjan Plaisier, eds. 2005. *Bijna goddelijk gemaakt: Gedachten over de menselijke gerichtheid op God* [Made almost divine: Thoughts on human directness toward God]. Zoetermeer: Boekencentrum.

Brinkman, Martien E. 2003. *The Tragedy of Human Freedom: The Failure and Promise of the Christian Concept of Freedom in Western Culture*. Amsterdam: Rodopi.

Brown, Warren S., Nancey Murphy, and H. Newton Malony. 1998a. *Scientific and Theological Portraits of Human Nature*. Minneapolis: Fortress.

———, eds. 1998b. *Whatever Happened to the Soul?* Minneapolis: Fortress.

Conradie, Ernst M. 2005. *An Ecological Christian Anthropology: At Home on Earth?* Aldershot: Ashgate.

———. 2011. *Creation and Salvation: Dialogue on Abraham Kuyper's Legacy for Contemporary Ecotheology*. Leiden: Brill.

Cooper, John W. 2002. *Body, Soul, and Life Everlasting: Biblical Anthropology and the Monism-Dualism Debate*. Grand Rapids: Eerdmans. Orig. pub., 1989.

Cortez, Marc. 2010. *Theological Anthropology: A Guide for the Perplexed*. London: Continuum.

Farris, Joshua R., and Charles Taliaferro, eds. 2015. *The Ashgate Companion to Theological Anthropology*. Farnham: Ashgate.

Green, Joel B., ed. 2004. *What about the Soul? Neuroscience and Christian Anthropology*. Nashville: Abingdon.

Grenz, Stanley J. 2001. *The Social God and the Relational Self*. Louisville: Westminster John Knox.

Gundry, Robert H. 1976. *Sōma in Biblical Theology, with Emphasis on Pauline Anthropology*. Cambridge: Cambridge University Press.

Jüngel, Eberhard. 1986. *Karl Barth: A Theological Legacy*. Translated by Garrett E. Paul. Philadelphia: Westminster.

———. 2014. *Theological Essays*. 2 vols. London: Bloomsbury.

Kane, Robert, ed. 2002. *The Oxford Handbook of Free Will*. Oxford: Oxford University Press.

Kelsey, David H. 2009. *Eccentric Existence: A Theological Anthropology*. 2 vols. Louisville: Westminster John Knox.

Labooy, Guus H. 2002. *Freedom and Dispositions: Two Main Concepts in Theology and Biological Psychiatry*. Bern: Lang.

Lamme, Victor. 2010. *De vrije wil bestaat niet: Over wie er echt de baas is in het brein*. Amsterdam: Bakker.

McFadyen, Alistair I. 1990. *The Call to Personhood: A Christian Theory of the Individual in Social Relationships*. Cambridge: Cambridge University Press.

Middleton, J. Richard. 2005. *The Liberating Image: The Imago Dei in Genesis 1*. Grand Rapids: Brazos Press.

Nee, Watchman. 1968. *The Spiritual Man*. 3 vols. New York: Christian Fellowship Publishers.

Nelson, James B., and Sandra P. Longfellow, eds. 1993. *Sexuality and the Sacred: Sources for Theological Reflection*. Louisville: Westminster/John Knox.

Neumann-Gorsolke, Ute. 2004. *Herrschen in den Grenzen der Schöpfung: Ein Beit-*

rag zur alttestamentlichen Anthropologie am Beispiel von Psalm 8, Genesis 1 und verwandten Texten. Neukirchen: Neukirchener Verlag.

Niebuhr, Reinhold. 1996. *The Nature and Destiny of Man: A Christian Interpretation*. Louisville: Westminster John Knox.

Pannenberg, Wolfhart. 1970. *What Is Man? Contemporary Anthropology in Theological Perspective*. Philadelphia: Fortress.

———. 2004. *Anthropology in Theological Perspective*. London: T&T Clark.

Plantinga, Alvin. 2011. *Where the Conflict Really Lies: Science, Religion, and Naturalism*. Oxford: Oxford University Press.

Reinders, Hans S. 2008. *Receiving the Gift of Friendship: Profound Disability, Theological Anthropology, and Ethics*. Grand Rapids: Eerdmans.

Roughgarden, Joan. 2004. *Evolution's Rainbow: Diversity, Gender, and Sexuality in Nature and People*. Berkeley: University of California Press.

Schnelle, Udo. 1996. *The Human Condition: Anthropology in the Teaching of Jesus, Paul, and John*. Minneapolis: Fortress.

Schoberth, Wolfgang. 2006. *Einführung in die theologische Antropologie*. Darmstadt: Wissenschaftliche Buchgesellschaft.

Schwöbel, Christoph, and Colin E. Gunton, eds. 1991. *Persons, Divine and Human*. Edinburgh: T&T Clark.

Shults, F. LeRon. 2003. *Reforming Theological Anthropology*. Grand Rapids: Eerdmans.

Spijker, Geert J., ed. 2010. *Vrijheid: Een Christelijk-sociaal pleidooi*. Amsterdam: Buijten & Schipperheijn.

Taylor, Charles. 1989. *Sources of the Self*. Cambridge, MA: Harvard University Press.

Turl, John. 2010. "Substance Dualism or Body-Soul Duality?" *Science and Christian Belief* 22:57–80.

Vanhoozer, Kevin. 1997. "Human Being, Individual and Social." In *The Cambridge Companion to Christian Doctrine*, edited by Colin E. Gunton, 158–88. Cambridge: Cambridge University Press.

Wolff, Hans-Walter. 1974. *Anthropology of the Old Testament*. Minneapolis: Fortress.

World Council of Churches. 2005. *Christian Perspectives on Theological Anthropology*. Faith and Order Paper 199. Geneva: WCC Publications.

Zizioulas, John D. 1985. *Being as Communion: Studies in Personhood and the Church*. London: Darton, Longman & Todd.

8 Existence Ravaged

Sin and Evil

AIM

This chapter deals with an awkward topic: we human beings stand in full view as wrongdoers. In the Judeo-Christian tradition this theme falls under a label that has become widely known without ever losing its specifically religious connotation: *sin*. What can Christian theology say about sin? In this chapter, we want to:

- define the similarity and difference between a phenomenological and a theological approach to sin (8.1)
- sketch some of the biblical-theological background of the doctrine of sin (8.2)
- categorize sin as an act, as a state, and as estrangement (8.3)
- show the place and knowledge of sin in the framework of the covenant (8.4)
- discuss what is meant by the doctrine of so-called original sin (8.5)
- explore how the concept of sin is related to the notion of tragedy in Christian doctrine (8.6)
- propose a theological approach to the issue of theodicy in the context of sin and evil (8.7)
- and, finally, say something about the "nonperson" of the devil (8.8).

MAKING CONNECTIONS

1. Take two minutes to jot down the associations that come to mind when you hear the word "sin." Can you give some examples of the way the media, politics, the people around you, and the church treat evil, sin, and victims?

2. What reactions do you see when a natural disaster occurs – on the part of the victims, in the media, in politics? Do you think these reactions differ from those of some fifty years ago?
3. Read and discuss the novel *Disgrace* by J. M. Coetzee (also made into a film and a play), or the classic *Crime and Punishment* (1866) by F. Dostoyevsky, or watch the film *The Kid with the Bike* (2011). How do they portray evil? Do they present a way out?

8.1. Sin as a Phenomenon and as a Theological Issue— a Preliminary Exploration

When we characterize creation as good, as we did in chapter 6, we did not mean to say that the world is perfect. Experience teaches us that it is no such thing; in fact, perfection is painfully absent. We want a solution for every problem and to find everything to be flawless and complete, but this is not the case. Life is often uncomfortable, problematic, cruel, or simply terrible. This reality surfaced already in chapter 6, when we pointed to the close intertwinement of what we read in the Bible about creation and redemption. Behind the Bible's statements about creation we discovered an awareness of chaotic powers that have been tamed by the God of Israel. The world as we know it apparently has a history in which God opposes destruction and chaos and creates space and order for Adam, the human being who has been created from the earth and is therefore vulnerable. But what is the role of us human beings in this story? Are we just victims and spectators of this vulnerability and evil, or does our involvement go further?

The uncomfortable aspect of the biblical story about sin is that it does not portray people as naive spectators or mere victims (not even in the book of Job). We play a key role in this drama, since we permit evil to continue. The Bible portrays us primarily as transgressors of God's commandments, that is, as sinners. In Gen 3 we see how Adam and Eve open the door to sin. In Gen 4 we find offender and victim in one and the same incident. Abel becomes the victim of his brother Cain, who is pictured as someone who cannot tolerate inequality. Cain gives free rein to his anger and kills his brother. This response was not unavoidable (Gen 4:7), but it happened nonetheless (v. 8). As we continue on in Genesis and beyond, we find that things go from bad to worse: from the

flood and the building of the tower of Babel, via the exile, to the crucifixion of the true Ambassador sent by God. In his Letter to the Romans
Paul powerfully declares what this all means: "All have sinned and fall
short of the glory of God" (Rom 3:23). The word "glory" (Gk. *doxa*) is
the equivalent of the Hebrew word *kabod* that is used for the glory and
majesty of God. The history that God wants to have with his human
creatures is in danger of running aground in mistrust and rebellion. Sin
is the loss of luster and glory. It is expressed in one word in the name
that Eli's daughter-in-law gives her newborn son: *Ichabod*, or "the glory
has departed" (1 Sam 4:21-22). The Bible in the final analysis tells about
the return of that glory (see Gestrich 1997, which develops the doctrine
of sin from this perspective).

This chapter begins with a few general observations before delving
into the essence of the doctrine of sin. Christians share the experience of
sin and evil with everyone else, including those who reject the Christian
faith altogether. They tend to give the phenomenon a different name
than do Christians, but they cannot avoid the phenomenon itself. This
commonality means that there is a kind of general phenomenology of
evil. Thus, when Christians develop a doctrine of sin, it is not out of some
special fascination for this theme that others do not understand and have
nothing to do with. Sin and evil are omnipresent in our world, and one
must have a rather superficial attitude toward life if one never thinks
about these topics. But if (whatever your terms for it) the experience of
sin and evil is general, so is the problem that it raises: how do we adequately deal with it? We therefore start our discussion on this general
experience and from there proceed to sketch some broad themes, before
focusing in on the specifically Christian approach.

We followed a similar method in chapter 2 and refer readers there for the reasons
behind this choice. Dogmatically, it would be possible to opt for a much more direct approach and define sin straightaway as rebellion against the God and Father
of Jesus Christ. This approach would result in a use of terms that differ from those
we normally employ to refer to moral evil. We will do this below, since the true
nature of sin will become clear only in the light of God's revelation. But this is not
our point of departure, since we believe there is a definite continuity between this
dogma and general human experience, which connection is important to view
from a theological and missiological angle. For the biblical background, see, for
example, the famous statement of Paul in Rom 2 that the pagans too have a sense
of good and evil, since "the law is written in their hearts" (Rom 2:15)—which,
however, does not imply that they also keep that law (1:21).

First observation: In our everyday language we interpret the concept of sin mostly as waste, a missed chance, or loss. We say it is "bad" when we drop a bottle of good wine on the floor, or when an expensive piece of clothing gets caught on barbed wire. This response expresses our regret that something is lost. We feel it is "bad" when we just bought a beautiful amaryllis and the flower falls off before we put it in a vase. The result we aimed for is not achieved. However, experiences of loss can be much more catastrophic. When a child dies or a young person falls victim to a fatal traffic accident, the experience is much more heart-rending. The Greek verb for "sin" (*harmartanō*) may cover this meaning; "to sin" may mean to miss or to fail. We could say that in this case sin presents itself as an evil that does not do justice to what we expected life to bring us.

Second observation: there are many forms of evil in which people play an active role. In many situations they cause it; they are the offenders. We have all experienced this form of evil, especially when we consider ourselves in the role of victim. This kind of evil can present itself in relatively unimportant matters: rude behavior, a stolen bike, disturbance by noisy neighbors. The issue may be, or seem, insignificant, but matters can escalate very quickly. Things are damaged or destroyed, with irreversible results. Think of broken relationships in families and between relatives, but also of traffic accidents, poverty, hunger, wars, or ecological disasters. People often play a crucial role here. In addition, sin has the tendency to spread and multiply, like germs. Relationships, the whole environment, and society at large may be affected by it—harmed, diseased, and irreversibly poisoned. Sin is like a computer virus that spreads in no time and eventually paralyzes the entire system.

There are plenty of examples from all domains of human life of such a spread and multiplication. Consider the atmosphere at work: if management is careless and knows little of what happens on the factory floor, an accident may gradually infect all levels of the company. Or an example in our personal life: gossip among friends creates distrust. Today this or that person is the target, but tomorrow it might be me. This spreading is not only synchronic (at a single moment), over space, but also diachronic, over time. The mistrust between Serbs and Croats dates from the Middle Ages and is passed on from generation to generation. For centuries this hostility has made the Balkans a continuous trouble spot. The fire may smolder for a long time and then suddenly burst into flames. Another example from the sphere of family and education: emotional neglect in childhood may go undetected for a long time but will emerge again and again in later years, like a plastic toy duck that cannot be kept below the water surface. This phenomenon often applies to victims of incest; incestuous experiences frequently lead to problematic relationships with one's own body and sexuality. These examples bring us to an aspect of sin we mentioned briefly above. Sin perverts and affects the environment. It is like a cancer cell that attacks other cells and results in a life-threatening tumor. There is no shortage of examples. Frustrations at work may come out in rude treatment of the first person at home who gets in our way. Frustrations experienced in childhood may affect a person's behavior into old age. The entire gamut of human reactions—from slight irritation to intense hurt—is characterized by the penchant for ceaseless repetition. It is like a row of dominoes set up so that one falls after another, with one domino imitating the one next to it. When the management of a company gives a poor example, employees readily replicate this behavior. When the government displays a lack of moral principle, the citizens tend to reflect this defect in their conduct. Entire societies may be eroded as a result.

Literature, theater, and film are rich sources for observing this kind of pattern, often in the realm of family and marriage. Besides the works mentioned above, see such classic plays as *Who's Afraid of Virginia Woolf?* by Edward Albee and *A Long Day's Journey into Night* by Eugene O'Neill. Displeasure and frustration lead to situations in which husbands and wives bully and belittle each other, demonstrating their own inability by destroying the potential of the other. Sin can take possession of a home, of mothers and daughters, fathers and sons, in such a way that the evil can hardly be stopped, if at all.

We refer to the type of action in which one person damages someone else as *moral* evil. In addition there is *physical* or *natural* evil: natural disasters, terminal diseases, or a serious handicap. The distinction seems clear, but it is not—and this indeterminacy is also characteristic, since sin and evil are never totally transparent; they are part of the realm of semidarkness that we will never fully grasp. For instance, it would seem that suffering as the result of natural disasters transcends any human involvement. Yet, when we look closer, human actions may play a definite role in them—think of how the poor suffered much more than the rich in Hurricane Katrina (2005). In some cases, of course, natural evil cannot be traced back to moral evil. Later in this chapter we will return to this issue in discussing the question of tragedy and theodicy (8.6 and 8.7).

Third observation: The question of the origin of sin remains a great dilemma for which we still seek some answers. Here are three different answers, to which we append our own thoughts:

1. *Sin is a matter of tragedy*, of fate. The world of antiquity believed in a cosmic coherence: every action has its consequences, and every evil

act must be avenged or compensated for. Greek tragedies connect evil with fate (*moira* in Greek, *fatum* in Latin), from which nobody will escape. Even the gods cannot escape it and cannot turn their fate around. Everything that happens is determined in a cosmic totality that demands balance and will therefore avenge evil. For their part, Eastern religions speak of karma. This tragic worldview is still found in the West today in literature, theater, and the life stories of people. Sin and transgression seem to be something inescapable.

2. *Sin is estrangement*. A second answer looks for the cause of sin and evil in imbalances of social and economic powers. That imbalance causes us to be estranged from each other and from ourselves. This answer has been (and still is) forcefully promoted by the Marxist tradition. In its classic form it sees a direct link between evil and control of the means of production. More broadly, we can think of the lesson of experience that "power corrupts." Usually, the possession of political or military power without any checks will make people arrogant, reckless, and egoistic, and when such power-hungry people have been successfully removed through resistance or revolt, their successors tend to be of the same kind. With the credit they have earned, liberators can turn into tyrants.

3. *Sin is natural behavior*. A third answer to the question of origins is that sin and evil result from the biological and evolutionary development of the human race. Humanity needs passions to procreate and cannot maintain itself without aggression. Moreover, human beings are limited by nature and have to learn by trial and error. The German language has a perfect word here: humanity is a *Mangelwesen*; that is, when compared with animals, we are very poorly equipped at birth. We require extensive growth and development. For many years a child is utterly dependent on the care and protection of parents and educators, and in this process much can go wrong.

Many aspects of our behavior may thus be linked to findings from neurobiology (nature) or to sociopsychological circumstances (nurture). Lately, neurobiological and cognitive scientific explanations of human behavior and consciousness have become quite popular, but attempts to reduce virtually everything to the level of brain waves (e.g., as in Dennett 1991 and Swaab 2014) can provoke sharp critique. Criminological research shows a definite tie between the environment in which an individual grew up and crime. Someone who has learned to survive on his own in childhood will subsequently pass this attitude on to others. However, the so-called nature-nurture debate immediately leads to a moral and, in the final analysis, theological question: does this dichotomy erase the concept of responsibility? If everything can be explained from genetics and milieu, the concept of sin ceases to be relevant.

This idea may take extreme forms and develop into total cynicism or intentional antihumanism (as with F. Nietzsche). On this approach there is no moral evil; there is only the power of one person over another. What we usually call evil is a social construct that gives a moral label to the experience of misery. This approach may be desirable from a social perspective but has no basis in reality.

What significance do these observations have for theology? In line with what we said in the previous chapter about human freedom, we suggest a few basic points that we will later develop further.

1. The Christian faith recognizes the existence of a relationship between evil and natural, social, and cultural facts but rejects the idea that this link offers a full explanation of evil in all its dimensions. Evil and human sin remain, in some ways, absurd and inexplicable.

2. It is a persistent misunderstanding that Christian dogmatics would want to, or is able to, provide an explanation for the origin of evil. The Bible shows remarkably little interest in the old question of where evil comes from—in the *unde malum* (whence evil?) with which the Manichaeans confused Augustine (*Conf.* 3.7). In fact, the Bible fails to give an answer. Therefore, Christian theology should recognize its limitations and resist the temptation to speculate about the cause of evil. Here we follow in the footsteps of G. C. Berkouwer (1903–96), who pointed out that every attempt to explain the existence of evil tends to be used as an excuse for ourselves (see Berkouwer 1971, 130–48, "The Riddle of Sin").

3. In dogmatics sin is first of all a *theological* and not a moral concept; that is, sin is rebellion against God and impacts our relationship with God. As we will see below, it involves a rift in trust, a breaking of a covenant relationship. Here we must pick up what we said in the previous chapter about human destiny: we are made with an inclination to live with God in love and trust. When we reject this path and lock ourselves into mere self-assertion, we abuse our freedom and miss the mark in a crucial way. We get entangled in ourselves; Luther spoke of human sinfulness in just this way (Lat. *incurvatus in se*, "curved in on itself"; see Jenson 2007 for an approach to a doctrine of sin that is built on this premise). We find this theological description of sin not only in the Old but also in the New Testament. In the Lord's Prayer the petitions for forgiveness of our sins and deliverance from the evil one are embedded in the perspective of kingdom, that is, the perspective of life as intended

by God. After the plea "Your kingdom come" and before we express our praise, "For yours is the kingdom, . . ." we ask:

> And forgive us our debts,
> As we also have forgiven our debtors;
> And lead us not into temptation,
> But deliver us from evil.

(Matt 6:12–13)

By emphasizing the theological character of the concept of sin, we oppose the often heard, and understandable, accusation that the Christian faith, in particular the spirituality of the Reformation, is guilty of creating an often somber and negative view of humanity. In this critique the church spoke far too much and far too often about sin and thus became responsible for the development of the extremely negative assessment that human beings are virtually incapable of doing any good. We cannot simply ignore this accusation. Quite often the confession that we are sinful has been explained as if it were an anthropological or psychological statement to the effect that human beings were capable only of bad things. This interpretation of the Reformation's doctrine of sin, however, is incorrect. Its emphasis on the radical nature of sin was theologically motivated: sin is a rupture in the relationship with God, and the guilt that results from this break cannot be annulled by any human being. We cannot pull ourselves out of the swamp by our own bootstraps.

Note the formulation of Heidelberg Catechism Q/A 8: "Are we then so corrupt that we are wholly incapable of doing any good, and inclined to all wickedness?" "Indeed we are, except we are regenerated by the Spirit of God." These words have often been interpreted as meaning that we are, in general, good for nothing and not able to do any good. Statements about humanity's corrupt nature that were theologically intended have over history received a psychological slant. We cannot deny that the psychological impact of this Reformed teaching has weighed heavily—and continues to do so—on a segment of the Reformed population. This response is not necessary. Remarkably enough, on this point Calvin makes a sharp distinction between earthly and heavenly things (*Inst.* 2.2.13). We have no problem when dealing with earthly things such as making arrangements for society, starting a company, finding our bearing at sea, or in science. However, we are not in and of ourselves able to restore our broken relationship with God. In that respect we are incapable. Adhering strictly to a theological interpretation will ensure that the statements in the Heidelberg will not have a depressive effect. See below, 15.2.

When we deal with sin primarily as a *theological* concept—as a concept that says something about our relationship with God—it becomes clear that it has nothing to do with pessimism. We might rather say that the localization and development of the theme of sin forms a barrier against a pessimistic view of life. For in the doctrine of sin human beings are not identified with the evil with which they are actively or passively involved. There is a fundamental difference between humans as creatures of God and as persons who are estranged from themselves and God. In brief: sin is additional, or *accidental*. In essence, it is not part of God's creation. The fall is not inherent in creation, and sin is not a natural category. This truth is expressed in biblical theology in the fact that Gen 1 and 2, the story of creation, precede Gen 3, the account of the fall.

For dogmatics, this conclusion implies that creation and fall must remain sharply distinct. In our nature we are free and fit for love. Sin is, theologically speaking, unnatural, for it does not accord with our destiny, a life in a relationship with God. As the American theologian Cornelius Plantinga stated: "Sin is an anomaly, an intruder, a nefarious uninvited guest. Sin is not part of God's world, but somehow has entered it" (1995, 88). This insight enables us, on the one hand, to receive our existence with gratitude, while on the other hand, to be realistic with regard to the elements of evil and sin that we meet in daily life and that cast a shadow across it. In all realism we can do damage control—getting evil under control and pushing it back, without falling into a general pessimism. For the fact that sin does not belong to the ontological structure of our humanness also means that we are *redeemable*. That conclusion, in the words of A. A. van Ruler (1972), is part of the "sunny side of sin."

We believe that these qualifications allow us to arrive at a "healthy" doctrine of sin. The Christian view of sin has very little to do with pessimism or optimism. It is fed by the conviction that God, in his dealings with us, makes a fundamental distinction between us and our sins and, in his free grace, does not pin us down to our sin or our estrangement. This insight is exactly the core of the doctrine of justification (see chap. 15). We may here refer to what we said earlier about revelation as verbal communication: God promises us that we may be his children. If God promises it and addresses us as such, then this is reality. God's speaking creates a relationship and is therefore performative. Thus, in his grace,

God creates the future. The Christian church speaks of sin within the framework of soteriology, of God's will to save us.

When we insist that being God's creature and being a sinner do not coincide in us, it means that we must retain the notion of the fall. The word itself is not found in the Bible and may create gnostic misunderstandings. But it correctly suggests that we have experienced a movement that may be qualified as downward ("fall") and that has caused us to be linked with evil. Contemporary scientific theorizing about the origin of the human species makes it far from simple, but not impossible, to present the fall as a historical event. The "monogenetic hypothesis," which says that the human species has descended from one single pair, has given place to "polygenism," the idea that the original human population consisted of more than one pair, perhaps as many as several thousands of people. However, these "Adamites" shared one common biotope and a common divine destiny (see Rahner 1967). With the awareness of this destiny came the possibility to willfully deviate from it. This falling away of the first "true" human beings from God's intentions by their choice to be independent and to follow animal passions rather than their divine calling is, we believe, the core of the fall into sin that is so forcefully described in Gen 3. For Roman Catholic comment, see Schwager 2006; from the Protestant side, Brink 2012. Earlier Berkhof (CF, esp. 192–94, 211–13) suggested a doctrine of sin that took evolutionary biology into account. Is it, in this light, still possible to speak of a *status integritatis*, a state of perfection? No, if we interpret this term as a more or less permanent state of moral perfection (note what we said in the previous chapter about the futuristic meaning of Eph 4:24); yes, if we grant that the earliest human beings must have had, before they began sinning, some primitive moral awareness that made them, however vaguely, conscious of good and bad in the light of God's commandment. See in this connection Shuster 2004, 15–16. But faith does not need these kinds of reconstructions. Therefore, they play no major role in dogmatics. They serve only as an auxiliary line for those who search for arguments against the view that the Christian doctrine of sin has been invalidated by contemporary science. What is decisive for the Christian faith is that, from a biblical perspective, sin is additional and accidental, not essential to human beings (see Ruler 1972). The classic work of the Oxford theologian N. P. Williams (1927) is critical with regard to the notion of a fall into sin, but it provides valuable insight into its religious-historical background and history.

8.2. Some Biblical-Theological Principles

An important conclusion in the previous section was that sin is primarily a theological concept; that is, it must be defined as a rift in our relationship with God. We now want to support this notion with some biblical-theological background.

God is depicted in the Bible as the one from whom all possibilities for our life originate. In Gen 1 and 2 God is the Maker of heaven and earth and the one who plants a garden for humanity: the Garden of Eden, where they get the space to live. The Garden of Eden is no Land of Cockaigne but a place given to humanity *to cultivate and to maintain* (Gen 2:15). The history of creation paints the world from a retrospective prophetic angle as it was made and intended by God. The world was full of potential for life, and God deserved to be trusted by his human creatures. Sin occurred when humans did not trust God and tarnished the relationship as intended by God.

As we already saw in chapter 6, we can express this whole picture in terms of the covenant. God creates the conditions for a life of dependence on him. The covenant implies that humanity will live in a way that takes God into account. We are made with a capacity for love, and to this end we receive the space of our freedom and creativity. However, the question remains whether we will respond positively to the covenant. In section 8.4 we take a closer look at sin as a rupture of the covenant.

In Gen 3 we meet the serpent, the most cunning of the animals that God created. It sows unrest and insecurity about God in the mind of Eve. Can God be trusted? Or is the command that humanity has received simply a pretext to withhold something good from them? (Gen 3:1–5). Already early in Genesis sin undermined trust in God; it is mistrust with regard to God's goodness. This attitude creates a distance between God and humanity, and that broken relationship becomes reality. For that reason Luther, on the basis of Rom 14:23b, describes the essence of sin as unbelief.

In the Old Testament sin is primarily the breaking of a commandment, or transgressing a limit that humanity was to recognize (*hatta'*). In this sense it may also refer to disobedience and rebellion (*pesha'*). Sin causes us to inflict damage on others, and that damage may be so extensive that we forfeit our own life. We not only break God's commandments but turn away from God himself. At the same time, it is clear that

God does not regard this trespassing as final. We see this grace especially when God makes a new start with humanity; from Gen 12 onward, God focuses his covenant on the people of Israel. The entire Israelite sacrificial cult is intended to give a future to life in the midst of sin and guilt. Where life is in danger of extinction, God gives, through the sacrifice, the possibility of restoration and of a way forward.

In the New Testament the concept of sin becomes more focused and distinct in the history of Jesus Christ. Here too sin is described as disobedience to God (Rom 5:19). Even more radically, as a result of sin, humanity becomes God's enemy (Rom 5:10). In the Pauline letters and the Johannine writings, sin develops into an all-encompassing concept; when humanity is referred to as flesh (Gk. *sarx*) or as carnal, it designates a mode of existence that is radically infected by the power of sin. Why this further intensification? It follows from the contrast with Jesus's ministry. In Jesus's presence his earliest followers experienced the overwhelming, overpowering goodness of God. The ministry of Jesus may be defined as the time during which Jesus freely gives a definitive presentation of God's love and of the trustworthiness of the covenant. The covenant that God made with Israel—"I will be your God and you shall be my people" (Lev 26:12; Jer 24:7; 30:22; etc.)—receives a new beginning and is fulfilled in the history of Jesus. That is, it becomes actual reality. Jesus not only proclaims a new regime, the eschatological kingdom of God, but he lives in it. When God ushers in his regime, blessing and life will again advance against the curse and death: the sick are healed, sinners receive forgiveness, community is restored, and the people are reconnected to the life-giving Torah of God (note the history of Zacchaeus, Luke 19:8). Thus we see in the ministry of Jesus the contours of the new covenant. The abundance of God's compassion comes to light. For this reason, the evangelist John can describe the life and person of Jesus Christ as the Word and the Life that is full of grace and truth (John 1:4, 14). The source of God's love flows into the life and ministry of Jesus (see John 7:38), which is to say: Jesus demonstrates that God is free in his life-giving love.

In the light of the reality of Jesus's ministry, the New Testament confronts us with some sharp contrasts. The totalizing qualifications of the human condition as sin and death, as flesh as opposed to Spirit, emerge from the discovery of Jesus Christ as grace and life. In the ministry and life of Jesus, the situation of humanity, of Adam, is seen in a different light. Adam, in whom we are all included, becomes the *first* Adam or the *old* Adam (Rom 5:12-21; 1 Cor 15:45). From the angle of systematic theology it is of utmost importance to recognize that this reference to Adam as the first Adam finds its origin in what the early church discovered in Jesus Christ. Jesus Christ is the ultimate divine Yes to God's good work (2 Cor 1:20). His life is de facto a restoration of the relationship between God and humanity. In Christ, God picks up the thread of the covenant that he initiated with Abraham in answer to the decay that started with Adam—but now in a new structure and with amazing power that guarantees its realization. Where the first Adam failed in the garden because he wanted to be as God and make his own decisions (Gen 3:5), the last Adam was willing to humble himself before God (Mark 14:36-42). For that reason God has "exalted him above every name" (Phil 2:9). This discovery and surprise led the earliest Jewish Christians to worship Jesus as Lord. They experienced in Jesus the overwhelming goodness and power of God. Against this new reality the existing reality lost its luster; what went before must be qualified as old in the light of the new (2 Cor 5:17; Heb 8:13).

In sum, against the background of the rejection of Jesus Christ and the failure to adequately react to the mission of the Son, the New Testament—particularly the writings of Paul and John—presents a very broad and radical concept of sin. Sin is not understood as a single act of disobedience but pictured as a power that encompasses and rules over the entire human realm. Under that power we are slaves or servants of sin. And this condition is true not just of some people but applies to all. Paul powerfully expresses this condition in Rom 3:23: "All have sinned and fall short of the glory [*doxa*] of God." As we said earlier, the glory is gone, the radiance is no more.

8.3. Sin as Act, Power, and State of Estrangement

After these brief biblical-theological comments, we introduce here a few distinctions about how to understand sin. Sin consists first in acts but may also present itself as a power or a state of estrangement.

1. *Sin as act*. Sin may, first of all, have the meaning of *committing* or *allowing* an evil act. In this sense, sin is disobedience to a prohibition or a commandment. When we speak of sin as acts, we tend to speak in the plural form. We usually speak of sins and may even make a list of specific sins. We encounter such lists explicitly in Paul's letters (e.g., Gal 5:19-21). Those who do such things are guilty. The characteristic feature of this approach is to view the problem of evil from the angle of the human as perpetrator.

2. *Sin as power.* Sin can also be viewed more comprehensively as a power. We might say that, when the same sinful acts are repeated so often and by so many different people, they become part of the sociocultural fabric and thus develop into a power that threatens us. We then become easily ourselves part of a system in which evil is entrenched. We cannot use this conclusion as an excuse, however. It may be difficult, but it is not impossible, to withdraw from such a poisonous system. It is very difficult, for almost everybody is involved in it, but it is not impossible; we can go against the flow. Otherwise, we would cease to be guilty, and sin would cease to be sin.

To further clarify this issue, we can begin with the experience of the victim. This perspective allows us to discover how universal and deeply entrenched evil is in human life and culture. When we think of victims, we must not limit ourselves to the victims of theft, robbery, or forms of personal abuse. There are also broader complexes in which people become the victims or perpetrators of superpersonal evil or evil that is caused by the culture. Slavery is a good example. For many centuries slavery and the slave trade were an accepted and defended practice in the Hellenistic, European, African, and American worlds. For hundreds of years people were part of a system in which this practice was accepted as normal by their society. Are such systems today a matter of the past? Hardly. With regard to our own time, we may think of economic systems in which the free movement of persons and goods is considered to be the highest good. The free market system has brought enormous prosperity to the world but has also led to serious abuses: exploitation of underpaid labor, the uprooting and forced migration of large groups of people, an irresponsible pressure on our natural environment, and advertising as a continuous stimulus for our egoism that is always in search of more—this is the reality of the political and social state of our contemporary cosmo-politan society. All the phenomena we mentioned are forms of evil in which people play a role, but we notice them only when we look at them through the eyes of the victim.

In this light the words we cited above from the Lord's Prayer are again significant: "Deliver us from evil" (Matt 6:13). We do well to remember that, although the Greek term *tou ponērou* is usually interpreted as "from the evil one," it may also be translated "from that which is evil." This ambivalence indicates that Jesus took evil very seriously as a power, as a sinful condition. Jesus himself would fall victim to the mechanisms of hatred and injustice that were, at the time, deeply entrenched in Jewish-Hellenistic society. Looking back from Jesus's perspective, we see that the Old Testament was already full of criticism of sins that had developed into structures of systemic idolatry, exploitation, and repression. Think of the angry protest of prophets like Amos and Hosea against the people in general and their spiritual and political leaders. However, when we look from the standpoint of the Gospels to the book of Revelation, we note that sin has led to dictatorial regimes in which people are repressed by godless tyrants—something that still happens in many countries around the world. Thus the Bible does not speak about sin as if it involved falling short of a kind of civil politeness. The raw desolation of many human lives that have been degraded, the structural injustices and unimaginable suffering that people inflict on one another—in one word, sin as the all-encompassing power that holds entire societies in its grip—is certainly not ignored.

We discover the problem of sin and evil and our own active role therein by keeping the elements of perpetrator and victim closely together and by constantly relating them to one another. In the Bible the story of the fall is followed by that of Cain and Abel (Gen 4). One brother, Cain, kills the other, Abel. In our culture the position of Abel, the victim of a brutal murder, often becomes the angle from which we look at evil. We tend to identify more easily with the victim than with the perpetrator. But the point of this story is not what happened to Abel but in the words God spoke to Cain: "Where is Abel, your brother?" We know the excuse and attitude of Cain from within ourselves: "Am I my brother's keeper?" (Gen 4:9). This inner distancing, the refusal to connect and to do justice to the element of brotherhood, is considered in this story to be the concretization of evil. In the same vein we might today call it sin to buy clothing or shoes that have been produced elsewhere in the world by child labor or under inhumane circumstances. It is not unlikely that a later generation will wonder how, at the beginning of the twenty-first century, so many people, including Christians, did so without giving it much thought, without being (or wanting to be) aware of doing anything wrong. Here sin has indeed become a power from which we can withdraw only with great effort.

3. *Sin as estrangement.* The reminder of the story of Cain and Abel also indicates that we might refer to sin under another, inclusive term: "estrangement." This gives not so much a broader but a deeper significance to what we mean by sin as an act. To speak of estrangement brings us to the real nature and background of sin as act and as power. People become strangers to each other when they violate the relational ties with which God has created them (see chap. 7). It divides them into the sepa-

rate categories of the perpetrators and the victims of evil. Estrangement thus is a relational concept that very poignantly describes how sin is understood by the Christian faith. It refers to a withdrawal from communion with God and others into isolation. As if we can live without each other! However, in situations where we do not generate blessings for but become strangers to each other, we pine away. By withdrawing into our supposed autonomy, we fail to do justice to people, relationships, animals, the environment, ourselves, and, above all, God.

We thus fail to meet the needs of others and ourselves, but also to meet the needs of the environment and even God. Sin in its deepest meaning has to do with the essential failing to meet a need. In the words of Augustine, evil is *privatio boni* (*Enchiridion* 8.24), that is, the taking away of what is good. In the final analysis, sin has to do with a turning away from God and the source of life toward emptiness, toward gods and powers that cannot fill our lives and will ultimately leave us empty. In this connection the Heidelberg Catechism speaks of our "misery" (Q/A 3). This word refers to a state of being away, far from home, homeless, and thus estranged. This line of thinking does not turn sin into something passive. Estrangement may take a very active form, namely, that of rebellion. When people intentionally persist in an attitude of turning away and continuing in emptiness, that is rebellion against God. It leaves us in the grip of sin as a destructive power. Destruction, torment, rape, killing, or humiliating becomes a pleasure. Sin has then devolved into being totally under the power of evil. When we speak of estrangement as the core of sin, this is not meant as a euphemism. Estrangement is the result of the baffling and totally serious event in which humanity turns away from God and from what is good, destroying itself in the process.

The story of Cain and Abel in Gen 4 is the primordial biblical story of estrangement. The estrangement between the two brothers is caused by the profound and puzzling estrangement from God that is described in Gen 3. Cain cannot stomach the fact that Abel's sacrifice is accepted while his is not. Cain turns away from God and breaks their relationship, which leads to Cain's estrangement from himself. The breaking of the covenant is repeated in successive generations like a row of dominoes. Cain loses his way, can find no rest, does not know where to go, and fears other people to the point of paranoia (Gen 4:14). Things become even worse in the case of his descendent Lamech (Gen 4:24). In the New Testament the parable of the prodigal son (Luke 15:11–32) is the clearest portrayal of sin as estrangement.

Estrangement as a description of sin has found wide recognition in modern times. It is the experience of a human being who feels lost in the universe but also in his or her own life, a human being who does not know the answers to the final and decisive questions of life and, for this reason, suffers from existential loneliness and lostness. For Hegel the concept of estrangement is a stage in the development of the divine spirit, while Marx applies it in a secular form to the social situation. Paul Tillich adopted it as a key concept in his theology. In the Dutch context we may refer to K. H. Roessingh (1886-1925) and G. J. Heering (1879-1955), representatives of a conservative modernism who called for more attention to the realities of sin and estrangement, in contrast to the optimism of nineteenth-century modernism. We find many examples of estrangement and lostness in literature and in the arts. See, for example, the work of twentieth-century painters like Francis Bacon and Edward Hopper, the pivotal modernist poem "The Waste Land" (1922), by T. S. Eliot, and perhaps supremely, *The Stranger* (1942), by Albert Camus. These works offer the possibility of using the category of estrangement to explain the biblical view of sin in such a way that nonbelievers too can perceive its relevance.

We summarize briefly. Sin as estrangement presents itself in four different ways: estrangement of a person (1) from other persons, (2) from oneself, (3) from one's environment, and (4) from God. These four relationships are not unconnected, their common root being a broken relationship with or a turning away from God. In all these relationships we note the breaking of the covenant, which penetrates as a power and as a condition into our entire existence.

8.4. Sin and the Knowledge of Sin in the Context of the Covenant

A Christian doctrine of sin must deal not only with questions about the origin and nature of sin but also with those regarding the knowledge of sin. How do we find out that we are indeed sinful? Theologically speaking, where does the knowledge of our sinfulness come from? To answer this question we must retrace our steps for a moment and remind ourselves of what was said above in 8.1 about sin as a theological concept and about the sequence of the Lord's Prayer. Here we are dealing with what is called the order of our knowing (Lat. *ordo cognoscendi*). With regard to the things we know about God, some things come first, and others follow suit. We should take care to begin at the beginning! The sense of guilt and failure is quite universal, but we come to learn about the absurdity of our sinful tendencies only when we place them in the light of God's loving condescension toward us in the covenant.

We have seen how closely, according to Calvin, the knowledge of God and the knowledge of self presuppose and impact each other—so closely linked that Calvin found it difficult to prioritize one over the other. But if he had to choose, he preferred to start with our knowledge of God (*Inst.* 1.1.1; see above, 4.1). In this chapter we have followed this lead and have emphasized that we cannot speak about sin without also speaking of our relationship with God. Now we add that *knowledge* of sin also originates in this domain of God's dealings with us, that is, in the realm of the covenant.

This orientation causes a shift with regard to our question, for where do we learn about God's will? If faith is indeed a relationship with God, and if we are made with an inclination to live in a love relationship with him, and if sin is a violation of that relationship, we are then faced with the question of where we actually meet God. How do we know what God demands from us and what is good?

In the dogmatic tradition this question is answered in different ways. Classic theology—both Roman Catholic and Protestant—tells us that we first acquire knowledge of God in his creation and in his commandments. In these domains he initiates contact with us, so this is also the domain where we learn about our sinful estrangement from him. In the Heidelberg Catechism knowledge of sin is therefore tied to the law. It should be noted that the authors of the catechism had the wisdom to present the twofold commandment of love as the essence of this law (Heidelberg Catechism, Q/A 4; see Mark 12:30-31). Our sinfulness consists, not primarily in what we do or fail to do, but in our failure, from the depth of our heart, to be oriented in love toward God and our neighbor. This answer is revealing. However, contemporary theology tends to follow Karl Barth and take its point of departure in a specifically christological approach, in the revelation of God in Christ. For precisely in the light of God's immeasurable love in Christ do we see, in sharp and ugly contrast, our own lack of love. God's revelation in Christ reveals that God has consistently and from the very first worked toward our salvation (see Eph 1:4-5). God wants us to live and is totally committed to this end. It is only from the perspective of this liberating and life-giving act of God in Christ that we discover what sin is—namely, that we cannot bear this yearning care of God to ensure our salvation. Astoundingly enough, we flee from it into the darkness of our own self (John 1:10-11; 3:18-19).

Whichever theological option we prefer, it is clear that in Christian theology words like "God" and "creation" are far from neutral. Both belong within the framework of the covenant, and within that framework we somehow acquire knowledge of sin. This claim needs some further explanation. The creation is more than what we today refer to as nature; it also implies that the world is the work of a life-giving God. In the Bible, even in Genesis, "God" is not a neutral term referring to some abstract higher power. Where God enters the picture, we are confronted with the unique name of the one who is present to set his people free (Exod 3:14; but this name YHWH makes its first appearance in Gen 2, where we read about the creation of humanity). Where God is present, he is active in creating space and possibilities for human life. From the very beginning God is active on behalf of humankind. This activity comes before we start talking about redemption and salvation; it is built into his creation. Earlier we referred to creation as an act of benevolence. From the moment we open our eyes and are part of this world, in God's rich and diverse creation, we are confronted with possibilities and structures that favor and optimize our life. We notice it already in the things we see and experience on a daily basis. The difference between day and night, the flow of the seasons, the way we grow and recover from being tired, the self-cleansing processes in nature—all these things can be regarded as tokens of God's benevolence. God's good work (Gen 1:31) becomes apparent in the life-giving possibilities that he creates.

We may summarize by stating that God, from the very beginning, made a covenant of life with the human race. In the light of this covenant concept, we must now give a more theological definition of sin. We meet sin when the life-giving possibilities that God offers are hidden, resisted, intentionally restricted, or cut off. In addition to the other characteristics of sin we discussed above, sin is also a breaking of the covenant. More precisely: sin as act, power, and estrangement are, from the very first, ways in which we violate the covenantal relationship with God. Whenever these life-giving possibilities are restricted or cut off, the Other, and the others are shortchanged. Sin is a matter of failing to abide by the agreements that God made with us through his commandments (as already in Gen 3, esp. v. 17); however, this commandment was intended to give us life. In our sins the nurturing of this life is inhibited or blocked, which means that there is no escape: we must "surely die" (Gen 2:17). Rather than fostering life and progress, we are brought to a standstill and begin to exude the fragrance of death. How harrowing this condition is truly sinks in only when we come face to face with the one who granted us life.

When in Luke 5:8 Peter stands eye to eye with Jesus and exclaims, "Depart from me, for I am a sinful man," this encounter does not happen after Christ has confronted him with his law but after Peter has seen how Jesus granted them two shiploads of fish—that is, gave them life. We apparently discover our own sinful condition in the experience of God's abundance. For a contemporary example, recall the experience of Peter Roelofsma that we referred to in 5.1. In the bright light of God's love he saw himself as wreckage, as a vagrant.

Sin at times may seem small or insignificant, but the crux of the matter is the spirit that inspires it. Modern readers may perhaps smile in amazement upon learning about Augustine's dismay when he recalled the moment when he stole a pear. Likewise, we find it hard to understand why eating a forbidden fruit in the Garden of Eden was such a big deal. But the issue here is the spirit that is manifested in such a sinful act. If this spirit is there, it will unavoidably manifest itself in other aspects of life. Sin will soon become less innocent, as we clearly see in the movement in Genesis from Adam, Eve, and the fruit, via Cain, Abel, and his murder, to Lamech and his sevenfold revenge, until there is such an accumulation of evil that the flood became necessary. So we have returned to the point we mentioned earlier in 8.1: sin perverts and infects the environment. Sin is like a malicious cell that attacks other cells and will finally grow into a life-threatening tumor. Using a term coined by René Girard (1923-2015), we might say that sin has a *mimetic* character. We ape one another. As a result, evil becomes so common that, only when contrasted with the totally different attitude that God shows to us, does it appear abnormal and create guilt.

Above, we outlined some options regarding the issue of our knowledge of sin. In essence, at least two views are possible: knowledge of sin is derived from the law, or it results from God's liberating and redemptive intervention, that is, from the gospel. Nowadays a third, eschatological option tends to be added. God's revelation tells us of his ultimate reign, in the light of which the true nature of sin is revealed. See, for example, the classic work of J. Moltmann, *Theology of Hope* (1967 Eng. ed.), where he argues that Christian faith proceeds from the hope of a future divine reign, and whenever we are not led in what we do by that hope, we are in the realm of sin.

The classic answer of Reformed theology is clearly expressed in Heidelberg

Catechism Q/A 3: "How do you come to know your misery?" "The law of God tells me." It should be noted that this law is not limited to the decalogue as found in Exod 20 and Deut 5 but is rooted in the law of nature (*lex naturalis*), which one meets in Greek antiquity, as well as in Rom 2:15. It may also be interpreted more broadly as the twofold commandment of love. This understanding implies that, to a certain degree, knowledge of sin is universal; every human being has a fundamental awareness of God and his will. Sin is a transgression of God-given commandments, and these commandments may be known, so far as their origin and content are concerned, from the law of nature (e.g., everyone has an innate sense that murder is wrong).

Roman Catholic theology, in particular, has given ample attention to the relationship between God's will and the law of nature. The most fundamental objections to the idea that we can know sin from the law came from Barth, who believed that it is impossible to know what sin is from nature, for it becomes visible only in the light of God's revelatory intervention, concretely in Jesus Christ. (After World War I, Barth had little confidence in human nature.) When the gospel is heard and God's grace is seen, our sinfulness becomes visible and knowable in our having turned away from God. At the same time, life gets a new orientation, and by God's redemptive intervention we are placed on the road that leads to a new life. At this stage, Barth argues, the law becomes meaningful. Not law and gospel therefore but gospel and law. In evaluating this radical reversal, we should not forget that Barth was also reacting against theologians with Nazi sympathies who believed that God's law told them, in particular, that Germany was for the (racially pure) Germans. These perversions led Barth to deal with sin and the knowledge of sin in CD IV, as part of the doctrine of the atonement in Christ. Only if we choose to truly belong to Christ can we know what God's law says and also know sin. We therefore conclude that it is not necessary to agree with Barth's reversal of the sequence of law and gospel to understand and appreciate what he was aiming for.

In chapter 6 we spoke of the covenant in referring to creation as existence granted by God. We now return to this concept as the umbrella term in our discussion of sin, defined as a violation of the covenant. In doing so, we join a long tradition in which the covenant concept held a structural significance for the entire unfolding of Christian dogmatics. This view of the covenant occurred particularly in Reformed theology. In the seventeenth century (though the roots of this idea reach far back into the sixteenth century), theologians gradually began to develop the relational character of the bond between God and humanity in covenantal terms. One of the foremost among these theologians was Johannes

Cocceius (1603–69), who was born in Bremen but worked mainly in the Dutch cities of Franeker and Leyden. The so-called federal theology (Lat. *foedus* = covenant) elaborated by him and others often distinguished a series of interconnected covenants (or dispensations) that all focused on our life and the restoration of our relationships. In paradise God made a covenant of works with humanity. That is to say, human beings were to obey the divine commandment not to eat from the tree of knowledge of good and evil. This test became the centerpiece in the relationship between us and God.

Disobedience to God led to a disturbance of this originally perfect relationship. Thus the doctrine of sin, the *locus de peccato*, is preceded by the theme of the demise of the covenant of works, the *locus de violatione foederis operum* (see Heppe, RD, chaps. 14–15). The state of perfection (*status integritatis*) is lost, and the humans are removed from paradise. Various successive covenants followed, initiated by God for the progress of life, each time with new conditions. God's first reaction to the new situation is the Noachian covenant, in which he promises that he will not allow the earth to perish as the result of its own wickedness (Gen 9:11). The rainbow that appears in the sky will be the sign of God's continuous care for his creation (Gen 9:12). The next step is God's covenant of grace (*foedus gratiae*), of which Christ is the head. This covenant had already been promised in God's words to the serpent, in Gen 3:15. It is further unwrapped in two steps, namely, in the covenant with Abraham and the covenant made at Sinai, where the Torah is the law that is added to this covenant. The covenant with Abraham is based, not on what Abraham does, but in God's gracious initiative; this pattern remains the case ever after. The mission of Jesus Christ, including especially his suffering, death, and resurrection, is the event in which God renews this covenant of grace with humanity, and this renewal also is based solely on grace.

The Reformed tradition has referred to the covenant that God made with humans at creation not only as a covenant of works but also as a covenant of life (e.g., see Genderen and Velema, CRD 395–96), a covenant of law, a covenant of nature, or as the "Adamic dispensation"; see Allen, RT 41–42. This multitude of names suggests some dogmatic uncertainty. History tells us that only with the passage of time was this covenant of grace distinguished from the one made with Abraham and his posterity (Gen 12). From an exegetical angle the discussion continues whether we may speak of a covenant in the first chapters of Genesis, since this term (Heb. *berit*) first occurs only in Gen 6:18 in connection with the Noachian covenant. Nonetheless, it would seem that, from the very first, all elements of the covenant are present in Genesis. There is a command that is linked to a promise (Gen 1:28) and that carries a sanction (Gen 2:17). Other biblical passages (Hos 6:7; Rom 5:12-21) seem to confirm the idea of an original covenant with Adam. In this covenant God acts as an ancient Near Eastern ruler does with his vassals: he gives them what they need (in the case of Genesis, an environment in which people can live and procreate) but also stipulates the conditions under which the relationship may continue (in this case by cultivating and caring for the earth). In addition, there are curses and punishments for disobedience and blessings as rewards (perhaps in Genesis, implicitly, the promise of eternal life).

"Covenant of works" is an unfortunate term, since it suggests a businesslike relationship between God and humanity, while in reality it involves a personal relationship of love and loyalty. In his treatment of Cocceius's doctrine of the covenants, Barth (CD IV/1:58-63) therefore opposed the notion of a covenant of works because of its suggestion that a relationship that was not mediated by Jesus Christ and, apparently, was not grace based preceded the covenant of grace. Moreover, the first generation of reformers (Calvin, Zwingli, Bullinger, Olevian) never thought in such terms and always insisted that the one covenant God made with humanity was to be regarded as a covenant of grace. In any case, we must take Barth's criticism to heart, that the covenant God made with humanity in the beginning must not be misrepresented in a legalistic way, as a businesslike work relationship with only one principle: *do ut des* (I give so that you will give). From the beginning there was a covenant in which faith, trust, and obedience were united; whatever name we give it, this covenant was violated by Adam's sin. For that reason we earlier referred to sin as a breaking of the covenant.

Barth took the notion of the covenant of grace as the point of departure for his entire theology, with the intention of getting an adequate view of all God's actions. God makes this covenant with us so that we will be able to live gratefully with God and to respond to God within the conditions of our vulnerable existence.

From this discussion of the doctrine of the covenant, we hold that God's relationship with us has been characterized from the very first by his goodness and grace. We observe a pattern in which, whenever this relationship is in danger or is violated by human sin, God searches for a way to continue it. We find this response as early as his reaction to the sin of Adam and Eve (Gen 3:22-25), in the ongoing protection of Cain (Gen 4:15), and in the history of Noah. After intense consideration God continues with Noah and enters into the Noachian covenant (Gen 9:8-17). God searches for a way to achieve his goal—an earth where shalom and blessing prevail. The covenant with Abraham inaugurates the way that

God wants to proceed, via Israel. In the Old Testament we notice a tension between the covenant with Abraham and the one at Sinai. In decisive moments we see a return to the first rather than to the second (Deut 9:5; 29:12; Ps 105:8-9, 42; Isa 29:22; Mic 7:20). We find the same duality in Paul. He places the righteousness that results from God's new initiative next to the righteousness provided by the law. In no way does Paul deny that we could reach a state of righteousness by obedience to the Torah (e.g., Phil 3:9; Rom 10:3-6), but the Sinaitic covenant is not final. Paul has discovered that, in sending Jesus and in Jesus's harrowing death on the cross, God has initiated a new arrangement for access to the covenantal relationship, based on a giving love that puts the preceding arrangement in the shadow. We thus see newness, as well as continuity, particularly with the Abrahamic covenant. In terms of the doctrine of the covenant, God confirms who he is, namely, the one who gives life by demonstrating his own being in Christ in a new way.

Placing our knowledge of sin within the framework of the covenant enables us to say something else about the nature of sin. We noted above that, as human beings, we cannot fathom the depth of sin and evil; we are simply not equipped to do so. However, we are creatures, which means that we are beings who can receive; we depend on what God gives us. Understanding evil is not part of this process (which seems to be the drift of the book of Job) and is not our task. God has taken this task upon himself in Christ, who has passed through the deepest depths of sin. In the tradition this aspect is often and aptly referred to as the *mysterium iniquitatis*, the mystery of sin.

When we place sin in the framework of the covenant, it means that we choose our point of departure in the goodness of the creation that we have been given, in the compassion of and redemption in Christ, and in a completion through the Spirit. In other words, the framework of the covenant has a Trinitarian design. We believe that this insight is a major gain. It does not enable us to solve the riddle of sin, but it provides us with a prism through which to look and with a directive for dealing with sin. To repeat: the Christian faith does not seek to solve the mystery of the existence of evil as an intellectual problem but is interested in deliverance from the evil that threatens our life. In creation, redemption, and completion God is invariably the initiator who turns toward his human creatures to give them life, and sin is our movement away from this divine condescension. This matter is serious, for "how shall we escape if we neglect such a great salvation?" (Heb 2:3). We do not commit ourselves to this divine condescension, and so we go our own way. For this reason, as we mentioned earlier, Luther characterizes sin as unbelief (*incredulitas* or *infidelitas*).

Luther interprets the first of the Ten Commandments ("You shall have no other gods before me") as a commandment to trust God. "For these two belong together: faith and God. I tell you, that whatever your heart desires and trusts is in fact your god" (Luther on the first commandment in his Large Catechism). This definition of sin as unbelief implies that the nature of sin is not primarily moral but rather relational. Sin is an encroachment on our relationship with God and may therefore be described as a breaking of the covenant. This characterization of sin as *incredulitas* or *infidelitas* is the other side of *sola fide*. Only through faith can we share in salvation. A similar approach is found in Calvin (*Inst.* 2.1.4).

The negations we continuously encounter in the doctrine of sin are a clear indication of the mysteriousness and absurdity of sin. In this connection Barth has described us as fallen human beings, as those for whom "the impossible has become possible" and "the unreal, real" (CD II/2:163-64). In view of God's intentions in his covenant and of the goodness of his creation, sin is impossible— but, yet, it exists. Sin is the ultimate emptiness, for it is not part of God's creative work, and all that exists has been created by God. Nonetheless, sin is real. Here our thinking meets an insuperable barrier.

Precisely in its mysterious negativity sin may assume various concrete shapes. It presents itself as distrust of God, as not accepting the limitations of creatureliness, as abuse of others, as hate or as a lust for the destruction of life and of God (a striking and fascinating survey of the many forms and variations in which sin presents itself is offered in Plantinga 1995). To use covenant terminology: sin occurs when humans step out of the circle of the light of the covenant and attempt to go their own way. By so doing, we take a step for which we are not equipped and which leads to a denial of who we are in the core of our being. Therein lies the self-destructive and destructive power of sin.

Our description of sin here differs from what we generally find in the tradition. Following Augustine, two basic forms of sin were usually distinguished: sin as pride (*superbia*) and sin as desire (*concupiscentia*). Augustine defined these concepts in his profound reflections on the nature of sin. He chose the redeemed life as his point of departure. We are supposed to be humble in view of the grace that we have been given; we must know our place before God. The essence of sin is the opposite of humility, namely, arrogance. When we lose God as the source of our life, it does not stop us from seeking the fulfillment of our desires. In our arrogance we not only seek salvation in the inner world of ourselves but also look with a lustful eye to the world outside.

With Augustine the driving force behind desire (*cupiditas*) and the aspiration to rule (*libido dominandi*) is gradually narrowed down to sexual desire. There human sin is concentrated. Localizing sin in one particular human passion has its historical roots in the Manichaean system, of which Augustine was an adherent for nine years. Manichaeism is a dualistic philosophy that posits good and evil as two powers that are eternally fighting each other and that situates evil in the material world. In Western theology Augustine's view of sin has resulted in a strong sexualization of sin, often with tragic consequences. However, this narrow view of sin was never given the status of an official church teaching. In fact, in 1341 it was explicitly condemned (Denzinger, ES, §1012).

Berkhof (CF 196) points to the remarkable fact that, traditionally, Christianity in southern Europe has given first place in sin to sexual desire, while in northwestern Europe and in North America (e.g., see Niebuhr 1941) this position went to pride and arrogance. The image of Faust, who wants to conquer the world and to this end concludes a pact with the devil, portrays sin as an unrestrained striving toward growth and dominance. Such a picture returned since the 1980s in theories that criticize the pursuit of unlimited economic growth (e.g., see Goudzwaard 1979 and Goudzwaard et al. 2007) and the concomitant ecological destruction (Conradie 2005).

Barth's doctrine of the atonement (CD IV) provided a creative redefinition of the concept of sin by presenting it as the flip side of redemption. In light of Christ's humiliation, sin is arrogance (CD IV/1); in light of Christ's glorification, sin is sluggishness (CD IV/2); and from the angle of the proclamation of the truth, sin is deception (CD IV/3). This trio describes sin as our inclination to deny and denigrate the work of God in Christ. In chapter 10, on Christology, we will return to the specific structure of Barth's concept of sin.

8.5. Original Sin

We turn here to an issue that many find even more difficult to digest than the doctrine of sin in general: the teaching of original sin. What is meant by this term? Is it true that sin is something we inherit from our ancestors?

If we want to understand what the doctrine of original sin is all about, we must start with what we wrote in 8.3 about sin as a state of things. We saw that this view of sin, as a power or sphere in which we live without Christ, is found particularly in the Gospel of John (note its contrasts between light and darkness, above and below, death and life) and in Paul's contrast between flesh and spirit (Rom 8). When we turn away from God, we live according to the flesh, but when we live through the Spirit of God and turn toward him, we are characterized as living "in the Spirit" (Rom 8:9). In the early centuries of the church this radical view of sin received less emphasis. The first Christians lived under the impact of the Sermon on the Mount and believed that the human will was free to live according to this new order. At baptism one was called to be the salt of the earth, a city on a hill, living in praise to God, and convinced that this life would not be too problematic.

The teaching of the British monk Pelagius (360–418), that sin is merely a matter of the (unnecessary) imitation of bad examples, should be understood against this background. If the Sermon of the Mount was, to a large extent, the guide for daily life, and if the disciples of Jesus are there challenged to be holy ("perfect") as God is holy (5:48), then human beings must be able to meet this challenge, for it would be meaningless if we were not ready to do so (PL 30:696).

Although initially Augustine also accepted this concept of freedom, he came to a more radical and comprehensive view of sin from his own life and pastoral experience. We might wish to do the will of God, but in real life we meet limitations that place a huge question mark behind our so-called free will. Augustine (re)discovered that sin goes deeper than just our acts. It does entail morality, but it is first of all a description of our state before God. Sin is an infringement not just on our will but on our whole being. In a certain sense we must say, *I am sin*. This admission does not imply that God's image in us is completely destroyed (see chap. 7); I remain a sinner, but I am also a creature, and therefore I have a sense of what is good. But I am sin in the sense that sin penetrates all aspects of my existence and pollutes my very nature.

This line of thinking led Augustine to make a few distinctions with regard to human freedom. In paradise Adam was still able not to sin (*posse non peccare*). After the fall this ability not to sin was lost, and thus we can no longer not sin (*non posse non peccare*). Only when we have reached our destination will we have, as it were, become fireproof to the possibility of sin (*non posse peccare*). For the present, however, there is no way of escaping its power. In this way Augustine put into words what down through the centuries became known as the Christian doctrine of original sin. Original sin means that human nature (esp. our will) has been infected, thereby making sin a collective and social phenomenon. Nobody is excepted. For this reason, original sin has often been referred to as hereditary sin, although the word is found only in Germanic languages and does not occur in Latin, let alone in the biblical languages. It is therefore better to speak of "original sin." This phrase denotes the universal inclination to do what is not good, an inclination so strong that no one is able not to give in to it time and again.

Romans 5:12-21 plays a major role in the debate about the precise way that sin spreads through the human species. Especially the interpretation of v. 12 has had significant consequences. The translation of the Latin Vulgate *in quo omnes peccaverunt* as "in whom all have sinned" led to the conclusion that in Adam all people have sinned. The Greek text allows for this phrase to be rendered differently, as "because all have sinned," but the Latin ignored that option. Therefore we must face the question how to understand this "sinning in Adam." Is it a matter of biological transfer (as Augustine was inclined to think) or of legal imputation? The first view is referred to as *realism*, the second as *federalism*. We find representatives of both positions in later Reformed theology. F. Turrettini (1623-87) was among the first theologians who supported the federalist approach, while American theologian William Shedd (1820-94) became an unrelenting realist (see McFarland 2010, 150-52). The realist suggests that, strictly speaking, all descendants of Adam were already present in his sperm, which makes them guilty of his act (a view that is supposedly supported by Heb 7:9-10). For the federalist, Adam is the representative ("head") of the entire human race, so that what Adam did is imputed by God to all people. This was allegedly supported by Rom 5, where Adam, in analogy with Christ, is represented as a "head of the covenant."

It is clear that both approaches have their problems. Bavinck (RD 3:110-17) searched for a synthesis to avoid either choice. Berkouwer regarded this issue as a dead end, however, and tried to overcome the dilemma in his detailed discussion of these problems (1971, 424-545) by concentrating on what the church wanted to say in its confession of original sin: "the overpowering and the total character of sin," from which we cannot escape to an untarnished, innocent, good side of our humanness (530-31). We prefer this latter approach.

The relationship between Adam and the sin problem, as presented in Rom 5:12-21, is best understood from the antithetical analogy with Christ. Paul sees in the cross and resurrection of Christ the eschatological judgment of sin. Analogous to this comprehensive finality of what God does in Christ, Paul refers to Adam as the one through whom sin entered the world. Thus, Adam receives a corporate meaning in the light of Christ. Adam and Christ stand for two assessments that each comprise all of humanity. This corporative approach of Paul is therefore of utmost importance for a sound understanding of his teachings of grace and sin. Paul and the early Christian church did not see God's act in Christ as a historical incident that affected only Jesus as an individual. What happened touched, in him, the entire state of humanity, whose prevailing situation was seen as having been decisively impacted by the "first Adam." It is therefore inadvisable to speculate about the question of how the sin of the first humans affected us without due regard for the shift in perspective that is brought about in Christ.

In contrast to the church of the West, this comprehensive meaning of sin gained no foothold in the churches in the East. Even today the churches of the East and Eastern Orthodoxy know of no doctrine of original sin. Athanasius maintained that all saints are without sin, and according to Cyril of Alexandria people are born sinless. Only the Western, Latin church saw a development toward a doctrine of original sin. The concept of "original transgression/defect" (*vitium originis*) emerged with Tertullian. It developed into the concept of *peccatum originale*, literally "original sin," which was considered to be transferable by inheritance (*peccatum haereditarium*). This view, of course, posed an enormous problem: how can people be guilty of sins that they have inherited? The Western church wanted to maintain the idea that we are all guilty because of our own acts, while at the same time stressing the communal and comprehensive aspect of sin. If inheritance is emphasized, there is significant danger that sin becomes primarily a matter of fate rather than of guilt. If, in contrast, the personal dimension is stressed, the corporate element entirely disappears. In practice, the church has attempted to hang on to both aspects. The Scholastics interpreted original sin as a kind of germ that is reactivated in every human life. At the same time, they went too far in trying to make this process transparent by distinguishing between original guilt and original blemish.

At times it is suggested that original sin is a typically Roman Catholic teaching. But Protestant confessional documents lay equal stress on this inescapable human condition. According to the Belgic Confession, original sin is "a perversion" of all nature, an inherited defect that affects even unborn children and that, "as from a root," produces all kinds of sin. It is ugly and detestable to God, which is sufficient reason to doom the entire human race. It is not even fully undone or "abolished" in our baptism, since "sin constantly boils forth as though from a contaminated spring" (art. 15). Even a person who believes and is baptized is not outside of the reach of the suction power of this human condition.

Original sin means, not that we are forced to sin, but that we cannot escape from it. In a statement that has become famous, Reinhold Niebuhr (1892-1971) said that the Christian view of human nature implies that the evil in us is "inevitable but not necessary" (1941, 150). This perspective may be seen as negative, but there is another, humanizing side to it. If original sin belongs to the package of Christian theology, it also means that we can no longer park sin and evil with one person or one particular group of people. By taking this radical concept of sin seriously, stigmatizing a group or individual becomes impossible. When push comes to shove, I am not better than anyone else, and if I do not, like some, make a total mess of my life, it is due only to accidental factors, behind which we may catch a glimpse of God's "general grace." The doctrine of original sin reminds us that collectively we have become enmeshed in the structures and complexities of sin and guilt. The classic view does justice to the social and structural character of evil. Sin goes deeper than morality and is totally intertwined with this life.

Remarkably enough, we find a new interest in the doctrine of original sin in contemporary theology and other disciplines. Partly it is because the idea of the hereditary nature of mutations in genetic material has become central in evolutionary thinking. But since this same theory of evolution has made the view that the entire human race descended from one human pair quite problematic, that theory may also provide reasons to deny the concept of original sin (see, respectively, Domning 2006 and Williams 2001). At the same time, the consequences of evolutionary theory might be rather limited (Blocher 1997). For other dimensions, see, among other recent studies, Jacobs 2008 and McFarland 2010. In a fascinating cultural-historical overview Jacobs demonstrates that Augustine has been unfairly accused of being most to blame for the concept of original sin. His approach had unmistakable roots in the early church (e.g., with Tertullian); moreover, he was a better interpreter of Paul than many are willing to grant. McFarland provides (see also his essay in Webster, OHST 140-59) a clear and creative reinterpretation of Augustine's line of thought regarding original sin in terms of the human will's increasing tendency to desire wrong objects, necessitating a liberation from this condition by the only Object that can truly satisfy our desires: God himself.

Earlier, McFadyen demonstrated in an important study (2000) how the Augustinian view of original sin provides, over against the empirical sciences, a unique language to speak adequately about experiences of severe person-directed violence, such as that encountered by victims of the Holocaust or of sexual abuse.

We referred to sin as a theological concept. Although modern science will never use the term "sin," contemporary empirical sciences have alerted us to reflexes and structures of sin that help us fathom the universal and the communal aspects of evil, which the concept of original sin expresses. Following in the steps of H. Berkhof, we may in this connection distinguish between superpersonal and subpersonal forms of inescapable evil (CF 211–15). The subpersonal realm is subject to our natural constitution and limitations. From the standpoint of biology, the human species belongs to the mammals, which means that appetite, lust for life, sexual instincts, staking out territory, and mechanisms of aggression and self-assertion form the basis of our biological, psychological, and social life. All these things belong to the natural substrate of our human existence and are connected to our experience of freedom.

The superpersonal factors include what the Epistle to the Ephesians refers to as powers (2:2–3; 3:10). When translated into the terms of our modern worldview, the term connotes the phenomena that are the object of sociological research: the superpersonal aspects of culture, money, fashion, codes of behavior, cultural myths, public opinion, Western or Eastern ideals, national pride, social media, and so forth. With all their positive potential, these powers also create addictions more than we often realize. They come with the air that we breathe. The ideals of eternal youth, of health and beauty, of the authentic self in every human being, and of unlimited possibilities are powers that have a dominant, often enslaving effect. The challenge to respond in freedom to God's love is therefore not situated in a vacuum but within a horizon where superpersonal as well as subpersonal powers exert a power of gravity and suction. The proper use of our freedom and the call to respond in love and loyalty will always assume the shape of concrete interaction with these realities within the framework of the covenant in which God calls us.

Even though anthropological, sociological, and cultural-psychological clarifications might give us a better understanding of "the powers," such empirical observations can never replace a theological view of sin. In theology—especially through the doctrine of original sin—we recognize the extent to which sin is interwoven with our creaturely and social makeup, but we do not identify sin with this makeup. A radical theological view of sin will find its point of departure in the new and surprising reality that appeared in Christ. The appearance of Christ opens a new reality and coherence that puts everything in a new light. This new cohesion is the result of God's life-giving love through forgiveness and a renewal of life, the first outlines of which are made visible in the key forms of Christian worship—the ministry of the Word, baptism, and communion. This worship creates a place where relationships dominate, where we receive a name and a place; in that habitat renewal can take its first steps. In contrast with this cohesiveness, we find what Paul identifies in Rom 5 under the label of Adam: a cohesiveness characterized by the break away from God, by sin as turning away from God, and by being cut off from the source of life.

The radical concept of sin that we find in Paul and that so strongly impacted the Augustinian tradition makes us very critical with respect to culture. If sin is an all-encompassing power, then, however accidental it may be, it is utterly impossible to locate sin precisely. Yet, we feel an urgent need to be clear about what sin is and where it is found; this is how our modern world deals with evil. From a deeply rooted belief that we can make and change our world, we think we must be able to find the reason for or culprit behind every form of evil. In public affairs this assumption often leads to a moralistic reflex. Our society and politics try to conquer evil by demanding new laws and regulations. What is the root cause of this reflex? Does the collective pressure to exclude every risk stem from the conviction that all evil is avoidable and occurs because of insufficient rules and control? Is it caused by uncertainty over how we will behave if we are left with too much freedom? Perhaps we should draw the following, paradoxical conclusion: on the one hand, our culture wants to believe in the essential goodness of humanity, but on the other hand, it treats people as if they need to be constantly distrusted and always controlled.

Whatever the case, this moralism may be avoided if we look for the source and essence of sin in the broken covenant relationship with God. When the relationship with God has been damaged, we refuse to seek our life, our safety, and our identity there; our relationship with the source of life has become murky. Instead of trust, distrust; instead of experiencing the closeness of God as the Living One, we end up in a state of cosmic loneliness. We are left alone with ourselves and necessarily regard everyone else with suspicion.

8.6. Sin and Tragedy—Guilt and Fate

In a previous section we spoke of sin from the angle of the perpetrator, of the victim, and of estrangement. We next examined these three elements in more depth by positioning them within the framework of God's Trinitarian covenant. Then we broadened our discussion by paying attention to the universal spread of sin as defined by the doctrine of original sin. In so doing, we touched on the question we must now face head-on: to what extent are we the ones who do evil, commit errors, do stupid things, or behave abominably? Is not our creaturely condition the real cause? Must evil be defined only in terms of individual or collective guilt, as if everything wrong in our life and society is somehow traceable to what we do? Or should theology and faith not also ponder the dimensions of evil that go beyond the human sphere?

These questions lead us to the relationship between sin and tragedy, guilt and fate. There is a reason why we have not introduced this problem until now. The order in which we discuss different questions is important. Only after having defined sin theologically as something that can be traced back to our own will may we ask the question about the extent to which this sinfulness is also tied to our creatureliness. If we had started at this point, it would have been too easy to come up with excuses for our behavior. But now that we have discussed the theme of original sin, the question of the role of tragedy presents itself quite urgently. If all people sin and no one can escape from it (even though sin is not necessary), does this sad reality not imply that there is a tragic component to our existence?

The Greek culture of antiquity had a strong sense of tragedy. People are the playthings of fate. The classical tragedies are about people who become the bearers of guilt without being aware of it; they carry a curse that only death can remove. The heroes in the tragedies of *Oedipus Rex* and *Antigone* unknowingly commit evil. Oedipus, the son of the king, is burdened with blood-guilt after he confronts and kills an attacker: it proves to be his father. Later, when he has delivered the city of Thebes from a monster, he is allowed to marry the queen-widow; thus, unknowingly, he marries his mother. Antigone is caught in this family drama and, for all her honesty and good will, succumbs to it. This theme of men and women as creatures who cannot make any other choice and who inevitably become guilty because of the limitations of life is also the subject of many modern theater productions.

In modern Western theology the finitude of creation has sometimes been largely identified with sin. Paul Tillich (ST 2:39-44) speaks of human beings as creatures who, in this life, miss the cohesiveness and unity that belong to God's essence. That is, we no longer know the unity of essence and existence, so that we cannot act authentically, in accord with our deepest being. From that angle the difference between

Creator and creature is indeed a rupture. We find this explanation of estrangement already in the nineteenth-century speculative philosophies of F. W. J. Schelling (1775-1854) and G. W. F. Hegel (1770-1831). Remarkably enough, we also find it in Hegel's prominent antagonist Søren Kierkegaard, in his book *Fear and Trembling* (see McFarland 2010, 154).

This approach left its mark on the theology of the early Barth. Initially, he saw creation as a downward movement, away from its sources, just as water rushes down along the side of a mountain, trying to find its way. In Barth (CD), this idea of the ambivalence of our finitude received further elaboration in the notion of *die Schattenseite des Daseins*, "the shadow side of our existence." According to Barth, the discovery of our finiteness (after all, we live only a short time), the anxiety about the purpose of life, and the experience of the fragility of our existence as we search and feel our way are not consequences of sin but are part of the shadow side of the existence that we have been given.

In *this* life, with all its risks and limitations, God wants to be worshiped and served by us. He has chosen this mode of existence, which at some time will be ended by our physical death (CD III/3:295-302). This shadow side of our existence must be distinguished from real evil. Evil is in its essence that which God has *not* chosen. Therefore, in this negative way (i.e., as that which God *not* wanted to be), evil is dependent on God (CD III/3:350-53). Evil is nothing but those things to which God has said No, and it is evil solely because God has said No to these things. In a starkly dialectical manner Barth synthesized these ideas in his (in)famous doctrine of *das Nichtige*—the nothingness that somehow nevertheless exists (CD III/3:289-368). Because of its speculative character and lack of consistency, this doctrine is often seen as one of the weaker parts of Barth's theology, as for example in the classic study of John Hick (1966, 126-44) about the problem of evil. For a profound analysis, see Krötke 2005. In contrast, upon closer study, Barth's view of creation is more positive and less ambivalent than has often been suggested (see Sherman 2005).

It is clear that Barth wanted to avoid any idea of suggesting that evil is an equally powerful opponent of God. However, the risk of such speculative theories about the origin of evil is that sin and evil may easily get the appearance of necessity. Since we must learn and grow, and since we are faced with limitations, the possibility of sin becomes inherent in creation.

Because of this significant risk we have chosen thus far not to deal with sin in the context of our tragic condition. We have resisted the strong trend in modern theology to place the fall outside history and to define sin metahistorically, as a consequence of our finitude (see above, 8.1). It is crucial that we do not make sin into something natural but clearly distinguish it as something that came later. Here the theology of Van Ruler (e.g., see his VW 4B:728–31) has been a source of great inspiration for us. Yet, we cannot deny that all kinds of evil (natural evil, such as sickness or handicaps, but also active evil, such as recklessness and a hot temper) have a biological or developmental-psychological substrate. In that sense the idea of tragedy is not irrelevant, for there is no answer to the question why some people face tragedy and others do not. The New Testament explicitly denies a direct connection between sickness or handicaps and sin (John 9:3), and the widespread idea that the suffering of animals and such natural disasters as earthquakes and tsunamis are the result of a "cosmic fall" in punishment of human sin finds no support in the Bible (as Blocher correctly points out, 2009, 165). We simply do not know why these things have a place in God's good creation.

Nevertheless, we cannot deny our crucial role as perpetrators and causes of evil. This is, we might say, the special contribution of the Christian tradition to this discussion. In this connection it is quite remarkable to note that the Bible gives no space to a tragic view of life. Even the book of Ecclesiastes, with its sharp eye for human limitations, finitude, and mortality, does not do so. Admittedly, it speaks in melancholy tones, but it deems wise those people who know how to receive life as a gift from God (e.g., Eccl 8:15; 9:7; 12:9). The beginning of wisdom is found in this attitude of respect for God (Eccl 12:13; see also Prov 9:10). This perspective leads us to the following proposition: Christian dogmatics must not be blind to the tragic elements that may play a role in our lives, but it must not define the essence of sin as a series of tragic realities. Theologically, it is decisive that God meets us and calls us in our situation and our eventual tragic circumstances. In other words, the deciding theological factor in dealing with these circumstances is to be guided by the covenant. God wants us to respond positively, to commit our life to him in the midst of evil and limitations.

From the very beginning God has addressed us, in spite of all our limitations, and he has taken us along in an adventure that we call "covenant," which finds its origin in his gracious love. In everything we encounter along this road, we remain able to ask, what does God want me to do in this situation? In other words, even when we are faced with misfortune, we retain the possibility of responding to God's call, at times perhaps even more distinctly than we might have done if all were well (2 Cor 12:10). For even if we have no answer to the why questions, we know that our life is "hidden with Christ in God" (Col 3:3). Therefore, there is no reason to withdraw in the defeatism of the tragic worldview. In this connection also note what we said in 6.7 about the doctrine of providence: we are not a plaything of fate but lie in the hands of the God and Father of Jesus Christ, which makes all the difference in the world.

Still, we do not deny that a contemporary theological reflection needs more terms and concepts to deal with sin and evil than those of personal and collective actions. A more nuanced approach is not only possible but necessary. For that reason we have described sin not only in terms of acts but also in terms of power and estrangement—the kind of language that tries to express what happens to us but surpasses our understanding. In the Bible the Christian tradition deploys an arsenal of options to seek adequate understanding of different situations of evil, sin, and guilt. At times the language of estrangement may be helpful to highlight situations in which persons or an entire society find themselves; sometimes the victim perspective or talking about a state of sinfulness may be useful; yet at other times talking about humans as actors, perpetrators, or collaborators may be relevant. What we need is the gift of differentiation. A person who finds himself or herself on the wrong path as the result of hunger, violence, or economic problems must be approached in a different way than will be an active actor in a consumerist culture or violent schemes, or those who show irresponsible greed. This point also applies to the way in which we treat those who are caught in a "sick" system, in which a new generation repeats the mistakes of their forebears. The Bible opens the possibility for such diversity.

In all of these considerations, we underscore that the uniqueness of the Christian concept of sin has to do with our relational involvement with God. The sin-concept reminds us that, with all the evil in which we are involved, as actor or as victim and as a link in a chain, we will eventually meet a personal God and his judgment. In the words of the title of Depoortere 1984, "We are yours with all our sinfulness."

8.7. Theodicy

The relationship between sin and tragedy also raises the question of theodicy. We will give this topic brief but explicit attention, especially as it pertains to the question of how all the suffering in the world can be harmonized with God's justice. (The word "theodicy" is derived from *theos* and *dikē*, the Greek words for "God" and "justice.") In the Western world and in theological discussions this problem has become ever more urgent. On the one hand, we face the age-old question of *how* the suffering of so many in wars, disasters, and sickness can be harmonized with faith in the goodness and justness of God. There is an immense quantity of misery that cannot be traced back to human acts. On the other hand, the question of the *why* of suffering has become more and more pressing.

But why? Although we have an increasingly firmer grip on our physical existence and have pushed back many evils by means of modern technology and medical science, and even though the standard of living has improved for many, we have not succeeded in protecting ourselves against disasters and misfortune. Those who have embraced modernism tend to think that sickness and misery can be overcome and life altered according to our wishes. But the belief in progress, which has proved to be such a mobilizing force ever since the Enlightenment, sooner or later gets stuck in our everyday life and may change into despair. Why has the kingdom of joy not yet been inaugurated? In what kind of world has God placed us, a world that cannot get rid of evil? Is God the culprit? God's only excuse, many say, is that he does not exist. But that may well be too easily said.

In his *Essais de théodicée sur la bonté de Dieu, la liberté de l'homme et l'origine du mal* (Essay of theodicy about the goodness of God, the freedom of man, and the origin of evil; 1710), Leibniz suggested a cosmological solution for the theodicy problem. Evil as such is inherent in the cosmic system, but viewed in its totality, that system appears to be the most optimal construction possible—we live in "the best of all possible worlds." In the theology of the twentieth century Leibniz's optimism has completely disappeared (even though contemporary philosophers suggest that he was not as naive as has sometimes been suggested). Especially since the 1970s the quantity of theological literature about God and suffering has become so immense that one cannot keep up with it. The process of coming to terms with the two world wars did not really start until the rebuilding of Europe was to a large degree completed. In the 1950s the relationship between faith and science topped the agenda, and in the 1960s secularization as a theological theme drew much attention. But then followed the decades in which theodicy came to the forefront (e.g., see Kushner 1978, and also the impressive book that proved to be the breakthrough of Beek [1990]). It was significant that the world gradually gained the sociopsychological ability to focus on the Shoah, the extinction of six million Jews during World War II, but it was not the only factor (see chap. 9). It also became possible from the angle of historical theology to put the question of God's presence on the agenda in a fundamental way. Already in Barth's early theology (see R2) the relationship of God to human culture had come under thorough consideration. God is not present by default, as a ferment in the history of civilization. He is not within our reach. But if God is not identical with what history presents to us, where is he? An impressive answer was given by representatives of the so-called theology of the cross: in the cross of Christ, God reveals himself in our own history of suffering. For good reason the Gospels find their apex in the shocking events of the death of the Son of God on the cross. Without any doubt, this event conveys an essential message about God and his presence among us. For example, see Jüngel 1972, Moltmann 1993, and Beek 1990.

We should also mention that in recent decades the problems of theodicy have been widely discussed by analytic philosophers. This treatment happened on a rather abstract level, from a desire to make things rationally clear, but without much sensitivity for the existential and pastoral aspects of the problem. In the past few years this focus has been changing, as this discussion has paid more attention to the theological tradition of reflection on the topic. For a selection of now almost-classic theoretical studies, see Adams and Adams 1990; for a fierce criticism of this approach, Surin 1986; and for an attempt at synthesis, Adams 1999.

When we listen to the Bible, we find that these questions are not totally absent (think of the book of Job), but they are assigned definite limits. In the Wisdom literature, to which the book of Job belongs, the questions about human suffering and human finitude do not receive any final answers; rather, we are directed toward the majesty of God (Job 38–41). Human complaints may be expressed, but the outcome of our debate with God remains uncertain. Theologically, this human dispute with God is of utmost importance. Christian theology makes it clear that we cannot find a final answer to the question of the origin of evil. However, when faced with suffering and decay, we have an address where we can go with our complaints: God. Thus, once again, we face our human role in dealing with the limitations of our existence. In connection with questions about sin and evil, it is important to determine how far we may go: what we *must* say, what we *may* say, what we can perhaps *say hesitantly*, or what we *must absolutely no longer say*. Here we must make some very careful dogmatic distinctions.

In the Bible we meet God as the one who wants to give us life and makes a covenant with us. This offer of God's must be the basis; this much we must make clear. In addition, we *can* and *may* say that God, in choosing this creation with its possibilities and limitations, has chosen a reality that is vulnerable—or, to use Barth's words, has a shadow side. This quality allows us to say that suffering (including suffering that is not inflicted upon us by other people) does not happen outside the will of God. But we *absolutely may not* say that God actually wants evil, let alone sin.

The importance of how we direct our questions has been touched upon earlier. We do not get a clear view of evil—also not of natural evil—by analyzing evil as such, but only by viewing it as a counterperspective to God's life-giving intentions. It is only when we have learned to look toward the triune God—as the Creator who gives us life, as the Redeemer who in Jesus Christ lets his compassion overrule his anger, and as the Spirit who makes us long for a better world (Rom 8:22–23; Rev 22:17)—that we can complain, ask questions, and remain silent in a Christian way.

The healing miracles in the Gospels (see chaps. 10 and 11) must be read as the concrete demonstration of the things that God opposes in his grace. Here we see the direction and the intention of God's revelation: God wants our salvation. People are reconnected with God as the source of life, and his salvation also includes physical, social, and psychological realities. It does not mean, however, that Jesus's ministry is the final realization of the new world. In Jesus's presence the kingdom of God is breaking through, and its silhouette becomes discernable, but it is not yet revealed in all its fullness. For that reason we must also consider evil from a pneumatological angle, that is, in terms of the Spirit of Christ, who comforts and leads us in the midst of atrocities, and who has been given to us as "a guarantee" of God's future (2 Cor 5:5).

8.8. The Devil as Unperson

We argued earlier that sin is not part of God's creation; it is a parasitic phenomenon that we can see clearly only when we begin with God's creation and his grace. As we saw, Augustine accordingly defined evil as *privatio boni*, a taking away of the good. This definition points to something very important. Sin is not an independent power opposing God but a parasite. Sin and evil feed on the good and rob the good of its reality. Because of the parasitic character of sin, we cannot regard sin as an independent power. That recognition impacts the praxis of faith. Christian theology cannot in any way support (faith) practices in which evil or the devil is approached with the same respect and deference as God. In this connection we must label fascination with the devil, evil, death, and horror, both in Christian and non-Christian circles, as an abnormal and unhealthy temptation to focus on, and to tame, these destructive and vicious elements.

This warning does not eliminate the place for the devil in Christian reflection on sin and evil. So far in this chapter we have hardly mentioned the devil, for good reason. For when we speak about sin and evil, we must first know how things are related and give first place to our own involvement in it. Here the Genesis story of the fall, where we meet a serpent and a strange voice that tempts Eve and Adam, points us in the right direction. In this story we are addressed as the responsible persons. The question is, which voice we will listen to: the word of God, or another voice that sows distrust with regard to God's trustworthiness? The emphasis in the story falls on the human role. Do we allow evil to proceed, or do we refuse to heed the voice of temptation? The history of Jesus's temptations in the wilderness stands in stark contrast to the story of the fall. Christ as the last Adam picks up the thread where the first Adam dropped it.

From the perspective of religious history, the figure of Satan is a latecomer. The oldest layers of the Old Testament provide no firm picture of God's relationship with evil. In the oldest layers Satan is not so much God's antagonist but stands in God's service as the accuser of humanity (e.g., see 1 Chr 21:1; Job 1–2; Ps 109:6; Zech 3:1). When David succumbs to the temptation to organize a census, this is attributed in 2 Sam 24:1 to God, who has become angry. But in the later book of 1 Chronicles it is attributed to Satan (21:1). This apparent correction shows how the Bible itself reflects the debate about God's relationship with evil. In the New Testament Satan has developed into the one who destroys and threatens God's work. However, this figure never becomes an equal opponent. The existence of the devil as God's antagonist is not denied, but his power is combated and brought low (Hoeven 1998, 175): "I saw Satan fall like lightning from heaven" (Luke 10:18). Satan is fallen and does not have power over heaven and earth. This is also the drift of the story of Jesus's temptations (Mark 1:12–13) and of the book of Revelation. Jesus is the victor and has conquered the power of evil; that is the true state of things. All entities and powers that manifest themselves are losers in view of the victory of Christ. The process by which Satan becomes an equal player occurs in Zoroastrianism and Manichaeism. There we have an absolute dualism, in which Satan has become the equally strong, opposite force to God as an independent person.

It is good to be absolutely clear at this point about the true state of things. Christians believe in God and do not believe in the devil. "Believe" here means faith in its theological sense. Faith is trust and commitment. When we consider God worthy of our trust, we cannot show the same respect for Satan, who is the antagonist; the same applies when respect develops into fear. That would be dualism. Nonetheless, this practical dualism has been very influential in parts of Christianity. For many, the devil actually plays the role of God's competitor and is an important element in the experience of their faith. However, we must be adamant that this is not the attitude of genuine faith. God alone is worthy to be worshiped; no opposing power is worthy of the same respect or attention.

This line of thinking is also significant for the ever-recurring question whether the devil or Satan is a person or a power. Is the devil a person? Or does that word give him too much honor? We cannot deny that Jesus spoke to the devil and chased the devil away. This incident might lead us to conclude that the devil has the characteristics of a person. In the past the general opinion has been that the devil is a person who opposes God. Contemporary systematic theology, however, would do well not to simply repeat these religion-historical and exegetical opinions as a dogmatic conclusion. Dogmatics must interpret the distinctive biblical data in the light of God's revelation in Christ in such a way that it is helpful in our relationship with God. This approach leads to a normative evaluation of these data and of the biblical evidence in view of the praxis of faith. We will therefore repeat the question whether Satan may be referred to as a person and will seek to provide a theological answer.

When the church prays to God in the name of Christ, it accepts him as person. Personhood here carries the character of responsiveness, responsibility, integrity, and goodness. In that sense Christian theology derives its understanding of personhood from the way in which Father, Son, and Spirit are persons. We saw in chapter 3 how this concept of personhood developed into a central category in the early church, particularly with the Cappadocian Fathers. It is truly significant to be a person. God is person in *optima forma*, and we are persons in an imperfect way as bearers of the image of God. God is therefore the original person (*analogans*); all other persons can be viewed as such only in a secondary sense (as being similar, or *analogata*). God is the ultimate person who, as the Giver of life, makes us into persons, into responsive and responding beings. This view makes personhood a meaningful theological and salvific concept. The figure of the Satan falls far short of this concept of personhood. The devil stands for disintegration, estrangement, emptiness, and curse, and he is therefore the opposite of God as a person. The devil is in the service of *depersonalization*. As such, he is, as God's antagonist, the personification of evil, as it were. The devil is "unperson" or "anti-person." Those who respond to Satan become depersonalized, become internally divided, and disintegrate. (See a novel by C. S. Lewis [1943] in which the devil takes possession of one of the characters; he is subsequently referred to as the Un-man and in the end speaks only gibberish.) With good reason the Greek word for the devil is *diabolos*, the one who "throws things into disorder."

We do not suggest that we wish, or are able, to avoid personal language when we speak about Satan. On the contrary, there may even be situations where we must address the devil as an identity and command him in the name of the living Jesus to come out. The early church was much more intensely involved in exorcisms (casting out devils) than we often realize. Admittedly, much depends on the culture and the worldview of the people involved. In Africa the power of evil becomes very concrete in the belief in spirits that influence and threaten life in many different ways. In many respects this culture is closer to the world of the New Testament than is our Western culture, where, since Kant, all spirits have been assigned to the religious imagination. The modern paradigm is useful for theology in that the responsibility of individuals and peoples can no longer be shifted to the influence of one or more evil spirits or Satan. It is we who allow ourselves to be made into an instrument of evil, or of the evil one. The Bible makes this responsibility clear from the very first. Moreover, we now have a better understanding of the pathological background of human actions, which must not be confused with demonic "possession." But these considerations do not allow us to declare the modern paradigm to be superior. The positive character of the older worldview lies in its taking the victory of Christ with utter seriousness. That victory was believed in, heart and soul. For us too, this turning toward Christ as the victor over Satan, the tormentor—over evil and over God's antagonist—is of the highest importance. In real-life situations this priority will determine the trend of pastoral conversations, of the proclamation of the church, and in particular, of prayers for healing and delivery.

In the meantime a precise description of the ontology of Satan has not emerged, and understandably so. As creatures, we are unable to provide an exact ontological definition of the opposite of God as the Giver of life. As the one who denies the Creator of life and who wants to turn God's good work into chaos, Satan falls outside the circle of light of the creation in which God is salvifically at work, bringing order, life, and freedom. Near God, as the source of life (Ps 36:10; see also 87:7), the creature can freely breathe, while outside the divine circle of life, the creature's breath is taken away. Such is what the devil, in fact, does. Fortunately, Christian theology has more to say about God than about the devil and his powers.

Not without reason Jesus taught his disciples to pray for delivery from the evil one. We already indicated that the Greek *tou ponērou* may be rendered in either a personal or a nonpersonal way. This uncertainty is typical for the shadowy sphere that surrounds the existence of the devil. The important thing is that, in this prayer, we address God the Father, trusting that he is ready and able to deliver us from the dark powers of death, also when these powers show very personal traits. This must be the direction of the Christian life of faith and of Christian theology. We are reminded of the old adage attributed to Pope Celestine I in the fifth century: *lex orandi lex credendi*, the rule for our prayers is the rule for our faith.

Once again we see the importance of not waiting to speak about grace until we first fully understand sin and evil. We should, rather, face evil and sin in the light of grace. This is, in fact, the only way in which we can bear to look at them. Therefore, we should once more remember that a Christian conception of sin cannot be separated from the covenant in creation and redemption. Here also the Lord's Prayer points the way, for the plea for deliverance from evil follows the request for the coming of God's kingdom. The church prays for delivery from all forms of evil in the light of the coming of the kingdom and the hallowing of God's name. Moreover, the one who prays is immediately asked to repeat what Jesus taught us to pray: "And forgive us our debts, as we have forgiven our debtors." We cannot think about evil, and certainly not pray against evil, without recognizing our own role therein.

In sum, we do not deny that we are confronted with many forms of evil and estrangement for which we are not personally guilty. Nonetheless, we cannot remain at a safe distance. The liberating knowledge that God in Christ stopped the power of evil and robbed it of its finality creates the space for us to recognize our own role in the complexities of sin and evil. This recognition has an important practical and public impact as well. Guilt and evil are not simply to be traced to one evil genius or to one segment of the population—usually a group to which we ourselves do not belong. Demonizing is utterly impossible, or evil. And for this reason a Christian doctrine of sin enables us to look at the concrete forms of evil, in both the individual and in society, to define them and, in the praxis of life, to proceed in wisdom to perform damage control. Such a realistic approach to sin and evil, in the light of the victory of grace, will help to make our entire society more humane.

References

Adams, Marilyn McCord. 1999. *Horrendous Evils and the Goodness of God*. Ithaca, NY: Cornell University Press.

Adams, Marilyn McCord, and Robert M. Adams, eds. 1990. *The Problem of Evil*. Oxford: Oxford University Press.

Beek, Abraham van de. 1990. *Why? On Suffering, Guilt, and God*. Grand Rapids: Eerdmans.

Berkouwer, Gerrit C. 1971. *Sin*. Grand Rapids: Eerdmans.

Blocher, Henri. 1997. *Original Sin: Illuminating the Riddle*. Leicester: Apollo.

———. 2009. "The Theology of the Fall and the Origin of Evil." In *Darwin, Creation, and the Fall: Theological Challenges*, edited by R. J. Berry and T. A. Noble, 149–72. Nottingham: Apollos.

Brink, Gijsbert van den. 2012. "Should We Drop the Fall? On Taking Evil Seriously." In *Strangers and Pilgrims on Earth*, edited by E. van der Borght and P. van Geest, 761–78. Leiden: Brill.

Conradie, Ernst M. 2005. "Towards an Ecological Reformulation of the Christian Doctrine of Sin." *Journal of Theology for Southern Africa* 122:4–22.

Dennett, Daniel C. 1991. *Consciousness Explained*. Boston: Little, Brown.

Depoortere, Kristiaan. 1984. *Wij zijn van U met al ons kwaad: Over zonde, verzoening en biecht* [We are yours with all our evil: On sin, reconciliation and confession]. Tielt: Lannoo.

Domning, Daryl P. 2006. *Original Selfishness: Original Sin and Evil in the Light of Evolution*. Aldershot: Ashgate.

Gestrich, Christof. 1997. *The Return of Splendor in the World: The Christian Doctrine of Sin and Forgiveness*. Grand Rapids: Eerdmans.

Goudzwaard, Bob. 1979. *Capitalism and Progress: A Diagnosis of Western Society*. Grand Rapids: Eerdmans.

Goudzwaard, Bob, Mark Vander Vennen, and David Van Heemst. 2007. *Hope in Troubled Times: A New Vision for Confronting Global Crises*. Grand Rapids: Baker Academic.

Hick, John. 1966. *Evil and the God of Love*. London: Macmillan.

Hoeven, Tobias H. van der. 1998. *Het imago van Satan: Een cultuur-theologisch onderzoek naar een duivels tegenbeeld* [The reputation of Satan: A cultural-theological study of a demonic counterimage]. Kampen: Kok.

Jacobs, Alan. 2008. *Original Sin: A Cultural History*. New York: HarperOne.

Jenson, Matt. 2007. *The Gravity of Sin: Augustine, Luther, and Barth on "homo incurvatus in se."* London: T&T Clark.

Jüngel, Eberhard. 1972. "Vom Tod des lebendigen Gottes: Ein Plakat" (1968). Chap. 5 in *Unterwegs zur Sache*. Munich: Kaiser.

———. 2001. *Justification: The Heart of the Christian Faith; A Theological Study with an Ecumenical Purpose*. London: T&T Clark.

Krötke, Wolf. 2005. *Sin and Nothingness in the Theology of Karl Barth*. Princeton: Princeton Theological Seminary.

Kushner, Harold S. 1978. *When Bad Things Happen to Good People*. New York: Schocken Books.

Lewis, C. S. 1943. *Perelandra*. London: John Lane (= *Voyage to Venus*. London: Pan Books, 1953).

McFadyen, Alistair I. 2000. *Bound to Sin: Abuse, Holocaust, and the Christian Doctrine of Sin*. Cambridge: Cambridge University Press.

McFarland, Ian A. 2010. *In Adam's Fall: A Meditation on the Christian Doctrine of Original Sin*. Oxford: Wiley-Blackwell.

Moltmann, Jürgen. 1993. *The Crucified God: The Cross of Christ as the Foundation and Criticism of Christian Theology*. Minneapolis: Fortress.

Niebuhr, Reinhold. 1941. *The Nature and Destiny of Man: A Christian Interpretation*. Vol. 1, *Human Nature*. London: Nisbet.

Plantinga, Cornelius. 1995. *Not the Way It's Supposed to Be: A Breviary of Sin*. Grand Rapids: Eerdmans.

Rahner, Karl. 1967. "Evolution and Original Sin." *Concilium* 26:61–73.

Ruler, Arnold A. van. 1972. "Zonnigheden in de zonde" [The sunny sides of sin]. In *VW* 3:361–63.

Schwager, Raymond. 2006. *Banished from Eden: Original Sin and Evolutionary Theory in the Drama of Salvation*. Leominster: Gracewing.

Sherman, Robert. 2005. *The Shift to Modernity: Christ and the Doctrine of Creation in the Theologies of Schleiermacher and Barth*. London: T&T Clark.

Shuster, Marguerite. 2004. *The Fall and Sin: What We Have Become as Sinners*. Grand Rapids: Eerdmans.

Surin, Kenneth. 1986. *Theology and the Problem of Evil*. Oxford: Blackwell.

Swaab, Dick F. 2014. *We Are Our Brains: A Neurobiography of the Brain, from the Womb to Alzheimer's*. New York: Spiegel & Grau.

Williams, Norman P. 1927. *The Ideas of the Fall and Original Sin*. London: Longmans, Green.

Williams, Patricia. 2001. *Doing without Adam and Eve: Sociobiology and Original Sin*. Minneapolis: Fortress.

9 Israel, the Raw Nerve in Christian Theology

The Doctrine of the Covenant

AIM

In this chapter we will study the topic of Israel in the context of Christian dogmatics. More specifically we want to:

- define what we mean by the term "Israel" and how the people, religion, land, and state that go by that name are interrelated (9.1)
- sensitize the reader to the close affinity that exists between church and synagogue by virtue of their common hope for God's kingdom (9.2)
- describe how Christian dogmatics has dealt with "Israel" in the past (9.3)
- indicate how the theme of Israel introduces a structural duality into Christian doctrine (9.4)
- try to gauge God's intentions regarding his covenant with Israel – for Israel itself and for the nations (9.5)
- outline the significance that the New Testament attributes to Jesus in connection with God's covenant with Israel (9.6)
- show that, at bottom, the difference between church and synagogue depends on their differing views as to the meaning of redemption (9.7)
- end with some conclusions about what we, at the very least, may learn from Israel (9.8).

MAKING CONNECTIONS

1. In 1958 the novel *Exodus* was published. Written by the American author Leon Uris, it takes its name from one of the ships that transported Jewish Holocaust survivors to Palestine after the Second World War. The novel is based on historical research into the establishment of the State of Israel. Boosted by the film that was made two years later, the book became a

bestseller. What stories, events, or traditions have shaped your view of the State of Israel?

2. Read the novel *The Chosen* (1967), by Chaim Potok. What does it mean to be chosen? How does this book relate to Zionism?

9.1. A Terminological Clarification

This chapter is about Israel. But what do we mean when we use this word? Discussions often get confused when it is unclear precisely which Israel we are talking about: the State of Israel? the strip of land that coincides with biblical Canaan? the Jewish people? If the latter, do we mean the biblical people of Israel or (also) today's Israelis? Or does "Israel" mean adherents to the Jewish faith, that is, Judaism? Contemporary theological studies about Israel frequently have Judaism in mind, but in that case we need to distinguish Judaism from the Jewish people, for not all Jews are religious, and if they are, they might be Christians or Hindus. In this book we try to be clear in each case which meaning we have in mind, whether historical or contemporary, whether religious, ethnic, or national. When we speak more specifically about the institutional form of Judaism, we will often use the term "the synagogue," just as we frequently refer to Christianity as "the church."

How does Israel figure in Christian theology? Our answer is, first, as the biblical people of Israel. Israel is a name that was given to a concrete people of flesh and blood. The Torah tells us that Israel as a people exists because God called it into being. God chose it and made it into a people (Gen 12:2) and has bound himself to it in such a way that it would not disappear in the bedlam of history (Deut 26:5–8; Hos 11:1–4). The entire Old Testament continuously affirms that Israel is the people that God has elected to be his special people (Exod 19:5–6). Why this people? The answer: because God loved them (Deut 7:7). We cannot give a rational explanation for this choice, however offensive it may be to us late-modern people, for "true love defies explanation" (Beek 2002, 149). So, when we speak of Israel, we speak first of all of this specific people, the "offspring of Abraham," as we meet them in the Hebrew Bible.

The Hebrew Bible (or Tanak) constitutes, as the First, or Old, Testament, an integral part of the Christian canon. This placement resulted from a fundamental decision made early on in church history when, in the second century, the church faced the challenge of Marcionism. The decision might have turned out differently, for already at that time a wide gap had developed between church and synagogue. But in its self-understanding the church realized its dependence on God's journey with the biblical people of Israel. The God whom Christians had come to know in Jesus Christ was the same as the one who in the past began with the people of Israel.

But Israel should appear in Christian theology not only as a biblical people. More is at stake than the history of this people as chronicled in the Old Testament and told in numerous children's Bibles. Letting Israel simply coincide with its appearance in the First, or Old, Testament relegates it entirely to the past and loses sight of the ongoing Israel. In dogmatics "Israel" also refers to living Judaism—to the Jewish community that, after the development of the Tanak and after the coming of Christ, has continued on through the centuries to interpret the Tanak and to regard it as the basis for its life. The first five books of the Tanak, the Pentateuch—or preferably the Torah, to use the Hebrew term rather than the Greek— occupy a particular place. After the close of what Christians call the Old Testament, the Mishnah was created as the oral and written exposition of the Torah, and then also the Talmud, a collection of commentaries on the Mishnah. These writings are the center for the Jewish people as a living faith community that survived even the Holocaust.

Thus we associate the name "Israel" both with the biblical people and with the ongoing impact of the Torah over time. But, third, we also associate the name with a country; that aspect is also firmly anchored in the biblical witness. When Israel as a people is defined theologically (i.e., from God's perspective), almost invariably the land—the *Erets Yisrael*—is also mentioned. As Gen 12:7 tells us, "To your descendants I will give this land." That promise is repeated over and over, confirmed, intensified (Gen 17:8: "for an everlasting possession"), and eventually realized. The promise to Abraham is unthinkable without the land of Canaan. The entire book of Exodus is full of the journey to the land that is "flowing with milk and honey" (Exod 3:8). Together with the rite of circumcision (Gen 17:9-14) and the law that was given to Israel on Mount Horeb, the promise of the land is an integral part of the covenant that God made with Israel. However, the oft-repeated question in Christian theological discussions today is to what extent this promise remains unchanged in the New Testament. The land is no more spoken of in the New Testament or, at most, only implicitly (Rom 9:4). Not the country but "the ends of the earth" (Acts 1:8) now forms the geographic horizon of God's salvific actions. So, has this promise of the land now been fulfilled or prolonged? Must it now be applied in a spiritual sense, or is it no longer applicable at all? Must it not be reinterpreted in the light of Christ's coming, since God's name no longer has its abode in a land with a temple but anywhere that two or three people come together in the name of Christ (i.e., in his church)? Or is this a faulty antithesis? Should we instead conclude from the silence of the New Testament that nothing with respect to the Old Testament has changed? Would we not have been informed if it were otherwise? We simply pose these much-discussed questions to highlight the degree to which Israel as a land is part of Christian reflection of faith.

Fourth, when we mention Israel we might think of the State of Israel as a political entity, as it was founded in 1948 under the leadership of David Ben-Gurion. This option raises the stakes. How can a contemporary political entity be the object of theological study? In the case of any other state, would this focus not immediately stir suspicions of religious nationalism—of a deadly mix of the "most holy faith" (Jude 20) with the glorification of one particular country, people, or race? History provides all too many examples of what this special treatment might bring. Especially from the combination of options that we have mentioned—people, religion, land, and nation-state—"Israel" proves to be a hot item for discussion. At one extreme we hear arguments in church and theology that completely detach the land and the state from Israel, recognizing only the biblical people and, at most, the present Jewish faith community. At the other extreme we find it asserted that the promise of the land is guaranteed only by the State of Israel and that support for Israel's politics is therefore a matter of faith obedience. Because of this lack of consensus the State of Israel cannot be avoided—at least in the form of a question—as a topic in dogmatics. For dogmatics has the task of reflecting on the problems and dilemmas that our faith evokes (there would never have been a Christology without a lack of consensus concerning Christ). For that reason we must address the State of Israel in a particular way—namely, in its relationship to "Israel" as a people and a land.

We choose to first regard Israel as a concrete community to which God revealed himself and gave his promises. This approach makes Israel both an ethnic and a religious entity. In the theological perspective of the writers of the Tanak, these two coincided, and this Tanak is the deposit of God's revelation to Israel. As we shall see, the covenant that God made with this people in Abraham has a central place, and from that angle Israel is not a free-floating notion—a cipher that with some effort might be applied to any (repressed) community—but a concrete nation. However, from the very beginning, the Tanak does not overlook other peoples. Or to put it in words that A. A. van Ruler might have used, the Tanak concerns Israel but is about the entire world. For "the earth is the LORD's and the fullness thereof" (Ps 24:1; e.g., see also Exod 19:5). But with this remark we have left the domain of terminology and now find ourselves in that of dogmatic reflection.

We begin this reflection with a short theological note about the relationship between the contemporary church and contemporary Judaism. The Old Testament and large sections of the New do not primarily speak about Israel and the church but about Israel and "the nations." Israel is described as the *ha'am* ("the people"), the nations as the *goyim*—always in the plural form and often in association with the gentile world. The relationship between Israel and the nations tends to be one of tension; the goyim appear more often as the enemy than as the friend of Israel. But in the eschatological expectation both come together under the blessing of the one name; see Ps 67 with its interaction between the "us" and the nations, also Zech 8:23 and Rev 21:26; 22:2. For a nuanced answer to the question whether and how the New Testament—as a continuation of the Old Testament—allows Christians to speak of the church as God's people and as a holy people, see Schoon 2006.

9.2. A Shared Expectation: "Thy Kingdom Come"

Article 1 of the Constitution of the Protestant Church in the Netherlands (PCN, founded in 2004 as a merger of three Protestant churches) reads as follows:

> In accordance with its confession the Protestant Church in the Netherlands is [a] manifestation of the one holy apostolic and catholic or universal Christian Church which, sharing in the expectation granted to Israel, looks forward to the arrival of the kingdom of God.

This statement signifies a major shift from older dogmatics. It refers to Israel as the people that received the promise of the coming kingdom of God. The church does not take the place of Israel but sees itself as a community that is privileged to share in the expectation that was given to Israel. That is to say, the expectation of the coming kingdom remains the horizon within which church and faith—and thus also Christian theology—operate. In previous chapters we have several times, and for good reason, emphasized the prayer that Jesus taught his disciples. In this prayer the "hallowing" of God's name and the petition for his kingdom hold center stage. The coming of the kingdom, a life in which God rules and where all will bow their knee before him, forms the overarching salvation-historical accolade that connects all themes of Christian doctrine. Whether it concerns creation, God's providential care for the maintenance of the world, the meaning of sin and grace, Christ and the Spirit, or renewal and completion—we can talk about none of these themes without touching on the relationship with Israel as the ethnic community to which the expectation of God's saving future was first given. Likewise, the church of today cannot, despite its perspective on Jesus of Nazareth differing from that of Judaism, regard Israel as a something of the past that is no longer relevant. Both Israel and the church cherish the expectation of a future in which God is recognized as the God of all nations and of the entire earth, as their universal perspective. Israel lived with this perspective before the church came into being.

We very intentionally begin our discussion about Israel by emphasizing the intimate link between the Christian faith and Judaism, a tie that is also present in the documents in which other Christian denominations describe their relationship with Israel. The Christian faith cannot speak of Judaism as just another of the world religions—in the same category as Islam, Hinduism, and Buddhism—because of the many elements that connect Judaism and Christianity at a fundamental level, in their deepest convictions, desires, and expectations. Christian views of Israel have too often emphasized points of difference, which do exist of course and will not be ignored in this chapter. But by allowing our view of Israel to be largely determined by these differences, a black-and-white model of thinking becomes almost inevitable. This approach fails to do justice not only to the common orientation of the two sides toward the same God (something that, as we saw, is more problematic in the case of Islam), but also to the church, historically, having its roots in Israel. The DNA of the Christian church continues to be more distinctly defined by Judaism than many realize.

Faith in Jesus Christ as the Savior is built on the infrastructure of the faith of the Old Testament and therefore displays many similarities. H. Berkhof (CF 19) enumerates some of these similarities as the transcendence and sovereignty of God, God's condescension toward humanity, the resistance of sinful human beings to this condescension, and the belief that a radical solution lies waiting in the future. This last-mentioned element involves the expectation of God's kingdom. We might add that we can perhaps no longer be certain that the role of the law differs fundamentally in the two religions. In any case, the idea that Judaism is totally based on salvation by works is too stereotypical for large segments of that community and has therefore proven to be incorrect. In the Old Testament the righteous person is challenged to live by faith (Hab 2:4), and the nature of faith as existential trust does not differ structurally from the Christian faith (e.g., see Isa 7:9). The difference is mainly that Christians believe that, in principle, the kingdom of God has already arrived in the life, death, and resurrection of Jesus Christ. This factor colors and changes the points of similarity we mentioned, but it does not annul them.

On the surface one might think that the expectation of the kingdom of God is only one aspect of the Christian faith, and perhaps of limited importance when compared to other elements. That would be a misunderstanding. Reading the Gospels and the New Testament epistles, one cannot escape the conclusion that this expectation occupies a central place, and the actual coming of Christ strengthens rather than weakens that expectation. In its essence, Christian faith is hope—hope for the fulfillment of God's promises as these have been transmitted by visionary prophets and Spirit-filled apostles. Christians share this essential characteristic with the Jewish community. For that reason this hope must be the starting point for our dialogue with Israel. The constitution of the United Church of the Netherlands continues with the statement that the church seeks "as a Christ-confessing community" (thus, without denying its identity) a dialogue with Israel "with regard to understanding the sacred Scriptures, in particular concerning the coming of the kingdom of God" (art. 17). Such a statement, we believe, is very appropriate.

We have intentionally opted for the term "dialogue." Our approach toward Judaism is not just one of mission, a strictly one-way traffic (in the past often expressed by the term "mission to the Jews"). In the New Testament, "mission" is primarily to be understood as a movement from Jerusalem and Israel to the gentile world; the apostles are literally "sent out" into the world. Of course, they also, even first, want to reach the Jews (wherever Paul went, he first visited the synagogue), but these apostles were themselves part of the Jewish people. Today, for representatives of the "nations" (the category that in the Bible stands in such a tense relationship with Israel) to use words like "mission" and "missionary" is inadvisable. Such words fail to do justice to what Israel has known about God since ancient times, and the relationship of Israel with God. In a (Socratic) dialogue we assume that the truth lies hidden within the dialogue partner and needs only to be brought to the surface. This is exactly the case with Israel: they have (not "had"!) "the covenants and the promises" (Rom 9:4). Therefore, nowadays the church and theology speak more modestly than in the past about seeking a dialogue with Israel. In a dialogue, participants listen to each other with genuine interest. We hope to learn from the other, for instance, about how the other sees himself or herself in relationship to God. This approach seeks to set aside preconceived ideas about Judaism. Furthermore, we also hope to share with the other what we ourselves have learned and received. For Christians such dialogue may also open possibilities to speak about the content of the New Testament, but the basis for the dialogue is what connects the two sides deeper down: the expectation of the all-encompassing kingdom of God, in which "steadfast love and faithfulness will meet" (Ps 85:10).

As early as 1951, the constitution of the Dutch Reformed Church opted for the term "dialogue." It was believed that the dialogue with Israel should focus on the Old Testament, not because the Jews do not accept the New Testament as authoritative but primarily because, as the influential Dutch theologian A. A. van Ruler said, most things are already found in the Old Testament. In that period Van Ruler was working on developing a high view of the Old Testament. His project reached its conclusion in a study of the Christian church and the Old Testament (Ruler 1971). Van Ruler referred to the Old Testament as "the real Bible" and regarded the New Testament as "not more than a list of explanations of difficult terms" at the back of the book. One must certainly call his approach courageous and to the point, if one realizes that he first suggested his view in a lecture in 1940 (VW 2:36), at a time when in Germany (partly under the influence of Nazi ideology) the Christian-theological significance of the Old Testament had been starkly reduced or even denied (e.g., see E. Hirsch, *Das Alte Testament und die Predigt des Evangeliums* [1936]). However, in retrospect, this radical form of Van Ruler's view proved to be untenable; the Old Testament helps us to understand the New Testament, but the New Testament certainly does add important matters. No doubt this was a factor in the decision not to reflect Van Ruler's strong emphasis on the Old Testament in the constitution referred to above.

Today churches of various traditions—Protestant, but also Roman Catholic—are working hard to define their attitude and their relationship toward the living Israel. Some will insist that the dialogue must have a witnessing character, while others maintain that this witness can take place only in the context of an honest and sincere dialogue. But most have said farewell to a past in which the church's approach to the synagogue was primarily a one-way traffic.

9.3. A Problematic Past and the Need for New Reflection by the Church

Given its importance, it is quite remarkable that attention to Israel as a theme in Christian dogmatics is only of recent origin. Theologians long regarded Israel as being only of historical significance; that is, once church and synagogue had split, Christians tended to see Jews as a group that had been left behind, stubbornly persisting in an outmoded faith. Furthermore, because of this "disobedience," the salvific role of Israel had supposedly ended, and the church had become the only legitimate continuation of Israel. The thought that those who believe in Christ are the true spiritual heirs of Abraham (e.g., see Gal 3:29) played a decisive role in this process. Behind this view lurks the idea of a series of successive periods (or "dispensations") in which the new invalidates the old, so that, in God's view, the Jewish synagogue and the temple cult have been replaced by the church. This theory of replacement or substitution is called *supersessionism* in English-language theology.

For supersessionism see, for example, the essay of Bruce Marshall in Gunton, CD 81–100. Beek (2002, 171–73) states that second-century Marcionism contains the basic structure of supersessionism in a radical form. Marcion identified the two eras of the Old and the New Testament with two different gods: the inferior God of the Jews, who thinks and acts in terms of law and revenge, and later the "strange" God of Jesus, who acts in love. An anonymous early Christian document *To Diognetus* (ca. 150 CE) develops this theme further, with the correction that, in fact, there is only one God. According to this document the Jews were so degraded that they believed that this God had to be satisfied with animal sacrifices and served with such peripheral things as Sabbath observance. In later forms of the replacement theory we meet this idea time and again. The Jews labor under a serious misunderstanding: they think they can please God by keeping the law and observing the sacrificial system. But because the church has accepted the gospel, it has become the new Israel that has replaced the old and surpassed it by virtue of its own superior morality. Supersessionist theology further suggests that the fulfillment of the covenant in Christ implies an invalidation of the law.

Over the centuries supersessionism has had enormous influence and consequences. Christians thought it annoying, even outrageous, that a faith that they believed had no further right to exist was still present. Furthermore, by the logic of replacement theory, even though they were God's covenant people, Jews were deemed not only as apostate but as the murderers of Jesus. The reaction of the Jewish leaders to Pilate's remark that he could not take the responsibility for the blood of the man who was about to be crucified—"his blood be on us and on our children" (Matt 27:25)—echoed long and loud in Europe and the Middle East. The common interpretation of this statement as a self-curse undoubtedly contributed to a cultural climate in which xenophobia and societal unrest could find a ready outlet by scapegoating Jews—the Jews had supposedly brought their misfortunes on themselves. Through the centuries this attitude led to anti-Semitic persecutions, which climaxed in the twentieth-century attempt to eradicate all Jews.

Admittedly, the ominous text in Matt 27 cannot simply be disposed of. It does not help, for instance, to stress that these words were shouted only by a handful of Jews (for only a small group would have fit in the court of the Antonia fortress), since Matthew very clearly treats this group as representative of "all the people" (v. 25; in v. 24 he refers to those who were literally present as "the crowd"). The evangelist may well have seen the destruction of Jerusalem as the result of the rejection of Jesus during his trial before Pilate. Neither should anyone suggest that, since the blood of Christ has saving power according to the New Testament, the people were subconsciously asking for this meaning of "blood." But it should also be stated that Pilate's words must not be seen as a form of Jewish self-cursing. Rather, the Jews who were present were simply transferring the legal responsibility for the death of Jesus from Pilate to themselves.

Is it, however, correct to think that Israel's role in God's salvific economy for this world has ended? Since the 1970s a new consensus has developed that supersessionism has no biblical basis but has its roots primarily in the ancient estrangement between church and synagogue. Israel as a concrete nation retains an enduring theological significance. As a result, attention to "the living Israel" increased. For a long time Christian sermons and catechisms referred to Israel only in the past tense: Jews believed, did, and thought so and so. Nothing was said about Jews who still believe, do, and think so and so, with the result that any encounter with current expressions of the Jewish faith tends to provoke misunderstanding and estrangement. Is it not an anomaly, a mere leftover from the past? It is therefore very important to discover Judaism as a continuing, living tradition and to see the ways in which it finds expression even today.

For a long time theology did not approach Israel as a living entity but merely as the type of a class of believers who were focused on the law. R. Bultmann modeled this approach, which was especially dominant in the Lutheran tradition. The Old Testament and the history of Israel, on the one hand, and the New Testament and the church, on the other, were presented as the matrix of law and gospel, poised in an antithetical relationship. As Bultmann said, the history of Israel was a *Geschichte des Scheiterns* (a history of failure), in contrast to the New Testament focus on the justification of the sinner as the gospel.

This typological approach to Israel also dominated Barth's thinking for a considerable time. The duality of election and rejection took concrete form in his *Römerbrief* (1922), in a typology in which Israel represented the one who is rejected. There still is an echo of this typology in Barth's doctrine of election in CD II/2:195–205 (which appeared in 1942!). Barth does, however, begin with the essential unity of Israel and the church. In the single act of God's election in Jesus Christ, Israel and the church constitute the one community of God, around the Messiah. Israel and the church are "under the arch of the [one] covenant" (Busch 1999, 491). Yet, the typological interpretation still predominates; in this one act of election Israel represents God's judgment, while the church represents God's compassion. It should be kept in mind, however, that for Barth, judgment is not the final word, since it is the judgment of a gracious God; therefore, from God's perspective, there remains a concrete future for the Jewish people. That is, Barth no longer adhered to supersessionist theology. From Switzerland Barth was also actively engaged (as was Bultmann) in rescuing persecuted Jews, so that when he simultaneously wrote negative things about "Israel," it was not about the concrete people of Israel but about Israel as a type of those who resist God's election. Barth uses the notions of Israel and the church in a typological sense, as two ways of viewing humankind, and even the Christian church. But the enormous risk remains that the concrete people of Israel are identified with the notion of God's judgment (and thus with the idea that this people is doomed to disappear). Such a theological use of the term "Israel" does not give space to the idea that the concrete people of Israel are the bearers of the promise and seek an eschatological fulfillment of this promise in their worship and striving for justice. In this climate the risk of violent caricatures cannot be excluded. Contemporary dogmatics is in search of new approaches.

Three historical events have prompted a new attitude toward Israel in contemporary theology: the attempt to exterminate the Jews during the Second World War; the return of the Jews to Palestine, followed by the founding of a Jewish state in 1948; and later—in fact, only from the 1970s onward—the ever-growing quantity of literature about what was from then on referred to as the Holocaust. This word was derived from the Greek *holokautōma* (*holokaustos* = fully burnt), which is frequently used in the Septuagint for "burnt offering" (e.g., Ps 40:7 [6]). However, since the persecution of the Jews in Hitler's days was certainly not a sacrifice offered to God (as if this might once again give meaning to meaningless evil?), many prefer to speak of the Shoah—a Hebrew word for destruction.

These events demonstrated how deeply anti-Semitism is entrenched in the history of Europe. Increasingly, the question was raised of how this attitude relates to the Christian faith. In any case, the background of hatred for the Jews can be traced back to the early church via Luther (*Von den Juden und ihren Lügen* [About the Jews and their lies, 1543]; in WA 53, trans. in *Luther's Works* 47) and the Middle Ages. Among the many anti-Jewish expressions were the eight aggressive "sermons against the Jews" (in PG 48) by John Chrysostom (345–407, a gifted preacher; his second name, a nickname, means "golden-mouthed"), and, even earlier, the infamous Easter sermon of Melito, the bishop of Sardis (161–80). Can we perhaps find this anti-Semitism already in the New Testament? That question must be answered in the negative, since anti-Semitism directs hatred toward all Jews (the Jewish race) while, except for Luke, the authors of the New Testament themselves were Jews. What about anti-Judaism, however, opposition to the Jewish faith? We find an echo of this not only in Matt 27:25, to which we referred above, but also in the Gospel of John (e.g., John 8:44). The question of whether this means the New Testament is a source of hatred for Jews has led to intense discussions. We should beware of any simplistic answers, if only because of the many positive texts about the Jewish people in the New Testament. In the same Gospel of John, which falls under so much suspicion on this issue, we can also read that salvation comes from the Jews (4:22). And Paul can call his fellow-Jews in one and the same breath "enemies of God, for your sake" but also "beloved for the sake of their forefathers" (Rom 11:28).

The discussion of whether the New Testament induces anti-Semitism was started by Ruether 1974, who argued the (too) radical proposition that the Christology of the New Testament did just that by prompting us to regard the Jewish people as disobedient. In the Netherlands, theologian Hans Jansen (b. 1931) wrote a substantial book about the traces of anti-Semitism in church history, and then added an even more shocking publication about "its New Testament roots" (Jansen 1981–85). In whatever way the question was answered, it precipitated an unprecedented process of consciousness-raising. It is clear that the anti-Semitism that led to Auschwitz and the Holocaust had deep roots in the Christian West. The church has no other option but to confess its guilt in shame and embarrassment. But it should not generalize it too much or even make it a Christian theologoumenon as a building block in a "theology of the suffering God."

For a good discussion of the distinction between anti-Semitism and anti-Judaism, see Keith 1997, 4–6, and Beek 2002, 79–81. This distinction should not be exaggerated (it makes little difference to Jews whether they are persecuted because of anti-Semitism or anti-Judaism), but neither should it be lost sight of or denied.

All these developments convinced many Protestants and Roman Catholics of the urgent need to take a totally new look not only at the past but also at the relationship with today's Israel. In the Netherlands this interest for the "Israelite," that is, living Judaism, has a long history, not least because, from early modern times on, the Netherlands has been a place of refuge for Jews who were persecuted elsewhere in Europe. Then too, by the end of the sixteenth century the Reformed branch of Christianity had become dominant in the Netherlands, and this tradition has a relatively strong interest in and appreciation for the Old Testament, that is, the Jewish Bible. Where Roman Catholic teaching saw the Old Testament foremost as a preparation for the higher stage of the New Testament, and where Lutheranism regarded it mostly as "the letter that kills" (see 2 Cor 3:6) in opposition to the liberating gospel of the New Testament, the Reformed tradition placed the Old and the New Testaments side by side as expectation and fulfillment. Calvin argued—not against Rome or Luther, but against the Anabaptists—that the old and the new covenants differ in their *administratio* (execution, implementation) but are one with regard to their *substantia* (essence, content). That is, while the Bible sometimes speaks of an old and a new covenant (e.g., in Jer 31:31; Heb 8:13), this actually refers to its implementation, for in final analysis there is only one covenant (or testament), not two.

The essence of the salvation that holds center stage in the Bible is communion with God in his eternal kingdom. The promise of this communion is, according to Calvin, already the substance and goal of the Old Testament covenant concept. It is affirmed in Jesus Christ and will become full reality in the completion of all things. However, the mystery of this communion has already become reality for those who embrace Christ. This view of the unity of the covenant stimulated great appreciation for the Old Testament, and also for the living Israel (the translators of the Dutch seventeenth-century *Statenvertaling*—the counterpart of the

King James Version in England—consulted rabbinical scholars to learn more about the meaning of Hebrew words).

In the nineteenth century the interest in Israel and in the Israelite background of Christianity within Dutch Protestant theology received a new impetus through the so-called Réveil (awakening). Especially the work of two Jews who had become Christians and joined the Réveil movement, Isaäc da Costa (1798-1860) and Abraham Capadose (1795-1874), was key in this connection.

In the twentieth century the Holocaust and then the founding of the State of Israel in 1948 led to a further theological rehabilitation of Israel in Dutch Protestant thinking. It was realized that Israel was a locus of lasting significance in Christian theology. According to theologians such as Hendrikus Berkhof, the return of the Jewish people to Israel had to be seen as a sign of God's faithfulness to his promises. In the same era, Protestant churches decided to employ the word "dialogue" instead of "mission" for characterizing their calling toward the Jews. It was sensed—rightly, in our view—that the central role of Christ as acknowledged by Christians can still be communicated in such a dialogue, provided that its Christian participants also listen to the witness of their Jewish partners. Moreover, it is very disagreeable to Jews to still be seen as the object of mission, after all the misery this attention has brought them through the centuries. On this debate, see Berkhof 1969.

Meanwhile, in international discussions the lasting significance of Israel for Christian theology is far from self-evident. Where some give ample space to Israel, others totally ignore the subject (e.g., Horton, CF).

A small but extremely interesting group are the Jews who confess Jesus as the Messiah. In their acknowledgment of *Yeshua* as the Messiah and, thereby, as the fulfillment of God's promises, and in their observance of halakah, the Jewish lifestyle, they keep alive the awareness that Jesus did not abrogate the law when he fulfilled it; rather, he demonstrated its full depth and essence. Likewise, the early Christians were Messiah-confessing Jews, who structured their life in conformity with the Mosaic law and, in so doing, followed other rules for themselves than did gentile Christians (Acts 15:24-29). Today, theologically and politically, this position is extremely controversial. Messianic Jews can count on a firm rejection from two sides: from most Jews and also from many Christians who regard their position as a theological anachronism and would rather have them abandon their Jewish background altogether. But gentile Christians would do well to think highly of the special position of Messianic Jews (as representatives of their "elder brother" in their midst), and to listen to them carefully.

All in all, Israel remains a raw nerve in Christian theology, as it involves so many interconnections and so many interests—political, legal, cultural, and religious. The topic of Israel is thus a thorny issue not only in the Middle East but also in the broader relationships among Christianity, Judaism, and Islam. The link between religion and country reminds us that God's revelation cannot be discussed as an idea that is fully detached from concrete history, and that we should not spiritualize the acts of the God of Israel into some eternal idea.

For descriptions of Messianic Judaism, see, for example, Harvey 2009 and Hocken 2009, 97–116.

There is a great danger lest Christian doctrine be simply idealized, that is, presented as something totally detached from our daily political-cultural reality. Neither Tillich's *Systematic Theology* nor Pannenberg or Jüngel pay any attention to the living Israel. Some exceptions in German theology on the Catholic side are, besides F. W. Marquardt (see below), especially F. Mussner (1984); on the Protestant side, B. Klappert (1980, 2000) and, to a lesser degree, J. Moltmann (Lapide and Moltmann 1981).

In the Netherlands, the works of Berkhof and van de Beek are among the exceptions to the rule. Berkhof broaches the subject in the context of what he calls "problems surrounding the covenant." He considers Israel as the laboratory where the covenant was experimentally tested. The problem, to which the later prophets often return, is the question whether eventually the covenant that God has intended for the entire world will succeed. For Berkhof, Israel is the failed experiment and Jesus the new initiative. As the last Adam, Jesus belatedly brings the promise to fulfillment.

Van de Beek also sees this universal significance in Israel. Israel demonstrates that a life with God is too big a challenge for human beings. The country is not cleansed from idols, life is not sanctified, and the Torah cannot be obeyed. God simply demands too much (Beek 2002, 398). Therefore, God himself comes to Israel to fulfill the law and the intent of the Torah. In so doing, God himself in Christ bears this breaking and broken life. If we want to be saved, we must give up the idea of self-realization.

Van de Beek stresses that this attitude also applies to the land. Israel must recognize that its only place is the Lord. In him lives the glory of God, and this Lord is in heaven. The notion of the land and the area (*maqom*) is not done away with but is radically repositioned in Christ. *Maqom* is not on earth but is hidden with Christ in heaven (see Col 3:3).

In the work of Friedrich Wilhelm Marquardt (1928–2002) the question of the significance of Israel after the Holocaust has been the driving force. Emerging from the Barthian school after the atrocities of 1933–45, this Berlin theologian sought ways to rethink the relationship between the church and Israel. It is impossible to summarize his complex and at times erratic arguments in just a few sentences. Put simply, Marquardt maintains that the Holocaust has been a shock of such a magnitude that Christian theology can no longer provide any suggestions, let alone firm answers; it can only ask questions. In this respect the title of Marquardt's three-volume eschatology is telling, "What may we hope for, if we were permitted to hope?" (1993–96). Whereas Moltmann gained popularity with his optimistic, forward-looking "theology of hope," Marquardt posed the perplexing question of whether there is, in fact, any hope left for Christians who experienced the Shoah in their midst. Only by asking questions will Christian theology no longer pose a threat to Jews, which Marquardt considered to be a nonnegotiable criterion for good theology. Our entire Christian theology must find a new basis. It is not enough to add a new locus to the traditional dogmatic scheme, in which the Christian-theological significance of Israel is discussed (as has happened here and there since Berkhof). Rather, Marquardt says, we need to rethink all loci, beginning with the question of whether theology's traditional claims can still be credible after Auschwitz.

Marquardt believes that such credibility can be reestablished only if the accent of theology is shifted from theory to praxis. It must be accepted that in Israel God mediates his covenant with the nations. Faith in the resurrection, for instance, can come alive only in the praxis of daily life, when we become obedient to the call not to acquiesce to all kinds of deadly powers but decide to go with Israel along the road of justice (halakah). It is impossible to say what a person who is connected with Christ misses if he or she does not believe in Christ's resurrection (Marquardt 1990–91, 2:133; 1997). Like Beek (2002, 19–20), we believe that, at this crucial point, Marquardt does not say enough. The resurrection does indeed have ethical implications, but in the Christian faith it does so as the concrete event in which the God of Easter raised his child Jesus from the dead. Precisely at this point the paths of church and synagogue have always split, and this dilemma is not quickly solved by denying or relativizing the Christian confession regarding God's eschatological intervention in and through Jesus. We will therefore have to find other avenues, and will do so by accepting the lasting duality that marks the relationship between church and Israel.

For an English introduction to Marquardt's work and a sample of his essays, including some in which he (audaciously but wrongly, in our view) advocates a political reading of Karl Barth's theology, see Marquardt 2010.

9.4. Structural Duality

The Israel theme builds into Christian doctrine a *structural duality* that is of fundamental importance and is manifested in many places. Taking our cue from Berkhof, we see that this duality registers both positively and negatively in the Christian perception of Israel—as recognition and estrangement. This *clair-obscur*, if we want to use that term, is mainly defined by Christology, in which we must do justice to at least two fundamental realities: (1) that Jesus knew he was sent by God to Israel and wanted to obey the Old Testament; and (2) that Jesus was rejected by the leaders of the people of Israel because they saw his claims and actions as contrary to the Old Testament (CF 226). The first element leads to a shared recognition by Jews and Christians of the Old Testament as the Word of God; the second element brings estrangement between the two faith communities. The Christian faith considers it of decisive importance that we see an essential link between the Old Testament and—in conformity with Jesus's own self-understanding (see 1)—the way and work of Jesus, so that we regard the latter as the continuation of the Old Testament. Jesus is the one who gives new life to the covenant, which, according to the Old Testament, had run into difficulties.

Following a frequently used image, we might say that the Old Testament has a tapered structure. Starting with "heaven and earth" (Gen 1) and proceeding through the misery of the flood and the building of a tower, the focus comes to concentrate on the people of Israel (Gen 12). When the attitude of a major part of Israel proves to be disappointing, the expectation shifts from the people of the twelve tribes to the kingdom of the two tribes of Judah and Benjamin, with Jerusalem at its center. But subsequently, Jerusalem is destroyed, and the people of the southern kingdom of the two tribes are exiled; now the hope is centered on a remnant that will remain (Isa 1:9; 7:3; Zeph 3:12) and ultimately return to the promised land. But will this remnant survive? In the end there is, in particular, the suffering *'ebed YHWH*, "servant of the Lord"; his redemptive work is the subject of dreams, songs, and prophecies. See the so-called songs of the servant of the Lord in Deutero-Isaiah, with its climax in Isa 53. With a shock the first Jewish Christians must have recognized the figure of this mysterious, vicariously suffering servant (Isa 53:4; see Acts 8:35) in Jesus of Nazareth. After this recognition we see how God's involvement with Israel begins to spread widely. Acts 1:8 tells us that the tapered structure is now reversed: beginning with Jerusalem and Judea, it spreads to Samaria and to "the ends of the earth." In this process Israel is not left out, but believers from the nations are added to the firstfruits from Israel.

It is of utmost importance to realize that God in Christ did not become just some human person in general, but that Jesus was an Israelite, someone with a Jewish ethnicity and a Jewish faith. Or as Paul says, a man "who was descended from David according to the flesh and designated Son of God in power according to the Spirit of holiness by his resurrection from the dead" (Rom 1:3-4). In God's act, *particularity* (Jesus as a Jew and a representative of Israel) and *universality* (Jesus as the representative of all nations) combine without nullifying each other. Paul considers the fact that the Jew Jesus was raised as the first of all who have died (1 Cor 15:20) has universal significance. For in the resurrection of Christ, God demonstrated his power over everything and made it clear that we now live in the new and final era that was announced by the prophets, a time in which the God of Israel becomes meaningful for all nations. The blessing once promised to Abraham and his posterity is now also available to the goyim (Gal 3:14).

Jesus's resurrection is of crucial importance for giving Israel its rightful place in Christian doctrine. As we will see in more detail in chapter 11, the resurrection is the moment when the identity of the Jew Yeshua is definitively disclosed. In the resurrection God confirms Jesus in his mission as Israel's Messiah (e.g., see Rom 1:3-4; Matt 1:21-23; Luke 24:25-27, 43-47). He is the Son, and in his ministry—so the New Testament tells us—the fulfillment of the history of the covenant with Abraham has begun, at least in a preliminary way. In the resurrection the role of Jesus is confirmed; he is the one who announced, in the name of the God of Abraham, Isaac, and Jacob, the arrival and breakthrough of the kingdom of God. He was right in what he proclaimed. From Jesus the light falls over Israel in two directions, which leads us to a second type of duality in how Israel registers in Christian doctrine (this theme has been clumsily labeled *Israelology*, the doctrine of Israel).

On the one hand, the light that Jesus emanates falls on the road that Israel has traveled. It is the road of the covenant, the relationship of God with his people, in which promise and commandment, return and restoration, play an essential role. Israel was chosen to live in a covenant relationship vicariously, on behalf of the nations. In and through Jesus this goal was at last achieved. For that reason the Old Testament has a lasting theological and practical significance. It shows the earlier journey of God with his people, the role human beings played in this process, and the difficulty the covenant partner repeatedly experiences in living a life of trust and obedience. But on the other hand, the light from Jesus's being "lifted up" also falls on the journey that Israel *has yet to go*. Israel and Jesus belong together, and even though this link may temporarily be rather opaque, things will change in the future. Paul tells us that God has not ceased his involvement with Israel because most of his fellow Jews have rejected the Messiah, but that, in some mysterious way, this rejection is part of God's plan: "I want you to understand this mystery, brethren: a hardening has come upon part of Israel until the full number of the Gentiles come in, and so all Israel will be saved" (Rom 11:25-26).

Much has been said about the meaning in this text of "Israel" and the word "so" ("then" in some translations) in the last sentence. We believe that this word ("so" in the Greek text) does include a temporal aspect (for exegetical arguments, see Horst 2000). As for "Israel," it seems to us that this term here must refer to the concrete people of Israel, as it does in the previous sentence. It would be incorrect in the latter case to think of some kind of "spiritual Israel," supposedly consisting of gentile Christians and individual Jewish Christians. Neither does Paul intend to say that Jews and Christians will each be saved in their own way. He probably thought of some massive future conversion of Jewish people who would belatedly recognize the Messiah in Jesus of Nazareth (note also the context of Rom 11:12). These words were thus interpreted by the pietistic Dutch Reformed theologians in the eighteenth century and served as their basis of hope for contemporary Judaism. God had not finished his work on behalf of the people of his first love; the synagogue was not abolished but was still awaiting a rich future.

Paul regards the current situation, in which the majority of Israel denies Jesus the title of Messiah, in the light of God's ultimate salvific intentions. In fact, because of this rejection the good tidings about Jesus could spread to the world of the nations (Rom 11:11). Moreover, just as the gentiles in the past were only temporarily disobedient to God's voice, so now the disobedience of many Jews is not the final word. "For God has consigned all men to disobedience, that he may have mercy upon all" (Rom 11:32). If we take this sentence seriously, we must conclude that postbiblical Israel, in its refusal to recognize Jesus as the Messiah, reminds us that God is not yet at the end of his journey. This perspective increases the stakes; it is all-important that the church now try to "make

Israel jealous" (Rom 11:11) by showing how the redemption that Jesus offers makes a crucial difference. And precisely at this point the church has often miserably failed.

It is not sufficient to repeat the negative statement that Jesus cannot be detached from the history of God with his people. A positive formulation is needed: we can understand the meaning of Jesus's mission and ministry only when we take this history and all its drama as our point of departure. This conclusion has enormous consequences for Christian dogmatics. The concepts that traditionally played a central role in God's dealings with his people, such as covenant, election, redemption, and sanctification, receive their true meaning in God's journey with this people and with Jesus Christ, who represents this people and forever connects the gentile world with it (see Rom 15:7–12).

In fact, in all loci of dogmatics we must pay attention to this duality if we want to avoid making Jesus an abstract person and relegating Israel to the margins. We find this duality, for instance, in *the doctrine of revelation*. From a Christian perspective, God's revelation occurs not only in Christ but also in the history of Israel and Christ. This duality is clear also in the Christian canon: admittedly, the New Testament may be read more frequently, but it is of prime importance that the church continues to fully recognize the Old Testament as a source of revelation. Here the journey of the God who chose Israel and his aim that Israel would serve the other nations are extensively documented. Thus the Hebrew Bible constitutes the Christian church's memory of God's journey throughout history. The term "Old Testament" may be misleading if it creates the sense that the period before Jesus is in the past perfect, without any significance for the present. In this approach the New Testament replaces the Old and might actually be sufficient by itself. We consider this rather common attitude a great danger for the Christian faith and for a correct understanding of the salvation that God provides in Christ, since the meaning of this salvation can be grasped only against the background of God's dealings with Israel.

Is there, then, a more suitable term to use instead of "Old Testament"? Should we speak of the Tanak, the acronym for the Torah (law), the Nebi'im (prophets), and the Ketubim (writings)? The advantage of this term is that it conserves the special character of the Hebrew Bible, but the disadvantage is that it moves the actual difference between church and synagogue into the background. The Tanak has its continuance in the Talmud, the haggadah, and the halakah. The Christian church has recognized the writings of the New Testament, as it now stands, as the legitimate sequel to the revelation given to Israel. Those who, as a compromise, prefer to speak of the First and the Second Testaments have also not fully understood the relationship between the two, and that relationship is what counts. Moreover, attempts to replace the traditional names of Old and New Testament have never succeeded, partly because, fortunately, the "old" in the Old Testament is usually not heard in a pejorative sense. We therefore stay with the traditional names without agreeing with the negative associations the adjective might sometimes carry.

It is important to stick with the sequence of the Jewish canon, which begins with the Torah, followed by the Prophets and the Writings. In some Christian versions of the Old Testament canon the sequence of Prophets and Writings seems to have been intentionally changed, with the idea of making the Old Testament open-ended. Thus it would appear as if the entire Old Testament terminates in the complete failure of the covenant. Berkhof nevertheless used this characterization to theological advantage—in our opinion, an unnecessary and uncouth move. Christians may also read the books of the Old Testament in the sequence of the Jewish canon so that it ends with fragments of unfaithfulness to the covenant in the Psalms and with the just in the Wisdom literature (Proverbs, Ecclesiastes, Job). This arrangement allows Paul, by also quoting the Psalms (14:3; 53:1), to say regarding the Jews and the gentiles that "none is righteous, no not one" (Rom 3:10). And this order also prompted us to speak above about the tapered structure of the journey of the covenant that God underwent with Israel in the Old Testament. However, none of these issues diminishes the fact that, by God's grace, individuals in Old Testament times were able to respond to God's intentions. For good reason many consider these sections (in particular Job, Psalms, Ecclesiastes) as their favorite passages of the Old Testament.

Without the history of Israel and the Old Testament, the salvation that Christ brought to the world becomes something abstract, an idea that is unrelated to the actual course of life on earth and to God's acts in history.

Finally, and not insignificantly, the duality we referred to also comes up in *ecclesiology*. We are, first of all, mindful of the duality of church and synagogue. The church recognizes the rights of Israel and the contemporary synagogue as the firstborn. God's election remains Israel's prerogative (Rom 11:28-29). This teaching does indeed cause a strong tension, for Christians believe that the righteousness that is sought in the Torah has been fulfilled in Jesus Christ. In line with Jesus's first Jewish followers, the church confesses that he is the one who was promised, the Son of God (Rom 1:4). "The same Lord is Lord of all and bestows his riches upon all who call upon him" (Rom 10:12). This Lord is Jesus, and the church cannot ignore this confession of the Messianic Jew Paul. The consequence is that the duality of church and synagogue will, from time to time, inevitably be experienced as a dichotomy.

The duality in ecclesiology is also visible in the "bi-unity" of Jews and gentiles in the Christian church. At this point we must not forget that the first Christians were Jews, either from birth or by entering the Jewish community as proselytes (etymologically, "someone who has joined"). At Pentecost, Jews from the diaspora were celebrating the Shavuot in Jerusalem and received the Spirit. "Real" gentiles joined the church only at a later stage (incidentally in Acts 8, and structurally from Acts 10 onward). The image that Paul uses in Rom 9–11 tells us that Old Testament Israel forms the trunk of the olive tree on which the gentiles have been grafted side by side with the Jews, who were always part of it. We might in this connection from the perspective of gentile Christians even speak of a *theology of incorporation*. We see this position as the biblical alternative to both supersessionism and the "two roads" view. In the former the church takes the place of Israel, while in the latter the church takes a detached position beside Israel, as a parallel pathway to God. The metaphor of incorporation in the olive tree makes clear that the Christians from the gentiles *have been incorporated in the already existing covenant* with Israel. Israel is the trunk of the olive tree, on which the nations are grafted after some of the branches—the Jews who refused to believe in Jesus—were broken off (Rom 11:17); supersessionists, it should be added, do not suggest that the root refers to Israel but to Christ—a view that, seen in this context, seems quite improbable. In this way the believers from the nations share, together with the branches that have not been broken off, in the promises that were given to Abraham and were fulfilled in Jesus Christ.

9.5. Covenant, Law, and Related Issues

In this section we look more closely at the nature of the promises given to Abraham. We do so by using an overarching term that we already encountered: *covenant*. Here we focus on the specific meaning of the covenant with and for Israel. In previous chapters we have seen "covenant" as a common theme through the history of God and humanity. But here, in the context of Israel, the concept acquires flesh and blood. A covenant is made with Abraham; it is accompanied by outward signs and is intended to regulate all aspects of the relationship between God and Abraham and his posterity (Gen 12:1–6). In contrast with the Noachian covenant, this covenant with Abraham does not disappear rather quickly from view but remains the central theme throughout the entire Old Testament. "Covenant" (*berit*) is a central concept not only for the church but also for the Jewish faith. At this point Christians think and believe just like Jews. However, the term "covenant" is hardly adequate to express its real meaning in the Old Testament. A covenant usually refers to two equal partners who reach a voluntary agreement, but the Hebrew Bible knows no such equality. The initiative is fully on God's side. In his covenant with Abraham, God constructs a life-giving and unbreakable arrangement in which Abraham is given a promise of a future and a blessing (Gen 12:2–3; 15; 17); from the covenant partner, God expects faithfulness and obedience. The covenant is thus unilateral in its structure, while it is bilateral in its content (see Berkhof, CF 234–35). (In technical jargon, the covenant is *monopleuric* in its origin and *bipleuric* in its implementation.)

See, for example, Ezek 17, where we learn of a *berit* between the Judean king Zedekiah and the Babylonian king Nebuchadnezzar. There is no freedom whatsoever on the part of Zedekiah. Originally, a covenant was often an agreement made with a vassal. A remarkable example of the indissolubility of the covenant is found in Josh 9, with its story of the Hebrews and the Gibeonites. The Gibeonites have tricked Joshua into a covenant that stipulated that they would be spared in the conquest of the land of Canaan (v. 15). Even when, subsequently, the deceit is uncovered (v. 16), it becomes clear that the covenant cannot be nullified (v. 19). History cannot be reversed. We find the same unilateral and indissoluble aspects in Gen 15 and 17, where God takes the full initiative and Abraham has no say in the matter. In Jer 33:20–21 the unbreakable nature of the covenant is even compared with the rhythm of day and night, with which God also has, so to speak, a covenant relationship. "If you can break my covenant with the day and my covenant with the night, so that day and night will not come at their appointed time, then also my covenant with David my servant may be broken." A little further on we read: "If I have not established my covenant with day and night and the ordinances of heaven and earth, then I will reject the descendants of Jacob and David my servant" (vv. 25–26).

Because of this unilateral and indissoluble nature, *berit* would be better translated "arrangement," a more adequate expression of the meaning of the concept. "Testament"—the term that many translations use for the Greek equivalent of *berit*—points to this unilateral nature, but in common parlance it is too exclusively linked to a document that regulates what must happen when someone dies. These remarks should be kept in mind when we continue to use the generally accepted term "covenant." A covenant has to do with the arrangement of a historical sequence. Paul is also conscious of the indissoluble nature of this arrangement (Rom 9:4; 11:1). For a detailed discussion of this issue, see Beek 2002, 183–86.

The covenant starts with God, but God also wants human beings to be partners who have a place in this relationship. The latter is not so much a precondition as an indication of the route along which the covenant may be realized (Bavinck, RD 3:229–30). The invitation that we respond to God's appeal comes with strings attached. Life is found in the keeping of the covenant. Beyond the boundaries of the covenant, life becomes chaotic; it threatens to disintegrate under the powers and forces that want to do anything that they please. Living within the boundaries of covenant and Torah brings blessing; outside of it, life is threatened by the curse. The twosome of blessing and curse not only forms a continuous line in the Old Testament but remains decisive in the New. The covenant calls us to live in harmony with the covenant, for therein we recognize God as God. The covenant succeeds only as long as we are willing to be guided by God and his Word, or (to use more traditional language) as long as we live in obedience to the covenant. Only then is the covenant realized in its twofold intention.

The outward signs that mark participation in the covenant, as well as the boundaries of the covenant community, are of great importance for its functioning: *the land, circumcision, the Sabbath*, and *the ceremonial and dietary laws*. We may follow James Dunn in referring to these as the identity and boundary markers of the covenant. At the same time, these markers point to the broad range of domains in which obedience to the covenant must be realized, namely, in the areas of *sacrificial worship, ethics*, and *justice*. All these spheres have to do with our relationship with God and our neighbor. Our neighbor cannot be viewed outside our relationship to God, for God is also the God of our neighbor (note the prototypical Gen 6:9). In the sacrificial worship of tabernacle, temple, and religion at home, the covenantal relationship with God is maintained and renewed. The realm of ethics regulates the relationship to the neighbor: family, property, slaves, the poor, and the foreigners. The legal instructions, such as the Sabbath year and the Jubilee, were intended to ensure equal access to the land and to combat long-term poverty over the generations. In the light of the later doctrine of the sacraments, we could consider the signs of the covenant as sacramental signs: they are concrete earthly signs of God's salvific involvement with his people.

The first concrete sign of the covenant is the land that Abraham's descendants are to receive for their use. But note: for their use—the land would never become their possession. It remains God's possession and functions as a sacrament, as a spatial concretization of God's faithfulness by which he ensures his people a place to live. The second sign is the circumcision of all male descendants. Each time a Jewish man looks at his genitals, he is reminded that God has accepted him into the covenant. There, where he is at once virile and vulnerable, his life is committed to God. The third sign is the seventh day as the day of rest, the Sabbath. This brings time, as well as space and the body, into communion with God in the covenant. Time is not poured over human beings as a random stream of water but receives structure as the result of God's creative design (Gen 1:1–2:3). In Exod 20:11 the Sabbath commandment is explicitly linked to the seven days of God's own creative activity. Just as God does not endlessly continue with creating and he himself rests, we are not to be busy with work and productivity all the time. The seventh day points back to creation as an act of benevolence. In addition, we must also mention the temple. God chooses a particular place, a spot (Heb. *maqom*) where he will be with his people. During Israel's sojourn through the desert this spot was the tabernacle; later it became the temple. Zion (= Jerusalem), with the temple at its center, is the place chosen by God to establish his name, as it is called in the Deuteronomic literature (e.g., Deut 12:21; 1 Kgs 9:3; 2 Chr 6:20; also Jer 7:10). Finally, we mention the ceremonial and dietary laws, which played an important role in the Mosaic legal system. They reminded Israel that all aspects of daily life are brought into the sphere of living with God in the covenant. We might refer to all these signs of the covenant as instruments of grace; they mediate and facilitate our communion with God.

Have all these signs lost their meaning for Christians? We must remember that Jesus stresses that he has not come to abrogate the law but to fulfill it (Matt 5:17). In the Sermon on the Mount he explained what this commitment implied. The radical nature of the Torah, in its most profound meaning, is love for God and neighbor. The New Testament tells us that it was a hot topic for debate in the early church whether these signs of the covenant were also incumbent upon the gentiles who had decided to confess Christ. The apostolic council (Acts 15) at this point decided No; the yoke of the law was not laid on the shoulders of the believers from the goyim (vv. 10, 29). Those who had come from the nations were not obliged to live like Jews. For them the Noachian commandments were the minimum of how human beings should live (Acts 15:29; cf. Gen 9:2–4). On this basis Christian theology distinguished between the ever-valid moral law (in the Ten Commandments and in several exhortatory passages in the New Testament that repeat these commandments) and the ceremonial laws, which were regarded as abrogated because Christ had fulfilled them, even though some priestly elements were still observed. While the Lutheran tradition viewed the law mostly in an accusatory role, the Reformed tradition emphasized the positive function of the Ten Commandments for the life of the believer and, in so doing, assigned a continuing role to the revelation given to Israel. In the Heidelberg Catechism the Ten Commandments are interpreted as the "rule of thanksgiving" (which is understandable in the light of Exod 20:1). This understanding, however, rendered the Sabbath commandment somewhat ambiguous, since it is, on the one hand, a sign of the covenant but, on the other, is also part of the Decalogue. With an appeal to the decisions of Acts 15 (and also Rom 14:5 and Col 2:16), the Sabbath commandment was generally thought to apply to Sunday. This was the position, for example, of Gisbertus Voetius. For the role of the law in connection with renewal and sanctification, see further chapter 15.

In light of the above remarks, gentile Christians should not object if their Jewish fellow believers still want to keep the signs of the covenant, such as circumcision and (Saturday) Sabbath observance—not as a legal requirement, but as a matter of thanksgiving. Thereby they do justice to the abiding character of God's covenant with the people of his first love.

The topic of the covenant is much discussed in Judaism. There, the divine-human duality mentioned earlier tends to be rendered in terms of correlation, meaning that while we depend, of course, on God, God depends just as much on us for the restoration of the world. In traditional Jewish circles the covenant was seen as something that could be fulfilled. The ancestors may have sinned, but their children can return (see Ezek 18). The covenant remains conditional, as the book of Genesis bears witness. On the one hand, Genesis tells us that once humans are expelled from paradise (Gen 3:23-24), they undergo regular testing. The story of Abraham in Egypt is an example (Gen 12:10-20). Forced by circumstances, Abraham leaves the country of promise and, in a difficult spot, tries to save his skin without putting his trust in the promise and help of God. At that moment Abraham becomes Adam, the person who listens to another voice rather than God's and thus tries to supersede the boundaries of his humanness. At the end of the book of Genesis, however, we meet Joseph, who, when he is under pressure, makes a very different choice. As vice-regent of Egypt and seeing a chance to take revenge on his brothers, who had sold him for money, he asked, "Am I in the place of God?" (Gen 50:19). Joseph differs from Adam and shows that we can choose not to pretend to be God. He is the righteous one who trusts in God.

This reading of Genesis demonstrates that in Judaism the story of the fall is read in a different way from the interpretation of the Christian church. According to Jewish tradition, we can always return to God, and the covenant can still succeed. The movement that worked to restore the temple under the leadership of Ezra and Nehemiah, and that later developed into various reform movements (e.g., the rise of Essenes and Pharisees), aimed to protect the holiness of Israel. Contemporary Judaism also thinks in terms of correlation. God seeks us out as his partner. The world may be saved when people strive for righteousness; those who save one person, in fact, save the entire world.

For the view that God searches out humanity so that we may fulfill our part of the covenant, see such classic studies as Buber 1937 (orig. pub. 1923) and Heschel 1955, but also the recent work of the British chief rabbi Jonathan Sacks (2005) and Dorff 2008. The dissertation that Miskotte (1933) wrote in just a few months in 1932 has become a classic description (and rejection) of the Jewish idea of correlation from a Christian perspective.

However, we can also clearly detect a different line in the Old Testament. In the first chapters of Jeremiah the key word is "return" (*teshuva*). Israel is called to return. Apostasy appears not to be definitive. God is still looking for people who act in righteousness. At this stage sin is not yet viewed as a human condition from which it is impossible to escape (cf. 8.3 above). But gradually the sense of the inevitable becomes more prominent, especially with the prophets. Israel's election demanded that the people would be fully committed to God, holy, and trusting in him. Israel was to respond to God's faithfulness by fulfilling the law, thus contributing to the fulfillment of the covenant and the coming of God's kingdom. But will it ever happen? Time and time again things seem to go wrong—because of idolatry, greed, social injustice, nationalism, and other forces that enslave the people. The Old Testament tells us that humanity's relationship to God, if not increasingly, at least repeatedly, suffers a new crisis that threatens the goal of the covenant: "I shall be your God, and you will be my people." This issue is a matter of life and death. In the book of Deuteronomy the recurring urgent question is whether God's covenant will succeed, and the people are confronted with the choice between life and death (Deut 30). Here the contrast between the faithfulness of God and the unfaithfulness of the people is constantly highlighted, with the burning question of how the drama will end. With Jeremiah the answer to the question gradually becomes clearer. It will depend even more on God's side. This answer leads to the vision—in one of the most beautiful passages of the Old Testament—of a time when God will write the Torah on the human heart (Jer 31:31-34). This is the only way in which the re-creation that comes from God will eventually be realized: "I shall be their God, and they shall be my people" (v. 33).

The eschatological (future-oriented) perspective of the covenant prompts the question of whether this blessing will ultimately be only for Israel or whether the other nations will also share in it. The Old Testament leaves no doubt that the latter will be the case. The nations form the horizon against which God's covenant with Israel takes shape. From the very first, in the key passage about the establishment of the covenant with Abraham (Gen 12:1-7), the inclusion of all people is clear. There is no doubt whatsoever that the promise includes the provision that, through Abraham, "all the nations" will be blessed (Gen 12:3). It does not mean that the nations of the world have an equal share in the covenant. God does indeed make a difference in favor of Israel, however irritating this choice has been to many. The covenant is restricted to Abraham and his posterity. But the *blessing* of the covenant flows over, so to speak, to the nations, to the extent that they will bless Israel and let themselves be inspired by the way in which God relates to Israel in the covenant. "All the families of the earth will be blessed through you" (Gen 12:3 NLT), Abraham is told—and this is a good translation, for the verb that is here employed may be taken as an imperative or as an indicative. This means that the people are called to mediate God's salvific revelation to the nations, with the promise immediately given that this mediation will be successful. The entire Old and New Testaments must be read in this light.

It is quite inadequate to call Israel God's experimental garden, as Berkhof does (CF 249), for this metaphor suggests too strongly that God's involvement with Israel was preliminary and experimental. Still, the Bible portrays Israel as representing all nations. Israel is the people with whom God has established his covenant, to whom he gives his blessings, but upon whom he also implements his curse when the covenant is disobeyed. Today this word applies in the same way to the entire community from all nations that have been incorporated into Israel (Rom 11:21-22; 1 Cor 10:11-12; Heb 4:11).

We may conclude that, out of all the nations on earth, God has elected Israel to live with him (Exod 19:5-6) in a covenant that produces blessing and life for Israel and, through Israel, also for the nations. Even before Gen 12 these nations were the object of God's special care. But things turned out badly, as we see in the flood story (Gen 8) and in the story of the building of the tower (Gen 11); now, apparently, God's choice of Abraham forms another route to reach the nations. In many different ways the Psalms and the Prophets express the hope and expectation that Israel may indeed understand how good and blessed it is to live in communion with this God. Psalm 80, for instance, is a concrete reference to the history of the exodus, and to the good times in which country and people thrived. In a situation of deep distress this longing is still alive, and we hear the prayer that God will restore his covenant and will make its blessing come true.

Using a metaphor from viniculture, Israel is compared to a vine that had been dug out from Egyptian soil and transplanted in Canaan. There this vine could grow into a lush vineyard, into a tree that would extend its branches from the sea to the big river (Ps 80:11)—not the Jordan, but the Euphrates! But this psalm also reminds the reader of the loss of this glory. "Why then hast thou broken down its walls, so that all who pass along the way pluck its fruit?" (v. 12). Israel is the cutting that God has planted, the child he himself has raised (v. 15; see Hos 11:3) but now abandons. Remarkably enough, this psalm does not attribute this abandonment to Israel's failure (which is not denied) but lays the entire unhappy situation before God. The vineyard lies before God in its withered state (v. 16), and he alone will be able to save it. Therefore, God is called upon to change the fate of Israel for the better and show his compassionate face.

The hope that God will show his compassionate face and will forever establish his righteousness is a crucial element in the expectation of the prophets. This expectation is found with both the Minor Prophets and the Major Prophets, and gradually it received universal scope. In the description of the role of the Messiah (e.g., in Isa 11:1–10), the new peace will be universal. The minor prophet Habakkuk (2:14) envisions a future when "the earth will be filled with the knowledge of the glory of the LORD, as the waters cover the sea." Through Israel, all the nations of this world will be led to the knowledge and service of the true God. All of Israel and the entire earth will see God's salvation and share in the blessing that has been given to Israel. The nations will share in these blessings when the God of Israel comes to establish his reign. The universalism of Ps 87 is but one example from a series of psalms that praise this global perspective (Pss 97–98, 100). In the prayer that Jesus taught his disciples, this universal expectation is affirmed: "Thy kingdom come!" In this expectation Jesus does not clash with Israel but himself personifies this prospect. Yet, we have to take one more crucial step: *In Jesus's coming and ministry, death and resurrection, the eschatological expectation of Israel—and thus the covenant—is in principle fulfilled.*

With this italicized sentence we appear to state what has, in fact, separated church and synagogue so tragically over the centuries, and what has become known as the great schism. Nonetheless, Jewish believers may see in the development of the worldwide movement of Christianity at least a partial fulfillment of Old Testament expectations and prophecies. For Judaism it is also a truly stirring fact that through one Jew, Jesus of Nazareth, many millions of people through the ages have come to learn about the God of Israel. The Jewish theologian Pinchas Lapide (1922-97), after approvingly quoting the words of Simeon in Luke 2:29-32, says (1983, 28-29): "Seeing that the West has come to accept monotheism by listening to a pious Jew, whom the evangelists address thirteen times as 'rabbi,' I can and must accept this historical effect as part of God's salvific plan, and the believing church . . . as an instrument that God wanted to use for the salvation of the world. Every other approach would, in the final analysis, be a denial of the universalism of the prophets of Israel and of the matchless love of God." Thus, the difference is not so much in the question of whether Jesus has become the "savior of the gentiles." You do not need a theologian, Lapide says, to determine this—"just looking around you suffices." The difference lies in the question of whether Jesus's work and person also have a salvific significance for Judaism. Is he also in this respect the fulfillment of the covenant with Israel?

9.6. The Significance of Jesus for the Covenant with Israel

We come now to the question of the significance of Jesus with respect to God's covenant with Israel. Should the church perhaps recognize that this significance applies only to the nations? The discussion touches on the themes of Christology and soteriology, which will be central in chapters 10 and 11.

For the early Christian church the ministry of Jesus was a transforming experience. In what Jesus brought to them, they felt a profound experience of the love of God that went beyond anything they knew. It compelled them to see that the appearance of Jesus bore a decisive significance; it signaled the breaking through of "these last days" (Heb 1:1), in which God himself came to his people. But does God come alone? The experience of their meeting with Jesus prompted the early Jewish Christians to go where the Spirit directed them (Acts 10:12, 17) and to believe in the unconditional and unlimited character of God's love. Along this line the New Testament explains the Christ-event as the fulfillment of the promises of the Old Testament for Jews and gentiles. And in that order—for Jesus came first of all as the Messiah of Israel.

This priority had already been made clear in Jesus's ministry. Jesus claimed to bring something new, the dawning of the time of the Messiah because of God's decisive coming to his people, Israel. Jesus does so by clearly reminding the people of the Jubilee, the "agreeable year of the Lord" of Lev 25, and by alluding to the coming of the reign of peace that was promised by the prophets (Luke 4:14-19). In that respect Jesus publicly distanced himself from John the Baptist (Matt 11:18-19), for John was still the prophet of doom who called the people to be converted in view of the coming day of judgment. Jesus no longer speaks of the ax that is at the root of the tree. Rather, he lived in the awareness and with the growing conviction (he was human in every respect) that in his words and deeds God himself was in the process of making his salvation concrete. Therefore, for Jesus the judgment no longer comes first (even though his work causes a separation, Matt 10:34); rather, he puts people in a life-giving relationship with God (John 3:17). For that reason he can present himself as the bridegroom whose coming brings all fasting to an end (Mark 2:19). This approach of Jesus must be interpreted within the framework of his intentions that were embodied in the covenant with Abraham and in the Torah that was given to Moses. When Zacchaeus accepts the invitation to be saved, it is because he is a child of Abraham (Luke 19:1-10); and in the story of poor Lazarus, the rich man is reminded that Lazarus belongs to the sons of Abraham (Luke 16:19-31). In brief, Jesus comes to bring to completion the covenant that God established with Abraham and his posterity, and he wants to unite the people around this covenant.

This focus on Israel as the goal of Jesus's ministry is also clearly found in other New Testament texts. In Mark 6 (see also Luke 9:1-6 and 10:1-24), Jesus sends his disciples two by two to proclaim the message of his imminent kingdom within the confines of Israel. We find a clear example of the focus of Jesus's mission in his meeting with the Canaanite woman; he says he has come for Israel. However, the woman, who recognizes Jesus's power to perform miracles, continues to call upon Jesus and pushes herself upon him, in spite of the efforts of the disciples to get rid of her. When at last she succeeds and stands face to face with him, the Jew Yeshua, he says: "I was sent only to the lost sheep of the house of Israel." What follows is also crystal clear: "It is not fair to take the children's bread and throw it to the dogs." But the Canaanite woman perseveres—Jesus does not easily get away from her—and she catches him at his own metaphor: "Yes, Lord, yet even the dogs eat the crumbs that fall from their master's table." The Jewish context remains visible elsewhere in the New Testament. Apparently, the Emmaus disciples and the more than five hundred brothers Paul refers to in 1 Cor 15:6 are Jewish people. Jesus has become a servant of those who have been circumcised, according to this same Paul in Rom 15:7. For that reason, during his missionary journeys Paul always first went to the synagogues. And Peter says in a sermon to his fellow Jews in Acts 3:26: "God, having raised up his servant, sent him to you first, to bless you in turning every one of you from your wickedness" (see Bockmuehl 2008).

We must conclude that Jesus's entire ministry takes place in the context of Israel. God's path goes via Israel to the nations, and in this journey, from the particularity to the universality of grace, the world will be blessed (see Gal 3:14). In Christian dogmatics we must follow this track. It is impossible for us to see Jesus as only sent to, and on behalf of, the nations of the world. Likewise, it is impossible to detach Jesus from his background in the history of Israel. In hermeneutical terms, we must read the history of Israel "alongside" Jesus if we are to understand his unique significance. When this aspect is ignored and Jesus is detached from Israel and the Jewish faith, the gospel becomes something abstract.

But we must inevitably also move in our reading from Jesus Christ back to the Hebrew Bible. From a hermeneutical point of view this is a reading, or rather a rereading, of the old texts in the light of this newer experience. We detect those two movements in Jesus's ministry. On the one hand, he found his way by following the law and the prophets; we might call this "reading alongside." For good reason Jesus is pictured in the Gospels as a student of the law (Luke 2:41–52), and in Heb 5:8 we are told that he had to learn obedience through the suffering he experienced. He was subject to growth and development. This process is mentioned also in the framework of the story about his early involvement in the "things of his Father" (Luke 2:40, 52). On the other hand, Jesus is pictured in the Gospels as the one who, on the basis of his own experiences and his own relationship with God, began to read and interpret the law and the prophets in a new way. Just think once more of the Sermon on the Mount as the converging and radicalizing interpretation of the Torah. This process of reading back and reinterpreting is characteristic of the entire New Testament and the early church (e.g., see Acts 8:32–35). The early church began to read the writings of Israel with new eyes, in the light of its experiences with Jesus Christ, especially his cross and the resurrection.

Often mistakes were made. In many places, for instance—at times through allegorical interpretations—people believed that they saw messianic prophecies or other christological interpretations in the Old Testament, when exegetically there was no basis for this. (An example is found in Ps 80, where older translations speak in verse 17 of the "Man at your right hand" and the "son of man"—using a capital letter to indicate that this person is the Messiah—while, very clearly, the people of Israel are meant.) For that reason it remains very important, in spite of what we referred to as the inevitable "reading back," to allow the Old Testament to speak in the first instance, as much as possible, for itself. Berkhof points to the correct method. When we are dealing with Israel, we must first allow the Old Testament to speak for itself; then we must look at the New Testament in the light of the Old Testament, and only then make the opposite movement (CF, §§30-31). But even this method offers no guarantee against mistakes, for when Berkhof finds in the New Testament mostly a confirmation of the main themes he discovered in his reading of the Old (262-63), we might remark that this was to be expected, since, subconsciously, we tend to read the Old Testament through our Christian spectacles (e.g., we note that Berkhof follows the Christian sequence of the canon and draws various conclusions from this order of the books). Nonetheless, Berkhof is right in suggesting that there is hardly any other methodological option. In this going back and forth, we should note what Miskotte calls the assets of the Old Testament—themes that are prominent in the Old Testament but disappear into the background in the New without, however, losing their theological significance. Miskotte points in this connection (1967, 173-302), inter alia, to God's hiddenness (which is so poignantly felt in the Psalms), to the experience of the mysterious closeness to God, but also to the political and even the erotic elements (e.g., see the Song of Songs, which is certainly not limited to a spiritual meaning).

We conclude that, when people read the Old Testament from the perspective of the Christ-event, they did not just find confirmation but also incurred a shift in the way in which they began to look at the atonement (through vicarious suffering), at redemption (now in principle, fully in the future), and at the resurrection (first one, later the others). New layers of meaning in the Old Testament message began to light up, and some aspects of the events around Jesus received an unexpected confirmation (the sense of surprise is palpable in texts like Luke 24:25-27, 32, 44-46). Not without reason we find that the Gospels and the Epistles are full of Old Testament quotations and the discussions they provoked (think of the so-called fulfillment quotations in Matthew).

Certain shifts also occurred in the attitude of the early Christian church with regard to the so-called identity markers of Judaism, even though the early Christians initially continued to normally participate in the temple worship (Acts 3:1). It is in light of discussions about the lasting significance of the law and the temple that we must understand the execution of Stephen (Acts 7) and the various debates that are echoed in the Pauline epistles (e.g., in Rom 14:2; 2 Cor 3; Gal 2–3). Once the universal significance of God's revelation in Christ is recognized, circumcision, for instance, is no longer regarded as a sign of entering into the covenant with the God of Israel. We might say that the rules of the game have changed. As the Father of Jesus Christ, the God of Israel has become accessible to all people, including for those who have come from the goyim. And this access comes through faith in Jesus Christ. Only by following this way—which, according to Paul (Rom 4) and the author of Hebrews (chap. 11), had always been central—do the believers from the nations become, in harmony with God's promises, heirs of Abraham (Gal 3:29). Here the universal scope of Israel's election is fully revealed.

In this fascinating process Jesus's crucifixion and resurrection become theologically decisive. In their close relationship to each other, these two must have played a central role. That Jesus himself saw his death on the cross as the fulfillment of God's covenant with Israel and as the inauguration of a new era of salvation is, most probably, seen in the words that accompanied the Last Supper: "This is my blood of the covenant, which is poured out for many for the forgiveness of sins" (Matt 26:28; in Luke 22 we find in the immediate context also such terms as "fulfillment" and "kingdom"). Through his resurrection from death Jesus's message and ministry were affirmed in an astounding way. Subsequently, this mystery of his life was publicly proclaimed (Acts 2:36). The early church was thus soon led to a short but shocking confession—*Iēsous Kyrios*, Jesus is Lord. This title, which points to his resurrection, expresses the conviction that Jesus could be confessed, called upon, and worshiped by his Jewish (!) followers as one with God the Creator. For *kyrios* was the Greek rendering of the name that was reserved for God alone (see Phil 2:9–10). Paul expresses this new title in 1 Cor 8 with a somewhat more elaborate confession that seems to have already become common in the circles of the Jewish followers of Jesus:

> For although there may be so-called gods in heaven or on earth—as indeed there are many "gods" and many "lords"—yet for us there is one God, the Father, from whom are all things and for whom we exist,

and one Lord, Jesus Christ, through whom are all things and through whom we exist. (vv. 5-6)

Here the Shema Yisrael ("Hear, O Israel"; Deut 6:4) is so interpreted that Jesus is part of God's identity. These Christians believed that the God of Israel and the crucified Messiah forever belonged together. In this history of the cross and the resurrection, God revealed himself to the people once more in a decisive way. What God wanted is not new in content, for it is still the saving communion of God with the people; but the way leading up to this goal is surprisingly new. What had already been at the core of the Torah—namely, to love God with all our heart, soul, and mind, and with all that we have—was practiced by Jesus at the cost of his own life. The love of God the Father was the power that led him to bring the supreme sacrifice, his life. This unconditional love is the basis for a new access to God. In spite of all unfaithfulness and defeat, the reconciliation between God and humanity breaks through. It is God who, through Christ, reconciled the world unto himself. The first people who saw this and shared in this development were the Jewish compatriots of Jesus. Only later, after Pentecost, was the circle widened to also include people from the gentiles. But what changes everything is that, already at this stage, a new, eschatological community is formed around the Messiah, just as the prophets had promised. At first it consisted of Jews, who after some time began to welcome gentiles in their midst. Most of the Jews at that time were unable to handle the high qualifications that were attributed to Christ, while the majority of the gentiles in and around Israel—no doubt quite casually—ignored him too.

Just a short remark here about the resurrection, running ahead of what we will say about it further in chapter 11. The difference between Judaism and Christianity is not that Jews—as opposed to Christians—would not believe in the resurrection and would not be able to give this a place in their belief system. Admittedly, in Jesus's days and the Judaism of his time, disputes were still going on about the resurrection; see Matt 22:23-33 and also Acts 23:1-10, where Paul cleverly pits the Pharisees, who believed in a resurrection, against the Sadducees, who were totally opposed to it. Yet, the expectation of a bodily resurrection of the dead at the end of time had by then become quite common in Israel. It was the capstone of a development of an ever-clearer awareness that God, as the Creator and Redeemer, truly has power over everything, and that for him death and injustice do not have the final word. Sooner or later God's righteousness would be revealed to, and realized in, this world (see Levenson 2006). Jesus's resurrection anticipates this future. The people were, however, faced with the question whether this was only a glorification of a Jewish martyr—contemporary Judaism believed that martyrs were especially destined to be resurrected—or whether this was a sign that the messianic kingdom had arrived. If we listen to the witnesses of the New Testament, the latter was the case: the messianic time has come, and around Jesus there develops a new community of Jews and gentiles. Remarkably enough, some Jewish thinkers can even go along with this view of Jesus's resurrection. Pinchas Lapide (2002) suggested that this resurrection was, in fact, needed to make the universal message of salvation and righteousness known to the nations outside Israel. Through Jesus the messianic hope and the Torah with the Ten Commandments have become common knowledge. It does not mean, he continues, that Christ also has theological significance for the Jews. But Lapide, with his remarkably sympathetic attitude to Jesus, certainly takes a new step in the Jewish-Christian dialogue. More generally, his writings helped (as did those of David Flusser [1917-2000]) many postwar Christians by his so-called *Heimholung Jesu* (bringing back of Jesus) to his original Jewish context and proceeding from this point as the basis for understanding him.

9.7. The Incompleteness of the Salvation

"Are you the one who is to come, or shall we look for another?" This question of John the Baptist (Matt 11:3; Luke 7:19) is typical for the most important issue in the dialogue between Judaism and Christianity, between synagogue and church. Jesus's answer indicates that he understood his own ministry within the context of Israel's messianic expectations. With his ministry the reign of God was breaking through; God was putting a claim on the lives of the people. In his answer to John, Jesus points to the signs that confirm that the kingdom is breaking through. But precisely this answer, which invites John to accept the messianic identity of Jesus, has been the reason that the greater part of observant Jews reject this claim. For Jesus's ministry did not conform in all aspects to the description that we find in Isa 11:1-10 and 25:1-8. Especially lacking is the *universality* of salvation.

In a famous discourse between Martin Buber and the New Testament scholar Karl-Ludwig Schmidt, on January 14, 1933, Buber formulated this objection as follows: "The church maintains that Christ has come as the God-given redemption for humanity. We, Israel, cannot believe this." With all the respect that Buber has for Jesus, he states: "We know in a profound and real way that the history of the world has not been broken open up to its foundations; that the world has not yet been redeemed. We experience the nonredeemed state of the world" (Buber 1963, 562). Similar statements have been made by Schalom Ben-Chorin: "The Jew knows that, in the final analysis, the world is still unredeemed and he does not recognize any enclaves of redemption in the midst of this unredeemed situation" (1956, 99).

The argument between church and synagogue is, as we have already seen, not about whether Jesus was resurrected. The roads diverge over the question of whether or not Jesus was the promised Messiah. Did he bring the new eschatological era, the "year of the Lord's favor," or were Jesus and his disciples, and later also the early church, mistaken in this conviction? The Christian church regarded the events of the cross and the resurrection, and also the Pentecost experiences, as the start of a new dispensation, a time in which God himself in Christ and in the Spirit provided a new way of access to communion with him and in which he fulfilled his promise. The Torah was not abolished, but the focus moved to the way in which Jesus had fulfilled it. The larger share of observant Jews was unable to agree with this conclusion, which has to do with their view of salvation. In the Old Testament and in the intertestamental period, salvation was seen as a world-encompassing, cosmic event in which God would come to his people Israel and restore it to its former glory (note still Acts 1:6). The crucial aspect for Israel's faith was that God would at that time establish his law and his righteousness over the entire earth. In the apocalyptic literature of early Judaism (usually referred to as the period of the Second Temple, between 350 BCE and 70 CE), as in 1-2 Maccabees and the book of Enoch, this restorative act of God is painted in cosmic proportions and colors. God would adjudicate between Israel and Israel's enemies and thereby bring a separation between the righteous and the unrighteous. It is crucial for Israel's end-time expectation that this event be total and comprehensive.

In the light of this all-comprising expectation, it is easy to understand that the resurrection of just one person—Jesus of Nazareth—was not recognized by the leaders of the Jewish people as the supreme end-time act of God. However, this faith persisted among Jesus's followers, in spite of their own expectations. They understood from the appearances of the Resurrected One that, in Jesus's life, God has granted a new, miraculous restart. For them these events meant, among other things, that God himself affirmed the life and ministry of Jesus, including the message he preached, as truthful (for a more detailed discussion of this point, see

11.1). In a theological sense, this understanding marked a discontinuity in the thinking about the resurrection of the dead. Because the one has already been raised, the resurrection of the dead has in fact already begun. For in raising this one, God has revealed his authority over death and also put Jesus's death on the cross in a new light. The early Christians may not have been sure how to interpret the resurrection, but they were in no doubt that Jesus, as the Son of God, was henceforth to be mentioned in one and the same breath with the Father.

In other words, a change was needed in the traditional Jewish view regarding the end-time redemption (Pannenberg, ST 2:345). On the one hand, there is the one, Jesus Christ, who was the first to be raised from the dead. He has gone ahead of the others. The Epistle to the Hebrews even tells us that, through the cross, he opened the door into heaven for all who followed him (Heb 9:11–12). The complete redemption at the end of time is separated from the opening of the way to God that has been realized through Jesus Christ. These two events are not simultaneous; an interim lies between them. Once again the structural importance of the doctrine of the Trinity surfaces. We do not know only of the drama of God and Israel, and the history of Jesus and the church. There is also the interaction between the Spirit and the world (John 16:8), which is still ongoing. Our communion with God in Christ must be distinguished from the ultimate redemption at the end of time. Or in a common summary of the theology of the New Testament, we must distinguish between the "already" and the "not yet" of the kingdom. Much is being said about reconciliation with God (2 Cor 5:18–21), but the ultimate realization of the redemption still lies in the future, which does not render it uncertain. Reconciliation is the event in which we are already, here and now, reconciled with God in Christ. We are already "in Christ," so nothing can separate us from our Lord (Rom 8:35–39). However, the redemption of the entire creation—the end and the re-creation of the world—is still in the future. These two moments do not eliminate each other but form a tension-filled unity that keeps on surfacing in the life of the believer and of the church. In this tension we will continue to deal with the questions of obedience to the covenant, sanctification, and renewal that are prominent in the Old Testament. This tension also determines how Christian theology must continue to reflect on Israel.

9.8. Some Important Takeaways

We conclude this chapter by summarizing what the church of today might learn from Israel (i.e., the synagogue or the community of observant Jews). Israel, its expectation, its search for the hallowing of God's name, and the identity markers of land, circumcision, Sabbath, and cult point us—at least—to the following:

1. *God is present in our daily life on this earth.* No theology that wants to give a place to Israel can ignore a positive appraisal of our earthly life. It is always possible to point to a concrete place where God is "hallowed." For Israel, it was the land of Canaan and, especially, the temple; for Christians, it is the place where God has come to live and where the covenant was personalized in the concrete person of Jesus Christ (John 1:14; Rom 9:6-10). We are told that he was raised and is seated at the right hand of the Father (Acts 2:25; Rom 8:34). He is not here, for he is risen (Matt 28:6). However, he remains Immanuel, God with us, who has promised to be with us always until the end of the world (Matt 28:20).

2. *The Messiah is the concrete locus of salvation.* Christians confess that, after his ascension, Jesus has been at the right hand of God and guarantees our life and our future. We can point to his place in heaven, which relativizes the localization of salvation on earth but does not deprive it of all significance. For God also lives where he establishes his name, that is, where two or three are gathered in his name. Therefore, the church as the body of Christ shares (in spite of all its sinfulness and ambivalence) in the local presence and concreteness of God's revelation. This concreteness also applies to the individual believer. Paul refers to the body of the believer as the temple of the Holy Spirit (1 Cor 6:19).

3. *The Spirit seizes us.* The work of the Spirit is not at variance with this concreteness and materiality but will always assume a particular shape and size upon times and places, individuals and communities. The preliminary contours of liberation and fulfillment are concrete. God seeks us in the geographic location where we were born and educated, where we learned a language and were taught to look for all kinds of things. There he approaches us and communes with us, in our own language (Acts 2:8). The church may learn a few things from Israel with regard to this concreteness. All too easily we allow faith to lose itself in abstract ideas and ideals. God seizes our life, space, time, language, and body. But he does so in the spirit of the Torah and of Jesus: not restraining, but permitting, giving life and space.

4. *The promise of the land does not evaporate or become frozen into*

just one possible mode of fulfillment. From this perspective, we look in two different ways at the signs of the covenant, especially at the sign of the land. On the one hand, these signs, in their materiality and concreteness, continue to have meaning within the context of God's covenant with Israel (and never in detachment from this). Here also we must beware of spiritualizing, broadening, and diffusing what God has promised very concretely (Gen 17:8). Thus, it is plausible to see the return of the people of Israel to their land in 1948 as a hopeful sign of God's abiding faithfulness to his covenant. On the other hand, this promise may never be used in a political sense. It is unclear how God will fulfill his promises eschatologically, but it is impossible to bring this fulfillment closer by human means, as some Orthodox Jews are well aware (note Gen 27 for the misery this effort will cause). In the spirit of the Torah and in the spirit of Jesus, believers have been called to manage their possessions with others in sight, and in their hearts. With respect to the land and the Palestinian conflict, this perspective means that, for the sake of justice and compassion, which both Torah and gospel demand, solutions and compromises must be sought on the basis of current international law.

5. *The church joins Israel in its prayer for the kingdom.* Together with the living Israel, the church prays for the kingdom of God. The perfect future has not yet arrived. Injustice and suffering continue, which prompts us to be pilgrims who live with a forward look. The Christian church, which consists of people from all lands, realizes in its forward-looking faith and desire that it is the younger brother, a branch that has subsequently been grafted into the olive tree. Israel was elected first as the one to which God bound himself forever. In the meantime, election and covenant have reached their goal in Jesus Christ, who came through David's posterity according to the flesh but appeared as the Son of God in power according to the Spirit (Rom 1:3-4). Nonetheless, even though redemption has not been completed, this prayer does not have less urgency.

6. *Christian theology must not return to any supersessionism.* It is of utmost importance that a structurally different approach to the role of Israel be anchored in Christian theology forever. If not, we run the risk of returning to the old sentiments of arrogance and contempt (note Rom 11:18-20). Latent anti-Semitism is never far away, and supersessionism often remains a well-known and attractive option to younger generations of believers and theologians. We have to be very clear in the way we restructure the traditional Christian theology of Israel, lest the deep-seated substitution doctrine will in the end prevail. We have to be all the more cautious now that most survivors of the Second World War have passed

away and the Holocaust is rapidly receding into the background of our collective memory.

7. *The church must be serious about the appeal for holiness.* In large part the Christian church consists of people who have been privileged to be grafted into the olive tree of Israel and who, in that sense, are receivers. We cannot look over God's shoulder to see how he moves and guides individuals and peoples. We are the recipients, and history is open-ended (1 Cor 10:12). Yet, these recipients have been given a task: the Christian church has been called to make Israel jealous (Rom 11:14). The warnings throughout the Letter to the Hebrews, addressed to those believers who forget and neglect their liberation, remain warnings to the entire church. For the Christian church and for theology, the theme of Israel remains an urgent invitation to live as people of reconciliation, to be holy, and to learn to practice justice. It is clear that this word represents an enormous challenge with regard to the way in which the Christian faith community conducts itself. But as long as this appeal remains unanswered, John's question of whether the Messiah has already come or whether we should expect someone else (Matt 11:3) will continue to sound from the circle of those who are guarding God's promises (Hab 2:1).

References

Beek, Abraham van de. 2002. *De kring om de Messias: Israël als volk van de lijdende Heer* [The circle around the Messiah: Israel as the people of the suffering Lord]. Zoetermeer: Meinema.

Ben-Chorin, Schalom. 1956. *Die Antwort des Jona: Zum Gestaltwandel Israels; Ein geschichtstheologischer Versuch*. Hamburg: Herbert Reich.

Berkhof, Hendrikus. 1969. "Israel as a Theological Problem in the Christian Church." *Journal of Ecumenical Studies* 6:329-47.

Bockmuehl, Marcus. 2008. "God's Life as a Jew: Remembering the Son of God as Son of David." In *Seeking the Identity of Jesus: A Pilgrimage*, edited by B. R. Gaventa and R. Hays, 60-78. Grand Rapids: Eerdmans.

Buber, Martin. 1937. *I and Thou*. Edinburgh: T&T Clark. Orig. German pub., *Ich und Du*, Leipzig: Insel-Verlag, 1923.

———. 1963. *Der Jude und sein Judentum: Gesammelte Aufsätze und Reden*. Cologne: Melzer.

Busch, Eberhard. 1999. "The Covenant of Grace Fulfilled in Christ as the Foundation of the Indissoluble Solidarity of the Church with Israel: Barth's Position on the Jews during the Hitler Era." *Scottish Journal of Theology* 52:476-503.

Dorff, Elliot N. 2008. *The Jewish Approach to Repairing the World (Tikkun Olam): A Brief Introduction for Christians*. Woodstock, VT: Jewish Lights.

Harvey, Richard. 2009. *Mapping Messianic Jewish Theology: A Constructive Approach*. Milton Keynes: Paternoster.

Heschel, Abraham J. 1955. *God in Search of Man: A Philosophy of Judaism*. New York: Farrar, Straus & Cudahy.

Hocken, Peter. 2009. *The Challenges of the Pentecostal, Charismatic, and Messianic Jewish Movements: The Tensions of the Spirit*. Farnham: Ashgate.

Horst, Pieter W. van der. 2000. "'Only Then Will All Israel Be Saved': A Short Note on the Meaning of καὶ οὕτως in Romans 11:26." *Journal of Biblical Literature* 119:521–25.

Jansen, Hans. 1981–85. *Christelijke theologie na Auschwitz* [Christian theology after Auschwitz]. 2 vols. The Hague: Bokencentrum.

Keith, Graham. 1997. *Hated without a Cause? A Survey of Anti-Semitism*. Carlisle: Paternoster.

Klappert, Bertold. 1980. *Israel und die Kirche: Erwägungen zur Israellehre Karl Barths*. Munich: Kaiser.

———. 2000. *Miterben der Verheißung: Beiträge zum jüdisch-christlichen Dialog*. Neukirchen: Neukirchener Verlag.

Lapide, Pinchas. 1983. *Hij leerde in hun synagogen: Een joodse uitleg van de evangeliën*. Baarn: Ten Have.

———. 2002. *The Resurrection of Jesus: A Jewish Perspective*. Eugene, OR: Wipf & Stock.

Lapide, Pinchas, and Jürgen Moltmann. 1981. *Jewish Monotheism and Christian Trinitarian Doctrine: A Dialogue*. Philadelphia: Fortress.

Levenson, John Douglas. 2006. *Resurrection and the Restoration of Israel: The Ultimate Victory of the God of Life*. New Haven: Yale University Press.

Marquardt, Friedrich-Wilhelm. 1990–91. *Das Christliche Bekenntnis zu Jesus, dem Juden: Eine Christologie*. 2 vols. Gütersloh: Kaiser.

———. 1993–96. *Was dürfen wir hoffen, wenn wir hoffen dürften? Eine Eschatologie*. 3 vols. Gütersloh: Gütersloher Verlagshaus.

———. 1997. "The Christian Confession of Jesus the Jew." In *Jews and Christians: Rivals or Partners for the Kingdom of God? In Search of an Alternative for the Theology of Substitution*, edited by D. Pollefeyt, 50–51. Leuven: Peeters.

———. 2010. *Theological Audacities: Selected Essays*. Edited by Andreas Pangritz and Paul S. Chung. Eugene, OR: Pickwick Publications.

Miskotte, Kornelis H. 1933. *Het wezen der Joodsche religie: Bijdrage tot de kennis van het Joodsche geestesleven* [The essence of Judaism: A contribution to the knowledge of Jewish spirituality]. Amsterdam: H. J. Paris.

———. 1967. *When the Gods Are Silent*. London: Collins.

Mussner, Franz. 1984. *Tractate on the Jews: The Significance of Judaism for Christian Faith*. Philadelphia: Fortress.

Protestant Church in the Netherlands (PCN). 2004. *Constitution 2004*. www

.protestantsekerk.nl/Lists/PKN-Bibliotheek/Churchorder-protestant-church
-articles-I-XIX-2004.pdf.

Ruether, R. Radford. 1974. *Faith and Fratricide: The Theological Roots of Anti-Semitism*. New York: Seabury Press.

Ruler, Arnold A. van. 1971. *The Christian Church and the Old Testament*. Grand Rapids: Eerdmans.

Sacks, Jonathan. 2005. *To Heal a Fractured World: The Ethics of Responsibility*. New York: Schocken Books.

Schoon, Simon. 2006. "'Holy People'—Some Protestant Views." In *A Holy People: Jewish and Christian Perspectives on Religious Communal Identity*, edited by Marcel Poorthuis and Joshua Schwarz, 279–306. Leiden: Brill.

———. 2009. "An Indissoluble Bond between the Church and the People of Israel: Historical Fact or Theological Conviction?" In *Interaction between Judaism and Christianity in History, Religion, Art, and Literature*, edited by Marcel Poorthuis, Joshua Schwartz, and Joseph Turner, 399–418. Leiden: Brill.

10 The Person of Jesus Christ

Christology

AIM

This chapter and the next deal, respectively, with the person and the work of Jesus Christ, and so belong together. In this chapter we want to:

- demonstrate why Jesus occupies such a central place in the Christian faith, and how closely his person and work are connected (10.1)
- make a deliberate choice in the controversy over the proper method of Christology (10.2)
- discuss the sources available for Christology (10.3)
- present some approaches that are used to define Jesus's identity (10.4)
- offer a bird's-eye view of the history of christological doctrine (10.5)
- review the biblical material behind christological doctrine by discussing how some of Jesus's most prominent titles throw light on his identity (10.6–7).

MAKING CONNECTIONS

1. Spend some time thinking about Christian holidays such as Christmas, Easter, Ascension Day, and Pentecost. What do they have to do with Jesus? Which one strikes you as most important?
2. In our culture people look at Christ in many different ways. Listen to a chorale of J. S. Bach's *St. Matthew Passion*, and then a song from the rock opera *Jesus Christ Superstar*. Note the differences.

10.1. The Central Meaning of Jesus's Person and Work in the Christian Faith

In this chapter we pursue the meaning of Jesus and his ministry. We will narrow down from the general importance of Jesus Christ that we saw in chapter 3, on the Trinity, to focus on Christology. In other words, we are probing the identity of Jesus. Jesus himself asked his disciples about his identity (Mark 8:27–29), and most of them gave an answer that placed him among the prophets. But Peter's reply went further: "You are the Messiah." In Matthew's version Peter's reaction was even more elaborate: "You are the Christ, the Son of the living God" (Matt 16:16). This answer includes two words, two titles, that try to express something about who he is, or his identity. Along with other words, like Lord (Gk. *Kyrios*) and Savior or Redeemer (Gk. *Sōtēr*), these titles have acquired enormous significance in the Christian faith. The Greek translation of Messiah (from Hebrew, "anointed one") is *christos*. Soon this adjective became Jesus's proper name: Jesus Christ. The term "son" developed in the course of history into the title that emphasizes the close bond between Jesus and God. On the lips of Peter it already has great significance, namely, that Jesus comes from God and is more than a prophet. "Son" became a key concept in the church's dogma. With this word we say that Jesus is of the same kind as God; he is "cut from the same cloth."

All these titles, in their own way, tell us who Jesus is. In him we meet with God's saving intervention. The previous chapter made clear that the Christian faith arose from the context of God's revelation to Israel. Faith in God as the Creator, who elects a people in Abraham and who wants to reach the world through this people, forms the seedbed of the Christian faith. Now we must take the next step and arrive at the core: faith in God's identity as the Saving and Redeeming One is defined in the Christian church by Jesus. We see this position clearly in the New Testament writings, in the documents of the early church, and in the songs and liturgical texts that, down through the ages, have been inspired by these writings. Here is our brief definition of that significance: *In Jesus Christ, God speaks and acts for our salvation. In Jesus as the Son, he offers his life-giving presence and his forgiving love in a definitive and irreversible way.* Christology and soteriology explore the content of this statement in a broad array of interconnected elements.

Jesus Christ's central place and high status in the Christian faith do not date from later times. Already in the earliest layers of the New Testament we detect that Jesus was worshiped. Numerous texts state that, in his resurrection, Jesus was "exalted" by the Father and that he is now seated at the Father's right hand. This is metaphorical language, of course, using the image of an Eastern ruler on his throne as described in Ps 110. Still, it has deep significance. Consider Rom 8:34; we find in it the same sequence of events that was later included in the Apostles' Creed:

> . . . Christ Jesus, who died,
> yes, who was raised from the dead,
> who is at the right hand of God,
> who indeed intercedes for us.

The image of Jesus seated at God's right hand illustrates how people regarded Jesus: *he shares in God's authority*. The same Jesus who walked about on this earth, proclaimed the kingdom, and was crucified is the Risen One, who, as the Son, now shares in the rule of his Father. But in the quotation from Romans we find a fourth element (besides cross, resurrection, and ascension) that indicates what Jesus, as the Living One, does: *he pleads for us*. In other words, he takes the place of guilty human beings. Jesus is still doing today what he did during his life on earth. His name is not just any name; it tells us what he does and who he is. Yeshua means "God saves."

The importance of this name is clarified in Matt 1:21, where Joseph is told by God to give the boy this name. This clarification points to an important fact: that Jesus and God are very closely connected. Put differently, in Christ, God *continues to engage himself* and to demonstrate who he is in the midst of human ambivalence, guilt, and estrangement. In this human being God demonstrates his majesty, his will for life and restoration. In the Son of Israel he stays with his covenant and demonstrates what a life is like that is brought under his rule. For that reason Christology is significant in two respects. On the one hand, it clarifies Jesus's identity as "God with us" (= Heb. Immanuel, Matt 1:23), as God's Emissary and Representative—yes, as the Son of God. On the other hand, it says something about the identity of Israel's God: no longer can the God of Israel be detached from Jesus. God's identity is definitively and irreversibly defined by Jesus. Anyone who wants to say something about God will also have to say something about Jesus. This image tells us about the high position Jesus held in the eyes of his first Jewish followers. In his bond with God, Jesus becomes someone upon whom people may call for help—someone who may even be worshiped. This high Christology has ancient credentials.

Numerous places in the New Testament allude to the imagery of Ps 110. See, besides Rom 8:34, also Mark 12:36; 14:62; Acts 2:34; 1 Cor 15:25; Eph 1:20; Col 3:1; Heb 1:3, 13; 8:1; 10:12; 12:2; 1 Pet 3:22. For a survey, see Hengel 1995, 119–225, and Roukema 2010. The early worship of Jesus is especially remarkable, given that contemporary Judaism was absolutely convinced that God alone was to be served, worshiped, and praised (Exod 20:3–5; Deut 6:13–15; 10:20; Matt 4:10); it was considered idolatry of the worst sort to worship a human being. How Jesus came to share so quickly in this worship remains a total anomaly unless we assume that his resurrection from the dead is the connecting link. Only then does it make sense (see 11.1).

This discussion so far does not yet enlighten us about the precise relationship between Jesus and God, which is the question Christology seeks to answer. In line with what we discussed in chapter 3, we can formulate the issue as follows: the New Testament testifies to a strong *union* between God and Jesus but, at the same time, to a clear *distinction*. We find these aspects close together in the prologue of the Gospel of John: the Word was *with* (therefore, apparently, different from) God, but at the same time the Word *was* God (John 1:1). The church has attempted to do justice to both this union and this distinction. The whole debate in the early church about the Trinity and Christology may be read as an attempt, via trial and error, to safeguard this biblical mystery and hand it on. This is precisely the role of doctrine in the church: to keep reminding us of this dual identity of Jesus. Not accidentally, the earliest doctrinal formulations concern the Trinity and Christology. From the recognition of the man Jesus of Nazareth as Lord (Kyrios, i.e., sharing in the identity of YHWH), the other doctrinal decisions follow suit.

We cannot say that the dogma of the church developed organically in a straight line from "Jesus is Lord." This romantic idea has proven to be untenable since Bauer's classic study *Orthodoxy and Heresy in Earliest Christianity* (1971; orig. pub., 1934). What was later regarded as orthodoxy often developed in reaction to opinions and practices that were rejected and, either then or later, labeled heretical or heterodox. In the fourth century the Christology of Arius nearly gained the upper hand. We simply want to say that this confession about Jesus was the driving force that led to elaborations and decisions in new situations. The relationship of Jesus to God demanded an answer (the Trinity), and so too did the relationship of the divine and the human elements in Jesus Christ (the doctrine of the two natures). From the angle of the history of dogma, we might say that even doctrines about Mary, transubstantiation, and infallibility developed from a desire for more precise definitions of these dogmas. The Reformation was defined in part by rejecting this ongoing development.

To summarize: Jesus, because of his divine origin and identity, has decisive significance for the Christian faith. But what precisely is this significance? Where does it lie? Answer: in Jesus being the *Mediator* (1 Tim 2:5). In different ways Jesus mediates between God and us. He brings us to God, and he mediates the Father's contact with us. This dual movement is expressed paradigmatically in the prayer that Jesus taught his disciples to pray. The Lord's Prayer teaches the disciples to address God as Father, *Abba*; Jesus takes them along in the same way he himself addressed God. In this announcement of God as Father, Jesus as the Son is himself the face of the Father. His sonship is evident in the manner of his own communion with the Father and the way he obediently implements the Father's saving will, to the very end. The word "Son" expresses this unique relationship between Jesus and God. As Son, he is also the Mediator. What he does and who he is are closely connected.

Most textbooks deal with who Jesus is under the heading "the person of Christ." What he does and how his acts affect us are usually referred to as "the work of Christ." We might perhaps say that Christology and soteriology are two-in-one; person and work, Christology and soteriology, cannot be separated. In what Jesus does we detect who he is, and who he is becomes clear from the course of his life and his exaltation by God. A study of this topic is, in fact, a quest for Jesus's identity. In this chapter we mostly deal with his person; in the next we will return to this topic from the perspective of his work, or "soteriology." However, this sequence is arbitrary and might just as easily have been reversed.

10.2. Choosing the Right Method

The early church's thinking about Jesus was strongly theological; it approached Jesus on the basis of his divine origin. For a long time this posed no problem, and christological questions were not among the church's main concerns. The theological debates around the Reformation, for instance, hardly ever broached the person of Christ and did not disrupt the broad consensus on the Trinity and Christology. The doctrine of grace was rather the central problem. How are we reconciled with God? How are we delivered from our state of sin and guilt and restored in our relationship with God? The question concerned, not the identity of Jesus

Christ, but the process of justification and sanctification by which the grace given in Jesus Christ reaches human beings. The authors of the Reformed confessions were keen to underscore their being fully part of the broad catholic tradition, as we see in article 9 of the Belgic Confession, which explicitly mentions and embraces the Trinitarian and christological decisions of the early church.

We see a shift only with the dawn of the Enlightenment. Some began to feel greatly troubled by the doctrine of Christ's two natures. Many found it more and more difficult to accept that God would enter time and space and intervene in our world. Moreover, there was fierce resistance to the idea that we need to be saved and cannot take care of ourselves; this too involved Christology and soteriology, but in reverse order.

The Enlightenment—at least, in its radical form that would determine its historical reputation—loved to define our world in terms of inflexible laws. In this scheme God is not part of that world; he belongs to the supratemporal sphere, which is not subject to time and space. Finding it more and more difficult to imagine that God would intervene in our reality, Enlightenment thinkers focused primarily on the moral function of religion and developed a thoroughly humanistic approach to history and culture. Under this approach, Jesus becomes our role model, someone who used his freedom to live a moral life. Kant is an exemplary case in point. He still maintained religion as a postulate; God's existence and an immortal human soul must be presupposed if one is to maintain that moral freedom truly exists. This move, however, turned faith and religion into the servants of morality and human development; that is, it "instrumentalized" faith. With this view of faith came the optimistic expectation that religion will educate people into adulthood. Humanity will learn to use its intellect and moral capacities in an adult manner, thus bringing the world to a state of bliss. This hopeful scenario for the future, often enthusiastically embraced, put religion in search of an interiorized faith under the ideal of human autonomy. This worldview reserves a place for Jesus as a great teacher, an example, a paradigm—but no longer the Son of God, who became human. Lessing and Kant had little use for the confessions of the early church, which spoke of a God who came to us from the outside and saved us from our lost state. For the Enlightenment this view was much too external: we have to free *ourselves* from our state of tutelage. Since the eighteenth century this intuition has become deeply entrenched in our culture. Today's dogmatics faces the challenge of preserving the deep biblical and Reformed conviction that God saves, while at the same time taking human subjectivity and renewal very seriously.

The rise of the Enlightenment put the classic theological method of Christology under great pressure. The schema of the Gospel of John, which dominated the doctrinal formulations, formulated the christological mystery in terms of the incarnation: Jesus was the Word, which was God, was with God, and became flesh (John 1:14). Jesus's identity thus came from "above," and to do justice to the secret of Jesus, we too must start from "above." The christological decisions of the fourth century and of later church councils maintained this approach. If Jesus's identity is grounded in his origin from God, methodologically we must start with God's initiative, with the sending of the Son. The Son descends to the depths of human history and, in Jesus, is among us, "with us." Jesus's secret is that God and humanity meet in him. This dual perspective on the one man Jesus Christ—truly God and truly human—formed the basis for the doctrine of the two natures.

Enlightenment criticism regarding this "Christology from above" labeled its product, sometimes derisively, as the "Jesus of the church," who most definitely had to be distinguished from "the real Jesus." What connection could possibly exist between the confession of the eternal Son and the Jewish rabbi Jesus of Nazareth, as described in the Synoptic Gospels? This criticism had major consequences for christological method. The point of departure had to shift; instead of beginning from above, we now had to start from below, with tangible historical data. The real Jesus must be found in history, in the time and space where he lived. Thus began the so-called quest for the historical Jesus.

The English literature divides the quest for a historical Jesus into a few different periods: a *First Quest*, a *No Quest*, and a *New Quest*. The First Quest—in the German of that period, the *Leben-Jesu-Forschung*—began with the posthumous publication in 1778 of the so-called *Wolfenbütteler Fragmente*, by Hermann Samuel Reimarus (1694-1768). Reimarus argued that Jesus aspired to be a political messiah. His disciples refused to accept this role for Jesus, however, and made him into a heavenly messiah. Thereby, Reimarus asserted, a gap developed between the real Jesus and what the church made him to be. The search for the historical Jesus became a very important theme in the nineteenth century. Various authors attempted to write a biography of Jesus by, so to speak, peeling him loose from the Gospels. The history of the historical-Jesus research became a subdiscipline of its own. Albert Schweitzer described the process in his *Von Reimarus zu Wrede* (1906), later rewritten as *Geschichte der Leben-Jesu-Forschung* (1913; see Schweitzer 2001). Schweitzer's volume was at once a monument for this research and its tombstone. The search suffered from a perennial weakness,

Schweitzer said; the various biographies of Jesus all tended to conspicuously reflect the ideal view of humanity held by the biographers themselves. Schweitzer wanted to show how Jesus's ministry and preaching were totally permeated with the proclamation of the imminent reign of God; that is, Jesus's words and deeds had to be consistently interpreted in the light of his eschatological consciousness. In this respect he is a complete stranger to us moderns, because such apocalyptic awareness has lost all meaning for us, or so Schweitzer maintained. Moreover, Jesus turned out to be wrong; God's reign did not arrive. All we can take from Jesus is his humanitarian spirit and respect for life.

After the failure of the First Quest there followed a period that we might, with Wright (1996, 21), label the No Quest. In his famous book *Der sogenannte historische Jesus und der geschichtliche, biblische Christus* (The so-called historical Jesus and the historical, biblical Christ, 1892; Eng. trans., 1964), Martin Kähler (1835-1912) argued that Jesus's identity must be sought not behind the biblical text but in the texts themselves. However, the New Testament texts are not intended as historical chronicles but must be seen as "tendency literature"; that is, they intend to communicate a certain message regarding Jesus—the kerygma. This message is so thickly intertwined with the texts that describe Jesus's life that his biography cannot be separated from it. However, the Christian faith is not in the least based on a scientific (and thus always provisional) reconstruction of Jesus's life. It is founded, rather, on the Christ as he is proclaimed by the New Testament witnesses. There is no other "real Jesus" than this historical-biblical Christ, the one who was crucified and is risen, as he comes to us in the Bible and operates in history through the proclamation of the church (Kähler 1964). Barth and Brunner were loyal disciples of Kähler to the extent that they too believed a search behind the text to be futile. Like Kähler, Barth and Bultmann rejected the route of a historical approach to Jesus's identity, since history cannot be the basis for our faith. Unlike Kähler, however, Bultmann denied that the evangelists described Jesus's life in a way that is accessible for modern people.

The New Quest of the post-World War II era once again embarked upon the search for the historical dimension—led by, of all people, some disgruntled disciples of Bultmann. Their concern was not to have another go at finding a historical basis for Jesus's identity, but rather to trace how the proclamation about Jesus as the Word of God (i.e., the kerygma) was linked with Jesus's own proclamation of God's Word (history). New Testament scholars such as Ernst Käsemann, Ernst Fuchs, Eberhard Jüngel, and Gerhard Ebeling believed that, even though historical research could not provide an absolute basis for this proclamation, it could still play a supporting role. We might refer to this endeavor as the *Second Quest*.

The Leben-Jesu-Forschung, or First Quest, was broadly criticized for detaching Jesus from his social, ethnic, and religious context. Recent attention to the earthly Jesus is scrupulously correcting that mistake; it takes seriously that Jesus was a Jewish man whose teachings and ministry cannot be separated from his Jewish context. Some have spoken in this connection of the *Heimholung Jesu*, Jesus returning home to his own people.

We regard the contemporary attempt to situate Jesus, in every respect, in the context of his own time—the Jewish-Hellenistic culture of the Second Temple era—as the *Third Quest*. While the First Quest focused primarily on the person of Jesus as an individual, the Third Quest is more interested in his socioreligious context. Even though today we know more about this context than a few centuries ago, as Kähler already surmised, this new quest has not led to unanimous results any more than did the first. In fact, opinions diverge with surprising breadth. One school of thought enmeshes Jesus thoroughly amid the many different factions and renewal movements in the Judaism of his time. Jewish scholars interested in Jesus, including Hans-Joachim Schoeps, Schalom Ben-Chorin, Pinchas Lapide, Geza Vermes, and David Flusser, have taken the lead at this point. In contrast, the so-called *Jesus Seminar*, a group of scholars around Robert Funk, which was quite popular in the United States in the 1980s, organized a series of meetings in which participants analyzed one Bible passage after another (sometimes verse by verse) and voted on their authenticity. Marcus Borg and John Dominic Crossan are the best-known names of this school. The outcome was a remarkably non-Jewish Jesus, who in many ways resembled a modern-day Wisdom teacher. At times extrabiblical sources (often gnostic in nature) were taken more seriously than were historically warranted. For a critical discussion, see Wright 1996, 28–82; for the topic in general, Keener 2009, 14-46, and Welker 2013, 55–94. We would suggest that the part of this Third Quest that connects Jesus with his Jewish roots is particularly relevant for today's dogmatics.

The attempt to describe Jesus against the background of Jewish history and religion has, besides its strong historical credentials, great significance for Christian dogmatics. For good reason we preceded this chapter with one about Israel. Attention to the historical background and the context of Jesus fits into the methodological approach from above. We simply cannot detach Jesus's ministry from the preceding history of God's relationship with his people. God persistently intervened in Israel's history by giving life and pardon, and always on his own initiative. According to the Letter to the Hebrews (1:1), God had spoken "of old" to his people through Moses and the prophets. Jesus's preaching cannot be detached from the words of the prophets. Jesus's mission is not separate from God's earlier acts, but his mode of action can change. God's journey with his people has twists and turns. Jesus's activities represented one such turning point, a totally new stage; the outpouring of the Holy Spirit would mark the next. When, subsequently, the disciples integrate Jesus so closely with his proclamation that John feels justified in defining him as the Word of God, it is clear that this new stage can never be disconnected from the previous steps but is an extension of the journey of God to which the Old Testament bears witness. In brief: we may not approach the person of Jesus simply from above and from below but also from "behind." That is, the only way to give Jesus his rightful place is to put him in the context of God's covenantal journey with Israel.

From the angle of biblical theology, the parable of the royal wedding (Matt 22:1–14) is very significant in this connection, as are the passages in the Gospel of John that speak about the Son as sent by God. In line with this Johannine "mission Christology," we sometimes refer to the missions (Lat. *missiones*) of the Son and the Spirit. The word "mission" implies that more than ordinary historical causality is at work; God himself is the one who acts. The Son is sent by the Father, as is the Spirit (for the involvement of the Son in this step, see 3.5). Therefore, we can speak of the mission of the Son and differentiate it from that of the Spirit.

Besides the approaches from above, from below, and from behind, we can add a fourth, which describes Jesus on the basis of his effects in world history—we might say, an approach from "in front." The appearance of Jesus has left impressions and traces in the world that have become embedded in cultures, norms, and laws. Compassion for the weak and the ideal of freedom are often mentioned as effects that can be traced back to the appearance of the gospel in the world—and justifiably so. We will say more on this approach in chapter 12, on the Holy Spirit. The disadvantage of these metaphors (above, below, behind, in front) is that they are quite formal and have little substance in themselves. Moreover, we can quickly get caught up in a false dilemma if we are forced to choose between one approach and another. We therefore prefer other terminology. The starkest contrast lies between a theological method and a nontheological (historical, sociological, religioscientific, or whatever) method.

As soon as we take God's actual speaking and acting into account, we are dealing with theology. This position in no way ignores or diminishes God's revelation coming to us interwoven with various cultural, ethnographic, and social factors that greatly affect our understanding. However, to methodically close our eyes to God's speaking and acting in the midst of all these factors would be to repress an essential dimension of the biblical witness. On the theological approach, we can defend the proposition that Jesus's true identity is time and again rediscovered in the present, in faith communities, among the poor, in families, among friends—everywhere "where two or three are gathered in my name" (Matt 18:20). If we are serious about our faith that Jesus is the Living One, the same yesterday, today, and in eternity (Heb 13:8), he can, by the power of the Spirit, make himself heard and be present.

Unfortunately, this theological perspective is often seen as problematic in contemporary discussions.

Since the 1960s, Continental theology has largely followed the critical, antitheological approach to ecclesial Christology. In dogmatics the trend began with Albrecht Ritschl and his disciples, of whom Adolf von Harnack is paradigmatic. Harnack maintains that confessing Jesus as the Son of God does not belong to the essence of Christianity; in his famous dictum (1901, 144), "The gospel, as Jesus proclaimed it, has to do with the Father only and not with the Son." Berkhof likewise asserts his fundamental objections in CF (§33) by rejecting the doctrine of Jesus's two natures. Jesus is foremost the ideal man. But at the same time Berkhof speaks of a new divine initiative, and he colors the image of Jesus so strongly pneumatologically that we see some "from above" qualities reappear, with the result that Jesus ends up as a kind of in-between figure, somewhere between God and a normal human. Simultaneously, in Great Britain an intense debate erupted over a book edited by John Hick (1977) entitled *The Myth of God Incarnate*. In many minds this book created the impression (erroneous, as we shall see) that high Christology was created by the later church. The basic idea was that, over the first centuries, the Jewish rabbi Jesus of Nazareth became overlaid with increasingly far-reaching "metaphysical compliments," with the result that, at the Council of Nicaea, he was finally identified with God himself. Contemporary Christian theology, however, should go back behind this development and stay with the much more sober *Religio Christi*—that is, with the Jewish faith that Jesus also adhered to (Kuitert 1999).

But is this developmental picture warranted by history? On this issue, see (among other authors) Gathercole 2006, Bauckham 2008, and Hurtado 1988, 2003. Moreover, from a purely historical point of view, we just cannot know whether or not Jesus's religion prohibited him from considering himself divine— so we either have to trust the New Testament witnesses here or remain agnostic.

See Os 2011 for a creative contemporary attempt to throw light on the "historical" Jesus by enlisting psycho-biographical insights.

In a three-volume study Ratzinger (2007–12) offers an excellent example of a different approach that does not play off the historical against the theological aspect. It respects and takes into consideration the uniqueness of the four gospels, while pointing up the limitations of the historical-critical method. The prime limitation concerns the absence of the canonical perspective, which reads the Gospels as the communal (and usually trustworthy) testimony of God's acts in Jesus the Christ in line with God's journey with Israel. It makes a great difference whether we are prepared to listen to all voices in strict isolation from each other or with an eye to their cohesiveness and interconnectedness.

Our problem lies in the doctrinal decisions of the fourth and fifth century—more precisely, in the kind of language they used and the conceptual framework it presupposed; the two together can leave these formulations alien to contemporary thought patterns. The incarnation— which, again, set the terms for church dogma on the mystery of Jesus's person and work, his identity—has God the Son "taking on flesh" (*assumptio carnis*). The famous two-natures doctrine of the Council of Chalcedon (451) insisted, further, that the divine and the human natures are united in the one person of Jesus Christ (the so-called *unio naturarum personalis*, or *hypostatic union*). This last concept, in particular, often seems in modern times to be at best difficult to understand or at worst simply indigestible for people who think seriously about their beliefs.

Criticism of the conceptual language of the dogma has been routinely repeated since Friedrich Schleiermacher. Schleiermacher argued (CF 392–93) that the concept of nature cannot be applied to God, since in modern times it is interpreted as including all aspects of "finite being." Indeed, the dogma does use concepts like nature (Gk. *physis*) and person (Gk. *hypostasis*), which at the time were part of Greek metaphysics. Does that mean they are unsuitable for Christian theology? We do not think so, but we hasten to add that they must be constantly reappropriated and reinterpreted in terms of new, contemporary concepts. In our time this process may entail translating concepts such as nature and person into terms of relationships and identities. Only then can they continue to function adequately as windows into the secret of how Jesus shares in God's identity. The need for reinterpretation applies to all theologians, both to those who want to be seen as liberal and to those who prefer to be viewed as orthodox. Orthodoxy too is subject to development and stays alive by a constant process of adaptation and reappropriation.

The challenge posed by concepts and language is no reason to think that the high Christology of the early church is outdated, much less outside the core of the Christian faith. Recent scholarship has shown that the worship of Jesus, as one who belongs to the sphere and identity of God, was not invented by the church of later centuries. The acknowledgment or confession that God revealed himself in Jesus's person and work finds a basis in certain New Testament texts, such as the well-known hymn about Christ in Phil 2:5-11 (see Hurtado 2003). The "high" elements mentioned in such passages also apply to the earthly Jesus. "High" and "low" are not opposing or mutually exclusive perspectives but, from a systematic-theological angle, can be seen as complementary.

Theology must pay attention to the historical dimension, even though history can never provide conclusive evidence for the truth of the Christian faith. The contribution of the disciplines of history and literature will never in themselves get beyond a premise embedded in their starting point, namely, that they are dealing with people who testify how they discovered that, in Christ, God was present in a unique way. Whether their testimony is true is another matter, for which there is no scientifically conclusive evidence. However, this specific, albeit limited, contribution must not be neglected. Contemporary theology does well to seek cooperation from history and the social sciences. It is indefensible—and also unproductive—for contemporary theologians to simply repeat the tradition and avoid the questions that arise from these quarters. We therefore formulate this proposition: historical research is not *foundational* for theology, but it is *relevant*; it enables us to discover the traces that Jesus and his disciples left behind in history. In that sense the historical and theological approaches supplement each other.

This interconnection is true even at the most fundamental level: the Christian faith in God lives in the sphere of history—the sphere of what happened concretely in space and time. As Berkhof succinctly put it, "Salvation depends on historicity" (CF 274). From a christological perspective, Jesus Christ is thus not the reflection of some general idea, as suggested in some gnostic or gnosticizing circles, but someone who appeared in history at a certain point in time. The Christian faith therefore cannot be broadened so as to include all kinds of Christlike experiences—ideas and stories that may be labeled messianic via a "hermeneutic of creative imagination." The point is that God has staged a saving intervention in our history, in the life and death of this particular Jewish man, whom we know as Jesus of Nazareth. The particular concrete aspect of his appearance may disturb or irritate people; in this connection the English literature often refers to the so-called scandal of particularity (following 1 Cor 1:23, where Gk. *skandalon* = "stumbling block"), the conviction that a specific person in a specific time and place has significance for all people. This scandal is the very uniqueness of the Christian faith, but it raises the question of what historical sources we have for our knowledge of the person of Jesus.

10.3. Sources

From what sources can we trace Jesus's identity? We mention three: the Bible, tradition, and, perhaps surprisingly, our current experiences.

1. The first source speaks for itself. We must rely on the books of the Old and New Testaments, in particular, the Gospels. These writings have been accepted by the church as authoritative and are even today the most important sources for our knowledge of Jesus and his message. They do not derive their authority from a decision of an emperor in later years but from the faith praxis of the earliest Christian communities. In dogmatics we must, for our knowledge and reinterpretation of Jesus, always return to the biblical, canonical sources.

The so-called apocryphal gospels, such as the Gospels of Thomas, Jude, and Philip, hardly tell us anything about the earthly Jesus. These writings, with their gnostic origin, date mostly from the second century. Despite their popularity—due in part to Dan Brown's *Da Vinci Code* (2003)—they play no role as a serious source for our knowledge of the person and the life of Jesus. We must beware not to be misled by popular literature, which often suggests bizarre conspiracy theories, as if the church intentionally obscured the "real Jesus." For a good survey, see Roukema 2010, 132–44 (with an unambivalent conclusion on 144), Gaventa and Hays 2008, 10–15, and Keener 2009, 46–70.

However, the biblical sources do not present a uniform picture. In fact, the New Testament writers offer a wide range of different images and perspectives to convey Jesus's identity. Nonetheless, they all find their unity in the supposition that God offers us salvation in Jesus and that Jesus's coming constitutes a definitive and irreversible point in God's intervention. With Jesus's coming, God began to complete his intentions and his work. Jesus's ministry inaugurated a new and decisive phase that we, in theological terms, refer to as the eschatological phase: namely, the last and definitive acts of God in and with history.

In the Gospels this basic element comes out in different and varying ways. Older theological reflection tended to focus on the Gospel of John, with its highly developed Christology. The characterization of Jesus as the Word (the Logos) or as the Son who came "from above" became one of—if not *the*—cornerstones of Christology. However, the New Testament describes Jesus not just in terms of the Word and the Son but also in terms of the Spirit and divine power. Jesus's very conception is connected to the Spirit (Matt 1:18; Luke 1:35). At his baptism Jesus is anointed with the Spirit (Matt 3:16-17), and from that point on he acts in the power of the Spirit (Matt 4:1; Luke 4:14). The uniqueness of Jesus may therefore be understood in the terms and from the perspective of the Spirit. Jesus is described as the ultimate bearer of the Spirit, and in his ministry we see many characteristics that we would today label as charismatic. In chapter 12, on the Holy Spirit, we will deal in more detail with the possibilities of a Spirit-Christology.

The biblical portrait of Jesus varies from one gospel to the next. In Matthew, Jesus is pictured as the faithful interpreter of the Torah, a second Moses who teaches righteousness to the new people of God and thereby saves them (Matt 5-7). He chooses twelve disciples (= the number of the tribes of Israel; Luke 6:12-19), which indicates that his work in the first place concerns the restoration of Israel. As a representative of the gentile nations, the Roman centurion confesses after Jesus's death that this Jesus was indeed a son of God (Matt 27:54). The Gospel of Luke, however, pictures Jesus as the true servant, a prophet who is led by the Spirit (Luke 3:21-22) and rejected and crucified by the Jewish leaders, but then raised by God and vindicated (24:7). In Mark, Jesus is the one who is sent and in whom the new reign of God breaks through with power; at the same time, it becomes clear that his followers must expect resistance and opposition. Beyond the Gospels, in the Pauline letters the focus shifts from the earthly ministry of Jesus to his status as the risen Lord. The church of Antioch inspired Paul to explain Jesus's rejection as God's emissary and his death on the cross to be God's confirmation that Jesus is the Lord who rules. All these images, metaphors, titles, and stories form a finely meshed web of signals that influence, interpret, and refine each other. They all throw light on who Jesus is, on his identity. One of the most concise descriptions of that identity is the primordial confession "Jesus is Lord" (Rom 10:9). Around these words the Christian confession developed into a norm for the faith (the so-called *regula fidei*—the early Christian name for the basic Christian truths). But dogmatics will never be able to capture all these biblical images and allusions in a single term.

In its reflection on what the church wants to say, dogmatics can function only as a reading guide. Jesus Christ himself is always more than the images that point to him, and certainly also more than the concepts of dogmatics that seek to bring some unity and cohesion to this web of signals.

2. Tradition is a possible second source for Christology, and there are strong arguments for using it. In the gathering of the church, in preaching, baptism, and communion, the concrete memory of Jesus is kept alive and transmitted. Christian liturgy, confessional texts, and the arts provide us an abundant arsenal of words, texts, images, concepts, and metaphors that we might call the faith heritage of the church. Dogma plays a very important role in the safekeeping and protection of this heritage. Therefore, a large segment of Christianity has decided to take this established tradition as the authoritative basis for thinking and speaking about Jesus Christ. In this respect the ancient churches of Asia and Africa, the Orthodox churches, and the Roman Catholic Church are united. The first two families accept only the decisions of the seven ecumenical councils as binding (and the six Oriental Orthodox churches only the first three such councils); in particular, they see the tradition of these conciliar decisions and of the liturgy that is based on them as the source of their christological reflection. For the Roman Catholic Church the faith heritage of the church is somewhat broader. The treasury of faith (*depositum fidei*) was entrusted to the apostles and their successors and has been handed down and protected across the generations, at times rephrased and made concrete through the papal teaching authority.

Faced with the overpowering role of rites and traditions, the Reformation wanted to return to "the Scriptures alone" (*sola Scriptura*) as the source and norm of faith in Jesus Christ. The Reformers believed that rites and traditions had obscured the clear picture of God, who offers himself in Christ and in his goodness, in which we may immediately share through personal faith. This direct access to Christ became the norm for Christology and soteriology. However, this conclusion did not mean rejection of the christological dogma of the early Christian tradition; as we already noted, the Belgic Confession explicitly mentions and affirms the decisions of the ecumenical councils. Protestantism thus has an ambivalent attitude toward the tradition: a grateful acceptance where it seems there is a legitimate development of the biblical essentials, but also a critical scrutiny and, if need be, a selective editing. In Protestantism the tradition is always subject to the criticism of the biblical sources. The Bible is the norm that establishes the norms (*norma normans*). We agree with this dual attitude of grateful acceptance and critical use, for Christology as well.

396

In a sense, and depending on where we currently find ourselves, the christological decisions of the fourth and fifth century are stations that we might have passed. We accept them gratefully while appropriating them critically. We need to pay attention to the underlying issues in the christological debate, to see where positions had to be guarded and why certain concepts that were introduced were needed. The conclusion of the Council of Nicaea that Jesus is of one essence (*homo-ousios*) with the Father, for instance, is much easier to understand when we realize that it was prompted by the desire to safeguard the thoroughly biblical idea that we cannot ensure our own salvation. God himself must become involved if the world—if we as human beings—are to be rescued from ruin, and for that reason Jesus must share the same "being," or essence, with God. We simply are not like the fictional Baron Munchausen who, according to a well-known story, was able to pull himself out of the mud by his own hair. In brief, we do not accept the formulas because they happen to be part of the tradition, but because we discover genuine biblical motives behind these statements and in what they want to signal. One could say that the christological decisions (Niceno-Constantinopolitan and Chalcedon) are the directives of a former generation for how to handle the gospel story, the message of the God of Israel, and the Father of Jesus Christ.

There also is an important theological reason to exercise this "hermeneutic of trust" with respect to the tradition's unifying message of the person of Jesus. Christ himself promised his disciples that the Spirit would lead them into all truth (John 16:13). It would be incredibly callous to suggest that the tradition is completely in the dark. At the same time, this promise gives no guarantee against the possibility of some obscuring or ideological manipulation of the gospel, whether presented in very high church or in popular forms. Therefore, we must always be critical in our dealings with the tradition; we must be selective on the basis of what the apostles and prophets have given us in the Bible.

When faced with the question of whether the tradition is a legitimate source for our Christology, we therefore give this dual answer. On the one hand, we gratefully accept the christological decisions of the church that came from the ecumenical councils. We thus abide by the course and the outcome of the christological debate. We move on, even though we realize that some alternatives might have been condemned at these councils owing to church politics and that the conclusions might well have turned out differently or have ended in the (often rather broad) margins of the church. But we trust that this is a case of *hominum confusione Dei providentia* (God's providence [may be executed in the midst of]

397

human confusion). On the other hand, our task is always to return to the biblical texts and, within their range of possibilities, take a critical look at the decisions and the terminology the councils used. Going back to the Bible this way is needed for several reasons. Something clearly present in the texts may have been lost in the process of debate; going back to the texts thus may represent an enrichment. But we also face a problem of comprehension when ancient languages become a stumbling block in a changed context, and we may need to reinterpret and reword the content of the dogma because of those changes. The struggles recent generations of believers and theologians have had with certain concepts of classic Christology represent a real problem that we may not simply brush away.

One example of a possible loss over the centuries is the New Testament's expression of Jesus's identity in terms of Spirit (power). As conceptual roadblocks, we once more point to problems with the way in which "nature" and "person" function in classic Christology. The confession that Christ is a person who consists in two natures presupposes by "nature" a static view of substance within the confines of Aristotelian metaphysics. Similarly with respect to "person." Today that word makes us think of a human individual who finds his or her identity only within a network of relationships with others. However, careful analysis shows that this current understanding also happens to have roots in early Christian thinking. Note what we remarked in chapter 3 about the unique concept of a person proposed by the Cappadocian church fathers.

In sum: we do well to heed the decisions and debates of the past, but must also always reread the Scriptures and try to discover how Jesus is described in the testimony of the New Testament writings.

    3. We briefly alluded above to a third possible source for Christology. May our own contemporary faith experience come into play here in addition to the Bible and the tradition? Various contemporary christologies that discover and emphasize particular aspects in Christ have made such a proposal. We might mention feminist theology, black theology, liberation theology, or charismatic theology, but also non-Western views of Jesus and Western art in which Jesus appears incognito. May we see all these so-called genitive theologies (theologies of women, of blacks, etc.) as more or less successful attempts to reword the classic Christian heritage of faith for new contexts? Or might these contexts, in turn, positively affect our current experiences with the living Lord? In any case, many such interpretations of Jesus are rooted in concrete communities and faith practices in which people have experiences with Jesus (for

informative surveys, see Brinkman 2009, 2013, and Kärkkäinen 2003, 189–285).

Such theologies raise the fascinating theological question whether these situations may show us faces of Jesus that we were hitherto unaware of (see also Brinkman 2013). The answer does not seem to be very difficult when we take the diversity of the Bible into account and recall our positive basic attitude regarding the development of Christian dogma. Time and again new aspects have been discovered in new situations. However, we must not forget that these were aspects of who *Jesus* was, the Crucified and Risen One of whom the biblical witnesses testify. Our attitude toward the experiences of people today must therefore have the same double structure as that toward the tradition: grateful recognition and critical reception. What else can we do in the light of the work of the Holy Spirit: "He will take what is mine and declare it to you" (John 16:14)? In other words, new experiences will unfold that we may gratefully recognize and appreciate, but they must ever be critically compared with what the church has been given in Jesus Christ, its Lord. Dogmatics should always teach about Jesus, but how this learning process takes place cannot be exactly predicted. Thus, in this secondary sense, current experience may be regarded as a source for christological reflection.

10.4. The Theme of Christology: Different Perspectives

After these introductory sections about method and sources, we now must try to determine the main themes of Christology. What actually is the purpose of Christology? First, let's try to organize the flood of biblical material about Jesus for simplicity's sake. Several summary schemes or perspectives have been offered to help us to get a grip on the vast amount of relevant material. These schemes are not meant to dictate our understanding but to give guidelines for charting the different perspectives on Jesus that are found in the New Testament. Three such schemes have found their way into Christology.

This aim of Christology—to simplify and, in the process, to place the multicolored biblical-theological material in a particular perspective—often provokes resistance, in particular, from biblical scholars. They prefer to let the Bible texts speak for themselves in all their diversity. Dogmatics does not oppose this concern. Indeed, the Bible can speak for itself, and its multitude of voices do not need to be streamlined or restricted. However, in light of how we formulated the task of dogmatics in chapter 1 (making sense of it all), we want to ask how all these various texts can be understood in their mutual relationships, and what total picture they might yield. Every Bible reader is confronted with this question, and so our aim is inevitable as well as legitimate. In fact, it leads biblical scholars themselves to write an "introduction to biblical theology," a "theology of the New Testament," or even a "Christology of the New Testament." Dogmatics listens carefully to these contributions, but (given the sources we discussed in 10.3) also considers the history of theology and contemporary experiences and debates.

1. First, we can follow a *temporal* model, especially in the Synoptic Gospels. This scheme sketches the life of Jesus in two consecutive phases. First we see Jesus as a prophet or messenger from God, followed by his death and resurrection. The first phase—as the second article of the Apostles' Creed indicates by way of summary—is one of increasing humiliation; the second phase begins with Jesus's resurrection and ascension. This temporal scheme can also be presented in a tripartite form. Here Jesus exists first of all as the eternal Word (preexistence), followed by the period of his earthly ministry, and finally by his state as the Risen One. We find this threefold sketch in the Gospel of John (see 17:5) and in the previously mentioned hymn about Christ in Phil 2:5-11. In classic Christology the two-phase variant of the temporal scheme translates into the concept of the twofold state (Lat. *status duplex*). The period of Jesus's earthly life from the incarnation on is seen as the state of humiliation (*status humiliationis*), and the resurrection as the beginning of the state of his exaltation (*status exaltationis*).

For this model, see Heppe, RD, chap. 19, and Muller, DLGTT 287-89. The idea of these states is of Lutheran origin but was soon accepted by Reformed Christians as well, although with some difference of opinion regarding the state of humiliation. Did Jesus, at his incarnation, waive his divine attributes (as Lutherans believe), or were these attributes merely hidden (as the Reformed thought)? This discussion revolves around the exegesis of Phil 2:7, which speaks about Jesus's self-emptying (Gk. *kenōsis*). Bultmann rejected the concept of the states as mythical (1984, 1-44), while Barth preferred to make them atemporal, two aspects of the same work of Christ (CD IV/1:78). For our part, we think that the temporality shows something of a phased process—of the turning points in God's saving intervention throughout history. What happens in time is theologically and christologically significant. This dynamic also offers clues for preaching: the community of believers may reflect on how each of these phases affects them (see Heidelberg Catechism 11-22). Over the centuries the concept of the states received a specific elaboration in salvation-historical forms of theology, which take their structure from the phased history of God's involvement with our salvation. Irenaeus's theology provides an early example of this approach; later instances come in federal theology (Johannes Cocceius) and the theology of Hendrikus Berkhof. This salvation-historical perspective also formed the matrix for theology and proclamation for such "liberated" Reformed theologians as Klaas Schilder and Benne Holwerda (1909-52). See further Genderen and Velema, CRD 468-72.

2. Besides the temporal scheme, note also the *perspectival* scheme. Jesus Christ may be seen from two directions: as belonging to God's order or to the human order. We find this idea in Paul when he states that we no longer know Christ according to the flesh but according to the Spirit (2 Cor 5:16). This scheme heavily influenced the christological dogma of the early church. The church confesses that Christ is truly God and truly human (*vere Deus et vere homo*). The Bible teaches us that Jesus and the Father are distinct but, at the same time, one. The result is two angles of vision that must be held together. The difficulty of doing so has caused a major challenge for making Christology consistent and has generated the major christological questions that we will deal with in the next section. For now, it is important to realize that the perspectival scheme has always remained dominant in dogmatic reflection, despite the Reformers' preference for the temporal schema. As a result, the incarnation became the dominant aspect of Christology, subordinating the temporal elements in Jesus's life.

3. Finally, we mention the *Trinitarian* scheme. This is the framework of this book. We saw in chapter 3 how the process of reflection that ended with the doctrine of the Trinity began with an examination of the saving significance, and so also the ontological status, that was to be assigned to Jesus Christ. In that sense we may say that Christology (reflection on Jesus Christ) is the key to the entire project of theology. It opens the horizon of our thinking about God's acts *pro nobis* (for us, with a view to our salvation). It receives a Trinitarian elaboration in the New Testament. The discourse about God the Father, God the Son, and God the Holy Spirit begins out of Christology, for if there is a very close relationship between Jesus and the God he called his Father, that says something about this God. The Nicene Creed was a christological but no less a theological confession: if we say that Jesus is one with God, it implies something dramatic and decisive about the identity of the God of Israel. As we saw in chapter 4, Christology thus opens the door to the doctrine of God, at least in its Christian form. But the reverse is also true: Jesus is the

Son because he received this title from his God and Father (Luke 3:22). This event clarifies his specific origin and function. In addition, we see that the disciples and others around him get involved in the interaction of Jesus with his Father. That experience also occurs for those—including for us, so many centuries later—who through faith share in the intimate communion between Father and Son. The New Testament tells us that this communion is mediated by the Spirit of Christ, who is also the Spirit of God. The pneumatological perspective thus completes the Trinitarian scheme.

For these schemes, see Dalferth 2015. As we detailed in chapter 3, over the course of time the Trinitarian scheme came more and more to lead a life of its own detached from Christology and soteriology. The strong focus on the so-called immanent Trinity caused it to largely lose its significance for reflection on the christological themes where it had originated. That focus also contributed to the dominance of the perspectival scheme. Karl Barth was the prime proponent of this dominance in the twentieth century. Although he brought the doctrine of the Trinity back to the forefront (CD I/1), his approach remained rather formal. George Hunsinger (2000, 129) showed convincingly how Barth's Christology continued to be modeled after Chalcedon. That is, Barth, in his attachment to the formula of Chalcedon, pulled apart the Alexandrian idiom (in which Jesus's divinity was central) and the Antiochian idiom (which emphasized Jesus's humanity) to the extent that the two, while not excluding each other, do not qualify each other either. Barth himself admits that this dialectical method can only place these two New Testament ways of speaking about Jesus's identity side by side; it does not help us to better understand the incarnation.

As already mentioned, the perspectival approach has dominated the historical debate about Christology: Jesus Christ is fully God, and he is fully human. It was an attempt to do full justice to two short propositions that both have a basis in the New Testament:

1. Jesus exists in a union with God the Father.
2. Jesus is distinct from God the Father.

In its doctrinal decisions the church wanted to retain these two lines. Based on what had been concluded at earlier church councils, these lines came together at the Council of Chalcedon (451) in the famous formula "truly God and truly man" (*vere Deus et vere homo*). At the same time, it was confessed that this duality was found in the one person Jesus Christ, and that this person is, in fact, the Son and the Logos, the Word that, according to John 1, was with God and is God.

10.5. The Christological Debate in History

In this section, we survey a few highlights in the history of the debates that led to the Chalcedon formulation, after which we will ask about the fundamental elements of Jesus's identity by looking at some of the biblical evidence. We have seen how the prologue of the Gospel of John played a decisive role in the classic christological debate, as it begins: "In the beginning was the Word, and the Word was with God and the Word was God" (1:1). In this passage Word and God are distinguished but also regarded as identical. This double approach is characteristic for the pattern of union-in-distinction of the evangelists' pictures of Jesus. But what exactly is the nature of this relationship? Is God one, or does he consist of two "parts" (Father and Son)? The third-century church father Origen played a significant preparatory role in answering this question by stubbornly insisting that Christ as the Word originated from the divine source, and that there is only one such divine source. This approach is called *monarchianism*: there is one alone (Gk. *monos*) who can be recognized as the originating principle (Gk. *archē*).

This answer certainly does not solve all problems. If Christ comes forth from the one God, does he keep this divine status, or does he lose it? Where is the dividing line between God and his creation, and where is the place of the Word in this arrangement? Origen believed that the Word was indeed God, but yet, as we saw (3.4), he was a little lower than the Father on the ontological ladder. This thought raised some questions, particularly about the close connection that was becoming increasingly apparent between this issue and soteriology. Is it not essential that we are saved by the one God himself rather than through an emissary, however divine he might be? In the twenty-first century we tend to be amazed about the ferocity of these old christological controversies and can appreciate it only when we understand the soteriological implications at hand: the question of Christ's identity is of crucial significance for our eternal salvation. It was seen as literally a matter of life and death to speak correctly about him. Justice had to be done both to the union between Jesus and God and to their distinctiveness. We limit ourselves here to the main players in the debate that resulted in the Trinitarian and christological dogmas: the erudite priest Arius and Athanasius, bishop of Alexandria, 328-73 CE.

10.5.1. *Arius and Athanasius*

Put most simply, Arius asked about the order to which Jesus, as the incarnate Word, belonged: to the order of God, or to that of created reality? Arius opted for the second and had some good arguments on his side. He read the Old Testament texts that speak of the unity of God: "Hear, O Israel, the LORD our God is one Lord" (Deut 6:4). If God, as the Father, is the first, then he must also be the only one, and besides him there can be only that which is created; thus Jesus belongs in that category. Nor can God exist in a double, a twofold (or threefold), manner, so Jesus is not a second God. The highest essence is not plural; God, as the only one, is by definition indivisible. This view does not so much make Arius a good Jew (as we mentioned earlier, Judaism in this era did not totally reject any plurality in God), but rather a good Greek. To the Greek mind, which is always in search of the unchanging primordial beginning (the *archē*), divisibility implies mutability.

Note Rowan Williams's striking description (2011) of Arius as a thinker who was, in fact, quite conservative and unwilling to take the revolutionary step of the Christian faith against the generally accepted view of God. Arius's course shows us how traditionalism may at times lead to heresy. It should be added that we actually know very little about the person and the theology of Arius, and most of the information we do have has been reconstructed from what his followers, and even more his enemies, ascribed to him.

To Arius, created reality does not originate so much in God's being but in his will, which is also true of the Son. Jesus resulted from a creative deed of God and therefore does not share in the same essence with the Father. He was "made" at a later point in time. Or to quote a famous phrase of Arius's opponent Athanasius made in summary of Arius's view: "There was a time when the Son was not." Some Bible texts might support this idea. For example, take Ps 2:7: "You are my son, today have I begotten you"; or again, the text from Proverbs about wisdom (8:22): "The LORD created me at the beginning of his work, the first of his acts of old." For this reason, the view of Arius has often been called *adoptionism*. Arius refers to the Son as God but clearly regards the Son, or the Word, to be the highest created element within the divine sphere of influence. He is something like the prototype of a new car featured in the automobile showroom. Other cars will be made just like that model. However, a gap separates the Maker from Jesus as the image or icon of God. In the garden of Gethsemane Jesus as the incarnate Word does not, when push comes to shove, attain to the glory of the inexpressible Father. What is true for all creatures is also true for the Son. He came into existence, and there was a moment when he did not exist, unlike the Father, who did not come into being at any point in time.

It is not hard to discern the soteriological implications of Arius's thinking. His Christology prescribes a focus on spirituality. If this one person, who is part of the created order, was able to proceed in the power of God along the road of salvation until he reached eternal redemption, that must be possible for his followers too. Jesus is our pioneer on the road to God (Heb 12:2). Arius's theology thus prompts us to strive for holiness. The question, however, is whether it leaves us too much to our own strength.

Athanasius felt strongly that it did. In opposition to Arius's position he argued that the relationship between the Father and the Son went beyond one of the will. The Son has his origin in the essence of the Father. The most obvious comparisons, which we also find in Origen, are those of fire, sun, and light. As fire is lighted by fire and becomes fire in all respects, the Son, and therefore the incarnate Word, can be fully identified with God. This view also clarifies the co-eternity of Father and Son. There is not a single moment when the sun does not produce light. Along this line, Athanasius interprets the repetitions in the Nicene Creed: "God of God, Light of Light, true God of true God." The importance of this statement is clear: with the coming of Jesus, this tarnished creation is no longer left on its own. Even the highest and the best representative of humanity cannot undo its defilement. To do so requires divine power, and for this reason Athanasius so strongly asserts that, in Christ, we are in a very real way dealing with God who has united himself with our human nature. This line of thought explains why the Council of Nicaea uses the concept of one-in-essence (*homo-ousios*). Let's explore in more detail the theological importance of this word for the divinity of Christ.

No human being exists in isolation. All men and women together compose humanity. With Adam's disobedience in paradise the human spirit got a bad orientation; we now face the wrong way. Instead of being directed toward God as the source of life, we have, ever since Adam, been oriented toward created things, the tempting array that the world has to offer. Thus did Adam, and we with him, lose immortality. We might also say that sin operates like a kind of virus that attacks the immune system and leaves the body highly susceptible to all sorts of nasty infections. The only remedy is a serum that restores our connection with the source of health. Athanasius was absolutely convinced that the Son would be unable to save us if he has divine power only by being allowed to share in it. A dead battery can get some power if it is connected to another battery for a while, but things get very problematic if many batteries need to be charged off this one. To get reliable help requires getting connected to the grid. So with our salvation. If we are to be truly revived, we need something more substantial than just a neighbor's battery.

We could say that at Nicaea the theology of Athanasius (who attended this council in 325 as a young deacon) was taken as the point of departure for reflection on the divine mystery of salvation. Christ does not just possess a divine power, but in him is God himself. This understanding is the core of the decision of the Council of Nicaea. Its intention was to honor our salvation as a work of God himself. This conclusion corresponds with what the apostle Paul says in 2 Cor 5:19 about the ministry of reconciliation: "In Christ God was reconciling the world to himself, not counting their trespasses against them, and entrusting to us the message of reconciliation." God continues to engage himself in the midst of a world of sin and transgression by initiating a work of reconciliation. That work, apparently, corresponds to who he is. In retrospect we may say that the doctrine of the divinity of Jesus Christ aims first of all to underscore our salvation as a gift of God himself. This fundamental goal is diametrically opposed to what Arius said. Well-meaning people, even saints, will ultimately not save the world. Only God can do so.

Arius and Athanasius both continue to attract and influence many minds even today. A recent Christology inspired by Arius can be found in H. Berkhof (CF, §33), but in the system of his successor, Abraham Beek (2002), Athanasius once again plays a decisive role.

10.5.2. Apollinaris and Nestorius: On the Mode of the Incarnation

After the Council of Nicaea in 325 the debate in the church about Christ's divinity abated. However, new controversies erupted over the question of how this divinity was related to Christ's human nature. Apollinaris of Laodicea (ca. 310–90) wondered how we should understand the unity of the person of Christ. His view is best grasped if we start with John 1:14: "The Word became flesh." How should we understand this sentence? Appollinaris argued that there is no way the Word could have united with a complete human being, as that would have resulted in some intermediate form of being, between God and man. He therefore suggested that in the incarnation the eternal Word took the place of what we normally refer to as the human spirit. This spirit is usually conceived as the principle of human consciousness and self-identity—and in Christ this spirit is replaced by the divine Logos. This is how God and man are fused together.

At first sight this seems like a perfect solution. It allows us to approach the incarnation in a rational manner. If the church fathers had placed all their cards on order and rationality, they should have warmly embraced Apollinaris. But they did not do so because Apollinaris shortchanges Jesus's human nature. For in his view the Logos united only with a body, leaving the *assumptio carnis* incomplete. If this is the case, our salvation also remains incomplete; once again the close tie between Christology and soteriology surfaces. Or is sin confined to the body, and is the human spirit *not* in need of salvation? Is salvation necessary only for human nature outside of its spirit, intellect, and will? The church rejected this option. Whatever stress the church fathers laid on Jesus's divine nature, at crucial moments they drew a clear line. During the Council of Constantinople (381) Apollinaris was condemned because of his failure to do full justice to Jesus's humanness. Anyone who wants to continue reading the story of Jesus as it is written, must beware of reducing his full human nature.

Gregory of Nazianzus concisely expressed the church's attitude toward Apollinarianism in what may well be his most famous statement: "What has not been assumed has not been healed . . . it is what is united to his [Christ's] divinity that is saved" (Ep. 101.7; PG 37:181). That is, in the incarnation God assumed the human spirit with all its weaknesses and all the anxiety to which that spirit is subject, as Jesus's life bears witness (e.g., see Matt 26:39; 27:46). This understanding of Jesus continues to be a comfort today for people who struggle with psychological problems; such issues do not indicate that such a person is handicapped or a misfit but is a normal human being, just like Jesus. Apollinaris's Jesus is, in the final analysis, an incomplete human being, and the church gradually grew in its understanding that it must confess the opposite.

If Apollarinaris's view proved to be inadequate, what was the alternative? The fifth century saw a search for a better formulation. A critical role in that process was to be played by Nestorius, who in 428 became archbishop of Constantinople. Nestorius—a representative of the so-called Antiochian school—was totally opposed to blending Jesus's divine and human elements on Apollinaris's model and turned in virtually the opposite direction. The human and divine in Jesus had to be sharply distinguished, he thought; it would be better to say that these two are connected in love than that they are fully united. In other words, their unity is moral rather than ontological. Jesus is indeed divine, but this quality is to be seen as supplementary and must always remain separate from his "normal" humanness. This view led Nestorius (or his chaplain), in a much-discussed sermon, to express serious reservations regarding the term *theotokos* ("the one who gave birth to God"), a popular title for Mary. If one accepts this term in every respect, one must also conclude that God was born, that at some point in time he was three months old, and so forth, which would obviously be absurd. This (quite carefully expressed) criticism stirred up a lot of opposition. Cyril of Alexandria, in particular, was very vocal in his views and had on his side the devotion to Mary that was already widespread at the time. To relativize the Marian title *theotokos*, he argued, was to tinker with Christ's divine nature. Rather than separating the two natures, they should be brought together in the most intimate unity, for in the final analysis Christ has only one nature, the divine, which has absorbed his humanity. Cyril managed to have Nestorius condemned during the chaotic Council of Ephesus (431). Nestorius's solution was untenable.

Still, Nestorius long remained influential both inside and outside the church. The church in the West would always retain some sympathy for him, particularly in its Reformed-Protestant branch, which was keener than the Lutherans to keep the divine and human natures clearly distinguished. For Nestorius and the Council of Ephesus, see Need 2008, 81–92, and for Cyril's Christology, Loon 2007. Beek 2002, 17–26 is very instructive about the broader context of the conflict between Nestorius and Cyril.

10.5.3. Chalcedon between Antioch and Alexandria

Must we divide Jesus into a part that is God and a part that is human? Or should we assume that his human nature is absorbed by Jesus's divinity? The Antiochians tended toward the former conclusion, the Alexandrians toward the latter. However, the lines established at the Council of Chalcedon, twenty years after the Council of Ephesus, rejected both solutions. It set a few boundaries for how we are to think and speak about the coexistence of the divine and the human in Jesus. It stipulated that there is one person in whom the two natures, the divine and the human, somehow converge. Remarkably enough, the council left it at that—and said that we should too. It fenced in the mystery of God's presence in Jesus by a number of exact coordinates, fixing the space within which we must stay but not trying to fully detail all that this space contained. To put it colloquially, it chalked out the pattern in which we play hopscotch.

On the one hand, Chalcedon was critical of the Antiochian school. Besides Nestorius, Theodore of Mopsuestia (ca. 350–428) also belonged to this circle. They may have passed into history as heretics, but it is important to recognize that they had some crucial insights. The Alexandrian tradition of Athanasius and his followers placed a strong emphasis on the eternal Son or Logos as the person-forming center of Jesus Christ. This Logos or Son is fully God. The Antiochians asked how the biblical statements about Jesus as a human being could then be taken seriously. Who, in fact, was born, grew up, and was overwhelmed by grief when Lazarus had died? Who was put in a tomb? Are we speaking of the eternal Son, the divine Logos, or should we in such instances make a much sharper distinction between the eternal Son and the human heir in the line of David? We have seen that, for the Antiochians, it was too much to say that the Son of God was three months old, grew up, or was laid in a tomb. For that reason they wanted to distinguish clearly between the two natures. When we read in Luke 2:52 that Jesus "increased in wisdom and in stature, and in favor with God and man," these words must apply to his human nature. But when he performed a miracle or silenced the storm at sea, his divine nature was at work. Chalcedon recognized that Christ's divine nature was indeed at work in the miracles, while his humanness became manifest when, say, he was tired. But both states and actions nonetheless point to the one person of Jesus Christ. He cannot be divided into different parts. In other words, there is more than just a connection, there is a "true" union of the two natures in the one person of Jesus Christ, the so-called *unio personalis*, or hypostatic union.

On the other hand, Chalcedon also criticized the Alexandrians. These thinkers did accept the hypostatic union as their point of departure but seemed to regard Jesus's human nature as almost totally absorbed by the divine so that, taken to the extreme, only the divine remained. Here we speak of *Monophysitism*, to which the name of Eutyches (ca. 380–456) will always be linked. Eutyches's view, in fact, implied that only one nature—the divine—endured in Jesus, for as a drop of honey is totally

THE PERSON OF JESUS CHRIST

dissolved in the sea, so in the incarnation the human nature was totally absorbed into the divine. But Chalcedon disagreed. The council rejected the idea that the divine and the human natures either become mixed or that this union resulted in a new kind of being the way that mixing yellow and blue produces green. The burning bush in the story of God's calling of Moses (Exod 3) served as a useful illustration. The bush was burning, but the fire did not consume its branches. The fire and the branches left each other intact, even though they were together. Jesus's divine and the human nature coexist in a similar way.

In its opposition to Eutyches the church threw the entire Alexandrian school into one pot. All who spoke of one nature were simply rejected without attention to the underlying issue. For the Alexandrians the concepts of nature and person belonged together. Every person has his own unique nature. For this reason, according to the Alexandrians, we must maintain that Christ has one nature (*mia physis*), the divine-human nature of the incarnate Word. Its emphasis on this one nature/person—the Suffering One in whom God was among us—underscored an important biblical motif. Jesus's secret is not that "the divine" and "the human" are combined in him in the abstract. Rather, it is this concrete person, Jesus of Nazareth, the Man of Sorrows, who is the mystery of God's compassion.

The early church tended to place more stress on the divinity of Jesus Christ than on his humanity. It remained difficult to give full cognizance to Jesus's humanness; this imbalance, in fact, proved to be the Achilles' heel of early Christian theology. For this reason, nowadays many try to follow the alternative route of Spirit-Christology. The confession that, in Jesus, God himself comes to us must be understood in every part and at every step in terms of God's Spirit. Jesus is born of the Spirit (Matt 1:20), in him the Spirit lives in all respects (Luke 4:18; John 3:34), and the exalted Lord is also the Sender and Giver of the Spirit (Acts 2:33; John 20:22). Quite often this Spirit-Christology has been dismissed because it was thought to make the distinction between Jesus and ordinary people purely quantitative, as if Jesus simply had a little extra of what we possess in more limited measure. This impression is indeed created in the proposals for a Spirit-Christology by H. Berkhof, P. Schoonenberg, R. Haight, and others. Their view rejects concepts like Christ's incarnation and preexistence, the Trinity, and Chalcedonian Christology. It replaces them with an adoptionist approach: in being anointed with the Spirit at his birth or baptism, Jesus was adopted as the Son of God.

Such a conclusion is not inevitable, however. Today we hear more and more voices that want to consider the subject in terms, not of either-or, but of both-and.

Can we perhaps understand Christ's uniqueness not only in terms of the Word but, in a supplementary way, also in terms of the Spirit? That way we do not need to say No to Nicaea and Chalcedon if we wish to do fuller justice to the Spirit-filled humanness of Jesus. Without the Spirit, Jesus could never have become the Christ. More developed proposals for such a complementary (rather than an alternative) Spirit-Christology tend to come from Roman Catholic authors like Ralph del Colle, David Coffey, and Thomas Weinandy, but there are also some Protestant moves in that direction, for example, by J. Moltmann. See Habets 2010 for surveys of replacement (194–200) and complementary (200–220) Spirit-Christologies, together with his own complementary proposal (220–80); and see Peppiatt 2014 for an exploration of the implications of Spirit Christology for Christian discipleship and mission.

The decisions of the Council of Chalcedon do not contain many positive definitions. Instead, they major in negatives. Positively, the council stated only that the two natures are united in the one person Jesus Christ. At the same time, it employed four negative adverbs: unconfusedly, unchangeably, indivisibly, and inseparably. The first two targeted Eutyches; the last two, Nestorius. Thus, the one person Jesus Christ is in his divine nature fully equal with God, and in his human nature fully a man. In Jesus we meet the one who is in all respects divine and human. However, this decision leaves us with a yawning gap that, in actual practice, is difficult to live with, so we often see attempts to bridge this gap in some way, by regarding the divinity or (more frequently) the humanity of Jesus as secondary.

However, Chalcedon offers us more than just a compromise between the various parties involved in these controversies. It added new and important insights to already-existing formulas to better deal with the complexity of the issues. It suggested that we halt before something that defies our further understanding, namely, the miracle of the union of the two natures. Unfortunately, this decision did not erase the distrust that remained on both the Alexandrian and Antiochian sides. While the current Eastern Orthodox churches accepted Chalcedon, the traditional Oriental Orthodox churches opted for *Miaphysitism* (Jesus has only a single nature). Only in the twentieth century have these traditions come closer together under the insight that the two parties at Chalcedon had different definitions of the concept of *physis*. Nonetheless, most denominations have recognized their faith in Christ by what was decided in Chalcedon (Berkhof, CF 291–92). Those decisions may be compared to comments in the margin of a musical score. Christ must not be divided into two persons. Neither should he be made into some kind of intermediate being. There is the one person Jesus Christ, in whom the divine and human fully converge. The divine and the human orders coexist and collaborate in this one person. How to explain this union remains unresolved. The point is that, in the union of the two in the one person of Jesus Christ, the eternal Son of God experiences everything and suffers to achieve our salvation.

Since many suspected a disguised protection of Nestorianism in the Chalcedon definition, there were subsequent efforts to emphasize even more strongly the unity of Christ's person and thereby his divinity. This unity was seen as a function of the eternal Word, the basic element in the person of Christ. Or as stated by the Second Council of Constantinople (553), the unity is a fact because "one of the holy Trinity, God, the Word, became flesh." Thus, the person of Christ was now seen primarily as the divine Word, while the human nature became concrete only in connection with this Word. This position is referred to as *enhypostasis:* the human nature has its personality in (Gk. *en*) the divine Logos. The opposite view is that of *anhypostasis:* the human nature in itself lacks personality and has no face of its own. In Christ, God did not become a concrete human person but rather assumed human nature in general. It cannot be otherwise, for only thus can all people—women, men, Jews, gentiles, and so forth—be saved by Christ. In concrete terms this *an-/enhypostatic* relationship means that nothing can be said about Jesus as a human being in detachment from the divine Word. Or, as A. A. van Ruler put it: there never was a Mr. Jesus of Nazareth.

Beek (2002, 77-89) has pointed out the remarkable difference between the West and the East in defining the christological dogma. Rarely does one hear in the West about the formula of Chalcedon as the *unio personalis:* the terminology of the doctrine of the two natures is preferred. For the Eastern church the one person is more important than questions about the two natures. Van de Beek explains this difference on the basis of the West's greater attention to people as independent persons, also in ethics. Whereas in the West the ethical imperative at times dominates the spiritual life, the spirituality of the Eastern church lives "entirely out of the indicative of the salvation that has appeared" (88). For instructive recent reflections on early Christian heresies, see the relevant contribution (originally sermons) in Quash and Ward 2007, 15-69, also 122-30.

Survey of the seven ecumenical councils

325   Nicaea I. Jesus is not a creature, but God; the Son of God is "very God of very God, begotten, not made, being of one substance (*homoousios*) with the Father."

381   Constantinople I. The divinity of the Holy Spirit is not explicitly but implicitly affirmed: ". . . who with the Father and the Son is worshiped and glorified"; this wording implies the doctrine of the Trinity.

431   Ephesus. Christ is one person, in whom the divine and the human are fully united. Mary may therefore rightly be called *theotokos* (the one who gave birth to God). Nestorius is condemned, as is (for other reasons) Pelagius.

451   Chalcedon. Provisional end to the christological controversy. Jesus Christ is very God and very man. He is one person with two natures. These two natures are unconfused, unchangeable, indivisible, and inseparable. The first two terms remonstrate against Monophysite tendencies, the other two against a Nestorian separation between God and man in Christ.

553   Constantinople II. One of the Trinity has become a human being. The emphasis is on the divinity of Christ and the hypostatic unity of the two natures.

680/81   Constantinople III. Did the fact that Jesus has two natures imply that he has one will or two? The council stays with the views of Chalcedon, where it was determined that Jesus, because he has two natures, also has two wills, but that, nonetheless, they are in the unity of his person unconfused, unchangeable, indivisible, and inseparable. It rejects Monotheletism and accepts Diotheletism.

787   Nicaea II. Grants the permissibility of image veneration and condemns iconoclasm. The underlying issue is, once again, largely christological: Christ's divinity is so strong that it can, as it were, pass along to images of him, his angels, and the saints. These images/icons may therefore be venerated but not worshiped – worship (*latreia*) is restricted to the pure divine nature.

Discussions about the meaning of the union of the divine and human in Jesus did not end at Chalcedon. Again and again questions were raised about the exact consequences of the hypostatic union—for the will(s) of Christ, for his actions, or for the veneration of material images of him. We mention briefly one of these ensuing discussions, since it later resurfaced in a new form. The doctrine of the hypostatic union raised questions about the consequences that this union had for the attributes of the two natures of Christ. If we take this union seriously, does that not mean that we must see these attributes as exchangeable? In other words, does this position lead to a form of mutual communication, or sharing, of what is essential in each of the two natures? This problem has become known by the term *communicatio idiomatum* (interaction of the properties of each of the natures).

Important elaboration on this issue (which in a certain sense is a direct result of Chalcedon) came from John of Damascus in the eighth century (*De orthodoxa fide* 2.3–4; PG 94:993–1006), and later from Thomas Aquinas (STh III.16a.1–12). The issue revived during the Reformation in connection with the doctrine of the Lord's Supper; and in the twentieth century, in connection with the doctrine of God.

Protestant orthodoxy distinguished various kinds (*genera*) of interaction (*communicatio*). See Muller, DLGTT 72–74, and Dalferth 2015. The *genus idiomaticum* was uncontested, which meant that all attributes (*idiomata* or *proprietates*), as well as all actions (*operationes*), were to be ascribed to the one person of Jesus Christ; they all refer to him. This conclusion enables us to say that the God-man Christ suffered and died as one person. However, the attributes and the actions remain idiomatic, that is, specific to one nature. In addition, the Lutherans also spoke of a *genus maiestaticum*, in contrast to the Reformed, who rejected this idea. The term "majestic kind" means that the human nature, because of its enhypostatic union with the one divine person of Christ, shares in the divine attributes. (Note that this is not just simple "transfer" between the two natures.) The main intention is to give full recognition to the attributes that express Christ's majesty, like his omniscience and his omnipresence. This variant is linked to the Lutheran view of the Lord's Supper: Christ's human nature shares in the omnipresence (the "ubiquity") of Christ's Godhead, and Christ is therefore bodily present in the communion bread. We must not look "above" for the Crucified One (as Calvin says; see chap. 4), since he is also present in the bread and the wine. The opposite of the *genus maiestaticum* is the *genus tapeinoticum*, or the kind of humility. Remarkably enough, this term dates only from the nineteenth century and betrays a switch from Christology to the doctrine of God. For if the statements about Christ's exalted state must also be applied to his human nature, should we then not conclude that, in reverse, the vulnerability of Christ's human nature also affects God's divinity? This conclusion gets particularly touchy when we speak of Christ's suffering and death. Must not these experiences also be attributed to his divine nature, and thus to God himself? This bold idea was too unwieldy for the classic doctrine of God, in which God's nature is regarded as immutable. It was impossible to say anything more than that Christ suffered in his human nature. But Luther protested against that restriction: "If I had to believe that Christ suffered for me only in his human nature, then Christ would be an insufficient Savior, who would, in fact, himself also need a Savior." In Christ, divinity and humanity are one single person. Therefore, even though we must say that "God himself does not suffer, yet the person who is God does, and we may therefore say that God's Son suffered" (WA 26:320, lines 10–14; 321, lines 5–10). This implication in itself seems to indicate that the *communicatio idiomatum* prompts us to say something about the divinity of Christ, and therefore also about the essence of God.

Whatever the case, the *communicatio idiomatum* also has a soteriological function. We detect this implication also with Calvin in *Institutes* 2.12.3 and 2.14.1, albeit in a form in which the divine nature empowers the human nature to gain the victory for us (see also Heidelberg Catechism, Q/A 17). This thinking gets very close indeed to the *genus maiestaticum*.

It may seem that the concept of the *communicatio idiomatum* is a theoretical abstraction, but as is often the case in dogmatics, upon closer inspection it happens to have an important soteriological function. That the eternal Son took on human nature so intrinsically that he even "carried it along" in his ascension guarantees our continuing communion with God (Heidelberg Catechism 49). In addition, reflection on this christological theme has contributed to a twentieth-century revision of the doctrine of God, which we dealt with above in chapters 3 and 4: if in Jesus God and humanity are so united, then God touches our history. It is therefore impossible for us to think of God in isolation from what Jesus Christ bears and experiences. This idea has implications for God's identity; we cannot think about God without also reflecting on the history of Jesus Christ, and on his journey through death.

10.6. Jesus's Identity as Demonstrated in His Ministry: A Few Contours

Having looked at the development of Christology in the tradition of the church, it is now time to go directly to the study of the biblical testimony regarding Jesus. To repeat: we may never skip this step, since the Bible is in a certain way always more than the tradition and should never be hermetically sealed off from it. Dogmatic concepts can be very helpful for reading the Bible but always have to be examined in its light and can never replace it. In this section we intend to scrutinize Jesus's identity by following some lines that are found in the New Testament and that are rooted back in God's revelation to Israel.

To point out a distinction that may be methodologically dubious but is inevitable in practice: in this chapter we collect and consult information from the evangelists and apostles about Jesus's life, with a view to his identity as a person. In the next chapter we will repeat this process but with regard to the salvific meaning of his work. Here we ask whether what Jesus did and experienced tells us who he is. There we will ask how we can be sure that what he did and experienced is relevant to us. Thus, an old distinction often made in the doctrine of God seems applicable here: we first focus on Jesus in himself (*in se*) and then on Jesus for us (*pro nobis*). We hope it will become clear how inseparable these two questions are.

First, we will see how in the Gospels Jesus is portrayed as an emissary from God. As such, he stands in a long line of many such messengers whom we meet in the Old Testament. Some of these Old Testament messengers were human prophets; others, in particular the angels that appeared as *mal'ak YHWH* ("messenger/angel of the Lord"), came directly from the sphere of the divine. Where does Jesus stand in this regard? How far do his speaking on behalf of God and his identification with God reach? In this connection, what can we learn about his origin and identity from his important titles (Messiah, Son of God, Lord; see 10.7)? Our answers will come in seven steps, divided over this section and the next.

1. We begin our survey with the oldest gospel, that of Mark. There we see how Jesus from the beginning is presented as *God's credentialed emissary*. His credentials are clear from his identification with God's rule in his proclamation of the kingdom and in his miracles. In all that he does, Jesus claims that the reign of God has arrived, and he identifies himself with God's acts in making this arrival happen. The familiar words at the beginning of Mark summarize this aspect of Jesus's identity:

> Now after John was arrested, Jesus came into Galilee, preaching the gospel of God, and saying, "The time is fulfilled, and the kingdom of God is at hand; repent, and believe in the gospel." (1:14–15)

In Matt 4:17 we find a similar statement that sketches a concise profile of Jesus's activities. Apparently, what Jesus does and says must be understood in terms of God's kingdom. It is clear that this kingdom does not refer to a particular territory and cannot be compared to a modern nation-state that encompasses a certain land area. We are here dealing with something much more dynamic that affects people much more intensely; it is a new regime, a way of life and communion that is determined by God's concrete saving power. *Jesus proclaims the nearness of this saving power of God*. However, his proclamation and ministry are not just a matter of speaking about this kingdom; this saving reign of God actually comes closer in Jesus's words and deeds. People come within the reach of this salvation-bringing power and the life and restoration it makes available, which is realized most specifically in the healing miracles and exorcisms. Where Jesus appears, darkness has to flee; the powers that destroy life are pushed back. In the very same opening chapter of Mark we read about a devil-possessed man who is freed from his unclean spirit. Immediately afterward, Simon's (i.e., Peter's) mother-in-law is healed, and then people come from all around to be delivered from their illnesses and troubles.

We notice right away that Jesus's approach as the liberator becomes a confrontation. The new regime is not automatically accepted but provokes resistance. Where God comes with his salvation, what resists or destroys his work also emerges. The dark opposition comes to light at the same time that it is being judged (Mark 1:22-26). God's judgment is an intrinsic part of his life-giving intervention. Judgment, condemnation, and punishment come with the process of salvation, because the world does not easily subject itself to God's rule. Instead, it seems to be under the authority of other powers. But Jesus accepts this confrontation with what imprisons the people, the physical misery and spiritual powers that torture them in the form of "unclean spirits." Modern Westerners find it difficult to think in these terms. We have learned to see and explain "evil spirits" as forms of mental illness, which is to be medicalized. It was different for Mark and his first readers. For them all things are interconnected; the boundary between sickness and the influence of evil spirits is fluid. Some things connect us with God, others separate us or turn us away from him. Sickness and evil spirits alike keep us away from life. In what he does and says, Jesus brings people back to God as the source of life. His being anointing with the Spirit (1:10) and his work as a healer portray him to be the deliverer from the powers of death. His ministry ensures that life flows once more. He reconnects people with God, with themselves, and with one another.

Isolation and reconnection are prominent motifs in the accounts of Jesus's healings. Take leprosy, for example. The Gospels show again and again that it led to being cut off from social life. Being touched and healed by Jesus not only means that lepers regain a healthy skin but that, once they are fully cured, they may rejoin society and visit the temple. Sickness threatens our ties with life even today. Sick people have the feeling that they are "out of it." Sickness is a rupture with normal life; when the illness is fatal, this break is complete. But God's regime, which breaks through in Jesus, does not stop at this point. A father gets his daughter back (Mark 5:21-24, 35-43), and a widow, her son (Luke 7:11-17). The widow, in particular, receives much more in the process; she escapes the shame and difficulties that a widow had to face in those days. Having to go through life alone was seen as a direct divine punishment, and economically, a widowed life was extremely hard. When Jesus sets people free from the powers of death, he does away with their isolation and reconnects them with the life-giving power of the Creator God.

All these activities give us a glimpse of who Jesus is. Seen in Old Testament perspective, they are deeds of the end time that had been announced by the prophets. Luke, in particular, profiles Jesus in this light. He describes the beginning of Jesus's public ministry in a detailed report of the sermon that Jesus preached in the synagogue of Nazareth. In this sermon Jesus applied the prophet Isaiah's eschatological message of salvation directly to himself:

> The Spirit of the Lord is upon me, because he has anointed me to preach good news to the poor. He has sent me to proclaim release to the captives and recovering of sight to the blind, to set at liberty those who are oppressed, to proclaim the acceptable year of the Lord. (Luke 4:18-19; cf. Isa 61:1-2a)

These words speak emphatically of anointing; the word "Messiah" (the anointed one) is derived from this verb. Is Jesus that Messiah, the long-expected son of David, who will bring Israel back under God's rule? Yes or no, he performs the works of the end time and indirectly claims to be the credentialed emissary of that time—the time of the Messiah.

2. The contours of Jesus's identity are further revealed in the Sermon on the Mount (Matt 5-7; cf. Luke 6:20-49). There we detect the parallel between Jesus and Moses—Jesus is portrayed as *the new Moses*. This identity signifies that his role somehow exceeds that of the prophets, for Moses had a unique function as mediator between God and the people. Just as Moses received God's commandments on the mountain, Jesus, while seated on a "mountain," teaches his disciples the law of the king-

dom. This law does not contradict the law of Moses; rather, Jesus deepens and radicalizes it (Matt 5:17–20). Jesus does not proclaim another god but leads his disciples to the heart of the Torah. He works like a prophet, for the Old Testament prophets operated in the same way. Jesus teaches his disciples to live on the basis of the covenant, which is the axis of the Torah. We see this emphasis clearly in the story of Zacchaeus. When Zacchaeus perceives his wrongdoing and promises to do what the law of Moses requires of him by way of restoration, Jesus says: "Today salvation has come to this house, since he also is a son of Abraham. For the Son of man came to seek and to save the lost" (Luke 19:9–10). Salvation and redemption are utterly concrete in this story: Zacchaeus is reconnected to God, who once gave his people the Torah. He learns again how he must live, the road he must travel in order to be a blessing.

The same theme comes through on the many occasions when Jesus has a conflict with the spiritual leaders, for instance, with respect to Sabbath regulations. Jesus profiles himself as the new Moses when he heals someone on the Sabbath (Mark 3:1–6), when his disciples are picking some grain (Mark 2:23–28) and thus, technically speaking, are working on the Sabbath. Even more: Jesus puts himself *above* Moses. He claims to get closer to the intention and meaning of the law by his ministry than all the nitty-gritty commandments and prohibitions of those days allowed. Thus, with regard to the concrete way of life under God's rule, Jesus profiles himself as the one with divine credentials. This not only put him in line with the prophets, who refer back to Moses, but with Moses himself, with all his crucial significance for the communion of God with his people.

3. The *parables* throw additional light on Jesus's identity as God's credentialed emissary. At first sight these are stories about very ordinary things in life; at the same time, they seem a little weird, with a marked tendency toward exaggeration. A woman loses a coin (Luke 15:8), something that happens every day. But this woman searches all day, leaving nothing in her house unturned, and when she finds the coin, she announces it to the whole neighborhood and invites everyone over for coffee. Or take the parable of the one sheep and of the shepherd who leaves his other ninety-nine sheep to search for this one. In such parables Jesus creates an alternative world. Is it not strange that this shepherd leaves all other sheep to search for the one that is lost? Jesus's audience knows very well what he is trying to convey—his own care for those who find themselves at the margin of society, where things are far from ideal or healthy. With such stories Jesus challenges his hearers to take a stand.

God has other preferences and options than we are used to. Just as it is natural for this weird woman to treat the whole neighborhood to cake and coffee, so it is for God and his angels to be excited when one of his children turns to him.

The parable of the royal banquet in Matt 22:1–14 tells us very clearly about the nature of Jesus's preaching and its appeal. There is a king who organizes a wedding feast for his son.

The king tells his servants to make a list of potential guests, but they all refuse to come. This response is a great affront. The invitees even physically abuse the servants when they arrive with the urgent invitation. In his anger the king sends out a punitive expedition to burn the town where the ingrates live. Not a very nice guy, this ruler! But his next move is equally resolute. He commands his servants to invite in everyone on the streets—good, bad, and indifferent. He must have a full house. Then the parable ends with the fearsome words: "Many are called, but few are chosen" (v .14). These words have frightened readers who have taken them to be referring to the doctrine of double predestination (see chap. 15); we have to wait and see whether we are chosen, but the odds are against it. In the parable, however, "being chosen" is far from a passive process. We can accept the invitation or not. Refusing it has dire consequences. It is an insult to the king and to his son.

What did Jesus mean by this strange story about this Eastern potentate? The potentate, of course, symbolizes the God of Israel, who is very keen to have people participate in the festive joy of his coming reign. He invites very generously, with Israel at the top of the list. Faithful Israel represents the chosen ones. But if they refuse to come, God goes to the rabble. The story is about God, but it highlights Jesus's own actions. His preaching of the kingdom, his interest in the outcast—in everything he is following the script of the story.

There is more here. The parables were vehicles that allowed Jesus to speak indirectly about himself. For instance, behind the well-known figure of the Good Samaritan (Luke 10), we can discern the contours of Jesus himself. His contacts with prostitutes, the impure, the collaborators with Rome, as well as his uninhibited invitation in searching for what is lost, his appeal to surrender to the royal rule of God—all of this is in the parables, and all of them indirectly identify Jesus's ministry with the coming of the kingdom. When he acts, God is at work. But what about the extent of this identification? Is Jesus one of the servant-messengers of the ruler in Matt 22, or is he perhaps the son?

4. The veil is lifted further by *the way Jesus deals with sin and guilt*. Here Jesus's mandate and identification with God appear to acquire a very special dimension. We see it in Mark 2, in what seems to be an ordinary healing story but, on closer look, turns out to have another point. Four men want to bring their paralyzed friend to Jesus, but a crowd blocks their way. When they cannot get close to Jesus, they make a hole in the roof and carefully lower their friend down into the room. Then we read:

> And when Jesus saw their faith, he said to the paralytic, "My son, your sins are forgiven." Now some of the scribes were sitting there, questioning in their hearts, "Why does this man speak thus? It is blasphemy! Who can forgive sins but God alone?" And immediately Jesus, perceiving in his spirit that they thus questioned within themselves, said to them, "Why do you question thus in your hearts? Which is easier, to say to the paralytic, 'Your sins are forgiven,' or to say, 'Rise, take up your pallet and walk'? But that you may know that the Son of man has authority on earth to forgive sins"—he said to the paralytic—"I say to you, rise, take up your pallet and go home." (vv. 5–11)

Jesus's healings revealed something of his identity, but here something else is at stake. The scribes are perturbed not so much by the healing of the paralytic but because Jesus also forgives this man's sins. In doing so, Jesus claims a prerogative that belongs solely to God. It can be said only of God that he forgives "all your iniquities" (Ps 103:3). The spiritual leaders rightly sense that something is awry here. If what Jesus said here is OK, they will have to thoroughly revise their view of Jesus. "Why does this man speak thus? It is blasphemy! Who can forgive sins but God alone?" Quite so, for also by forgiving sins, Jesus identifies himself as the authoritative emissary of God. Apparently he can make that pronouncement in the name of God.

The characteristics of God appear to dominate Jesus at other moments as well. Take the story in Luke 5:1–11. Jesus encourages Simon to go fishing, but Simon objects that they have been fishing all night and have caught almost nothing. When Simon finally accedes to Jesus's instructions, he hauls in an unbelievably big catch—the nets are full to bursting. When Peter sees the situation, he falls at Jesus's feet and exclaims, "Depart from me, for I am a sinful man, O Lord." Why, of all things, does Peter fall to the ground and speak of his sinfulness at this point? What is going on here? Peter suddenly realizes the total otherness of Jesus. For an instant, Jesus's majesty comes unbearably close. In the final analysis, sin is not a moral but a religious concept. Jesus shares in the majesty of the eternal God; in him the majesty of God is present. This sense creates in Peter a sense of enormous distance.

However, this account does not mean that we can simply place an equal sign between God and Jesus. For Jesus is also distinct from God in heaven. Look at how Jesus reacts with shock when someone calls him good: "Why do you call me good? No one is good but God alone" (Mark 10:18; see above, chap. 3). This same response is seen also, if more implicitly, in the very indirect character of his identification with God—he will never confirm this relationship unequivocally, since he wants to focus everybody's attention on the Father (see above, chap. 3). Even the Gospel of John, which most explicitly speaks of the union between Jesus and God, maintains this distinction. Yet, Jesus at the same time presents himself as the right hand of God, also with regard to misfortune and guilt. He and God form one enterprise and share the same job; they are one in what they seek to accomplish. This is an important principle of Christology: Jesus is at God's side and identifies his acts with the acts of God.

10.7. Messiah, Son, Lord

The first four contours from Jesus's ministry—Jesus as God's emissary, the new Moses, a teacher of parables, and one who deals with sin and guilt—lead inevitably lead to associations with the concept of Messiah. The Gospels abound with rumors and discussion to this effect. When we get close to Jesus, the contours of the messianic times become visible. His own life was totally involved with God. The content of the covenant—I will be your God and you will be my people—will be fully realized only in the coming kingdom but is already concretely manifested in Jesus's life, and it breaks through in those who listen to his appeal and turn toward God (Luke 17:21: "The kingdom of God is among you"). At these moments Jesus's God-given mandate breaks through, and his unique mission as God's emissary becomes visible.

5. In addition, are we entitled to describe this mission as the sending of the Messiah, that is, of the anointed one who would come in God's name at the end of time to sanctify and deliver his people? Down to the present, this question is answered in the negative by most of Jesus's (also believing) fellow Jews. We can understand this response when we notice how little joy Jesus's followers often show at being saved. Yet, precisely the Jews from Jesus's immediate surrounding began to respond positively

to the question of his messiahship, and through the centuries this answer has been echoed among Jews and gentiles.

The New Testament makes it impossible to speak about Jesus as the Messiah as if this title was self-evident. Even John the Baptist had major doubts about it (see Matt 11:1–6). Jesus's journey from humiliation to exaltation was an "unpredictable synthesis" of Old Testament expectations (Berkhof, CF 258), for it did not, as John had expected, bring an immediate end to all sorts of injustice, sin, and violence. Still today, in spite of Christ's coming, the world is not redeemed. Christians who nonetheless have come to recognize the Messiah in Jesus must have empathy for the Jewish inability to agree with them. Perhaps we can find a third way between traditional arrogance and postmodern indifference in our attitudes, and "as a Christ-confession community of faith . . . seek a dialogue with the Jewish people concerning the understanding of Holy Scripture, in particular as regards the coming of the kingdom of God" (Constitution PCN, art. 1.17).

This brings us to one of the most prominent titles given to Jesus, one that developed from an adjective into a proper name: Messiah, or the corresponding Greek term, Christ. The Messiah is the God-appointed and Spirit-equipped implementer of the eschatological redemption. The term has royal associations. The Messiah is the Son of David, who brings the people back to the liberating rule of God, and therefore must be discussed in the context of Jesus's life and work. In a situation in which Jesus's true identity still remained vague, the people who met him were quick to speculate about who he was. Some of their ideas were superficial: "Behold, a glutton and a drunkard, a friend of tax collectors and sinners!" (Matt 11:19). The disciples, however, thought that Jesus's identity was to be found in the Old Testament. Mark tells us how Jesus himself started a discussion on this point:

> On the way [Jesus] asked his disciples, "Who do men say that I am?" And they told him, "John the Baptist; and others say, Elijah; and others one of the prophets." And he asked them, "But who do you say that I am?" Peter answered him, "You are the Christ." And he charged them to tell no one about him. (Mark 8:27–30)

The other disciples' reactions connect Jesus to the prophets who belong to the end of time. But according to Matthew (16:17), Peter gives the correct answer by explicitly referring to Jesus's messiahship. But then comes the injunction to keep silent about this title. Jesus's response has a profound meaning. The road that lay ahead of Jesus was completely lacking in the national-political aspirations and agenda that were usually connected with the title of Messiah. These images and expectations had to be drastically revised, and the true nature of Jesus's messiahship would become apparent only from the journey he has yet to make. Only in retrospect, after the resurrection, will the title no longer lead to misunderstandings; then it can be freely proclaimed (Acts 2:36).

Much has been said by New Testament scholars about the so-called messianic secret in Mark ever since 1901, when Wilhelm Wrede coined the term. Wrede argued (and in his tracks also Bultmann, ThNT 4.4) that Jesus neither was nor wanted to be the Messiah; only later did people make him into their Messiah. Wilhelm Bousset went furthest in this direction. He saw the worship of Jesus as Christ and Lord gradually developing under the influence of the Hellenistic mystery religions, until he acquired the status of a cultic god. This hypothesis is revived every once in a while, but it lacks any basis. For a pre-Easter use of the title "Messiah" after, but in continuity with, Old Testament Judaism, see the reflections of Goppelt, ThNT 168–72. More generally, recent scholarship provides evidence that the high view of Christ had very early Judeo-Palestinian roots and was not a later development under Hellenistic influence. See, for example, Sanders 1977 but, in particular, the important studies of Hurtado (1988, 2003), which discuss early Christian devotional practices to prove that the worship of Jesus as divine must have been caused by an early explosion (Easter?) and not by some gradual development. See also Roukema 2010.

There is a direct link between Jesus's title "Messiah" and his anointing by the Holy Spirit. We know that the Old Testament prophets received their mandate from the Holy Spirit even without having been anointed; they had, as it were, stood under the Spirit's shower. The Synoptic Gospels define Jesus's messianic mandate as the result of his explicit anointing with the Holy Spirit. We therefore have a solid theological basis to see Jesus as the Spirit-bearer. In a brief profile of Jesus in Acts we read how God "anointed Jesus of Nazareth with the Holy Spirit and with power; how he went about doing good and healing all that were oppressed by the devil, for God was with him" (Acts 10:38). God's being with Jesus, as well as Jesus's being anointed with the Holy Spirit and with power, form the background for his "going about doing good." Jesus's communion with God is expressed in terms of the Holy Spirit, so does Jesus's ministry therefore belong in the line of other prophets? If so, we must speak of him as a human being and say at most that Jesus just had a bit more of the Spirit and a little more power than others. Or does Jesus's anointing with the Spirit and power allow us to speak of a bond with God that differs from that of earlier prophets? We choose the latter option: Jesus's identity cannot be formulated only in terms of the Spirit. He belongs to God in such a special way that we can say that his origin is with God, that he is part of the life of God himself. The same cannot be said of any other human being. For that reason he is called the Son of God. This brings us to yet another perspective on his identity.

6. At the Council of Nicaea (325) Jesus was confessed as:

[the] one Lord Jesus Christ,
the Son of God, begotten of the Father
[the only-begotten; that is, of the essence of the Father,
    God of God,]
Light of Light,
very God of very God.

The term "Son of God" as a title for Jesus predates the New Testament. It is found in the Old Testament in a more general sense, where "son of" may simply mean "belonging to." A son of a prophet is not a biological descendant of that prophet but belongs to the circle of the prophets. The same concept may be applied to the people of Israel. Exodus 4:22 refers to Israel as the firstborn son. It stands to reason that in this connection God is called Father. "Is not he your father, who created you, who made you and established you?"—so we read in Deut 32:6. The title is also later applied to the king of Israel. In Ps 2 the king says after his coronation:

I will tell of the decree of the LORD:
He said to me, "You are my son,
today I have begotten you."

(v. 7)

Also, 2 Sam 7:13-14 speaks of the relationship between God and the Davidic dynasty in similar terms; it says of David: "He shall build a house for my name, and I will establish the throne of his kingdom forever. I will be his father, and he shall be my son." Here sonship has a more restricted content. It is applied to someone who has a unique relationship with God and the right to rule on that basis.

What does the expression mean in the Gospels? We start with a text that attracts our attention because it stems from the final showdown between Jesus and the leaders of Israel; as the Gospels relate it, the high priest asks Jesus: "Are you the Christ, the Son of the Blessed?" (Mark 14:61; Matt 26:63). Note that "son of the Blessed" further explicates what "Messiah" means; the two concepts apparently are intertwined. Jesus's miracles, parables, and authoritative approach ensure that they evoke each other. Their content is not defined by what they mean in earlier writings; they have received a decisive new meaning from their connection with this person. Thus, we cannot say that the term "son of God," having been used for others, carries no special meaning, for it is abundantly clear that the conflict with the Sanhedrin concerns the messiahship of Jesus. It is in that context that the high priest asks whether Jesus is the Son of God. In other words, does Jesus have the authority to represent God because of a special relationship with him? The concept of sonship now clearly carries a heavier load.

This deeper meaning also comes to light in the reports about Jesus's baptism in the Jordan River and his glorification on the mountain (Mark 1:11; 9:7); there "son" refers to Jesus's unique intimacy and loving bond with the Father. It also shines through in Jesus's prayer practice. Jesus addresses God as Abba, the Aramaic word that was widely used by both children and adults for addressing their father (Mark 14:36). In this act of prayerful surrender to his Father, Jesus wants to be subjected to his rule. By obediently surrendering to the Father, and through his desire to live fully in him and for him, Jesus demonstrates that he is the Son. In the New Testament "sonship" clearly bears connotations of obedience and servanthood. By teaching his followers to address God as "our Father," Jesus opens the possibility for them to understand themselves as sons or children of God. Paul explicitly tells the Roman Christians that they "have received the spirit of sonship" and so may "cry, Abba! Father!" (Rom 8:15-16). In many places Paul speaks about Jesus as "the Son of God" in a unique sense, while John often refers even more succinctly to "the Son" (e.g., John 5:19-23). It seems that the difference between Jesus and everyone else is found in his obedience and dedication to the Father. This relationship—and not the suggestion that he would never have killed a fly—is the reason why the church began to speak of Jesus's *sinlessness* (see Heb 4:15). We find the term "son" used in this absolute sense not just in John, Paul, or the Letter to the Hebrews, with their high Christologies, but also in the Synoptic Gospels. There the father-son relationship refers to the way in which Jesus experienced his own relationship with God. Of extreme significance in this connection is Matt 11:27 (for its meaning, see Schillebeeckx 2014, 216-18):

All things have been delivered to me by my Father; and no one knows the Son except the Father, and no one knows the Father except the Son and any one to whom the Son chooses to reveal him.

The title "Son of God" underscores that Jesus belongs with God in a very special category. The exact nature of this uniqueness cannot be directly distilled from the tradition-historical background of this concept but becomes clear when we study Jesus's whole journey. Ultimately, Christ's sonship is determined and clarified by three pillars: (1) in his ministry as God's emissary, when Jesus claimed that God himself acted and spoke in what he did and said; (2) in his path of suffering and death; and finally, (3) through God's affirmation of that path in Jesus's resurrection.

But exactly when did Jesus become the Son of God? The church has refused to point to a specific moment, as adoptionism did. Jesus's sonship did not begin with his resurrection, baptism, or birth, but is from eternity. Here we touch on Jesus's preexistence; his existence as Son predates all time and is rooted in the depths of God's being. For biblical support the church pointed once again to the prologue of John's Gospel and also to the hymn about Christ in Phil 2. This hymn of praise, which Paul came across in the earliest practice of Christianity, shows how old the belief is that Jesus is part of God's eternal being. Jesus's existence thus has a three-phase history: his preexistence, his life on earth, and his "postexistent" exaltation with God.

[He] who, though he was in the form of God, did not count equality with God a thing to be grasped, but emptied himself, taking the form of a servant, being born in the likeness of men. And being found in human form he humbled himself and became obedient unto death, even death on a cross. Therefore God has highly exalted him and bestowed on him the name which is above every name. (Phil 2:6–9)

In this passage Jesus is presented as both God and a human being, thus laying out the core of the christological dogma early on (as, rightly, Hengel 1995, 389). For discussions of the doctrinal and biblical-theological questions about Jesus's preexistence, see Gathercole 2006 and Roukema 2010. We feel that Berkhof (CF 292–93) dismissed statements about Jesus's preexistence too readily, but this move was inevitable, given his Christology. The stories about Jesus's virgin birth (Matt 1:18; Luke 1:34–35) are connected with the belief in Jesus's preexistence. For a defense of the historicity of the virgin birth that merits consideration, see Beek 2002, 148–57.

7. One of the most common titles that offers a key to understanding Jesus's identity is "Lord" (Gk. *Kyrios*). In the Greek world this title was used to address or refer to a superior. Today we would say that a *kyrios* is our chief or boss. In the Roman Empire it was also employed for the highest person of all, the emperor. In the Septuagint the name of God is translated as Kyrios. Significantly, this title is applied to Jesus all through the New Testament. In numerous Old Testament quotations that were originally about God, Paul substitutes Jesus Christ (Hurtado 2003, 112). In brief, Jesus becomes the Kyrios. The most telling example is, once again, the hymn about Christ in Phil 2 that we just discussed. The "name which is above every name" that Paul applies to Jesus is, without any doubt, YHWH, the name of God that is never uttered. The honor that belongs to God is in this passage also attributed to Christ. The Septuagint version of Isa 45:23 says that every knee will bow before the Lord; Paul now applies this prophecy unreservedly to Jesus. The identification that follows is straightforward: "every tongue [will] confess that Jesus Christ is Lord, to the glory of God the Father" (Phil 2:11).

In 1 Cor 8:6 we also have confirmation that Jesus is the revelation of YHWH. There Paul writes: "Yet for us there is one God, the Father, from whom are all things and for whom we exist, and one Lord, Jesus Christ, through whom are all things and through whom we exist." Paul is here alluding to the Shema Yisrael (Deut 6:4), while at the same time recognizing a differentiation in the concept of God: apparently, Jesus shares in the power of God to create and to rule. He was already present at the time of creation. We could add many other such texts, as, for instance, 1 Cor 12:3 and 2 Cor 8:9. In these passages, which often echo a liturgical setting, we detect traces of the faith praxis of the first Christians. They confessed Jesus of Nazareth as the Kyrios, and in so doing gave him the highest conceivable honor. As Lord, Jesus should be worshiped. According to Larry Hurtado (2003, 117), these texts prove (1) Jesus's high authoritative status, (2) Jesus's future role as the one who will come to judge, and (3) Jesus's place in the devotion of his earliest followers. All testify to the high position Jesus had in the earliest forms of Christianity.

This conclusion has great significance for Christology and for the doctrine of God. If Jesus Christ is portrayed as the Kyrios who was, and is, fully involved in God's creative work, then whenever the church speaks of God the Creator, it cannot do so without also bringing in Jesus Christ. Henceforth all reflection about God stands in the light of Jesus. Moreover, the Hebrew Bible must now be read in the light of Christ's appearance. The earlier must be seen in the light of what came later—of what was recognized as the decisive moment in God's revelation. From now on, the history of God with his people is read and interpreted on the basis of the revelation in Jesus Christ.

We could well treat the doctrine of God at this point rather than in chapters 3 and 4. The way in which God's turn toward us has been realized in the sending of Jesus has fundamental importance for the reflection of classic dogmatics on the divine attributes (God's virtues or characteristics). God is who he is in his turning toward us, in his condescension toward humanity.

We thus can see the immense importance of Christology for the doctrines of God and the doctrine of the Trinity. The one who manifestly played a vital role in history can be portrayed only as the one who was present from the very beginning. Or in dogmatic lingo, what is eschatologically decisive affects the protology. In this connection we often speak of the "cosmic Christ." The cosmic significance of Christ also implies that he must be considered as preexistent. We discover the idea that Christ has been appointed as the head of all creation (Eph 1:10, 22), particularly in the Letters to the Ephesians, to the Colossians, and to the Hebrews, and also in the Apocalypse. Jesus is the image (*eikōn*) of the invisible God (Col 1:15), and all things exist in him (Col 1:17). He is the first and the last (Rev 1:17). Such wording places the meaning of Jesus Christ in a cosmic framework, as decisive for all reality. This is the step from the economic to the immanent Trinity that we described in chapter 3—in this case, the step from Jesus as Lord and Son of God to Jesus as God the Son. The Trinitarian scheme becomes the mold that shapes the entire history of salvation. The Father, the Son, and the Spirit existed from the beginning. What appears before our eyes in time is actually a manifestation of what God already is—of the eternal, triune God.

How does the temporal model of salvation history relate to this Trinitarian structure? Any attempt to reconcile the two or combine them into one image will be unfruitful. A contemporary dogmatics must do full justice to the drama of salvation history, God's invitation, and the failures of humanity; at the same time, it must fully recognize that Jesus Christ determines in every respect our reflection on who God is in his essence. Christ is therefore not of secondary importance but belongs to God in an essential manner—another way of saying that he is part of God's (Trinitarian) being. The two images aim to express God's rule over time (the horizontal axis) and space (the vertical axis). Jesus's acts in time manifest who God is. The manifestations of his Lordship in time affirm and clarify the identity that he has always had.

In the previous pages we have not inventoried all the special titles that the Bible attributes to Christ—for instance, such well-known terms as "Son of Man" and "servant (of the Lord)." However, we want to note that different titles often share similar meanings or a degree of overlap. This is certainly true of titles such as "son," "servant," and "anointed one" (see Berkhof, CF 289 in reference to Ps 89:20-37), but also of "Christ" and "Lord." We think the titles discussed above adequately clarify Jesus's identity.

References

Bauckham, Richard. 2008. *Jesus and the God of Israel: "God Crucified" and Other Studies on the New Testament's Christology of Divine Identity*. Grand Rapids: Eerdmans.

Bauer, Walter. 1971. *Orthodoxy and Heresy in Earliest Christianity*. Philadelphia: Fortress. Orig. German pub., Tübingen: Mohr, 1934.

Beek, Abraham van de. 2002. *Jesus Kyrios: Christology as the Heart of Theology*. Translated by Okke Postma. Zoetermeer: Meinema.

Brinkman, Martien E. 2009. *The Non-Western Jesus: Jesus as Boddhisattva, Avatara, Guru, Prophet, Ancestor, or Healer?* London: Equinox.

———. 2013. *Jesus Incognito: The Hidden Christ in Western Art since 1960*. Amsterdam: Rodopi.

Bultmann, Rudolf. 1984. *"New Testament and Mythology," and Other Basic Writings*. Edited by Schubert M. Ogden. Minneapolis: Fortress.

Dalferth, Ingolf U. 2015. *Crucified and Resurrected: Restructuring the Grammar of Christology*. Grand Rapids: Baker Academic.

Gathercole, Simon J. 2006. *The Preexistent Son: Recovering the Christologies of Matthew, Mark, and Luke*. Grand Rapids: Eerdmans.

Gaventa, Beverly R., and Richard B. Hays, eds. 2008. *Seeking the Identity of Jesus: A Pilgrimage*. Grand Rapids: Eerdmans.

Habets, Myk. 2010. *The Anointed Son: A Trinitarian Spirit Christology*. Eugene, OR: Pickwick Publications.

Harnack, Adolf von. 1901. *What Is Christianity?* New York: Putnam.

Hengel, Martin. 1995. *Studies in Early Christology*. Edinburgh: T&T Clark.

Hick, John, ed. 1977. *The Myth of God Incarnate*. London: SCM.

Hunsinger, George. 2000. "Karl Barth's Christology: Its Basic Chalcedonian Character." In *The Cambridge Companion to Karl Barth*, edited by John Webster, 127-42. Cambridge: Cambridge University Press.

Hurtado, Larry W. 1988. *One God, One Lord: Early Christian Devotion and Ancient Jewish Monotheism*. London: SCM.

——. 2003. *Lord Jesus Christ: Devotion to Jesus in Earliest Christianity*. Grand Rapids: Eerdmans.

Kähler, Martin. 1964. *The So-Called Historical Jesus and the Historic, Biblical Christ*. Philadelphia: Fortress. Orig. German pub., 1892.

Kärkkäinen, Veli-Matti. 2003. *Christology: A Global Introduction; An Ecumenical, International, and Contextual Perspective*. Grand Rapids: Baker Academic.

Keener, Craig S. 2009. *The Historical Jesus of the Gospels*. Grand Rapids: Eerdmans.

Kuitert, H. Martinus. 1999. *Jesus: The Legacy of Christianity*. London: SCM.

Loon, Hans van. 2007. "The Christology of Cyril of Alexandria: Milestone on the Road to Chalcedon." PhD diss., Culemborg, Netherlands.

Need, Stephen W. 2008. *Truly Divine and Truly Human: The Story of Christ and the Seven Ecumenical Councils*. London: SPCK.

Os, Bas van. 2011. *Psychological Analyses and the Historical Jesus: New Ways to Explore Christian Origins*. Edinburgh: T&T Clark.

Peppiatt, Lucy. 2014. "New Directions in Spirit Christology: A Foundation for a Charismatic Theology." *Theology* 117:3–10.

Quash, Ben, and Michael Ward, eds. 2007. *Heresies and How to Avoid Them: Why It Matters What Christians Believe*. London: SPCK.

Ratzinger, Joseph. 2007–12. *Jesus of Nazareth*. 3 vols. San Francisco: Ignatius.

Roukema, Riemer. 2010. *Jesus, Gnosis, and Dogma*. London: T&T Clark.

Sanders, E. P. 1977. *Paul and Palestinian Judaism*. London: SCM.

Schillebeeckx, Edward. 2014. *Jesus: An Experiment in Christology*. London: Bloomsbury. Orig. pub., 1975.

Schweitzer, Albert. 2001. *The Quest of the Historical Jesus*. Minneapolis: Fortress. Orig. German pub., *Geschichte der Leben-Jesu-Forschung*, 1913, = 2nd rev. and exp. ed. of *Von Reimarus zu Wrede*, 1906.

Welker, Michael. 2013. *God the Revealed: Christology*. Grand Rapids: Eerdmans.

Williams, Rowan. 2001. *Arius: Heresy and Tradition*. London: SCM.

Wright, N. T. 1996. *Jesus and the Victory of God*. London: SPCK.

11 "What a Friend We Have in Jesus"

Jesus Christ as Victor, Redeemer, and Mediator

AIM

This chapter is also about Jesus Christ but focuses less on his person and more on what is traditionally referred to as his work. The main issue is the significance of Christ's work – of what he did but also what he experienced – for us today across the gap of so many centuries. Why was Jesus's work so important that it can define and determine our life in such a decisive way? In close connection with what we said in the previous chapter, we now hope to provide insight into:

- the significance of Jesus's resurrection as confirmation of who he is (11.1)
- soteriology's unique standing in being both linked with Christology and yet distinct in and of itself (11.2)
- the different methods that can be used to discuss the saving work of Christ (11.3)
- the role of Christ as Mediator and how this role affects the theory of the threefold office (11.4)
- the classic view of Christ's work of reconciliation as a victory over the powers of evil (11.5)
- the Anselmian and Reformed doctrine of the "atonement through satisfaction" (11.6)
- the subjective theory of atonement, and how this may complement the other two (11.7)
- the specific salvific meaning for us of the different phases of Jesus's journey: first in his life and ministry (11.8)
- then in his death on the cross (11.9)
- and finally in his resurrection and ascension (11.10).

MAKING CONNECTIONS

1. Find a digital collection of religious art, such as the one at Princeton University (http://ica.princeton.edu) or the Rijksmuseum in Amsterdam (www.rijksmuseum.nl/collectie). (If need be, ask the librarian of your school to provide access to such an art collection or to suggest alternatives.) Find four paintings of Jesus's crucifixion. How can you tell the particular way in which Jesus was important to the painter?

2. Read Lord's Days 4 through 6 in the Heidelberg Catechism and jot down your impressions on three points: what caught your attention, what touched you emotionally, and what struck you as strange or repulsive?

3. Soteriology plays an important role even in popular culture. For example, a popular Dutch praise song, "Hand in Hand with Jesus," has a line that reads (in literal translation), "Jesus Christ, Victor, my Redeemer, Mediator." Do these three concepts convey the same meaning, or does each of them convey a different aspect of the salvation that Christ brings?

11.1. The Resurrection as the Link between Jesus's Person and Work

In this chapter we continue our search for the identity of "the man who fits no formula" (Schweizer 1971, chap. 2) by looking especially at Jesus's (saving) significance for us. That is, we are moving here from the person to the work of Christ, with the proviso, again, that this step is quite indefinable. The work of Christ, his saving intervention, forms the basis that confirms and further clarifies his identity as a person. Who Jesus is simply cannot be detached from what he does for us and in us.

That is, it became clear who Jesus was and is from what he did and the way that God affirmed him. Theirs was, we might say, a history of mutual identification. In his ministry Jesus identifies himself with God and his reign, while God identifies himself with Jesus the Son. Here we come to a topic we did not yet consider in discussing the person of Jesus Christ: the resurrection. The resurrection—or, using a broader term—the exaltation of Jesus may be seen as the connecting link between the questions of who he is and what he did. Put simply, in the resurrection Jesus is *definitively affirmed as God's Son*.

Toward the end of the previous chapter we remarked that it is very difficult to mark exactly the transition from person to work. As Berkouwer writes, "There is such an inseparable connction between his person and work that any separation causes us to go astray" (1965, 19). The close link between the two becomes evident when we begin this chapter about Christ's work (soteriology) with his resurrection. In a biblical-theological sense Jesus's resurrection is, first of all, God's affirmation, or "justification," of Jesus's work. This resurrection makes it possible at last to give a sensible answer to the question about who Jesus was and is. In his resurrection he is "designated Son of God in power according to the Spirit of holiness" (Rom 1:4).

In our reading of the Gospels it is important to always remember that they were written *after* Easter and *because of* Easter. The evangelists did not produce biographies in which, like modern historians, they proceeded carefully from one decade to the next in their account of Jesus's life. Their concern was to transmit the good news about Jesus—his significance for our salvation. For this reason, from the very beginning, the light of Easter shines over what they write, and in their story of Jesus's ministry they want to ensure that this light is reflected as much as possible. The miracles of Jesus, for instance, are not clever tricks but acts by which he inaugurates a new era as the one in whom the kingdom of God is being realized. It has become clear that the kingdom is indeed being realized in Jesus himself—that he in fact personifies this kingdom—in a special way through the divine stamp of approval in his resurrection at Easter.

The best way to clarify this point may be as follows. We may wonder whether Jesus was right in what he did and in the claim that was implied in his work. Does not his untimely death suggest, as Albert Schweitzer for one argued, that he was a failed idealist, thwarted in his expectation of God's intervention? No! The Christian church emerged from the testimony that Jesus truly was the man whom God sent to us and who was confirmed by God as having spoken the truth. The New Testament writings tell us that God gave this confirmation by ensuring that, in Jesus's case, death would not have the last word—by raising him from death. The testimony of Jesus's resurrection belongs to the core of the New Testament message. "God raised Jesus from the dead" is the recurrent formula (Rom 4:24; 10:9; 1 Cor 6:14; 15:4; see also Acts 2:24, 30, 32; 4:10). The early church community mentioned God and the resurrection of Jesus in one and the same breath. The Christian faith stands or falls with this historic confession: witnesses can testify that God identified himself with Jesus in a radical way. The resurrection provided the proof and confirmation of Jesus's messiahship and uniqueness. Everything Jesus proclaimed and did was in the name of God. In his ministry we discover what God wanted to do in our midst, and after his rejection by the leaders of Israel, Jesus's resurrection is the demonstration by which God the Father points to him as the one in whom the promises for Israel and for the world will be fulfilled.

When these witnesses see Jesus alive (Luke 24:39-43; John 20:27) or even clothed with divine majesty (Acts 9:3; Rev 1:13-18), it implies the Yes of the Father to the one who was rejected by the people. Therefore, the theological significance of the resurrection as an act of God on behalf of Jesus holds fundamental importance for the Christian faith. It means that Jesus cannot be viewed as an idealist who sadly failed. His life is not just another incident but occupies a crucial place within the framework of God's turning toward Israel and, through this people, to the world. God has affirmed him as the Messiah and has rehabilitated him. He made him a Kyrios and a Christos, a Lord and an Anointed One (Acts 2:36). By raising him from the dead and clothing him with divine glory, God, as it were, positioned himself beside Jesus and said: "This man belongs with me" (see Rom 1:4). We might describe this as the occasion on which God and Jesus, as the Father and the Son, were both differentiated and identified. The Father now identifies himself with Jesus, who always has been distinct from the Father and has subjected himself to him as his Son (Mark 10:18; John 5:19; 14:28-20:31; see Pannenberg, ST 2:372-79). Thus the resurrection signifies an extraordinary rehabilitation of the crucified, and thus accursed, Jesus (Gal 3:13). This central turn is a fully and unavoidably Trinitarian event: the Father raises the Son through the Spirit (1 Tim 3:16; 1 Pet 3:18), in whose power he indeed rises (Rom 1:4).

Do these events imply that Jesus was not, from the very beginning, the Son of God, the Messiah? Had he not from all eternity shared his Father's home (see Prov 8:22, 30)? We must here return for a moment to the question of Christ's preexistence, which we posed in the previous chapter and which has generated so much discussion. As we saw, Berkhof understood preexistence as just an idea (CF 293-94); texts as John 1:1-14, Rom 10:6-7, 2 Cor 8:9, Gal 4:4, Phil 2:5-6, Col 1:15-20, and Heb 1:1-4 intend only "to exalt the divine initiative . . . in the creation [*sic*] of Christ." We, however, think these biblical statements (whatever may be their precise background in the historical tradition) must be understood in an ontological sense, as a *reality*, derived from the real appearance, and especially the resurrection, of Christ. In the context of the resurrection Jesus's messianic titles receive their most intense and specific meaning: "God has *made* him to be Lord and Christ." This act also provides the opportunity to confess, while looking back, that Jesus satisfies God's intention in all respects; to put it even more strongly, that he is the image of God (Col 1:15; Heb 1:3) and reigns together with the Father (1 Cor 15:24-25). If Jesus must therefore be included in God's identity and determines who God is, and in a hidden state always was, the statements about preexistence fall into place. This preexistence ultimately means that Christ comes, with the salvation that he brings, from the being of God himself. How deeply, then, is our salvation anchored in God!

As we noted in chapter 9, about Israel, belief in the resurrection was part of Israel's prophetic and eschatological expectation. At the end of time God will demonstrate his power; Israel will be restored, and the dead will be revived. That is, the New Testament testimony is not unique in its affirmation of the resurrection of the dead per se. When in 1 Cor 15 Paul speaks of the resurrection of Christ, he is convinced that his readers already share in the expectation of a resurrection of the dead at the end of time. "If there is no resurrection of the dead, then Christ has not been raised" (1 Cor 15:13, 16). The new and different element is that this resurrection has first of all been realized in *Jesus's* return from death and is not yet a universal event. For that reason Christ is referred to as the firstfruit (Rom 8:29; 1 Cor 15:20, 23; Col 1:18). What happened in Christ was the beginning of the "last days" (Acts 2:17), and in these last days the other believers will also experience what has already happened to Christ.

We intentionally referred to "other" believers to underline that Jesus himself was a believer (and according to Heb 12:2, in a very special way). In the context that we just sketched it becomes very meaningful to see Jesus in this way. Particularly in the Pauline writings we find more allusions to this idea than has often been acknowledged; many contemporary exegetes believe that the Greek genitive constructions *pistis Iēsou* and *pistis Christou* in Rom 3:22, 26, Phil 3:9, and Gal 2:16, 20 probably denote "the faith *of* Jesus/Christ" and not "faith *in* Jesus/Christ," as it has often been translated. For a good dogmatic basis and further development of this issue, see Allen 2009.

For the Jewish end-time expectation we refer to Lapide 2002, Levenson 2006, and Pannenberg, ST 2:346-53. "Resurrection" is, in actual fact, a figurative expression: as a person is awakened by someone from his or her sleep and suddenly "looks alive," so God will raise the dead. In the background we may detect texts from Jewish apocalypticism and from Dan 12:2; Ps 13:3; Job 3:13; 14:12; Ezek 37. However, the idea that a raising of the dead is possible because of a miraculous divine intervention is older than Jewish apocalypticism (Levenson 2006, 132); for example, see Isa 25:8 and Hos 6:2. God is able to do something beyond all expectations. The resurrection means that, against all expectations, God persists in a sublime demonstration of his power, providing justice and creating a new world. In Second Temple Judaism, belief in a resurrection of the dead was accepted by the Pharisees but rejected by the Sadducees (Acts 23:7-8).

The meetings with the risen Lord were interpreted within the framework of Old Testament end-time expectations. At the same time, they were thoroughly modified by Jesus's followers; what had been thought of as a universal event was initially realized only in Jesus. He is the firstfruit of the eschatological reign of God. There is thus an interim between the time of Jesus's resurrection and that of the others.

What does it mean that Christ was raised from the dead? How exactly must we define Christ's resurrection? What did the disciples experience at Easter? We very intentionally began this section with the theological significance of Jesus's resurrection in the New Testament because that perspective often remains undertreated. Now we must take a further step and ask the oft-discussed question about the ontological aspect of the resurrection.

The many answers to this question can be reduced to three main options (see Hunsinger 2004):

1. Jesus's resurrection is a historical event that becomes plausible by employing historiographical methods.
2. "Resurrection" is a word for the inner conviction of the disciples that Jesus continued to have a significant meaning after his death.
3. Resurrection points to an eschatological act of God that we cannot really understand because, in its newness, it is so totally different from everything that is historically imaginable.

That is, the resurrection may be viewed as an objectively verifiable event, as a subjective experience, or as an eschatological act of God.

A few remarks about how the resurrection can be conceived and imagined. This topic has been hotly debated in the Western world since the Enlightenment, but the dispute may have started much earlier. In Hellenistic culture the idea of Jesus's bodily resurrection was used as an argument to dismiss the Christian message as nonsense. That humans have eternal souls was acceptable because it is conceivable, but that God's faithfulness would also include the the material aspects of our being ran counter to the common thinking of antiquity. Their approach to life made a resurrection from death inconceivable and therefore unimaginable. Note the reaction of those who listened to Paul's speech on the Areopagus in Acts 17:32. The debate about the reality of the resurrection keeps recurring.

1. The first view mentioned—the resurrection as a historic event—regards Christ's resurrection as the ground of Christian faith. At times the idea is used in a strongly apologetic mode, based on the conviction that we must accept that Christ was raised if we simply let the historical facts speak for themselves. That is, using conventional historical methods, this approach attempts to demonstrate the plausibility that real people had real encounters with the risen Christ. In our time Pannenberg and Wright, among others, have tried to prove the historical reliability of New Testament testimonies about Jesus's resurrection on the basis of this model.

See Pannenberg 1968, 53–114, besides his work that was published in 1991: ST 2:343–63, and Wright 2003. Pannenberg deals, in his characteristic fashion, with the frequently heard objection that Jesus's resurrection was only handed on by believers and that any independent verification is impossible. He argues that the fact that the witnesses were believers does not show that they interpreted events on the basis of their preexisting convictions (he points to the experience of Paul, who wanted to have nothing to do with Jesus prior to his encounter with him), but rather that no one who actually experienced an encounter with Jesus could remain an unbeliever (ST 2:345). Wright believes that neither the empty tomb nor the stories of the appearances of Jesus provide sufficient proof in themselves but that, together with a third argument, they do. This argument, which Wright regards as decisive, is that the prevailing Jewish ideas of the resurrection would never have changed if there had been no empty tomb and actual appearances. The stories about the empty tomb and Jesus's bodily appearances are best explained, therefore, by assuming that these appearances did indeed happen. Wright does not require a watertight proof for the resurrection but is looking for an "inference to the best explanation" (2003, 716): how do the pieces of the puzzle most naturally fit together? About Wright, see further Brink 2008; and for more extensive surveys, Thiessen 2009 and Welker 2013.

2. The second view differs radically from the first: the resurrection was not an objectively verifiable event in time and space but was primarily a change that occurred in the disciples, that is, in the human subject. Together, they discovered how important Jesus's message had been for them. The resurrection stories bear witness to this inner change.

We find a classic example of this position in Schleiermacher, CF, §99. Already during Jesus's life the disciples were deeply impressed by his intense sense of the divine. The stories of the resurrection and ascension did not add to this sense in any way but merely underlined and illustrated it. Bultmann's programmatic study *New Testament and Mythology* (1941) was also extremely influential. He believed the resurrection to be a symbol of the lasting significance of Jesus's life and his death on the cross; more briefly stated, the resurrection "expresses the meaning of the cross" (Bultmann 1954, 31). It is a historical event in the sense that Jesus was resurrected in the faith experience of his followers and thus in the kerygma of the early Christian faith community. The reality of the resurrection is completely absorbed in the reality of faith and becomes dependent on it. In the background of his position (beside the problem of our inability to conceptualize it, which we mentioned above) lies Bultmann's fear that our faith will rest on a barren fact, detached from any faith commitment—in particular, detached from the appeal of the proclamation on us. It would, as it were, be possible to be a good Christian by simply affirming Jesus's bodily resurrection. However, the correlation between revelation and faith in Bultmann's manner of thinking is totally shifted to the side of faith. We find the same emphasis on the role of faith and experience in Schillebeeckx (2014a, 90). The resurrection is a matter of revelatory grace that cannot be recognized without an act of faith, although the notion of God's acting in the earthly Jesus is maintained. Thereby Schillebeeckx distances himself from Bultmann (Schillebeeckx 2014b, 61); for good reason, the original Dutch title of Schillebeeckx's first Jesus-book was *Jezus, het verhaal van een levende* (Jesus, the story of a Living One). Yet, in this book he develops his thoughts in a way that we find difficult to accept, saying, for example, "An eschatological, bodily resurrection, theologically speaking has nothing to do, however, with a corpse" (339). This position brings him back close to Bultmann, as Wright (2003, 701) correctly remarks.

3. The third position is the view that the resurrection is an eschatological event. "Eschatological" in this context means that the resurrection points to a definitive and decisive act of God that goes beyond our comprehension and that we can hardly imagine, but that nevertheless touches, qualifies, and transforms our reality. Christ's resurrection points to something totally new, incomprehensible, and surprising that God does in Jesus. Because it belongs to such a different category, the resurrection cannot be equated with historical events that happen in time, but saying this does not reduce it to a mere idealistic possibility. It is rather the decisive reality that supersedes our reality and ultimately determines it.

Examples of the eschatological view are found in Barth, R2 280–81, Moltmann 1990, and Dalferth 2015. Discontinuity with existing reality dominates this eschatological interpretation. For this approach, see also Beek 2008, 146–47. The eschatological interpretation strongly emphasizes that the resurrection is an act of God that we cannot approach with our usual historiographical tools. Or to cite a frequently used metaphor, if someone had been able to take a picture of the resurrection, it would certainly have been overexposed. Still more, the resurrection changes the character of what we henceforth may call history, for it marks the beginning of a new era that directly connects us to the end of time (1 Cor 15:23–24). The passive verbal forms that the New Testament prefers when it describes Jesus's post-Easter appearances (e.g., 1 Cor 15:5 and Luke 24:34) make it clear that this "daybreak of the new creation" (Hunsinger 2004, title) is due to a very special divine intervention, namely, the raising of the Lord. The emphasis falls on the unusual and on the living Lord as the acting subject.

We agree with position 3 that, because of its transcendent origin, the resurrection cannot be categorized as an "ordinary" historical event. With position 2 we agree that we cannot sensibly speak of Jesus as the Risen One if we take faith out of the equation, since fact and significance cannot be separated (note the end of 1 Cor 12:3 and the strong focus on the meaning of the resurrection in Heidelberg Catechism Q/A 45). But we also agree with position 1 that Jesus's resurrection does indeed disturb the physical substrate of earthly reality. However difficult it is (and has always been) to imagine the resurrection, if we allow it to evaporate into a purely spiritual event, we cut all ties with the early Christian confession (e.g., 1 Cor 15:12–17). It cannot be denied that Christ's resurrection involved a corpse, for Scripture tells us that Jesus did not remain a corpse (Rev 1:18).

We want to add just a few words about the eschatological view, since it is undoubtedly the least known and most problematic option. Most supporters of this view do not deny that the resurrection is an empirical and physical event, but they believe it cannot be scientifically verified and must be accepted only by faith. A person does not become a Christian by acknowledging Jesus's resurrection but only by allowing himself or herself to be resurrected to a new kind of life (Rom 6:4; also Eph 2:5). The ground of this faith is not an objectively verifiable resurrection but a personal encounter with Jesus as the Living One, who indeed was raised from the dead. This conviction therefore does not depend on a historical evaluation of its probability (as with Swinburne [2003, 214], who reckoned the probability of the theory that Jesus, as the incarnate Son of God, was bodily resurrected at approximately 97 percent).

The eschatological view reflects the peculiar tension between appearing and withdrawing that we detect in testimonies about the resurrection. On the one hand, the risen Lord can be touched and seen, but on the other, he does not allow himself to be "caught" (Welker 2013, 124-26). In his encounter with Mary in the garden, she does not recognize Jesus until he calls her by her name and she realizes she is being addressed (John 20:16). There follows the warning that she must not try to keep him there (v. 17). In the story of the Emmaus disciples the identity of the strange Guest becomes clear only in the breaking of the bread, after which he immediately disappears (Luke 24:30-31). When, a little later, he appears to his disciples, they first think they must be seeing a ghost until he eats some broiled fish before their very eyes (Luke 24:37, 42-43). Ontologically, these testimonies display a structure of appearing and withdrawing. The risen Lord wants to be involved in the material life of the disciples, but at the same time he remains distant. This behavior demonstrates the freedom of God's glory, which introduces a new eschatological order and gives it its brilliance. This is not to say, however, that the New Testament testimony about the resurrection is unambiguous. The story of the empty tomb in the Gospels (Mark 16:6 and pars.) underscores God's concrete intervention with regard to the dead Jesus. "He is not here"—these words indicate that the resurrection is a bodily event. Paul, however, does not mention an empty tomb, even though we believe such is implied in 1 Cor 15:4. He sees the resurrection as a transformation to an incorruptible mode of existence (1 Cor 15:35-49). But the way in which this transformation is realized and how the corruptible changes into the incorruptible remains like a seed that is hidden in the soil and thus hidden from human sight and comprehension.

The core of the biblical resurrection-faith is that God intervenes to give Christ new life. This divine act is not just of symbolic value but indicates a real progression in God's dealings with the earthly Jesus. What God realizes in the Jesus who had died is not a return to this life—there is a huge difference, for instance, between the raising of Lazarus (John 11:43-44) and the resurrection of Jesus—but a sharing in the glory of God the Father. It is a step toward, and a definite sharing in, the glory of God the Father. Despite the discontinuity in the nature of Jesus's physical appearances, there is a continuity of identity. It is the same person who was there and now is here. Berkhof rightly speaks of the resurrection of Christ as a "boundary event" (CF 315-16). Christ preceded us. He is where we, who still live on this earth, are not yet.

In the New Testament the resurrection of Christ is therefore the first realization and affirmation of the redemption that God makes available to us in Christ. In Christ our salvation is realized, and for that reason Paul can speak of Christ, in an all-encompassing way, as wisdom, righteousness, sanctification, and redemption (1 Cor 1:30).

11.2. Soteriology and Christology: Difference and Interconnectedness

The rest of this chapter zeros in on redemption. But exactly what is this saving work that is realized by Jesus and that provides redemption? Here we shift our emphasis from Christology to soteriology and view the significance of Jesus's work from the perspective of his resurrection.

When theologians have wanted to explain what salvation in Christ means, they usually speak very concisely about the *work* of Jesus Christ. This work encompasses the meaning of such great themes as reconciliation, redemption, deliverance, and eternal life. But we may also approach the question on the basis of the doctrine of sin: from what calamity does God save us through Christ's work? What is this salvation (Gk. *sōtēria*) that the Savior (*Sōtēr*) accomplishes? We described the substance of what Jesus does (10.1) in the terms of life-giving presence and forgiving love. Just as Jesus as the Son is totally oriented toward God the Father and lives in his life-giving presence, so he is oriented toward us. His person and his life will benefit us. Soteriology and Christology mutually presuppose each other. The Nicene Creed brings this confession of Jesus as the Son of God to a peak in powerful words:

> . . . who for us men, and for our salvation, came down from heaven, and was incarnate by the Holy Ghost of the virgin Mary.

This formulation is striking by its focus. The incarnation is not just a miracle in itself but has our salvation as its point and meaning. In other words, the incarnation is soteriologically motivated. It would not have occurred had there been no need to save us from the powers of sin and death (see Berkouwer 1965, 19-34, for a discussion of the persistent train of opposing voices on this point, from Duns Scotus via Andreas Osiander to J. H. Gunning, BidO 3:132).

We want to develop this connection further, but this task is far from easy. The entire Christian tradition presupposes a salvific linkage between the story of Jesus (his life, cross, resurrection, and ascension) and our life. The deep conviction of the *pro nobis* (for us) has been expressed in liturgical texts and in Christian teachings in many ways—in proclamation, song, confession, and reflection. But how exactly we should describe this positive relationship is much more puzzling. What is it in his life, suffering, death, and resurrection that benefits us? What fruit does his life produce for us? Does redemption happen *because* of the suffering of Christ, or *in spite of* it?

A word about our posture or tone in answering this question is in order here. First, we must do so in all humility. Second, we should not labor under the impression that we are dealing here with simple formulas or some type of arithmetic. Quite often the doctrine of atonement has been treated in the Western church as a bald form of accounting or as following some self-evident logic. "Of course, Jesus died for our sins so that we might go to heaven." However, this atonement was in no way self-evident. We may not forget, for instance, Paul's words about the curse of the cross in Gal 3:13, in which we can still hear an echo of the bewilderment caused by this death. How can someone who underwent the curse of death on a cross be the source of joy for others? If there is a positive relationship between Christ's suffering and human salvation, it is not a matter of calculations that can be made beforehand; it is a fact that we can ponder only subsequently (that is, a posteriori) in utter amazement. The connection between the death on the cross and our salvation is a surprise after the event, which forced some fundamental rethinking. No one could have imagined it (note 1 Cor 2:8). Therefore Christian dogmatics, in speaking on this topic, must always reflect the surprising, overwhelming character of God's saving act in the death of Christ. Soteriological reflection comes in hindsight, based on what has been received in Christ; it respects the journey God takes in dealing with our guilt and estrangement. We have no right to suggest to God how he should have demonstrated his forgiving nature. In soteriology we are always to speak as recipients, as grateful receivers of God's salvation.

The Bible and the tradition offer a multitude of metaphors and images to express the substance of the salvation that Christ provides. He has become flesh (John 1:14), has reconciled us (2 Cor 5:18), is a ransom for us (Mark 10:45), gave his life for us (Luke 22:19), died for us (Rom 5:8), made himself an offering (Heb 10:10), conquered death and purified us (Heb 2:14-15), delivered us from slavery (Rom 8:15), and made us children of God (Rom 8:21). A superabundance of images and expressions! Should we perhaps single out one of them, or should we try to synthesize them all into one model? Neither. It is the task of dogmatics to show, with constant reference to the Bible, how these images provide access to the different dimensions of the salvation that Christ brings. We take a closer look below at some of the most prominent images and concepts. It will become clear that we cannot say everything in a single statement or that any one metaphor can suffice. There is good reason why the Bible offers such a plethora of images and metaphors: they all aim to give us more insight into the "manifold wisdom" of God (Eph. 3:10) that is revealed in the work of Jesus Christ. Nonetheless, we cannot avoid searching for some kind of common denominator to clarify the cohesion between the various aspects of that work.

The word "soteriology" is derived from the Greek word *sōtēria* and poses an awkward terminological problem. How should it be translated? The related word *sōtēr* is usually rendered "savior" or "redeemer." *Sōtēria* itself has a broad range of meanings: saving, delivering, setting free, and making happy. The term we choose as an umbrella concept makes a big difference. In Protestant textbooks the present topic is usually dealt with under the heading of *atonement*. Jesus Christ's work as Mediator consists first of all of the reconciliation that he accomplishes. But that choice may have the disadvantage of fully identifying the work of Christ with just one of its facets, and one that is central in the Arminian doctrine of atonement (see below): the removal of the guilt of sin.

In order to make it clear that there are other aspects at hand as well—for instance, the gift of eternal life because of Christ's victory over death—we will mostly use the word *redemption* as an all-encompassing term and will thus view soteriology as the doctrine of redemption/atonement. The New Testament gives us strong arguments for this choice. It portrays the salvation that Christ brings as a particularly eschatological event that breaks into history at a given moment but, at the same time, inaugurates and comprises the "end of time." It is therefore one and the same divine movement that encloses present and future. We prefer "redemption," since it points to the broad spectrum of total deliverance (atonement, inner healing, sanctification, glorification) in Christ and emphasizes the unity of these aspects.

Within this one eschatological movement of salvation we need to differentiate between those aspects of Christ's work that have already been realized and unfolded and those that will be completed at the end of time. We will use *atonement* for the first and most important phase of Christ's salvation in the present. Atonement is a function of redemption and provides the basis for the work of the Spirit that finds its completion at the end of time.

We will further discuss the broader aspect of redemption (and thus of soteriology in its fuller sense) in chapters 15 (esp. 15.1) and 16 below. For these issues, see Beek 2008, which sharply differentiates (or even totally separates) atonement as a reality in Christ and its effect now from (and at the expense of) eschatological redemption; on the terminological distinction between atonement and redemption, see also Bavinck, RD 3:452–54.

Church history, like Scripture, has also used a multitude of images and concepts to describe the salvation that Christ provides. While the many biblical presentations of the concept provided a footing, they were usually linked as well to the circumstances of the people who received them. Perhaps we can compare the process with looking at an enclosed garden through many different windows; we see the same garden but from different angles. We should not play these various perspectives off against each other, for they all provide a view of one and the same garden. By analogy, the different windows are the various receiving contexts or cultures. It makes a considerable difference whether the light of Christ enters a Germanic context, in which heroism is a central idea, or an African context, in which veneration of the ancestors is all-important, or modern western European culture, in which the ideal of personal identity predominates. Context determines, at least in part, the choice of central concepts and metaphors for redemption or atonement. Successful ones are often borrowed from the receiving culture and then filled with biblical content—also in the hope that the cultural garb will be criticized and transformed.

We cannot—and should not—remedy this disadvantage by simply restricting ourselves in dogmatics to biblical terms, for the point of dogmatics is to translate these texts and concepts in order to make them understood. Like it or not, our understanding is culturally conditioned. Paul clearly recognized that, with respect to God and his salvation, on this side of the grave we will always know only "in part" (1 Cor 13:12). There is no theological reason why this limitation should surprise us. It is part of the work of the Holy Spirit that what happened in the life, death, and resurrection of Jesus Christ can always be translated in new ways, depending on context and culture. Through his Spirit, God draws people toward his salvation. The substance of that salvation does not just hover above people and their ability to understand; rather, the Spirit provides a link between God's salvation and the new situation. We see this already in the Bible. Biblical concepts like reconciliation and redemption are already the result of appropriation and interpretation; the biblical authors use these terms to make connections with events in their own world and with traditions that may serve as eye-openers. The work of the Spirit, just like his character, is multifaceted and multivocal. This multiplicity of voices is heard in the wide range of concepts and images in the Bible, as well as in the Christian tradition that expresses the meaning of salvation in Christ. In soteriology we thus face a fabric of concepts, metaphors, expressions, and stories that at times stand in isolation but often mutually influence each other. This mixture provides a reservoir of possibilities that enable us to reflect in a more or less cohesive manner on the content of salvation in Christ.

The concepts and images we use thus become a matter of considerable importance. Not every image is adequate. We may well ask ourselves what happens when we apply the image of a Germanic hero, a guru, or a healer to Christ. Here dogmatics has a critical and selective task. Quite often the images and metaphors themselves change when applied to Christ. Briefly put, a new culture uses new concepts that, under the influence of the gospel, assume a different color. This process we may therefore call a double transformation.

This dynamic poses the urgent question for Bible translators of whether they should use "Christ" in place of a title like "Son" in versions that are intended for Muslims because of the connotation of sexuality and procreation that "son" has for Muslims. From the standpoint of dogmatics, it must be maintained that "Son" has too central a significance for Jesus's connection with God to be avoided; it will have to be used and explained.

The arts provide an instructive mirror of the shifts in soteriology that have transpired over the centuries. In the catacombs in Rome we find Christ represented as a shepherd carrying a lamb on his shoulders, which depicts how God seeks the lost and brings them home (Luke 15:1-7; John 10:1-18). In later iconography the accent shifts to Christ as the powerful King (the Pantokrator, or Ruler of everything), who, like the Roman emperor (who now is a Christian), reigns over his kingdom. In the Middle Ages, beginning in the twelfth century, the accent is on Jesus as the Man of Sorrows. He is portrayed as an emaciated figure who carries the sins of the world. His humanity, poverty, and total identification with the human condition stand in the foreground, as in, for instance, the crucifixion scene of the Isenheim altarpiece painted by Matthias Grünewald (early sixteenth century). We also repeatedly see the suffering Christ in the work of Rembrandt, but he always places his own contemporaries in the foreground. At times painters even include themselves in his picture as if to say, we are part of this as witnesses and participants. (Possibly Mark himself did something like this, as he was the only evangelist who did not place angels but a young man—himself?—in the empty tomb of Jesus, Mark 16:5; see also 14:51.) In twentieth-century art Christ is often depicted as a figure hanging on the cross in total loneliness. He suffers the fate of desolate humanity in a cruel and empty universe.

For the process of double transformation, see especially Brinkman 2009, Beek 2002, 195-276, and Kärkkäinen 2003, 189-285. It is telling that the church has not delivered any dogmatic statements about soteriology. We look in vain for the doctrine of atonement in the Apostles' or Nicene Creeds, for there were no controversies that led to sharp divisions on this question in the early church. This lack of attention is perhaps due to the ever-changing windows through which the salvation of Christ is viewed. In popular parlance we hear of "the dogma of the atonement," often in a pejorative sense, but this use of the word is incorrect. "Dogma" designates a truth that is set in concrete and is not open to discussion (see Bavinck, RD 3:340-41).

11.3. Methodological Questions

Given that the salvation provided by Christ has so many facets, what is the best method for comprehending it? A contemporary position needs to weigh the most common approaches of the past.

1. We could follow the *temporal* order of the Apostles' Creed by dealing in sequence with Christ's birth (incarnation), his condemnation and crucifixion, his death, his descent into hell, his resurrection, and his ascension. This is, in fact, the approach that the Heidelberg Catechism takes to Christ's work; its Lord's Days 11–19 take their point of departure from the Apostles' Creed and simply add at every step of the way the question as to what salvific meaning may be at hand for us. Berkouwer 1965, 88–252, and Beek 2002, 133–93, give further examples of this method.

2. We could opt for a more *functional* description of Jesus Christ as Mediator between God and humanity. This is another approach within the Reformed tradition, exemplified by Calvin, who recognizes three aspects in Christ's mediatorial work: prophet, priest, and king. These are not three different offices but one threefold office (Lat. *munus triplex*) and may serve as a guide to clarify the most important aspects of Christ's ministry.

3. We could also decide to use the so-called doctrine of the *states* of

Christ as our structuring principle. This method adapts the temporal method, recognizing consecutive periods in God's intervention in the history of Jesus Christ. Following such passages as John 1, Phil 2:5-11, and the Letter to the Hebrews, this approach divides Jesus's ministry between a "state of humiliation" and a "state of exaltation." Sending the Son into the world creates a situation of "emptying" (Gk. *kenōsis*), while his exaltation by God the Father in the resurrection and the ascension restores Christ to glory (see John 17:5).

4. We could choose the doctrine of the *atonement* as our point of departure and discuss the various concepts of atonement that have had a strong influence in the history of the church (esp. in the West): reconciliation through victory, satisfaction, and reconciliation through transformation.

Each of these historic approaches focuses more clearly on one particular aspect of the story than on others. For this reason, we prefer to combine them. In what follows we first briefly discuss Calvin's view of the offices and the way in which Karl Barth combined it with the doctrine of the states. Then we present a survey of the models of reconciliation that, each in its own particular way, vividly describes the salvation that Christ brings. Finally, we devote considerable space to the various aspects of Christ's work as moments and dimensions of his mission to the world. In the previous chapter we described Christ's ministry as the sending of the Son, by which God gives us access to his life-giving presence. In this movement, this *theo-drama*, we see confrontation, rejection, suffering, judgment, and death. In the resurrection of Jesus, however, God perseveres in his purpose to save us and the world. This salvation, this redemption, can become visible and understandable only via a kaleidoscopic range of images. The custom of following the sequence of the Apostles' Creed gives us a handle on the overall subject, so we deploy it in the final sections. Thus, by the end, all four methods we have mentioned will prove to be useful.

The term *theo-drama*, derived from the work of Roman Catholic theologian Hans Urs von Balthasar (1905-88), has proven to be ecumenically fruitful in recent years. Among the Reformed theologians who have embraced and further developed the idea are Kevin Vanhoozer (DD) and Michael Horton (CF). Even though the contexts and motifs of the various authors may differ, the key idea of theo-drama is to underline the reality of the dynamic history of God's dealings with us as human beings. "Salvation history" is not a play that is performed but a real event in which God invests himself through Christ and the Spirit, with all the ups and downs that this condescension involves. The term "theo-*drama*" aims to tell us that this history is an extraordinary, serious, and exciting sequence of events, in which human choices and decisions play a vital role, while the initiative always remains with God (thus *theo*-drama). A theology that is serious about the notion of the covenant is particularly suitable for a theo-dramatic approach—probably the reason why Reformed theologians like Vanhoozer and Horton have welcomed this concept.

11.4. A Functional Approach: Jesus as Mediator

Let's begin with the more functional description of the work of Christ in terms of his mediating role. A key text for this approach is 1 Tim 2:5: "For there is one God, and there is one mediator between God and men, the man Christ Jesus." The question of how Jesus mediates between God and humans is answered by referring to the three Old Testament offices of prophet, priest, and king that we also applied to Christ in the New Testament. The Old Testament offices give us a prism that better displays the various roles Christ plays in his relationship to us. Calvin, in particular, did pioneering work in this area (*Inst.* 2.12 and 2.15). Long before the Reformation each of these offices was applied to Christ. Eusebius of Caesarea (263-339) came close to affirming this threefold office (*Historia Ecclesiastica* 1.3.8; NPNF[2] 1:86), but Calvin (in the last edition of his *Institutes*) developed the various facets more systematically into a more or less cohesive theory. "If we want to know why the Father sent Christ, and what he did for us," Calvin writes, "we must specifically note three things: his prophetic, priestly and kingly office (*Inst.* 2.15, heading). The Heidelberg Catechism adopted this motif and applied it in a practical way (Lord's Day 12) to the life of the Christian, who, after all, is called to the discipleship of Christ. The concept of the threefold office has proven to be of great ecumenical value; it has since been accepted by Roman Catholics: "Jesus has fulfilled the messianic hope of Israel in his threefold office of priest, prophet, and king" (*Catechism* 1994, §436).

This approach to the work of Christ has a number of major advantages. In Israel's history the prophets, priests, and kings represented the most important functions that were to mediate God's dealings with his people. Starting from this view of the offices thus provides us with a powerful impetus to fully appreciate the role of the Old Testament in disclosing the ministry of Jesus Christ from the perspective of its historical lineage. Moreover, the concept of the offices shifts our attention from the person of Jesus to his roles and functions, and thereby to his practical and soteriological significance for us. This emphasis does not necessarily contradict what early church Christology said about the person of Jesus (and what was also affirmed by the Reformation). The person and the work of Jesus form an inseparable unity. However, emphasizing the offices has the advantage of putting the spotlight on the content of the salvation that God provides in Christ. It is as Philipp Melanchthon, a good friend of Calvin, stated in a famous sentence: "To know Christ is to see what he did for us, and not to understand his natures" (LC, Intr. 13). This statement points up the strong soteriological interest of the Reformation, for its Lutheran (Melanchthon's one-liner was based on Luther's ideas; cf. WA 1:362; 5:108), as well as its Reformed, branch. The Reformers, who had become fearful of all kinds of metaphysical speculations about Christology and the Trinity, often turned fiercely against all sorts of scholastic arguments (usually without pointing to particular persons). They wanted to concentrate fully on the existential and practical question as to how Christ's work redounds to our benefit.

Let's briefly trace the most important lines that delineate Jesus's threefold office. As *prophet*, Jesus follows in the tracks of the Old Testament prophets and proclaims God's reign, calls us to repentance, and explains our situation. He proclaims the truth. That is to say, he shows us the extent to which we have become estranged from God and reveals God's purpose, the establishment of his kingdom. But as he brings and proclaims God's kingdom, he meets resistance, which demonstrates how humanity has been caught up in its estrangement. In this confrontation Christ assumes more and more *priestly* characteristics (which are, in particular, developed in Heb 7–10). Christ himself is brought down by the power of sin. This does not happen because he is a passive victim, however. Rather, out of his love for humankind and because of the will of God the Father (Mark 14:36), he is willing to put his life on the line. In so doing, he is simultaneously the sacrifice and the one who brings it. In this movement from priest to sacrificial lamb, the deepest mystery of the forgiveness of sin is revealed. In Christ's reconciliation the power of death, our estrangement and rebellion against God, are judged and are robbed of their definitive character. In all of this work, finally, Jesus figures as *king*. This is not just the case after his resurrection but also applies very clearly during his earthly life, not only when his kingship is announced (Luke 1:32-33) and acknowledged (John 1:50), but also when people attach all kinds of concrete expectations to it (Matt 20:20-21; John 6:15). In the end, Jesus enters Jerusalem as a messianic aspirant to the throne, not on a horse but on a donkey (Matt 21:6-11 and pars.)—a sign of humility and servanthood and in response to Jewish expectations of Israel's restoration (see Zech 9:9). From then on, the controversy around Jesus finds its center in the question of the nature of his kingship (Luke 23:2-3; John 18:36-37; 19:14-15), until he is ultimately mocked as "the king of the Jews" (John 19:2-3) and crucified (John 19:19). Only after the resurrection does the true nature of Christ's kingship become clear. In the emerging kingdom of God, Jesus is the Lord, which leads to a situation in which life is made whole and reconciled in all respects, and divine shalom governs all relationships. It is this Jesus Christ, who reigns on God's behalf (1 Cor 15:25-27), who will be the judge and to whom has been given all power in heaven and on earth (Matt 28:18). He is the Messiah who was anointed with God's Spirit and who announces, realizes, and maintains a new mode of existence.

These short remarks must suffice. In sections 11.8 and 11.9 we explore further the threefold task of Jesus, followed by our own portrayal of the soteriological significance of Jesus's life and death, based on the biblical-theological data.

As we mentioned in passing, Karl Barth forged his doctrine of the atonement (CD IV) as a dynamic reinterpretation of this concept of the offices, in close connection to his doctrine of sin and his views regarding the states of Christ's passage. The teachings about the states, the offices, and sin all come together so as to demonstrate the dynamism of God's self-revelation in Christ as an event that is aimed at our salvation. Barth thereby clarifies the close link between the person and work of Christ, on the one hand, and human sin, on the other. He shows the extent to which Christology, soteriology and hamartology constitute a unity so that, for example, when we learn to know Christ, we also get a better understanding of the nature of sin.

In his doctrine of the atonement Barth portrays the history of Jesus Christ as an interplay of powers in which God acts for the good of humanity. We can approach this position from different angles. Each angle offers a new perspective, but all perspectives gaze on the same reality—the reality of Jesus Christ, in whom God is with us and for us. The following scheme summarizes Barth's thought:

	CD IV/1	CD IV/2	CD IV/3
Office:	priest	king	prophet
State:	humiliation	exaltation	witness
Human sin:	pride	inertia	deceit

In the first part of his doctrine of atonement (CD IV/1), Barth describes a path from above to below. Chapter 14 thus carries the title "Jesus Christ, the Lord as Servant." The sending of the Son is described as a journey into a foreign land ("Der Weg des Sohnes Gottes in die Fremde"). Barth thus succeeds in connecting the priestly office to the state of humiliation. At the same time, we see mirrored in this phase of Jesus's life-journey the nature of human sin as pride. We do not want the place that we have been assigned; in contrast with the Son of God, we want to move up rather than down.

In the second part (CD IV/2) Barth looks in the opposite direction, from below to above. Chapter 15 has the title, "The Servant as Lord." Here the exaltation of Jesus Christ is depicted as the return of the Son of Man. In this perspective we see Jesus as the Kingly One, which is also the promise for Jesus Christ's fellow human beings. It is the coat they may put on. In this way the state of exaltation is linked to the royal office. At the same time, we detect in the nearness of this divine intervention another core element of human sin: inertia. We do not in any way measure up to the reality God has provided in Jesus; we lack the trust and the drive to follow Christ in a kingly fashion, doing good.

The third part of Barth's doctrine of the atonement (CD IV/3) focuses on the prophetic office. Chapter 16 has as its heading "Jesus Christ, the True Witness." Jesus Christ himself is the witness who presents himself to the people in the power of the Spirit. He mediates himself; no one else can take this role in his place. And here we find a third side of sin—deceit. We reject what is true. Jesus Christ is the truth, the light, and the life, but we are inclined to obscure it. Yet, we also see the result of being a witness of Jesus Christ, a faith community that senses its call to live with him and to bear witness of this hope and expectation to the world.

In the next three sections we will explore in more detail what this salvation—which was realized in Christ as prophet, priest, and king, in his humiliation and exaltation—has accomplished for us. We treat this topic under the heading of *atonement*, and (following the fourth of the methods listed above) we distinguish between three models of atonement that have become known through the work of the Swedish Lutheran theologian and bishop Gustav Aulén (1879-1977). We use this scheme because it has become widely accepted and continues to offer a useful framework for reflecting on the various elements that are part of Christ's work. Following Aulén 1931, we can distinguish three models of the substance of Christ's salvific work and its benefits for us:

1. Atonement through victory
2. Atonement through satisfaction
3. Atonement through transformation.

Aulén developed an essay that he earlier published in the *Zeitschrift für Systematische Theologie* into a modest book that became quite famous and remains influential even today: *Christus Victor* (Swedish, 1930; Eng. trans., 1931). He intended this study as a corrective to the ideas of liberal historians of dogma like Adolf von Harnack and Reinhold Seeberg (1859–1935). Aulén argued that the earliest view regarding the saving significance of Christ's work was that Christ fought against and conquered the evil powers that enslave humankind—the tyrants of sin, the devil, and death. God in Christ thus reconciles the world with himself (2 Cor 5:19). Salvation must therefore be defined in terms of victory rather than as a satisfaction we have to render to God or as a moral transformation in us. On this account, these two latter theories, particularly that of transformation, give people too important a role in the process of reconciliation. But in fact, everything in the atonement depends on what God does in Christ. Aulén referred to this victory model as the classic view of atonement, since he believed it was dominant in the early church. It is also often referred to as the dramatic model of atonement, since it gives central place to the drama of Christ's struggle and victory. Aulén saw Luther as one of the representatives of his model, and following in his tracks (Aulén was a Lutheran himself) he included the law of God with the evil powers that were conquered by Christ.

11.5. Atonement through Victory: Jesus Christ Victor

The first model of atonement tells us that the salvation that Christ provides is the result of his victory. Christ conquered the powers that hold the world and humanity in their grip and so became their Liberator. This theme is found in many places indeed in the New Testament. In Jesus's ministry we see how the powers that destroy human life, in body and spirit, flee when Jesus comes close. His proclamation of the kingdom is no empty word, as Jesus demonstrates in his power over the evil spirits (e.g., see Mark 1:21-28 and 5:1-20). The theological significance of these stories is not so much Jesus's confrontation with demonic powers that make his life difficult, but rather the totally *asymmetric* relationship between the two. Wherever Jesus appears and makes the kingdom a present reality, these powers must recede—and they know it. Wherever God comes, they are close to destruction and disappearance. In a surprising way the entire New Testament testifies of this conquering power. In Luke 10 we notice that the evil spirits are even subject to the disciples who have been sent out, and in a vision Jesus sees the devil fall from heaven (v. 18). In brief, where Jesus appears, the powers of evil must depart. In this vein we can read the healing stories in the Gospels as signs of the liberation Jesus brings. Where he comes, we are delivered from the powers that cause illness. The images of struggle, delivery, and victory frequently occur outside the Synoptic Gospels as well (John 12:31; 16:11; 1 Cor 15:24; Eph 1:20-22; Col 2:15; Heb 2:8; Rev 12:1-17). Even its impact on the church and its faith may be implied (Rom 8:37; 1 John 5:4).

The metaphor of Christ as Victor acquired a dominant place in the doctrine of the atonement in the early church. It put the death as well as the resurrection of Christ in a central place. Through his death and resurrection Christ was victorious over the power of the devil and over death and hell. In an ancient eucharistic prayer, attributed (Schwager 1986, 32) to Hippolytus of Rome (170-235), we read that Christ voluntarily subjected himself to suffering in order to break the chains the devil had used to bind him and to deliver the just. This image confronts us powerfully with the status of the powers and our deliverance from them. In early Christian liturgy the themes of death, hell, devil, and victory are closely intertwined. Baptism thus implies that the baptismal candidate is being delivered from the power of the devil.

Baptism has to do with being claimed and incorporated into a new community. In the form used in many Dutch Reformed churches, for instance, we read that in our baptism the triune God "lays his name upon us and brings us under his redemptive reign," and in the baptismal prayer we say, "May [the child] during its entire life serve you with joy and gratitude, fight with perseverance, and victoriously, against the devil and his entire rule, so that, at some future time it may, being comforted, depart from this life and appear without fear before the judgment seat of Christ" (appendix in *Liedboek* [Dutch ecumenical hymnal, 1973], 21, 24). For similar notions of turning away and turning toward, in which we can hear an echo of the praxis of exorcism, see the order for baptism as in use in Reformed churches in America (both RCA and CRC): "The minister addresses the candidates and, if children are being baptized, parents: Beloved of God, I ask you before God and Christ's church to reject evil, to profess your faith in Christ Jesus, and to confess the faith of the church. Do you renounce sin and the power of evil in your life and in the world? *I renounce them.* Who is your Lord and Savior? *Jesus Christ is my Lord and Savior*" ("Celebrating the Baptismal Covenant," in: *Worship the Lord: The Liturgy of the Reformed Church in America* [2015]).

Much less obvious, however, is the answer to the question of how this victory is realized. Clearly there is a victory, but how could the death of Christ play such a crucial role in that victory? In general, we can distinguish three explanations in the early church: Christ brought salvation by (1) his descent into hell, (2) catching the devil at his own game, and (3) offering an appropriate exchange or ransom.

1. The idea that, after his death, Christ descended into the netherworld is based on such texts as Matt 12:40, Acts 2:24 and 31, Eph 4:8–10, and 1 Pet 3:18–20. In itself this idea is unrelated to struggle against the devil, for originally the descent into the netherworld was related to the fate of the Old Testament believers. Would they share in the victory of Christ? According to Heb 11:40, God had determined that "apart from us [the early Christians] they should not be made perfect." The intent of Christ's descent into hell was, apparently, to proclaim the good news that the victory was won, to free souls from the waiting room (*limbo*) where they were bound, and to take them with him into heavenly glory (see also Heb 12:23, about "the spirits of just men made perfect"). To this idea of proclamation and deliverance the motif of struggle and war is added. Apparently, the delivery of the prisoners from the netherworld was not without difficulty but was accompanied by a fierce fight. Many icons depicting the resurrection show Christ seizing the gates of hell (for the idea that the hell has gates, see Matt 16:18). Whatever the case, in this view Jesus's descent into the realm of the dead (or "the descent into hell" or "the harrowing of hell") underlines how all-comprising and decisive was the victory that he won in his death and resurrection.

That Christ rattles the gates of the netherworld and, at last, uses his power to crash them is an ancient motif in Christian preaching. The idea that Christ brings order to the netherworld first appears in an official ecclesial document with the Confession of the Synod of Sirmium (in today's Serbia) in 359. We meet this motif even earlier in Eastern Church documents that resemble confessions of faith. Only later is the formula *descendit ad inferna* (he descended into hell) found in the *textus receptus* of the Apostles' Creed. Today, among other documents, the Roman breviary reads *descendit ad inferos* (he descended into the netherworld), referring not to the place of those who are doomed but to the shadowy sphere of the realm of the dead (the Sheol of the Old Testament). Why this "descent into hell" was later inserted into the creed can no longer be determined, but the place of insertion leaves no doubt that the descent into hell occurs after Christ's death, that is, after his "finished" work (John 19:30). In any case, the fact that Jesus's death—just like the death of any other human being—signifies a descent into the realm of the dead places it in the context of his victory. The Apostles' Creed does not speak of the devil in this connection (see below, 2 and 3). See Kelly, ECC 378-83, and Schwager 1986, 33-34.

In Calvin's explanation (*Inst.* 2.16.10-12) the descent into hell undergoes a fundamental shift in meaning. He views it as part of Christ's suffering on the cross, as the very culmination of what happened there. The descent into hell—the place of the absolute absence of God—represents all aspects of the pain that Christ suffered in his godforsakenness (Mark 15:34). For Calvin this step is no longer a part of Christ's victory but entails the deepest dimension of his suffering on the cross, his abandonment by God. The Heidelberg Catechism follows this explanation in Q/A 44, which well captures the depth of Christ's suffering and the comfort it yields. It assigns Christ's descent a vicarious character; this, too, he did for us.

We feel that the victory motif has stronger biblical-theological credentials than is often recognized. The New Testament positions this victory particularly in Christ's death and resurrection, but its witness is further supported by Christ's descent into hell (see, in addition to the text already mentioned, Rom 10:7; Col 1:18; 2:15) and his ascension into heaven (Luke 24:51; Acts 1:9; e.g., see also 1 Pet 3:22, in parallel with 3:19 about the descent into hell; in both cases the same verb for "going" is used). It should be noted that the Reformed tradition strongly emphasizes the importance of Jesus's bodily ascension—first to underscore that Christ, in his humanity and bodily existence, is now in heaven and therefore cannot be present in the bread and wine of the communion (see Farrow 1999 and his essay in Alston and Welker, RT 351-71). By contrast, Jesus's descent into hell has been spiritualized ever since Calvin. From a biblical-theological perspective Calvin's move was justifiable, for hell is where one is totally forsaken by God (as in the Old Testament Sheol or the realm of the dead, Ps 6:5; 30:9; 115:17). But when this view excludes other aspects (which has its own motives in protest against softening representations of death and the netherworld, as in the idea of the limbo; *Inst.* 2.16.8–9), we do insufficient justice to the sequence of the Apostles' Creed and the New Testament data already referred to. Admittedly, texts such as 1 Pet 3:18–22 are difficult to fully comprehend. First Peter 4:6, which is often linked to this doctrine, has another meaning; it is about the fate of loved ones who have died—maybe those on whose behalf some (as we read in 1 Cor 15:29) belatedly wanted to be baptized, if that had not happened during their lifetime.

The theological significance of all this discussion is the important point, however, which is not obscure. Texts about Christ's descent into hell and his ascension tell us that Christ's victory over the powers of evil is no mere insignificant incident; rather, it reverberates to the most distant corners of the universe. In terms of the Old Testament worldview of three layers (Exod 20:4), in heaven above, the earth below, but also in the netherworld, the message of Christ's victory is heard and celebrated (see also Matt 27:51–53). To keep this cosmic scope of Christ's resurrection in mind, it would be good if the descent into hell and the ascension would receive more attention, just as they do in the Apostles' Creed, as parallel witnesses that accompany and support the gospel of Easter. At this point Eph 4:8–10 leads the way. Jesus did not just ascend to heaven. He also descended to hell, that is, to the realm of death, where any contact with God is impossible. Of course, these two representations need not be expressed in terms of an outdated cosmology but ought to be translated in terms of our contemporary multidimensional worldview to make them intelligible for today. In this light, there may be good reason for the church, and possibly society at large, to celebrate not only an Ascension Day but also a Descent-into-Hell Day.

2. Early Christians also explained how Christ's death signified victory by the notion of the devil as the deceived deceiver. The devil gained his hold over the earliest human ancestors, Adam and Eve, by deceiving them and leading them into temptation (Gen 3:13; for the identification of the serpent with the devil, see Rev 12:9). Ever since, the devil has been the ruler of this earth. The victory over the devil now results, according to a widespread and popular idea, from a clever plot. The bait is the humanity that the Son of God takes upon himself; the devil is the fish that goes after the bait; he swallows it and is thus caught.

On this account, the Son of God, by being sent in human flesh, gives the devil the impression that in Jesus of Nazareth he is faced with a weak human being. By having Jesus condemned to death, the devil plans to get Jesus in his power. The opposite transpires, however. Jesus's divinity hooks the fish in the mouth, and the devil chokes on it. The devil cannot keep his victim under his power; he is himself overpowered. We see this motif in many sermons!

One example is the following extract from a sermon that tradition has attributed to John Chrysostom.

> I [Jesus] speak these words not from fear of death: "Father, if possible, may this cup pass from me." I am rather speaking of a hidden mystery. These words are as a bait for the devil. With these words I must entice him toward the bait. The devil saw me do many signs. How I was healing the sick by laying my hands on them, and how, with one single word, I dismissed legions of devils. Such deeds inevitably showed him that I am God's son, and he had to consider that my death on the cross would be his destruction, my descent into the netherworld would break his iron lock and crash his strong gate. If he considers this, he will flee and will not crucify me.
>
> What must I do now? As a good fisherman I use my craftiness. I will pretend that I fear death and say: "Father, if possible, may this cup pass from me." Such humble words should make him think that I am afraid and want to escape from death. These words must prompt him to erect, in the center of the earth, the mystery of the cross. I must come up with a ruse, as an experienced fisherman would; I must endure everything to save the lives of all people. So, the devil thinks: "Yes, he is also a human being! I have devoured Abraham, Isaac, Jacob, the patriarchs and the prophets—I will also devour this man." However, when he devours Christ, he will also find me in his stomach with the power of God. The deceiver is deceived. (PG 61:753-54, quoted in Schwager 1986, 35)

3. A third variant of the victory motif casts the end result not so much as a matter of deception but as the payment of an adequate price. The devil attacks Jesus, while Jesus—in contrast to all other people—is sinless. This means that the devil made a fateful mistake and has thus lost his right to rule humanity. In this mode of thinking, Jesus's life is the price paid to ransom the human race. Often, as for instance with Origen and Gregory of Nyssa, this image was combined with that of the deceived deceiver. It is suggested that the devil had agreed to accept Christ as a ransom for the souls that he kept as prisoners, but when the exchange took place, he found that he had brought the power of life into the home of the dead. And where the Light enters, the darkness has lost (see Green and Baker 2000, 121-23, also for the point that the early church was all too familiar with hostage taking and paying ransom).

The idea that our salvation may be the product of crafty deceit or paying the devil ransom might seem rather bizarre and fanciful to us at first sight. And indeed, even though the image of a ransom payment, in particular, has some support in the New Testament (Mark 10:45 and 1 Tim 2:6), when measured by the scarcity of detail in the Bible, these notions are very speculative. Nonetheless, they contain biblical elements that are important for today's dogmatics (see Migliore, FSU 183). In the first place, the motif of deception points to the hidden ways of God's love. God does not win through brute power or violence. Acording to Paul, in fact, it is incomprehensible—it is outright foolishness—that the cross is God's ultimate means of realizing his plan of salvation (1 Cor 1:18-31). To the powers of this world, salvation through the cross was a totally unexpected outcome (1 Cor 2:8). Second, it is true that the evil powers not only destroy others but themselves. The powers that employ a terror of lies and deceit in the end fall on their own sword (see Matt 26:52).

Ever since Aulén introduced it, many have followed him in reconsidering the victory motif. In this rethinking the New Testament "principalities and powers" (Col 2:15), over which Christ also triumphed, are often applied to all sorts of repressive regimes. It is exegetically dubious whether this interpretation is correct, for the phrase seems primarily to point to powers of a demonic (e.g., Stott 2006, 271) or a cosmic (Kooten 2003, 121-35) nature. There is no need, however, to reduce the gospel to a political statement in seeking a warrant for this application. Paul states that the cross of Christ runs contrary to "the wisdom of this age or of the rulers of this age, who are doomed to pass away" (1 Cor 2:6). Jesus himself fell victim to these rulers (v. 8), but they do not have the final word. Seen in that light, the victory of Christ remains for contemporary Christians an important source of inspiration not to simply submit to repressive and dictatorial regimes that enslave people, for these powers and structures have already been unmasked by Christ and have no future (Wink 1999).

But there is more that makes this motif of struggle and victory relevant and useful. While modern people have become convinced that we are no longer part of a world of powers and demons, we know full well that we are in the grip of all kinds of laws, mechanisms, and seemingly irresistible patterns of development. These may assume the form of collective addictions (such as the drive to consume), cultural myths (such as constant growth and progress), mass anxieties (islamophobia, xenophobia), nationalism, fashion, or the pressure to be healthy and successful. A focus on good health and vitality can quickly become an idol when it becomes the principal obsession of people and cultures. Instead of trusting God, we court other powers and soon find ourselves in their grasp. The idea of being devil-possessed may not be so alien when we consider how much we have lost power over our own lives. The petition "Deliver us from evil" in the Lord's Prayer remains utterly relevant.

An important variant of the victory motif is referred to in the literature as the physical doctrine of salvation, as found especially in Athanasius. This views the victory of Christ as primarily a victory not over the devil but over death. Athanasius argued that, by turning away from God, the source of life, Adam was left with the vulnerability and the corruptibility that belong to human nature. Salvation is accomplished by the Son, who, through his divine nature, so penetrates and transforms our human nature that in the resurrection of the dead we can share in his immortality. He, the Logos, became human so that we might become deified (*De incarnatione Verbi* 54; *Contra Arianos* 1.39). In his movement from high to low, Christ takes upon himself the humility, guilt, and subjection to mortality, so that in a countermovement from low to high, he may clothe us with his glory and immortality. In this connection we sometimes speak of *theōsis*, a Greek term that we will examine in more detail in chapter 15. The literal meaning is deification, which is misleading. It does not intend to say that we "become God" but that, through God's grace, we may share in incorruptibility and glory.

In the death of Christ two elements, our malaise and God's glory, converge in such a way that we may share in the divine glory. The motif of the "miraculous exchange" we meet later in Luther and Calvin. Whereas the Eastern Church traditionally expressed this exchange mostly in terms of death and life, or of corruptibility and incorruptibility, the church of the West focused more on sin and grace, guilt and forgiveness.

Note the straightforward expression in the classic Reformed communion form. "He was bound in the garden, so that he would set us free. He suffered immeasurable abuse, so that we would never be put to shame. While innocent he is condemned to death, so that we would be acquitted in the judgment of God. He took the curse of us all upon him, so that he would fill us with his blessing. On the cross he humbled himself in body and soul unto the deepest depth of rejection and the terror of hell, when he cried with a loud voice: 'My God, my God, why have you forsaken me?' (Matt 27:46) so that we would be accepted and never be forsaken by him. And finally, through his death and the shedding of his blood, he completely fulfilled the eternal and new covenant of grace and reconciliation, when he said: 'It is finished' (John 19:30)." In contemporary forms of the theology of the cross, we see how the Eastern accent on death and life has often been adopted, for instance, in the motif of the death of death (*mors mortis*). Although this motif can be found in Luther, it came to more prominence in recent Western theology; for example, see Jüngel 1974.

11.6. Atonement through Satisfaction: The Hard Core of Redemption

The soteriology that became very influential in the West is inextricably connected with the name of Anselm of Canterbury. The key word in his view of atonement is *satisfactio*, usually translated into English with the similar word "satisfaction." Reconciliation is accomplished through the vicarious sacrifice of Christ for the sins of humanity. The word "satisfaction" has contributed to the bad reputation that this view has acquired for many people. Does not this approach portray God as someone who is out for revenge and demands satisfaction? Does it not make reconciliation a kind of cosmic business transaction without any involvement on our part? Or does this model express something that must indeed be counted as the hard core of the Christian doctrine of atonement, namely, that Jesus Christ is not just a model for us to imitate but vicariously does something for us in his life, suffering, and death? We believe the latter is the case. Christ does something in our place—something we do not and cannot do.

The model of atonement through vicarious suffering has unmistakable biblical roots. With the history of Jesus as a vivid memory, the early Christians reread the prophets and could interpret what Isa 53 said about the Suffering Servant only as a striking prophecy of Jesus (note Acts 8:32-35). In Gal 3:13, Rom 3:23, and the Letter to the Hebrews we find traces of an interpretation that places the significance of Jesus's death against the background of the sacrificial cult. Jesus is the sin offering that suffers vicariously for the sins of the people. The people are acquitted as the lamb is slaughtered. In the sacrificial cult we see a movement for the benefit of the sinner. By what he or she has done, the sinner has lost the right to live and is separated from God, the source of life. But in the provision of a sin-offering God gives Israel a path toward restoration (e.g., see Lev 17:11). God does not want us to die but to live, and for that reason he offers us a way of escape.

For the ritual to work, the one who brings the sacrifice must identify himself with the sacrificial animal (*identification*, or consecration, is often symbolized by the laying on of hands, e.g., Lev 16:1-28); the sacrificial animal is then slaughtered (*mactation*), and then the blood of this sacrifice is applied to the altar (*incorporation*). In this confrontation with the sacred a decisive turn occurs, the turning around that God himself wanted and realized (see the seminal essay on atonement in Gese 1981, 93–116).

Anselm laid out his view of atonement in his book *Cur Deus homo* (Why God became man, completed in 1098). It is set against the background of medieval feudal society, which was characterized by an elaborate system of rankings, relationships, duties, and rights. Anselm rejects the popular idea that, as a result of our fall into sin, God lost his right to reign and the devil became the actual ruler or owner of the earth instead. One might say that Anselm contrasted this view with the words of Ps 24:1: "The earth is the LORD's and the fullness thereof." Being accustomed to a society in which each member has his or her proper place, Anselm states that man has not given God what is his, that is, his honor (Lat. *honor*), even though man owed it to God (*debitum*). Is it actually possible that God in his majesty is dishonored by man? No, Anselm replies, God is too lofty for that. Nevertheless, something has gone awry in the relationship. The web of mutuality (the *ordo*) has been damaged. In the relational system each person has his or her specific place, king as well as subject. Therefore, it is not fitting that God would simply accept the consequences of the fall. God wants to replace the fallen angels with human beings; he wants creation to attain its purpose.

So how will God bring restoration? Will he do so by condemning us to capital punishment (*poena*)? Or is there a possibility that we will restore the damage and bring things to order? This second possibility is what Anselm refers to as satisfaction (*satisfactio*). God opts for the path of satisfaction, which is quite different from destruction. Satisfaction does not equal revenge. We should rather see it as a reciprocation by which the sinner restores the relationship. We might compare it to the modern method of punishment that requires community service. The transgressor is given an opportunity to return to his or her place in society by demonstrating good faith. Next, Anselm discusses how this satisfaction is realized. On the one hand, the debt must be paid by the person who has incurred it, but on the other hand, it is clear that an ordinary person is unable to perform what is required as an adequate compensation for the weight of sin. A person who dishonors God commits a sin for which no mortal can ever compensate. For this reason, compensation must be rendered by someone who is human but at the same time has divine power. This person is the God-man Jesus Christ.

Jesus does not merely demonstrate the obedience that was required of him as a human being, but he also yields up his life—voluntarily. This immeasurable act of love produces an infinite reward, because through the *unio personalis* (see chap. 10) it is the Son himself who does the act. One particular human being earns such a great reward that all of us may borrow from it and offer it to God. Anselm's argument has been defined as a judicial theory of atonement. We do not agree with this label if judicial is understood as a mere arrangement of rights and duties. Rather, Anselm is attempting to define the relationship between us and God as a sociopsychological system in which mutual relationships not only bear an external significance but are also internally meaningful and binding.

For recent Anselm studies that lead to a new appreciation for his theory of atonement in this regard, see especially Greshake 1983, Gäde 1989, and Plasger 1993. For a contemporary English translation of the text of *Cur Deus homo*, see Anselm 1998, 260-356.

The Heidelberg Catechism (HC), Lord's Days 4-6, replicates the reasoning of *Cur Deus homo* (CDH), but with some noteworthy differences that prompt us to review the whole topic in light of its biblical contexts. The argumentation of the Heidelberg Catechism seems to render God's justice and compassion as opposites; God can be compassionate only if his justice has been satisfied (Q/A 11). The last section of this answer seems to have lost sight of the Old Testament testimony that the path to reconciliation is initiated and offered by God himself. Nonetheless, the HC also indicates in its own way that God is the giver and initiator of the atonement. In the climax of its argumentation we read that the Mediator "was given to us . . . by God [*qui factus est nobis . . . a Deo*]" (answer 18). In other words, God does not have to be persuaded to change his mind. Still, the HC can stand some biblical-theological improvement. Studies of the Old Testament concept of *tsedaqah* (justice, righteousness) over the last century have shown that justice and compassion are not opposites but complementary. Even though it does not lack a retributive-corrective aspect, God's *tsedaqah* primarily expresses his faithfulness to his acts and thus to his goodness and compassion. Therefore (to the amazement of Luther), the psalmist could write, "In your righteousness deliver me and rescue me" (71:2). A frequently heard objection against the Heidelberg Catechism is that it erases the difference between punishment and satisfaction that is still found in Anselm. Anselm argued on a basis of a theory of merits, while in the Reformation, with its stress on the personal aspect of the relationship with God, this framework falls away. As a result, the context for interpreting Christ's death shifted from the principles of civil law to those of criminal law. Moreover, it has been argued against this view of atonement that, in both the HC and Anselm, God seems to be bound to a law that is superior to him. But this interpretation of CDH no longer finds support, while in the HC God is first and foremost bound to his own justice and not to something outside or above him. The structure of God's actions in creation and redemption are fully dependent on God himself.

Therefore, although there are differences between CDH and the HC, there is certainly no major rift. Behind diverging verbal expressions we find strongly related concepts. For instance, the concept of justice in the HC, like the concept of honor in CDH, clearly conveys that God cannot simply ignore sin because he feels insulted and because of any external law. He cannot ignore sin because of himself and his creation! Moreover, it is also clear that, for Anselm, satisfaction and punishment are not identical: since in the Bible human sin must be punished by death (Rom 5:12; 6:23; see also Gen 2:17), Jesus has, through his satisfaction, undergone our death and thereby also borne our (not his!) punishment. Even though this point remains implicit with Anselm, it does lie in the background. Today, more than in the past, we realize the extent to which the evil that destroys good relationships calls for correction and compensation, as well as forgiveness. CDH and the HC each formulate this awareness, when it comes to the relationship with God, in biblical terms. Both want to say that we are dealing with "another kind of grace" (Gäde 1989) than the dubious form that can ignore sin. This other kind of compassion and grace—as Christ's incarnation, suffering, and death demonstrated—receives full emphasis in the HC. And in the final analysis, this tenderness does not stand in contrast to God's justice, for also in Q/A 16–18 of the HC, its first intent is to restore humanity in our relationship to God. In sum, in both the CDH (2.19) and the HC (Q/A 18), the intent of "satisfaction" is our salvation.

Thus, behind the formulations that may cause misunderstandings, we also recognize the important biblical notions in the HC. They include a strong awareness that sin is no stray action but involves a destruction of right relationships; it demands not only repentance but also a concrete correction and compensation. It also firmly asserts that Christ has accomplished that correction on our behalf, which is implied in the New Testament affirmation that Christ "died for us" (see Rom 3:23–28; 5:8–9; Gal 3:13, also the Letter to the Hebrews). Christ has become the sin offering that covers human guilt and thus destroys the power of death.

Christ's work is here described as something that happens outside of us, *extra nos*, but that has been done for us (*pro nobis*) and for our benefit. This is the reasoning we find with the Reformers: one human being, Jesus Christ, suffers the penalty for sin, the burden of capital punishment, and God considers this punishment of suffering to be one for all of us. But only Christ can undertake this substitutionary task, since he is not only human but also the Son of God, and thus has an enormous capacity for suffering (HC 17). This is the road along which God's saving intent and grace are realized. Could it have been otherwise? We really should not try to answer that question, since it can easily lead to all kinds of speculation. Of fundamental importance, in any case, is the conviction that salvation, as the restoration of relationships, comes from outside of ourselves. Being just before God does not originate in us; our own good will is not adequate to realign our relationships. Forgiveness is a gift, an offer of progress, of new life, which never can be forced. Luther therefore spoke of a joyful exchange. Christ bears the punishment while we are acquitted; Christ suffers death while we receive the promise of eternal life.

The term "forensic theory of justification" is often used in this connection. The new relationship realized by Christ, which puts us aright—being righteous—is a righteousness that we do not owe to ourselves. It is a "strange" kind of righteousness (Lat. *iustitia aliena*). By counting this righteousness of Christ from outside of ourselves as ours (*imputatio*), God henceforth sees us as belonging to Christ. What is true for him is now also true for all those who are "in him." For the implications, see also chapter 15.

The thought that Christ bore the penalty for our sins is one of the main pillars of Calvin's theology (*Inst.* 2.15.6). In his priestly office (see 11.4 above), Christ obtains reconciliation and thereby removes God's righteous anger. Here Calvin is part of a long tradition that began with Athanasius (Edmondson 2004, 20-21) in which humans must bear and suffer God's anger. Does this mean that God was angry toward humanity until the moment that Christ intervened? Calvin struggles with that question, but at last suggests that "God the Father, by his love, prevents and anticipates our reconciliation in Christ." Yes, since he first loved us (1 John 4:19), he subsequently reconciled us with him (*Inst.* 2.16.3). God already loved us while, because of our sins, we were still his enemies (*Inst.* 2.16.4). However, full acceptance by God becomes a fact only when Christ has united us with him. This happens—and here we find, just as in HC 20-21, a pneumatological extra in comparison to Anselm—only through an act of personal faith. Through the gift of faith the Spirit connects us with Christ, and thus we can actually share in his "benefits." Or, as Paul wrote, "Since we are justified by faith, we have peace with God through our Lord Jesus Christ" (Rom 5:1).

Ever since it was composed, the satisfaction theory of the atonement has met with much criticism. It is often faulted for having been excessively conditioned by the medieval feudal system of Anselm's day. But the theory has always had its ardent supporters as well, so it would seem that the debate is not simply a function of cultural shifts. Peter Abelard (1079-1142) stressed other elements, even though he was Anselm's contemporary. At the time of the Reformation, Faustus Socinus (1539-1604) and his followers strongly resisted the idea that God could not "simply" decide to forgive, without compensation for the evil that has been done. In the history of Dutch theology the critical attitude of H. Wiersinga (1971) and C. J. den Heyer (1998) repeatedly led to intense controversies in their denomination. In these disputes others defended the Anselmian view with even greater fervor. Ironically enough, the dogmatics of reconciliation have often become a bone of contention, with all too little willingness for reconciliation displayed among the contenders. It should be noted that similar discussions were (and are) also taking place in other countries; see Holmes 2007 for a good overview of the Anglophone evangelical world.

The satisfaction theory of atonement has strong credentials. It has never been a point of dispute between Rome and the Reformation but is accepted on both sides. The only controversial aspect involved how we as human beings share subjectively in the atonement. We believe the Anselmian-Reformational view of atonement clarifies a number of key elements in the New Testament's testimony about the significance of the work of Christ. The most difficult issue—one in fact covered by the Reformational and not, or at most only implicitly, by the Anselmian variant—is undoubtedly the thought that, in his suffering and death, Christ bore in our place the wrath and penalty of God. Nowhere in the New Testament is this literally stated, and the self-evident way in which the formula is often used fails to do justice to its staggering meaning. But texts like John 3:36, Rom 8:3, and especially Gal 3:13, with Isa 53:5 in the background, come very close to this notion (see also Berkhof, CF 309-11). Proposals for a theory of atonement that try to avoid such concepts (e.g., see Weaver 2011) are therefore not very convincing from a biblical-theological point of view.

The persistent criticism that the satisfaction theory has attracted down through the centuries stems (if we see it correctly) from the fact that its proponents detach this aspect of redemption in Christ from other aspects that are just as important. Its advocates can give the impression that, because of Christ's vicarious role, it is possible for us to live in a right relationship with God without demonstrating a forgiving attitude ourselves, that it is irrelevant that we ourselves reflect the love of Christ to others who may have offended us. As if this was not the test of truly sharing in Christ's reconciliation (see Matt 18:21-35)! This is really a critical misapprehension that does not justify criticism of this theory of atonement, but it does make that criticism more understandable.

11.7. Atonement through Transformation: What the Way of Jesus Does with Us

The third classic model focuses on us as partners in the process of reconciliation. Reconciliation is at stake when a person experiences a transformation whereby he or she undergoes a process of inner change and is thus turned around. Not until we respond to God by choosing a life without injustice and violence can reconciliation take place. Peter Abelard is usually seen as the originator of this model and is thereby taken to stand in archetypal contrast to his contemporary Anselm. That picture is incorrect to the extent that Abelard also saw Christ's submission of his life as a sin offering for us. But he did place greater emphasis on the example Jesus gave in this submission, an example that should inspire us so that we ourselves live a life characterized by love and a forgiving spirit. This approach is often referred to as the subjective, or effective, theory of atonement. Other well-known representatives of this model are Faustus Socinus (with his book *De Jesu Christo Servatore* [1594]) and Albrecht Ritschl (*Die Christliche Lehre von der Rechtfertigung und Versöhnung* [1870-74]).

The multitude of names and definitions for the various theories and models of atonement can get rather confusing. The so-called objective theories do not always claim that God is the object of the atonement (i.e., the one who needs to be reconciled in order to free himself of his wrath) but rather that the atonement between God and humanity is primarily realized in an objective reality outside of us. God intervenes in a concrete way to deal with the sin problem; Jesus's sacrifice takes care of our guilt. This action happens totally outside of us and may be further clarified in terms of *satisfaction* or *penal substitution*. Such theories are also at times referred to as the constitutive approach: Jesus's self-surrender, including his suffering on the cross, constitutes the atonement. Subjective theories explain atonement primarily as *a positive change in the human subject*. Wiersinga (1971) spoke in this connection of the "shock-effect" that Jesus's persevering love may have on us. The real atonement is not in Jesus's act but in our conversion that follows as its effect (which is why we also speak of effective theories). In the Anglophone world this model is most often referred to as the *moral influence theory*, secondarily, as the *exemplary theory*. Jesus's example exercises a moral influence on us, and as a result we experience conversion; thus we sometimes hear of the *conversion model*. In this view God's actions in Christ are not constitutive of our atonement, for there is nothing to be compensated for or corrected. What God does in Christ demonstrates that he does not wish our destruction but rather a restored relationship in which evil is conquered by what is good. It might be added that Christ's suffering on the cross shows how far God will go in his love to pay the price that is demanded for the unconditional forgiveness he offers us (e.g., Brümmer 2005, 78, 87).

We feel that the contrasts that are often created between these various models are rather artificial, for each of them can appeal to biblical motifs and backgrounds. Much better than playing them off against each other would be to reflect on them in conjunction with each other.

This transformational, or conversion, model can also claim to be firmly anchored in the Scriptures. It focuses on the purpose of God's turning toward us and on his love. The reconciliation process is complete, and its purpose achieved, only when we respond to God's love with our love. This response presupposes a process of transformation on our part. This third model fits well with the world of the Gospel and Epistles of John, and with Augustine's spirituality. We find in this literature many references to the sinful woman in Luke 7:47, who, we read, loved Jesus and anointed him. We may point to the anxious responses and questions of the people who heard Peter preach his sermon in Acts 2:37: "What shall we do?" And we can refer to 2 Cor 5:19-21, where Paul argues that, in Christ, God was reconciling the world unto himself—and then follows up with an appeal: "Be reconciled to God!" For Paul, the factuality of the salvation that God has realized in Christ does not preclude our being exhorted to open ourselves to this reality.

In short, the transformation model with its biblical roots has excellent theological credentials. It does not have to be seen as excluding the model of atonement through satisfaction, even though in practice it has often and unfortunately been characterized as an approach in opposition to the Anselmian model. Playing off these two against each other as subjective vs. objective theories of atonement fails to do justice to the biblical testimony regarding reconciliation. Together with the victory model, they form a totality of biblical perspectives that are dogmatically supplementary and must not be reduced to a single concept. Their different emphases reflect the differences between the christological and the pneumatological perspectives. In Christ a new reality has arrived, the reconciliation between God and humanity; in the Spirit we are led into this mystery and transformed to a new life as we follow Christ. Any Trinitarian theology that bases itself on Jesus and the Spirit as the two hands of God will employ at least three themes when it speaks about the atonement: (1) the death and resurrection of Christ are the axis of the event in which God the Father conquers the power of the devil and death, (2) Jesus Christ bears and removes the guilt of sin, and (3) the Holy Spirit changes us into new people who have died with Christ and have been raised to a new life.

A more recent example of the transformation model is the theory of the *scapegoat mechanism* as elaborated in a number of publications by cultural anthropologist René Girard. Girard maintains that violence lies at the very base of human culture and is evoked by the mechanism of mimetic desire. The fact that someone else possesses a particular object makes me want it. I might not want the thing as such, but since the other possesses it, an urge arises to imitate—I want what the other person has. The first owner thus becomes a model for me, and as a result we become rivals. This mimetic process (Gk. *mimēsis*, "imitation") may become so intense that the rivals become totally obsessed with each other, deriving their identity from the other. My very identity is then determined by what the other has and what I do not. Spread across an entire community, such tensions may build to the point that violence erupts, targeting a group or an individual as a scapegoat (Lev 16). A particular category of people (e.g., Jews, witches, redheads, Muslims, foreigners) is seen to be the source of all misfortune and misery. By banning, excluding, or destroying them (see Lev 16:9-10), all suppressed feelings of frustration and unrest become focused on one spot. The scapegoat becomes a symbol for the rival. Atonement rituals in such cultures help maintain social equilibrium and prevent the escalation of violence. Girard calls this the scapegoat mechanism that has been unmasked in the history of Jesus. The death of Jesus Christ reveals the violent character of human culture and serves as a brake on mimetic violence. In Christ's death a radical, nonviolent God is confronted with violent people. Understanding this scapegoat mechanism puts the ax to the roots of violence, leading to transformations. For a summary and criticism, see Boersma 2004, 133-51.

In the most recent reflections on the atonement, we see a great sensitivity to the need to speak of God's reconciliation in Christ in a way that refuses to promote violence. This tendency usually also leads to an emphasis on moral transformation as the aim of Jesus's atoning work, even though at times the victory model is also brought into the equation. For a specific application from a Mennonite (i.e., pacifist) source, see Weaver 2011; for further discussion and criticism, see Sanders 2006, especially 1–46.

In sum, we make a strong plea not to let the three classic ways of speaking about redemption and reconciliation in Christ compete against each other, but to keep them together and allow each to complement the others. In that way we may somewhat better comprehend the length, breadth, and depth of Christ's love and be filled with God's perfection (Eph 3:19-20). Christ delivers us from the deadly forces that dominate our life. He atones for the guilt of sin and inspires and transforms us through his Spirit to a new way of facing life. Only by allowing for these different voices in our theological reflection can we do justice to the plurality of metaphors—borrowed from the military, judicial, economic, and cultic domains of life—that the Bible uses to speak about God's atonement (see Gunton 1988, Green and Baker 2000).

A question that we have thus far left aside is whether the salvific significance of Christ's work is specifically found in his suffering, death, and resurrection, or also in his life and ministry. Accordingly, in the last three sections of this chapter we will sketch the soteriological meaning of the different phases in the journey that Jesus undertook, as the Gospels record it. We will briefly examine how Jesus's life, followed by his suffering, death, and resurrection, may be understood as different aspects of the salvation that he has brought.

11.8. The New Humanity: Jesus's Life

In the previous sections we have briefly reviewed how people have thought in the past about the salvation that Christ provides. Now we take another look at our topic, proceeding on the basis of the life of Jesus as the one who was sent by the Father. We intend to stay as close to the Bible as possible and will refer less to secondary literature.

What, in brief, is the new piece that Christ adds? Or in classic terminology, what is the soteriological significance of his life and ministry? Recall from the previous chapter how Jesus told his disciples, in the prayer that he taught them, to address God as "our Father." What Jesus has achieved is to make it possible for people to respond to his invitation. They get involved in the communion between him and the Father, and they may also address God as Father. Jesus lived on the basis of total orientation and freedom toward God. Recall again that this freedom, as well as his openness to people, was the result of Jesus having been anointed with the Spirit. The Spirit of the Father being upon him makes him the Anointed One, the Messiah. Our salvation flows from the life-giving communion with the Father that Christ wants to share with those who are his. In this way he proclaims the kingdom of God as the new regime, the new dispensation that is about to break through. In its wake everything that is in discord with this saving reign of God and with living in his communion will be overcome. This is the messianic character of Jesus's ministry (see Matt 11:5 in connection with John the Baptist's question in 11:3).

Classic dogmatics has often undervalued how the kingdom of God plays a central role in the preaching and ministry of Jesus as the fulfillment of prophetic expectation. In Dutch theology this situation was remedied by H. Ridderbos's important study (1962) of this theme. This lack of attention stems from undervaluing the salvific significance of Jesus's life in comparison with his suffering and death. By contrast, contemporary pleas for a rehabilitation of the kingdom tend to view the message about the kingdom and the message about atonement as mutually exclusive alternatives (possibly to be ascribed to Jesus and Paul, respectively). We believe there is no reason for this separation, since the Gospels, as they gradually unfold the story, show that "the motif of suffering was one of the most constitutive factors in determining the meaning of Jesus's kingdom proclamation" (Ridderbos 1962, 169–70, who points out that a denial of this connection is "one of the main reasons for all kinds of one-sidedness and aberrations in the exposition of Jesus's preaching of the kingdom of heaven"). Particularly in the passages about the Last Supper we find a close link between soteriology and eschatology, between the atonement and the kingdom. Jesus's suffering and death is the pathway for "many" to a full communion between him and those who are his in the kingdom of God (see Mark 14:24–25). Jesus's atoning death on the cross appears to be the pathway along which the kingdom on earth takes shape. Note the extensive and largely convincing work of N. T. Wright on this field (e.g., 1996, chaps. 10 and 12).

As we seek an answer to the question about the substance of the salvation that Jesus brings, we will not restrict ourselves to the cross and the resurrection. We must see the cross and the resurrection in connec-

471

tion with his life. The ministry of Jesus and his proclamation led to his execution by crucifixion, followed by the resurrection. In that sense we may say that the cross and resurrection became the zenith of his life. But this point of culmination also sheds light on what went before, and the events that followed (esp. Pentecost) are also to be viewed in this light. Life, cross, and resurrection belong together and cannot be separated.

The text of the Apostles' Creed may easily create the impression that Jesus's life is unimportant. Right after "born of the virgin Mary" the text jumps to "suffered under Pontius Pilate." The Heidelberg Catechism interprets this jump by suggesting that his entire life was a form of suffering (Q/A 37). In classic theology the life of Jesus is characterized by the concept of active obedience (*obedientia activa*), meaning that Jesus followed the path of obedience to the Torah, as he was supposed to do in his humanity. This was distinguished from the passive obedience (*obedientia passiva*) that he showed in taking upon himself the suffering for the guilt of the world, which was laid upon him by the Father (see Heppe, RD, chap. 19). If this wording established a potential connection between the two aspects, in practice, attention tended to focus rather exclusively on the passive obedience.

We can put the matter differently: Christian soteriology is anchored in the life of Jesus. The communion Jesus experienced with the Father, the source from which he lived during his earthly existence, is the salvific means par excellence that God uses in his invitation to us. God works in Jesus and reveals himself in him. Here is a life that is lived in communion with God, which leaves no space for any distance from God or for any mistrust. Here is realized what the Father intended from the very beginning, namely, a life in communion with him. In Jesus the blessing promised to Abraham is completely fulfilled. In the previous chapter we therefore spoke about Jesus's sonship. The term "Son" refers to the ultimate identity of Jesus Christ. In all respects he lived in and for God as his Father. Now we want to explore what this reality means for us. What does it open up for us, and what are the dimensions of this liberating and life-providing reality?

When we find our point of departure in the communion that Jesus experienced with his Father, we notice first of all how this relation was reflected in an unexpected and abundant humanity. In his ministry and proclamation Jesus realizes a form of humanity that does not create isolation from God and is not inspired by fear and mistrust. He lives fully on the basis of this relationship with God, and as a result, God's love is revealed in an astounding way in what he does. Jesus crosses boundaries that in his context and culture seemed impossible to transcend. Precisely because he is so intimately connected with God the Father, he can touch sick people who were ceremonially unclean. He was a Jew but was accessible to gentiles. He was a man but related to women in a way of total integrity that did them justice. What is demonstrated around him and through him is an atmosphere of *righteousness* that enables people to step forward and flourish. The gospel descriptions make clear that Jesus's actions had a public character; they were for everyone to see. Things happened right before their eyes. In this respect he shows himself to be the Prophet of the divine kingdom; he tells his compatriots publicly what God intends for them. Christian tradition has thus referred to his prophetic office. We are furthermore confronted in the gospel, and in the same public manner, with the fierce reaction this telling could trigger, including disapproval and scorn: "This man receives sinners and eats with them!" (Luke 15:2; see also Matt 11:19). Jesus associates in great freedom with all the various groups in society, with all their prohibitions and prejudices. His approach of enabling people to come into their own and of doing them justice is liberating. The theme of freedom and deliverance, which has deep roots in the Old Testament (esp. in Exodus and Deutero-Isaiah), is very present in the Gospels.

The open, inviting, and fruitful character of Jesus's ministry as the Messiah is demonstrated in the way in which Jesus invites people, or rather urges them, to respond to God's appeal. People who have lost their way, who have become estranged from God and from themselves, are urged to participate in this new, eschatological community in which God's righteousness and peace will suffuse all relationships. Thus Jesus fulfills the promises regarding the Messiah and introduces the messianic dispensation of the new covenant (Jer 31:31). The hospitality Jesus manifests and realizes on God's behalf tells us that he makes room for people who are estranged from, who even violate, his work and intent—in other words, for sinners. It also means that he was very critical of those who wanted to maintain the status quo with a religion that was focused on external things and that obstructed the way to the kingdom for others (Matt 23:13). The long diatribes against "the Pharisees and the scribes" occupy a sizable portion of the Gospels (see Matt 15:1–20 and Matt 23 and pars.). This dual approach of Jesus impressed his disciples and certainly also a wider circle of followers. Reading the gospel stories, we discover the impressions that Jesus left behind (e.g., Matt 11:18–19). There is no way we can say that Jesus is portrayed as an ordinary person.

We see both amazement and a lack of understanding in the reactions of his audience.

The words in which Jesus summarized his own mission (Luke 4:18-19) sound not so much like a program but like an attack on the normal course of affairs. "The Spirit of the Lord is upon me, because he has anointed me to preach good news to the poor. He has sent me to proclaim release to the captives and recovering of sight to the blind, to set at liberty those who are oppressed, to proclaim the acceptable year of the Lord." We can read this text from the perspective of the threefold office. Jesus's ministry has prophetic, priestly, and kingly/ liberating characteristics—and these three are closely interconnected. To these we can connect love, hospitality, and liberation, respectively, as the key concepts to describe the ministry and humanity of Jesus. He heals the sick, touches the lepers in order to heal them, and makes the deaf hear. These are the signs that are part of the coming of the messianic kingdom; they show that an attack has been launched on the aspects of human existence where destruction, isolation, and dissolution do their disintegrating work.

In the power of the Holy Spirit, Jesus is making visible the restorative work of God. Therefore the forgiveness of sins is now implicitly, now explicitly, present in Jesus's ministry and preaching, for his ministry deals with our separation and estrangement from God and the disintegration that ensues. Jesus ensures the progress of the work by which God brings people home into his kingdom and gives them their real life. The forgiveness of sins and its positive result, justification, are elements of the Christian message that do not appear only in the Pauline epistles but form an integral part of Jesus's ministry. This emphasis underscores the soteriological significance of his ministry. In and around him the contours of God's regime become visible, which are so new and unusual that, on the one hand, they precipitate strong emotional reactions (e.g., Mark 14:1-9) but, on the other hand, also provoke strong resistance, since they are so at odds with current relationships, boundaries, and rules. Think of Jesus's radical interpretation of the law in the so-called Sermon on the Mount (Matt 5-7)—an interpretation that went so much against everything people saw, and see, as normal that it continues to astonish and shock us even today

From a salvific perspective we may say that, in his love for, and freedom before, God and the people, Jesus picks up the thread where Adam dropped it. He is the Son of Man who perseveres where Adam failed and gave in to distrust. He wins the victory where Adam fell victim to the tempter. Jesus is the new man, the last Adam, who does right what Adam did wrong and brings things to a victorious conclusion (1 Cor 15:20–22, 45). The passages about the temptations in the wilderness (Matt 4:1–11; Luke 4:1–13) very specifically point to Gen 2 and 3. Jesus is led by the Spirit into the wilderness where, just like Adam, he is confronted with voices that come from elsewhere. But while Adam and Eve were open to the suggestion that God perhaps could not be trusted, Jesus rejects the idea. In the wilderness he is surrounded by wild animals (Mark 1:13), an image that reminds us of the Garden of Eden, where Adam gave the animals their names and ruled over them.

In all these settings, Jesus acts in royal freedom. In this context "royal" means generous, with inner freedom and an awareness of his mandate. The tradition is therefore correct when it speaks about Christ's kingly office. The new humanity Jesus brings in as the Messiah is not fed by fear or distrust but is confident and untouched by cynicism. In the sphere of royal freedom Jesus's humanity flourishes, and what was crooked becomes straight. The powers that enslave or destroy human life are now placed under the authority of a new regime; they are bypassed and finally placed in the service of God's love. God perseveres in his covenantal work in the history of Jesus Christ, beginning with his life and ministry, and thereby reshapes it. This work comes at a high price. In the parable of the vineyard, the son, who was the last person to be sent, was killed by the tenants (Matt 21:33–46 and pars.). The price is as high as life.

11.9. The Salvific Dimension of the Cross

In the previous section we explored the salvific dimension of the life of Christ; in this section and the next we focus on the cross and the resurrection. What is the salvific scope of these two events? We start with Jesus's death on the cross as the culmination of his path of suffering. How does the cross relate to our salvation? How do cross and salvation belong together? Did God perhaps plan the death of Christ? If so, what does this say about God? If we want to somehow understand these things, we must once again begin with Adam, the first human, and with the purpose of the covenant. The New Testament portrays Jesus as the last Adam, the new human in whom God fulfills the intent of the covenant as given in the Torah. In Jesus's ministry we discover the love of God. His mission constitutes a new phase in God's involvement with Israel in which the people, who have lost their way, are offered a new relationship with God (see John 1:16-17). This offer needs to be accepted, however. At this point a big conflict erupts. God's offer in Jesus is not understood; it is even rejected. As the prologue of the Gospel of John puts it, "The light shines in the darkness, and the darkness has not overcome it" (John 1:5; see also Luke 19:28-44 and pars.). The people—especially the leaders of Israel—had become so entangled in their own patterns and expectations that they did not recognize and accept Jesus as the Messiah and failed to perceive God's new act in Jesus's ministry. This refusal led to a bitter conflict and ultimately to Jesus's crucifixion.

If we want to gauge the theological and soteriological dimension of Jesus's death on the cross, we must take this salvific course of events with utter seriousness. The biblical data give us no justification for explaining the death of Jesus on the cross as, first of all, an intentional plan of God that makes the people involved into unwitting executioners and marionettes in some theater. When we use such an interpretation of the texts that speak of "God's plan" in the path that Jesus traveled (e.g., Acts 2:23, spoken, not coincidentally, after the Pentecost experience), we fail to register the dramatic perspective of the gospel record of these events. We live and act in the realm of this history, and in considering this experience and the actual course of the events, we may join the Bible in speaking about God's ruling and arranging. But this way of talking does not provide theology—as a work in progress—any a priori access to God's mind, or any Archimedean angle of insight. We will have to hold on to both angles of vision. On the one hand, we have access to the historical perspective. On the other hand, in the perspective of the resurrection the Christian church recognizes God's sovereignty in all aspects of history—and, therefore, most certainly also with regard to the events that Jesus underwent. This perspective leads in the Bible to such doxological statements as we find, for instance, in Eph 1:3-11 and Rom 11:33, in which the profundity and majesty of God's reign over everything that happens is recognized, from beginning to end, including the bewildering event at its center, the crucifixion of God's beloved Son. *The doxological statements surround and clarify the drama of salvation history but do not remove the reality of the drama.*

Why is it so important to repeatedly return to the historic context of biblical statements to consider how they fit the timeline? It is because otherwise we might easily be inclined to make a caricature of the way in which the Father is involved in the death of Jesus. Green and Baker (2000, 141) give an example of how things may go wrong—for instance, in the way the story is often told to children. In trying to explain the significance of Jesus's death, the comparison has been made with a railway signalman whose son is playing on the track as a train is approaching with alarming speed. The signalman has the option to quickly, in the nick of time, switch the train onto another track, but that choice would result in a derailment that would certainly kill many passengers. Hence, he chooses not to change the signal but to allow his own son to be crushed by the train. Similarly, so the moral of the story goes, God allowed his son to die a horrendous death on a cross, since this event would save many others. Admittedly, some texts can be found (e.g., Isa 53:10) that would seem to support this way of telling the story, but it constitutes an irresponsible short-circuiting and undoubtedly (esp. with children) raises the question of whether the gospel of reconciliation is truly good news.

From the beginning, the rejection of Jesus and his death on the cross shed a sharp and revealing light on *our* reality, in which injustice and violence so often reign supreme. Think of Caiaphas and Pilate—but also of oppressive structures that enslave many people today. We see no lack of military and economic designs to make other people mere instruments of the perpetrators' interests. Jesus entered such a world, where extortion and abuse, belittling and humiliation, are the order of the day. In this world with its deeply entrenched evils, God's perfect love in Jesus would inevitably meet with fierce resistance, rejection, and opposition. We cannot endure so much light, since it challenges our preference for the twilight. When God's eschatological order enters this perverted world, the Servant of God inevitably becomes the Suffering Servant. When we are told that Christ's suffering was necessary (Luke 24:26), it first of all has this meaning.

We cannot simply conclude that the end of Jesus's life was a regrettable mistake. The cross reveals the resistance Jesus evoked, and various announcements ahead of time of Jesus's suffering indicate that Jesus foresaw it. We opt for a third road between the historical-critical view that we regard these announcements as *vaticinia ex eventu*—prophecy from the event (i.e., "predictions" added later to the text to match what already occurred)—and the hyperorthodox view that Christ was speaking exclusively in his divine nature. For in the end he is condemned as a blasphemer who had no right to claim to act on behalf of the Most High. Here we should note that, already early on, the significance of the cross apparently posed a problem and became a subject of intense reflection in Christian theology. Early Christians did not regard the death of Christ on the cross as something to be proud of and to tell others about. Initially, it was a very uncomfortable element in their faith that the one they honored and worshiped as Lord (Kyrios) had met his end naked and in a most repulsive way as a criminal. Not without reason the first Christians did not use the cross as a symbol, as is so common today. In the Roman Empire crucifixion was regarded as *mors turpissima* (the most opprobrious kind of death), an excruciating and humiliating form of execution by which the authorities demonstrated their deep contempt for the condemned person. This form of execution was mostly reserved for runaway slaves, murderers, and rebels who wanted to overthrow the existing order. One did not speak of crucifixion in civilized company; it was simply too barbaric (see Moltmann 1993, chap. 2.1).

The bewilderment about the cross echoes in texts we have already mentioned (Acts 2:23 and 1 Cor 2:8-10). At the same time, in these texts we discern an awareness that this event is somehow rooted in God's "plan and foreknowledge" and in the "depths of God." An important Old Testament parallel, which the early Christians found very enlightening, was the story of Joseph in Gen 37-50, with its climax in 50:20: "You meant evil against me; but God meant it for good, to bring it about that many people should be kept alive." This perspective enables us to take the next step.

In Jesus's death, second, the cross is regarded not only as a revelation but also as bringing atonement. Atonement means, again, that God condemns sin but provides a future and life for the sinner. This word takes us to the question of the specific salvific meaning of the cross. Is there redemption for us *in spite of*, or *because of*, the death of Jesus?

We do well to observe that *both* perspectives are present, and are ever intertwined, in the New Testament interpretation of Jesus's death (Barth 1992). Let us first look at "in spite of." In the parable of the vineyard, the tenants (i.e., the leaders of Israel) kill the son of the owner (Luke 20:9-19). We cannot find anything positive in the death of the son; we see a horrendous act for which the tenants are to blame. In other places of the New Testament we sense this same awareness that the death of Jesus on the cross is a disaster (we may perhaps also point to Gal 3:13). In view of the symbolic meaning of crucifixion, this response is understandable. The cross was a matter of shame, and neither the Jews nor the Greeks could imagine what to think of a crucified Lord. We must therefore clearly state that the crucifixion as a violent elimination of Jesus was, first of all, a terrible injustice inflicted upon him. In this act the Romans and the leaders of Israel were no worse than other people at other times, but they do serve as a paradigm for what happens when God approaches the world with his salvation. Jesus is crucified in the name of the God-given Torah because his ministry and claims were considered blasphemy and could not be tolerated. At its core the suffering of Jesus is the result of the violence, dishonesty, cowardice, and treason of the people toward him. In fact, as Reinhold Niebuhr put it, "Human striving can do no better than the Roman law and the Hebrew religion"; yet it was through these, "both the highest of their kind . . . through which the Lord was crucified" (Niebuhr 1971, 20). His death was desired by the highest religious authorities and ratified by a legal government. This is the first perspective: people got rid of Jesus because he was in their way. We cannot dress up this rejection in nice soteriological terms, for it manifests no saving or redeeming aspects.

Yet, there is more to say. In the New Testament what God does is decisive, not what people do, for God does something with the acts of the people. God remains the Lord of history, even when the people commit injustices. He uses the people's rejection as instruments in his own action plan. When Jesus dies as a discarded sinner, something happens that the judges and executioners did not reckon with. When God intervenes, the human condemnation becomes a decisive judgment on humanity and the world. In terms and images that refer to God's eschatological acts, we are told that, in the crucifixion-event, God pronounces his condemnation of sin. The Gospels mention three hours of darkness as an apocalyptic sign (most emphatically in Matt 27:52–53). Jesus himself did not simply experience his execution as a rejection by the chief priests and scribes. It certainly was a rejection, but more important are the words that express how he saw this event as one between himself and the Father. Jesus endured his mission from the Father unto the very end. Even in the garden of Gethsemane he placed the will of the Father above his own (Mark 14:36 and pars.). Yet, at the same time, he felt forsaken by his Father. The words on the cross that express this sense of being forsaken (Mark 15:34 and pars.) must be taken with utter theological seriousness. The Son *is* forsaken by the Father. This was not just Jesus's subjective experience; it was absolute reality. The Father's judgment over the power of sin and over death falls on Jesus. Jesus gauges the depth of godforsakenness and indeed suffers absolute separation from God. We have seen how in Reformed theology this severance has rightly been linked to Jesus's descent into hell. In this forsakenness God puts Jesus in the place where sin would have brought Adam (i.e., humanity), if the last Adam had not assumed his place.

Nonetheless, the dying Jesus perseveres in his dedication and submission (Luke 23:46). In this submission Jesus is empowered by the Spirit.

Hebrews 9:14 affirms that it is indeed the power of the Spirit that enables Jesus to persevere in his dedication to the Father, even when condemned and in a state of godforsakenness. Here we see the clear Trinitarian character of the event of the cross: Father, Son, and Spirit are each involved in their own way. In this process Jesus the Son occupies the place where the powers of sin and disintegration dominate. In so doing, he joins us. In other words, he takes our place before God and as a result is confronted with God's absolute rejection of sin—with God's wrath. Jesus's work and position are what is meant by vicariousness or representation. It is an act of ultimate love and sacrifice for the other.

The extent to which God must be considered an active agent in the death of Jesus remains a point of intense discussion in contemporary theology. Did Jesus only *subjectively* experience this desolation as being forsaken by God, or did the Father really forsake him at that moment? This latter view was defended not only by Luther ("God forsaken by God! Who can fathom this?") but also by Calvin and, in the twentieth century, by K. Barth, W. Pannenberg, J. Moltmann, A. van de Beek, and H. Boersma. Others—in particular, Roman Catholic theologians—have argued that the infinite love of the Father for the Son preempts the possibility of seeing wrath as a real predicate of the Father. The Father does not really punish the Son, but the Son subjectively experiences the loneliness on the cross as such. See, for example, H. Urs von Balthasar, E. Schillebeeckx, R. Schwager, and A. Houtepen (cf. Schneider, HdD 1:418-19); in the Protestant camp see Berkhof (CF 306-7), who contended (we believe wrongly) that we would do well to avoid applying the term "godforsakenness" to Jesus. For a discussion in the American context, see Weaver 2011.

The fact that something decisive occurs in this death remains the mystery of redemption and atonement. We may explore this mystery in our theology, but we cannot get a firm grip on it and make it rationally comprehensible. God absorbs the acts of people in his own acts (see Berkouwer 1965, 142). In these acts, in his judgment over sin and evil, there is a movement toward what is good. A change takes place because God himself acts and has placed himself in his Son in the dark hole that has been caused by sin. The destructive power of death must surrender when God appears, and thus the guilt of humankind does not remain the final and decisive reality. Death is about to crumble; through the power of God, death itself is eliminated. The resurrection is the *mors mortis*, the death of death. There is a way forward, and not just in spite of Christ's death, for precisely through this death the power of sin is definitely judged and broken. And thus we may also speak of salvation *because* of the death of Jesus.

In this positive, salvific significance of Jesus's death, we meet the priestly office of Jesus, which we will now explore a little further. Particularly in the Letter to the Hebrews, the significance of Jesus is portrayed in images of the temple and the sacrificial cult. Jesus is not only the high priest but also the sacrificial lamb. The death on the cross is pictured as the once-only and ultimate sacrifice that fulfills, and thereby ends, the entire sacrificial cult (Heb 10:10; for this latter aspect, see also Matt 27:51). This sacrifice, this shedding of blood, is the definitive sacrifice through which Christ as the high priest makes God's presence with us irreversibly effective. The execution that the people demand is a sacrifice that has been offered in heaven. Because Jesus remains obedient to the saving will of his Father, he falls victim, as a sacrifice, to human treachery and violence. But he does not undergo this sacrifice of his life as a blind fate or as something that, in final analysis, the people inflict on him. His words on the cross express his surrender to the Father. And thus he shows himself to be the priest who brings his sacrifice with a view to restoring the relationship between God and humanity.

According to the Gospels, this identification with the sacrificial lamb is already presupposed in Jesus's last meal with his disciples. Jesus there portrays his death in terms of the broken body and the shed blood of such a lamb and characterizes his approaching execution as the ultimate sacrifice of life (Matt 26:20-29; Mark 14:12-25; Luke 22:14-23). Therefore, it is possible in Rom 3:25 to describe the death on the cross from the opposite perspective of the Father, as an event in which God himself appointed Jesus as the means of atonement, or as the covering of the ark (Gk. *hilastērion*), the place where God himself realizes atonement for the sins of the people. For did God himself not institute the sacrificial cult? In this image the focus is no longer on what people do to Jesus but on what God does by using these human acts. On Golgotha the burden of sin as estrangement from God is laid on Jesus and is conquered through the power of the Spirit, who at this moment of highest tension is the connecting link between Father and Son. This is the Trinitarian movement from the cross to the resurrection. In Jesus's surrender of his own life, the victory over death is realized. Thereby he achieves what remained beyond the reach of the people in the Old Testament; he fulfilled the covenant that had become derailed. "For this is my blood of the covenant, which is poured out for many for the forgiveness of sins" (Matt 26:28 and pars.). The renewed covenant has Christ at its center.

It is confirmed through the sacrifice of his life, which is accepted by the Father.

In the previous section we intentionally used blood-terminology. Even though in our modern urban culture we have (despite the arrival of many Muslims) become estranged from anything that has to do with slaughtering and blood, and although a mere reference to the blood of Christ often arouses discomfort or disgust on the part of many, there are solid arguments to maintain this metaphor in spite of all objections. It is a broadly based biblical metaphor that underlines the objective nature of our salvation, as well as our existential involvement in it. Especially in the communion liturgy ("This is my blood . . ."), it points to the structure of salvation: outside of us, for us, and in us (*extra nos, pro nobis, in nobis*). The blood of Christ in a liturgical context signifies that Christ totally surrendered himself on our behalf; it shows something of the preciousness of this gift. Blood coincides with life. In receiving the bread and the wine, we appreciate how this gift involves us. The wine we drink is the blood of Christ. This metaphor stands for the concreteness, the solidity, and the radical nature of our salvation. Therefore it is totally out of order to soften the words of institution and, for instance, to speak of "the wine of the kingdom." Ever since Jesus's death on the cross the cup of the covenant is indissolubly linked to the sacrifice of his life. See Hunsinger 2000, "Meditation on the Blood of Christ."

In sum, the New Testament often uses sacrificial terminology to speak of the saving significance of the work of Christ. Jesus himself spoke this way during the Last Supper. Paul employs this terminology in his epistles, and the Letter to the Hebrews puts Jesus's entire life journey in the perspective of the temple cult. In Christian liturgy and theology, sacrificial terminology has exerted great influence. But we may wonder whether this metaphor is still appealing today. Therefore in this chapter we have consciously chosen not to speak exclusively in the idiom of atonement and sacrifice. Yet, stories in which a man does what he can for someone else, even to the point of sacrificing his own life, have as much appeal today as in the past.

This is clearly the case in popular culture. As a fitting example, consider the film *Saving Private Ryan* (1998), in which the officer who must search for Ryan and keep him alive does so at the cost of his own life. Just before he dies, he says to Ryan, "See that you live up to it." The film begins and ends with Ryan as an elderly man standing at the graveside of the officer, wondering whether he had indeed done so. Compare also the story of Aunt Riek and Frits de Zwerver (pseudonyms for Mrs.

H. Kuipers-Rietberg and Rev. F. Slomp), two well-known members of the Dutch resistance during World War II. When Aunt Riek asks Frits to start an organization to help people to stay in hiding, he protests at first. He has a family and is already on the list of people the Germans are looking for. "It may cost me my life," he says. She straightens her back and replies, "Man, would it be so terrible if you lost your life if thousands of boys could be saved?" (www.johannesterhorst.nl/ds_slomp_en_de_LO). We could immediately put texts such as John 13:15 and Rom 5:7-8 alongside this story.

The temple cult with its sacrifices offers an impressive context that helps us understand what happened between God and humanity in Christ's death. In the Day of Atonement ritual (Lev 16), the high priest arranges for the atonement for the sins of the people. In 11.6 we spoke of a sequence of identification, slaughter, and incorporation. Paul turns this sequence around. As he looks back on the cross of Jesus, Paul sees God incorporating the acts of the people in his own judgments (Rom 3:21-25 and 2 Cor 5:19-20). God has already incorporated us in the sacrifice of Christ, and in faith we affirm this relationship. We thus have the inverse sequence of incorporation, slaughter, and identification or consecration. By God's act the entire condition of human estrangement is accumulated in Christ. God incorporates all in the one. And then the moment of forfeiture and of access to life converge. The moment of identification takes place from Easter, and especially from Pentecost on, as people begin to understand what Christ did for them. In faith we open ourselves to his already having died for us and thus to our being able to share in the salvation he accomplished. This is the most complete analysis the New Testament offers us, and it is the most profound answer we may give to the question of how the work of Christ benefits us.

In the Pauline writings two concepts are used for the atonement. On the one hand, we hear of *katallassō* or *katallagē*, "[bring into] friendship with," to describe the completeness of the restoration that God brings about (2 Cor 5:18-20), including the moment of identification. In Latin translations this word is rendered as *reconciliatio* (reconciliation). But we also find the words *hilasmos* and *hilastērion* (Rom 3:25; Heb 9:5; see also 1 John 2:2 and 4:10), which may be translated respectively as "atonement" and "means of atonement." In Latin this root is rendered *expiatio* (expiation). Atonement as *expiatio* refers especially to the actual removal of sin. Behind the term *hilastērion* is the Hebrew word *kapporet*, which denotes the cover of the ark of the covenant, where the blood of the sacrificial animal was sprinkled (Exod 25:17). This is the place where forfeited life and divine holiness converge and where, as a result, life is provided. For the inversion of the sequence of identification, slaughter, and incorporation, see Dalferth 2015.

One final remark needs to be added in this connection. The three-some of identification, slaughter, and incorporation indicates that, in the Bible, atonement is primarily a matter of restoring relationships; yet, the moment of judgment and expiation is not absent. Because God is life and wants us to live, his judgment is elicited by whatever opposes life. Whatever destroys God's love and threatens his intentions comes under his judgment and will be removed from his sight. And not just from his sight; when God comes with his righteousness, everything lacking in righteousness will lose its place. However unpopular these concepts may be in church and theology, wrath, punishment, and penalty must be seen as forms of God's faithfulness and love. They follow God's grace, just as shadows are brought forth by the light. Wrath and judgment do not exist independently but, as we saw in chapter 4, constitute the reaction that follows the resistance God meets in his love.

11.10. The Salvific Significance of Christ's Resurrection and Ascension

We began this chapter with a question about the significance of the resurrection for Jesus's identity, which gave us a natural opening wedge to speak about the salvific meaning of his work. Christology and soteriology were shown to be closely intertwined. Jesus is called the Son of God only because God's acceptance of Christ's sacrifice was affirmed in the resurrection, and only because he has always been the Son of God could he bring his sacrifice. Now, finally, we must explore the significance that Christ's resurrection has for us. Thus we come full circle. What does it mean for us that, since his exaltation (i.e., his resurrection and ascension), Jesus has preceded us and is sitting at the right hand of God?

First, we must say that the exalted Lord *represents us with the Father*. In Jesus we have someone who is human, just as we are, and in whom God's covenant is a reality. His vicarious role did not end with Good Friday and Easter. Romans 8:34 tells us that he continues to represent us before the Father. In dogmatic terms we call this his *intercession*. Here the New Testament enlists the entire language of the temple cult. He is the priest who works with the Father on our behalf. His sitting at the right hand of God is, first of all, a saving representation.

In the last century the significance of this aspect of Christ's work has been scrutinized by the influential Scottish theologian T. F. Torrance (1913-2007), notably in his theory of the *vicarious humanity* of Christ, in which Eastern and Western approaches (esp. of Athanasius and Calvin) converged. In the incarnation God assumed our human nature, and with this nature he gave God, on our behalf, the perfect answer of active and passive obedience. In this way he saved and healed our human nature through his redemptive work. In his ascension he took his human nature with him into heaven, where he continues to represent us before the Father as our high priest. For that reason Torrance (1993, 43) regards the bodily character of Jesus's ascension as a sine qua non. For if Jesus is not in heaven "in the fullness of his humanity, we have no anchor behind the veil [Heb 6:19-20] and there is no hope for people of flesh and blood [Col 1:27]." Jesus still offers the Father worship and prayers in our place and thus perfects our inadequate prayers (for this reason we pray "in Jesus's name"). In fact, Torrance takes with utter seriousness what the Heidelberg Catechism says, in Q/A 49, that, because of Christ, we "have our flesh in heaven." See, for kindred notions, the work of his younger brother James B. Torrance (1981).

A second element of Christ's exaltation is his sharing in God's reign, which is exactly what "sitting at God's right hand" means. This notion has its roots in Ps 110 and eventually found its way into the Apostles' Creed. Jesus sharing in God's rule also implies that he works for the benefit of the world. He not only represents us with the Father (see the first point); *he also represents, through his Spirit, the Father with us.* For he has received—no doubt from the Father—all power in heaven and earth (Matt 28:18). The powers of the world no longer have the final word. Admittedly, his kingship is hidden. Even though in faith we see Jesus crowned with majesty and glory, "we do not yet see everything in subjection to him" (Heb 2:8). But whatever our darkness, despair, and bitter uncertainty, the Bible assures us that this Lord has broken this deathly power down to its roots. This Lord is the Alpha and Omega, the beginning and the end of world history (Rev 22:13).

A third element of this hope is that the exalted Lord is *with his church* in a very special way (Matt 28:20). As the Good Shepherd (John 10:11), he continues to lead and to call his sheep. However small the church might become, and whatever pressures it may have to endure, the Lord knows those who are his (2 Tim 2:19). On the one hand, this assurance gives us strong encouragement to stay near to him; on the other hand, it allows us to trust that he will always call people to build and protect his church. The New Testament can therefore affirm that the Holy Spirit leads the church into all truth, but just as clearly that Christ himself protects and keeps it.

Apparently, there is no contradiction: Christ does the work through his Spirit and his Word.

Fourth and finally, in Christ's resurrection we also have the *pledge of our own resurrection*, as the Heidelberg Catechism phrases it (Q/A 45). If Christ precedes us and if he is the Firstfruit, his resurrection offers a vista of life in his presence where we humans not only are saved from death and judgment but also are glorified. Here concepts like heaven and eternal life fit into the overall picture. God's faithfulness toward humanity holds enormous promise for the future. He does not let go of what his hand has begun but finishes it. In this eschatological passage the Bible does not mince words. It intends a deliverance from all the powers that still enslave us, and a glory and blessing that exceed all expectations. The eschatological glory will be greater than its prototype (1 Cor 15:46-47; cf. 1 Cor 2:11). The theological implication is that Christ's work provides not only atonement but also exaltation (an aspect that has often been more clearly enunciated in Roman Catholic than in Protestant theology). The unimaginable glory that we see in the exalted Christ at some future time awaits all God's children (see Rom 8:16-21; Col 3:4).

How do we become and do we remain involved in this work? How can we be sure that we will share in this salvation and in this future? These questions lead us to pneumatology and the loci that are connected with it—the doctrines of the church, of the Scriptures, and of spiritual renewal—that explain our participation in our salvation.

References

Allen, R. Michael. 2009. *The Christ's Faith: A Dogmatic Account*. London: T&T Clark.

Anselm of Canterbury. 1998. *The Major Works*. Edited by Brian Davies and G. R. Evans. Oxford: Oxford University Press.

Aulén, Gustaf. 1931. *Christus Victor: An Historical Study of the Three Main Types of the Idea of the Atonement*. Translated by A. G. Hebert. London: SPCK. Orig. Swedish pub., Den kristna försoningstanken, Stockholm, 1930.

Barth, Gerhard. 1992. *Der Tod Jesu Christi im Verständnis des Neuen Testaments*. Neukirchen: Neukirchener Verlag.

Beek, Abraham van de. 2002. *Jesus Kyrios: Christology as Heart of Theology*. Zoetermeer: Meinema.

———. 2008. *God doet recht: Eschatologie als Christologie* [God does justice: Eschatology as Christology]. Zoetermeer: Meinema.

Berkouwer, Gerrit C. 1965. *The Work of Christ*. Grand Rapids: Eerdmans.

Boersma, Hans. 2004. *Violence, Hospitality, and the Cross: Reappropriating the Atonement Tradition*. Grand Rapids: Baker Academic.

Brink, Gijsbert van den. 2008. "How to Speak with Intellectual and Theological Decency on the Resurrection of Christ." *Scottish Journal of Theology* 61:408-19.

Brinkman, Martien E. 2009. *The Non-Western Jesus: Jesus as Bodhisattva, Avatara, Guru, Prophet, Ancestor, or Healer?* London: Equinox.

Brümmer, Vincent. 2005. *Atonement, Christology, and the Trinity: Making Sense of Christian Doctrine*. Aldershot: Ashgate.

Bultmann, Rudolf. 1954. "New Testament and Mythology." In *Kerygma and Myth*, edited by H. W. Bartsch, 1-44. London: SPCK.

Catechism of the Catholic Church. 1994. New York: Doubleday.

Dalferth, Ingolf U. 2015. *Crucified and Resurrected: Restructuring the Grammar of Christology*. Grand Rapids: Baker Academic.

Edmondson, Stephen. 2004. *Calvin's Christology*. Cambridge: Cambridge University Press.

Farrow, Douglas. 1999. *Ascension and Ecclesia: On the Significance of the Doctrine of the Ascension for Ecclesiology and Christian Cosmology*. Grand Rapids: Eerdmans.

Gäde, Gerhard. 1989. *"Eine andere Barmherzigkeit": Zum Verständnis der Erlösungslehre Anselms von Canterbury*. Würzburg: Echter.

Gese, Hartmut. 1981. *Essays on Biblical Theology*. Minneapolis: Augsburg.

Green, Joel B., and Mark D. Baker. 2000. *Recovering the Scandal of the Cross: Atonement in New Testament and Contemporary Contexts*. Carlisle: Paternoster.

Greshake, Gisbert. 1983. "Erlösung und Freiheit: Zur Neuinterpretation der Erlösungslehre des Anselms von Canterbury." In *Gottes Heil, Glück des Menschen: Theologische Perspektiven*. Freiburg: Herder.

Gunton, Colin E. 1988. *The Actuality of Atonement: A Study of Metaphor, Rationality, and the Christian Tradition*. Edinburgh: T&T Clark.

Heyer, Cornelis J. den. 1998. *Jesus and the Doctrine of the Atonement*. London: SCM.

Holmes, Stephen R. 2007. *The Wondrous Cross: Atonement and Penal Substitution in the Bible and History*. Milton Keynes: Paternoster.

Hunsinger, George. 2000. "Meditation on the Blood of Christ." In *Disruptive Grace: Studies in the Theology of Karl Barth*, 361-63. Grand Rapids: Eerdmans.

———. 2004. "The Daybreak of the New Creation: Christ's Resurrection in Recent Theology." *Scottish Journal of Theology* 57:163-81.

Jüngel, Eberhard. 1974. *Death: The Riddle and the Mystery*. Philadelphia: Westminster.

Kärkkäinen, Veli-Matti. 2003. *Christology: A Global Introduction; An Ecumenical, International, and Contextual Perspective*. Grand Rapids: Baker Academic.

Kooi, Cornelis van der. 1997. "Dankzij of ondanks de dood van Jezus?" [Thanks to, or in spite of, the death of Jesus?]. *Nederlands Theologisch Tijdschrift* 51:281-97.

Kooten, George H. van. 2003. *Cosmic Christology in Paul and the Pauline School*. Tübingen: Mohr Siebeck.

Lapide, Pinchas. 2002. *The Resurrection of Jesus: A Jewish Perspective*. Eugene, OR: Wipf & Stock.

Levenson, John Douglas. 2006. *Resurrection and the Restoration of Israel: The Ultimate Victory of the God of Life*. New Haven: Yale University Press.

Moltmann, Jürgen. 1990. *The Way of Jesus Christ: Christology in Messianic Dimensions*. Minneapolis: Fortress.

———. 1993. *The Crucified God: The Cross of Christ as the Foundation and Criticism of Christian Theology*. Minneapolis: Fortress.

Niebuhr, Reinhold. 1971 (orig. 1937). *Beyond Tragedy: Essays on the Christian Interpretation of History*. Freeport, NY: Books for Libraries Press.

Pannenberg, Wolfhart. 1968. *Jesus—God and Man*. Philadelphia: Westminster.

Plasger, Georg. 1993. *Die Not-Wendigkeit der Gerechtigkeit: Eine Interpretation zu "Cur Deus homo" von Anselm von Canterbury*. Münster: Aschendorff.

Ridderbos, Herman N. 1962. *The Coming of the Kingdom*. Philadelphia: P&R Publishing.

Sanders, John, ed. 2006. *Atonement and Violence: A Theological Conversation*. Nashville: Abingdon.

Schillebeeckx, Edward. 2014a. *Interim Report on the Books "Jesus" and "Christ."* Translated by John Bowden and Ted Schoof. Collected Works 8. London: Bloomsbury. Orig. pub., 1978.

———. 2014b. *Jesus: An Experiment in Christology*. London: Bloomsbury. Orig. pub., 1975.

Schwager, Raymund. 1986. *Der wunderbare Tausch: Zur Geschichte und Deutung der Erlösungslehre*. Munich: Kösel.

Schweizer, Eduard. 1971. *Jesus*. Translated by D. E. Greene. London: SCM.

Stott, John. 2006. *The Cross of Christ*. Nottingham: Inter-Varsity. Orig. pub., 1986.

Swinburne, Richard. 2003. *The Resurrection of God Incarnate*. Oxford: Clarendon.

Thiessen, Jacob. 2009. *Die Auferstehung Jesu in der Kontroverse: Hermeneutisch-exegetische und theologische Überlegungen*. Vienna: Lit.

Torrance, James B. 1981. "The Vicarious Humanity of Christ." In *The Incarnation*, edited by T. F. Torrance, 127–47. Edinburgh: Handsel.

Torrance, Thomas F. 1993. *Royal Priesthood: A Theology of Ordained Ministry*. Edinburgh: T&T Clark. Orig. pub., 1955.

Weaver, J. Denny. 2011. *The Nonviolent Atonement*. 2nd ed. Grand Rapids: Eerdmans.

Welker, Michael. 2013. *God the Revealed: Christology*. Grand Rapids: Eerdmans.

Wiersinga, Herman. 1971. *De verzoening in de theologische diskussie* [Reconciliation in theological discussion]. Kampen: Kok.

Wink, Walter. 1999. *The Powers That Be: Theology for a New Millennium*. New York: Doubleday.

Wright, N. T. 1996. *Jesus and the Victory of God*. Minneapolis: Fortress.

———. 2003. *The Resurrection of the Son of God*. Minneapolis: Fortress.

12 Holy Spirit, Giver of Life

Pneumatology

AIM

This chapter deals with the person and work of the Holy Spirit, that is, with "pneumatology" (derived from Gk. *pneuma*, "spirit, breath, wind"). This is the first topic that the Apostles' Creed lists in its third group of articles. That group itself is sometimes referred to as the third article, to underline the basic Trinitarian structure of the creed. The third part of the creed, and also of our book, asks what Christ's saving work means for us and for the world, and how we might share in it. Our remaining chapters will answer that question, step by step, in more detail. Chapter 13 focuses on the Bible; chapter 14, on the church, its offices and sacraments. Chapter 15 treats the renewal of humanity, while chapter 16 wraps things up with the renewal of the world, or "eschatology." All of these topics are connected with the work of the Spirit.

   This chapter sets the foundation for the rest by exploring the person and the work of the Spirit. In the following sections we intend to:

- explain why the chapter on the Holy Spirit is placed here in this book (12.1)
- learn what biblical theology has to say about the work of the Spirit (12.2)
- indicate how, from a biblical-theological perspective, the Spirit is related to Christ (12.3)
- try to explain the theological and spiritual importance of the conceptual pair "Word" and "Spirit" (12.4)
- explore what is meant by the fruit of the Spirit, the gifts of the Spirit (the charismata), and baptism by the Spirit (12.5)
- elaborate how the Spirit, as the creator of relationships, is not only involved with individuals but also calls for a new community (12.6)

- ask the question of whether the Spirit has an even broader impact on culture and history (12.7)
- investigate the factors that have raised pneumatology to such a prominent place on the ecclesial and theological agenda (12.8).

MAKING CONNECTIONS
1. In church tradition, only a few prayers are directly addressed to the Holy Spirit. Why is that? Is it justified?
2. Listen to Martin Luther King's famous speech *I Have a Dream*, given in Washington, DC, in August 1963. Could King's words have anything to do with the Holy Spirit and prophecy? Jot down your impressions and discuss this question in a small group.

12.1. Introduction

Placing the chapter about the Holy Spirit after Christology and soteriology may cause a misunderstanding, namely, that the work of the Spirit flows only out of the work of Christ. Such a view fails to do justice to the testimony of the Bible and the church. For good cause we have already discussed the Spirit at earlier points in this book, especially in connection with the doctrine of the Trinity (chap. 3), in our treatment of Christology (chap. 10), and in the context of the doctrine of creation (chap. 6). Note well that in the history of salvation, the activity of the Spirit precedes that of Christ. Nonetheless, for the Christian church the work of the Spirit centers in the history that has been inaugurated by Jesus Christ. The Spirit helps us to relate to the saving work of Jesus Christ; through the Spirit, God ensures that what has been given in Christ will have its full impact on us and the world. The Spirit generates a lot of movement and dynamism. The well-known sentence in the Lord's Prayer, "Thy kingdom come," releases the restraints on our life and the world and sets us on the road toward God's future. The Spirit at once propels us forward and draws the future into the present.

It is often complained that Western theology has not given pneumatology adequate attention. Referring to an adage of Martin Heidegger, who lamented philosophy's *Seinsvergessenheit* (ignoring the topic of "being"), some theologians have criticized their own field's *Geistvergessenheit* (forgetfulness of the Spirit;

note Kärkkäinen 2002, 16–17, a passage in which the Holy Spirit is called "the Cinderella of theology"). However popular it has become, we question whether the accusation is justified. True, in many theology textbooks the person and the work of the Holy Spirit have not been treated as a separate topic (e.g., Berkhof, CT; Genderen and Velema, CRD). Traditionally, the Spirit is discussed under the doctrine of God, in connection with the doctrine of the Scriptures, and especially with respect to the appropriation of salvation—that is, in connection to questions about the *ordo salutis* (see chap. 15). Historically, separate attention to the Spirit has quickly aroused suspicions of uncontrollable fanaticism, as if interest in the Spirit betrayed an inclination to extreme and spectacular phenomena. As a result, Western theology has not duly recognized the full scope of what the Bible has to say about the Spirit. In that respect the complaint of insufficient attention for the Spirit is justified.

Yet, there is another side to the story. The Western church has given other topics in the domain of pneumatology significant attention, particularly the salvific activities of the Spirit in and on behalf of humanity. Led by such church fathers as Tertullian and Augustine, the church in the West excelled on the practical side of things (as the East has on the mystical). It showed great interest in the conduct of ordinary Christian life, giving it clear organization and structure. Spirituality and theology reflected long and hard on the concrete meaning that faith in God has for us, which was expressed, for example, in the development of the doctrine of grace in the Middle Ages. What happens to us when God approaches us in Jesus Christ? How do we share in this grace? This question was answered in the doctrine of the sacraments. Interest in our personal life of faith increased as time went by. Calvin shifted the accent from the sacraments as channels of salvation to the personal work of the Spirit in the human heart. As a result, he has sometimes been called the theologian of the Holy Spirit. Puritanism and Pietism, Methodism, the Holiness movement, and Pentecostalism have, in different ways, further explored the work of the Spirit in relation to the individual believer's walk of faith. They all shared as well in Western culture's increasing interest in the human being as subject. This focus led to a wide range of, but essentially also interconnected, questions. What does the Spirit do in us? What happens when the Spirit touches us, opens us, lives in us, and transforms us? Do we play some role in the process? More recently the question of transformation has also become a question about the transformation of society. Does the work of the Spirit have any meaning for the communities and society to which we belong? We will also explore this question.

For a comprehensive overview of biblical, historical, and contemporary reflection on the Holy Spirit—and as such, a clear sign of the ongoing "pneumatological renaissance"—see Thiselton 2013.

In the doctrine of God (chaps. 3 and 4) we discussed how both Jesus Christ and the Spirit play a role in the drama of salvation history. To return to the metaphor of Irenaeus: Christ and the Spirit are God's "two hands" in dealing with us. In a Trinitarian theology we do not consign the work of God to just one person of the Trinity. Father, Son, and Spirit each represent particular aspects of the saving actions of the one God. The Spirit's particular role is to ensure our connection with Christ, and thus also with God. The Spirit leads us into communion with what God does on our behalf. This connection happens in many different ways. He was already active in creation, in the history of Israel, and in Jesus Christ and his work of atonement; but in a very special way, he is the one who ensures that God's work will come to completion.

For that reason we want to pay systematic attention to the work of the Holy Spirit after having treated Christology and soteriology. Some topics that we have already dealt with will inevitably reappear, but we will now look at them from the angle of the work of the Holy Spirit. The work of the Spirit is, as it were, the apex of God's involvement with us. In the Spirit, God himself touches us, which is the grand mystery of creation, atonement, and redemption. The Holy Spirit might very well serve as a canopy under which we can place our entire theology. Even so Christocentric a theologian as Karl Barth recognized this possibility and seriously considered developing this approach further. Such a capacious treatment of the work of the Spirit is indeed quite defensible, particularly when we take into account the numerous ways in which the Bible speaks of the Spirit of God.

12.2. The Spirit of God and His Activities: Biblical-Theological Core Elements

The following survey is certainly not intended as an exhaustive study of the biblical-theological material on the Spirit. We simply take a look, with the interests of systematic theology in view, at three important aspects of the work of the Holy Spirit that we encounter in reflecting on the biblical data. These three are the Spirit's involvement in the creation, redemption, and the completion of this world.

12.2.1. *The Spirit as Creator of life*

The first and fundamental thing we must say is that the Spirit brings life. The wider background and significance of the biblical term "Spirit" are found in its connection with life and breath. The Hebrew word *ruach*, as it occurs in the Bible, as well as the Greek word *pneuma*, each bear the original meaning of "breath" and "wind." The fundamental idea is a sense of movement and life.

It should be noted that, grammatically, *ruach* is feminine and *pneuma* is neuter. But a term like *paraklētos* (comforter, solicitor; John 14:16) is masculine. This mixed usage clearly indicates that the Spirit supersedes any form of sexual differentiation. Fearing Gnosticism (in which the Spirit is seen as feminine) or feminist theology, the church has in practice tended to refer to the Spirit with masculine pronouns. To do justice to the diversity in the original biblical grammar, we would do well to sometimes use feminine pronouns in our discussion of the Spirit.

These original connotations of breath and wind have never been completely lost. Spirit or breath is what ensures that something or someone is alive. In the Old Testament *ruach* is presented as the Spirit of God who brings life from the outside and on whom all life depends (Job 34:14-15; Ps 104:29). Spirit or breath allows a being to breathe, pulsate, receive vitality. But the flip side is that this same Spirit can be a mighty wind bringing judgment and condemnation (Isa 4:4; Jer 4:11-13; Ezek 13:11-13). We find a beautiful example of this usage in Ps 104:29-30, where the Spirit of God is referred to as the mystery that makes creation come alive and the small green shoots to sprout—but whose withdrawal also causes living things to die. Calvin referred to this contribution as the "hidden work" of the Spirit in nature (Comm. on Gen 1:2; CO 23:16).

This Spirit is active in what modern people call nature, as well as in history. Again, this activity can be constructive and ordering, but it might also be destructive. The Spirit awakens life (Job 26:12-13; 33:4) but also disperses and confuses (Gen 6:3; Exod 15:8-10; Isa 40:6-7). The book of Genesis shows the close tie between human vitality and God's activating power in history, as is demonstrated in the story of the blessing of Jacob and Esau (Gen 27). Isaac must first eat and receive energy before he can bless. The words he speaks then show their force in history; they accomplish something. Blessing is an important Old Testament theme. It has vital importance and is linked to growth, prosperity, progress, posterity, energy, and power. The other side of the coin—curse—is also evident.

When the Spirit of God draws back and goes missing, the curse descends. Life comes to a standstill and shows no progress: no harvest, no children, no health (Frettlöh 1999, 55–57).

12.2.2. *The Spirit as Liberating Power*

The Hebrew Bible characterizes the work of the Spirit also as a liberating power. We see this function in the stories of Moses, the judges, and the early kings. Of some of them we read that the Spirit of the Lord fell upon them (Judg. 3:10; 6:34; 11:29), enabling them to deliver their people. The Spirit makes men and women into what we would today call "charismatic leaders." The Spirit equips people for God's intended work so as to establish God's reign over human lives.

We intentionally place the term "charismatic leaders" in quotation marks. The use of "charismatic" as an adjective dates back little more than a century and is unknown in the Old and the New Testaments. In our time this adjective suggests that we are dealing with a personal quality, but this sense is not found in the Bible. People receive the charismata, but they do no become "charismatic" as a result.

The Old Testament often links the liberating work of the Spirit to the phenomenon of prophecy. The Spirit is the Spirit of prophecy (Num 11:17–30). To prophesy is not primarily to predict (as is often thought) but to give a true account of the current situation; it delivers a message of God for the times in which the prophet lives. When the Spirit of the Lord takes hold of Saul, he begins to prophesy; that is, he publicly explains the will and the work of God. Note here that the appearance of the Spirit may at times be highly unusual, even indecent; when the Spirit came upon Saul, we read that he "lay naked all that day and all that night" (1 Sam 19:24). We cannot restrict the activity of the Spirit; it may be somewhat uncouth, confrontational, and going beyond set boundaries. The somewhat startling saying spread in Israel: "Is Saul also among the prophets?" (1 Sam 10:10–11 and 1 Sam 19:23–24). Apparently, sometimes this rude quality was necessary; the gift of the Spirit equipped Saul to proceed with power and courage. When the Spirit touches people, they become restless and take initiative. Gideon, and later Saul, helped the Israelites rise from their lethargy. We strongly emphasize in this connection the *communal* effect of this gift; personal empowerment serves to instigate a liberating work in and for the community. Thus God's salvation touches the way people, the polis and politics, live together.

The Old Testament Major Prophets tend to lay greater stress on the eschatological nature of Israel's hope regarding God's acts, that is, national restoration and the manifestation of God's justice before the eyes of the nations (as in Isa 48:16). God will provide escape and salvation through a future event, such as the intervention by King Cyrus (Isa 45:1–8). In the eyes of the prophets and of others who have been touched by the Spirit, God's creative work is continuing in his *liberating* and *life-saving* acts (Ezek 3:14; 11:5, 24). This process is far from easy; the Spirit constantly meets with resistance and rebellion. We read of "hearts of stone" (Ezek 36:26). But those hearts can change. Here we are faced with the incredible drama the work of the Spirit accomplishes. God lets himself be heard; he arouses people, interrupts their life, and demands an answer. The end remains uncertain. In the biblical drama the appeal to say Yes is first addressed to Israel. God wants to use Israel as a channel to reach the nations. Thus the Spirit is portrayed as the one who brings God's reign nearer and who is active in the ultimate liberation of Israel. Ezekiel even says the activity of the Spirit leads to the resurrection of Israel (Ezek 37:14); the vision in this pericope is primarily applicable to Israel and not to the church! And so the panels shift. The Spirit is no longer the one who operates in creation as the giver of life but is the liberating power on the path to the future.

Finally, the Spirit himself becomes the *content* of the prophesied future, as the ultimate divine gift that will lead to a restoration of relationships and a renewal of the covenant (Isa 32:15–16; 34:16; 57:16). In the end time all people will be touched by the prophetic Spirit of God, and then the covenant or the new community that God intends will be realized (Isa 59:21; Jer 31:31–34; Ezek 36:28), and the time of salvation will arrive (see Joel 2:28–32 = 3:1–5 in the Hebrew Bible). The New Testament sketches the eschatological fulfillment of these announcements, beginning with the powerful outpouring of the Spirit recounted in Acts 2 (see vv. 16–21). Not just with, but also after, this event the Spirit keeps propelling history forward in the direction of God's kingdom.

In the Netherlands Oepke Noordmans, in particular, called for attention to the dynamic, uncharted aspect of the work of the Spirit. The Spirit prompts the faith community not to seek its growth in all kinds of established structures or models of a political, ecclesial, or liturgical sort, but to let itself be carried along on the unknown path of God's future. The Spirit does nothing but break through.

Noordmans based his conclusion especially on the events in the book of Acts. He summarized the turn in salvation history that he discerned there in a striking expression: "Paul comes, and Peter goes" (see Blei 2013, 174-75). Peter represents the church in Jerusalem as preferring to keep things as they were in the past (see Acts 10:14), but in Acts he gradually disappears from sight (only to return in a negative light in Gal 2). Paul, whose name is not mentioned in the Gospels, represents the Spirit-inspired movement toward the world. This direction proves to be the future, and so the rest of Acts and the Epistles are to a large extent about Paul's activities.

12.2.3. The Spirit as Gift of Renewal

Thus far we have considered the Spirit as a power in history. From Pentecost on, this power acquires stronger personal traits; it appears as God's special gift of the end of time that connects people with God's salvation. More precisely, the Spirit connects people with the Son and the Father. The Spirit establishes our relationship with Christ and thereby leads us to participate in the new life. Thus, *the Spirit is the gift of renewal*. In the Gospel of John this idea is developed in the figure of the Paraclete (John 14 and 16). This word is often rendered "Comforter," but such a translation might convey connotations that are too restrictive. "Paraclete" means "called to be present"; it might refer to a lawyer who pleads and speaks on behalf of the accused. In that respect, translating "Paraclete" as "Comforter" may be applicable. The Spirit is the Comforter who actively applies the work of the Son and extends it further to those who stayed behind (John 14:26; 16:15).

However, the Spirit is not only a gift (Rom 5:5) but is also clearly a subject, a person. In the book of Acts and in the Johannine writings, the Spirit is the one who assists, leads, and shows the way. This does not first of all apply to individuals; rather, it is communal. The Spirit descends on the multitude that has come together, and in John 20:22 we see how the disciples collectively receive the Spirit. The Spirit comes to live in the body of Christ. Again, this living is broader than just an experience of individual believers; the church as a whole takes first place. In summary, we may say that the Spirit now is the power that leads people in history, corrects them (John 16:9), gives them new insights, and renews them. In a theological sense we therefore regard the church and its people similarly, as a Spirit-led community. Can the circle be widened even further to the domain of culture and politics? Can we say that it is due to the work of the

Spirit that, under the influence of the gospel, the sense for a truly humane and livable existence increases in a society? At this point opinions differ, and we hesitate. We will return to this issue later in the chapter. For the time being we conclude that the Spirit leads people to participation (Gk. *koinōnia*) in the communion between Jesus and the Father.

Another, and exciting, question we must answer is, how are we to understand this participation? What does it mean concretely when we say that the Spirit leads us to participate in Christ's saving work and thereby renews us? A biblical image for this participation is that of *indwelling* (John 14:17; Rom 8:9, 11). The image warns us not to indulge too rosy an idea of what this entails. We quote a statement that A. A. van Ruler made at a time (1964) when a housing shortage in the Netherlands in some cases forced different families to live together in the same house: "Like all forms of 'indwelling,' this one inevitably causes controversy" (Ruler, VW 4A:378). It seems as if the fire of the Spirit will entail some purification. Renewal is not just pleasant; the Spirit brings a lot of unrest to our life. He makes us sigh and suffer together with the creation, which is subject to so much senselessness and pain (Rom 8:20–23).

Yet, the New Testament also makes clear that the presence of the Spirit gives the experience of a new life as the first installment of what, at the final completion, will be a perfect reality. The Greek term used for this function in the Pauline writings is *arrabōn*, which means something like "earnest," "security," or "down-payment" (2 Cor 1:22; 5:5; Eph 1:14; cf. Rom 8:23, where another metaphor with the same meaning is used). These are flashes of the light that is to come, a small sample that gives a foretaste of the feast to be served. By referring to the prophecy of Joel 2:28–32, the book of Acts (2:17–21) signals that, in principle, this future has already arrived. The present is part of the last days that the prophets spoke of. The end of time is not something still awaiting us, as is often suggested in evangelical circles; it already began a long time ago, namely, when the Spirit was poured out. From that moment on, a new community has existed that proclaims the mighty acts of God and is equipped with the Spirit to be a witness. Compared with its depictions in the Old Testament, the Spirit in the New Testament is profiled with increasing clarity. The result of the Spirit's activities is henceforth determined by the history of Jesus Christ. The Spirit has become "Christomorphed." We might say that she is now made available to Jesus Christ, and that she lets us enjoy what has been given in Christ so that it has its full effect in our lives. We may therefore speak in this connection of the *transformative function* of the Spirit. This transformation, or renewal, takes its substance from

Christ but unfolds in a widening range of effects (1 Pet 4:10). The Bible speaks about the fruit, work, power, and gifts of the Spirit. In the next few sections (and also in chap. 15), we will explore these effects further.

Augustine particularly emphasized the aspect of the Spirit as gift (or *donum*, in his Latin). As a result, he was less clear about the personal character of the Spirit—quite less so than the Cappadocians. For Augustine, the Spirit is first of all the bond (*vinculum*) of perfect love between the Father and the Son, and because the Spirit is subsequently also given to us, this love is also poured out in our hearts (Rom 5:5), so that we share in the divine communion. See above, chapter 3.4. Thus we begin to understand how in the Middle Ages—in line with Augustine's pneumatology—our sharing in God's love was seen in terms of the *sacraments* of the church (which were either poured over or into the people). In this view pneumatology could be hidden behind ecclesiology. We can say that the Reformation brought pneumatology back into the full light; both the personal character and the activities of the Spirit (two accents that usually go together) once again received due attention. The Spirit renews us by letting us personally share, through faith, in Christ. This leitmotif became so strong in Protestantism as to sometimes eclipse the renewing spiritual power of the sacraments.

12.3. The Spirit and Jesus: A Threefold Relationship

We remarked above that pneumatology in fact comprises all of salvation history, from creation to completion. From this angle we should not be surprised to see how the New Testament outlines for us a threefold relationship between the Spirit and Jesus: the Spirit precedes Jesus, rests upon him, and is handed on through him. Or to reverse the angle: Jesus proceeds from the Spirit, bears the Sprit, and as the exalted Lord, sends the Spirit. At the center stands the figure of Jesus as the bearer of God's Spirit. That is, the eschatological, liberating power promised by the prophets rests on him and enables him to live fully from and for God. We may summarize this relationship in the image of an anointing with the Spirit, which has its roots in Isa 61:1 and explains why Jesus is described in Luke (4:18) as the Messiah; he is the one who is anointed with the Spirit. In the book of Acts Jesus's profile is largely determined by this terminology of anointing by the Spirit (e.g., see 10:38). The mission of Jesus combats our estrangement from God, the broken covenant. God resumes his project in sending Jesus, and in this mission the Spirit plays a leading role. The Gospels of Luke and Matthew very specifically link

Jesus's birth with the Spirit, and as the eschatological bearer of God's Spirit, Jesus can hand this Spirit on (John 20:22; Acts 2:33).

In so characterizing Jesus, the New Testament makes clear that being the bearer of the Spirit is not to be confused with blissful enjoyment. Once again we come up against the confrontational aspect of the matter. Immediately after Jesus is baptized with the Spirit, he is driven by this same Spirit into the wilderness (Mark 1:12-13). The baptism with the Spirit is accompanied by movement, conflict, and drama. Jesus's temptations may be explained as a recapitulation, a "makeover," of the journey of the first Adam. This God-given Man withstands the tempting suggestion that, when push comes to shove, we must take care of ourselves. Here Jesus is presented as the true Son; the relationship between Jesus and God proves to be one of incessant dependence and trust. Through the Holy Spirit, Jesus ultimately submitted himself as a sacrifice (Heb 9:14). Sonship and being the Spirit-bearer—in the terms of later dogmatics, Logos and pneuma-Christology—are not opposites but mutual affirmations.

In this book we can refer to only a few of the New Testament data about the work and functions of the Spirit. Mark mentions the Spirit as the one who descends on Jesus at his baptism in the Jordan (Mark 1:10). This is Jesus's first public appearance and, according to Mark, comes with a voice from heaven: "Thou art my beloved Son; with thee I am well pleased" (v. 11). In other words, Jesus stands as the bearer of the Spirit par excellence. He passes through the country in the power of that Spirit, preaching the message of a new order of salvation that is about to break through. The Spirit equips Jesus for this work. What we see in Mark we also find in Matthew and Luke, only these writers trace the role of the Spirit further back than Mark does. They describe Jesus's conception as something that happens through the Spirit of God (Luke 1:35; Matt 1:20). In various ways the point is thus underscored: the life and ministry of this Messenger or Prophet rests on a unique, divine initiative. Jesus proceeds from the Spirit. From the Old Testament (see Isa 11:1-5; 61:1-3) we see what great significance this anointing or equipping with the Spirit bears; it implies that all of Jesus's activities must be seen as God-initiated.

In this connection two interrelated matters call for further clarification: (1) the personality of the Spirit and (2) the relationship between the Spirit and the exalted Christ.

1. Opinions differ about whether the Spirit must be regarded as a person. Since the concept of person almost automatically makes us think of a separate individual, many theologians have opted for an alternative term such as "mode of existence" (Barth) or "power in history" (Berk-

hof). Even though we have made our own opinion clear (see chap. 3), it is far from simple to resolve the matter. Significantly, the debate on this issue did not reach a preliminary conclusion until the second half of the fourth century. Under the influence of the Cappadocian Fathers, the Council of Constantinople (381) declared that, just as we are dealing with God in the Son, so we are dealing with God when we speak of the Spirit, and that the Spirit has his own personality. For them this did not mean that the Spirit is a person in the modern sense of an individual; rather, they emphasized that the Spirit, in an indissoluble unity, acts in a personal way, just as the Father and the Son do.

The equal status attributed to Father, Son, and Spirit in the baptismal command in Matt 28:19—a text that has been constantly referred to since Athanasius—played a dominant role in the discussion of those days. In addition to this biblical argument, there was the theological case: if we can be saved only through the Spirit, the Spirit must also be God, for only God can save us. Here the same reasoning was applied to the Spirit that had been decisive for the confession of the *homo-ousios* in Christology (see chap. 10). Third, the Cappadocians had a deeply spiritual argument, one rooted in the collective experience of monastic life. They felt that their own faith experience and the renewal of their lives involved no mere impersonal power or influence but, for a third time, God himself.

Indeed, we meet God in the Father who created us, in the Son who became incarnate, and in the Spirit who brings us life and transformation. God is not only above us and with us but also in us. This step is both overpowering and diminutive. The Spirit makes himself small as he points to Christ and to the Father. We see this humility in the prayers and the liturgy of the church. Besides the hymn *Veni, Creator Spiritus* (Come, Creator Spirit, a ninth-century hymn for Pentecost that was rewritten and recommended by Luther), there are few prayers that address the Spirit directly. In principle, Christians pray to the Father through the Son in the Spirit.

2. But is the Spirit really "someone other" than Christ? Could we not simply say that, today in any case, the Spirit coincides with the exalted Christ? Indeed, some passages in the New Testament seem to suggest this (esp. 1 Cor 15:45 and 2 Cor 3:17). However, if we were to extend those lines any further, it would become impossible to ever separate Christ and the Spirit, and we must say that most of the textual material in the New Testament does not permit such a division. Incidentally, the Spirit who operates on earth and in the lives of human beings may be identified with Christ who lives in us, but a clear distinction is too often

made between Christ and the Spirit to let us take such identification as theologically determinative. The Corinthian texts (if they are relevant at all—see the note below) refer to a marginal situation, a focusing on the ultimate common aim in the work of the Son and of the Spirit. Admittedly, the risen Christ and the Spirit are both intimately linked to the same eschaton, but the nature of their involvement is different. In Christ the eschaton has already been realized; through the Spirit it is being realized in and for believers.

For this point see, in particular, Versteeg 1971, which concludes that the New Testament texts leave no room for an identification between Christ and the Spirit. For some time H. Berkhof (perhaps in part from an anti-Trinitarian motive) tried to defend that identification (1976, 25-26, where he speaks of the biblical-theological "discovery" of the identity of Christ and the Spirit), but subsequently he had to admit that he could not substantiate this case (CF 331-32). In the meantime an increasing number of exegetes read 2 Cor 3:7-18 (the most important proof text for such an identification) as a midrash on the Septuagint rendering of Exod 34:29-35, which supposedly indicates that the Kyrios is not Christ but YHWH (see Fee 1994, 311-14).

A. A. van Ruler articulates the distinction between Christ and the Spirit in terms of a wide range of *structural differences* between the christological and pneumatological perspectives. The most noticeable of these is that, christologically, we "remain outside," since Christ did his work for us but without us (as expressed in the concept of *vicariousness*). Pneumatologically, however, we do not remain outside but are involved; for instance, the Spirit does not testify instead of us but together with our spirit (Rom 8:16). We discern a God-directed mutuality, or in Van Ruler's idiom, a "theonomous reciprocity." "The most characteristic aspect of the work of the Spirit is, that it puts us to work." See Ruler 1989, 35. We agree with Van Ruler's plea for the uniqueness of the pneumatological point of view. For further discussion on the Roman Catholic side, see McDonnell 2003 (which borrows its title from Irenaeus's striking metaphor). For an intricate defense of the distinctive personality of the Spirit developed on the basis of the doctrine of the Trinity, see the dissertation of the Syrian-born theologian Najeeb Awad (2011).

This distinction fits with what we said earlier about the two missions (*missiones*). The first mission is that of the Son, the second that of the Spirit; both are equally important (McDonnell 2003, 197). To clarify the similarity and the difference: in the mission of the Spirit we are involved in what has been accomplished in the mission of the Son. The

Gospel of John keeps the two missions carefully separated (John 7:39). In John 20:22, when Jesus breathes on the disciples, it is as if the breath of God is felt for a second time, this time not as the beginning of creation but as the beginning of a new communion brought about by Christ. The risen Christ is the one who gives the Spirit. Only after his exaltation does the living water start to flow (John 7:38–39). Not until Jesus has withdrawn himself to the Father is there room for the Spirit (John 16:7). The dispensation that now begins is no less important, no poorer, than that of the Son; in its breadth and scope it is even greater and richer. Hence, particularly in view of the Gospel of John, the participants in the debate about the relationship between Jesus and the Spirit have come to refer to the two missions.

We may never neglect the distinction between the two movements that proceed from God: that of the Son and that of the Spirit. If we fully identify the mission of the Son with the mission of the Spirit, or reduce the one to the other, we run the risk of no longer doing justice to the biblical story and our own experience with it. In dogmatics we must regard the christological and the pneumatological as the two perspectives from which to understand our life. The Bible speaks of the life of Jesus as a life that has reached its completion; God exalted him and placed him at his right hand (Acts 2:33–34; Eph 1:20; Heb 1:13). This imagery points to a kingship that is already being exercised (cf. 1 Cor 15:25 with Ps 110:1, once again in the background). It signifies an unbreakable bond between the Father and the Son. Christ entered the reality of God as the last Adam, who precedes us. The Bible references this movement in terms of an incorruptible inheritance that is prepared for us (1 Pet 1:4). The work of the Son not only has been completed but was done "for us." From the christological perspective we discover the moment of something definitive, a decision that God will not revoke; thus, it is said of those who hope on Christ that their life is hidden with him in God (Col 3:3). In the Protestant tradition this truth has been further developed in the doctrines of justification and election (see chap. 15).

But also the work of the Spirit connects us with this completed work of Christ. Here we see a different structure. The Spirit works "in us," in the lowliness of our existence. The work of the Spirit in us is a work in progress. The Spirit does not lift us above our existence, which all too often is enmeshed in controversy and confusion (Rom 7), triggering sighs and prayers (Rom 8). The Spirit is characterized by closeness, and in this closeness things may happen that we ourselves cannot control. Or as Augustine said (*Conf.* 3.6.2), "God is closer to me than I am close to myself."

The link between the christological and the pneumatological contains a tension between the complete and the incomplete. God is affected by that tension. Through the Spirit, whom he has sent, God is involved with the sufferings of the present. Paul even states that the Spirit intervenes "with sighs too deep for words" (Rom 8:26). What an intense and sensorial image! It tells us that the Spirit operates in the midst of our existence and shares in all the ambiguity of our actual life in time. Experiences of great joy alternate with times of heart-rending sadness. Terrible emptiness may be filled again and again with God's grace by a small token of life. The Spirit is connected with all these things. Christ is above, the Spirit is below. Christ pleads for us before God (Heb 7:25), the Spirit prays for us on earth (Rom 8:26-27). When we no longer know what we should pray, what we should say, because we really are at our wits' end, the Spirit meets us and gives us a voice. In other words, when we call on God, we find the Spirit beside us. She is already present within the mystery of God's condescension toward us.

This systematic-theological distinction between pneumatological and christological perspectives exemplifies how theological reflection is not a goal in itself but aims to provide guidelines, in second-order language, for our relationship with God. It gives us tools to detect the presence of God and his quiet guidance in the midst of our everyday experiences, in moments of need and loneliness, but also in seasons of joy when things seem to fit together—and having found God, also to find the courage to call upon him and to trust him. Pneumatological reflection helps us in responding to God.

12.4. How God Relates to Us: Word and Spirit

We need to explore how God relates to us a little further along the lines of Reformed Christianity. Here, the Spirit's focus on the human person has always occupied a central place. The Spirit not only works to ensure salvation for the individual person by, as it were, a "home delivery" of salvation, but also works for a person's renewal. Or in the classic terminology that we will examine more closely in chapter 15, the Spirit is the motor behind justification and sanctification. This focus on the individual has enormous power but at the same time is an Achilles' heel, a weak spot where Protestantism has proven to be very vulnerable. When the relationship with the community is demoted below the bond with the individual, the single person may acquire a weight that in practice can scarcely be borne. We have ample evidence of the real risks of subjectivizing and individualizing the Spirit's work.

For a historical survey of this syndrome, see, for example, Anderson 2004, 19-38. The danger of overemphasizing the subject is that the reality of salvation becomes completely determined by our human appropriation. God's acts seem to become real and present only when, through the Spirit, the believer touches that reality and is enabled to appropriate it as his or her own. Or in theological language, the work of Christ is completely absorbed in the work of the Spirit. The objective aspect becomes marginal and may entirely lose its color beside the subjective: "If I have not experienced it, it has no meaning for me, for only what I feel is true." The danger of such a theology is clear. When the objective aspect (Christ, God's intervention, the biblical message) is absorbed by the subjective aspect (my journey of faith, my faith assurance), the human subject begins to revolve around its own axis. Eventually, all that is left is my own subjectivity, so that my own experience must provide me with something to hold on to. However, such experience cannot function as our anchor. We cannot do without a history and a word from outside ourselves (*extra nos*) that is determinative and that qualifies our experience. If only self-determination and self-development remain, *what* is actually determining and developing itself? Of course, this kind of subjectivism lies at the extreme. But it is far from imaginary in a culture where greater stress is put on presentation than on content, and where truth and values must often give place to good feelings. In some ways the emphasis on religious experience in the conservative branch of the Reformed family and the evangelical feel-good culture fit nicely with the postmodern cult of experience. Both might seem to be more resistant to secularization than other forms of faith, but they may eventually fail for not anchoring faith in the objective Word (i.e., Christ, the Bible, and preaching as promise-filled assurance).

This is the reason why we appeal here to the strong points of Protestant pneumatology, approaching the discussion of the Spirit in close connection with the (objective) Word. When the pneumatological perspective is controlled by the "in us," by "indwelling" and "coming to our assistance," we might be on a road characterized by searching and groping. Does the Spirit confirm our thoughts or rather contradict us (see Acts 16:7, 9-10)? However, we should not deny that the Spirit is at work with us. In close connection with the canonical witness regarding God's involvement with humanity, the Spirit helps us to gradually get to know God better. The Reformed dogmatic tradition utilizes a particular word-pair to describe this work; it may be referred to as *mystagogical* (introducing us into the "mystery" of the human relationship with God). This pair is "Word and Spirit." The boundaries of Word and Spirit form, as it were, the space within which our human relationship with God is realized, with all that is thereby entailed in terms of light and darkness, searching and avoiding, resistance and surrender, relapse and growth. In this chapter we mention a few preliminary points before further developing the subject in the next few chapters.

1. The use of this word-pair tells us first of all that we cannot have the Spirit by himself. The Spirit is connected to the Word, with Christ, and cannot therefore be combined with just anything. What we said earlier about the threefold relationship between Christ and the Spirit returns on the level of salvation history and of the Bible. The prophets and apostles spoke as they were "moved" by the Holy Spirit (2 Pet 1:21), which is what we call *inspiration*. The Spirit points us to the revelation, to the Bible as a collection of books that have the status of the Word of God, of *revelation*. The Bible is therefore not a dead letter; God reveals himself through the Word. The Spirit proceeds on this basis with his work of enlightening people, which is called *illumination* (see 2 Cor 4:6). The Bible as the deposit of the human relationship between God over the ages is the fruit of the Spirit, and so is what the Bible does. The Reformation has therefore kept Word and Spirit closely together. It attempted a middle way between the theology of the existing church of Rome, with its accent on the objectivity of the sacraments, and the spiritualists, with their emphasis on the subjective experience of the "inner light."

We point here in passing to a subtle but significant difference between the Lutherans and the Reformed. Lutherans saw the Spirit at work "through the Word" (*per verbum*). This wording could create the impression that the Spirit was, as it were, locked up in the Bible so that it would suffice if the Bible was read and proclaimed. But Calvinists referred to the work of the Spirit "with the Word" (*cum verbo*). This wording created some critical distance that allowed people to ponder whether the Spirit was indeed at work when the Word was opened. The correct middle position is embodied in the church's prayer of epiclesis (Gk. *epiklēsis*, "invocation, calling down from on high"), a pleading to God that, when the Scriptures are opened, God will be present, as promised, with his Spirit where even "two or three are gathered" in his name (see Matt 18:20).

In chapter 13 we study further the topic of inspiration and illumination in connection with the Bible. For the illumination of the Spirit, see Webster 2011.

2. Second, the reverse is also true: just as we cannot detach the Spirit from the Word, so the Word may not be separated from the Spirit. In that

sense the pairing of Word and Spirit qualifies the rather formal term "revelation." It points to the dimension of power in our relationship with God as it is mediated by the Bible. The Word does not simply provide some information. No, the Spirit ensures that, through the Word, something happens with us and in us. We develop this thought further in chapter 15 in terms of faith, participation, and transformation. We cannot control this process, precisely because we are dealing with the Spirit, who blows in the direction of his choice (John 3:8). But we can move with that wind by allowing ourselves to become actually involved with the community around Christ; the light will then shine from the outside to the inside. *In concreto*, this process requires participating in worship, in the various elements of the liturgy, joining in prayer, "placing ourselves under the Word" (as the classic expression says), and submitting to a daily discipline in our service and obedience to God. This is where the light shines, and anyone who wants to learn how to have faith must go there. In brief, Word and Spirit point to a praxis of faith that has an outer side of rituals, customs, and acts (that can easily be labeled "empty rites") but that, in their outward dimension and materiality, also have an inner dimension. We experience an osmosis between external and internal; we are "porous." Sharing in prayer and song, celebrating the Lord's Supper, kneeling to receive the blessing, joining in singing Handel's *Messiah*, caring for the sick—all these actions inevitably affect us. In these acts we are, first and foremost, receivers, but at the same time we become active participants.

3. The first two aspects bring us to a third: God's Spirit *enlists* people who have been touched by the Word; to use the words of Paul, we become colaborers with God (1 Cor 3:9; cf. 2 Cor 6:1). This term points to a dynamism that is difficult to fathom but should not for that reason be ignored. The difficulty is that we cannot precisely indicate where God's work stops and ours begins. God works, in his own way and at his good time, in the activities of people, educators, coaches, and in a wide range of pastoral and diaconal functions in churches, organizations, networks, and up-to-date "databases." Yet, we must repeat again that the indwelling of the Spirit (both in the body of Christ and in individuals) has its uncomfortable side too. Individuals as well as organizations can grieve the Spirit, go backward, sleep, or just keep the door shut.

In summary, the pairing of Word and Spirit recognizes that God wants us to become alive through all the objective gifts of Bible, story, and the work of the church in its proclamation, rites, and diaconate. Detached from this life-giving work of the Spirit, all these media remain inert, and Christ remains outside of us, disconnected. The Spirit brings

Christ toward us; rather, the Spirit brings us to Christ and incorporates us in the body of Christ (see Calvin, *Inst.* 3.1.1). The Spirit of God thus ensures that the Word of God, the promise, the new life, comes to us. The Spirit ensures the experience of being touched, of an existential relationship, of participation and encounter. The Spirit does not rest until we are truly involved in God's turning toward us and respond to it.

Here all sorts of experiences can play a mediating role. Encounters with people, a hymn, an image, a dream, experiences of horror or of being deeply moved may play a role. The Christian church has typically been rather reluctant to grant such experiences a place in God's relation with us. This hesitancy is understandable, but it may also feed a practical agnosticism, even a functional atheism: we no longer meet God in our daily lives but only in the Scriptures. In fact, modern rationalism has overtaken the traditional view of inspiration, restricting God's revelation—in the sense of his way of relating to us—to the Bible. We wish to be entirely clear: the Bible as the Word of God is normative, but it does not exclude other means whereby God relates to us. The Spirit blows where she wants and can use anything. More about this follows in chapter 14.

12.5. God's Ways of Relating to Us: The Fruit of the Spirit, the Gifts of the Spirit, and Spirit Baptism

The previous paragraph ended with a few remarks about the life-bringing work of the Spirit, which we will explore further in chapter 15. This aspect of the Spirit's work was strongly emphasized in the Reformed tradition over the past few centuries, usually under the heading of the new birth. In actual practice the new birth often came to be viewed as the only really important work of the Spirit. But that view fails to do justice to the broader perspective of the New Testament, which does not allow us to reduce the richness of the work of the Spirit to one element. For the Spirit is active not just in the beginning of our relationship with God but also in its progression. In this connection we briefly explore the Spirit's continuing involvement with the believer in three specific areas: the fruit of the Spirit, the gifts of the Spirit, and baptism with the Spirit.

1. First the *fruit* of the Spirit. In Gal 5:22–24 Paul identifies a number of virtues as the fruit of the Spirit. His use of the singular fruit—not "fruits"—indicates that these virtues cannot be received one by one but belong together (see also Eph 5:9). This cohesion is also affirmed in the pas-

sages of exhortation where Paul speaks of the renewal people experience by the power of the Spirit (e.g., Rom 12:2; 13:8-14; Eph 4:17-32; 5). Those who allow themselves to be led by the Spirit already live in a different order, the order of the Spirit of Christ, with its disposition of life and peace (Rom 8:6). However much Paul realizes that this renewal is not yet complete, that he is still "away from the Lord" (2 Cor 5:6), he believes that it is already a reality. The indicative of the new life determines the imperative; the fact that the Spirit has initiated a relationship with Christ ensures that Paul can genuinely exhort us to live henceforth in accordance with that relationship.

Christian theology may therefore count on the evolution and growth of virtue. The recognition that we are sinful beings may not lead to a mentality of skepticism and distrust. Such an attitude would shortchange the power of the work of the Spirit, who ensures the fruit by ever strengthening the believer's bond with Christ. Moreover, concrete expressions of the renewal of life have largely been responsible for the growth of the Christian church, not just in the early centuries but also later in the many places where the gospel has been preached.

Using the metaphor of fruit to help explain this complex of moral virtues has deep roots in the Old Testament. We find Israel described as God's special vineyard (e.g., Ps 80). Again and again God looks for the fruit of people concretely turning toward him and, concurrently, away from other gods and the powers of social injustice. See, for example, Isa 5:1-4, with the "application" in v. 7, and the surprising turn in Hos 14:8: "From me comes your fruit." In the New Testament the metaphor reappears prominently in John 15:1-4, where it is applied to Jesus's followers. There the text also uses "fruit" in the singular. It is no accident, therefore, that the Pauline epistles speak of "the fruit of the Spirit."

In this context we want to point out in passing that the rather musty image of the concept of virtue has recently been thoroughly refurbished because of the revival of so-called virtue ethics (e.g., see Besser-Jones and Slote 2015, with a survey of its contemporary Christian varieties by Jennifer Herdt, 223-36) . This approach argues that moral actions may best be understood not in terms of rules for and consequences of our actions, but rather in terms of character formation. Virtues are to be understood as positive dispositions, that is, character traits that allow for further growth. Christians do not deny that others can develop these kinds of virtues, but nonetheless they see our orientation toward Christ and the workings of the Spirit as the main source.

2. Second, there are the *charismata*, or the *gifts* of grace. Here, quite intentionally, we find the plural form: there is a diversity of gifts which (in

contrast with the fruit of the Spirit) are not all given to every believer. The New Testament's consistent theme is that a wide range of gifts exist, but that the Spirit distributes these as he sees fit (1 Cor 12:11). The paradigm that Paul so impressively develops in 1 Cor 12:12-31 is of one body with many parts.

In New Testament times the Greek loan word *charisma* was not yet the technical term it would later become. It is to be translated "gift of grace." To get a balanced perspective we should realize that the New Testament does not limit the gifts of the Spirit to extraordinary phenomena, such as healing, prophecy, and tongues (also often referred to, from the Greek original, as glossolalia). These three are on the list but are not alone. As gifts of the Spirit, the Pauline letters list rather common things that we would classify with the offices of the church. Romans 12:6-8 enumerates prophecy, service, teaching, exhortation, contributing, giving, and compassion; in 1 Cor 12:8-10 we read of speaking with wisdom, faith, gifts of healing, working of miracles, glossolalia, and distinguishing between spirits. These are summaries of examples and are not meant to be normative. The main point in 1 Cor 12-14 is that all these activities can serve as instruments of God's grace. They are given by God to equip and guide the faith community in its journey.

This broader perspective is still important today. In the Pentecostal movement (more on this below), the concept of the charismata has been incorrectly reduced to tongues, prophecy, and gifts of healing. The overall impression of Scripture, rather, is that the Spirit somehow makes a person into a channel of God's grace and love. A charism is most definitely not a personal attribute (as it is, for instance, in the adjective "charismatic" that Max Weber [1864-1920] coined for a particular personality type), and it does not always refer to something extraordinary. We may speak of a spiritual gift when God lifts "ordinary" people above their possibilities so that their contribution becomes a divine gift to the community. This gifting often happens in a way that tallies with a person's natural talents; the Spirit of renewal is the same Spirit who was active in creation. However, this broader understanding of the concept does not mean that theology should deny or suppress the specific gifts of tongues, healing, and prophecy.

For a historical survey of the concept of charisma (and also baptism with the Spirit), see Baumert 2001 and 2004. The gifts of the Spirit, or *charismata*, involve the equipping, guidance, and encouragement that God gives his people on their pilgrimage. These are gifts for the journey, not intended for individual persons but for the entire faith community—sometimes for the entire world! For this last aspect, think, for instance, of Martin Luther King's prophetic "I Have a Dream" speech delivered at the March on Washington in 1963.

There has been much discussion about whether the charismata are linked to natural gifts we already possess. Pentecostals often point to the radically new, liberating, and often surprising character of what the Spirit arouses in us. Without denying that view, we agree with others that God does not suppress our humanness but enlists it in his service. We should no longer think dualistically about the relationship between pneumatology and anthropology, like between creation and redemption. As Bavinck argued, God's grace restores and perfects nature but does "not add to existence any new creatures or introduce any new substance into it" (RD 3:578).

3. Third, we mention the *baptism* with the Spirit. Here we notice a similar pattern as with the charismatic gifts. Whereas in Mark this baptism serves as an all-encompassing term for the dedication to God prompted by the Spirit (see above, 12.3), it acquired a much more specific connotation in the Holiness movement that grew out of Methodism during the nineteenth century. The baptism with the Spirit came to be regarded as the Spirit's most important work, a most singular experience of being touched, fulfilled, and sanctified, which led to being filled with God and unreservedly ready to serve him. In the Pentecostal revival at the beginning of the twentieth century this so-called Spirit-baptism was further defined and restricted to the experiences of speaking in tongues and the gift of prophecy. So, whereas initially baptism with the Spirit was a rather broad and fluid concept for everything that the exalted Christ bestows upon people and that empowers them in the service of his kingdom, the concept became theologically reduced to one specific kind of experience. The specific forms of "tongues" and "prophecy" became the spectacles through which "baptism with the Spirit" (Baumert 2001, 2:282) was understood, and anyone who had not received this baptism was seen to be an incomplete—if even real—Christian.

Baptism means immersion, thereby suggesting abundance. Such an abundance became available at the outpouring of the Spirit on Pentecost in Jerusalem (Acts 2), and subsequently also in Caesarea, when for the first time gentiles received the Spirit (Acts 10:44-46). The well-known words of John the Baptist point forward to that occasion: "I have baptized you with water, but he will baptize you with the Spirit" (Mark 1:8 and pars.; note also Jesus's reference to this baptism in Acts 1:5). As Jesus himself was baptized with the Holy Spirit, so would his disciples be.

Both cases involve an "anointing" (Acts 10:38; 1 John 2:20, 27), with the result that a person will continue to be led by the Spirit (John 1:32; 14:17). There is only one reference to a baptism with (or in) the Spirit, namely in 1 Cor 12:13. Gordon Fee (1994) provides an excellent discussion of this text. He concludes: "Paul's present concern is not to delineate how an individual becomes a believer, but to explain how the many of them, diverse as they are, are in fact one body. The answer: The Spirit, whom all alike have received" (178).

Baptism with and in the Spirit may therefore be understood to mean the same thing as being filled with or through the Spirit, and it is also linked to being sealed with or by the Spirit (2 Cor 1:22; Eph 1:13; 4:30). All three terms denote an intense experience of God's nearness, grace, and power, in which we may receive particular charismata, as well as the assurance of salvation. Does this reception coincide with the moment when a person first becomes a believer, or does it refer rather to a "second blessing"? This question has caused a lot of debate. Charismatic and Pentecostal Christians, but also some currents in the Reformed tradition, have preferred the second option. Likewise, the distinction between infant baptism and confirmation in the Roman Catholic tradition can be traced back to the idea that, at various points in time, a person may receive this grace. Indeed, the New Testament sometimes refers to a certain lapse of time between the moment a person first becomes a believer and the time he or she receives (the baptism of) the Spirit (in particular, cf. Acts 8:14-17 and 19:1-7). This Spirit-baptism is sometimes, but not always, accompanied by a laying on of hands, speaking in tongues, and receiving the gift of prophecy. But in other testimonies they all coincide—possibly with water baptism as well (e.g., Acts 10:44-48; 1 Cor 12:13). It would be wrong to play Luke and Paul off against each other, even though, admittedly, they stress different points: Paul tries to keep things together soteriologically, while Luke appears at times to spread them out charismatically (see Thiselton 2013, 54-62, 129-30, also for recent developments within Pentecostalism on the interpretation of the relevant texts).

Whatever the case, we must be careful not to force everything into one system. Apparently, the Spirit works with people in different ways and—independently of their character, spiritual development, or communal context—is able to give them, at a certain moment in time, an important new impulse, an intensification of a conscious life in the Spirit, so that they "grow up in every way into him who is the head, into Christ" (Eph 4:15). In this context it is important to keep in mind the basic New Testament principle: all believers share in the Spirit and in full salvation in Christ. The Holy Spirit is "the identity marker of the converted" (Fee 1994, 88). Therefore, there is no reason to differentiate between two categories of Christians: those who have received the baptism, infilling, or sealing with the Spirit and those who have not (yet).

12.6. The Spirit as the Founder of a New, Global Community

We described the work of the Spirit as instigating relationships and participation. Thus far we have applied this mostly to individuals, in keeping with the line laid out at the Reformation. We have alluded here and there to the fact that these individuals have, from the very start, also belonged to a community, the body of Christ; now we want to explore that matter a little further. The Spirit does not just work in individual people but establishes a community around Christ and so gives shape to the "new covenant"—in fact, the church. Here again a few remarks will have to suffice, pending further elaboration in chapter 14.

The first thing we need to say about the church is that the initiative for this new community comes not from us but from the living Christ. In the history of Jesus Christ, God has unfolded the mystery of history. This same God who started small with Abraham and remained true to his promise through everything that occurred to the patriarch and his posterity—this God has now provided everyone access to him in Jesus Christ (note Gen 12:3b). In other words, the path of the Spirit of God proceeds not outside of history but within it, along the tracks of Israel's history. Jesus is God's big Yes with respect to his promises to Israel (2 Cor 1:20), and from this resounding Yes, the non-Jewish nations may now also benefit. The mystery of God's saving acts now stands revealed; all may join in the covenant, in the eschatological community.

This worldwide scope has an enormous importance for the way we look at God's operation in history. It certainly was an astounding discovery for Paul, who grew up with the conviction that God gave Israel a very special treatment. His utter astonishment still resounds in his epistles: "The mystery was made known to me by revelation, as I have written briefly. When you read this you can perceive my insight into the mystery of Christ, which was not made known to the sons of men in other generations as it has now been revealed to his holy apostles and prophets by the Spirit; that is, how the Gentiles are fellow heirs, members of the same body, and partakers of the promise in Christ Jesus through the gospel" (Eph 3:3-6).

This topic brings us to the *boundary-crossing* character of the work of the Spirit. In his efforts to let the entire world share in Christ, the Spirit propels people over lines they had never thought they would cross. Paul himself is one of these, but the book of Acts provides other impressive examples. Peter is urged to put aside Jewish dietary laws; the persecution of the early church results in the gospel spreading to many places outside Israel. Admittedly, all these movements are accompanied by much confusion and suffering. For dogmatics, it bears repeating: as in the Old Testament, so in the New, the work of the Spirit is often confusing, creates unrest, and rarely follows straight lines. This insight can yield great comfort; confusion, resistance, and misfortunes in the advance of the gospel message do not prove that the Spirit has lost his way. Even persecution may have unintended consequences, though—and this again seems confusing—it is not a fixed rule. It would be sentimental to pretend that the saying "the blood of the martyrs is the seed of the church" always proves true. At times persecution and violent displacements of Christians have apparently been very effective in elimating the presence of believers and churches. However, such results never mean that the Spirit has met a dead end, for the Spirit is not easily caught off guard.

Globalization, the shifts of economic power in the world, enormous streams of migrants, the shift of the church's numerical strength to the Southern Hemisphere, the growing influence of Islam in Europe—all of these developments may confuse us, but in pneumatological perspective, they might stand in a different light. They are possibilities where the Spirit may penetrate. The church must pray for the gift of discernment. For that reason our ecclesiological reflection must be very empirical. We can discern where the church is, where the Spirit is leaving his tracks, only by constantly reconnoitering our global, multicontextual reality. However, unexpected good news appears surprisingly often; for instance, the church is currently undergoing strong growth in China, which has always tended to be closed to the gospel.

The new community around Christ is *worldwide* and *diverse*. Apparently, Christ is revealed in many divergent creations of the Spirit, but all faith communities find their unity and common bond in Christ. For all their diversity and provisional character, these communities form a revelation of the one body of Christ. The crucial text in this respect bears repeating, 1 Cor 12:13: "For by one Spirit we were all baptized into one body—Jews or Greeks, slaves or free—and all were made to drink of one Spirit." A few verses earlier (v. 3) this same apostle presents the confession of Jesus as Lord to be the first and most important work of the Spirit. Paul immediately sees the boundaries and divisions that must

513

be surmounted by the work of the Spirit, yet the very people who earlier "were led astray to dumb idols" (v. 2) are now prepared to confess "Jesus is Lord." This confession has a binding, not a separating, effect. The Spirit does not establish a new sect, another schism, or a new religion but brings very different persons and groups together as God's new people. The work of the Spirit may be recognized precisely in this unity-forging process. The separation between the Jews and the people from the nations is removed, since in Christ those two categories have been reconciled (Eph 2:13-22). "For through him we both have access in one Spirit to the Father" (v. 18).

Nonetheless, within this all-encompassing spiritual unity we find enormous cultural, ethnic, and social diversity. It is crucial to ensure that this diversity works in a centripetal and not a centrifugal way. Paul himself had to take up this vital task, as we note in his relentless efforts to combine unity and diversity, and to make this diversity fruitful for the community. His most impressive contribution in this regard is undoubtedly the image of the church as the body with many parts (1 Cor 12). But even when Paul gets somewhat agitated in his epistles, it is almost always because he feels that the gospel—and thereby Christian unity—is in danger of being negated in the faith community.

For Paul, truth and unity are not polar opposites but belong together. A clear example comes in his confrontation with Peter, narrated in Gal 2:11-14. Peter was close to destroying this unity through his inconsistent ways of dealing with gentile Christians. Paul's condemnation of Peter's actions stems from his deep conviction that there is no gospel other than that of the "grace of Christ" (Gal 1:6), in which both the Jews and the people from the nations may share. Therefore, even an epistle that seems to be rather doctrinal and that powerfully stresses the importance of purity seems to have a practical ecclesiological focus: the unity of the church is constituted by its faith in Christ and nothing else. Paul undergirds that unity pneumatologically: "Let me ask you only this: Did you receive the Spirit by works of the law, or by hearing with faith? Are you so foolish? Having begun with the Spirit, are you now ending with the flesh?" (Gal 3:2-3). A new awareness forcefully emerges in this Epistle to the Galatians: in light of the only truly new fact that has ever occurred—the coming of Christ (4:4)—history has been given a new direction. We are no longer to live under the tutelage of the law or the powers of the world (4:3, 9) but are redeemed by Christ from the curse of the law (3:13) to live an emancipated life in the freedom of the Spirit (5:13-18). It is unthinkable that one would regress to a premodern world of enslavement, disempowerment, and coercion!

A remarkable Paul-renaissance has been occurring in recent years in Continental philosophy, with such authors as Giorgio Agamben, Alain Badiou, John Caputo, and Slavoj Žižek; for a survey, see the special issue *The Apostle Paul in Modern Philosophy* (= *Bijdragen* 70.2 [2009]). These scholars are impressed that Paul apparently cannot do without metaphysics but also (esp. Badiou) with Paul's universalism. They do not mean that Paul envisioned all people sharing in salvation at the last day, but that Paul deliberately broke through all ethnic, political, and social boundaries. His Spirit-inspired message takes into view all people, whom he apparently considers equals, without exception. Admittedly, this approach separates Paul from what specifically makes him a Christian, but it is nevertheless remarkable that his vision continues to resonate even in our postmodern context.

The Pauline image of the church as one body united by the Spirit should occupy the mind of today's Christians much more strongly than it does, certainly considering that the church in the West seems to have almost succumbed to individualism and the tendency to divide. The Spirit does not let people believe in isolation or only in a small group that shares certain desired social characteristics. On the contrary, the Spirit unites us across social and cultural boundaries, gives us to each other, and translates all differences into a community: the *familia Dei*, the family of God; see also Mark. 3:31–35; 10:28–30.

We do not need to travel far to find examples of diversity. In virtually every metropolis in Europe and North America, we find the worldwide diversity of Christianity. For an example, see Gornik 2011. In fact, we have come full circle, and after a long period of relative cultural homogeneity in Constantinian Christianity, we have returned to the extremely pluriform cultural and religious situation of the world of the New Testament and early church. Our Western world is no longer the world of the 1950s. This change should not frighten us; apparently, it is the new road the Spirit wants to go. He offers new opportunities to meet and to undergo an osmosis with Christians of non-Western origin. A Christianity gone lethargic can, if it is ready to break through its own historical limitations, be reinvigorated by such a new input.

In short, the Spirit does not limit her work to creating and sustaining individual faith but draws her circles much wider, in and with the Christian community. Remember, the Spirit has been promised as the Paraclete, or Comforter, who would be sent to stay with the church and guide it. He is the Spirit of truth who "will not speak on his own authority, but whatever he hears he will speak, and he will declare to you the things that are to come" (John 16:13). This prophecy signifies continuity, so that the church may live in the promise that the Spirit will lead it through all time. Protestants tend to regard this statement with some distrust, for it seems only a short step to thinking in terms of ecclesial infallibility or triumphalism. But this potential should not detract us from the promise of Christ. The assured assistance of the Spirit helps us to bear up when the church gropes to find its way amid new challenges without ready-made solutions. It also helps us to trust that the Spirit will always point us to passable roads as we proceed through history.

12.7. The Work of the Spirit in Culture and History

So far we have mainly discussed the work of the Spirit in the life of the individual (12.4 and 12.5) and the significance of the Spirit for the church and community (12.6). But can we go further? Can we also discern the Spirit at work beyond the church and the individual believer in the wider circles of culture and society? Can the Spirit also perform his healing and sanctifying work in official structures like the state and via the informal mechanisms that regulate how people deal with each other? Or are earthly culture and human history just being prepared for the judgment? If the Spirit is indeed at work in culture and history, how could we tell? May we say, for instance, that the work of the Spirit is behind the recognition of human equality or in our arrangements for health care? Is there any link between God's Spirit and democratic forms of government, in which the authorities are held responsible and may be dismissed? Or are these at most riverbeds with some rifts and shallows that occasionally fill with water but may suddenly go dry, leaving just a memory of a stream? What may be said about a culture that claims to have been influenced by Christianity? These themes touch on questions that are usually handled under the heading of church and state. However, we choose to sketch some broad outlines here in this survey of the work of the Spirit. The chapter on the church (14.10) will develop the topic more fully.

We can distinguish between three options or models of the relationship between church and state (or, more broadly, society and culture). The first posits a far-reaching identification, the second a complete separation, and the third a stance of critical discernment. The first model calls for a strategy of optimistic trust, the second for critical distance, and the third for prayer and testing the spirits. We want to say something about each approach. (A volume in Dutch on the entire topic is Borgman et al. 2008.)

12.7.1. *From* "societas christiana" *to* "societas humana": *Identification*

For many centuries Europe saw itself as a *societas christiana*, a Christian society, in which government and church were to converge. This ideal of unity reached its peak in the eleventh and twelfth centuries around the Investiture Controversy, in which emperor and pope argued about who had the right to appoint bishops (investiture = clothing, i.e., with episcopal authority). Whatever their actual conduct, their abuse of power, and their usurpation of regions and possessions, the princes and lords of church and state believed they had a common goal: a Christian society. This ideal of a *corpus christianum* marked the era of Christendom.

That ideal remained alive after the Reformation. The Ten Commandments were not regarded as the exclusive domain of the church but were thought to have a place in public life. Besides its other functions (see chap. 15), the law of God had a political role, the *usus politicus*. Ideally, only the God of the Bible was to be worshiped in society, and only as he himself had commanded (i.e., from a Reformed viewpoint, not in a Roman Catholic or Anabaptist manner). We find this "theocratic ideal" in the controversial article 36 of the Belgic Confession (1561), which affirms that the earthly authorities have the task to "destroy all idolatry and false worship" (OF 65). Should we call this ideal "identification"? It did not go quite that far. Civil authorities did indeed have the *ius circa sacra* (rights concerning the church's externalities) but not the *ius in sacra* (the right to deal with internal church matters). Attempts at complete identification were thwarted by the theory of the two kingdoms, which originated with Martin Luther and was later adopted by Calvin. Both Luther and Calvin leave us in no doubt that human beings are citizens of two different kingdoms or regimes: one that deals with eternal salvation, and another that cares for our earthly well-being. They were well aware that the Holy Spirit, the Spirit of Christ, was not to be identified with what people do on this earth, but they had a theologically motivated confidence that the civil authorities, if they perform their task as they should, have a role in facilitating our earthly pilgrimage. Theologically, this idea was based on the ancient notion of natural law, the idea that the moral law has been implanted in every human being—in the conscience—so that, even people who are not Christians know what is good and what is bad. For further analysis, see, for example, David vanDrunen, *Natural Law and the Two Kingdoms* (Grand Rapids, 2009).

The magisterial Reformation (i.e., Lutheran, Calvinist, and Anglican) held a high opinion about the role of the government as God's instrument to help us on our way to our eternal destination. Calvin treats the topic of the government in the fourth book of his *Institutes* (4.20), where he refers to the "external means that God uses to invite us to enter into communion with Christ, and saves us therein." That is, like the church—the first and most important means—the government belongs in the sphere of pneumatology. When Calvin deems civil government to be one of the external instruments of God, he connects its acts with the work of God's Spirit. When the authorities punish evil, they promote the quality of life and guarantee a safe environment; such responsibility makes government a servant of God (see Rom 13:1-7). Note that, in Calvin's usage, "external" does not mean inappropriate. The identification of "internal" with authentic and of "external" with inauthentic dates from later times.

The nineteenth century brought a second high point in the link between Spirit and culture, but now of a totally different order. The atmosphere around German philosopher G. W. F. Hegel and his followers was one of astonishment and joy at human progress. Witnessing the growth of knowledge, the spread of culture, the sharing of power, improved morality—one can almost feel their enthusiasm about the times and the course of human achievement. For Hegel, history could be comprehended as an ascent along a dialectical route of thesis and antithesis that would climax in a grand synthesis. Moreover, human beings—in particular, the philosopher—took an initiating, commanding role in this process. We observe the multicolored stream of reality not from the outside but right in the midst of it. The world unfolds itself in the human mind, as was being demonstrated most clearly in science and the ever-stronger call for assertive citizenship and rational governance. Indeed, Hegel thought that in human history the Spirit of God comes into his own; the divine Spirit had already exerted so much influence on modern consciousness and culture that an intimate link had been established between the human spirit and the Holy Spirit. The nineteenth century lived in this confidence, that the Spirit of God works immanently in culture. If Barth would later label Hegel's a philosophy of self-confidence, an earlier theologian in Hegel's line, Richard Rothe (1799-1867), advocated the desacralization and socialization of the Christian faith—that is, that the church be absorbed by the state. If the ideals of the kingdom of God have shaped laws and institutions, then justice and compassion have become the rule in society, and we can do without the church.

This so-called cultural Christianity provides a perfect example of the identification model. The question is not whether the Spirit impacts culture and history, for he is nowhere more active. The working of the Spirit does not depend on a conscious belief in God but on humanity's objective progress along the road to the kingdom of God—a progress that demands our recognition.

These patterns of thought are particularly evident in the liberal theology of the nineteenth and twentieth centuries—for instance, with scholars like Rothe, J. H. Scholten (1811–85), and, in the twentieth century, H. M. Kuitert (b. 1924), T. Rendtorff (b. 1931), and H. J. Adriaanse (1940–2012). E. Troeltsch (1865–1923) definitely belongs to this tradition as well, but he became increasingly pessimistic about the sustainability of the synthesis between Christianity and culture; toward the end of his life he feared that European culture was turning in a nihilistic direction. (Here is a clear example where we may justifiably speak of the charisma of prophecy!) See Berkhof, 200YT 50–60 (on Hegel), 66–68 (Rothe), 98–103 (Scholten), 150–62 (Troeltsch), and 212–28 (Kuitert). In this tradition the close connection between the Spirit and Christ, which prevailed in the New Testament, has largely disappeared; what remains is the thought that our culture has been saturated with Christian values. This is the lasting value and significance of Christianity. Western culture may be compared with a rocket that has left its booster engine behind and now flies on its own power. But will this vessel succeed?

Barth, after World War I, as well as postmodernism, after World War II, had some very hard-hitting comments about this progress-optimism, especially after the horrors of war that ravaged so-called enlightened Europe.

In the identification model the essential notions of the gospel have been translated into cultural values. The notion of a humanity created in God's image was transposed into the principle of equality, with important positive consequences in practical application. After centuries of hierarchical social rankings and classes, we now see the determination to accord maximum possible equality of political, social, and economic rights to all people. The legal basis for a social safety net, equal access to education and health care, and the degree to which these advances have become axiomatic are regarded as a result of the gospel, of the Spirit of Christ. Indeed, much has changed since the Middle Ages! Gradually the ideal of a *societas christiana* has shifted to that of a *societas humana*: a state with the rule of law, or a union of nations in which every attempt is made to safeguard the ideals of freedom and justice in laws and institutions.

However, so explicitly positive a view of the cultural transformations resulting from the impact of the gospel on Western culture was not limited to liberal theologians. It became quite common also among Protestant theologians of various backgrounds. We may point, for instance, to Abraham Kuyper, who developed the concept of common grace into a positive evaluation of human cultural development. Herman Bavinck followed in his tracks; for example, see his work *De katholiciteit van Christendom en kerk* (The catholicity of Christianity and church [1888]). Later in the twentieth century as well we find a very high estimation of the influence of the gospel on European culture in A. A. van Ruler ("History is the work of the Spirit par excellence," IB, chap. 33) and Berkhof (CF 503-15). As time went on, Berkhof developed reservations, as he saw how our society was "cutting down the gospel tree from which it is picking the fruits" (518), but he still maintained that not only individual persons but also structures may be sanctified (511-12). The question has been asked in criticism of Berkhof whether the word "sanctification," with its personal connotations, may indeed be applied to structures. In any case, we may say that structures can reflect God's intent for society to be marked by justice, compassion, and peace. But structures themselves are never holy. They are possibilities, pools that must remain filled, and must therefore be used and protected by people who are called to be just and compassionate. Without connection to the roots of the gospel, structures that were intended to give people freedom may suddenly change into new powers that will take this freedom away. Continental philosophy called this specter the "dialectic of Enlightenment" (T. Adorno).

12.7.2. *Separation*

A second model for the relationship between the Spirit and culture is that of contrast and separation between the two. In this approach the Spirit is considered to be at odds with the societal and cultural status quo. This was a strong motif in the theology of the 1970s, which prided itself on social critique. It nearly insisted that the church or Christians stand against the existing order. Instead of continuity or even identity between our reality and God's kingdom, as in the first model, the supporters of the second emphasize the rift, a tearing between the two. This approach at times generated attitudes of distance and asceticism, as with John H.

Yoder and Stanley Hauerwas; sometimes, however, the realization of discontinuity opened opportunities for intense interest and unprejudiced participation. At other times it led to fierce social criticism, often rooted in a neo-Marxist, politically colored engagement. (This last option disappeared, however, soon after the fall of the Berlin Wall in 1989.)

These different attitudes may be carrying on the rupture between Christian faith and culture that Barth inaugurated in his commentary on the Epistle to the Romans (1919; 2nd ed., 1922). In this book Barth argues that God's kingdom is of a completely different order than the world known to us. This world is and ever remains the world. What we meet in the Bible is an eschatological reality that touches and cuts through our world, but the world never shares this reality. Grace, resurrection, justification, the Spirit—everything that comes from God—arrives at the gates of our existence, knocks on them, keep us awake and restless, but does not abide with us. The Word indeed reveals itself but does not remain incarnate; it does not live among us except perhaps incognito by negation—the denial that something of the Spirit might find a place in this life. The work of the Spirit should make us hunger and thirst, show sympathy with the burdened and distressed, and so far as politics is concerned, opt for the side of protest. These are the basic outlines of a theology that definitively refuses any identification between Christendom and the Christian faith. Christendom is a cultural phenomenon, a historical complex of half-hearted attempts, a cemetery of ideals, and a theological impossibility. Barth's critical theology signified a break with every form of Eurocentric thinking.

Wir stehen tiefer im Nein als im Ja (We stand more deeply in the No than in the Yes), Barth stated in his famous Tambacher speech, "Der Christ in der Gesellschaft" (The Christian in society [1920]; for a translation, see Karl Barth, *The Word of God and the Word of Man*, trans. Amy Marga [London, 2011], 60). However, Barth did not stop at this point. When he declared in *Christengemeinde und Bürgergemeinde* (The Christian community and the civil community [1946])—that is, right after World War II—that the Christian community must be an example for society and points to God's love as the ultimate basis of civil liberties, negation and separation are not predominant, but a critical loyalty toward society as it is portrayed in the prayers of the church. Quite clearly, in this Barth provided the theological space in which we may respond creatively to God's voice. In the obedience of human acts we may see analogies with God's kingdom, one of which is the democratic state with its rule of law. This analogical thinking prepares for the possibility of a more constructive relationship between Spirit and history. Nonetheless, the essential structure of Barth's separation model remained intact; we must sharply distinguish between what God does and what people do in response, between God's Spirit and the human spirit. These two never simply coincide, as was thought in the nineteenth century, and it is extremely dangerous to mix them—that is, to try to win God's approval for our deeds. This does not mean that the sanctification of our lives will always fail, but it will be realized only in an attitude of prayer and total dependence.

In short, under the influence of dialectical theology, many began to define the Spirit-culture relationship in terms of criticism and separation. There was great fear of the kind of theology of glory that many saw in Kuyper and his followers, and that we may nowadays detect in forms of *civil religion* and the *health-and-wealth gospel*. This separation model also characterizes most liberation theologies, also sometimes referred to as genitive theologies, since they define liberation from a particular perspective (gender, race, repression, environment, poverty, physical suffering). In these approaches the Spirit is the one who interrupts and disturbs the status quo in a critical and salvific manner; but does the Spirit ever finally find a place to "land" and become visible? There is good reason to remember that, after the flood, Noah released a dove—in the Bible a symbol of the Holy Spirit (Luke 3:22 and pars.)—only to have it return in the first instance, since it found no place to land (Gen 8:8-9).

12.7.3. *Testing and Distinguishing*

Can we find any theological warrant for the notion that, still today, God is present through his Spirit in faith, fruit, and gifts, without getting trapped in a naively optimistic theology of glory? This is the direction we ourselves want to suggest regarding the work of the Spirit in history and culture.

We must therefore distance ourselves from both of the other notions considered thus far. Our theological point of departure is the fundamental distinction between the new order that has been realized in Christ and all the other orders in which people live together. We must learn to distinguish between situations in which the Spirit is at work and situations where other spirits call the tune. We plead for a pneumatology that does not warrant just anything, yet does recognize the fragmentary but real work of the Spirit in the era between resurrection and second coming. This demands a theology that is conscious of the need to test and distinguish. As we said earlier, theology may never see the gifts as personal property or the assured possession of the church. But we may pray for these gifts and aspire to them, and for this one as well.

We find the New Testament basis for our proposed model in the notion of "distinguishing between spirits"—which, according to 1 Cor 12:10, is itself a gift of the Spirit! The most relevant application of this gift in the New Testament church involved evaluating prophecies that were presented in the meetings of the church (see 1 Cor 14:29). This was a critical issue, as it had been already in Old Testament Israel (Deut 18:21-22; Jer 29:8-9). But the necessity of testing and distinguishing extends further to what occurs outside the Christian church (for this more general importance, see Matt 7:15-18). In this connection we should also read 1 John 4:1-3 with regard to the need for "internal" distinctions (in this case between gnostic and nongnostic interpretations of the gospel), and Phil 4:8 regarding the good things that can happen outside of the Christian milieu. Paul refers to the "unusual kindness" shown to him and his companions on the island of Malta (Acts 28:2). Even outside the circle of the gospel light we may find institutions or patterns of actions that reflect God's intentions for human society.

The main thing, therefore, is to face the world with open ears and eyes. On the one hand, we must be critical with respect to all things that are clearly wrong—after all, Barth and his followers were not tilting against windmills. But on the other hand, we must be open to new situations where the work of the Spirit may somehow appear. The Spirit works in unexpected, multicontextual, and pluriform ways (Welker 2006, 229). Fortunately, the church does not have to look on with empty hands. In Bible, liturgy, confessions, stories, and prayers, it has a treasure that can point the way in any situation. This belief is our normative basis. The Spirit continues to conform himself to the Word (see 12.4). God continues to speak, so amid flux and change we may pray for and intervene in our neighborhood, city, country, and continent. Even when a society has become totally Babylonian, we are still called not to turn away from it but to seek its peace and do what we can for its benefit (Jer 29:7). The Christian community will look with joy at the things in society that are good, genuine, and clean, and it will facilitate whatever makes life better; but where and when required, it will also serve as a counterculture.

In this effort we cannot take a priori positions that are detached from concrete historical events and render judgment from outside. We are always to carefully observe the signs of the time and evaluate them. Here too we are recipients and not directors. The process of appropriating, testing, and distinguishing the working of the Spirit in history takes place while we stand with our boots in the mud. We cannot find some suprahistorical point of view.

12.8. Background to the Newer Approach in Pneumatology

Finally, we explore the remarkable new interest in pneumatology that has arisen in various quarters over the last half century. As with the doctrine of the Trinity (chap. 3), we might speak of a renaissance here too (see Kärkkäinen 2002, 11-19). The Holy Spirit is no longer the Cinderella of theology, the girl who has to stay home while her older sisters go out and have fun (16). We see renewed interest in and expectations about the work of the Spirit from a number of different angles. Even though we cannot give any simple explanation, a range of motives and backgrounds seems to be in play, some more prominent in one sector of Christianity, others in another. However, we can detect some links with more general cultural developments. In line with what we said about the Spirit and culture, perhaps these links are among the traces the Spirit has left outside of the immediate environments of church and Christian circles. Whatever the case, we briefly discuss how four factors have played a role in the recent revival of pneumatological interest.

1. We can point first of all to the renewed *interest in transcendence* and the search for meaning that emerged in the Western world toward the end of the twentieth century, which was connected with the shift from modern to postmodern ways of thinking. However much continuity there may be between those two, for instance in their mutual emphasis on individual autonomy, they also show an important difference. The modern climate with its focus on science increasingly came to feel hard and cold, especially outside academic circles. It no longer seemed to satisfy the deeper levels of our humanity. Some dominant traits of our culture, like rationalization and instrumentalization, led to a systematic neglect, even disintegration, of essential human needs. As a result, there developed an intense longing for meaning, for coherence in life and inner fulfillment. Many once again became open to the "more things between heaven and earth" that Hamlet posited against Horatio's philosophy. In this climate, pneumatology has more to offer than Christology for those seeking direction in the Christian faith. God, or the divine, is especially pursued in terms of the Spirit that undergirds all existence, and on whom all living things depend. In contrast with a theology that seemed to lock

God up in the past, now space opened up for a theology that takes the presence of the divine, of God or the Spirit, as its point of departure. God is no longer spoken of as the one whom we come to know in Jesus but as the cosmic Spirit, who is globally present in creation and in all religions, inspiring and life giving. Such an approach can take the form of a consistent *pneuma-theology*, in which pneumatology does not follow Christology but precedes it. In this model the doctrine of God is fully defined by pneumatology, for God as Spirit, *pneuma*, forms the basis of all reality.

In the theology of the 1960s and 1970s, the so-called God-is-dead theology dominated attention. The expression meant to say that God as an acting person had disappeared from modern spiritual experience. "Modern man," it was said, could no longer reckon with an invisible God far above us, determining our future. In response, a range of theological proposals followed that all started from the earthly history of the cross of Jesus. If God is anywhere to be seen and related to our reality, it is in the history of the concrete historical Man of Nazareth. The Sermon on the Mount, the cross, and/or the resurrection (depending on where the emphasis was put) were seen as the decisive moment. Such concepts, however, leave us with questions about the present. Can God really be seen today? Is the present empty? Do we live in a desolate wilderness where God is absent? This climate led to a shift in the final decades of the twentieth century toward transcendence, Spirit, and God (or at least "the divine") once again being "in," while Jesus simultaneously went "out" and "became an ever decreasing blur in our rearview mirror" (Okke Jager). Once more we see how crucial it is not to play the christological and pneumatological perspectives off against each other but to think of them together in all their distinctiveness.

The interest in pneumatology fits well with a fundamental sense of the word "spirit." Spirit, or *ruach* in its original meaning, points to the mysterious reality that in some elusive and yet unmistakable way bears upon human existence and makes it concrete; it alludes to a community and creation. In the meantime we have seen quite a number of "pneuma-theological" proposals emerge, especially but not exclusively from theologians who have their roots in the liberal tradition. The question always remains whether these do justice to the Trinitarian and christological foundations that have been accepted by the church, and whether they therefore may be considered to be fully Christian.

Schleiermacher and Tillich offer classic examples of pneuma-theology; more recent cases are the proposals of Houtepen and Küng (Küng 1995, 42-44). Berkhof's CF may, to some extent, also be characterized as pneuma-theology; Berkhof defines the Spirit as "God's active presence" (326). We should note that, for Berkhof, "God" represents particularly what the tradition referred to as the Father (in his view the Son is not part of the Godhead). A variant concept that seeks to connect the work of the Spirit with the Trinitarian dogma is found in the Pentecostal theologian Amos Yong (2002).

Pneuma-theological concepts often offer the possibility of approaching world religions positively, as workings of the one Spirit of God. But can we maintain this view without doing injustice to the identity of the Christian religion as defined by the status of Jesus Christ as Lord and Redeemer? For that question, see chapter 5. The connection between Spirit and life also provides a framework for treating ecological issues. For this, see, for example, Moltmann 1992 and Bergmann 2005.

2. A second factor that has increased attention to the work of the Spirit is the *ecumenical movement*, which promotes Christian unity across confessional and institutional borders. The mission conference in Edinburgh in 1910 was mostly attended by young leaders who developed initiatives for mission, faith, and order. One outcome was the founding of the World Council of Churches in 1948. The ecumenical movement hit an institutional crisis at the end of the twentieth century, but its boundary-crossing effects live on. One of them is the recognition that the Spirit of God is active in other Christian faith traditions besides one's own. Ecumenical encounters have resulted, for instance, in more knowledge of and appreciation for the Eastern Orthodox and the historic Asian and African churches.

In the Eastern tradition the role of the Holy Spirit in liturgy and theology is different from, and more prominent than, in the West. The sense of the universality of the Spirit facilitates a mystical experience of reality. The high point of the Eucharist is not the formula of institution but the epiclesis, understood as the invocation of the Holy Spirit over the emblems. Easter, which is prefigured in the Transfiguration on the mountain, represents the glorification of our entire life. For the question of how far these distinctives may be explained by the absence of the so-called *filioque* in the Eastern variant of the Nicene Creed, see above, chapter 3.

3. Simultaneous with the ecumenical impulse was the rise of the *Pentecostal movement* in the twentieth century. This movement has seen global expansion and influence for over a hundred years, with no sign of

abating today; it is currently the fastest growing Christian family in the world. The Pentecostal influence is not limited to the "free" churches and groups of believers but, through a process of so-called evangelization, has come to permeate churches and traditions that were long very negative toward Pentecostalism. Many official Western manuals of dogmatics still ignore it—at times rather arrogantly—but there is no reason to do so. Instead, we should explore the dogmatic relevance of what this movement represents, also for mainstream churches.

Pentecostalism is best viewed as a renewal movement that brings special attention to the Spirit's work of *equipping*. Pentecostal movements claim that the Spirit does not stop when someone starts to believe but wants to equip the believer with special spiritual gifts—in the New Testament referred to as charismata. The classical Pentecostal movement places special emphasis on the more spectacular charismata—such as tongues, prophecy, and faith healing through the laying on of hands—as gifts that should be had by every true Christian and in every faith community. Beginning in the 1960s, these ideas penetrated the established churches (in particular, the Roman Catholic, Presbyterian/Reformed, and Methodist families) in the form of the so-called charismatic renewal. This movement differed from the first in not regarding the most remarkable charismata as the sole evidence of having the Spirit, but appreciating them alongside with other, less extraordinary gifts such as hospitality, wisdom, and the gift of teaching (i.e., of the transmission of the faith).

The charismatic renewal is thus an implicit recognition of the theological importance of Pentecostalism. Indeed, the work of the Spirit is not limited to the new birth or to our sanctification, however important these experiences may be. It also includes equipping us, in the present, with the New Testament spiritual gifts. We therefore conclude that the kind of theology that draws a line after the New Testament or (more often) after the period of the early church with respect to the special gifts is not defensible from a biblical-theological perspective. Nowhere in the New Testament are these special charismata restricted to a certain period. We may desire to receive all the gifts of the Spirit, as long as we keep in mind that the Spirit is free to distribute these gifts to whomever and whenever she wants.

Like the ecumenical movement, *Pentecostalism* crossed many borders. Classical Pentecostalism, which began in Los Angeles in 1906 in the so-called Azusa Street Revival, was a transnational movement with roots in African culture. One of the key persons of the first hour was William Seymour (1870-1922), the son of a freed slave, who became a Holiness preacher. Having taken Bible studies from Charles F. Parham, he became convinced that the gift of tongues was the necessary proof of being baptized with the Spirit. He became the spiritual father of the revival in North America. Apart from the question of whether we should see Parham or Seymour as the founder of contemporary Pentecostalism (Robeck 2006; if it was Parham, the beginning must be dated to January 1, 1901, the first day of the twentieth century), it must in any case be recognized in all respects as an impressive renewal movement. The characteristics of the Azusa revival fit with what we said earlier (12.2.2), on the basis of biblical theology, about the liberating work of the Spirit. Boundaries that until then had been impossible to cross were removed, as the Spirit broke through fences that human beings had erected. The first revivals saw a defiance of racial segregation; white and black participated together in the communion service. Likewise, the social rifts between rich and poor and between male and female were done away with. As in the Holiness movement, women at first were allowed to have a prominent role. Theologically speaking, this behavior reminds us of the road sketched out in the book of Acts. The Spirit propels people beyond the borders that must be crossed for the sake of the kingdom of God (e.g., Acts 10; see also the summary description of this event in Gal 3:28). At first the Pentecostal movement was rather anti-intellectual and anti-theological, but since then it has matured (or is at least in the process of maturation). For a survey of Pentecostal theology, see Duffield and Van Cleave 1987; for the origin and development of Pentecostalism, Hollenweger 1997; and for the full picture, also Anderson 2004.

We add a few explanatory remarks about the impact of the charismatic movement in more traditional churches. It introduced a spiritual phenomenon or, perhaps, a particular kind of spirituality. In the Netherlands the charismatic renewal movement began to get organized toward the end of the 1950s. At first the organization was quite fluid and very ecumenical. The pioneers remained members in their own denominations. This choice demonstrates an important theological conviction that we also see in the pioneers of Pentecostalism. They were of the opinion that attention for the work of the Spirit, including attention to the gifts, should be part of normal church life and not lead to denominational splits. In fact, they fought for the recognition of some elements in the biblical and Christian tradition that the Pentecostal churches had demanded.

However, suspicions of European academic theology against Pentecostalism have not yet disappeared. Positive exceptions in Germany include H. Mühlen, N. Baumert, J. Moltmann, and M. Welker (see Welker 1994, e.g., 7-15). In the Netherlands J. Veenhof (1989) and M. Parmentier have played a pioneering role. The Roman Catholic world has always found it easier to relate to renewal movements, stimulated by the close theological bond between Spirit and church and centuries of experience with renewal movements. As happened before with the monastic orders, the charismatic movement found a slot in the ecclesiastical framework. It would seem that the original ecumenical forms of the charismatic renewal, which was so characteristic at the beginning, are now something of the past. It has settled into existing confessional and denominational structures. At the same time, we see, on both national and international levels, a wide-ranging exchange of practices, hymns, and methods across institutional boundaries. See Klaver 2011.

4. As the fourth and final element behind the recent interest in pneumatology, we can mention a *renewed reading of the Bible*. More and more people have become convinced that the biblical texts not only demonstrate the fruit and gifts of the Spirit but that the Spirit himself is the eschatological gift par excellence. There has been an increasing awareness that early Christians did not regard the Holy Spirit as primarily a concept or an object for reflection but saw him within very concrete experiences of God's presence and liberation. As the Bible speaks of these gifts in terms of outpouring, baptism, and being filled, the gift of the Sprit defines our time as the end time. With Joel 3, the outpouring of the Spirit was seen as the final step by which the earth would be filled with the knowledge of God. When we are filled with the Spirit, our communion with God is restored, our existence reaches its full potential, and we are freed from enslavement and imprisonment (Rom 8:18-27). In that sense the Spirit is a herald of the kingdom.

This is an extremely important insight for dogmatic reflection. In a particular way this became the central category in so-called liberation theology (G. Gutiérrez and others). Inspired by Western theologians such as J. Moltmann, it subjected the present to the criticism of the messianic future. Once a person has tasted this liberation, he or she wants more of it. We find this pattern also in other forms of contextual theology. The common characteristic of the theology for the poor, feminist theology, ecological theology, *and* charismatic theology is found in their eschatological orientation. These are actually all forms of liberation theology, and over the past few decades they have been drawing closer together. Charismatic and evangelical Christians are now inspired by their faith to be more involved in social projects, while ecumenical and progressive Christians are rediscovering the indispensable value of prayer and Christian spirituality. Even those who do not want to immediately carry these insights over to a social application may be impressed by the close link between pneumatology and eschatology. Van Ruler, a Reformed theologian, once said: "As the scent-dog Kees could smell every trace of gas in the houses in Utrecht, likewise the Spirit is the all-important sense-organ for the eschaton, for the future and the ultimate destiny of the world. Thus we begin to long for it" (IB, chap. 33).

From this chapter we can draw some links, not only to the next three, but also to chapter 16. Note the way in which the third cluster in the Apostles' Creed (its division into three articles is more fundamental than into twelve!) immediately follows the confession of the Holy Spirit with that of the church, personal renewal, and the eschaton. (In the Nicene Creed, mention of the church is preceded by the inspiration of the prophets and of Scripture.) The New Testament regards the outpouring of the Spirit, together with the resurrection of Christ, as the main eschatological events that completely shape the further course of history. From heaven the resurrected Christ sends the Spirit, on the very day when the Jews brought the firstfruits of their harvest to the temple (Acts 2:1; see Lev 23:15-17). In this way the earth is blessed and time is marked off as harvest time, the time of the breakthrough of the Spirit. History is therefore not a black hole where we must simply kill time or search around for some sort of meaning. It is a time of harvest that leads to God's future, the space in which the Spirit manifests herself and gives us life. The Spirit of Christ manifests himself in the witnesses who publicly announce that the crucified Jesus is the living Lord. God is already present in their prophetic words and actions, and his presence brings life. The Spirit seeks a dwelling place, materiality, corporality. These features happen first of all in the faith community where God is called upon, where ministers preach their sermons, where church members praise God without ceasing, where people intercede in prayer for one another, and where the church rediscovers its missional task. It happens even more intensely when in this dynamic people are touched and experience renewal. And it is completely realized when eternal life becomes a reality in the ultimate eschaton.

References

Anderson, Allan. 2004. *An Introduction to Pentecostalism: Global Charismatic Christianity*. Cambridge: Cambridge University Press.

Awad, Najib George. 2011. *God without a Face? On the Personal Individuation of the Holy Spirit*. Tübingen: Mohr Siebeck.

Baumert, Norbert. 2001. *Charisma—Taufe—Geisttaufe*. 2 vols. Würzburg: Echter.

———. 2004. "'Charism' and 'Spirit-Baptism': Presentation of an Analysis." *Journal of Pentecostal Theology* 12:147-79.

Bergmann, Sigurd. 2005. *Creation Set Free: The Spirit as Liberator of Nature*. Grand Rapids: Eerdmans.

Berkhof, Hendrikus. 1976. *The Doctrine of the Holy Spirit*. Atlanta: John Knox.

Besser-Jones, Lorraine, and Michael Slote, eds. 2015. *The Routledge Companion to Virtue Ethics*. New York: Routledge.

Blei, Karel. 2013. *Oepke Noordmans: Theologian of the Holy Spirit*. Translated by Allan J. Janssen. Grand Rapids: Eerdmans.

Borgman, Erik, et al. 2008. *De werking van de Heilige Geest in de Europese cultuur en traditie* [The effects of the Holy Spirit in European culture and tradition]. Kampen: Kok.

Duffield, Guy P., and Nathaniel M. Van Cleave. 1987. *Foundations of Pentecostal Theology*. Los Angeles: L.I.F.E. Bible College.

Fee, Gordon D. 1994. *God's Empowering Presence: The Holy Spirit in the Letters of Paul*. Peabody, MA: Hendrickson.

———. 1996. *Paul, the Spirit, and the People of God*. Peabody, MA: Hendrickson.

Frettlöh, Magdalene L. 1999. *Theologie des Segens: Biblische und dogmatische Wahrnehmungen*. Gütersloh: Kaiser.

Gornik, Mark R. 2011. *Word Made Global: Stories of African Christianity in New York*. Grand Rapids: Eerdmans.

Hodgson, Peter C. 1994. *Winds of the Spirit: A Constructive Christian Theology*. Louisville: Westminster John Knox.

Hollenweger, Walter J. 1997. *Pentecostalism: Origins and Developments Worldwide*. Peabody, MA: Hendrickson.

Kärkkäinen, Veli-Matti. 2002. *Pneumatology: The Holy Spirit in Ecumenical, International, and Contextual Perspective*. Grand Rapids: Baker Academic.

Klaver, Miranda. 2011. *This Is My Desire: A Semiotic Perspective on Conversion in an Evangelical Seeker Church and a Pentecostal Church in the Netherlands*. Amsterdam: Pallas Publications.

Küng, Hans. 1995. *Christianity: Its Essence and History*. The Religious Situation of Our Time. London: SCM.

McDonnell, Kilian. 2003. *The Other Hand of God: The Holy Spirit as the Universal Touch and Goal*. Collegeville, MN: Liturgical Press.

Moltmann, Jürgen. 1992. *The Spirit of Life: A Universal Affirmation*. Minneapolis: Fortress.

Robeck, Cecil M. 2006. *The Azusa Street Mission and Revival: The Birth of the Global Pentecostal Movement*. Nashville: Nelson.

Ruler, Arnold A. van. 1989. *Calvinist Trinitarianism and Theocentric Politics: Essays toward a Public Theology*. Translated and edited by John Bolt. Lewiston, NY: Edwin Mellen Press.

Thiselton, Anthony C. 2013. *The Holy Spirit in Biblical Teaching, through the Centuries, and Today*. Grand Rapids: Eerdmans.

Veenhof, Jan. 1989. "Charismata—Supernatural or Natural?" In *The Holy Spirit:*

Renewing and Empowering Presence, edited by George Vandervelde, 73–91. Winfield, BC: Wood Lake Books.

Versteeg, Johannes Pieter. 1971. *Christus en de Geest* [Christ and the Spirit]. Kampen: Kok.

Webster, John. 2011. "Illumination." *Journal of Reformed Theology* 5:325–40.

Welker, Michael. 1994. *God the Spirit*. Minneapolis: Fortress.

———. 2006. "The Spirit in Philosophical, Theological, and Interdisciplinary Perspectives." In *The Work of the Spirit: Pneumatology and Pentecostalism*, edited by Michael Welker, 221–32. Grand Rapids: Eerdmans.

Yong, Amos. 2002. *Spirit-Word-Community: Theological Hermeneutics in Trinitarian Perspective*. Aldershot: Ashgate.

13 The Book of God and of Humans

The Doctrine of Scripture

AIM

Anyone who thinks that contemporary society has little interest in the Bible is mistaken. In many different ways the Bible remains a source of inspiration, study, and discussion. The appearance of new translations sparks new interest in the Bible. New research projects on the origin and history of the biblical text regularly win grants from national institutes for scholarly research. More dramatically, when militant Muslim leaders appeal to the Qur'an in defense of some sort of violent action, people ask what the Bible, the book of the Christians, might have to say on such matters. Does it not include similar statements? Is it like the Qur'an or a totally different book?

In this chapter we want to:

- summarize the classical Protestant view of the Bible (13.1)
- review the crisis that arose from the findings of modern Bible scholarship (13.2)
- show how this crisis shifted and was intensified by postmodernism (13.3)
- describe how the Bible developed into the canon in early church history (13.4)
- plead for a theological interpretation of the Bible (13.5)
- situate biblical exegesis within a Trinitarian framework of hermeneutics (13.6)
- on this basis, discuss questions about the authority and interpretation of the Bible (13.7).

MAKING CONNECTIONS

1. Do you think you can find some central message in the Bible, a kind of

common thread that runs through all its books? If so, try to summarize this message in a few words. If not, what makes the Bible into some definite entity nonetheless — is it pure chance or something else? If you belong to a group that reads this book, take a few minutes to share your answers to this question and discuss any disagreements that might arise.

2. If you were to write a book on dogmatics, where would you deal with the Bible — at the very beginning, toward the end, or somewhere in between? Why do you think this chapter about the Bible comes where it does in this book?

3. Find a painting or two of a woman reading the Bible: for instance, one by Rembrandt (https://www.rijksmuseum.nl/en/collection/SK-A-3066) or Gerard Dou (http://www.wga.hu/html_m/d/dou/1/old_read.html). What grabs your attention in these images? What would be some reasons why such a painting is so characteristic of Protestantism?

13.1. The Bible in the Protestant Tradition

Christian churches regard the Bible as canonical, that is, as the source and norm for faith and the conduct of Christian life. When, for instance, the United Protestant Church in the Netherlands was formed in 2004, the very first article of its church order declared that it would recognize the Scriptures as "the only rule for the proclamation and service of the church" (art. 1.3). Other denominations subscribe to similar formulas. In these churches the Bible has always been essential for their very being as a church; Protestants cannot imagine a church without an authoritative Bible. In the Roman Catholic Church the situation is different; the church does not depend on the Bible for what it says, but the Bible depends (for its correct interpretation) upon the church. However, since the Second Vatican Council (1962–65) Catholic attention to the Bible and awareness of its great significance have increased. More than in the past, the Catholic Church today insists that the content of the Bible be made available so that its adherents can learn more about the ramifications of their faith.

The basic Christian claim about the Bible is actually quite simple: the church was born from the Word and abides by the Word, because it will not listen to the voice of a stranger (John 10:4–5). For that reason the church sees human regulations to be binding only to the extent that they are anchored in the Bible (Theses of Berne, 1528; see Faulenbach et al., RB 203). No explicit doctrine or theory or view of the Bible is at work here; rather, a deep sense from far back in the Christian tradition that is rooted in and reflects the almost self-evident way in which the New Testament attributes authority to the Old Testament (Matt 4:4-10; 19:3-6; Acts 13:35; Heb 3:7). Classic Reformed confessions (such as the Augsburg Confession, 1530; the Genevan Catechism, 1545; and the Heidelberg Catechism, 1563) so completely take for granted that the Bible is the norm for faith that they do not even mention the topic. Some other documents from that period, however, do open with a passage about the constitutive significance of the Bible for faith (e.g., the First Swiss Confession, 1536; the Belgic Confession, 1561), which became customary as time went on.

Particularly after the Council of Trent in 1546 established the authoritative status of an oral apostolic tradition besides the Bible ("Scripture and Tradition"), Protestants emphasized ever more strongly the unique significance of the Bible. The expression *sola Scriptura*, which was coined by Luther (WA 7:98), began to function as a slogan and war cry of the Reformation. It was Luther's decisive insight that the Bible could speak for itself. To understand what the Bible means to say, we must constantly analyze its texts and not depend on all sorts of preexisting interpretations. By doing just that kind of reading in the years leading up to the Reformation, Luther discovered the liberating significance of the biblical view of God's righteousness and on that basis declared that Scripture "is in and through itself absolutely certain, clear, transparent, and its own expositor" (1520; WA 7:97).

Calvin expressed this thought in his own way by speaking about the *autopistia* of the Scriptures: in and from itself (*autos*), Scripture is worthy of our faith (*pistos*). It does not require any external ratification; barring interference, the reader will be directly impressed by its unique power and meaning (Belt 2008). In this connection Calvin points to the special involvement of the Holy Spirit; the Spirit ensures that, as we read along, the Bible's message resonates in our hearts. Thus we become convinced that, through these words, God himself addresses us. For Calvin this factor is important not only for understanding the biblical message but also for being assured of its trustworthiness. We come to trust the Bible and become completely certain that it connects us with God. This assurance is not due to any ecclesiastical stamp of approval or primarily to a range of rational arguments for its divine origin, but to the internal testimony (*testimonium internum*) of the Holy Spirit in our hearts.

With the second generation of Protestant theologians, however, this argument began to be used to support the nature of the Bible itself.

It was as if appeal to the work of the Spirit meant skating on thin ice. These theologians were eager to demonstrate that we have good arguments for the objective truth of the Bible, and so they laid increasing stress on rational arguments proving its divine origin. In addition, the high qualities that the young and ecstatic Luther attributed to the Bible now developed into a list of the official "properties" of the Scriptures: authority (*auctoritas*), sufficiency (*sufficientia* or *perfectio*), and clarity (*claritas* or *perspicuitas*). These words were intended as positive declarations in their own right but, of course, must also be understood as part of the Protestant polemic against the Roman Catholic Church. That is, the Bible's *authority* does not depend on any judgment by the church; its *sufficiency* for our salvation means that it does not need any amplification by tradition; its *clarity*, or *perspicuity*, means that, for all the obscure and perplexing passages it might contain, we do not have to rely on some official ecclesiastical pronouncements (the teaching authority, or *magisterium*) to understand the Bible's message. On the contrary, as Luther put it, the Scriptures are their own interpreter (Lat. *sui ipsius interpres*), a formula that would become widely accepted in the Reformation.

All these features are found both in Lutheran and in Reformed Scholasticism. For a survey of the properties that Reformed theology has attributed to the Bible, see Heppe, RD, chap. 2. There were conscious attempts to make the doctrine of the Bible parallel to the doctrine of God, with its range of properties or attributes (see chap. 4). Theologians therefore pointed, without hesitation, to the divinity (*divinitas*) of the Scriptures. A twentieth-century discussion of the main properties of the Bible appears, for example, in Berkouwer 1975, 240–326. Ascribing such properties to the Scriptures was characteristic of the so-called magisterial Reformation, which undertook the reform of church and society in close cooperation with—or even at the initiative of—the civil authorities (the magistrates); thus, Luther, Zwingli, and Calvin had close ties, respectively, with Wittenberg, Zurich, and Geneva. The radical Reformation of the Anabaptists and Spiritualists recognized private faith experience (the "inner light") as authoritative along with the Bible.

As time went by, discussions about the Bible and its authority followed a very clear trend of narrowing and formalization. Where initially, as in John 1, the expression "Word of God" was applied to Jesus Christ and the gospel message that he brought to us, it was soon directly identified with the biblical text (Rohls, RC 35). That text, naturally, needed to be carefully defined, resulting in long lists of the canon in the confessional documents of the time, dry enumerations of all the books that belong to the Bible. While for Luther the Bible still derived its authority from the living voice (*vox viva*) of God that he heard in its words, later the authority of the Scriptures was increasingly made to stand on its own as a formal basis more or less detached from the content of the biblical message. We might even say that a gradual reversal took place. At first the Bible was placed on a pedestal, since people felt the incredible power of its content; later, the quality of the content was said to derive from its place as a document of divine inspiration.

A certain *intellectualization* became evident. The Bible was no longer seen as the vehicle for the one central message of how the Father, through the Son and in the Spirit, leads us to communion with him and thereby to our destiny. Rather, it was viewed as an extensive collection of individual proof texts for a range of doctrines on many different issues. Dogmatics was to neatly order all these texts and draw logically correct conclusions from them. In this connection theologians have often spoken of the *loca probantia* (i.e., proof text) method for dogmatics. This approach is characterized by quoting many Bible texts to undergird particular doctrinal positions, while often expending little to no effort to gauge what these texts might mean in their own intrabiblical context. This method was characteristic for many Protestant theologians in the seventeenth and eighteenth centuries, but also for Herman Bavinck and even more so for Charles Hodge (ST) in the nineteenth.

The process of formalization and intellectualization is most clearly discernible in the doctrine of inspiration, which developed increasingly into a rational and intellectual system. The Bible early on was deemed to be inspired by God's Holy Spirit. Calvin and the earliest Reformed confessional documents applied inspiration especially to the way God enlisted the prophets and apostles in his service to transmit God's words— that is, to God's saving activity in history. For instance, the Belgic Confession states, "We confess that this Word of God was not sent nor delivered 'by human will,' but that 'men and women *moved by the Holy Spirit* spoke from God'" (art. 3; see OF 27, italics supplied). The confession stays close to the Bible, for most of this sentence is a direct quotation from 2 Pet 1:21. In 2 Peter, however, God "commanded his servants, the prophets and apostles, to commit this revealed Word to writing." That is, all emphasis falls on what God does and how he makes himself known to us in his mercy. As a result of God's special care for our salvation, the Bible provides a later-recorded testimony to God's work.

Gradually, however, inspiration began to function as a property inhering in the Bible itself as a guarantee of its divine origin. In the process, the efforts multiplied to stipulate how exactly inspiration operates and how far it extends, so as to remove every possible trace of doubt. Not just the general intent of the message but the very words of the biblical authors were thought to be directly inspired by God's Spirit (i.e., the position of "verbal inspiration"). Those authors had no need to engage in any research—they were simply clerks who wrote down what God dictated! This theory was later somewhat uncharitably referred to as the mechanical view of inspiration, as if the biblical authors were no more than automatons, instruments in the hand of the Spirit without any will of their own. We find the climax of this development in the Helvetic Consensus Formula (1675), which stated that even the letters and vowel points of the Hebrew text of the Old Testament—the so-called Masoretic text, dating from the eighth century CE—were Spirit-inspired.

These extreme attempts to protect the text of the Bible against all human influence soon made the orthodox Protestant view of the Scriptures very vulnerable. The rise of the Enlightenment awakened a historical awareness in Europe that generated new points of debate. People increasingly realized that the Bible did not fall ready-made from heaven but went through a long and complex process of development in which human hands played a significant role. That is, the Bible is the product of a human journey. Gradually there developed a sense of two sorts of distance between the Bible and the reader: first, a historical distance, and later, a hermeneutical distance. This realization convinced many that the Bible's words cannot be simply identified with the events they refer to. At the very least it had to be acknowledged that the Bible puts these events in a very special light, gives them a specific order, a particular interpretation, a certain spin; indeed—as Calvin could rather casually admit—the Bible might even contain some mistakes! Most recently, still another form of distance has come into play, as postmodernism discredits any possibility of establishing one interpretation that remains permanently valid.

In 13.2 we will further explore the (historical) distance between event and text, and in 13.3 the (hermeneutical) distance between text and exegesis. From the eighteenth to late in the twentieth century—the period we usually refer to as modernity—the first distance caused a major crisis in the Protestant view of the Scriptures; this crisis further deepened under the conditions of postmodernism beginning in the late twentieth century. If modernity discredited the authority of the Bible, postmodernism denied the possibility of arriving at any unequivocal interpretation.

More and more people feel that the Bible's content simply does not co-incide with our faith experience and contemporary theology. However much we may be able to learn from Abraham, we are not Abraham but live in a totally different culture; as a result, we have other questions and problems and experience our faith differently, and we bring these differences along as we read and interpret the Bible. We thus must face the question of whether, with the church of all ages, we can still speak about the Bible in a dogmatically adequate way.

Three remarks on this point:

1. For a survey of the development of the doctrine of biblical inspiration in the various Reformed confessional documents, see Rohls, RC 29–45. Rohls pays careful attention to the subtle but sometimes theologically important differences between the various formulations, and to the gradual development of the doctrine of the inspiration of the Bible as described above. Muller (PRRD, vol. 2) places much more emphasis on the continuity between the various documents and positions from the time of the Reformation on.

2. Scholars do not agree on whether Calvin had a detailed theory of inspiration. At times he connects inspiration mainly with God's original revelation to prophets and apostles and not so much with the biblical authors (e.g., *Inst.* 1.6.2). Nevertheless, he sees the Bible writers as the "secretaries of the Holy Spirit," who, "in a certain sense," dictated the words to them (i.e., the apostles) (*Inst.* 4.8.8–9). We do not find in Calvin, however, any specific reflection on the nature and extent of the inspiration of the Bible. He rather seems to consider it as self-evident that God is the active subject and we are the receivers who listen.

3. For the use of the term "crisis" with respect to the (Protestant) principle of Scripture, see Pannenberg 1970. While failing to clearly define what he means by the "principle of Scripture," he convincingly argues that this crisis is due to the dual distance we mentioned: between history and text, and between text and contemporary reader (6–7). For a broader and more recent survey of the history of the changes in the Protestant view of Scripture in the light of this crisis, see Lauster 2004. The American theologian David Kelsey (1975) has shown, in what has become a classic study, how diverse and divergent our ways of dealing with the Bible became in the nineteenth and twentieth centuries.

13.2. The Challenges of Historical-Critical Bible Scholarship

Throughout the ages the Bible has been read as the testimony of God's great acts in history. In the Bible these acts are described and are the object of song, confession, doubt, memory, and expectation. With the rise of a more pronounced historical awareness in the seventeenth and especially the eighteenth century, more and more questions came to be asked about the Bible's historical trustworthiness. Gradually, a critical or differentiating attitude developed. Not all Bible texts seemed to carry the same weight. The products of the various Bible writers seemed to each have their own style and vocabulary. Tensions between smaller and more extended textual units were discovered—more accurately, were taken more seriously because such discrepancies, of course, had not escaped the attention of precritical readers. Biblical passages that seem to contradict each other (which Johannes Polyander in 1621 "briefly explained and harmonized") were now no longer regarded as just "seemingly" contradictory. Explosive questions emerged. Did everything really happen as described in the Bible? Or had the church just forced people to believe that it did, from honorable or not so honorable motives? In particular, Spinoza in the seventeenth century voiced doubts about the miracle stories in the Bible.

Even more, these doubts radicalized and resonated with an increasing number of scholars. Among the most radical was the German scholar H. S. Reimarus, with his polemic *Wolfenbütteler Fragmente* (1774-78), published posthumously and without attribution by the Enlightenment philosopher Gotthold Lessing. These writings portray the gospel evangelists as deceivers who, after the death of Jesus, could not accept that they had been mistaken and decided to give a positive spin on their life with him. From such efforts arose the resurrection story. Official church teaching allegedly was based on the quicksand of this sort of wishful thinking by the disciples. Reimarus himself was not a church member, but even scholars who were churchgoers developed a critical attitude toward the ecclesiastical tradition of the Bible.

It did not stop with individual voices and opinions. Over time, a "historical-critical" *method* emerged, that is, a more or less systematic approach to the exploration of (biblical) texts with the aim of determining their sources and mode of transmission. The first principle of this method was to dispense with the notion of the Bible's divine inspiration and to start instead from the presupposition that its origin and content must be explained like that of any other book, without any appeal to supernatural actors—in other words, without God's involvement. Whereas through the ages the church had understood the Bible as God's revelation, the new approach insisted that the Bible be seen as a collection of writings from the ancient Near East that tell us what people in those days believed.

Those people were first of all the ancient Israelites, and later also the earliest followers of Jesus of Nazareth. In principle, we can study how they thought, lived, and believed without "involving God." By following the historical-critical method—by carefully sifting what is and is not historically reliable in the biblical witness—we can discover "how things really were." Starting from the biblical text, the scholars searched for the history behind the text and concluded that there might be considerable discrepancy between those two.

The course of historical-critical scholarship has often been described. Among the important general studies with respect to the Old Testament is the work by Kraus (1984); with respect to the New, that of Kümmel (1972). We should not forget that the roots of this method are already present in humanism (with its motto "back to the sources") and the Renaissance of the sixteenth century. In addition, the Reformation's accent on *sola Scriptura*, together with literalist exegesis of the Bible, led to increased interest in the factual backgrounds of the biblical text. Calvin, who was educated in a humanist climate, already wondered on grammatical and stylistic grounds who in fact had written such New Testament epistles as 2 Peter and Hebrews.

The erudite analysis of Hans Frei (1974) of modernity's consequences for our dealings with the Bible is extremely intriguing. Prior to the Enlightenment, Frei argues, average Europeans felt, as a matter of course, that they were part of the biblical story. Just like the important biblical characters, they lived their life under an open heaven and felt very close to Abraham, Moses, David, and Paul. They intuitively interpreted the world around themselves in terms of the biblical story. But after the Enlightenment this framework for the biblical story was obscured (hence Frei's title, *The Eclipse of Biblical Narrative*). Rather than understanding our own time in the terms of the Bible, we now try to understand the Bible within the context of our own, modern times. As this task proved to be increasingly difficult, the rift between the biblical story and our own lives widened further and further. Frei, and very many others, thus developed what is usually referred to as a postliberal theology and went in search for ways to once again allow the Bible to determine the climate in which we live, rather than vice versa. Another description of the discontinuity between the biblical story and modern consciousness in the emerging Enlightenment is an older study that is still very worthwhile to read: Hazard 2013 (orig. pub., 1935).

Although the results of historical-critical studies are still far from unanimous, we cannot deny that they have provided us with much knowledge and insight into the origin and transmission of the biblical text. Even more strongly, they have given us insight into the ways in which texts have moved around and thereby have confronted us with something theologically significant. The complexity of texts and their history apparently is the road along which God makes himself heard. We will return to this idea at the end of this chapter, when we speak about the authority of the Bible. This theological appreciation, however, does not diminish the fact that historical-critical scholarship was often much less neutral than it pretended to be. It was accompanied by considerable antichurch, as well as often also anti-Jewish, sentiments. For instance, everything that resembled later Judaism and that differed from the message of the prophets was labeled legalistic and cultic, and therefore deemed unoriginal. It was also argued that the Bible could hardly be studied objectively so long as dogmatic traditions determined how it was to be understood. For that reason the enlightened biblical scholar wanted to "free" the Bible from its imprisonment in ecclesial-confessional chains. From then on, biblical scholarship and the theology of the church have increasingly gone their separate ways. Even biblical scholars who saw themselves as Christians got used to leaving their faith at the door as soon as they took up their work. For, it was argued, in this discipline one must proceed objectively and without preconceptions, thus without allowing your own faith or the opinions of the church to interfere in any way. One does not need the Christian faith to discover the meaning of biblical texts!

Most Christian theology, however, continued to seek its point of departure in the faith of the church of the ages. It continued to see the Bible not just as any collection of writings but as the sacred Scriptures, as canon. One might say that this strategy was one of survival: Christian faith would not survive if it considered the Bible to be simply a collection of ancient Eastern documents on a par with all kinds of other expressions of religious experience. Even more, the content of the Bible gave the church a strong argument not to simply give in to the historical-critical approach. *For the biblical writings contain a foundational message about God and his relationship with people.* As readers, we are constantly directed toward this message and so implicitly, if not explicitly, face the question: does this not also apply to us? This incessant appeal in the Bible cannot be without consequences for its interpretation. If you are interested in Isaiah's or Paul's *concept* of God but not in their God, you detach them from the only thing in which they were passionately interested, namely, how they encountered exactly this God in their experience (cf. Brink PST, 151). We might even say that it betrays a lack of scholarship to seek to know everything about Isaiah or Paul except whether they were right in their claim that their ministry was based on God's actions and words.

In this connection we may also quote the famous words of Karl Barth: "I believe the critical historian ought to be more critical!" (Barth, R2 14). Barth means that the critic should also ask what the biblical writers actually wanted to say. To establish "what it says" and how it came about is only the beginning; we must understand what the Bible wants to assert by way of content, and we must deal with it. "What do people mean by understanding and explaining, if there is hardly any effort in that direction? . . . Or do these scholars, whom I do respect as historians, have no idea that that there is something, a crucial matter, a Word within the words?" (14-15)

Yet, this methodical restriction to nontheological aspects became the accepted praxis in modern biblical scholarship. This decision resulted in the already-mentioned rift between the so-called objective biblical scholar on the one hand and, on the other, the church-related systematic theologian, who might even be bound to a particular confession. Often there is only sporadic contact between the two groups. This rift is very regrettable. For theology must be done in close connection with the reading of the Bible and therefore also with the findings of those whose discipline is the study of the Bible (see Bockmuehl and Torrance 2008).

The rift between biblical scholarship and theology runs more or less parallel with that between the academy and the church. Besides the historical-critical approach, other methods of interpreting the Bible have developed at the universities: literary-critical and symbolic, feminist and womanist, those of depth-psychology and social criticism. Usually these methods are quite inaccessible to nonspecialists because of the knowledge and skills they presuppose. In addition, the historical-critical method of interpreting the Bible has disadvantaged the believer in many ways, in spite of the useful insights it provides with respect to the history and background of the biblical text. The denial of the historical trustworthiness of many Bible stories created the impression that, since the humanness of the Bible was so clear, the Bible could not be a divine book. This was often either implicitly suggested or explicitly stated. Historical criticism thus impoverished the believer's relationship with the Bible as a book for our existential orientation. And because believers, understandably, wanted to retain such a relation with the Bible, many opted for an antischolarly or biblicistic approach. In this sense historical criticism has probably been counterproductive.

As in pre-Reformation times, the correct interpretation and the general use of the Bible have come to be reserved for a select group of experts—not the clergy any more, but academic Bible scholars. But how could the church use the fruit of this scholarly effort without hurting its own identity? The main problem lay not in the modern critical method's desire to reconstruct the history and composition of the biblical text but in its presupposition that the biblical text is a purely human product. This presupposition, if initially perhaps applied to methodology, gradually carried over to matters of factual content. How is it possible, then, to read the Bible as it was clearly intended, as the decisive testimony of God's acts?

Reformed theology has devoted a lot of reflection to this question. For a long time, many struggled to do justice to the human contribution in the Bible's origins. Was not the historical approach a direct attack on the authority of Scripture? What divine aspect remained besides the human elements in the Bible? Increasingly, discussions about the Bible also became drawn into questions about the certainty of our knowledge of God. With the rise of the Enlightenment, people thought that all our epistemological claims must be grounded on a foundation of indubitable certainties. Dogmatics accordingly gave first place to the doctrine of the Bible as the foundation for the certainty of faith. First and foremost we had to be sure about the authority of the Scriptures; then everything else would fall into place.

This climate explains the intense interest in the doctrine of Scripture on the part of A. Kuyper and H. Bavinck. They tried to solve problems concerning the human aspect of Scripture by introducing the concept of *organic inspiration*; the biblical authors were "moved" by the Spirit in such a way that their own character, style, and context remained visible but without any errors. By way of contrast, they characterized seventeenth- and eighteenth-century theories of inspiration as *mechanical*, according to which the Bible writers were used as instruments but without any contribution of their own. However, Kuyper and Bavinck—like their kindred spirits Hodge and Warfield at Princeton—stayed with the literal inspiration of the Bible, or its *theopneusty* (its quality of being breathed through by God). Bavinck preferred this term, since it not only says something about the origins but also points to a permanent property of the Bible: it breathes God (Keulen 2003, 115). In this view inspiration is not limited to the person of the authors (à la Schleiermacher) or to its religious-ethical content, as was defended by such proponents of ethical theology as D. Chantepie de la Saussaye (1818-74) and J. H. Gunning Jr.

(both of whom were, consequently, much more open to historical criticism). Kuyper and Bavinck were primarily concerned about the reliability of the Bible as the given Word of God; their concept of organic inspiration wanted to do full justice to the fact that the Bible comes to us through human channels. However, eventually it proved to be unsatisfactory to define the authority of the Scriptures in a way that differed from that of the early church (see 13.4)—that is, to attempt a definition without further reference to the content of the actual texts.

The concept of organic inspiration made it possible to recognize that the biblical authors were people of their own times—for instance, in their cosmological beliefs. This possibility was lost, however, when the Bible presented itself as *history*. An important parallel was drawn between the *incarnation* of the Son and the process of *inscripturation*, whereby revelation was put in writing. Bavinck referred in this context to the "servanthood" of the Scriptures (RD 1:435). We do not accept this close parallel between Christology and the doctrine of Scripture because in dogmatics the doctrine of the Scriptures belongs under pneumatology (Brinkman and Kooi 1997, 123).

Van Ruler was remarkably relaxed with respect to the doctrine of the Bible: "This may be our motto: Let us therefore not waste our time and energy in a controversy about the nature of the Scriptures—whether or not it is developed into a broad theory—but let us rather listen to what the Bible says and live accordingly" (VW 2:355). Van Ruler argues that the orthodox view of the Bible of post-Reformation times "has proven at some points wrong and untenable" and that any formal theory will land us "in a lot of difficulties" (356). In practice, the Bible will continue to exert its authority: "The Bible goes its own sovereign way" (357).

13.3. Postmodern Approaches to the Bible

Today the high tide of historical-criticism in the Enlightenment mode has passed. The rise of postmodernism brought its pretenses under suspicion. Was the modern scholarly approach as objective, neutral, and value-free as its supporters claimed? Was it not in fact just as prejudiced as classic church exegesis, only from the opposite corner? Was not its first axiom—that we can obtain objective results by employing unprejudiced reason—almost as dogmatic as long-derided church claims for its confessions? In any case, many of its findings proved to be less "hard" than was often asserted. An example is the so-called source-theory, which long served as the flagship of historical-critical scholarship. This theory claims that the Pentateuch consists of materials from a number of distinct sources. Mainly on the basis of the names that each source used for God, one could presumably distinguish between the work of a Yahwist, an Elohist, a Deuteronomist, and also a Priestly code (J [for German Jahwist], E, D, and P). Recent research has questioned this hoary, seemingly unassailable theory. Can the different sources in the Pentateuch indeed be so precisely distinguished? Can we be sure that such sources really did exist in the form of underlying documents? New, alternative hypotheses have emerged, but they have not provided absolute certainty either. There is a real prospect that scholarly research on these matters will never be able to move beyond a multitude of theories and more or less probable interpretations.

In a certain way it is characteristic of our postmodern era that the historical-critical method has gradually lost its glamour while being dissolved into a multitude of diverging interpretations. We postmoderns are deeply conscious of the inevitable *plurality* of all things, but this awareness has not diminished the distance between biblical scholarship and theology, between academy and church. On the contrary, one crisis in biblical interpretation is followed—or perhaps complemented—by the next. The postmodern paradigm for dealing with the Bible assumes that it contains a cacophony of mutually incompatible voices and thus must be subject to a broad range of very divergent theological interpretations. "In vain I have searched for any form of unity and cohesion. . . . The Bible is a book for discussion" (Heyer 2007, 150-51). Such a conclusion may easily serve as an excuse to ignore the Bible, to fall back on one's own religious agnosticism, and to limit oneself to questions that belong to the sphere of the secular study of religion.

In addition, we should note that postmodern approaches allow no universal criteria to decide which of the many competing interpretations of the Bible may be right or wrong. Because of developments in philosophical hermeneutics—for example, see the work of H. G. Gadamer (1900-2002) and J. Derrida (1930-2004)—interpretation seems to be determined, in part or entirely, by our point on the timeline of history, by our own cultural context. *Reader-response* theories afford a prime example of this approach. They direct our attention less to what may lie behind the text historically or to its literary structure and narrative patterns and more toward what lies, as it were, ahead of the text. What reactions has the text evoked, how has it been received, and what meanings does it still provoke among the very different groups that read it? Behind this approach lies the assumption that texts contain a "surplus of meaning"

(P. Ricoeur 1976, title), so that meaning is not totally fixed in the text. Since we are to attend to the way in which individual or groups of readers receive the text, we as readers also subconsciously fill in certain blanks in the information that the text provides. We simply cannot avoid how our ideas are conditioned by our culture, class, gender, and certain interests that we may be consciously or (more often) subconsciously pursuing—for instance, our desire to either belong to or distance ourselves from a certain group. We might be searching for certainty or (like the founders of the historical-critical method) for liberation from some traditional bonds that torment us. No one is immune to such processes. And therefore we cannot give any sensible answer to the question of which interpretation of the Bible or of a particular Bible passage is correct. Unprejudiced exegesis is an impossibility, as is a definitive interpretation of "the" biblical message. Our reading always brings ourselves along, which always shapes the way we read the Bible. We cannot pull ourselves out of the swamp of subjectivity by our own bootstraps.

And a swamp it is, indeed. If we can say that the modern crisis led to a rift, the postmodern crisis evokes the image of a quagmire. Our interpretations emerge from the morass of history, culture, language, and traditions, but there they also get stuck, and there they will someday disappear. Modernity exploded the classic Protestant view of the divine authority of the Bible; postmodernism erodes the conviction that the Bible has a clear message that leaves no one uncertain about what God wanted to convey in the Bible. The Bible cannot be its own interpreter; it is subject to the inevitable arbitrariness of the reader.

In such a climate, is it still possible to hear in the Bible a single, decisive testimony of God's great acts? Or must Christian theology, in responding to these developments, set off in search of a view of the Bible that is totally different from the one that prevailed in the church for so many centuries? If we want to answer to these questions, we should first go back to the beginning—to the texts themselves, their transmission and their history. How, in fact, did we get the Bible? Is it not intriguing that early Christians had to do without a Bible as we know it today? They had Moses (the Pentateuch), the Prophets, and the Writings, plus an assortment of epistles and gospel stories that would later come to constitute the New Testament. So how and why was it that, in the first few centuries of Christianity, the Bible gained its unique status and significance?

13.4. Canon around Kerygma, Dogma, and Creed

The Christian church is rooted in a fundamental conviction that can be summarized in two Greek words: *Iēsous Kyrios*—Jesus is Lord, that is, the one who, after his scornful crucifixion, was resurrected from death by the God of Israel. This confession became the center and norm of the biblical canon. As the Resurrected One, Jesus received the name that is above all other names (Phil 2:9). By committing themselves to the bearer of that name, people can share in the eschatological salvation of God. Because of the Spirit of God, who, shortly after the resurrection, was poured out as a fulfillment of old prophetic expectations, many began to entrust themselves to Jesus and became convinced of the message of the apostles. For "no one can say 'Jesus is Lord' except by the Holy Spirit" (1 Cor 12:3). In other words, people became Christians as the result of the Spirit-inspired confession about salvation in Jesus Christ. This confession determined the boundary lines. "Every spirit which confesses that Jesus Christ has come in the flesh is of God, and every spirit which does not confess Jesus is not of God" (1 John 4:2-3).

The act of God in Jesus Christ through the Spirit touched people in the deepest layers of their existence and enabled them to find a new direction for their lives. It usually also prompted them to get involved in spreading the message of the apostles about this salvation. We refer to this message regarding the decisive significance of Jesus Christ for our ultimate bliss as the kerygma. This message originally could be summarized so succinctly as "Jesus is Kyrios." However, as we saw in chapter 10, this formula soon demanded further explanation, clarification, and demarcation. The term "Kyrios," for example, was used in the Septuagint as the equivalent for the Old Testament name for God (YHWH). Therefore, when we confess Jesus as Kyrios, are we saying that he may be identified with YHWH? Or is he (for early on the title "Son" became common) a mode in which YHWH existed? How, then, are we to understand the relation between Jesus and the God he addressed as his Father?

After concluding that many answers given to these questions failed to do justice to the Christian message of salvation, the Councils of Nicaea (325) and Constantinople (381) at last agreed on a few principles that did. These dogmas, formulated in the *credo* (the confession of faith) of the church, therefore constituted a further clarification of the kerygma, as well as a protection against deformations and errors. The so-called rules of faith, or rules of truth, had a similar function; they were summaries of the content of the Christian faith based on the apostolic writings that in time would constitute the core of the New Testament. The early church used these rules of faith in its struggle against heresies (esp. of the gnostic kind), that is, against those who did not seek the basis of salvation in the incarnation, cross, and resurrection of Jesus Christ. The first of these rules of faith, a text of about twenty lines, is from the second-century church father Irenaeus, but variants of this rule already circulated at an earlier date. They served as the norm for a correct interpretation of the kerygma.

At about the same time, an even wider circle emerged around the kerygma, which eventually led to the canon of the New Testament.

The Greek word *kanōn* (canon) originally meant "measuring stick." It can also mean "list, catalog." The two meanings coincide: we are dealing with a list of books that together may serve as a measuring stick for the content of our faith. Around the beginning of the Christian era most Jewish groups seem to have considered the Old Testament canon as "closed." This canon typically comprised the thirty-nine books that also define the canon for Protestantism. Yet, it could be more (for Qumran) or less (for the Sadducees) than thirty-nine. The so-called apocryphal books seem to have been added later to the Septuagint in Christian circles. Nowadays, this extension of the canon is regarded as a consequence of the growing estrangement between church and synagogue; since Christians believed these books contained prophecies about Christ, they were eager to include them in "their" canon. Through the Septuagint this broader canon gained authority in the Western church. The Protestant Reformers came up with a wise, Solomonic judgment: following Jerome, they decided to retain the original canon but continued to regard the apocryphal, or deuterocanonical, books as instructive and inspirational at a lower level.

For a survey of contemporary research on the Old Testament canon (which has largely discredited the so-called Council of Jamnia theory), see McDonald and Sanders 2002, part 2.

The canon of the New Testament consisted of those writings that, in conformity with the preaching of the apostles, underlined the unique significance of Jesus as the Christ. After the apostles' death, their writings were preserved, assembled, and read in the meetings of the Christian communities. The apostles had been the direct eyewitnesses or (in Paul's case) contemporaries of Jesus, and therefore their witness was regarded as unique and invaluable. The formation of the canon is indissolubly linked to the way in which these writings functioned in the local churches, in their practices of reading, hearing, baptism, and Eucharist.

549

In the second century a corpus of writings gradually developed that were assumed to be of apostolic origin. For quite some time uncertainty hovered around certain of these writings; for some (e.g., the Epistle to the Hebrews), it was not clear that they had been written by an apostle, but because of their christologically pure content, they were accepted as part of the New Testament canon. However, there is no example of any apostolic document that did not get into the New Testament. If in our day a document was found that was judged to be genuinely apostolic, would it be added to the existing canon? All we can say for now is that such a question is entirely hypothetical.

A much more important question, and one that has caused theological controversy through the ages, is whether the canon was (1) consciously demarcated or (2) received over time by a process of ever further clarification. The Roman Catholic Church defends the first option, while most Protestant denominations support the second. Even today the debate continues. Robert Jenson (ST 1:27-28)—a catholicizing Lutheran—argues that the canon must be regarded as a "decision of the church," which thereby manifests its authority (see Jenson 2010 for an account of the subtle interplay between canon and creed he posits in this connection). John Webster (2003a, 63-64), in contrast, defends the idea that it was primarily "an act of confession and submission" with respect to something that impressed the church. The church thus derives its authority from its obedience to the canon (see also Webster 2003b, 121, and Weber, FD 1:269-74). We believe that history shows that Webster is right—there was never a council or synod that officially decided what belongs to the New Testament canon. The canon as we know it dates back to a summary by Athanasius, preserved in his thirty-ninth Easter letter, dated in 367. Theologically, we maintain that the church had its origin in the Word—the kerygma of the apostles—and not vice versa. We are the recipients of the canon. At the same time, we must not forget that the New Testament writings contain the Spirit-inspired answer to the witness regarding Jesus Christ; in that sense the canon cannot be considered in detachment from the community of the church (Gaventa and Hays 2008, 6-17). Note Kruger's (2013, 22) criticism of the "extrinsic model," according to which "the idea of a canon, and the beginning of the canonical process," should be "laid at the feet of later ecclesiastical figures (or groups) who sought to solidify their power." Instead, he rightly sees the canon as more "innate to the early Christian movement."

In this book we have intentionally placed this chapter about the Bible after those on Christology, soteriology, and the Holy Spirit. In our view, the doctrine of the Bible does not belong in an epistemological framework but is connected to pneumatology. It was the Holy Spirit who, after Easter and Pentecost, prompted the apostles to go out into the world with the message of the salvific significance of Jesus Christ. This same Spirit, early Christians (e.g., Clement of Rome and Irenaeus) commonly believed, inspired the writings in which the apostles recorded their message and applied it to all kinds of concrete situations. They reread the Scriptures they already possessed—the Law (i.e., the Pentateuch), the Prophets, and the Writings—which they considered as authoritative and of utmost importance. They remembered that Jesus had understood himself and his life's journey as the fulfillment of "the Law and the Prophets," that is, what we refer to as the Old Testament (see chap. 9). For that reason the Christian church initially accepted the Hebrew Bible without much controversy as part of its canon. Only after Marcion did this decision have to be emphatically defended.

Theologically considered, therefore, reflection about the significance of the Bible must follow upon consideration of the significance of the Holy Spirit. The doctrine of the Bible finds its place in the context of pneumatology; the Bible and the canon are means to facilitate our understanding of the salvation and reconciliation with Christ, which comes to us through the work of the Spirit. The Bible is the instrument par excellence by which the Spirit keeps us close to the kerygma of salvation. God brings us the testimony of our salvation along a road of the emphatically human transmission, rereading, appropriation, and interpretation of texts.

We cannot say that the Bible is the only instrument in this connection. Just as with the kerygma and the creed (i.e., the rule of faith), we must ask how the canon is to be interpreted, for regarding the canon, too, many heretics emerged early on with their own erroneous ideas. To clearly distinguish the core of things, the church once again looked to the creed and official dogmas as extensions of the kerygma. In sum, the canon, the creed, the rule of faith (*regula fidei*), and the underlying kerygma form the poles of a common field of coordinates and interpret each other in a back-and-forth movement. The Reformation's *sola Scriptura* implies that no decisive authority may be attributed to tradition (whether secret and oral or not) in interpreting the Bible, but that we must let the Scriptures speak for themselves. This slogan does not imply, however, that the church may not have any other authoritative documents that, as extensions of the apostolic message, can direct us to find the correct course in the Scriptures. The Reformation itself unequivocally created such writings in the form of its confessional documents. Yet, these writings are intended to explain the Bible and should not aim to say something that is not already present in the Bible. These writings must be read and, if necessary, corrected by always keeping the Bible in mind.

For the situation in the early church, see also Williams 2006. Some consider the offices of the church (i.e., church officers) to be a third instrument of authority in the church, besides the canon and the creed (dogma, rule of faith). It is good to underline the important role of the church offices. Nonetheless, we are of the opinion that the offices (like the church itself) derive their authority only from their obedience to the Word and may not be viewed as a separate source of authority for the correct interpretation of that Word. The offices are so important in the church precisely because they must *keep us close* to the Word; they must serve the Word. See chapter 14 for a further discussion of church offices.

The *sola Scriptura* of the Reformation was directed against the duality of Scripture and tradition as it had developed in the medieval church. In the first few centuries tradition (*traditum* = the content of faith as transmitted) was equated with the rule of faith, the *regula fidei*. During many centuries the definition of Vincent of Lérins (d. ca. 450) was regarded as the correct expression of the *conserving* function that the concept of tradition served: "Everything that has always, and by all, been believed" (*Commonitorium*, from 434, §2.6). In the late medieval period, however, the tradition was invoked to justify all kinds of elements that could not be found in the Bible; here, tradition assumed a *productive* function. Besides the Bible, there allegedly existed a separate oral tradition of things that Christ had said and that had been handed down from the apostles to the present day. The Council of Trent legitimized this view of tradition by requiring that it should be accepted and honored "with equal piety and reverence" (Denzinger, ES §1501) as the Scriptures. This position placed the Bible and the tradition beside each other as two sources. The First Vatican Council maintained this view and made it more explicit by determining that only the pope could decide on the content of this tradition. The declaration of papal infallibility on July 18, 1870 (Denzinger, ES, §3073), with the provision that the pope is infallible only when he speaks *ex cathedra*, gave this power a stronger basis. Vatican II (1962-65) interpreted tradition as one stream in the transmission (*transmissio*) of God's revelation but clearly emphasized that the church does not find its certainty about all that had been revealed in the Scriptures alone (*Dei Verbum* 9; Denzinger, ES, §4212). The explanatory role remains with the pope. Roman Catholics believe that just one institution in their church possesses the teaching office, or magisterium, and may decide what the revelation means today (*Dei Verbum* 10; Denzinger, ES, §4214).

It is important to stop for a moment and clarify that, in view of what we have just said, the church has not received the Bible as a kind of manual in which God provides us with all sorts of interesting information (to mention just one example: the age of the earth). Neither does the Bible give us an assortment of general religious truths about God and the world. Rather, the church has received the Bible as a gift from the Holy Spirit to keep us close to the message of the apostles and prophets—close to the kerygma about Jesus Christ as our Lord and Savior. In all the complexity of the history of God with his people, the Bible testifies of God's struggle to establish his covenant with us. In earlier chapters we have studied this covenantal history from different angles. In this history, which leads to the history of Jesus Christ, we continuously see who God is and how he provides salvation and redemption. The Bible must always be understood, explained, and applied in this way—from the perspective of the history of Jesus Christ. Martin Luther expressed this principle in a superb and virtually untranslatable way by stipulating that the Bible is about all *was Christum treibet* (what drives home Christ [to us]; WA DB 7:384). Accordingly, he severely criticized books in the Bible in which he failed to immediately detect Christ in his saving role—for example, the Epistle of James. In such a situation Luther could exclaim, "We use Christ as an argument against the Scriptures" (WA 39/1:47; see also Zwiep 2009–13, 1:281). We think this criticism goes a step too far, since we must always remain open to the possibility that Christ is present in a veiled way in places where we cannot immediately see him. With Calvin and the Reformed branch of the Reformation, we would rather remain with *tota Scriptura:* the entire Scriptures are important, including those passages that, for some reason or another, do not appeal to us. However, we do feel that Luther's *was Christum treibet* shows a fine intuition for what really matters in the Scriptures, and why they are given to us; they are the testimony to the living Lord. Many Christians, even today, believe that the Bible is the foundation of the Christian faith. That is wrong, for the Bible itself (1 Cor 3:11) reserves that distinction for Jesus Christ.

It is extremely important to understand this point, for here lies the defining difference between the church and all forms of fundamentalism that see the Bible (more or less in parallel with the role of the Qur'an in Islam) as a collection of truths that dropped down from heaven and provides us with the materials to construct a perfect and complete edifice of Christian teaching. Protestant orthodoxy has often created this impression, for instance, by placing the doctrine of the Bible in the prolegomena of dogmatics (see Brakel, CRS; Heppe, RD; but also recent authors, e.g., Kreck, GD; Berkhof, CF; Kraus, ST). Modern and post-modern biblical scholarship has shown how vulnerable this positioning makes the cause of faith. Instead, we should go back to the role the Bible had from the beginning, as the special instrument through which the Holy Spirit keeps us connected with the apostolic message about Jesus Christ, the one who was crucified but also resurrected.

13.5. The Theological Interpretation of the Bible

What are the implications of this discussion for our concrete interpretation and use of the Bible? We answer by pointing to the so-called theological interpretation of the Bible, an approach that has recently developed into a very productive movement in biblical hermeneutics (a few representatives are Stuhlmacher 1992–99 and 1995, Watson 1994, Fowl 1997, Talstra 2002, Vanhoozer 2005, Billings 2010, Volf 2010, Jenson 2010, and, as an important precursor, Childs 1985). Since this term is liable to misinterpretation, let's first indicate what it does *not* mean. First, it does not mean that the Bible should be read from the perspective of a predetermined kind of theology. That approach would signal a return to a dogmatic way of reading where dogmatics in effect dominates the Scriptures, rather than vice versa. Rather, the theological interpretation of the Bible has adopted the insight of postmodern hermeneutics that our dealings with the Bible are never neutral. We never come to the Bible as blank slates or without any value system. We always read it in the light of our own experiences, expectations, and presuppositions. Some things will especially strike us as we read the Bible, while other things may remain vague or completely escape our attention. This approach, however, is quite different from reading the Bible from the angle of a particular theological tradition. The latter approach enchains the Bible with a tradition—something the Reformed, following *sola Scripture*, have fought against, for good reason.

Second, the theological interpretation of the Bible does not aim to be the latest product in the warehouse of biblical methods, a new alternative to the many approaches we already have. On the contrary, it wants to benefit from everything that is true, insightful, and helpful in each and all of these, whether they search out what lies behind the text, the literary form or the narrative plot of the texts, or the sociological aspects of the reading communities "ahead" of the text. At the same time, the theological interpretation of the Bible would keep our dealings with the

Bible from being restricted to just one of these approaches. Our aim in reading the Bible is to come into contact with *God* and his acts, through the Scriptures. Christians believe that God was active in the history behind the biblical text, also in the origin and development of the text, and also in the faith communities that have interpreted the Bible in particular ways. It is essential, therefore, to pay due attention to each of these three aspects—yet only because, and to the extent that, such attention helps us better see how the God of the Bible addresses us. At the same time, we should view the complexity and diversity of the text, along with the debates to which it has given rise over the centuries, as theologically important, not as something troublesome that is to be avoided or neutralized or quickly left behind. All this complexity and diversity says something about the actual way in which God allows himself to be heard.

To put it into one sentence: the theological interpretation of the Bible is the interpretation that takes the professional process of biblical exegesis with total seriousness by following the indications that these texts provide and by proceeding with our questions *until we reach God*. In this approach, therefore, God does not just pop up in a nonscholarly epilogue where we add a few private thoughts after having completed our "real" exegetical and hermeneutical work. Rather, the basic premise of this method is that, as these texts themselves claim to say something about God and about our position in relation to him, so present readers of these texts may not ignore their claims. The key to unlocking the biblical text is our willingness, our determination, to hear God's voice there.

But is God's voice not always the echo of our own voice? Do we not always hear what we *want* to hear? Two answers may be given to this question. First and foremost, the theological interpretation of the Bible is guided by the conviction that God stands prior to the biblical text and its historic and cultural contexts. This is the first pillar of a theological interpretation. We must uphold the basic principle that God does not just serve the interpretative interests of a particular faith community but precedes them as the one who addresses us at the level of deeply rooted experiences and basic convictions. In this realm nothing can be proven; at most we may refer to something that simply happened to us in our experience with the Bible. Everything begins with either our human subjectivity or with God. Christian reflection on our faith opts for the latter, which has consequences for the expectations we bring to our dealings with the Bible.

Second, the theological interpretation of the Bible most emphatically includes theological criticism. Unlike what happens in historical-critical scholarship, however, this criticism is not directed to the biblical text but to the reader. To avoid mere self-projection it is crucial that we allow the Bible to constantly *disturb* us, in the images and thoughts we have formed about God, the world, and ourselves. With good reason the call to repentance and the renewal of our mind—so that we will not become decentered—hold center stage. If our aim in reading and interpreting the Bible is to get to know God better and to live for him, we will not just attempt to find confirmation for our own ideas there or follow the trajectory of our own wishes; we will be willing to run the risk of being made uncomfortable by what we do not like.

Why is the theological interpretation of the Bible a better method than the common alternatives? The strongest answer to that question is that, as we saw in 13.2, God is the central issue in the Bible. This point is so easy to see that we might miss it. Nonetheless, the principle is of vital importance. It is evident already in the variety of genres the Bible contains: gospels (accounts of the good news of God's acts in Christ and the Spirit), prophecies (appeals to turn toward God's will in view of the future), psalms (hymns that sing about our relationship with God), and apocalyptic texts (which in creative language describe God's ultimate victory over the powers of evil), and so forth. To do justice to the Bible in and through all this variety, the reader must first be interested in God—that is, the reader must have a theological interest. To repeat, the texts themselves indicate that they must be read with God in view. We will do them justice only if we read these texts, which testify to God as the decisive reality in our lives, as believers, with a receptive heart. Only in so doing do we not force our own agenda or ideology on the Bible but demonstrate our willingness to listen to what the Bible wants to tell us (Talstra 2002). For a slightly more critical account of this theological interpretation of Scripture, see Zwiep 2009-13, 2:114-18 (and note also Zwiep 2016).

This orientation has the important consequence of retrieving the authoritative interpretation of the Bible from the monopoly of scholarly specialists. Getting to know God is not a purely academic exercise; rather, it is what the church throughout the ages (at least at its best moments) has aimed for: to help people get to know God through the Bible. The theological interpretation thus lodges most naturally in the community of the church. Here is its second pillar: the Bible is not just the book par excellence about God; it is also the book of the *church*. Not that the church owns the Bible and may therefore determine its message and its interpretation. Nor that the Bible has nothing to say outside the church and cannot exert its influence there. No doubt, the Bible can also be profitably read outside the church. The implication is, rather, that the church in some way originated from its contact with the biblical testimony. The church is *creatura verbi* (a creature of the Word) in the sense of being a community of people who have begun to look in the direction to which the Bible points, namely, the direction of God and his kingdom (see Matt 6:33). For this reason, the Bible has its most natural habitat in the church, for there we find those who want their entire mode of thinking and acting to be guided as much as possible by the message of the Bible. In that sense we may say that the Bible functions optimally in the church—at least ideally so, when the church allows itself to be led by the Bible. For this leading to happen, however, the Bible must be constantly reinterpreted and made real. The church is therefore first and foremost a community of interpretation, of people who help one another to understand the meaning of the Bible.

When we say "church," we must in this context not think of a specific denomination but of the holy catholic church, the church of all times and all places. "Together with all the saints" (and not just with some of them), we are able, Paul says, to understand the breadth, the length, the depth and the height of Christ's love (Eph 3:18). For this reason, the interpretations of Jewish exegetes and church fathers, of medieval Bible commentators and the Reformers, and also of the contemporary world church remain so important for us. In light of contemporary methods, we may raise an eyebrow about the Bible interpretations of premodern theologians, but for a fully theological interpretation of the Bible, we must also approach them with great openness. Church fathers, Reformers, and other spiritual authors from the past were especially eager to read the Bible to discover what it teaches us about God and God's relation to us and our world. In that sense they were great theological interpreters; some would argue that their exegeses are therefore superior to the interpretations that have been produced in the last two hundred years (e.g., D. Steinmetz in Fowl 1997, 26–38). In any case, we stand on their shoulders when we read the Bible in our search for God today.

Much the same holds for the way in which the Bible is currently read and interpreted, worldwide and in many denominations. A theological interpretation of the Bible does not aim to safeguard a typically Western way of reading the Bible but welcomes enrichment, and possibly correction, from non-Western forms of Bible reading and exegesis.

Consider just one example: in the West we usually see the point of the parable of the good Samaritan (Luke 10:25–37) to be that we must, like that Samaritan, help needy people who cross our path. In Tanzania, however, many intuitively feel that the parable wants to tell us something else: if you are in need, you must not be picky but must be ready to accept help from anyone, possibly even from your enemy. They read the parable through the eyes of the injured Jewish man who is willing to accept treatment from a Samaritan. This is an example of an interpretation that brings us closer to the intention of Luke and thus enriches our understanding of such a well-known biblical passage. See further Wit 2004.

The theological interpretation, we might say, represents a homecoming (*Heimholing*) for the Bible. The Bible is brought back to its original and most natural context, the church, and in the process is rehabilitated as canon, as a collection of books that derive their meaning from being recognized as true pointers to God. Such an approach offers no room for automatism, as if each Bible book, or part thereof, formed a closed textual unit. Rather, the separate biblical passages can become clear only when they are read against a much wider background—ultimately against the grand story of the Bible in its entirety.

It is no mere coincidence that the various books of the Bible became part of one collection, nor is this arrangement incidental to their correct interpretation. Both formation and interpretation center in the theological content and spirit of all these writings. That *these* very books came together invites us to compare them with each other, to lay them side by side. Do they not refer to one and the same God? Is the God of Israel not the same as the Father of Jesus Christ and the Sender of the Spirit? Can the books of the Bible not be optimally understood in light of each other, and especially in the light of the kerygma and the creed around which they are grouped? In any case, the Bible is not an ordinary collection of texts, like any other; the canon makes them into the sacred Scriptures (Watson 1994, 4). We might here indeed apply the doctrine of sanctification: the special position that God gave these writings sets them apart from all others and gives them a very special status (see Webster 2003a, 17-30).

In principle, everyone may join the discussion about how God lets himself be known through the Bible. One does not have to be a biblical scholar or the graduate of a theological program to contribute to a theological interpretation of the Bible. The reader must simply be prepared to follow—in faith and in his or her thinking—the route to which the texts point. This approach does justice to the central conviction of the Reformation, namely, that, in principle, the Bible can speak for itself and may never become the exclusive domain of an elite group of experts to whom correct interpretation may be entrusted. This is the awareness behind

Gerard Dou's painting of a simple woman reading her Bible. All of us may find God through the Bible, and other people may learn from those who have.

The same rule applies to the various subdisciplines of theology. No one, including professional exegetes, should avoid the theological task. To arrive at a good theological interpretation of the Bible, it is important that church and theology profit from the way in which experts use modern and postmodern tools to clarify the meanings and backgrounds of the biblical texts. The theological interpretation of the Bible does not aim lower than the other professional methods, but higher. It wishes to have those methods contribute to an interpretation that helps people to get to know God and his saving acts. No method, therefore, can be regarded as autonomous, as if it would arrive at a neutral or "purely scholarly" meaning of the text, for this is a fiction. Academic tools provide us with better insight into the history of texts and textual units, into the transmission, the selection, and appropriation of texts. They clarify the theological questions that are at stake: who is God? what is our role? what is Israel's role? will God's covenant be successful? In this way they may provide clarification to help us understand the Bible as the God-given Word. Only when something significant can be said about these questions will the interpreter be ready with his or her work.

In addition to "ordinary" believers and professional biblical scholars, the various specialties in the theological guild can contribute to this theological interpretation of the Bible (see Vanhoozer 2005, 21–22). *Biblical theologians*, for instance, will analyze what the different biblical authors thought about God and his relationship with us (i.e., what their theology was) to determine whether any common theme can be found in their writing(s), and if so, what it looks like. To do so, they will have to leave the safe haven of their supposed objective and neutral study of the Bible and ask further questions about how the results of their work influence how people hear God's voice today. Certainly *systematic theologians*, who study dogmatics and the doctrines of the church, must not ignore their own journey with the Bible. This separation has often been the case as the rift between Bible and dogmatics widened. Dogmaticians often encounter considerable suspicion when they make statements about the Bible; at the same time, they have often manifested too little trust in the usefulness of biblical scholarship, preferring philosophy as their primary discussion partner instead. In this textbook the biblical basis holds a prominent place for good reason. If it is part of the task of dogmatics to provide an account of what can be said about God here and now, it must always do so by carefully listening to the biblical testimony about the salvation that has been given in Christ. The Bible is the source for the Christian faith, and we must allow the Bible to serve as our point of orientation—and our prod of disturbance.

Finally, *practical theologians* will also naturally get involved in the interpretation of the Bible. They will likely look at the reactions the Bible evokes in contemporary readers and thus will be focusing on the world ahead of the text. A theological interpretation of the Bible is not ultimately just a matter of words; it reaches its goal in the praxis of faith, where the biblical orientation toward God gets a practical dimension. Practical theology studies the domain of the praxis of faith and may come up with creative proposals for ways of our being the church that do justice to the biblical message.

Our sketch treats the theological interpretation of the Bible as a more or less homogeneous movement. In reality, its representatives place different accents at different points. Generally speaking, some (e.g., Vanhoozer) attribute more significance to the reality behind the text, others to the history of its origin and development (Talstra) or to its final form (Frei). Still others (such as Fowl) emphasize the reading and interpretation by today's faith community, a process that Christians believe is also guided by the Spirit (see John 16:13a). In fact, the recent movement for the theological interpretation of the Bible is not really a new phenomenon; the giants in church history have always tried to read the Bible this way. Augustine's reiteration of the radical nature of God's grace in his controversy with the Pelagians, Luther's insistence on the significance of the concept of God's righteousness, and Barth's *Commentary on Romans* are all examples of a strict theological interpretation. Surprises could flare up along the way, for God's speaking was not always found to be an extension of our own thoughts. It sometimes proved to be totally different, and very positive. In particular, *Karl Barth's* doctrine of Scripture has been formative to the rise of theological interpretation. For an instructive collection of older and newer essays on Barth's theory and practice of reading Scripture, see Hunsinger 2012.

In sum, a theological interpretation can free the Bible from the shackles that held it enchained since the Enlightenment. If the Bible was analyzed by rationalist scholars until its message was completely obscured, it can now once again become the book of God and humanity. And we use the singular form "book" quite freely—not from a naïveté with regard to the plurality of voices in the Bible, but because of the common focus that supersedes this plurality. It does not require a nonscholarly or antischolarly attitude to see the Bible primarily as one unit, the unity of the canon. We might refer to this attitude as a "second naïveté" (Ricoeur).

13.6. The Bible as a Function of God's Trinitarian Acts

Having considered the theological interpretation of the Bible, what can we say about the classic questions of the authority and exegesis of the Scriptures (13.7)? Before we can adequately address these questions, we must first take a closer look at the Bible's background and origin in God's saving acts (13.6). In this section, then, we examine the position that the Bible holds in the Christian church. To say that the Bible is the Word of God—the sacred Scriptures—says first of all that the Bible is a function of God's acts. At the same time, it says something about our use of the Bible. We offer the following remarks about this double function.

1. The Bible itself is the fruit of God's *acting and speaking in history*. God's dealings with humanity led, as we have seen, to a deposit in texts, a diversity of documents that have come down through history and are now available to us as canon. Still today, the church treats these texts as God's Word, as the channel through which God addresses us. Not the text but the God to whom these texts point is the final authority that takes effect on us. The conviction that God has spoken (*Deus dixit*) is directly linked to the expectation that God will speak, and on that basis the Reformation could regard the proclamation of the Word as an instrument of salvation (see chap. 14). This belief has immediate consequences for our *use of the Bible*; as "sacred" Scripture, the Bible has a prominent place in church worship, in the home, and in our personal relationship with God.

2. The reference to God's acts points to God's *identity*. We intentionally decided to deal with the doctrine of the Trinity in this dogmatics directly after the prolegomena. That doctrine tells us about the one to whom we want to relate. When we now state that the Bible is a function of God's action, we bracket the reading of the Bible for a moment so as to point to the identity of God who is the subject of salvation history. In previous chapters we have discussed different aspects of God's identity— with Israel's belief in God as the Creator of the world, and with the Old Testament's theme of the covenant that God established with Abraham. In the covenant with Israel, God was in search of a lasting love relationship; both the Old and the New Testaments testify of this search. In the New Testament we discover how God stretches his two hands toward us

(Irenaeus) in Jesus Christ and the Holy Spirit. Christian theology deals with the history of this drama under the heading of reconciliation and redemption. This search of God manifests his desire to involve humanity—he wants our response; he wants to save and transform us and his world. For our use of the Bible, this aspect of God's will implies that we may and must continue to ask where our place falls in the story (in classic jargon, the question of the application of the Bible). That moment may occur at different times: in hearing the Word preached, in a hymn, in Bible study and meditation, in silence, or in bibliodrama (the performance of biblical stories in small groups of Bible readers).

3. The Bible as a function of God's acts also points to a *progression* in those acts. We fail to do justice to the Bible when we use its texts as a source for general statements about God or to simply illustrate human sentiments or situations. The Bible as canon serves as the church's collective memory, reminding us of the progressive stages of God's dealings with Israel and the church. Accordingly, we must be aware of *our* place in history. We are not part of the people of Israel in the wilderness, and we do not live in Babylon. When we feel culturally estranged, it does not mean that our situation is the same as that of the exiles in Babylon. Likewise, the suffering of Jesus Christ may not be used as a general illustration of human suffering in the present. That sort of reversal makes the Bible into a picture book from which we can pick stories at random. There is a progression in God's acts that we must remember as we read and interpret the Bible. Too often Christians use passages from the Bible as agenda, model, action program, or illustration. This is both too easy and insufficient. The church lives in a time *after* the suffering and resurrection of Jesus Christ and is itself the fruit of the outpouring of the Holy Spirit. We live in the time of the Spirit, in which God, through his Spirit, wants to involve us in the blessing and fulfillment of the covenant through Christ. In sum, in our journey through the Old and the New Testaments, we look back at the distance that has already been covered. We are set on that path at our baptism but always in a forward direction.

What does this factor mean for our use of the Bible? Does it erase all forms of personally relating to the Bible? Should the Bible reader first sit for an exam with people who have studied theology? Not at all. Everyone may read the Bible and seek to come in contact with God through these sacred Scriptures, in its texts, hymns, and prayers. At the same time, we must realize that these texts are not our individual possession. As we read, we are in the communion around Jesus Christ, in the church, which means that our interpretation and conclusions are always subject, first, to the Bible in its entirety and, second, to the "distinguishing of the spirits."

We find a beautiful explanation of our point in a passage by Berkhof (CF 252–53) that speaks about "cultural-historical distance." Berkhof notes that many themes in the Bible (esp. in the Old Testament) give us cause to wonder, such as the custom of casting lots, the identification of God's voice with the thunder, the wars in which YHWH engages, the role of retaliation and revenge, the polygamy of Abraham and his contemporaries, the inferior position of women, and the almost total lack of an expectation of life after death. These things come to look different, however, when we do not isolate them but place them along the route that God has traveled with his people. That is, these texts are in themselves not normative. "Normative in the sense of a revelation and as being decisive for us is the journey that Israel was to make with its God and the experiences the people had with him and with themselves during that journey. We must appropriate these in a spiritual sense and express them in a new manner in the world in which we live" (253). That is, we must not focus on the specific place of these texts but on their progression.

4. Taking the Bible to be a function of God's acts also entails *expectation*. As the church uses the Bible, it believes it is dealing with the same God as the one of whom these writings testify. That is, the power that has been deposited in these texts as a reality and as a history that has transpired may be realized in the present. The same mistakes Israel committed are still a very real threat to the church today (note 1 Cor 10:1–12). At the same time, the God who, in his dealings with Israel, always searched for a way out so as to keep the covenant alive and to fulfill his promises, is the God who still helps his people survive their moments of despair. There are always new readers who find comfort in these ancient words. In chapter 9, about Israel, we saw an example of this reading from the New Testament: Paul allows himself to be led in his expectations of the future by the promise given to Abraham in the distant past (Gal 3; Rom 4). He accepts what was revealed to Israel. The church believes that Jesus Christ—the same person who dwelt on earth and healed the suffering—now shares in God's rule and has been given the task to judge our history (see Matt 28:18; 1 Cor 8:6; Rev 1:7–8). This faith is the dome above our expectations. Moreover, believers in the New Testament experienced the power of the Spirit as a real force by which God came close and manifested his presence. For our use of the Bible, this experience implies that we are dealing with the same God as Abraham, Isaiah, and Ezekiel,

and with the same God who has been "exegeted" for us in the ministry of Jesus Christ (note John 1:18: "the Son *exēgēsato* [i.e., has made known, 'exegeted'] the Father"). The blessing of the life-giving communion with God that was once promised to Abraham now stands available to those who have come in from the nations.

13.7. The Authority and Interpretation of the Bible

At the start of this chapter we cited what the Dutch Protestant Church officially says about the authority of the Bible. To this subject we now return. The Bible is "the only rule for the proclamation and service of the church." This statement assigns the Bible a status that has received broad recognition in the Christian tradition. But what exactly does this authority mean, and what is implied by recognizing the Bible as the Word of God?

To answer this question, first a quick review. We have seen that the Bible has authority in the church because it testifies to the saving acts of God in Israel, in Jesus Christ, and in the Spirit. Around this testimony originated the canon, a list of authoritative books. The authority of the Bible is grounded in its recognition by the church. *The acceptance of this list of books in the fourth century was a matter of taking stock of the actual situation, of the pattern of practice that had developed in the reading and liturgical use of these writings.* All theorizing about the authority of the Bible and its inspiration, or theopneusty, were of later date. That is no problem, and we do not say this with the intention of depreciating any reflection about the authority and inspiration of the Bible. But this is how theology works—it follows reality.

Likewise in the practice of baptism. It began with the praxis of faith, a concrete act by which people were added to the circle of Jesus Christ's followers. Theological reflection followed later. Initially, reflection on the Bible as one unit (our canon) was unnecessary and even impossible. Until the third century most Christian communities possessed, at most, only one or a few biblical writings. Manuscripts were rare and costly. Locally, the church existed as a small community with certain practices and orally transmitted memories (Wolter 2003, 51). In the meantime the church perceived that the writings that were read and used exerted authority.

We also saw (13.4) that a document had to be apostolic to have authority. Originally, the concept "apostolic" meant having a link with the apostle as a person; the writings had to be authored by a direct disciple of Jesus. The meaning of "apostolicity" arose directly from this connection. To be read and acceptable for liturgical use, a writing had to conform to the teachings of the apostles, exhibiting continuity with the teachings of Jesus's apostles on the points of salvation, sin, redemption, and the renewing work of the Spirit. The authoritative canon emerged in parallel to the rule of faith; the norm developed as the content was being formed. Whatever diversity we may find in the Bible, it is the permanent source-book that the Christian church recognizes when dealing with the questions of who God is for us, who we are, and what our future holds. Behind and through this entire process stood the church's faith and confession in the one God of Israel, the Father of Jesus Christ and the Sender of the Spirit. All epistles, gospels, and other writings have been agglomerated around the recognition that the God who acted in Jesus Christ is the same as the one who revealed himself in the history of Israel.

The element of apostolicity proved to be functional by virtue of its content. Various gnostic writings, such as the Gospels of Thomas, Jude, or Peter, did not meet this criterion. The distinction between canonical and noncanonical is not based on a decree of tyrannical bishops (as many conspiracy theories want us to believe) but is the result of the praxis of reading, selection, and appropriation (see also 10.3).

The authority of the Bible therefore rests on the salvific character of its content; its authority is soteriologically determined. If we can say that God is spoken of in the history of Israel and in the history of Jesus and the Spirit, then the Bible is the book in which this speaking is reduced to a written form. We can read it ourselves, others can read it to us, it can be read afresh by new readers, translated anew, understood in a new light, and can make itself heard when people present it as the "word." Paul expresses this ground of biblical authority when he says of Jesus in 2 Cor 1:19-20, "in him it is always Yes. For all the promises of God find their Yes in him." In that sense we have solid reason to refer to the Bible as the inspired Word of God and to agree with Herman Bavinck that these Scriptures are "theopneust," breathed through by God. The pneumatic qualifications of inspiration and theopneusty come into their own in light of the process of origin, borrowing, transmission, selection, appropriation, loss and recovery, and reinterpretation by which the Bible came to be. God did not feel embarrassed by these thoroughly human, historical, and receptive processes by which he allowed people to speak of him. Where two or three are assembled in his name, the power of these words may once again be heard and come alive. Thus, no literary-critical qualities but rather theological qualifications give these texts their indisputable warrant as belonging to the canon of the church.

From this soteriologically determined authority streams the proper *interpretation* of the Bible in proclamation and service. The conviction that the Bible testifies to God's saving acts in Jesus Christ provides the crucial norm for the canon as a whole and for the proclamation of the biblical message. Theologians in the past spoke in this connection of interpreting by analogy to faith (*interpretatio secundum analogiam fidei*) and by analogy to the Scriptures (*interpretatio secundum analogiam Scripturae*). Both rules have their roots in the basic Protestant principle that the Bible interprets itself (*sacra Scriptura sui ipsius interpres*). This notion implies that obscure things must be interpreted in light of what is clear. That rule risks leading people to think that the Bible is one big block that fell from heaven. Our pneumatological approach aims to avoid that impression. The Bible, the canon of the Old and the New Testaments, has come to us via a long and often rather cloudy history. However, it is clear that the process of canonization was always connected with the actual practices of the temple, the synagogue, and the culturally diverse Christian communities. There always existed a community that worshiped God, prayed to him, ensured the continual offering of praise, and thereby experienced God's faithfulness.

This last remark shows the *link between liturgy and the biblical writings*. That relationship already existed in Israel, where the Law and the Prophets were authoritative sources. In the footsteps of Jesus the early Jewish-Christian church read Israel's writings, recited and reinterpreted them, and sang the Psalms in the light of the cross and resurrection. Thus the basic structures of Israel's worship—the focus on the Scriptures, the offering of prayers, thanksgiving and praise, and the recitation of Psalms—entered the liturgy of the early and medieval church in the midst of enormous diversity. The canon reflects the wide range of cultural and social contexts in which the confession of Jesus as Kyrios was introduced. That confession served as the new "identity marker" of the books that were accepted as part of the canon. Although that acceptance involved a long process, once the canon was recognized, the authority of the Bible became a self-evident part of the Christian faith. Therein, we might say, lay the Bible's formal authority.

This formal authority (the *auctoritas*) is accepted not only in the Protestant tradition, where a special doctrine of the Scriptures was developed, but was already asserted in the medieval church. The Reformation did not invent the principle as a protest against Rome but did make it more explicit. Later Protestant orthodoxy began to distinguish between the formal and material authority of the Bible. This idea, derived from Aristotelian metaphysics, is plausible and useful to a certain extent. But it may also easily lead to a rationalistic decision as to what kind of authority a given biblical passage has. As a result, things that belong together get divorced. Moreover, normative and historical authority might have to be distinguished, so that—for instance—the words of Satan at Jesus's temptations (Matt 4:1–11) are clarified as being historically but not normatively true. They are part of the Scriptures, but not everything in the Scriptures is binding.

Such attempts to identify normative substance in the Bible make sense and are to some extent inevitable, but at the same time can easily evolve into means of making the Bible say what we want it to say. In this book we too have practiced selectivity among many texts and pericopes, for instance, in treating Christology and soteriology. We might even say that every theologian (and probably every believer) has some favorite biblical passages, Bible books, or hymns—a "canon within the canon." Recall Luther's adage: *was Christum treibet*. It was very significant that Reformed theology never adopted such a principle. All Scripture is of importance, including the parts that trouble us or leave us bewildered— for instance, the texts that appear to sanction divine violence during the Hebrews' conquest and occupation of the land of Canaan (Josh 10–11) or the punishment of Ananias and Sapphira (Acts 5:1–11).

Other notorious texts of violence include the endings of Pss 137 and 139 and a lesser-known text like Rev 6:10. These passages may be understood as expressions of legitimate anger on the part of the believers, who are not silenced by God but actually receive a place in the canon.

The authority of the canon has been established and affirmed time and again in the actual praxis of its reading and use. In this process the entire span of the canon is useful, even what seems marginal or less relevant today. We do not feel the need to make any further distinction between margin and core. Berkhof still indulges this somewhat rationalistic practice when he speaks about four circles in Scripture bearing different degrees of authority (CF §17). We do not deny a layered aspect in the Bible with their attendant differences, but we find the modern suggestion that we can make a reasonably sharp distinction between core and margin, or form and content, to be rather debatable. Form and content are often directly related. Moreover, what is considered marginal or mere form at one moment might appear to be of much more importance in a different time and culture.

Can we in fact speak of unity when confronted with all the diversity in the canon? There have been five ways of dealing with that question:

1. *Elimination.* A notorious example is Marcion, who composed a list of the books (only Luke and ten Pauline letters) that he felt were consistent with the God of love. He thus rejected the Old Testament in toto.

2. The distinction of a *canon within the canon.* This strategy seems less radical than the first but is actually quite similar in rendering some parts of the Bible to be virtually ignored. Luther's adage *was Christum treibet* is the classic example. In his line an impressive series of Lutheran theologians declared the justification of the sinner (Romans, Galatians) to be the critical core of the canon (e.g., E. Käsemann, E. Jüngel).

3. *Harmonization.* The differences between texts are eliminated in order to yield up a cohesive version. An ancient example was the attempt to make a "harmony of the gospels" as, for instance, Tatian's *Diatessaron* (second half of the second century). Quite often, in debates about the historicity of the Bible, the harmonization process was applied to arrive at a clear and unequivocal picture of what actually happened. Such attempts are, in themselves, certainly justifiable; the Bible refers to events at a particular place and time. The problem comes when harmonization devolves into ignoring or twisting parts of the text.

4. *Search for deeper unity.* Here we could mention attempts by many biblical theologians (as B. S. Childs, G. von Rad, R. Rendtorff, T. C. Vriezen, H. Gese, and P. Stuhlmacher) to find a consistent or connecting line or center in the Bible. Even though this approach to the canon has been heavily criticized for its holistic presupposition (Barr 1999), it usually leads to valuable insights that systematic-theological reflection can fruitfully use.

5. *Diversity as virtue.* We must not attempt to eliminate or neutralize the diversity of texts and perspectives, for it shows the richness of perspectives on Christ and salvation. In theological language: complexity reminds us that we are the recipients of revelation and that God's salvation unfolds itself from various angles. An important argument in favor of this view is offered by the history of the canon itself. The church did not embrace just one gospel or a harmonization of the gospels but four gospels (Barton 2003, 23). An important example of the diversity-as-virtue approach with respect to the Old Testament is Brueggemann 1997. In this book we follow options 4 and 5.

The issue of the question of authority in the midst of diversity becomes most acute in the realm of ethics. The same was true in Judaism, where considerable diversity of opinions was tolerated, but not regarding halakah. Early Christianity was faced with the burning question of the salient Jewish "identity markers" maintained for gentile believers, as is clear from the discussion at the apostles' council (Acts 15). Other examples of controversies about the halakah in the New Testament appear in Gal 2:11-14 and 1 Cor 10:23-33. They show that, in the history of the church, the search for a Christian way of life in the footsteps of Jesus Christ was a slow and often painful learning process. Later examples include the abolition of slavery in the nineteenth century, a new view of poverty as social injustice, the position of women in society and church, and ideas about marriage, fertility, relationships, physical and mental handicaps, and ecology.

On these kinds of issues, the actual answer to the question of the authority of the Bible seems to flow from a constant interaction between culture, context, and the Bible. In this process believers seek to be obedient to the Bible and to let that source be decisive. However, as we have argued above, the Bible is not an autonomous entity, not a code of law, but a function of the actions of Father, Son, and Spirit. Here we may claim the promise of John 16:13-14: "When the Spirit of truth comes, he will guide you into all the truth; for he will not speak on his own authority, but whatever he hears he will speak, and he will declare to you the things that are to come. He will glorify me, for he will take what is mine and declare it to you." This text in no way allows for a rank and lazy subjectivism. It points readers and disciples to their relationship with Christ. We cannot deal with the question of biblical authority without this concrete attitude of faith. We are reminded of Berkouwer's "correlation principle" (see Keulen 2010) and once again refer to the role of doctrine and confessional documents. They are the relative authorities that try to protect the content of the gospel in a particular time and place. Most concretely we receive training for this disposition in the prayer that Jesus taught us. In the Lord's Prayer the disciples are instructed to focus on making God's name holy and on the coming of the kingdom. We can give a satisfactory answer to questions of authority only when that prayer is our reality.

References

Barr, James. 1999. *The Concept of Biblical Theology: An Old Testament Perspective.* London: SCM.

Barton, John. 2003. "Unity and Diversity in the Biblical Canon." In *Die Einheit der*

Schrift und die Vielfalt des Kanons, edited by J. Barton and M. Wolter, 11-26. Berlin: de Gruyter.

Belt, Henk van den. 2008. *The Authority of Scripture in Reformed Theology: Truth and Trust*. Leiden: Brill.

Berkouwer, Gerrit C. 1975. *Holy Scripture*. Grand Rapids: Eerdmans.

Billings, J. Todd. 2010. *The Word of God for the People of God: An Entryway to the Theological Interpretation of Scripture*. Grand Rapids: Eerdmans.

Bockmuehl, Marcus, and Alan J. Torrance, eds. 2008. *Scripture's Doctrine and Theology's Bible: How the New Testament Shapes Christian Dogmatics*. Grand Rapids: Baker Academic.

Brinkman, Martien, and Cornelis van der Kooi, eds. 1997. *Het calvinisme van Kuyper en Bavinck*. Zoetermeer: Meinema.

Brueggemann, Walter. 1997. *Theology of the Old Testament: Testimony, Dispute, Advocacy*. Minneapolis: Fortress.

Childs, Brevard S. 1985. *Old Testament Theology in a Canonical Context*. Philadelphia: Fortress.

Fowl, Stephen, ed. 1997. *The Theological Interpretation of Scripture*. Cambridge, MA: Blackwell.

Frei, Hans W. 1974. *The Eclipse of Biblical Narrative*. New Haven: Yale University Press.

Gaventa, Beverly Roberts, and Richard B. Hays, eds. 2008. *Seeking the Identity of Jesus: A Pilgrimage*. Grand Rapids: Eerdmans.

Hazard, Paul. 2013. *The Crisis of the European Mind, 1680-1715*. New York: New York Review of Books. Orig. French pub., Paris, 1935.

Heyer, Cornelis J. den. 2007. *Twee testamenten: Reden tot vreugde of bron van tegenspraak*. [Two Testaments: Reason for joy or source of dispute]. Zoetermeer: Meinema.

Hunsinger, George, ed. 2012. *Thy Word Is Truth: Barth on Scripture*. Grand Rapids: Eerdmans.

Jenson, Robert W. 2010. *Canon and Creed: Resources for the Use of Scripture in the Church*. Louisville: Westminster John Knox.

Kelsey, David. 1975. *The Uses of Scripture in Recent Theology*. Philadelphia: Fortress.

Keulen, Dirk van. 2003. *Bijbel en dogmatiek: Schriftbeschouwing en schriftgebruik in het dogmatisch werk van A. Kuyper, H. Bavinck en G. C. Berkouwer* [Bible and dogmatics: View of Scripture and use of Scripture in the dogmatic work of Kuyper, Bavinck, and Berkouwer]. Kampen: Kok.

———. 2010. "G. C. Berkouwer's Principle of Correlation: An Attempt to Comprehend." *Journal of Reformed Theology* 4:97-111.

Kraus, Hans-Joachim. 1984. *Geschichte der historisch-kritischen Erforschung des Alten Testaments von der Reformation bis zur Gegenwart*. Neukirchen: Neukirchener Verlag. Orig. pub., 1956.

Kruger, Michael J. 2013. *The Question of Canon*. Downers Grove: IVP Academic.

Kümmel, Werner G. 1972. *The New Testament: The History of the Investigation of Its Problems*. Nashville: Abingdon. Orig. German pub., 1958.

Lauster, Jörg. 2004. *Prinzip und Methode: Die Transformation des protestantischen Schriftprinzips durch die historische Kritik von Schleiermacher bis zur Gegenwart*. Tübingen: Mohr Siebeck.

McDonald, Lee Martin, and James A. Sanders, eds. 2002. *The Canon Debate*. Peabody, MA: Hendrickson.

Pannenberg, Wolfhart. 1970. "The Crisis of the Scripture Principle." In *Basic Questions in Theology*, 1:1–14. London: SCM.

Ricoeur, Paul. 1976. *Interpretation Theory: Discourse and the Surplus of Meaning*. Fort Worth: Texas Christian University Press.

Stuhlmacher, Peter. 1992–99. *Biblische Theologie des Neuen Testaments*. 2 vols. Göttingen: Vandenhoeck & Ruprecht.

———. 1995. *How to Do Biblical Theology*. Eugene, OR: Pickwick Publications.

Talstra, Eep. 2002. *Oude en nieuwe lezers: Een inleiding in de methoden van uitleg van het Oude Testament*. [Old and new readers: An introduction to the methods of interpretation of the Old Testament]. Kampen: Kok.

Vanhoozer, Kevin J., et al., eds. 2005. *Dictionary for Theological Interpretation of the Bible*. Grand Rapids: Baker Academic.

Volf, Miroslav. 2010. *Captive to the Word of God: Engaging the Scriptures for Contemporary Theological Reflection*. Grand Rapids: Eerdmans.

Watson, Francis. 1994. *Text, Church, and World: Biblical Interpretation in Theological Perspective*. Edinburgh: T&T Clark.

Webster, John. 2003a. "'A Great and Meritorious Act of the Church'? The Dogmatic Location of the Canon." In *Die Einheit der Schrift und die Vielfalt des Kanons*, edited by J. Barton and M. Wolter, 95–126. Berlin: de Gruyter.

———. 2003b. *Holy Scripture: A Dogmatic Sketch*. Cambridge: Cambridge University Press.

Williams, Daniel H., ed. 2006. *Tradition, Scripture, and Interpretation: A Sourcebook of the Ancient Church*. Grand Rapids: Baker Academic.

Wit, Hans de, et al., eds. 2004. *Through the Eyes of Another: Intercultural Reading of the Bible*. Elkhart, IN: Institute of Mennonite Studies.

Wolter, Michael. 2003. "Die Viefalt der Schrift und die Einheit des Kanons." In *The Unity of Scripture and the Diversity of the Canon*, edited by John Barton and Michael Wolter, 45–68. Berlin/New York: Walter de Gruyter.

Zwiep, Arie W. 2009–13. *Tussen tekst en lezer: Een historische inleiding in de bijbelse hermeneutiek* [Between text and reader: A historical introduction to biblical hermeneutics]. 2 vols. Amsterdam: VU University Press.

———. 2016. "Bible Hermeneutics from 1950 to the Present: Trends and Developments." In *Handbuch der Biblehermeneutiken / Handbook of Bible Hermeneutics*, edited by Oda Wischmeyer, 941–1016. Berlin: de Gruyter.

14 Renewal of God's Community

Ecclesiology

AIM

In our previous two chapters, on the Holy Spirit and the Bible, we discussed some ways that God draws us into his salvation. This drawing implies participation on our part. Having explored the Bible's role in this process, in this chapter we discuss a number of other elements that can be seen as instruments of salvation, namely, the church, the sacraments, and church offices. Our participation will be just as important here. We want to:

- consider what the concept of the church means theologically (14.1)
- define the essence of the church by examining the relevant biblical images (14.2)
- provide a survey of the most important models of "being the church" (14.3)
- determine the relationship between the church and the kingdom of God (14.4)
- introduce the notion of the means of grace, and show how the proclamation of the Word of God is the first of them (14.5)
- explain the nature and meaning of the sacraments (14.6)
- broaden the concept of the sacraments and discuss three guides that help structure the church as a faith community: baptism, communion, and pastoral visitation and instruction (14.7)
- introduce the principal issues pertaining to the offices of the church (14.8)
- clarify the four characteristics of the church that have creedal status: one, holy, catholic, and apostolic (14.9)
- discuss the role of the church in the public domain (14.10).

MAKING CONNECTIONS

1. When you attend church services, what in particular do you notice? What are the most important ingredients of a worship service? How much participation do you see there? Who is (or are) in charge? Are the attendees mainly spectators or something more? For each of your answers, ask "Why?"
2. The institutional church has lost much of its popularity. Could we do without the church? Are other forms of Christian community possible, like Taizé and social media?
3. Watch the film *Babette's Feast* (1987) with some friends and think about what sacraments mean through the lens of this film.

14.1. Initial Exploration: The Church as Eschatological Community

This chapter deals with the church, church offices, and the sacraments. We could have introduced this topic much earlier, for faith and Christian theology can never be separated. Faith is usually experienced in a community of people and originates in communion with others. This interconnection was clear in the chapter on prolegomena, when we moved from a broader to a narrower range. That is, besides formal theology, we took notice of the wide range of experiences and practices that have their place within the Christian community. The church is the place where we pray, sing, tell stories, are baptized and celebrate communion, and learn how to share with others. All of these are *activities*; faith has to do with the *praxis* of life. Even so, we have opted for the usual approach and are treating the church under pneumatology. It is the Spirit who bridges the gap between the Father and the Son on the one hand and, on the other, draws us into the Father-Son relationship. For this reason, we elaborate on "ecclesiology" following our treatment in chapter 12 of the Holy Spirit.

Historically considered, ecclesiology is a latecomer in dogmatics. In the classic systems that were dominant until the Reformation, the church belonged to the study of faith, the sacraments, and church offices; its connections to the means of grace remained mostly implicit. See, for instance, book 4 of Peter Lombard's *Sententiae*. By contrast, the Reformation gave the church a much more central place; it was the place where the Word was proclaimed and the sacraments were administered.

This approach was intended as a criticism of the medieval sacramental church.

Ecclesiology was further elaborated only in the nineteenth century, when, under the pressures of social modernization, the church became just one community and institution among many others. Much more than before, the church now had to consider its public place and task without the self-evident and dominant role it had earlier. As a result, Christendom now consisted first and foremost of the institutional church.

The twentieth century saw much more written about the church. On the Roman Catholic side we mention Küng (1967); Ramsey (1990) gives an Anglican view, and Kindler (1958), a classic Lutheran treatment. Reformed contributions include, for instance, Torrance 1993 and Berkouwer 1976; the free-church perspective is represented by Littell (1958) and Volf (1998). In the ecumenical world the discussion about church, sacrament, and church office was greatly stimulated by the World Council of Church's study *Baptism, Eucharist, and Ministry* (1982); see, for example, Borght 2007. A later report in which the World Council of Churches (WCC) took a major step toward a common understanding of what it means to be church is also of great importance: *The Church: Towards a Common Vision* (2013). On the church as a "contrast community," see Hauerwas 2001.

In our chapters on Christology and pneumatology we noted how a new community originated around Jesus Christ. Christ calls his disciples; then after the resurrection he appears to them and sends them into the world. The essence of the church is found in its communion with its living Lord. We also discussed how the Holy Spirit provides access to this community. The Holy Spirit is the one who pulls people into the communion that exists between the Son and the Father. The Spirit makes them participants in the salvation that Christ has provided; he gives life (Nicene Creed). This role of the Spirit encapsulates the church's most essential aspect. It is important to maintain the christological and pneumatological dimensions in any discussion of the church, the sacraments, and church offices. The Trinitarian motif indicates that the church did not originate by human initiative but, in the final analysis, is grounded in God's own acts. Even though, by the work of the Spirit, the church has deep roots in human history, this factor does not define its origin—or its destiny. The church is the eschatological community that is gathered as a harvest before God already in the present, the interim between Pentecost and the second coming. It is a place created by the triune God himself, where we may learn to live in the covenant under the renewed conditions we learn from the New Testament.

More concretely, the church is where believers assemble, proclaim Christ, and remember his atoning death. All who belong to this new community around Christ are invited to his table and may be called children of God; Paul even uses such lofty words for us as "heirs" and "co-heirs" of Christ (Rom 8:17). Through faith we share in the salvation that God offers. In baptism our name is connected with him, and as adopted children we have a place at the table. The concept of participation thus plays a prominent role in this chapter. At the same time, we must carefully differentiate the relationship that exists between Jesus Christ and the Father from our communion with the Father and the Son (Torrance 1993, 37). Our participation is qualitatively different from their relationship. As participants, we are recipients, and so we will always remain. Our participation in salvation does not depend on our own actions but on what we receive. When speaking of the church—of how the church leads us to God's salvation and of the church's mission in the world—it is decisive for us to remember that, no matter how active we may be or may become, we are on the receiving end.

Our position as recipients of God's salvation was uniquely expressed by Mary, Jesus's mother, in her response to the angel's announcement that she would become pregnant (Luke 1:38): "Let it be to me according to your word." Mary subjects herself fully to the Word; she accepts what she is told and is willing to be used. If Protestants have any place for devotion to Mary, it would be here. In fact, we note an interesting rapprochement between Roman Catholicism and Protestantism with regard to Mariology. Vatican II placed Mariology within ecclesiology, ending the tendency that began in the tenth century to make it a part of Christology instead, which granted Mary a structural role in the work of redemption. The promulgations of 1854 (immaculate conception) and 1950 (Mary's ascension) are the fruit of that older model, which was based on an analogy between Christ and Mary. In the more recent approach the person of Mary represents our receptivity and the response of the church to Christ. She does not have a place next to Christ but bears an important function for the church that is en route. (For recent systematic reflection on Mary in the Roman Catholic Church, see Elizabeth Johnson's essay in Fiorenza/Galvin, STRCP 431–59). For an interesting defense of why a Protestant might say the Ave Maria (not as a direct prayer but as a request for intercession, just as we may ask fellow believers to pray for us), see Beek 2012, 174–76.

Under the influence of so-called Radical Orthodoxy, the concept of participation has received increased attention in the Anglophone world. In contrast with the secularist emphasis on this life as our only concern, Radical Orthodoxy advocates a return to the Platonic-Christian synthesis that suggests that all earthly things somehow point to, and share in, heavenly things. See, for instance, Milbank 1990 and Boersma 2009 and 2011. However, the concept of participation remains rather vague and demands more specificity. We therefore stress that, in any form of participation, ours is first and foremost the role of recipient. Only on that premise may we take up the suggestion that we ourselves have an active role in this participation, that the human self is activated (Immink 2014, 59). The status of recipient is abundantly clear in the notion of the covenant; through Jesus Christ we share in the promise of God's ultimate and all-encompassing—that is, eschatological—community. Compare Acts 2:39 and Gal 3:14.

The new community in Christ has its origin in a divine initiative. Through the Spirit, God opens himself up for us and invites us to live around, and in a close connection with, Jesus Christ. This work of God helps us to see that the essence of the church is the visible presence of the new, eschatological salvific community around Christ. The church is closely connected with Christ but not identical with him. There is proximity, but that very proximity presupposes a distinction. *He* has died and has risen, which is for *our* good. And this difference brings us life. The church is what it is because of Christ's continuous presence through the Spirit and the gift of his communion. The church is the creation of the Spirit of Christ. We take the difference between Christology and pneumatology very seriously; neither the church nor believers as a community are the fruit of incarnation. The *incarnation* happened once and for all in Jesus Christ. The *church* is created by the Spirit, who gathers people upon its foundation: Christ. For that reason we treat the church under the heading of pneumatology.

The high view of the church, as resting in a divine initiative, is still visible in the preposition "in" (*eis*) that is found in the original text of the Nicene Creed (381): "I believe in one holy, catholic, and Christian church." In later versions this preposition was omitted in an attempt to more clearly distinguish between our confession of faith in the divine persons and a belief concerning a creaturely phenomenon such as the church. For a strong emphasis on this divine initiative with regard to the church, see also the Heidelberg Catechism, Q/A 54.

> *Question*: What do you believe concerning "the holy catholic church" of Christ?
> *Answer*: I believe that the Son of God through his Spirit and Word, out of the entire human race, from the beginning of the world to its end, gathers,

protects, and preserves for himself a community chosen for eternal life and united in true faith. And of this community I am and always will be a living member.

It is important to note that the Heidelberg Catechism, just as the Belgic Confession, article 27, does not point to Pentecost as the beginning of the church but also, without hesitation, includes Old Testament Israel. This understanding agrees with the "incorporation theology" that we discussed in chapter 9.

The wording of the Heidelberg Catechism hints that the church's continued existence in this world should not be taken for granted; it needs protection and support from God. We must remember this need, and not only in circumstances of explicit physical and political persecution. When the church follows its Lord, it will often have to bear its cross and face cultural and political oppression. See John 12:26. In modern Western culture the Christian faith and the institutional church are coming under increasing pressure. The question about its social manifestations is more and more acute. Especially when we look at the phenomenon of church empirically, it is essential to hold on to this theological motif of divine faithfulness. It stimulates us to keep our eyes open for new and emerging manifestations of the church as the body of Christ, and not to let feelings of defeatism and surrender have the final word. A recent study of such new manifestations is Doornenbal 2012.

14.1.1. *Visible and Tangible*

The visibility of this new community in history has often been a topic of debate. Under the pressures of historical circumstances, a distinction was made between the visible and the invisible church. Augustine posited a difference within the visible community of the church between those who have been elected to eternal life and those who have not. He did so to counter the Donatists, who believed that the church must consist only of visible saints. Augustine insisted that only God knows who really belong to the church and who will be saved; mere human beings must refrain from judgment on the eternal salvation of others. Later, this distinction between the visible and the invisible church became a controversial issue in Puritanism. Jonathan Edwards (1703-58), for instance, required the visible sanctity of all church members. John Smyth (ca. 1570-1612), one of the founding fathers of the Baptist movement, likewise saw a visibly new walk of life as the basis of being the church. The majority of Reformed theologians have followed Augustine. The church is a community where the wheat and the tares are intermingled; it is a *corpus mixtum*. In the nineteenth century Abraham Kuyper made grateful use of the visible-invisible distinction to help justify the institutional diversity of the churches. The true church is the invisible church, the community of the saints and the elect. The various institutional forms of the church represent this one, undivided but invisible body. Kuyper also employed this argument to recognize the Roman Catholic Church as a true Christian church, unlike many other Protestants, and to justify the existence of "free" churches next to the traditional national churches in Europe. However, the distinction between visible and invisible was also used, or rather abused, as an argument to consider divisions among the churches as normal, to accept it as simply a fact of life (see the critical reaction of Berkouwer [1976, 51-76] to Kuyper's views on the "pluriformity of the church"). The visibility of the church finds its fiercest defense in Roman Catholic theology and is least emphasized in congregationalist circles. Roman Catholics see the church as the visible representation of God's grace in the world; it may even be called the sacrament of the world (*sacramentum mundi*, LG 2.9; cf. GS 45). According to official Catholic teaching, the church has its christological and soteriological core in the ordained priestly office and in the Eucharist, which is administered by the priests. There the earthly church, which is still on its pilgrimage, is one with the church of heaven (e.g., see LG 49 and the encyclical *Ecclesia de Eucharistia* of 2003). In congregationalism, visibility is linked not to a church office or an institution but to believing individuals who gather in local faith communities.

14.1.2. *A Dual Dynamism: Ingoing and Outgoing*

By saying that the church is a primary visible form of the community around Christ, we have also said that this community exists by invitation to participate in the communion between the Father and the Son. The church has a fundamental dual characteristic of both in-going (*communio*) and out-going (*missio*) movement.

First, the in-going movement, or invitation. The Word connects us with Christ, and as a result we receive a new identity. To use a biblical image, we become children of God (Rom 8:16) or members of his body (1 Cor 10:16; 12:13). Many of the biblical metaphors for the church are directly related to this movement toward Christ. The christological is always connected with the pneumatological. Christ himself is the one who calls and gathers (Rom 1:6; 10:8-17; John 10:3, 16). In the communion with the triune God believers may even share in the qualifications that are reserved for Christ; the Bible speaks in this context of wisdom, righteousness, sanctification, and redemption (1 Cor 1:30). In the new era all may share in the anointing with the Holy Spirit (Acts 2:17). From then on, the Spirit no longer elects only individuals; the entire community is now addressed as a holy and royal priesthood (1 Pet 2:5, 9). Compared with the Old Testament, this status represents an enormous expansion and broadening of the work of the Spirit. What was only local during Jesus's life, now, since his exaltation through the Spirit, has a global spread. This anointing and its gifts remind us of what God's turning toward us produces in terms of spiritual values: faith, hope, and love. And finally, we are reminded of the range of concrete evidences of grace that bring us into the sphere of God's salvation, including everything that Paul could cluster under the one heading of spiritual gifts: teaching and explaining, governance and assistance, and the gifts of prophecy, healing, and liberation. They are all gifts of grace (*charismata*, 1 Cor 12:1-11), through which God pulls us toward himself and for which we should, first of all, thank him.

Faith, hope, and love (charity) were early categorized with the Christian virtues, but because of its moral connotations the term "virtue" no longer suffices. It may be used only if it is understood in its broader, more general meaning of the disposition and direction of life of the human individual.

These remarks themselves suggest that this focus on Christ immediately results in a second, out-going movement. Those who have been saved are now sent into the world (*missio*); once again the gifts of grace are the tools for this movement. Together, these two movements ensure a twofold dynamic that is the foundation of the church, its offices, and the sacraments: people are connected with God, and as a result they all share in their own way in the sending of the Spirit into the world. The Spirit-inspired gifts of grace become operational in the movement toward the outside world. They are usually categorized under three Greek concepts of *martyria* (witness, proclamation), *leitourgia* (worship, baptism, communion, and prayer), and *diakonia* (assisting people and a sense of community).

This may be the place to say something about the methodological renewal in ecclesiology. Ecclesiology increasingly makes use of empirical social-scientific methods from sociology, anthropology, psychology, and studies of ritual. Religious practices such as church services and prayer groups, a liturgy for the home, Taizé services, and mass gatherings (youth congresses, festivals, conventions)—these all share in the character of concrete practices that can be studied with the tools of the social sciences. The empirical perspective reminds us very concretely that the church is not primarily an idea or a concept but praxis. In this way the threat of Docetism in ecclesiology is reduced. Faith is not, first and foremost, a web of interconnected ideas but is lived out in an active relationship with God. Seen from that angle, a worship service has the character of a performance in which the reality of the gospel is actualized (Immink 2014, 24). It is an utterly physical and sensorial reality. With our physical and spiritual capacities we are pulled into the community around Christ and find our direction and its forms in a concrete praxis. The church is not primarily a place to exchange ideas but a place for the practice of prayer and song, praise and worship, and celebrating the Lord's Supper. It is a place for sanctification, for being shaped by the Word of God, for learning to listen to God. This is not just a matter of the head or the heart; it has visible, physical, spatial, and social components. Customs, ways of acting and reacting, are practiced and cultivated. This climate results in a culture in which people are enlisted as acting persons. This concrete, empirical reality also implies that questions about diversity of culture, ethnicity, race, and gender cannot be avoided in talking about the church.

Berkhof (CF 348) noted the highly "docetic" character of ecclesiology and urged attention to its empirical elements. We agree with this emphasis. In recent years the role of empirical studies has increased—at least in the Dutch context (this "empirical turn" is still largely absent in the otherwise excellent handbook Mannion and Mudge 2008); for example, see Borght 2009, Klaver 2011, Paas 2012, and Immink 2014. The empirical focus provides opportunities for fine-tuning our ecclesiology so that local possibilities and limitations become more clearly visible.

14.2. What Is the Church?

What, in fact, is the church? When hearing the word "church," many people instantly think of an institution: a building, an organization with a particular kind of hierarchy, church services, rules, and rituals. In other words, the church is something visible that can be described. However, in our day people are so disgusted with the institutional church that newer groups prefer not to use that label but rather call themselves a community. This change is understandable as an effort to ward off certain negative preconceptions. At the same time, it is regrettable that, in doing so, the distance between institution and community, and between church office and charisma, is affirmed. Every community needs an organizational form; this also applies to the church as the body of Christ and the people of God. In the Pauline letters we do not yet find the sharp distinction between what was later referred to as church office and charisma (or organization and community). Both have their basis in the work of the Spirit of Christ, and they are closely connected. Only later, when the unity of the church and its continuity with the witness of the first apostles came under threat, was the charismatic de-emphasized in favor of the episcopal. It is good to note that current theological work is making concerted efforts to restore the proper correlation between charisma and office.

One effect is the recognition of gradations in the institutionalizing of the community of Christ. There are more places of "church," where the Spirit is at work, than just established churches and their services, even though the latter will always play an important role as the axis in a network of connections. In this book we stay with the traditional word "church," which forces us to first of all explore the theological content of the word. To do so, we now turn to the Bible.

In the New Testament we find numerous metaphors for the church (note the survey in the classic study of Paul Minear [2004; orig. pub., 1960]). A well-known image is that of the body of Christ (1 Cor 12:27), in which Christ is the head and church members are the body with its many parts. This same connectedness with and dependence on Christ is also found in the Johannine picture of the vine and its branches. Believers are connected with Christ like the branches are with the vine; they derive their life from him (John 15). This comparison has ancient credentials back in Ps 80, where Israel is called the vine. Our close tie with Christ and our human dependence on him are also apparent in the powerful image of the church as the bride (Eph 5:23–32). In addition, we find the church compared to a building or a house (Eph 2:19–22), which teaches that the church must also be seen as the work, the creation, of Christ, with its foundation in him. The church does not build itself; its members allow themselves to be used as stones for the building (1 Cor 3:9–10, 16; 1 Pet 2:5), Christ himself being the cornerstone. In brief, these metaphors point to our close connection with Christ—to communion, *communio*, with him. They also point toward the out-going movement, the *missio*. Many images and metaphors express the idea that the church is sent into the world. This out-going movement is evident in the metaphor of the vine's branches and in the images of the church as a letter of Christ (2 Cor 3:2-3) and as the salt of the earth (Matt 5:13). The dual dynamic of belonging to and of being sent converges in the image of the people of God that he has made his own so that they might proclaim his mighty deeds (1 Pet 2:9). It pictures the church as an eschatological community, the fruit of the covenant that God established with Abraham and that now has come to a new realization. This community must demonstrate the presence of God's salvation in this world. For that reason believers are called priests and kings and are given a prophetic task (1 Pet 2:5-10). The fact that the visible community is a preliminary form of that communion around Christ comes into sharp focus in the image of believers as "strangers and exiles" (Heb 11:13).

However, the very word "church" is not without significance. It is derived from the Greek *kyriakon* and points to the Lord (Gk. *Kyrios*) of the church. Nowhere does this church exist in a vacuum. The precise way in which it receives a visible form around Christ depends in part on social, cultural, and political circumstances.

Forming a community or being the church meant something different for the first generations of Christians in the Roman Empire than it did for the Germanic tribes that were later "christened." Likewise, contemporary conditions of increased mobility and new information technology provide another cultural matrix and pose a challenge different from that at the beginning of the nineteenth century. The church in post-Napoleonic Europe was forced to position itself as an institution next to other social institutions. Modern governments now required that churches become associations or societies as the only way they could acquire legal status. Ever since, the word "church" connotes for many people an institution dominated by legal rules and lacking the dynamic that is still heard in the word "community." The same negative valuation applies to other social institutions. The word for church, however, evokes the notion of a community that has been called out of the world, for which the Greek word is *ekklēsia*. For good reason, many ecclesial and ecumenical documents emphasize the concept of *communio*, community, as the fundamental category for understanding what the church is at its core. This term shows how important it is to avoid any one-sided identification of the church with its institutional aspect. The community around Christ can assume a more flexible shape, for instance as a network, or become visible in events that transcend boundaries. The increased attention given to "fluid" or "emerging" forms of community formation is directly related to the changed role of the church in our society. From having a monopoly position, churches now find that they must engage in "marketing." They must convince people why the church, and belonging to a church, is important. In fact, this change holds true for all traditional institutions. However venerable they may be, the monarchy, different levels of government, politics, trade unions, science, and medical doctors must all prove their usefulness. For that reason the questions of church and Christian community formation are nowadays at the center of attention. Pete Ward (2002) refers to "liquid church."

There is no reason to look with arrogance at the institutional or visible church or community. To the contrary. Our theological point of departure is that everything the church does by way of organization, offices, sacraments, rituals, arrangements of time and space, music, and missional-diaconal work has a clear aim: to mediate the salvation that Christ has given his church. Everything else is less important. The aspects and functions we just listed are gifts and means. They operate in the dual dynamic of in-going and out-going (*communio* and *missio*) that are the core characteristics of the church. Sermon, sacraments and offices, hours and locations, customs and gestures are all part of the worship service, which, according to Paul, is no more than our "reasonable" sacrifice, in view of what Christ has done as a sacrifice for us (Rom 12:1). Each of these ecclesial practices in its own way says that the church belongs *to* Christ and is sent into the world *by* Christ. *Communio* and *missio* are as directly linked as breathing in and breathing out. The church operates and lives in the connectedness and dynamic of these two movements.

14.3. Three Models of the Church

If we start from the premise that the church is a community around Christ that originated by the work of the Spirit, we can proceed to the question that is asked again and again in history and in the church today. Does ecclesiology begin with the individual or with the community? We do well to distinguish three positions that together present the spectrum of answers to that question. These are:

1. the Catholic, episcopal model,
2. the presbyterian, or Reformed, model, and
3. the congregationalist model.

The churches of the *Catholic* or *episcopal* type start from the primacy of the community, represented in its unity by the bishop (Gk. *episkopos*, "overseer"). In this model the individual derives his or her full identity from the community to which he or she belongs; one's personal faith is not the main concern. Recall that the origin of the church is in Christ. He called the disciples to him, appeared to them, and charged them as apostles to go out into the world and to baptize people. Christ is the essence of the apostolic community; he gives himself in the priestly office and the sacraments. As a result, the priestly office acquires a decisive role in the mediation of salvation. A person belongs to Christ and to the community around Christ by participation in the sacraments and in the liturgical life of the church.

A good example of this view of the church appears in the encyclical *Ecclesia de Eucharistia* (2003), which locates the essence of what it means to be church in the eucharistic communion, in which Christ offers himself. Participation in the Eucharist presupposes full participation in the communion of the church. This is to say, it implies recognition of the ordained church office as rooted in the mandate given by Christ himself (Matt 16:18-19; John 20:21-23; 21:15-17). One's personal faith is not the primary factor—participation in the sacraments is. The visibility of the (priestly) office and the sacrament of the Eucharist are the core of being the church. These are understood in a sacerdotal sense, that is, in terms borrowed from the Jerusalem temple and the Old Testament priesthood. From a dogmatic point of view Christology and ecclesiology are put on one straight line, even at the risk of becoming identical. The office culminates in its sacerdotal function, in its authority to give saving communion with Christ via the Eucharist (*potestas in corpus eucharisticum*; Denzinger, ES, §1326; see also *Ecclesia de Eucharistia*, §8).

At the opposite end of the spectrum we find the *congregationalist* model, which deems the church to be a community of confessing believers who have assembled on the basis of their faith. The priesthood belongs to all believers; joining the church community is a decision of one's own free will and proceeds by one's own confession of faith. Baptism upon confession makes a person a church member. This understanding turns the church into a historical phenomenon that has its origin in a human, not a divine, initiative. Numerous evangelical, Baptist, and Pentecostal churches have adopted this congregationalist model.

Very often this "free" model of the church is linked with the teaching of "believer's baptism." A person joins the church upon his or her own confession of faith and as the result of a personal decision to become a believer. Some free-church circles hold the conviction of the invisibility of the church so strongly that the relationship between baptism and the visible church is underdeveloped or even nonexistent. Often a person is baptized without joining a church. For a description of this type of Baptist free-church tradition, see Volf 1998. Volf lays greater stress on the pneumatological basis of the church as a community of believers (*communio fidelium*), but he retains the element of the free decision of the individual members (175-77). In this model as well, Christology and ecclesiology can overlap, but in contrast to the episcopal model, participation in Christ comes not through the bishop but through each believer as an individual person.

Between these two extremes lies the Reformed, or presbyterian, church model. The Reformed model is (to use a saying of Berkhof) the daughter of the Catholic and the mother of the congregationalist model. Ever since the Reformation, the Reformed model has appealed to the notion of the covenant, as a result placing a strong emphasis on the community of the church as the matrix in which the faith is received. The origin and essence of the church are thus not found in history but in a divine initiative; God establishes his covenant, and Christ calls those who are his through the Spirit. That is, through the Spirit, we already enjoy communion with Christ; at the same time, we feel a strong eschatological pull. The Spirit connects us with Christ, but communion with Christ will be completely fulfilled only in the eschaton. The church is now still en route, on pilgrimage. This view implies a strong, inherent tension between the "already" and the "not yet," between our present communion with Christ and its future completion.

In its intermediate position the presbyterian model gets tugged toward the two ends of the spectrum as soon as the question comes up of who belongs to the church and what the nature is of its offices. Take, for instance, discussions about baptism. Many larger Protestant churches follow in the track of the episcopal model, where covenantal notions remain dominant. Yet, debates about infant or believer's baptism shows that congregationalist ways of reasoning have gained a significant, or even a self-evident, place.

Ambivalence toward the proper model of the church is also reflected in approaches to church offices. The resistance to sacerdotal views of the priestly office led to an emphasis on the priesthood of all believers. Luther declared that everyone who has passed through the baptismal waters may be called a priest (*To the Christian Nobility of the German Nation*, with an appeal to 1 Pet 2:9). The Heidelberg Catechism,

Q/A 32, also states that those who believe in Christ participate in his anointing. This pneumatological dimension is accompanied by a powerful plea for the church "to be governed according to the spiritual order that our Lord has taught us in his Word" (Belgic Confession, art. 30; OF, 56). In actual practice this desire has meant an important role for the church council or church board (*presbyterium*).

This development gave the board of elders (*presbyterium*)—rather than the bishop—an important role, especially for the minister to whom the preaching of the Word and the administration of the sacraments were entrusted. At the same time, it is clear that nothing and no one may intrude between the believer and Christ. Jesus Christ is "the only universal bishop, and the only head of the church" (Belgic Confession, art. 31). In fact, the christological, representative dimension of the ministerial role never completely disappeared in Reformed/ presbyterian polity and has fully returned in contemporary discussions. See, for example, Beek 2012, 205, and section 14.8 below.

The Reformed model allows for emphasis both on the church as the community that precedes us and on the importance of the believer as an independent subject. Calvin refers to the church as "mother" (*Inst.* 4.1.1 and 4.1.4) and takes a firm hierarchical line in his approach to church offices. God rules and instructs us through his servants, so these hierarchical structures may not be abandoned. At the same time, his focus on personal faith and emphasis on election—that is, election of the individual person to salvation—betray a tendency toward individualism. This dual focus has created a continuous tension in Reformed Pietism and across the spectrum of Reformed Protestantism. When push comes to shove, the individual person comes first, and the notion of the covenant carries less theological weight.

We find a typical example of this ambivalence toward the church in Calvin. He sees the covenant as "something in between," a *quiddam medium* (*Inst.* 3.21.7) between double predestination and salvation. Not everyone who belongs to the covenant is effectively elected to eternal life. This distinction implies a tension between covenant and election—a tension that is effectively solved in ultra-Reformed Protestantism either by evacuating the covenant of all salvific meaning or by equating its scope with that of election (for the latter option, see Engelsma 2011).

In the Belgic Confession, article 27, we read that the church does not start at Pentecost: "This church has existed from the beginning of the world and will last until the end, as appears from the fact that Christ is eternal King who cannot be without subjects. And this holy church is preserved by God against the rage of the whole world, even though for a time it may appear very small to human eyes—as though it were snuffed out." This is a strongly eschatological view of the church.

This survey brings us back now to the question with which we began: does the community or the individual come first in ecclesiology? The question itself betrays a modern approach, in regarding the two as opposites. In this book we try to stay close to the Reformed church model. Once again we find our point of departure in the Lord's Prayer, in which Jesus leads his disciples into communion with God the Father. Christ invites his disciples to form a community around him, which takes its most concrete visible form around the communion table. The initiative toward visible community and church formation does not lie with a group or with a single individual but with Christ. Christ is the source of the church and connects us with the Father through the Spirit. Therefore, we cannot beforehand decide whether the individual or the community comes first; this remains a sterile debate. Each presupposes the other and needs the other. When we come to Christ, we find our brother and sister already there; "community" is never something abstract but consists of a community of people who have preceded me and on whom I, in fact, depend. A community of people needs a structure or order to clarify relations, tasks, and responsibilities. Not without reason did Calvin therefore refer to the church as our mother, and the church fathers underline the indispensability of the church. In fact, the church with all its regulations and its offices has always been the milieu, the breeding ground, where faith could originate and be formed.

We must understand the following statement by Cyprian in that sense: "Habere iam non potest Deum patrem qui ecclesiam non habet matrem" (He who does not have the church as his mother cannot have God as his Father; *De ecclesiae catholicae unitate*, 6; CCSL 3:253).

Because of the twofold dynamic of an in-going, gathering movement and an out-going, sending movement, it belongs to the very nature of the church to transcend boundaries. This dynamic underlies and explains the apostolic nature of the church. The church that developed from the community around Christ did not stop with his first Jewish disciples. It soon crossed borders and went to the goyim, the heathen. The dynamic of the kingdom does not stop before the boundaries of gender, race, class, or ethnic descent but will always transcend them. It does not mean that these distinctions must or can be ignored. The characteristics of gender, language, descent, race, ethnicity, being educated within a certain social class—all these are factors that affect the possibilities and make-up of life. But they do not separate us from Christ. Christ's community with those who are his must determine the way in which those who are his interact with one another (Borght 2009).

The boundary-transcending character of this out-going missional movement is not self-evident in the church itself. Often people become prisoners of their own forms and actions. The book of Acts tells us how the Spirit is the actor who can use even confusion and persecution to spread the good news beyond the church in Jerusalem. The Spirit pulls Peter over the line to baptize Cornelius, the Roman centurion. In a night-time vision Paul is called to move beyond the border of Asia Minor into Europe. The first and real actor is the Spirit of God.

14.4. God's Kingdom and the Church

"Jesus preached the kingdom, and we got the church." This famous statement (not intended to be cynical) by A. Loisy from the early twentieth century reflects the criticism many people harbor about the institutional church. It also points to the contrast that, especially since the nineteenth century, has been seen between the church and the kingdom of God. That realization has a long history, however; there has always been a tension between God's reign and the church. The kingdom of God does not coincide with the church but goes far beyond it. When Jesus sends his disciple on a mission to proclaim God's kingdom, and when, at the end of the Gospel of Matthew, he gives the charge to make all people his disciples, it demonstrates that the movement that began in Jesus and his ministry has a universal thrust. The kingdom of God is the purpose for which the disciples are sent out; this is the framework in which a person becomes an apostle. The church does not exist for its own sake but for God's kingdom. Itself the fruit of the mission of the Son and the Spirit, the church seeks to be obedient to this apostolic assignment. In Matt 28:18-20 the risen Lord says, "All authority in heaven and on earth has been given to me. Go therefore and make disciples of all nations, baptizing them in the name of the Father and of the Son and of the Holy Spirit, teaching them to observe all that I have commanded you." In the New Testament the kingdom of God is not a territorial but a spiritual category that refers to God's rule over all aspects of life. People reach their purpose under the impact of God's life-giving love, and everything that seeks to obstruct this love will meet with God's judgment. This life-giving love also implies that people will allow others to flourish. As a result, a new community comes about. The church is the initial, provisional form of this new community, not yet its realization. The church is aware of this difference.

In church history, groups emerged quite early in criticism of the existing church and its failure to assume its evangelical task. The desert monks are a good example. They believed that the ideal of perfection could be reached only on the margin of, or even outside, the inhabited world. The strong development of monasticism in the fourth century would not have been possible without the church's having become legally acceptable at the time of Constantine. The Middle Ages saw many attempts to renew the life of the church and its members. Most of the monastic orders must be seen as critical renewal movements that tried, each in its own way, to follow the evangelical ideal of Jesus. Francis of Assisi is a well-known example who wanted to live as Jesus had lived. The poverty that he practiced was not a goal in itself but a way of demonstrating his dependence upon God.

In Eastern Orthodoxy the saints rather than the clergy serve as the church's focal point. Even if they may be regarded as fools, saints are a window into heaven. In an Eastern Orthodox church the iconostasis, with its icons of saints on all sides, is for good reason the wall of separation between the holy space and the area for the laity. In the Eastern Orthodox view the church on earth exists only because of its participation in the liturgy already being celebrated in heaven. The holy is above but radiates toward us here below. This view has immediate structural and organizational consequences: every local church is in all respects a revelation of the body of Christ. It is therefore contrary to the Eastern Orthodox ecclesiology to locate the church's unity—as Roman Catholics insist—in one bishop as the vicar of Christ. That is, although the Eastern Orthodox churches share in the episcopal model, its structure does not have the hierarchy of the Roman Catholic model (Bulgakov 2002, 262-63). The Reformation refused to establish separate orders and monasteries and, consequently, the setting apart of saints. The sanctification of life was not to be left to separate groups who lived according to monastic rules, but it was to take place in everyday routine. The city, the polis, was to be sanctified, and all aspects of life were to be brought under the discipline of a "godly" regimen. Max Weber referred to this ideal of sanctification as *innerweltliche Askese* (asceticism in the world). This view obliterated the difference between life in the monastery and life in society. Our entire life must be sanctified and fashioned according to God's reign.

To what extent is the church itself a realization of the kingdom of God? The defining element in Eastern Orthodox liturgy is the sense of participating here and now in the heavenly sanctuary. In Roman Catholic theory we also find a strong awareness that the church has its ground and its existence in Christ himself. Still today Christ makes himself visible and shows himself to be present in the chain of Peter and his successors. The church finds its center in the priestly office and the Eucharist. From the viewpoint of systematic theology, we thus find in Roman Catholic doctrine a strong continuity between Christology and ecclesiology. Can we say that, in actual fact, Christology and ecclesiology coincide? Are tactility and actual presence the final consequence of the incarnation?

Pope Pius XII wrote in his encyclical *Mystici Corporis Christi* (1943) that the church of Christ is, in fact, the Roman Catholic Church (Denzinger, ES §3809); the two are identical. In *Lumen Gentium* (1964), from the deliberations of Vatican II, the verb *subsistere* is used to describe the relationship between the body of Christ and the church. According to many experts on Vatican II, by using this word the council sought to break with the claim of exclusivity. Borrowing terminology from the doctrine of the two natures of Christ, it says: "The society structured with hierarchical organs and the Mystical Body of Christ are not to be considered as two realities, nor are the visible assembly and the spiritual community, nor the earthly Church and the Church enriched with heavenly things; rather they form one complex reality which coalesces from a divine and a human element. For this reason, by no weak analogy, it is compared to the mystery of the incarnate Word. . . . This is the one Church of Christ which in the Creed is professed as one, holy, catholic and apostolic. . . . This Church constituted and organized in the world as a society, subsists in [*subsistit in*] the Catholic Church, which is governed by the successor of Peter and by the Bishops in communion with him, although many elements of sanctification and of truth are found outside of its visible structure. These elements, as gifts belonging to the Church of Christ, are forces impelling toward catholic unity" (*Lumen Gentium* 1.8).

It is clear that this approach regards the essence of the church to be analogous to the incarnation. The result is heavy emphasis on the visible church in its social form and on the sacraments as the means through which God lets us participate in the new life in Christ. At the same time, this view clearly does not allow for other churches to be called church. They do have elements that may be seen as characteristics of the church of Christ, but unity is found only in Peter and his successors. In Roman Catholic eyes other churches are not church and not catholic. In other words, the apostolic succession serves as the central nerve of the church as the body of Christ.

Vatican II has undoubtedly placed some new accents on traditional Roman Catholic teaching. Rather than regarding the church merely as a hierarchically led imperium or company, or as a sheepfold with the pope as its shepherd, it gave much more space and attention to the concept of the church as the people of God. The greater involvement of laypeople in the work of the church and their endowment with the charismatic gifts once again received a place next to the offices. The apostolic character of the church as a whole stands much more boldly in the foreground.

As opposite the episcopal model of the church, the congregationalist model also posits a dramatically different view of the relationship between the church and the kingdom of God. Recall that the church here is seen to be fundamentally a gathering of confessing and committed Christians. Its defining elements are personal faith, conversion, and active involvement—active for the world as God's world, in combination with aspirations to live a holy life in accordance with the Sermon on the Mount. In other words, the relationship between the church and the kingdom of God also focuses on individual involvement. Depending on the place of these congregationalist, or free-church, groups in society, they may at times exert a major public influence. Significant examples are found in churches of Anabaptist or Mennonite origin. The emphasis on the sanctification of life may, on the one hand, lead the group to withdraw into isolation away from the menacing world (note the Amish in North America) or, on the other hand, to powerfully emphasize the calling of the church in the world. In any case, the church is challenged to be a messianic body, in stark contrast with the ways of the world. It is something of an avant-garde elite who have heard the first sounds of God's kingdom and are on their way toward it.

Representatives of this line of thought include Barth in CD IV/2 (§§71-72), John H. Yoder, Stanley Hauerwas, and Jürgen Moltmann. For some time J. C. Hoekendijk's theology of the apostolate has been influential in the Dutch Reformed Church in the Netherlands. H. Kraemer's classic *The Christian Message in a Non-Christian World* (1938) served as an important source in discussions about the relationship between church and world. Hoekendijk (1966) went so far as to call the church a function of the apostolate, but that reduction of the church to just one function was not tenable. The church is indeed the firstfruits, the body of Christ, a house where God wants to live. But it is also missional, directed toward the world that surrounds it, because this world is God's world and the people are God's creatures. See Berkhof, CF 417-19.

The *presbyterian* church type also occupies a middle position on the relationship between the church and God's kingdom. Theologically, neither apostolic succession nor personal conviction is decisive here; the living Word that is present in all aspects of the work of the church is the point of departure. What makes a church, church, is in the first place the pure proclamation of the Word of God and the proper administering of the sacraments (Belgic Confession, art. 29). This explains the emphasis on the Bible as the Word of God and on the proclamation as the "ministry" of the Word. In this concept the church is first and foremost the community that is addressed by the Word, that remembers Christ's saving death, and that becomes the bearer of the promise.

In this view, although the faith community is connected with the kingdom through Word and sacrament, the two do not coincide. Here again, the eschatological expectation is strong. The church to which we belong does not coincide with God's kingdom but is the ship in which God's people are protected. This is not a self-evident proposition. History is full of examples of how the church on this model can become a very cozy and self-satisfied place. However, the image of the church as pilgrims on their way to the kingdom can also have a very positive effect, especially when it faces social and political oppression. The church realizes that it lives on the basis of Christ's promise and, in all its activities, is but on its way toward the perfection of the kingdom.

The eschatological tone is aptly expressed in a Dutch Reformed form for the communion service (*Katern* [1981], 36): "Moreover, at the communion table we may with great anticipation look for the return of Jesus Christ and to the supper of the Lamb in the perfection of God's kingdom, where God will be all in all." In times of acute political and cultural pressure the image of pilgrimage may serve as a reminder that the church is God's people en route. Without this pressure, however, the image can easily serve to excuse apathy about one's own culture and environment. At such times the church must remember that it is this world that God wants to win in the sending of his Son and of the Holy Spirit. In this connection classic theology has utilized the distinction between the church militant and the church triumphant (*ecclesia militans* and *ecclesia triumphans*). The latter consists of the saints gathered around the throne of Christ as the Lamb of God, while here on earth the church is still en route and its confession "Jesus is Lord" is accompanied by struggle and suffering.

14.5. How God Involves People: Word and Spirit

To summarize what we have covered thus far: The church is the provisional form of the body of Christ. Christ himself gathers his people through Word and Spirit into the unity of the church. Therein lies the identity of the church. Its center lies, therefore, not in institutional forms, organization, and offices, nor in active and engaged persons, but in the action that issues from God himself. Through his Spirit, God establishes our connection with Christ. Crucial to that connection are what classic theology refers to the means of grace, the *media gratiae*.

The Reformation primarily thought of these means as the preaching of the Word and the administration of the sacraments; in ecumenical parlance we may divide them into three basic categories: witness (*martyria*), worship (*leitourgia*), and service (*diakonia*). We begin this discussion, however, by returning to the word-pair that we examined in the chapter on the Spirit, now using it to view the church from the perspective of God's reign: God rules over us in his church through Word and Spirit. Through the Word, people are brought close to God. In the Word that is spoken to us at *baptism*, in *preaching*, and *around the table*, we find out who we are and to whom we belong, and the Spirit nurtures us in this new community. These practices provide structure for our life in the church and are thus indispensable. Note that in all three of these practices the Word is the undergirding and binding element, because Christ himself, as God's Word, personally presents his salvation in them. They are the essentials. But around them we find other practices that in one way or another provide more concrete expression to what is given in these basic forms. We can think, for instance, of counseling, governing, the services of the diaconate, prayer and intercession, brotherly love, the interaction of the charismata, praise, and song and music. All these may be the channels through which God approaches and turns toward us and may become part of the mediating structures in the service of Christ and of his Spirit.

These ways and means all have their ground and norm in Jesus Christ as the Word of God in person. The identity of the church, its essence, is the risen and exalted Christ. This identity may therefore never be qualified as external. That is, Word and Spirit are never the property of the church or of individual believers; they are and ever remain a gift of him who has promised us his presence. We believers are recipients. We live on the basis of the promise that we have been accepted in Christ as God's children. Yet, at the same time, this Word also has consequences. It penetrates our life and, if all is well, will shape ("sanctify") it.

In the remainder of this section we first discuss proclamation as a means of grace. Then (14.6) we deal with the concept of sacraments. Next we focus on a few particular means of grace—baptism and communion, instruction and dialogue (14.7); and, finally, we study the offices of the church and the role of prayer (14.8). At every step we are addressing the means or instruments that God uses to draw us to his salvation.

The central notion of the Word. What, in fact, do we mean by the Word? Because this is such a central notion, we look at it more closely here. People often make the mistake of identifying "word" with a thought, something cerebral. However, this understanding is far too limited. Word is address and communication in the fullest sense; it may be a gesture or a way of looking at someone. This broad meaning of Word becomes immediately clear when we look at John 1:14. There we read that Jesus Christ is the incarnate Word. In the Bible and in worship, we meet Christ as Word in person.

Following what Karl Barth proposed in his doctrine of revelation, we may speak of the threefold form of the Word (CD I/1:116-18). God's revelation is the first and most fundamental form on which everything depends. The church lives from the presupposition that God has already spoken at the time of the prophets, has fully revealed himself in Jesus Christ, and still speaks today (*Deus dixit*). The church confesses that it does not live on the basis of historical memories but through the presence of Jesus Christ as the Word of God. He remains the same yesterday, today, and forever (Heb 13:8). The second form of the living Word, which depends on the first, is the Bible. As a written document, the Bible testifies of the saving acts of God in history, of his faithfulness to the covenant, and of how this faithfulness was realized in Jesus Christ. For this reason, concentration on and communication with the Bible is so immensely important. When we study it, we discover the foundational structures of the covenantal drama and God's continuous involvement with humankind. This conviction explains why the open Bible is an important symbol in the Protestant worship service. We live on the basis of this public, revealed mystery. In the Bible we find the testimony concerning Jesus Christ, and this testimony is heard again and again whenever people become hearers of that message. They are drawn into the Word, and it becomes the basis of their existence, their expectations, their self-image, their hopes and actions.

This brings us to the third form of the Word of God: the proclamation. In the last few volumes of his dogmatics Barth abandoned the sacramental view of the proclamation of the Word. Thereafter he qualified proclamation as witness (CD IV). In Dutch theology K. H. Miskotte (1973) stands out as a theologian who emphasized the great importance of preaching. Miskotte sees preaching as proclamation in the succession of the apostles: "Nowhere in the New Testament is there a question of a church that can look back to this *kēryssein* as the origin of its existence but now no longer needs it; the kerygma remains the dominant factor that turns the speaking of the apostles into a unique witness. . . . Christ is not merely to be considered as a foundation on which to build further. He cannot be approached through reasoned discourse and he cannot be left behind with rational conclusions. He is to be proclaimed! His rule is announced at this moment in time" (223). Miskotte was writing against the background of the secularization that was already apparent in his days. He continues: "The estranged person does not realize that in the worship service something of indispensable value happens, and that this is administered by those who serve with ultimate seriousness—the same seriousness that, for instance, was seen when the people of antiquity brought their sacrifices, and was apparent in the gravity of the Day of Atonement, or in the execution of a work of art or a meeting of the workers' movement." (298)

For good reason the churches of the Reformation have so strongly emphasized the proclamation, making the sermon, in fact, the center of the church service. "The preaching of God's Word is the Word of God," according to a famous statement by Heinrich Bullinger (*praedicatio verbi Dei est verbum Dei*, in *Confessio Helvetica posterior*, 1566). The proclamation or sermon is not simply an exercise in interpretation or an informal meditation; it is an appeal with the expectation that, through his Spirit, God will use what is human (and often all too human) to bring hearers from a state of being lost into the kingdom of Christ (note Col 1:13) by giving them faith.

One might say that the sermon is itself a sacrament. The sermon is not first and foremost about what people sense and experience but a testimony of the message of Jesus Christ who lived, died, and rose for our salvation. Paul refers to this message as "the word of the cross" (1 Cor 1:18). That description is the short summary of the entire history of cross and resurrection. It comprises the movement and drama of God's involvement with humanity. It is clear that this proclamation cannot only consist of explanation; it bears a message and is addressed to specific people. And as in every good speech or discourse, those who are addressed are included in the communicative event. They are challenged to find their place in the new constellation that has formed in the coming of Jesus Christ.

Is this proclamation limited to the sermon? Protestant theology has become increasingly convinced that proclamation also includes the communion service, or Eucharist (lit. giving thanks). In the Bible, communion and proclamation are so closely connected that they cannot be theologically separated. The apostle Paul insists that the proclamation of the "word of the cross" has its focus on what happens around the table: "For as often as you eat this bread and drink the cup, you proclaim the Lord's death until he comes" (1 Cor 11:26). Scripture and table belong together as the two foci of an ellipse. We cannot detach the table from the proclamation or the proclamation from the table.

This is the first step toward clarifying the importance that proclamation holds in the Reformed tradition; God leads his people through his Word. But in chapter 12 we discussed how, on this point, the Reformed tradition speaks with two words: God directs us through his Word and through his Spirit. This phrasing does not mean that God directs *either* through the Word *or* through the Spirit, but that Word and Spirit are closely related. The Word proceeds from the work of the Spirit, and the Spirit brings that Word to us.

We explore this point further with regard to the church service or the gathering of believers as the central event of the church. We must pause here to repeat what we said earlier about the church's external identity; we can never own the Word and the Spirit. But that caution ought not prevent us from regarding all elements of a worship service as means that can be used by God. In principle, these means include everything and all: all who have an active role in the church service (minister, elder, deacon, worship leader, musician, and congregation) and all who accept being involved, each in their own role. "Everything" includes whatever comprises the environment, location, design, music, and actions of worship (Klaver 2011). Empirically speaking, worship is a "per-formance" in which the people, individually and collectively, are "formed" and directed toward God.

Participation in the experience of salvation takes place through a process of mutual communication (Immink 2014, 27). In this process the church service and the sermon are not unilateral; in a good sermon the audience becomes involved, and the people, with all their life experiences, become active partners. Therefore, the church service totally depends on, and expects, the working of the Holy Spirit. This expectation is expressed in the *epiclesis*, the prayer that calls upon the Holy Spirit. The congregation prays for enlightenment by the Spirit, and all services in classical Genevan style therefore begin with a so-called *votum*—a benediction formula in which the promise of God's presence is proclaimed with the words of Ps 124:8.

The worship service is thus set off as a space in which we expect everything from the living Lord. What we said earlier about the Spirit as the great bridge builder also applies here. Therefore, preaching can never simply repeat what has been said before. Every context will provide new features, since the Spirit interprets the Word to people everywhere and to all generations in their own times and circumstances. The Spirit is closely connected with the Word; he explains the Word, but he is not identical with the Word. Reformed believers therefore have always said that the Spirit works with the Word (*cum verbo*), while Lutherans were more inclined to let Spirit and Word coincide: the Spirit works through the Word (*per verbum*).

The promise of Christ's presence is not limited to the proclamation of the Word or the sermon but must concern all aspects of the worship service. All its elements—preparation, ministry of the Word, praying, singing, celebration of the sacraments, and the offerings—share in the promise of the Spirit. But the promise goes further still: where people speak in obedience to the Bible, engage in Bible study, meditation, *lectio divina* (a meditative approach to Bible reading), bibliodrama (the theatrical performance of biblical stories), communal singing, or dialogue, the underlying secret is that Christ himself addresses us and speaks his Word to us. Throughout, Christ remains in command of his Word. No minister or preacher can claim that he or she owns the Word; at best, the preacher is the servant of that Word (the *verbi divini minister*). The *votum* at the beginning of the service indicates that the entire service is dependent on Christ and rests on the promise of Christ's own presence. Consequently, the entire service, including the ministry of the Word in the sermon, may acquire a sacramental character.

For an intriguing attempt to start the entire theological enterprise from the church's liturgy and to explore its implications for our understanding of God, see Wolterstorff 2015.

14.6. The Theology of the Sacraments

The term "Word" is particularly useful for making immediately clear that God is interested in communication and relationships. Word equals communication—not only as passing along information but also in the sense of performance. Language, word evokes and forms reality and leads to a relationship. Language is a conduit. This phenomenological analysis helps us to understand that the category of Word is not just about the proclamation of the Word; it also includes other conduits

597

that mean to lead us to Christ. The traditional term for this function is *sacraments*.

The Bible does not provide us with a full sacramental theology; that developed only later. What we do find in the Bible are a few customs and structure-providing practices that acquired a more or less permanent place in the life of the church and gave form to the worship service. In Acts 2:42 we read, "And they devoted themselves to the apostles' teaching and fellowship, to the breaking of bread and the prayers." Here we recognize the three ancient elements of testimony, celebration, and service, or Word, sacrament, and diaconate. One verse earlier we read about the practice of water baptism that sealed inclusion into the eschatological people of God (see also Rom 6:3–5 and 1 Cor 1:14). These are practices for expressing communion with God and one another. Reflection on these practices eventually led to the development of a sacramental theology. In these sections on the place and function of the sacraments, we are not forgetting about those later developments, pretending to start from scratch. We want to be led by the simple realization that the early church already knew certain customary practices that guided them and allowed Jesus's disciples to share in God's salvation and grace.

The word "sacrament" has become a loaded term because of debates about the Lord's Supper, especially in Reformation times. For Protestants, baptism and communion are the only legitimate sacraments, but Roman Catholics draw a wider circle. They recognize seven sacraments and also *sacramentals*, material objects or actions blessed by the church. Partly because of the historical connotation of these terms, Berkhof suggested that we no longer speak of sacraments at all. He wanted to focus on what serves as a conduit and promotes our participation in the experience of salvation. He even coined a Dutch term to refer to elements that serve as "mediators" (CF 350–51). Berkhof's proposal points us in the right direction. It opens our eyes to the many ways and means through which communion with God is established. Nonetheless, we will continue to use the term "sacrament," especially in view of the eschatological connotation of baptism and communion: "The sacraments are expressions of eternal life . . . and no one can do without them: there is no Christian without baptism, and no Christian life without the Eucharist" (Beek 2012, 266–67). These practices mark our entrance into the new, eschatological community around Christ. A person who decides to be baptized and who partakes in the meal swears allegiance to Christ as Lord.

Tertullian introduced the Latin word *sacramentum* to translate the Greek word *mystērion*, and this translation has become standard. In the

New Testament the word *mystērion* was still used to refer to the unveiling of the end of history, for example, in 1 Cor 15:51 and Rom 11:25, so its meaning has first of all to do with the history of Jesus Christ. His appearance and life are the divine mystery (1 Cor 2:2, 7-8 and Col 2:2). In general, the term *sacramentum* points to the sphere of the holy. In civil affairs *sacramentum* was the oath or pledge of loyalty that a soldier swore to the flag. This prompted Tertullian to use *sacramentum* to define baptism. Baptism and confession initiate believers into the Christian faith. The person being baptized puts his or her full trust in Christ and swears allegiance to the crucified Lord.

An essential aspect of the classic sacramental concept came to be defined by Augustine's semantics. He begins with the difference between sign (*signum*) and object (*res*). A sign points to something. The presence of deer tracks tells us that a deer has passed, just as smoke points to fire. A distinction is to be made between natural signs (*signa naturalia*), such as deer tracks and smoke, and conventional signs (*signa data*). A flag, a handshake, and a red light are conventional signs; they are based on a conventional, or agreed-upon, meaning. Sacraments are excellent examples of conventional signs. The visible tokens point the believer to something invisible; baptism points to forgiveness of sins. The sacrament always consists of an element (a thing or an act) and a word that accompanies it. The word that is spoken with the act is decisive for the Christian understanding of the sacrament.

Calvin cites an extensive range of Old Testament signs that were given to affirm God's promises, including the tree of life (Gen 2:17), the rainbow in the story of Noah (Gen 9:13), circumcision (Gen 17:10), and the fleece of Gideon (Judg 6:37). In all these cases an element taken from concrete reality is turned into a sacrament by the Word of God to become an instrument of his grace. The word is of fundamental import. Pouring water over a human being without any accompanying words is meaningless. The baptismal formula that accompanies the pouring of or immersion in the water makes this act full of meaning. In Augustine's words, "What is water other than water, if you take away the word? The word is joined to the element and this results in the sacrament, and thus it is, as it were, a visible word" (*Joh. Ev. Tract.* 80.3, CCSL 36:529). For the Augustinian approach to semantics, see *De doctrina Christiana* 2.2.3 (CCSL 32:33).

By making words and formulas determinative, Western theology acquired its own flavor vis-à-vis the theology of the East. In the Eastern church the substance is already present in the image or sign and is much less dependent on the word. Peter Lombard gave much attention to the sign but also to the question of the cause (*causa*) of the grace at hand (*Sent.* 4.1.4), and this question of causality dominated the discussion in the West. Is the causality or effectiveness inherent in the sacrament itself, or is it based on a promise of God? In Thomas Aquinas, God remained the causal agent. The divine activity thus became grounds for the notion of *ex opere operato*—the view that the sacrament operates irrespective of the faith of the believer. Roman Catholic theology places the greatest weight on the objectivity of the grace that is given in the sacrament. The sacrament contains what it means, and the sacrament is the instrument of grace (*Continent quod significant. Sacramentum est instrumentalis causa gratiae*; STh III.62.4). It sometimes seemed as if grace was a kind of substance that could simply be handed out.

The medieval church had a great number of sacraments. Before it was fixed at the holy number of seven in the early thirteenth century, the list varied from five to seven, twelve, or even thirty sacraments. Roman Catholic sacramental theology manifests an anthropological orientation. The sacraments guide the individual in his or her journey through life, and through these means one is led into a state in which one can become justified before God. Grace is interpreted as a life-giving power through which a person is transformed into someone who is justified. This goal is reached through baptism (*baptismus*), confirmation (*confirmatio*), the Eucharist (*Eucharistia*), auricular confession (*poenitentia*), marriage (*matrimonium*), priesthood (*ordo*), and anointing (*extrema unctio*).

The fact that faith in God presupposes a relationship receded completely into the background, even though the Council of Trent argued, in response to the Reformation, that the individual needs to come to the sacrament with the appropriate disposition. The Reformation was highly critical of the idea of *ex opere operato*. It seemed as if one could participate in God's grace without any personal engagement. By emphasizing faith and grace in a given relationship, the Reformation brought the receiving person more to the foreground. This move raised the risk, however, that the efficacy of the sacrament would become dependent on the believer.

This change developed to a greater degree in the denominations of the free-church, congregationalist type. Baptism and communion assumed primarily the character of a testimony, leaving hardly any theological room for the notion of sacraments as instruments of grace. However, actual practice proves to be different. It shows very concretely that, even in evangelical and free-church groups, many are looking for means of grace that touch human beings. Many things that at first sight seem to be external means and adaptations, such as the design of the worship space, the kind of music, the opportunity for personal testimonies, gestures and body language, and the use of the voice, are implicitly recognized as means that help to form and transform a person. They are used on the expectation that they can be instruments of grace. Today these groups tend to have a heightened sense of sacramentality. It should not surprise us therefore that, in Baptist circles, for instance, we see a "sacramental switch" (see Cross and Thompson, 2003-5). Empirical—that is, anthropological, sociological, and psychological—reflection on the faith praxis of different groups of believers can help us understand the theological concept of sacrament in a new way and reduce its docetic character. The Spirit uses a multitude of ways to gain entrance into our lives.

In Roman Catholic sacramental theology the main emphasis has traditionally fallen on the objectivity of the salvation that is provided to us and on the office of ordained clergy as the avenue through which the saving benefit is provided. Lutheran theology adopted the first aspect but broke with the second. It strongly asserts that sacraments are indispensable for attaining salvation; baptism and communion are themselves saving events. In the Eucharist the body and blood of Christ are truly and genuinely present and are truly shared in the bread and the wine (Formula of Concord). This view remains very close to the medieval doctrine of transubstantiation.

For Zwingli and Calvin the believing subject plays a more significant role. Zwingli sees the sacrament as something through which a person testifies of his or her faith. For Calvin the promise of God comes first, but at the same time he clearly states that the sacrament remains without effect if it is not received in faith. The Reformed tradition thus developed in the direction of a sacramental parallelism: what water, bread, and wine are for the body, the Spirit is for the soul. The sacraments are called signs and seals (Heidelberg Catechism, Q/A 66). In time, this labeling led to a devaluation of the physical and sensorial nature of the sacrament. Its essence came to be identified in the believer's reflection and remembering, that is, in the human subject. "Remembering" thus became a category of thought, a cerebral exercise. In this chapter we want to stress that the entire person is involved in baptism and communion, with the senses and the physical facilities playing a role.

Calvin still underlined the sacrament as a God-given visible sign of his promise. He defines a sacrament as "an external sign, by which the Lord seals on our consciences the promise of his good-will toward us, in order to sustain the weakness of our faith, and we in our turn testify of our piety toward him, both before himself, and before the angels as well as men" (*Inst.* 4.14.1). At the same time, this formulation sounds like a concession to the limitations of our physical nature. This dualistic anthropology tells us that the body is the weaker part in comparison to the human spirit, which, on its own, has accomplished more. For this reason, the Reformers and the Belgic Confession have often interpreted the gift of the sacraments as a concession. God adapts himself to the limitations of our earthly-bodily condition. (See *Inst.* 4.14.1; Belgic Confession, art. 33.)

In view of contemporary anthropology, which pays much more attention to the connections between our physical, mental, and spiritual dimensions, we no longer accept such negative qualifications. The language of concession was inspired by a hierarchical worldview in which the spiritual and nonphysical were considered to be closer to the divine, while the physical belonged—literally—to the terrestrial sphere. We have abundant reason to no longer accept this worldview and to regard the entire human being—body, soul, and spirit, or however else one may define human beings (see 7.5)—as the object of God's involvement and favor. The physical, sensorial, and sensory capacities participate fully, together with all our cognitive, mental, and spiritual facilities. The Spirit of God is able and willing to involve all of it. He "broods" over creation and connects it with God.

14.7. Means of Grace I: Baptism, Communion, and Pastoral Care

Under the Reformation, the proclamation of the Word was no longer seen as preparation for the Eucharist but was itself considered to be a central means of grace. Christ turns to us in the sacraments; they are themselves a form of the Word. The sacraments could be described as the visible word (*verbum visibile*). Thus, on the one hand, the sacramental concept was maintained, while on the other, the number of sacraments was reduced to two, on the criterion that a sacrament had to have been instituted by Jesus himself. Indeed, it is easy to point to the biblical basis for the Lord's Supper, or the Eucharist. The Gospels tell us that, when Jesus celebrated the Passover for the last time, he emphatically related it to his own imminent death (Matt 26:26-28; Mark 14:22-24; Luke 22:17-20). Baptism was warranted by the command in Matthew (28:19-20).

However, one may wonder whether this criterion is not rather biblicistic and whether a broader foundation might be possible. We should keep in mind that the Reformation developed its argument in critique of the ritualism of Rome and in an attempt to refocus on the gospel. Instead of building on a few more or less isolated texts, however, it might be better to give a broader foundation to the meaning of baptism and communion as structure-providing acts. We should look to Jesus's own ministry and the mediatorial work of the Holy Spirit, and can do so for both historical and substantive reasons.

1. First a historical argument. Both baptism and communion/Eucharist are faith-based practices or rituals that were firmly anchored in the life of the church from the very first. The believers told others of their faith in Jesus, and they baptized and celebrated the Lord's Supper in line with the meals Jesus had with his disciples.

2. The second, biblical-theological argument concerns the substance of sacraments. In baptism and the Eucharist we perceive the meaning of the new reality that Christ has opened. They are not simply wordless signs; both are themselves proclamation. The central point is that in baptism and communion God involves us, through his Spirit, in the drama of Christ's history. In other words, he incorporates us into the body of Christ. This incorporation is especially evident in baptism as the sign of the death and resurrection of Jesus Christ, and in communion as the eschatological community around the Lord, who gives himself for those who are his. We find a broad biblical foundation for the connection of communion and baptism with the cross and the resurrection (Mark 14:22-24; Matt 26:26-28; Luke 22:19-20; 1 Cor 11:23-26). As signs, they allow us to share in the death and resurrection of Christ. They are meaningful acts that clarify, first of all, that Christ is the one who provides salvation, and second, that people are the recipients of that salvation and thereby become witnesses of it. What the disciples already experienced during Jesus's life is confirmed in the appearances of the risen Lord: God does not relinquish his claim on humankind. This truth means forgiveness, liberation, acceptance into the eschatological community, mutual love, and servanthood.

If we anchor proclamation, baptism, and communion in the mediatorial work of the Spirit and understand sacraments as the "visible word," we can see possibilities for widening the circle of the sacramental. We have in mind practices that, besides those already mentioned, have found recognition as conduits of God's salvation. In close relationship with the classic *media salutis* (means of grace), let's look at some new elements that may be placed around these two.

In this broadening we agree with Berkhof, but still stick with the sacramental concept because of the eschatological connotations of baptism and communion. In baptism and communion we share in the community with Christ, and believers fully entrust themselves to Christ and pledge him their allegiance. Berkhof argued that the word "sacrament" has become totally unsuitable because the classic sacramental concept is derived from the kind of thinking in which God's salvation is primarily seen in terms of substance and materiality (CF 352–53). Berkhof measures the traditional sacramental theology by what he takes to be its core: the encounter. The sacramental has become a conduit, perceived exclusively in relational terms. We argue, however, that this approach constricts community with Christ into individualistic categories. Human beings are always partly determined by broader contexts, and their humanness must, even in its sensorial and affective possibilities, be thought of as porous rather than as a walled fortress. The Holy Spirit can use these possibilities to bring us into communion with Christ. Mediation, transfer, and reception do not occur nonphysically.

A broader view of the sacramental also enables us to see the anthropological, psychological, and social aspects that are in play when we speak of the means of grace. From an anthropological perspective, a sacrament has the character of a ritual. A ritual not only illustrates a doctrine we have been taught; it is itself an important means of communication (Rappaport 1999). It involves the senses, feelings, and emotions. Rituals follow a more or less established pattern of acts and words, a script that is enacted in a drama. Words are not always all-important; gestures and movements have communicative and performative significance too. In their direct, physical, sensorial nature, together with the formulaic words uttered, they give a concreteness to baptism and communion that is not fully captured by the word "sealing." Word and action interact as they accomplish our involvement in the salvation of Christ. In their mutual involvement they form a ritual that is to be regarded as a communicative event in which we are first of all recipients of God's salvation but are also enlisted as acting persons. That is to say: in baptism and communion we not only receive but also thank God for offering his life; we confess our faith and commit ourselves to God.

14.7.1. Baptism

Besides proclamation and communion, baptism is among the oldest, most fundamental, and still most stirring faith practices of the Christian church. In baptism the one being baptized is placed under the umbrella of the triune God. Baptism tells us that we do not find our identity inside but outside ourselves. We must be "christened." The believer lives because of Christ and unto Christ, as the Word that addresses him or her. His identity is *ex-centric*, derived from Christ, the new life-center. The person being baptized is visibly immersed in the water, and the words that are spoken turn the baptismal act into a dramatic event: "I baptize you in the name of the Father, of the Son, and of the Holy Spirit." (The alternative practice of sprinkling with water is not heretical, but it has lost much of the evangelical radicalism that is depicted in the act of immersion.)

The person being baptized is addressed by name and is connected with the triune God. From an anthropological angle, baptism is a rite of initiation. However, it finds its true meaning in what it is *theologically*: the entrance into the new eschatological saving reality of Christ. The acts that are part of the baptismal event—question and answer, reading the baptismal form, immersion into and being lifted out of the water—point to the death and resurrection of Jesus Christ. This human being stands in the light of the gift and the promise that the church has received in the life, death, and resurrection of Jesus Christ.

In baptism God's promise has first place. Baptism marks the once-only incorporation, the entrance, into the body of Christ. A man who is baptized now no longer belongs to the world, to himself, or to his history; his life is now brought into a definitive relationship with Christ. Baptism thus means, first, dying to the world and forgiveness of sins. For a gentile, Christian baptism is a break with paganism and all the gods that we craft. The damage this idolatry has inflicted upon us and the stains we have received must be washed away before we get new clothes. We are no longer shut up in ourselves but live from our new center. We might even say that our ownership has been transferred. A baptized woman is no longer what she appears to be, a mortal in the grip of all sorts of powers and in a cruel and arbitrary universe; she is the object of God's gracious turning toward humanity. It puts a stamp on who this person now is. It marks her identity, and people may now look at this person with that expectation. She is a christened human being and stands under the power and promise of God's covenant.

Who are the actors, or the acting persons, at baptism? This is an important question in the discussions of this sacrament. We recognize three actors in this one, single act: first there is God, then the one being baptized, and third, the one who performs the baptism. All three take part but in very different roles. Theologically, it is decisive that God acts on behalf of the person being baptized. The baptismal candidate is addressed in the name of Father, Son, and Spirit, which underlines and affirms his or her subjectivity. Then there is the one being baptized, who connects his or her life with Christ. Third, there is the minister, who has been mandated by the church and called by Christ to perform the baptism, and who acts as a servant of Jesus Christ.

Baptism's historical origin is difficult to discover, but even in the oldest layers of Christianity we meet the practice of baptizing in Jesus's name. There are probably direct links with the ritual washings known in the Old Testament (e.g., see Num 19:1-20) and with proselyte baptism. A proselyte was someone who came from paganism and wanted to be circumcised in order to become a Jew. There is also a very direct link with the baptism by John. According to John 1:29-34, Jesus too underwent this baptism. But being baptized in the name of Jesus Christ is fundamentally different, since it looks back to the judgment that was executed in the cross of Christ. John still anticipated the judgment, while Paul looked back on it. Paul connected baptism with the death of Christ (Rom 6).

Jewish and non-Jewish submission to baptism have very different structures. Therefore, it is wrong to simply state that circumcision has been replaced by baptism (Heidelberg Catechism, Q/A 74). By baptism a Jew returns to the God of Israel, whom Israel is already serving by keeping the Torah and who has made Jesus Christ his or her definite dwelling place. For those who come from the nations (the goyim) and submit to baptism, baptism is a rite of initiation. They now join the people of God, are cleansed from their sins, and will receive pardon for their sins in the final judgment.

The Lutheran view of baptism puts all emphasis on God as the actor. Through baptism God makes the baptized person his property. Therefore, the Lutheran confessional documents teach that baptism is a prerequisite for salvation and that children must be baptized (Augsburg Confession 9). The Reformed tradition also speaks of a requirement, but does so with an explicit appeal to the covenant. See Heidelberg Catechism, Q/A 74. This wording was later softened, with "requirement" giving way to "privilege."

The connection with Christ that is marked by baptism also has the character of a rite of *disownment*. The person is drawn away from the world, out of the grip of the power of sin and death, and into the life-giving presence of God. Or to use covenant terminology, baptism marks the entry into the covenant that God gives. For this reason, it is good that the wording of the baptismal rite has retained allusions to the exorcist practices of the ancient church. God does something, the individual does something, and the congregation or church does something. In the Lord's Prayer, Jesus taught his disciples to pray for deliverance from evil. Appealing to him who has broken the power of evil and of estrangement from God, the congregation may pray this prayer at every baptism.

What we said above implies that baptism may never be seen as a kind of rite of passage or festival of birth. Such terms suggest that baptism is an initiation into a particular culture or extended family, a view that must be regarded as the remnants of a Germanic popular culture that survives in our contemporary middle-class life.

But the biblical notion of the covenant is quite relevant. This notion is fully theological in that divine initiative and human response provide the structure. Likewise, circumcision in Israel had a spiritual focus—the circumcision of the heart—and may therefore not be identified with the natural ties of family or group. Just as circumcision was a sign of God's claim on those whom he accepted into the covenant, so baptism signifies the entrance into the eschatological community of Christ. What we earlier stated with regard to the covenant also applies here: the relationship between God and humanity reflects the asymmetry of grace. God initiates his covenant; he opens it, invites us, and calls us to faith and to a response to him.

Baptism, as the transfer from death to communion with Christ, does indeed symbolize a dramatic event. The minister who performs the baptism should not be afraid to use a lot of water for fear that the person being baptized might feel uncomfortable. If a (young) person cries while being baptized, that is fully in order: this is, after all, a life-shaking event.

From a theological perspective, then, baptism upon confession of faith is the basis of Christian baptism. Baptism must be received, and the faith of the baptized person is important. But how is this importance to be expressed? The answer depends on how we understand the subjectivity of the baptized person.

The baptismal ritual makes our role as recipients in the relationship with God very visible. The person submits to baptism; it is an act that is performed. No one baptizes oneself. First, baptism appeals to God's promise of salvation and affirms it: "I connect my name to this person." This human being, God says, no longer belongs to the evil powers; he or she belongs to me." This element of receiving and of deciding to be baptized presupposes that the person being baptized has a role as a believer. The person receives salvation and allows himself or herself to be surrounded by it. This is an active attitude that represents both a testimony and a promise. It is an activity within the asymmetric relationship of the covenant. The covenant that God made available demands a response and calls for faith and obedience, which do not happen overnight. This response and obedience span one's entire life, as the Yes that was given at baptism demands confirmation, time and again. A reminder or confirmation of baptism is valuable for reiterating its significance for us. The Holy Spirit pursues us with our baptism.

What does this line of thought mean for *infant baptism*? Usually this discussion focuses on the question of how infant baptism can be possible if faith is a correlate of baptism. Can parents or godparents speak on behalf of the infant who cannot speak for itself? Our position is that infant baptism is a secondary practice that finds its justification by appeal to the covenant that God has established with his church. God's relationship with his people must not be seen as purely individualistic, which is emphasized in the words of Peter in Acts 2:39: "The promise is to you and to your children." The call of God, his loyalty and initiative, carry far and wide, further than we can imagine.

This confidence in the free and never-ending initiative of God becomes visible in the practice of communal faith and prayer. Baptism—both of adults and infants—presupposes a concrete community (congregation, baptismal witnesses, a group of friends) in which people are seen not as separate individuals who must take care of themselves, but as people who are the treasured objects of attention, care, and prayer. The role of the responding subject is therefore not limited to the baptized person, not even if he or she is an adult, but overflows the edges of the person's own subjectivity.

In a theology of the Holy Spirit we do not deal with "closed" subjects but with fellow human beings who, as communal beings, must be regarded as "porous" and open to the mysterious work of the Spirit of Christ. For many who have this hope in God and his gracious freedom, infant baptism indeed becomes a source of comfort when children choose to leave the way their parents had envisioned when they had their infants baptized. The application of this view of God's covenant and his faithfulness will differ depending on one's culture and the circumstances. In an environment that underscores the communal aspect of faith, infant baptism will be a more prominent and enduring practice than in a culture where the individualizing tendencies affect—and increasingly determine—entrance into the faith community. The more baptism is experienced as a break with the current situation, the more likely the practice of believer's baptism, or baptism on confession of faith. If the church wants to maintain the notions of God's initiative in his covenant, it must react wisely and above all protect the sanctity of baptism from all modern forms of superficiality.

In the section above we stressed the asymmetry of the covenant and broadened the role of the responding subject. The subject, the person being baptized, is never isolated from others but must be seen in the context of his or her environment. This environment is, first of all, the local church, the community of faith, and also the family as part of that faith community. We find an example of this broadening in Mark 2:5, where Jesus heals a paralytic because of the faith of his friends who brought him to Jesus. The faith response is here fully conditioned by the environment. This is, however, not a plea to baptize just anyone; that would lead to some kind of covenantal automatism. The covenant is never automatic; it demands a covenant community that journeys along the road of faith, prayer, and obedience. The church is a covenantal community with interrelational and intergenerational obligations. Only when these aspects are duly present may we may have the courage to baptize a little child in the conviction that this human being is the object of the gracious acts of Father, Son, and Spirit.

We have thus followed the track of a Reformed concept of baptism (see Berkouwer 1969, 90–188). It agrees with the Roman Catholic view in its presupposition of an actual functioning community of faith (the church as mother). The church baptizes on the assumption that the lifetime of the person will show growth in faith and grace. However, where the faith community no longer functions, infant baptism can easily turn into an empty ritual.

This perspective significantly strengthens the critical opposing voice of the Anabaptist and Baptist tradition. In the twentieth century Karl Barth became one of the most pronounced critics of infant baptism. According to Barth, baptism with the Spirit is God's work, and water baptism is the human response. In it we testify to the completed work of Christ. Barth positions baptism within the context of ethics. The follower of Christ obeys his or her calling, and baptism is the act that is part of this testimony. We are the actor in water baptism. In the Baptist perception biblical baptism always presupposes the personal faith response of the person being baptized. That is, infant baptism has no value or is at best defective, though it can be remedied through a new baptismal ritual (McClendon, ST 2:396). The latter marks a change from the older Baptist view in which the rejection of infant baptism led to a resolute denial of the ritual that had once been performed on the infant. For a survey, see Kerner 2004.

In baptism the Spirit of God connects us with Christ. Therefore, baptism is christologically and pneumatologically defined. Spirit baptism and water baptism cannot be theologically distinguished; Acts 19:1–6 offers too little basis for such a separation. For Paul, the Spirit leads to the confession of Jesus as Lord (see chap. 12). We do not interpret what the Bible says about baptism with the Spirit as referring to a one-time event, however. Being filled with the Spirit occurs across our entire life, in different phases and impulses. This event also presupposes a believing and praying community. In a community where God is served and sought, people may be sure that the Spirit will fill them, in many ways, under different circumstances, and in new forms. And so our baptism follows us through life.

14.7.2. Meal—Communion—Eucharist

Celebrating communion (or the Eucharist) and proclaiming the Word are the two foci of Christian worship. In Dutch, communion is referred to as the evening meal (*Avondmaal*). This word reminds us of the Passover meal that Jesus ate together with his disciples on the night before his death on the cross, and it accentuates the reconciliatory nature of his death. The word "mass" is simply derived from words in the Tridentine Rite (which are actually rather unclear), that are spoken by the deacon at the end of the service: *ite, missa est* (go, you are dismissed). The term "Lord's Supper" indicates who is the Host at the meal. The word "Eucharist" is also very acceptable in the context of Reformed theology. It refers to giving thanks for Christ's sacrifice of his life.

Whatever name we prefer, in the ecumenical dialogue of the past few decades a consensus has clearly developed regarding the importance of intercommunion. Celebrating communion is a central event in which the gathered believers experience the meaning of salvation in Christ in a comprehensive way. Our remembering (the so-called anamnesis) is not just a matter of head and heart; in eating and drinking our whole being is included in the salvation that God gave through Christ's death and resurrection. The communion service demonstrates, through the use of our senses, the significance of Christ's salvation: freedom from the power of sin, reconciliation, and acceptance by God into a new community of people with whom we are connected in unity and equality (Welker 2013, 290–303). Moreover, the celebration of communion is based on an emphatic word of Jesus that is recorded in a number of places in the New Testament (Mark 14:22–24; Matt 26:26–28; Luke 22:19–20; 1 Cor 11:23–26). We cite the wording of Paul:

For I received from the Lord what I also delivered to you, that the Lord Jesus on the night when he was betrayed took bread, and when he had given thanks, he broke it, and said, "This is my body which is for you. Do this in remembrance of me." In the same way also the cup, after supper, saying, "This cup is the new covenant in my blood. Do this, as often as you drink it, in remembrance of me." For as often as you eat this bread and drink the cup, you proclaim the Lord's death until he comes. (1 Cor 11:23–26)

With these words Jesus qualified participation in this meal as *communion*, our coming together with him as the one who gives his life for those who are his. For the early church and for the church of all ages, sharing in this meal is therefore perceived as participation in the new covenant that God made available in Jesus Christ. In breaking the bread, drinking the wine, and reciting these foundational words, the Lord of the church comes to us. The real presence of Christ in these signs is essential.

Celebrating the communion, or Eucharist, means *eating together*. The small piece of bread and the mouthful of wine symbolize the sharing of a meal. Sharing a meal with others has physical, social, sensorial, psychological, and ritual aspects. In communion all these aspects play a role through the meaning that Christ himself attached to them: the establishment of a new covenant. In the communion service we have before us the structural duality that we referred to in chapter 9, about Israel. Together with his disciples Jesus celebrates the Passover meal as a remembrance of the exodus from Egypt, and he connects the sacrifice of his own life with the bread and the wine. This association gives new meaning to the acts of breaking the bread and drinking the wine: they are connected to the suffering and death of Jesus Christ and with the new covenant.

Jesus thus follows the worship model of Israel but reconfigures the covenant. The characteristics of a covenant are abundantly clear. Establishing a covenant was always sealed with a meal. We read in Isa 25 how the eschatological future is pictured by the image of a feast for all peoples. We discover God's inestimable hospitality in Jesus's own ministry. He sits at the same table with the high (note the leaders he confronted in Luke 14:1–24) and the low; that is, also with those who, through their conduct, had placed themselves outside the community of Israel (Matt 11:16–19). Tax collectors, prostitutes, and notorious offenders *had* in fact turned their back on the covenant. They no longer belonged to it and had strayed away as sheep without a shepherd. In his invitation, for example, to Zacchaeus (Luke 19:1–10), Jesus brings them back. He liberates them from the vicious circle of greed, fear, and isolation. They are invited to share in the new eschatological community.

In the communion service the essential notions of the gospel converge: liberation, redemption, reconciliation, invitation, covenant, and future. This rich deposit of meaning places the celebration of this meal by the church in an eschatological tension with the completion of all things. The one who was crucified and exalted now sits at God's right hand; he already shares in God's rule.

In this meal the church is reminded of what God has done in Christ. It gives thanks for Christ's sacrifice of his life, which makes the term "Eucharist" very applicable. The remembering that takes place during this meal is not to be equated with a memory that we recall; it is an act that ensures our involvement in what happened then and there. The living Lord, the story of his cross and resurrection, surround us and tell us who we are. In this way our unity with Christ (*unio cum Christo*) is realized, and Christ is present through the power of his Spirit.

At the same time, this meal is not yet identical with the supper of the Lamb, which will take place only in God's eternity when he is all in all. The communion that we celebrate is a meal on our journey. We have not yet arrived. Surely, we sit down as "members of the household of God" (Eph 2:19), but then we must get up again and continue our pilgrimage. The Israelites ate their meal in haste, ready to move on! (Exod 12:11). This eschatological tension is characteristic of the Reformed way of celebrating communion. Listen to a Dutch version of the classic Reformed form for the communion service: "Give us also your grace, that, being comforted, we may take our cross upon ourselves, deny ourselves, confess our Savior, and in the midst of all sadness expect with our head held high our Lord Jesus Christ from heaven, where he will make our mortal bodies like his glorified body and take us into his eternity" (Barnard et al. 1998, 342–43).

The Reformed view of communion is strongly pneumatological. The Holy Spirit creates the bridge and gives the power (*virtus*) and the life of Christ in the elements. Calvin holds the view that we must recognize a real presence of Christ (*presentia realis*) in the elements, even though we cannot comprehend how this presence is realized. He says that the presence must be conceived of as *spiritualiter*. His Lutheran critics interpreted this word in a spiritualistic sense, by which, they argued, Christ's presence was reduced to an object of remembrance and contemplation—and thus a cerebral affair. But by *spiritualiter* Calvin meant that the Spirit guarantees Christ's presence. This meaning is very different from restricting it to our thoughts. According to Calvin, being the church is concentrated in the visible community that celebrates this meal. However, over time, this Catholicizing element has virtually disappeared from Reformed spirituality, which developed in a more Zwinglian direction (Kooi 2005, 191–95). For Calvin, celebrating communion is still firmly connected with a holy community. Celebrating the communal meal requires a form of confession and discipline.

From the perspective of historical theology, the debate over communion is both interesting and complex, reflecting how the presence of Christ's salvation has been perceived in ages past. We detect a more or less materialist approach in Justin Martyr and Ignatius of Antioch, who described the Eucharist as the "food of immortality" (*pharmakon athanasias*). With Irenaeus we find a tradition that understands communion against the background of christological doctrine. That is, through the prayer for the Holy Spirit, the bread and the wine may be seen as something other than normal bread and wine, even though the taste remains the same.

The idea that bread and wine would change in their substance or essence became prominent only long after Augustine, at the high tide of Scholasticism. Here the idea of a repetition of the sacrifice is important. Christ allows himself to be sacrificed in the present for the sake of life in this world. We find a fully developed form of this idea in Paschasius Radbertus in the ninth century. What is sacrificed on the altar becomes the concrete body and blood of Christ. His contemporary Ratramnus stayed with the more symbolic view of Augustine. But this approach lost out when, in 1059, Berengarius of Tours was condemned for his support of this interpretation. With the Fourth Lateran Council (1215) this view became referred to as the doctrine of transubstantiation. The Council of Trent both resisted this sacrificial realism by speaking of the *repraesentatio*, *memoria*, and *applicatio* of the sacrifice of the cross in the sacrifice of the Mass, and referred to what happened in the Mass as a real atoning sacrifice. The Reformation especially opposed the idea of the Mass as a repetition of the bloody sacrifice of Christ, since Christ had died once and for all.

The Catholic position is usually called transubstantiation, while the Lutheran view is referred to as consubstantiation: Christ is really present with and under (*cum*/con) the elements of bread and wine. Catholic spirituality strongly stresses the consecration (commitment, ordination) that occurs through the epiclesis (the plea for the presence of the Spirit of God), by which the bread and wine are changed and Christ is present.

Reformed spirituality emphasizes communal eating and drinking. In our sharing of the meal, we are in communion with Christ. This community is not just a mental construct but is embedded in Christ's real presence. Through the power of the Spirit we come into the presence of Jesus Christ. For this reason, the *sursum corda*, the lifting of our hearts to the Lord, is not a unilateral act in which we attempt to climb upward but a plea to receive the Holy Spirit, who unites us with Christ (*unio cum Christo*). See Immink 2014, 224-51. For further elaborations, see also Welker 2000 and Beek 2008, 322-92. Van de Beek proposes that we use the term "Eucharist."

In the communion service we *are united with the risen and exalted Christ*. This thought implies that communion is not a funereal meal and ought not be celebrated in such an atmosphere. The church "proclaims the Lord's death," but such wording means that it testifies of the risen Lord, who has suffered and has gone through death on our behalf. Looking back to this event, the church is inspired for its life ahead.

However, it is significant that, as we share in the communion, we "proclaim the Lord's death" and are reminded of the "night in which he was betrayed" (Barnard et al. 1998, 230). This is a delicate part in our collective Christian memory (Welker 2013, 297-300), for it is a somewhat veiled allusion to our own role. The structural difference between the Jewish Passover celebration and the Christian communion service is that, in the former, the danger came from without, but the Christian church knows well that the threat may come from within. Both Judas, who was to betray Jesus, and Peter, who would deny him three times, participated in the Last Supper. This fact points us to the role that we, as the people around Jesus, may play. Before we know it, we may belong to those who turn away from Jesus or betray him out of ignorance, cowardice, or indifference. Therefore, it is good that the celebration of communion comes connected with the appeal to sanctify our life and live together as reconciled people. Given that connection, the communion meal puts life in the church under tension.

The requirement of a holy life and of prior repentance had an important place in the classic Reformed communion liturgy. It was emphasized to the point of often obscuring, and in fact blocking, the invitation to participate in the communion service. The requirement of a sanctified life was the basis for the custom—which in many congregations, unfortunately, has fallen into disuse—that the church board conduct a *censura morum* (a mutual evaluation of the conduct of the members of the church board). This was (and is) an orderly instrument to ensure that the church is blessed by unity and progress.

14.7.3. *Pastoral Care and Catechesis*

We have discussed two modes of our participation in salvation: the sermon and the sacraments. Now we briefly discuss two more: pastoral care and catechesis. Here again communication and information play an important role.

First, *pastoral care*. A pastoral visit brings people into the sphere of the Word in a different way. The person who is visited is at the center of the conversation as the one in whom God is interested, just as Christ was interested in people wherever they happened to be. In this pastoral contact people are challenged to open themselves up, not by pretending to be better or stronger than they are, but with all reluctance and hesitancy, and also in all honesty. A thoughtful conversation offers people the opportunity to leave their comfort zone, to see themselves in a new light, and to have their life story or situation connected with the gospel. Such interaction permits the current situation to be reconfigured, and the person's story to be retold on the basis of the gospel.

Biblical examples of conversations that have a sacramental function are found in the Gospel of John: Jesus's conversations with Nicodemus (chap. 3), with the Samaritan woman (chap. 4), and with the man born blind (chap. 9). These examples show the hurdles that may have to be cleared in a conversation, how old ideas may have to be revised, and how a person may come to a moment of prophetic insight. Such a pastoral interaction—nowadays also often referred to as spiritual guidance—takes place with the expectation that the Good Shepherd himself will speak. This confidence is also expressed in the pastor's prayer; it lays things out before God, and the human pastor withdraws to leave space for the *Pastor Bonus*, the Good Shepherd.

Speaking of pastoral care and instruction makes us think of—besides the classic forms of catechesis—discussion groups, the Alpha Course, mass gatherings such as international youth conferences, retreats, Taizé services, worship services on television, *lectio divina*, and the use of the Internet and the social media.

Catechesis as church-initiated instruction amounts to an ongoing process of Christianizing, so limiting it to the religious socialization of the young is a tragic reduction. In catechesis the church instructs current as well as future members about what it means to be baptized and to be part of the new community around Christ. This learning process is never completed.

To think of catechesis only as instruction for the youth is an outmoded idea belonging to the Constantinian era. Instead, catechesis is the ongoing dialogue of learning about what is true and what is worthy of commitment. What different kind of perspective on life may we discover as participants in the death and resurrection of Christ? Which views may we develop toward birth, death, work and occupation, money, sexuality, the environment, politics, justice, aging? Every generation and each stage of life needs christening. Catechesis as the medium of transferring the faith may be infused with new life by arranging it intergenerationally, based on the view that the church is a covenant community in which several generations meet and depend on each other.

Special events and new (social) media must be explicitly mentioned and given due place in this regard. These are contemporary means of creating community and facilitating mutual communication, by which people get their "cultural education" (e.g., see Smith 2009). The new media are instruments to use for the spiritual nurture of people, to point them to salvation and to anchor them in it.

All means and forms—established, institutional, newly created (liquid, emerging, and missional)—must obtain their life from the biblical source. To the extent that they remain attached to that source and allow themselves to be guided by it, they are modern forms of proclamation, *praedicatio Dei verbi*. Christ, as the Word, uses human instruments, including digital messages and tweets. They shape our existence. The communication of conceptual content is embedded in all sorts of contacts, appeals, connections, and things we have in common. God's voice is heard in the living voice of a minister, a friend, a singer, and in *sound bytes*.

Thus, around the centrality of the Word lies a wide circle of realities that we may include in our discussion of communication in the broadest sense. The circle includes music, space, artifacts, design, and architecture. The Reformation acquired the reputation of being so solely focused on the Word as to become iconoclastic, that is, of wanting to remove everything that smells of ornament and image. But the open Bible on the pulpit and the communion table are also symbols that direct and form our spirit. Architecture, music per se and in its different styles, cultures, building design, the use of space and light, the voice of the minister—all of these are the creaturely garb in which God meets us. These definable, empirical realities have theological significance.

14.8. Means of Grace II: Ordained Office and Ministry

In all that that we have said thus far about the mediation of grace, the official posts of the church—the "offices" to which certain people are ordained—have been implicitly present. In this section we treat these offices as a separate topic. Church offices are theologically anchored in the twofold dynamic of church life, its in-going and out-going movements (*communion* and *mission*), and are enmeshed in its christological and pneumatological dimensions. We therefore begin with God; it is God who calls and sends. This calling and sending concern, first, the entire faith community. As the body of Christ, the entire faith community shares in the anointing by the Spirit and may therefore be called apostolic.

But we must also take the next step. Some people are called by God to perform a specific task (*vocatio*) and are confirmed in their calling by the community. The first aspect, vocation, is the office of all believers; the second is the special office that is connected with the proclamation of the gospel and the administration of baptism and communion. This office has its particular place in the context of the church's mission. The church may give a special task to certain people who feel called by Christ; this mandate is given to further the church's overall mission.

The gospel's call for proclamation and witness can be directly traced back to Jesus himself, who makes the disciples witnesses of his resurrection and sends them into the world, charging them to proclaim the gospel and to make other people into his disciples (Matt 28:18-20; see also Mark 16:15; Luke 24:47; John 20:21-23; Acts 1:8; Rom 16:26; 2 Cor 3:4-6; 12:1-10). Jesus selects twelve disciples (Mark 3:13-19), reminiscent of the twelve tribes of Israel in their function for the entire world. Paul is very clear about the link between proclamation and calling: "But how are they to call upon him in whom they have not believed? And how are they to believe in him of whom they have never heard? And how are they to hear without a preacher? And how can they preach unless they are sent? As it is written, 'How beautiful are the feet of those who preach good news!'" (Rom 10:14-15).

Ordained offices did not develop as a separate order in the church until the second century, in response to the crisis of that era. Marcion and the broad movement of Gnosticism made the search for the identity and sources of the Christian faith urgent. In the context of this debate, creed, canon, and office (episcopate) developed into instruments that were to protect the unity and identity of the church (Beek 2012, 338); meanwhile, the charismatic element diminished. From the lists of the gifts and tasks that Paul gives in 1 Cor 12 and 14, we may conclude that the offices and the charismata were closely intertwined; they all serve for the building up of the body of Christ. Together, the exalted Christ and the Holy Spirit are the active agents in the life of the church. Yet, the Bible also differentiates between calling and mission. Both come from Christ; empowerment comes from the Spirit. In 1 Tim 4:14 Timothy's ministry is linked to a specific prophetic word that was confirmed by a laying on of hands by an elder. This duality of calling by Christ and anointing by the Spirit has come to structure the approach to the offices in the church and is widely accepted in contemporary discussions.

The role of the *church* in calling and ordination (consecration, confirmation) was documented by Hippolytus of Rome (early third century). He recounts that the bishop (*episcopos*) is elected by the entire congregation, while neighboring bishops lay their hands on him (*Traditio apostolica* 2). The laying on of hands is the gesture of the epiclesis, the prayer for the Holy Spirit. The bishop will have to lead the church as shepherd; he must administer the Eucharist and receives the mandate to consecrate priests. This set of functions is usually seen as an early indication of the bond between the individual, the collective priesthood, and the entire church community. The bishop represents the unity of the church (David N. Power in Fiorenza/Galvin, STRCP 298-300). We also find this connection in the WCC's so-called Lima Report, entitled *Baptism, Eucharist, and Ministry*.

From a historical angle we can say that a threefold structure of offices developed in the early church: bishop, presbyter, and deacon. The bishop was the overseer in a particular territory or diocese and represented the church's unity. The presbyter served as the local leader, and the deacon served at the table. The Reformation broke with the sacerdotal emphasis of the office, that is, with the idea that the priest receives the mandate to administer the Eucharist, to distribute the body and blood of Christ, and to forgive sins. This view implied a personal-ontological quality in the priesthood that thereby acquired a dominant role in the allocation of salvation. On the basis of Acts 6:1-6 the Reformation supported a twofold structure, that of presbyter and deacon. The office of presbyter (minister and elders) was to keep the church focused on the Word of Christ, while the deacons were to ensure that no one would be severed from the community because of shortage or need. In actual church practice, however, the priestly-liturgical approach continued to be felt, particularly in the spirituality that developed under Calvin's influence.

Undeniably, the churches of the Reformation have always harbored an acute fear that church offices will usurp power that belongs only to Christ. As a result, the topic is often, and unfortunately, reduced to questions of power (Borght 2007, 413-14). But church office involves much more; it deals with the question of how God keeps us safe in his grace.

To this end he uses people—mortal and fallible people with their limitations—and structures; the latter imply influence, authority, and thus power. But human limitations, authority, and power are in themselves phenomena that must not be seen as negative or remain hidden. They must be used to benefit the church and the world, with all the risks this effort involves. That is the criterion for everything church offices entail. For good reason they are often referred to as service, or with the appropriate English word as *ministry*, from the Latin *ministerium*.

A few words must be said about the diaconate, which is often rather neglected in discussions about church offices. Traditionally, the diaconate has been assigned care, assistance, and works of love—*caritas* in the fullest sense of the word. These descriptions, however, may undervalue the place of the diaconate in the total life of the church, locally and worldwide. The diaconate involves the mutual care of people who sit together at the table of the Lord and there learn what God's peace, reconciliation, justice, and mercy encompass. From the nineteenth century the modernization of Western society resulted in care for the poor being largely taken away from the church and addressed by social legislation instead. The loss of this function may lead to the perception that the government takes care of justice and the church takes care of mercy. However, such a dichotomy, along the lines of the doctrine of the two kingdoms, is contrary to the conviction that our entire existence, our religious teachings and our actual life, are affected by God's promise and appeal. Just like the other offices, the diaconate is part of the ministry of the Word of God (church order PKN 4.1, ord. 8). Its essence is ministry through listening; in each case, in ever-changing contexts, we must learn anew what kind of service is needed and to whom a specific task must be given. Together with missional work, the work of the diaconate is the portal to society, and in the interaction between the communion table and society, we must again and again learn what justice and shalom mean. For literature, see Wolterstorff 2011 and Goheen 2011, 208–26. The seven classic works of mercy (feed the hungry, give people drink, clothe the naked, provide hospitality to the stranger, care for the sick, visit the prisoners, and bury the dead; see Matt 25:35–36) may suddenly become surprisingly relevant in our life today.

In practice, the Reformed break with the sacerdotal led to a more functional approach and a stronger accent on the minister as the "servant of the Word" (a literal translation of *Verbi divini minister*). The elder has a supervising task. The renewal Calvin brought, when compared with what Zwingli proposed, was to no longer entrust the supervision of the church to the state or civil authorities but to put it into the hands of the *consisterium,* the church council or board. The mayor was a member of this board but, upon entering its meeting, had to leave his staff of civil office at the door.

For Calvin the key element is that church officers have a calling, a *vocation*, from Christ. For him, rule in the church would constitute a "christocracy" along strong aristocratic-hierarchical lines. Alongside this model, however, there emerged in the Reformed tradition a pneumatological line that was present, though underdeveloped, in Calvin. It was more prominent with his contemporary John à Lasco and later with Schleiermacher, Kuyper, and Noordmans. The pneumatological approach starts from the gifts that the Spirit distributes to everyone and uses for the well-being of the church; it thus highlights the charismatic character of the church in all its facets and the contribution that all its members can make. Within the context of the body of Christ, God gives a range of gifts for the building up of the church and the salvation of the world. Nonetheless, the pneumatological dimension must be entwined with the christological dimension. Again, it is wrong to make the offices and the gifts compete against each other. Both emerge from the work of the Spirit, both are needed in the church, and both are christologically defined.

We also find the pneumatological approach in Vatican II, where the hierarchical priesthood is connected with the common priesthood of all believers (see 1 Pet 2:4-10), with the cautionary note, however, that these differ "in their nature, and not just in their order of importance. . . . The person with the priestly office instructs and governs through the sacred authority that is invested in him" (LG 10). Likewise the Lima report on BEM tries to do justice to both aspects. The calling of the entire people of God and the pouring out of the gifts of the Spirit precede the discussion of ordination. Ordination to office is a special expression of the gift of the Spirit and thereby carries special authority and responsibility. The report recognizes that opinions differ with regard to the concrete ways in which the different offices are arranged. We can conclude that there is broad support for the view that the offices and ordination practices are rooted in, and intertwined with, the life of the faith community as a whole.

It is appropriate within a Trinitarian theology, which emphasizes both the christological and the pneumatological perspective (Ruler, VW 4A:369-91), to pay attention not only to church office—which is a gift in itself—but also to the ways in which the gifts of the people are used; at the same time, we must be open to incidental and at times extraordinary spiritual gifts that are given for the benefit of the church and the world. About such gifts, see in particular 12.5.

The dialogue on this issue between the churches in the North and the South, and between theology and science, has hardly begun. Attitudes toward the charismata differ, for instance, depending on culture, worldview, and time (e.g., see the report *Experience in Faith and Life* [2012]. Over its long history the Roman Catholic Church has gained more experience and has developed a more relaxed attitude toward the extraordinary aspects of some spiritual gifts. As an example, witness its attitude, past and present, toward Francis of Assisi and its strict policies regarding reports of miracles.

Clearly, church offices hold a different position in the Reformed tradition than in Catholicism. Church office exists to serve the ministry of the Word, and calling to that ministry is based on a calling by Christ himself. At the same time, that call is heard in the affirmation by a local congregation. This dual basis places the office in a christological as well as a pneumatological context.

The role of ecclesiastical offices is to point the church to its salvation and its calling in the world. The community around Christ is established and maintained as an event defined by the Word. Christ is present in the Word. Appropriately then, in the Reformed perspective we find the spiritual focal point of the church right here, where the congregation assembles for the reading of the sacred Scriptures and to listen to the preaching of the gospel; for the administering and celebration of baptism and communion, the worship in praise and prayer, and the works of mercy and justice—that is to say: in the local congregation. There is the heart of the church. A regional, national, or international church, or whatever supralocal form of organization there may be, must primarily serve this concrete manifestation of the body of Christ.

This view entails a tension that is unavoidable in any presbyterian ecclesiastical structure. The question of how local churches must relate to broader organizational echelons, such as the presbytery/classis, regional umbrella organizations, and the general synod, remains a point of debate with very practical consequences.

The Reformed model is different from the Roman Catholic model, where communion with Christ is mediated through the mystical body of the church as concentrated in the Eucharist and ordained priesthood. While the Reformation did not totally do away with the priestly order as a mediating authority, it significantly relativized its importance, moving it from an ontological to primarily a liturgical status. In faith the individual person stands directly before Christ, and although the mediating authorities continue to be instruments of God to establish connections, they are not essential for the divine-human relationship as such.

Toward the end of the twentieth century discussions about church offices heated up in Protestant circles, especially under the influence of the Lima report *Baptism, Eucharist, and Ministry* (1982), with its plea to regard ordination as more than a functional, organizational feature. Catholicizing forms of Protestant theology point out that the unity of the church is particularly represented in the episcopal office, and so make pleas for it (Borght 2007, 231, 417–19; Jenson, ST 2:237–49; Beek 2012, 195–274).

In contrast, we hear voices, often under the influence of Karl Barth, which argue that, as a matter of principle, the Spirit remains free from what is human. In free churches, ordination is not related to the essence of the church (*esse*) but at most to its *well-being* (*bene esse*) (Volf 1998, 152). This tradition fears that an understanding of office and Word that posits more than a purely functional relationship between them and assigns the office a symbolic role of representing Christ will lead to abuse of power.

We may well question, however, whether anxieties about that abuse have not been exaggerated and can lead to a suspicion toward church offices as such. We think so. Possible abuse does not exclude proper use. The church needs a form or order that sustains it in its faith in Christ and encourages it to discover, develop, and use the gifts of the Spirit for the good of the church and of the world.

Ordination, therefore, does not just serve the church's well-being but most definitely belongs to its essence. A church board, together with its minister, has the task of keeping the church connected with Christ and with its calling; this task requires the ability to provide guidance and assumes a mandate that, in the final analysis, rests in a calling by Christ himself and empowerment by the Holy Spirit. Church office must function for that task, which implies that there are moments when officeholders may, or even must, act with authority. This mandate originates with Christ himself and applies wherever the Word is proclaimed, prayers are offered for and with the people, and the sacraments are administered. The mandate can never become the personal property of the officeholders; it accompanies the execution of the ministry (*ministerium*) or task (*officium*) that is entrusted to them. At such moments the minister acts on behalf of Christ and may be regarded as a representative of Christ. But the mandate remains a gift. Even the person with an office is first of all a recipient.

A question that we have not dealt with so far concerns the criteria that determine whether someone may be confirmed in an office. If it is the task of officeholders to keep the church close to Christ, they must have the required gifts and capacities, an adequate education, and a record of unblemished conduct. The matter of age and education requirements depends to a large extent on culture and social circumstances.

In this context we must also deal with the topic of the ordination of women. Is gender a proper criterion for officeholding? Or is it irrelevant when we speak of the task of keeping the church close to Christ and his Word? In churches around the world this question is answered in many different ways. In most denominations of the episcopal type, ordination is reserved for men. The Roman Catholic Church maintains its belief that only males can represent Christ, since the Son became incarnate as a male (*Presbyterorum Ordinis* 2 [1965]). The Anglican Church has allowed women's ordination since 1994; the Old Catholic Church, since 1998. In churches of the presbyterian type we find very divergent positions, all of which appeal to the Bible. Some clearly reject it (e.g., on the basis of 1 Cor 11:1–15), while others have fully accepted it (e.g., with an appeal to Gal 3:28). We conclude that the theological argumentation moves between two extremes. To the extent that ordinands are taken to represent Christ and the maleness of Christ is seen as part of that representation, it becomes more difficult to give women a place in the proclamation of the Word and the administering of the sacraments. But when it is emphasized that women were, in fact, the earliest witnesses and proclaimers of the resurrection of Christ, a totally different picture may emerge. However, there are exceptions to this rule, as with Beek (2012, 271–72), who has a high view of church office but also believes that, dependent on the cultural context, women may hold office and represent Christ ("In every situation we must ask: Who is the best candidate?" 271).

But being called and receiving a mandate are not limited to offices that require ordination—to the work of priests, pastors, elders, and deacons, who by their office have been formally called to pray for others, to administer the sacraments, to pronounce forgiveness (absolution), and to assist with various needs. All members of the church may be called to such acts, depending on circumstances of life, time, and place. Here we may think particularly of intercessory prayer and pronouncing a blessing. These are not restricted to the church but may have a meaningful role in other circumstances (at home or at work, among friends, at larger events like festivals or conventions). Calling and mandate may differ in nature, depending on the context and the relationship between the people involved. Intercessory prayer and blessing are two acts whereby one may bring another person into God's life-giving presence. See, for example, Frettlöh 1999 and Greiner 1999.

14.8.1. *Prayer and Intercession*

Besides the instruments studied thus far, here we look at some other measures that may qualify as conduits of grace. In this book the Lord's Prayer has helped provide structure, so it is natural that we pay attention to prayer, especially in connection with Word and office. What is the role of prayer in worship? Jesus himself taught his disciples to pray and thereby identified prayer as an avenue to God. In prayer human beings speak with God. It happens on the presupposition that in prayer God has already spoken to us and continues to do so. Prayer is the setting for the contact of the human with the divine and of the divine with the human. In prayer we listen, and as we listen, we pray. In prayer we stand in God's presence. In its prayers the congregation demonstrates that it is not just thinking things up but that its existence and future, its faith, hope, and love, are founded outside itself. God's appeal to us comes first; human responses come second.

Since God's appeal is to us collectively, prayer is not only to be practiced in a private, spontaneous manner (Immink 2014, 20–21). We are not alone in the community of the saints, and we do not pray in isolation from others. We are carried along by words and prayers that have proven their meaning, have real substance, and do not run unnecessarily long. The Lord's Prayer itself is the paradigm of prayer that Jesus Christ, as its Lord, has given the church. This prayer shapes our own prayers by its petitions for the "hallowing" of God's name and for the coming of his kingdom. It rises above daily concerns and intervenes in them.

These features make prayer—in the church service, as well as in small groups, in a pastoral encounter, and in the privacy of one's room—in all respects a characteristic of the church and often also an instrument of God's grace. This understanding affects the official role of ministers, elders, and deacons. Their task is not just to care for the organizational matters of a congregation, but also to guide and keep the church in a living communion with God. Prayer is part of this guiding and keeping. In our contemporary Western world we often notice a great deal of hesitancy regarding this task, which belongs to the core of church office. A minister or elder is not primarily someone who provides good ideas, even though that is expected of one in this office; every such leader is called to facilitate contact with God, and thoughtful prayer is a part of the means of doing so.

14.8.2. *Anointing the Sick*

To intercessory prayer and giving a blessing we can add anointing the sick as a special means of grace. This act is not to be interpreted as a sacrament for the dying but as a meaningful act of prayer with and for the ill, as indicated in Jas 5:14–17. It is a ritual of intercession and laying on of hands but does not imply a *theologia gloriae* (theology of glory, such as in the so-called health-and-wealth gospel; see 12.7.2-3), as seems to be the case in some healing practices.

The theological basis for anointing the sick is to be sought in the promise of the kingdom rather than in some isolated texts. Christ's rule covers our entire life, and our salvation concerns body and soul—the entire person. In our culture anointing the sick can serve as an antidote to the medicalization of disease and can underline the bond—physical and psychological—between the suffering person and the living Lord and the church. Such a ritual, applied in a wise manner, resists the fragmentation of the human person.

Anointing the sick is widely practiced in Anglican and Episcopal churches, the Roman Catholic Church, and numerous charismatic circles. The worship manual of the PKN also includes a liturgy for such anointing.

As we said earlier, the circle of sacraments as conduits of grace may be drawn wider than the Reformation did in its attempts at evangelical renewal. There is a wide array of means proposed to serve as such conduits. We already referred to music and song, which have a place within a pneumatological perspective, since they can be means by which we are touched by God's salvation. We would like to add marriage and sexuality as well. The Roman Catholic Church does indeed have biblical arguments for attributing sacramental power to marriage. The images of God and his people, also of Christ and his church, as bride and groom, appear frequently in the Bible and are eschatologically charged. If we are to believe the apostle Paul, everything in this relationship, without exception, speaks of our relationship to God. Desire, dedication, vulnerability, self-sacrifice, enduring commitment, joy and pleasure, beauty and tenderness: everyday life in all its unruliness is a sacrament of God's grace.

14.9. Attributes of the Church

How do we recognize the church? In the early centuries four marks, or "notes" (*notae ecclesiae*), were mentioned in the Nicene Creed: unity, holiness, catholicity (i.e., universality), and apostolicity (apostolic succession). These attributes served an apologetic function to set the true church off against heretical, sectarian groups and movements. Likewise, Cardinal Bellarmine (1542–1621), one of the most prominent apologists of the Roman Catholic Church after the Council of Trent (1545–63), argued that the true church had to be as visible and tangible as the Roman senate, the Kingdom of France, or the Republic of Venice. The Reformation reduced the number of marks to two or sometimes three: the proper proclamation of the Word and the correct administration of the sacraments (Augsburg Confession 7); in the Reformed tradition censure or church discipline (Belgic Confession, art. 29) was added, emphasizing obedience and ethics. Luther enumerated a few more attributes, among them prayer, the singing of psalms, and bearing one's cross. More recent dogmatics (e.g., Bavinck, RD 4:305–7) have removed discipline, believing that it is unrealistic to make the church's purity a binding characteristic.

The history of the church demonstrates that, in themselves, the four classic marks are insufficient and quite ambiguous. They nevertheless may still serve as a prism that allows us to see, once again by way of self-criticism, what the church is all about. That is, the function of the marks has shifted; whereas they once served as a means to differentiate a true church from others, they have now become a guide for careful self-reflection.

Moltmann 1977 reinterprets the church as messianic community. Attention to the church as a "contrast community" also fits with the image of social-critical reinterpretation (Hauerwas 2004). Even Pope Benedict in 2000 (at the time still Cardinal Ratzinger) spoke of the church as a creative minority (Jenkins 2007, 114).

14.9.1. Unity

The first characteristic that the Nicene Creed lists is unity. The obvious divisions in Christianity seem to give us little reason to put this mark first. Nonetheless, confessing the unity of the church has great theological and practical importance. Its essential unity is found in the unity of God. The unity of Father, Son, and Spirit defines in a fundamental way what the spiritual unity of the church (Eph 4:4-6; John 17:11) entails. The unity of the church does not imply uniformity but unity in direction and dynamic. In the Spirit, Christ connects us with the Father. The New Testament pictures Jesus as the Shepherd, who gathers his followers into one flock (John 10:16). Quite clearly, confessing the unity of the church functions as a critical norm amid all our diversity and divisiveness. We tend to think first about the divisions among the major church families that follow the principle of episcopacy. Besides the Roman Catholic Church—which functions more than the others as a true world church—we find the Anglican, Eastern Orthodox, and the ancient Asian and African churches. In these bodies unity becomes visible in the Eucharist and ordination. The Eucharist can be celebrated only where we find the fullness (plenitude) of communion. By focusing on the visibility of the offices and apostolic succession, it has become difficult, if not impossible, for the Roman Catholic Church to recognize other faith communities as part of the church.

At great distance from the major episcopal bodies, which have much in common, we see the colorful conglomeration of Protestantism, of the presbyterian as well as the congregationalist type. Their institutional differences and divergences on church office are most apparent. Protestantism too confesses the unity of the church in Christ but is less concerned that this unity be visible. The term "Protestant" recalls the wound that was inflicted upon Christianity at the time of the Reformation, when it proved impossible to reform the medieval church—the rupture occurred that endures to this day. Protestantism originated as an emergency measure to reform the church. Even though an awareness of this emergency character has survived in some circles (note the life of John Henry Newman and Cornelia de Vogel), the view gradually emerged in congregationalism that the church is an association of believers in which the offices play a theologically secondary role.

The early Reformers made it very clear that they considered their movement to be an emergency measure, aimed at restoring the church as a community around Christ. See the strong language in article 28 of the Belgic Confession: "But all people are obliged to join and unite with it, keeping the unity of the church by submitting to its instruction and discipline, by bending their necks under the yoke of Jesus Christ, and by serving to build up one another, according to the gifts God has given them as members of each other in the same body. And to preserve this unity more effectively, it is the duty of all believers, according to God's Word, to separate themselves from those who do not belong to the church, in order to join this assembly wherever God has established it, even if civil authorities and royal decrees forbid and death and physical punishment result."

We may wonder: are the reasons for prolonging this state of division still valid? The ecumenical movement of the twentieth century is one of the most remarkable signs that the division of Christianity is not a state to which we must simply resign ourselves. Numerous bilateral and multilateral dialogues have brought real progress in mutual understanding. For a congregationalist view, see Volf 1998. We find a strong emphasis on the unity of the church in Beek 2012.

However, the unity of the church must not be sought only in supralocal organizations; it also needs to be realized locally, in all kinds of forms, in our own congregations and networks. Church unity is not a state but a process, a direction that first needs to receive shape and form close to where people are. The worship service, where people join in one community, in singing and by gathering around the communion table, is a concrete expression of this unity. Around the table we meet with people we may not have chosen as friends. But they have been chosen by Jesus Christ; the unity is in him.

Clearly, what we just said stands in critical tension with all kinds of plurality and diversity, which may stem from particular forms of spirituality or clear differences in how people confess their faith. But very often they can be traced to circumstances of cultural, social, and ethnic diversity. The latter traits may not become an excuse to avoid reaching out to one another or to hold one's own identity as the highest aim.

Such a criticism regarding pluralism has been advanced in Reformed circles in the twentieth century by, for example, Schilder (Wentsel, D 4B:69) and has been applied by Borght 2009 to cultural, social, economic, and racial diversity.

14.9.2. Holiness

We must also start with God when we speak of this mark. When we refer to a holy church, we are not speaking first of all of the moral quality of the church or its members. Rather, holiness is christologically defined: "He is the source of your life in Christ Jesus, whom God made our wisdom, our righteousness and sanctification and redemption" (1 Cor 1:30). Holiness is not an inherent quality of believers but indicates that the church receives its identity through its communion with Christ. Church members are recipients of the self-giving love that exists between the Father and the Son, which is the meaning of the expression "communion of the saints" (*communio sanctorum*). Traditionally, this expression has been interpreted in two ways: first, as the communion of believers with Christ and with one another; second, as participation in the "holy things," or sacraments. However, the qualification "holy" must certainly be read as an imperative as well: "Be holy, for I am holy" (Lev 11:44-45; 1 Pet 1:16). Just as the people of Israel were called to dedicate themselves to God and to live according to the Torah within the framework of the covenant, so the people of God, gathered around the Messiah, are expected to live by the rule of the kingdom (Matt 5-7). "You, therefore, must be perfect, as your heavenly Father is perfect" (Matt 5:48).

First Peter 2:5 tells us that the church has been called to be "a holy priesthood, to offer spiritual sacrifices acceptable to God through Jesus Christ." This appeal for sanctification must not be conceived of primarily in terms of all kinds of deprivations and cultural isolation, even though sanctification might indeed entail such behavior. Holiness is primarily an active characteristic. Just as God offers his life-giving love and initiates a bond with us, the community of the believers is called to learn and practice justice and mercy.

We may at this point refer back to what we said earlier (10.7) about the sinlessness of Jesus. Sinlessness is not a kind of colorless decency but an activist attitude that does justice to God and neighbor and does not shy away from confrontation. Sinlessness and holiness are action-oriented. To be holy is not to be bland but to live as free human beings according to the shalom and righteousness tasted by those who gather around the table. They are admonished not to let themselves be pushed around by the powers, but to live in such a way that God is praised by friend and foe.

The First Letter of Peter is an example of Jesus's followers, though they may be very few, being called to live according to the good news that they have recently accepted: "Maintain good conduct among the Gentiles, so that in case they speak against you as wrongdoers, they may see your good deeds and glorify God on the day of visitation" (1 Pet 2:12). We learn this holiness and justice around the communion table, in an atmosphere of sacrifice and thanksgiving. Communion teaches us that Christ has invited all people and that he shows an unparalleled hospitality that offers a future for all. Around the table—around the sacred emblems—the fundamental notions of shalom and justice are visible and practiced. In the practice of eating together and experiencing community, believers are called to reflect God's holiness in their actions and to respond in a creative way. This practice and response has consequences not only for our personal life but also for the public sphere. See Hauerwas 2004 and Wolterstorff 2011.

14.9.3. *Catholicity*

Catholicity is a translation of the Greek word *katholikos*, which combines the words *kata* (over) and *holos* (whole, entire). It refers to something that encompasses both time and space. Interestingly enough, every denomination wants to be called catholic, but the way the term is interpreted varies greatly. The classic definition was provided in the first half of the fifth century by Vincent of Lérins in his *Commonitorium*, where he stated that we must remain with what has been believed everywhere and by all, for that is genuinely catholic (see also above, 13.4). This is first of all a quantitative definition that strongly emphasizes visible unity; for Vincent, unity lies in the content of the faith, the creed. Later, the apostolic succession and the sacraments were added. As we noted earlier in this chapter, according to Vatican II only the Roman Catholic Church is entitled to the predicate "catholic." Protestants, however, do not regard catholicity as a characteristic of one particular organizational structure as much as the universal meaning of the one gospel that has been entrusted to the church. In this perspective the qualitative aspect of catholicity dominates the quantitative; catholicity concerns faith in the salvation that lies most fully within our reach in the gospel of Jesus Christ. But the gospel affects all aspects of our life, and it applies not only to the church of the present but to the church of all times, everywhere.

In the Reformed tradition the qualitative meaning has emerged as most important. Christ must affect our entire existence. We might therefore define catholicity as a claim to the universal scope of the effects of the gospel; there is not a square inch that Christ does not claim for himself. If the church is truly catholic in this sense, it must demonstrate an active intent to place all areas of life under God's regime. In the Lord's Prayer we pray that God's kingdom may come. Whoever joins in this prayer moves in the catholicizing current. God wants to involve those who until now have stayed aloof; see, for instance, the parables in Luke 15, whose common theme is this divine intention.

In modern Reformed spirituality the inherent universality expressed in the word "catholic" has been significantly expanded with regard to culture. Examples are the address of H. Bavinck about the catholicity of Christianity and church (1888), and the famous statement of A. Kuyper in his address about sphere sovereignty (1880): "There is not a square inch in the whole domain of human life, of which Christ, the Sovereign of all, does not exclaim: 'Mine!'" Protestants also claim the title "catholic." Note the title (in Eng. trans.) of Kronenburg and de Reuver 2007: "We Are Also Catholic: On Protestant Catholicity."

14.9.4. *Apostolicity*

The fourth commonly mentioned characteristic of the church is apostolicity. In a preliminary search for its meaning, we should keep close to the Greek verb *apostellō* (send). The true church traces its origin back to Christ's mission charge to the apostles. Apostolicity thus refers to the witness of the church in the world, which in its essence corresponds to the gospel of Jesus Christ (Rom 10:14-15). How is this apostolicity to be guaranteed? Where do we locate the unity with the witness of the apostles?

The Roman Catholic Church connects apostolicity with the historical succession proceeding from the apostle Peter to his successors. This apostolic succession (*successio apostolica*) constitutes a concrete and visible chain of bishops who interpret the Word and guard the treasury of the faith. Thus the teaching authority (*magisterium*) is placed with the bishop and, in the final analysis, with the pope.

By contrast, the Reformed tradition argues that trustworthiness is not anchored in the visibility of a historical chain of officials but in the faithfulness of the church to the gospel. The Word of the cross must be handed on and safeguarded. This way to say it makes content rather than form the main criterion. However, it also implies that apostolicity must be conceived of as diachronic, stretching over time, for the task of safe-keeping the truth must be assigned somewhere. In the Reformed model the magisterium, the continuity of the apostolic witness, is entrusted to the local council of minister and elders. In the free-church model this task rests with the community as a whole, at the risk of leaders seizing the initiative and founding new groups of believers.

In the last few decades a growing consensus has emerged for a dynamic interpretation of the concept of apostolicity, as the result of numerous bilateral interchurch dialogues and, in particular, of the BEM report, with its multilateral origin. The starting point for our reflection on this issue is that the Spirit sends people to be witnesses of Christ in the world. In the Bible the term "apostle" is not reserved for the twelve apostles as eyewitnesses of the Lord but is applied to a much broader group. The church as a whole must be apostolic.

There is no reason to reintroduce the office of apostle, as happened in some so-called apostolic circles in the nineteenth century and also in some groups today, as if the original situation was the ideal model valid for all ages. Such a view fails to recognize that the tasks and functions listed in Eph 4:11-16 serve as examples. The point of that pericope is the building up of the church, by means of the various tasks and functions mentioned.

Finally, when we speak of the church, we do well to remember the person of Peter. His life story is not straightforward. Church leaders—also within Protestantism—may suddenly become traitors who need to be called anew by Christ and drawn back to live under his forgiveness and reacceptance. These marks—its unity with its Lord, its holiness, its influence on all spheres of life, and its apostolicity—the church does not possess of itself but because of God's creating and calling Word. The identity of the church is *ex*-centric. Apostolicity is well described in article 5.1 of the church order of the PKN: "The public office of Word and sacrament has been given by Christ to the church, that it may remind the congregation of the good news of salvation and of its calling in the world." This formulation maintains the church's connection with Christ, the priority of its having been called by God, and the public nature of its task in the forum of the world.

14.10. The Church and the Public Domain

In chapter 12 we discussed the relationship between the Spirit and culture. We now want to expand on that topic by talking specifically about the relationship between church and state, or more broadly, about the church's place in public life. In line with our Trinitarian approach, we can say that every other human community in which people have organized their lives stands in the critical light of God's coming kingdom, in which ultimate authority has been given to the crucified and resurrected Lord. But rising from the communion table, we realize that, although we are citizens of the heavenly kingdom, we are also en route on this earth and continue to be part of earthly arrangements. This awareness of a dual citizenship is known theologically as the doctrine of the two kingdoms.

The classic expression of the doctrine of the two kingdoms is found in Augustine's *City of God* (*De civitate Dei*). He wrote it between 412 and 426 CE to answer accusations that Christianity was to blame for the demise of the Roman Empire. The word *civitas* ties our word "civic" to the ancient urban community as a political entity in which people live together—and which claims the allegiance of all citizens. That is, this issue entails from the start, and in all its profundity, the question of where final authority rests. Following in the track of the church of the martyrs, Ambrose and Augustine saw the church community as embedded in the coming kingdom of God, the *civitas Dei*, where love for neighbor and forgiveness must rule.

To Augustine, the (Christian!) emperor represents the earthly state (the *civitas terrena*), which enacts and enforces laws, governs, and implements decisions—if necessary, by use of force. Civil authorities have a monopoly on the use of force in order to restrain evil. Augustine's distinction was generally accepted in the Middle Ages and was also adopted by Luther and Calvin to differentiate between the two "regimes" under which the people live (*regimen spirituale* and *regimen politicum*).

From the nineteenth century on, it became customary to speak instead of three domains—church, state, and society—reflecting the modernization of society. After the formal separation of church and state (in the Netherlands in 1796), society was recognized as a separate entity next to the church and the state. Church and the state continued to recognize each other as important players in the life of the society. But since the 1960s this recognition of the church as a player in the public domain has largely evaporated on the argument that religion and church pertain exclusively to the private sphere. In the last few decades the distinction between private and public has gained support as a fundamental line of demarcation and, in public discussion, often appears to confine faith and church to the private domain. But from the angle of faith and theology, the church's proclamation, prophetic role, and service definitely have a public character. The church is convinced that, after Easter, everybody may and should know what has happened. In that sense all theology is public, and the church is so unapologetically.

Today the conceptual trio of church, state, and society is no longer adequate. It is too static and does not sufficiently underline the strong interaction among the various domains. Below we will use more general historical and sociological terminology to reflect how the various domains touch, contain, and penetrate each other. Between the state and politics on the one hand, and the domain of private life on the other, we see an intermediate domain of the market and public life. None of these domains stands in isolation; in the civic and the political realm international agreements and treaties (NAFTA, NATO, UN) increasingly direct our lives. We understand the public domain in a broad sense as comprising everything outside of government and the private sphere: businesses, educational institutions, service organizations, banks, insurance companies, health care institutions, the entertainment industry, the media, and so forth. Often these domains are themselves part of transnational entities or international consortiums.

Nobody in the church can avoid this dual citizenship, and we must all determine how to relate to the public domain. But how should we view and shape this relationship? The theological approach implies that, in any case, we cannot shield the church from the public domain, as if our faith would be only a private matter. The Christian faith claims to have discovered that the gospel of Jesus Christ bears universal meaning and is important for all people. This conviction makes it impossible to ignore the question of its relationship to public life. We can sketch a spectrum of options falling between two extreme positions: the *theocratic* idea that the spheres of the church and the public domain fully overlap, and the ideal of the total *separation of church and state*.

Theocracy. At one end of the spectrum lies the theocratic ideal that serving God defines and encompasses all elements of public life. It has found fertile soil in Reformed spirituality, in which the law of God held, besides its civil and spiritual roles, a lasting normative function for all our life (for this "threefold use of the law," see further, 15.7). That is, the law has continuing significance first of all for the lives of individual Christians and the church, but also more broadly for the operation of a Christian society. The theocratic ideal of a city, state, or nation that seeks its direction from God's law and commandments has a long history in the Reformed world. We may think of Calvin, of the Puritans in New England, and of men like Groen van Prinsterer (1801-76), P. Hoedemaker (1839-1920), and J. A. Wormser (1845-1916) in nineteenth-century Netherlands—men who still firmly believed in a christening of society. But we also find the theocratic ideal in Barth, when he states that the community of Christians knows something that the civil society does not know of itself.

The separation of church and state. At the other end of the spectrum we find the Anabaptist alternative—the view that our heavenly citizenship must be distinguished as sharply as possible from the earthly. The desire for a holy church on the model of the Sermon on the Mount inspires this resolution. Throne and altar, in this view, have nothing in common, and Christians should shun politics, as well as military service. We find examples of this position in the early church and in the Reformation among the followers of Menno Simons (1496-1561), but also among Protestant intellectuals today. An outspoken proponent of this standpoint is the Methodist Stanley Hauerwas (b. 1940), who calls for a Christianity that does not seek to rub shoulders with the existing powers but finds its strength in a praxis formed and nourished by the gospel.

Besides Hauerwas we can mention J. H. Yoder (1927–97). In his best-known publication, *The Politics of Jesus* (1994; orig. pub., 1972), he takes issue with Reinhold Niebuhr, who defended the possibility of a just war. In his challenging style and uncompromising appeal, Hauerwas continues in the line of Yoder.

While Reformed theology discussed the relationship between heavenly and earthly citizenship in theocratic terms, Lutheran theology approached the issue under the heading of *law and gospel*. But in essence they live under the same tension. God not only speaks to us in the gospel, but he also claims us (as we read in Rom 13) through the authority of earthly powers. The intention of the law-gospel distinction does not differ in principle from the Reformed aim; both seek to bring all of human life, including the social and political, under subjection to God's commandment. Church and state are neither to patronize nor to dominate each other. The law-gospel distinction certainly did not intend to make the state totally independent, detached from any divine norms, but rather to underline its value as an instrument in God's service, while rejecting (Catholic) papalism and (Reformed) theocratic dominance. Throne and altar must be distinguished, without totally separating the two regimes (Pöhlmann 1985, 314).

For many, the doctrine of the two kingdoms has fallen into disrepute because of its association with the way in which the law-gospel distinction was interpreted by a number of Lutherans before and during World War II. That distinction is based on the Lutheran concept of revelation, which stipulates that we are connected to God in two ways. "Law" represents our obligations and brings us under judgment; "gospel" stands for whatever elevates us (Pöhlmann 1985, 42). In both cases God is involved. The controversial interpretation was forged by F. Naumann (1860–1919) and E. Hirsch (1888–1972) in the first decades of the twentieth century. They regard God's law as residing not outside of time but within the concrete structures of every period of history. They particularly point to such universal institutions as civil regulations, family, race, nation, and state. This approach turned the law into something completely independent, detached from the sphere of the gospel (the justification of the sinner, the church, the love of God), which eventually served to justify the Deutsche Christen (the German

Christian movement that reinterpreted church and theology in line with Nazi ideology).

But in many other cases the doctrine of the two kingdoms has been used to maintain a critical tension between God's kingdom and earthly regimes. The way that Ambrose, as the bishop of Milan, called Emperor Theodosius I to account for slaughtering the population of Thessaloniki during a military expedition in 390 is paradigmatic. Theodosius was banned from the Eucharist and readmitted only after he had shown remorse and had taken measures to ensure a more humane treatment of the rebel population. Ambrose, in other words, respected the distinction between church and state, but it did not cause him to turn a blind eye to earthly affairs. For the way in which the Reformed tradition has dealt with the doctrine of the two kingdoms from Calvin on, see VanDrunen 2009.

There are a number of intermediate forms between the extreme poles of total theocracy and radical separation between church and state. We refer here to a few examples from Dutch history that illustrate various efforts to find a road between ideal and reality. We stress that these examples apply to the Dutch situation; every country provides us with its own picture.

1. *The public domain as arena.* Kuyper emphasized the plurality of worldviews in Dutch society and promoted an organization of public life along these lines. This step led to the development of various subcultures (the various "pillars" of Dutch society: Roman Catholic, Reformed, socialist, liberal, and so forth). In this way Calvinism, through the initiatives of its members, could make its voice heard and influence public affairs. In a sense this effort relocated the theocratic ideal: the church remained at a distance from the formal state yet could manifest even stronger influence in public life as an "organic" spiritual power. In the Netherlands, from the 1960s on, rank-and-file Reformed church members experienced a pulverization of their own subculture under the weight of secularization. On the right wing of the Reformed world the organizational structures became more and more a way of withdrawing from the public domain in order to survive within one's own subculture. As we see it, however, this falling apart of the Kuyperian ideal was largely due to external cultural forces rather than being necessitated by any internal deficiencies.

2. The church as a *Christ-confessing church for all people.* After the Second World War the Dutch Reformed Church promoted the ideal of a Christ-confessing church for all people; in this way it tried to connect distance from and commitment to public affairs. The model followed Barth's proposal that the church, by its proclamation, should fulfill a pub-

lic role for the common good. This "theology of the apostolate" has also been referred to as *proclamation-theocracy*: the church does not directly interfere in the government and does not attempt to usurp its powers but rather, on the basis of the Bible, holds up a prophetical-critical mirror before those who govern. The ideals of the World Council of Churches and other efforts to have the church assume a prophetic role in the world also belong in this category. The supporters of this view were optimistic about its possibilities, but in the Netherlands their attempt failed because the forces of secularization were stronger than expected.

3. The church as *servant community*. When the lofty ideals of the theology of the apostolate were shipwrecked because of the process of secularization, the image of the church as a servant community emerged. The church was to function in public life as a source of social engagement and "social capital." The church must first of all show its presence and should cooperate with the authorities as closely as possible. This aspiration reflected a desire to be socially relevant and rested on the assumption that the church is a powerful, vital community with a clear identity that enables it to get involved in a pluralistic society. But the self-image of a servant community also showed its limits when the church's attempts to speak through official pastoral publications and position papers proved ineffective. As a rule, we can say that such statements will matter only if they are rooted in the local activities of a community, as suggested by the next model.

4. The church as a *counterculture* or *contrast community*. A recent and popular image for the church's role in the public domain proposes that it be a "contrast community" (Yoder, Hauerwas; but also more and more theologians from mainline Protestant churches feel attracted to this model; e.g., see Bruijne 2012). That is, the church is not primarily an association with some good ideas; its vitality is found by living under a new life order, namely, that of the kingdom. This kingdom produces its own politics, a structure of practices in which people bless each other, wish each other well, forgive each other, and reject all forms of violence. It not only *bears* witness of the heavenly kingdom but *is* itself a witness through its praxis. This praxis, in fact, answers the question of how the church may speak.

This position strongly emphasizes the difference between the church and the world; it may indeed be called Anabaptist to the extent that the orders of heavenly and earthly citizenship are kept far apart. Practically, it leaves the political order to its own devices. But it can also take a more Reformed or Catholic shape through a new appreciation of

637

the Augustinian doctrine of the two kingdoms—by recognizing, in other words, that in real life the two realms cannot be totally separated. They are intertwined here below and will be separated by God only in the eschaton. (see Matt 13:29-30). In this world Christians must live with this tension. When they try to escape and eliminate that tension (as in the Anabaptist view), they withdraw from the ongoing course of history, in which God ordains that his church live. A real continuity connects the fallen world and redemption, and the work of the Holy Spirit is not confined to the domains of church and believer; it seeks to have an impact upon the world. What we noted in chapter 8 about a responsible doctrine of sin is relevant at this point. It enables us to take a realistic view of the world and to implement damage control from the perspective of God's new reality. This attitude differs from that of older Protestant positions in consciously leaving behind the quest for relevance, and with it the majority strategy that for many centuries burdened and plagued the church in the public domain.

Whatever our answer, the tension between our heavenly and earthly citizenship is unavoidable. Indeed, it is arrogant or even dangerous to suggest that theology can take a safe position that guarantees that we will be on the right side. The Reformed tradition has always sought a middle road between theocracy and world-avoidance. That is, we tend to be ambivalent about the recent revival of the so-called two-kingdoms doctrine in Reformed circles. Though this doctrine was not, as traditionally assumed, exclusively Lutheran but found acceptance also in the Reformed tradition, it cannot and should not be used to promote world-avoidance. Such world-avoidance is rarely as apolitical as is suggested, since in fact it supports the status quo in society, which in the West is characterized by liberalism, unbridled capitalism, individualism, and consumerism. We think that the Dutch Kuyperian tradition with its "social program" and its strong link between theology and society is to be preferred here. One of the most exciting developments in recent American Protestant theology is the adoption of this tradition and the attempt to make it fruitful for the contemporary cultural landscape in the United States.

See especially the work of Richard Mouw (2012) and his students in this connection; and see Bratt 2013 (esp. 215-58) for the historical backgrounds in the life of Abraham Kuyper.

We met the tension between our heavenly citizenship and our earthly calling in chapter 7, when discussing humanity as the image of God. Whether we define the image of God by using kingdom (Ps 8; Gen 1) or relational terminology, in either case we are dealing with the way in which people must relate—to other people, animals, the land. Human society, in the broadest sense of the word, is placed in the light of God's righteousness. In Ps 72 we find the ideal of the just ruler. There is good reason why the Torah pays so much attention to treatment of the neighbor (laws about marriage, inheritance, foreigners, the land, and agriculture) and why various sacrifices are stipulated to restore things that have gone wrong. In the Sermon on the Mount, Jesus, as a second Moses, develops and radicalizes the Torah for his disciples (Matt 5–6). He teaches his disciples to pray for the kingdom of God. Everything is related to this reality, even the attitude toward the Roman authorities. In Rom 13 Paul views the current Roman government in the light of God's reign. He does not deify Roman rule. On the contrary, the recognition of Jesus as the Kyrios results, from the very first, in a critical distance from all other authorities. This critical attitude becomes more pronounced when a government demonstrates more and more anti-Christian and antihuman traits. Revelation 13, in which the anti-Christian state is pictured as "the beast from the abyss," stands in contrast to the picture of the state in Rom 13. A Christian view of the state must maintain the tension between these two chapters rather than make one subsume the other. Or to put this in Johannine language: the Christian calling is to be fully *in* the world without becoming *of* the world (John 17:6).

The Christian faith refuses to recognize any authority that claims to be autonomous. It sees its true nature and moves beyond it, toward God. It recognizes God in Christ as the highest authority, as the Kyrios, to whom all power has been given in heaven and on earth (Matt 28:18). This understanding gives the texts about our heavenly citizenship their structuring significance (Eph 2:19; Phil 3:20; Col 1:13). Next to this highest level, all other authority can be regarded only as secondary and derived. The church recognizes the authority of the government out of respect for government as a tool used by God to promote just and peaceful relations among people, and to harness evil. Without that governmental role, society would soon deteriorate into anarchy, where people behave like wolves toward each other (*homo homini lupus*) in a war of each against all in which the strongest prevail. That is, we might well have discussed the role of the government in chapter 8, on the doctrine of sin; there, we would see that governments have the task to restrain evil and to promote justice, including social and economic justice.

Whatever the case, in Christian theology our view of the government is not primarily determined by sociological or historical but by theological arguments. Church members must enter the public domain

639

vigorously and loyally, regarding it as part of the world in which God has placed them and challenges them by his Spirit. This conviction implies proactive answers to questions that people might put to us, the will to be engaged and, if possible, actively involved, even if such a commitment results in dirty hands. Therefore, prayer for the public domain in general and for the authorities in particular is an essential task of the church community. But we cannot pray for the government if we are not prepared to personally and concretely make our own contribution.

At this point we disagree with Beek (2012, 123-26), who recognizes the value of praying for the world (and for the government?), but when all is said and done, he rejects any political responsibility on the part of Christians. For him, the decisive argument is that a Christian can never assume any responsibility for the use of violence or, ultimately, for the death of another person (126). But we feel we cannot get off so easily. If, for instance, we fail to participate in an Amnesty International signature campaign, we may become *coresponsible* for violence and the death of another human being. Refusing to get involved in the activities of the government does not guarantee clean hands. It is better to look for the best options for the *civitas terrena* in concrete circumstances, also, when feasible, by assuming political responsibilities.

The form of government. One last question remains with regard to the state and society. Is there a particular form of government or political model that may be called specifically Christian? We feel that, for reasons already mentioned, we ought to be extremely cautious at this point. Every form of government has advantages and disadvantages, but this admission does not stop us from choosing the model with the fewest disadvantages. The church has lived and served under different cultural, social, and political circumstances. We will briefly review a few forms for which some biblical arguments may be adduced.

1. *Monarchy* (authority centered in one person). In the past, Christians have preferred a kind of government that most closely resembled Old Testament kingship. We already mentioned Ps 72, with its image of the righteous ruler. In both Catholic and Protestant circles this kind of regime received most support well into the twentieth century. Royal rulers may be held accountable for being good rulers of their subjects, as David was with Israel.

2. *Aristocracy*. The presbyterian form of church government represents an oligarchic or aristocratic type of regime in which Christ is professed as the only sovereign but in which, in practice, a small elite

bears responsibility. Calvin preferred this model. The American Revolution (Declaration of Independence) began as an aristocratic rebellion but gradually developed into a popular democracy, even though it might be argued that today a capitalistic elite—that is, a plutocracy—actually holds the most power.

3. *Democracy.* The theme of humanity bearing God's image might perhaps serve as a biblical foundation here. The doctrine implies several values that can be best realized in a democratic model. All people bear the image of God and are called to respond in freedom to God's appeal to enter into relationships and assume responsibilities. From the New Testament we might warrant democracy from the Holy Spirit's having been given to all, with the corollary that therefore all can contribute something. This idea has exerted a powerful influence in Reformed and Congregationalist circles. We find this inclusive model for human community with Schleiermacher and later with Abraham Kuyper.

In sum, there is no single model that may be called specifically Christian. All of them may be abused, and all of them offer possibilities to be used for the common good. The democratic model provides the best possibilities for controlling the power of the rulers. The need for checks and balances and for a certain distance toward earthly authorities is based on God's being the highest and the only real authority. Theologically, we should add that Christians must remain alert and awake so that they pay attention to the appeal for justice heard in the gospel message. Moreover, they must be ready to do what they can within the context of their time, culture, and political circumstances.

References

Barnard, M., et al. 1998. *Dienstboek—een proeve: Schrift, maaltijd, gebed.* Zoetermeer: Boekencentrum.

Beek, Abraham van de. 2008. *God doet recht: Eschatologie als Christologie.* Zoetermeer: Meinema.

———. 2012. *Lichaam en Geest van Christus: De theologie van de kerk en de Heilige Geest* [Body and mind of Christ: The theology of the church and the Holy Spirit]. Zoetermeer: Meinema.

Berkouwer, Gerrit C. 1969. *The Sacraments.* Grand Rapids: Eerdmans.

———. 1976. *The Church.* Grand Rapids: Eerdmans.

Boersma, Hans. 2009. *Nouvelle Théologie and Sacramental Ontology: A Return to Mystery.* Oxford: Oxford University Press.

———. 2011. *Heavenly Participation: The Weaving of a Sacramental Tapestry*. Grand Rapids: Eerdmans.

Borght, Ed A. J. G. van der. 2007. *Theology of Ministry: A Reformed Contribution to an Ecumenical Dialogue*. Leiden: Brill.

———. 2009. *Sunday Morning—the Most Segregated Hour: On Racial Reconciliation as Unfinished Business for Theology in South Africa and Beyond*. Amsterdam: VU University, Faculty of Theology.

Bratt, James D. 2013. *Abraham Kuyper: Modern Calvinist, Christian Democrat*. Grand Rapids: Eerdmans.

Bruijne, Ad de. 2012. "'A Banner That Flies across This Land': An Interpretation and Evaluation of Dutch Evangelical Political Awareness since the End of the Twentieth Century." In *Evangelical Theology in Transition*, ed. C. van der Kooi, E. van Staalduine-Sulman, and A. Zwiep, 86–130. Amsterdam: VU University Press.

Bulgakov, Sergius. 2002. *The Bride of the Lamb*. Grand Rapids: Eerdmans.

Cross, Anthony, and Philip E. Thompson, eds. 2003-5. *Baptist Sacramentalism*. 2 vols. Studies in Baptist History and Thought. Milton Keynes: Paternoster.

Doornenbal, Robartus J. A. 2012. *Crossroads: An Exploration of the Emerging-Missional Conversation*. Delft: Eburon.

Engelsma, David J. 2011. *Covenant and Election in the Reformed Tradition*. Jenison, MI: Protestant Reformed Churches of America.

Frettlöh, Magdalene L. 1999. *Theologie des Segens: Biblische und dogmatische Wahrnehmungen*. Gütersloh: Kaiser.

Goheen, Michael. 2011. *A Light to the Nations: The Missional Church and the Biblical Story*. Grand Rapids: Baker Academic.

Greiner, Dorothea. 1999. *Segen und Segnen: Eine systematisch-theologische Grundlegung*. Stuttgart: Kohlhammer.

Hauerwas, Stanley. 2001. *With the Grain of the Universe: The Church's Witness and Natural Theology*. Grand Rapids: Brazos Press.

———. 2004. *Performing the Faith: Bonhoeffer and the Practice of Nonviolence*. Grand Rapids: Brazos Press.

Hoekendijk, J. C. 1966. *The Church Inside Out*. Translated by Isaac C. Rottenberg. Philadelphia: Westminster.

Immink, F. Gerrit. 2014. *The Touch of the Sacred: The Practice, Theology, and Tradition of Christian Worship*. Grand Rapids: Eerdmans.

Jenkins, Philip. 2007. *God's Continent: Christianity, Islam, and Europe's Religious Crisis*. Oxford: Oxford University Press. Repr., 2010.

Kerner, Wolfram. 2004. *Gläubigentaufe und Säuglingstaufe: Studien zur Taufe und gegenseitigen Taufanerkennung in der neueren evangelischen Theologie*. Norderstedt: Books on Demand.

Kindler, Ernst. 1958. *Der evangelische Glaube und die Kirche: Grundzüge des evangelisch-lutherischen Kirchenverständnisses*. Berlin: Lutherisches Verlagshaus.

Klaver, Miranda. 2011. *This Is My Desire: A Semiotic Perspective on Conversion in an*

Evangelical Seeker Church and a Pentecostal Church in the Netherlands. Amsterdam: Pallas Publications.

Kooi, Cornelis van der. 2005. *As in a Mirror: John Calvin and Karl Barth on Knowing God; A Diptych*. Leiden: Brill.

Kraemer, Hendrik. 1938. *The Christian Message in a Non-Christian World*. London: Edinburgh House Press. Repr., Grand Rapids: Kregel Publications, 1956.

Kronenburg, J., and R. de Reuver. 2007. *Wij zijn ook katholiek: Over protestantse katholiciteit* [We are also catholic: On Protestant catholicity]. Heerenveen: Protestantse Pers.

Küng, Hans. 1967. *The Church*. London: Burns & Oates.

Littell, Franklin H. 1958. *The Anabaptist View of the Church*. 2nd ed. Boston: Starr King.

Mannion, Gerard, and Lewis S. Mudge, eds. 2008. *The Routledge Companion to the Christian Church*. New York: Routledge.

Milbank, John. 1990. *Theology and Social Theory: Beyond Secular Reason*. Oxford: Blackwell.

Minear, Paul S. 2004. *Images of the Church in the New Testament*. Louisville: John Knox. Orig. pub., Philadelphia, 1960.

Miskotte, Kornelis H. 1973. "Het waagstuk van de prediking" [The bold venture of preaching]. In *Om het levende Woord: Opstellen over de praktijk der exegese*, 221–370. Kampen: Kok. Orig. pub., 1948.

Moltmann, Jürgen. 1977. *The Church in the Power of the Spirit: A Contribution to Messianic Ecclesiology*. London: SCM.

Mouw, Richard J. 2012. *The Challenges of Cultural Discipleship: Essays in the Line of Abraham Kuyper*. Grand Rapids: Eerdmans.

Paas, S. 2012. "Ecclesiology in Context: Urban Church Planting in the Netherlands." In *Evangelical Theology in Transition*, ed. C. van der Kooi, E. van Staalduine-Sulman, and A. Zwiep, 130–47. Amsterdam: VU University Press.

Pöhlmann, Horst Georg. 1985. *Abriss der Dogmatik*. 4th ed. Gütersloh: Gütersloher Verlagshaus.

Ramsey, Michael. 1990. *The Gospel and the Catholic Church*. Cambridge, MA: Cowley Publications. Orig. pub., 1936.

Rappaport, Roy A. 1999. *Ritual and Religion in the Making of Humanity*. Cambridge: Cambridge University Press.

Smith, James K. A. 2009. *Desiring the Kingdom: Worship, Worldview, and Cultural Formation*. Grand Rapids: Baker Academic.

Torrance, Thomas F. 1993. *Royal Priesthood: A Theology of Ordained Ministry*. Edinburgh: T&T Clark. Orig. pub., 1955.

VanDrunen, David. 2009. *Natural Law and the Two Kingdoms: A Study in the Development of Reformed Social Thought*. Grand Rapids: Eerdmans.

Volf, Miroslav. 1998. *After Our Likeness: The Church as the Image of the Trinity*. Grand Rapids: Eerdmans.

Ward, Pete. 2002. *Liquid Church*. Eugene, OR: Wipf & Stock.

Welker, Michael. 2000. *What Happens in Holy Communion?* Grand Rapids: Eerdmans.

———. 2013. *God the Revealed: Christology.* Grand Rapids: Eerdmans.

Wolterstorff, Nicholas. 2011. *Hearing the Call: Liturgy, Justice, Church, and World.* Grand Rapids: Eerdmans.

———. 2015. *The God We Worship: An Exploration of Liturgical Theology.* Grand Rapids: Eerdmans.

World Council of Churches. 1982. *Baptism, Eucharist, and Ministry.* Faith and Order Paper 111. Geneva: WCC Publications.

———. 2013. *The Church: Towards a Common Vision.* Faith and Order Paper 214. Geneva: WCC Publications.

Yoder, John Howard. 1994. *The Politics of Jesus: Vicit Agnus noster.* 2nd ed. Grand Rapids: Eerdmans. Orig. pub., 1972.

15 Renewal of the Human Being

Justification and Transformation

AIM

In the Lord's Prayer we say, "Forgive us our debts, as we forgive our debtors." This petition is just one line, yet it puts us on high alert. Is Jesus saying that God will consider forgiving our sins only if we have demonstrated our willingness to do the same toward others? Some translations of the prayer seem to imply exactly this connection. Does that make God's forgiveness conditional? Or is the reverse more likely, that when we have received God's forgiveness, we too will show a forgiving spirit? This reading implies that changes occur when God enters our life. This chapter will deal with two of the most important of these changes, the forgiveness and renewal (or justification and sanctification) of the individual person, with all the issues that these actions entail. In particular we want to clarify:

- the role that individual renewal plays in dogmatics (15.1)
- how the notions of guilt and repentance (or conversion) are presupposed in Christian reflection about human renewal (15.2)
- how and why justification is the foundation of the renewal of our life (15.3)
- the nature and meaning of faith in relation to justification (15.4)
- why the doctrine of justification has been revived in recent theological discussion (15.5)
- how the believer's participation in Christ constitutes an organic tie between justification and sanctification, or transformation (15.6)
- how the transformation of the believer is the complement to justification in terms of a concrete renewal of life (15.7)
- whether, and if so how, we can persist and progress in our new orientation of life (15.8)

- how and why God's election may best be discussed as the capstone to the concept of renewal (15.9).

MAKING CONNECTIONS

1. Read the text of the hymn "Amazing Grace," written by John Newton, a former captain of a slave ship. What does this text say about renewal and transformation?

2. The themes of guilt and forgiveness or renewal play a fascinating but complex role in much of nineteenth- and twentieth-century literature. Read one of the following novels with this factor in mind: Nathaniel Hawthorne's *The Scarlet Letter* (1850) and its twin, George Eliot's *Adam Bede* (1859), François Mauriac's *Thérèse Desqueyroux* (1927), Graham Greene's *The Power and the Glory* (1940), Ian McEwan's *Atonement* (2001), or Khaled Hosseini's *The Kite Runner* (2003). Better yet, read several of them and compare how they treat guilt, forgiveness, and change.

3. Some conservative evangelical and Reformed churches insist on a personal experience of conversion as a condition for church membership. Here, everything is focused on the questions that this chapter deals with. If you are not familiar with this type of Protestantism, attend one of their services and note the role these elements play in the sermon. What thoughts and emotions do the sermon, hymns, and prayers evoke in you? If possible, discuss this experience with students who are well acquainted with this tradition.

15.1. What's It All About?

The topics of this chapter are viewed quite differently by the various Christian traditions. In large swaths of Roman Catholicism they hardly figure at all apart from the matter of personal sanctification. Likewise, liberal Protestants have great difficulty understanding why these questions and concerns should be important. In contrast, in major sectors of evangelical and Reformed Protestantism they have received so much attention over the past few centuries that they have pushed other issues in dogmatics into the background. We still see examples of people who struggle their entire life to "make sure that they are saved," but without ever finding assurance on the matter. We will take questions about the personal appropriation of salvation, and living on this basis, most seriously, but not as the only important questions. We need to discuss these things but should not get lost in the discussion; they should not derail the entire dogmatic order.

The labels for what we are talking about get complicated. Traditional names for it are *applicatio salutis* and *ordo salutis*—respectively, the "application" (or "appropriation") of salvation and the "order" of salvation. They presuppose that salvation (and its concrete history, the *historia salutis*) is not just part of the past and that we must deal (only?) with the question of how this salvation is "applied" to individuals in the present, and possibly to people collectively. Although, on this understanding, the history of salvation happened once for all, its application takes place with each person anew, in a more or less established order. The problem is that this approach creates a dichotomy that we do not find in the Bible. Scripture gives the sense that we are touched and carried along by one, world-encompassing movement that God began in Israel and carried forward in Jesus Christ and the Holy Spirit, which explains why such terms as *applicatio salutis* and *ordo salutis* emerged only in the seventeenth and eighteenth centuries, when people no longer experienced themselves and the world as being embedded in God's saving acts.

The term *ordo salutis* is usually traced back to Rom 8:29–30, where Paul speaks of people who have been "called according to his [God's] purpose":

> For those whom he foreknew he also predestined to be conformed to the image of his Son, in order that he might be the firstborn among many brethren. And those whom he predestined he also called; and those whom he called he also justified; and those whom he justified he also glorified.

This passage has been called the golden chain, a sequence of divine acts for the benefit of humanity that work like links in the chain of salvation. We indeed find here a certain *order* in the acts by which God adopts those who are his into communion with his Son. From foreknowledge the process proceeds via predestination to calling, justification, and glorification. Other biblical passages use other terms, such as repentance/conversion, faith, new birth, adoption, and sanctification, and not surprisingly, attempts have been made to harmonize these with the text in Romans. However, we may well ask whether this effort succeeds and whether in fact any such sequence was intended. In any case, different lists were drawn up that varied substantially, not only between confessional families, but also in one and the same ecclesial tradition. Lutheran lists gave priority to repentance/conversion (Lat. *poenitentia*); Calvinists tended to see everything from the perspective of predestination, forgetting that Paul also referred to foreknowledge; a typically Arminian *ordo* usually did the opposite. All such differences triggered fierce arguments, since the correct sequence was seen as decisive for the question of who truly shares in God's salvation.

It is believed that the term *ordo salutis* was coined by two Lutheran theologians, J. F. Buddaeus (*Institutiones theologicae dogmaticae* [1723]) and Jacob Carpov (1737), against the background of emerging Pietism. However, the matter had been put on the agenda much earlier by Reformed theologians. Calvin's successor, Theodore Beza, proposed a schematic representation (his famous *Tabula* [1555]) of the various stages of the life of faith within the comprehensive framework of God's election (it has rightly been emphasized, however, that Beza's "table" did not serve as a paradigm for his theological system; see Muller 2012, 196). Beza's disciple William Perkins (1558-1602) designed a similar table and summarized his complete theology in a title that directly referred to the order of salvation: *A golden chaine; or, the description of theology. Containing the order of the causes of salvation and damnation, according to God's Word* (1590). Such a title reflects an international development—in England (Puritanism), Germany (Pietism), and the Netherlands (Further Reformation; cf. Lieburg 2014)—toward subjectivizing and psychologizing the content of faith, so that experiencing the various stages of the *ordo salutis* became increasingly important. It is significant that Calvin knew nothing of a fixed "order of salvation," even though we see some elements that "after him served as building blocks for a more or less systematized *ordo salutis*" (Graafland 1984, 244; Muller 2012, 169, sees more continuity between Calvin's views and later developments in Reformed theology). The same is true also in the Lutheran camp, for instance, in Luther's *Small Catechism* 2.3. For the differences in the lists within Reformed circles, see Honig, HGD 535-36, which surveys the sequences of Gomarus, the Leyden *Synopsis Purioris Theologiae* (1625), W. à Brakel, J. à Marck, C. Hodge, A. Kuyper, and H. Bavinck. The two last mentioned even varied the sequences in their own publications.

The term *applicatio salutis* is found with Heppe (RD, chap. 21) and was taken up in the twentieth century by Van Ruler, whose lectures of many years about this theme were recently made available for the first time (VW 4B:25-26, 312-74).

But do the relevant biblical passages indeed intend to stress a fixed temporal order? This idea is difficult to maintain when we compare the "golden chain" of Rom 8 with similar sequences such as the one in 1 Cor 1:30 ("Christ Jesus, whom God made our wisdom, our righteousness and sanctification and redemption") or 6:11 ("you were washed, you were sanctified, you were justified"). In one case righteousness/justification precedes sanctification, but in the other case it follows it. This example indicates that one should not try to distill any fixed order of salvation from these biblical texts.

It would also be problematic to point to a causal connection between the different elements, for in all cases God is clearly in charge. Being called does not automatically lead to justification; in fact, we read that *God* also justifies those whom he has called. The golden chain and the other texts that summarize what God or Christ does for us in the realization of our salvation are strongly doxological in nature. They do not present a complete systematic-theological list of the various steps that God takes (and the believer must experience) but aim to praise God for the many acts by which he adopts us into his communion. There is, of course, a certain logic in the order, but we should beware of making it inflexible. Particularly when people want to add other links to the chain, we see endless (and usually fruitless) discussions about whether faith must precede justification or vice versa. In Scripture, apparently, the main idea is to mention certain constitutive aspects of God's dealing with the individual person, which for didactic reasons may be differentiated from each other and be placed in a certain order. Through the prism of the Spirit, the light that appeared in Christ is refracted into a broad spectrum of multicolored rays.

The Latin terms mentioned above might cause misunderstandings but can nonetheless be defended to some extent. In any case, they show we must say more than just speak of the "appropriation" of salvation. To quote Van Ruler: "The application of salvation differs from its appropriation. Moreover, it is such an important event that a reference to faith does not suffice. The Holy Spirit must play a role. He must apply the salvation that Christ has provided" (VW 4B:737). Taking the Trinitarian perspective seriously, as we do in this book, creates space for a relatively independent discussion of the work of the Holy Spirit in and on behalf of the individual person. We should note that this connection is already found with Calvin. By giving a Trinitarian structure to his *Institutes*, he was able to devote an entire section (book 3) to the Holy Spirit. Even though he does not support the idea of a fixed order of salvation, he treats the subject in great depth. That is, for him (contrary to what would often happen later), the focus does not shift from God's acts to human experience, suddenly making humanity the center. Especially in Reformed theology the realization of salvation is seen as strictly theocentric; we are always dealing with what God does on our behalf—in this case through his Spirit—and not with the human contribution to the process of salvation.

Berkouwer 1954, 25–29, provides a good survey of the pros and cons of thinking in terms of an *ordo salutis*; his key statement reads: "The ways along which God leads man to His salvation are so richly varied that it is impossible to circumscribe them all in fixed stadia" (27). Berkouwer prefers to speak of "the way of salvation" (*via salutis*). This notion is currently emerging again in practical theology, for example, with Immink 2005, 107–15: "The linkage with salvation history should not lead us to view the unique life of every human being as of little importance" (106).

More recently, authors have applied other terminology to this point, with their own pros and cons. O. Weber (FD 2:229–407) and J. A. Heyns (D 291–328) speak, respectively, about "the work of the Holy Spirit" and "the person and work of the Holy Spirit." This wording ensures a proper theocentric and Trinitarian emphasis but brings up the whole cosmological and ecclesiological work of the Spirit. Both authors maintain a good theocentric balance but treat ecclesiology as a separate issue of a somewhat lower order. This approach fails to do justice to the close connection between Spirit and church that we find, for instance, in the Apostles' Creed. Others, such as Genderen and Velema (CRD 539–72), speak of the "doctrine of salvation" or "soteriology." This choice very nicely keeps the locus close to the person and work of the *Sōtēr* (Greek for Savior, Redeemer), Jesus Christ. But therein lies the problem: soteriology is usually (see chap. 10) defined as including the work of Christ, particularly the atonement, an important aspect of our salvation! But the appropriation of salvation by the individual person must be understood within a different, pneumatological category.

We also want to refer to the terminology used by Honig (HGD 529), who speaks of the "benefits of the covenant." This phrase has the advantage of keeping the application of individual salvation from becoming isolated from the broader context of covenant and community, for it is within those broader collective structures that the individual may participate in salvation. It seems to us, however, that this terminology is too archaic to be of much service to contemporary dogmatics.

At this point we join Berkhof (CF) and Vlastuin (2014), who speak of human renewal. We see this as a unique work of the Spirit, along with the renewal of the community (chap. 14) and the renewal of the world (chap. 16). In developing this theme, we will focus on three biblical-theological notions that constitute its core: guilt and repentance/conversion, justification and faith, and sanctification and perseverance/election. This threefold emphasis aims to do justice to the central place of justification. In justification we find the center and focal point of God's mediation of salvation on behalf of the individual. If we add too many other elements, we risk diminishing the liberating power of this event by reducing justification to just one link in the chain of conditions we presumably must fulfill. Surreptitiously, our attention may once again shift from what God does to what must be done by, and to, the human subject. This is a disastrous path.

Yet, we cannot maintain that renewal is limited to God's justifying judgment. Something must precede and follow God's acquittal. Something happens to us, and for us. What precedes may be put under the heading of guilt and repentance; what follows may be labeled transformation and persistence. At the same time, we admit that speaking about "preceding" and "following" is not really adequate, for we are not dealing with three different stages in our experience. All three of these moments remain significant for the entire span of the Christian life. Nonetheless, it would also be artificial to completely negate the thought of temporality and some kind of sequence. From the earliest days of church history the spiritual life has been pictured as a road. Throughout the ages mystics have spoken of the three phases of enlightenment, purification, and unity. The Heidelberg Catechism memorably categorizes the life of faith as misery, redemption, and gratitude. Whether these three are seen as phases or as facets, the image of a pilgrimage road undeniably lies in the background. John Bunyan (1628–88) developed this metaphor further in his unsurpassed *Pilgrim's Progress*. Still today the same image shapes reflection by mystics and others on the individual's spiritual journey through life. The image prods us to ask, how have my experiences with God and others made me the kind of person I now am? What things did I have to forsake? What progress have I made, and what development do I see? How can I know whether I have grown and become more spiritually mature? There was a time when such questions immediately aroused suspicions of an unhealthy introspection and a self-absorbed view of salvation. Today, however, there is a far greater risk that we run too fast; we may be doing injustice to ourselves and others by no longer asking these kinds of questions. We therefore plead for a rehabilitation of what Roman Catholics have always referred to as spirituality, and what

651

Protestant circles called the spiritual life or spiritual road: establishing a pattern for living in a relationship with God, aided by a concrete rhythm of prayer and meditation.

How does such a spiritual life become Christian? In itself, spirituality is a general religious phenomenon and can easily deteriorate into a generic discourse more or less detached from any specific faith tradition. It is quite understandable, then, that Barth and his followers treated these categories with suspicion, or even totally rejected them. Yet, "spirituality" is derived from *Spiritus* and is therefore connected with the Spirit of God. As we have seen, this Spirit is also the Spirit of Christ. Christian spirituality derives its uniqueness from being linked to the movement of Father, Son, and Spirit toward us; it simply traces this move, as it were, in the opposite direction. The Spirit brings us into communion with Christ, and thereby in communion with the Father. A Christian gives meaning to his or her life by interpreting it as a journey toward the threefold life of God (Higton, CD 137), responding, in so doing, to the act by which God in Christ reconciled the world to himself (see 2 Cor 5:19). In this process, "as they journey along," Christians are themselves renewed and transformed into the image of Christ.

We agree with Berkhof (CF 430-31) that the ultimate goal of our renewal should be to become like Christ. But contrary to Berkhof, we do not regard the order of salvation as a mirror of the history of salvation, as if the individual believer must repeat the journey of Christ through its various stages. In fact, Berkhof himself cannot consistently maintain this idea, as he cannot find anything analogous in Jesus's life for the notions of judgment and repentance. He therefore depicts these steps as the flip side of Israel's journey as described in the Old Testament. The concept of renewal then returns as a negative symbol, a token of guilt and disloyalty. Yet, in the Old Testament we also find Israel as the object of God's forgiveness and sanctification (e.g., with Hosea, Zechariah, and in Ps 130). We therefore prefer to picture the road of salvation as analogous to the basic Trinitarian structure of the biblical testimony. Believers are convicted of sin by the Holy Spirit (John 16:8-9); they are justified in Christ, and they are brought by the Father to their ultimate destination in his act of election. But because these three are one, we should not make this pattern too constrictive; we are dealing with differentiations, not separations. For a beautifully consistent Trinitarian approach to the "summa" of theology and thereby also to the goal of the Christian life, see Higton, CD. The image of the road the Christian must travel is aptly expressed in the subtitle of Horton, CF.

Barth places all his emphasis on the objectivity of the atonement provided in Christ. The Spirit, as the subjective side of God's revelation, acquaints us with this saving reality but does not have to validate it (CD I/1:449–50; IV/3:353). For Barth, ethics is very important; we are challenged to start living in accordance with this new state of affairs between God and humanity. This is a lifelong exercise that has its basis in prayer. It is striking to see how Barth develops what was supposed to be the capstone of his doctrine of atonement—that is, his ethics—as an interpretation of the Lord's Prayer (see Barth 1976, now also included in Barth, GA 7). The Christian life is, first of all, an exercise in truly living in fellowship with Christ. See further the last section of 16.6.

Recently, much has been published about (Christian) spirituality. See, for a Roman Catholic view, the extensive survey of Waaijman 2002, and for Protestant perspectives, Willard 1988 and Sittser 2007. We believe it is essential, also today, for the church, on the basis of its age-old experience in providing guidance on the journey to God, to point people in the right direction and assist late-modern and postmodern people in their spiritual quest. Hence a Christian doctrine of renewal remains of utmost importance.

15.2. Guilt and Repentance/Conversion

All world religions share the sense that things in life are often not what they ought to be. They all share the core belief that life is poisoned by evil and misery, yet that a better future is a real possibility. All agree that humans are at least part of the problem, and they all want to see positive changes in the individual person. But they differ on many counts as to how this change must come about and what the road from evil to good looks like.

Unlike other religions (e.g., Greek and some Eastern religions), the Jewish-Christian tradition does not primarily define human failure in terms of tragic fate but as guilt. Old Testament hymns like Ps 32 and, especially, Ps 51 are typical of Jewish-Christian spirituality in this regard—texts that over the centuries have had an influence on people that can hardly be overestimated. In them we hear the voice of people who have learned no longer to point an accusing finger toward their environment, who have become deeply impressed by the evil that lives within them. In chapter 8 we studied the topic of evil and categorized it as sin. Here we again pick up the thread, now mostly in terms of the awareness of sin. We employ the more general term "guilt," however, partly because its associations with guilt-consciousness or guilt-feelings make it clearer what the issue is.

The Bible and the Christian faith tradition have always paid due attention to human guilt. In the Old Testament we need think only of the elaborate sacrificial rites, with their detailed rules for the restoration of the broken relationship with God. Likewise, the New Testament story of God's saving presence in Christ and the Spirit makes sense only against the backdrop of human guilt. This is so, even when we realize that God's plan of salvation includes more than restoration and renovation, and moves on to the fulfillment and perfecting of God's original intention for humanity (1 Cor 15:45-49; 2 Pet 1:4). The *historia salutis* can be understood only against the background of our guilty estrangement from God and our intended destiny. This separation applies no less in a subjective sense: the *ordo salutis* and the salvation that God provides can be experienced only against the background of our recognition, or at least our awareness, of an estrangement caused by guilt. The collective dimension—the fact that all human beings share in this estrangement—cannot annul the individual dimension, the recognition of *my* personal part in this development.

Interestingly enough, the Bible does not have a separate term for this awareness of personal guilt and failure. But it does have some important key concepts for the entire package of human remorse and its accompanying change in mentality. *Teshuvah* is an important Old Testament term. It refers to a turning around or returning and is most frequently found in forms of the verb *shuv*. In the New Testament the word *metanoia* and its cognates are prominent; they denote a change in attitude or mentality. Momentously, the Latin Vulgate (mis)translated this word as *poenitentia*, which became a prominent part of the theological vocabulary. It is important to know that these terms refer to the objective as well as the subjective side of the question. Most languages do not have a single term to express those two aspects, so we often have to choose between what we inwardly feel and what is outwardly observable. This brings us, in the first case, to "repentance" or "remorse," and in the second case typically to the word "conversion." But these translations are rather misleading, for they cannot help but underemphasize one side of the matter or the other. In the Bible the subjective and objective aspects are indissolubly connected: conversion is genuine only when it results not from outward compulsion but from an inner change in mentality; likewise, repentance has significance only when it leads to an actual change in conduct (see 2 Cor 7:8-11 about "mourning" and "grieving into repenting").

Various parables in the Gospels are relevant here, particularly, of course, the parable of the prodigal son in Luke 15 (vv. 11-32, esp. 17-19). In this passage remorse, penitence, and conversion all clearly have a place within the larger context of the covenant, in which the father's love is not only experienced but undoubtedly to some extent determines the son's depth of remorse.

Because the Vulgate mistranslated the New Testament *metanoeite* (Mark 1:15 and pars.) as "doing penance" (*poenitentiam agite*), when the Greek actually means something like "changing one's mind," a strongly practical emphasis became dominant; at its extreme, it ultimately led to the trade in indulgences.

Along this line, the medieval practice of confession and penitence required three preconditions for receiving absolution (annulment of guilt): oral confession (*confessio oris*), a contrite heart (*contritio cordis*), and satisfaction through certain actions (*satisfactio operum*). In this way word, deed, and mentality were kept together. Gradually the tendency grew to be content with *attritio* (regret) rather than to insist on *contritio* (remorse). Regretting something ("I wish I had not done that") usually results from the negative consequences I suffer rather than from a distaste for the sinful act as such. The Council of Trent saw such regret as a good start, but Roman Catholics who were heavily inspired by Augustine—such as Cornelis Jansen (1585-1638) and his supporters, including the French philosopher Blaise Pascal—did not. They believed that salvation was at risk of becoming very superficial, since grace does not remain real grace—namely, a surprising and undeserved acquittal by God—but is reduced to a benefit acquired by some sort of commercial transaction. The Jansenists argued that it was less important to see as many people as possible participating in the Eucharist, as Jesuit priests were promoting, than genuine remorse on the part of those who did. More generally, the Jansenists wanted to see a genuine life of faith, a sober lifestyle, with ample emphasis on prayer and study. However, their reform program triggered much resistance, leading to a fierce battle between the Jansenists and the Jesuits that did not abate, despite various papal interventions and condemnations. Eventually, it led to the Schism of Utrecht and to the origin of the Old Catholic Church (1723).

Among Protestants of the time the relationship between repentance and grace went off the tracks another way. The pietists of the Second Reformation heavily stressed the need for repentance, and they premised it emphatically upon the seeker realizing the full extent of his or her personal guilt before God, so that this awareness became an absolute precondition for sharing in God's salvation. In fact, repentance was placed outside of the real faith relationship. We agree with Calvin that being conscious of our own failures is an integral part of that relationship and not some kind of anteroom to it. "While Luther, Martin Bucer [1491-1551] and Melanchthon had located penitence before faith, Calvin made a rigorous decision to place repentance within the context of soteriology" (Vlastuin 2014, 32).

See *Inst.* 3.3.1-10: "What we want to show is that a person can only seriously engage in *poenitentia* when he knows he belongs to God" (3.3.4). Clearly, Calvin does not intend to make the sense of guilt and remorse a precondition of the Christian life, but to show that they are an integral part of it. Unfortunately, later generations of Protestants did not persist in this lofty idea but, surreptitiously and unintentionally, made it into something that must come before faith, with the rather obvious conclusion that we ourselves have this work to do. This change represented a structural return to the deterioration of the late medieval practice of confession and penitence, in which the penitent had to do (or pay) something to get access to salvation. The deplorable part of this relapse was that the character of salvation as absolute grace—the first principle of the Reformation—could easily get lost in the process. "True repentance totally denies any idea of ability and meritoriousness on man's part" (Berkhof, CF 433).

Initially the *Lutheran* tradition saw this danger very clearly; the first of Luther's famous Ninety-Five Theses against the trade in indulgences (1517) even suggested that Christ had intended the *entire life* of the believer to be devoted to penitence. But also in Lutheranism the notions of a sense of guilt and remorse could become detached from the life of faith because they were from the start tied to the law, whereas the gospel was credited with an origin in faith. We detect this structure already with Melanchthon (*Apology* [1531], art. 12), even though he still kept law and gospel close together. However, since law and gospel were seen as opposites, as God's "real" vs. God's "strange" work (*opus proprium* vs. *opus alienum*), it was practically unavoidable that faith and repentance drifted apart. Remarkably enough, because of the imputed superiority of the gospel, this development led to few spiritual problems in the Lutheran tradition, while its adoption on the *Reformed* side often did cause anxiety, discouragement, and spiritual indifference, as many never got any further than the first step, the law, with its correlate, "misery."

The Heidelberg Catechism followed misery with two other steps: redemption and gratitude. In this famous triad the catechism defined all of soteriology in a practical-pastoral way. But it gave rise to discussions of whether the three facets were to be understood as phases, that is, as a chronological sequence. This issue might well be a later retrojection. As a matter of fact, in the Heidelberg Catechism knowledge of one of the three aspects somehow presupposes knowledge of the other two, which is made clear by subtle interconnections between the three aspects; for example, "there is already a hint of gospel in part 1 on the law and much more than a hint of law in part 2 on the gospel" (Bierma 2013, 33). It seems to us, then, that the three leading motives should be seen as integral parts of the Christian life rather than as temporal stages in the Christian's experience. It is telling in this connection that the discussion of the three aspects is preceded with the impressive words of Lord's Day 1, which teaches that, with all we are and have, in life and death, we belong to Jesus Christ our Savior.

Yet, integrating a sense of guilt and repentance as part of our faith must not be used to relativize its importance. God's fundamental concern about the mess we have made—in biblical idiom, God's wrath and judgment—is only too real. In God's law we see a mirror of our own failures (Rom 7:7-13; note Heidelberg Catechism, Lord's Day 2); and lest we think that the picture is not so bad, we should remember the deepest intentions of the Torah, which still remain valid and were reasserted by Jesus in his Sermon on the Mount (Matt 5-7). We must not measure ourselves against our own mediocrity but on the basis of the ultimate destiny God has in mind for the human family. Our failures become, if possible, even more painful when we compare our life with that of Jesus Christ. Human guilt is so immense that Jesus—the only person who, according to the New Testament, did not in any way share in it—would die because of it, and in order to deal with it. His undeserved death on the cross shows the absolute bankruptcy of all *human morality*; the cross and the resurrection sealed, once and for all, God's judgment over what we have done and failed to do. Jesus had to suffer so that he could break the power of sin and guilt (see 11.8). A person whom the Spirit had led into communion with Christ will apply this judgment personally, and will at times experience the bewilderment about his or her own irreparable failings.

This bewilderment, however, does not lead to utter despair, since the gospel tells us that, paradoxically enough, Christ's death on the cross is also a power to salvation, and that his resurrection has become the basis for our justification (Rom 4:25). In Paul's letters in particular, we are taught that our sinful self died with Christ so that legally (*de iure*) it no longer exists; at the same time, we have been raised with Christ from death and so have escaped judgment (e.g., see Rom 6:4-11; Gal 2:20; Col 2:12). This fundamental communion with Christ—the New Testament refers to it several times as "being in Christ" or, even more intimately, as "Christ being in us"—makes the knowledge of our sins bearable, knowing

657

that God's judgment over our life, however radical it may be, is not the final word.

In the meantime, we must be careful not to simply translate these theological concepts into psychological categories. To speak theologically about the need for a sense of guilt and repentance is not to suggest that we should dislike ourselves, regard ourselves as worthless, or any such thing. (The words in the classic Reformed communion liturgy that tell us to be "displeased" with ourselves can easily cause misunderstandings.) God created us "good" (Heidelberg Catechism 6), and we are therefore basically worthy. The startling statement of the catechism that we are "wicked and perverse" and Calvin's teaching of "total depravity" (*corruptio totalis*)—which is not literally, but in substance, found in *Inst.* 2.1.9—must not be taken in a psychological sense. These statements concern our relationship to God, whom we have come to know in Christ as our Father (Heidelberg Catechism 1). This relationship has been corrupted not only with regard to our bodily existence but also in our mind and spirit, that is, in our total being (the statement of Calvin is, in fact, remarkably anti-Platonic). The Christian faith does not prod us to detest ourselves and should not lead to any feelings of depression or inferiority, but it does assert our total dependence upon God's mercy because of our radical failures. In ourselves we are utterly unable to restore this rupture, even in a small way. A transgression of one commandment means that we have broken them all (Jas 2:10) and have corrupted everything. This is not to say, however, that we cannot do any good in our dealings with others, or that our guilt is a fate that has befallen us, or that our self fully overlaps with our sinfulness. (Note in this connection Canons of Dort III/IV.4, about "some degree of natural light" that has remained in us.)

At first glance, it may seem far from easy for people today to grasp the meaning of these notions, simply because most of us no longer worry much about our sins. Previous generations did. When a disaster occurred, they would immediately ask what they had done wrong, whereas in the West today, most of the evil that comes our way is by definition irrational. Evil strikes us as an unfair disruption of our privacy, given our assumption that we have a natural right to happiness. Contemporary theologians like Rahner and Tillich have pointed out that we have traded the question of guilt for the question of meaning. Our main problem is no longer how to live a moral life or how to get OK with God; rather, we question the meaning of our existence and whether God actually has a role in it. We sometimes hear in this connection that, if we do still feel guilty, we tend to simply offer excuses for ourselves in what we may perhaps refer to as a "sorry-culture." If that effort does not work, we can have our degree of responsibility assessed—and any compensatory measures arranged—by the courts. It would appear, at least superficially, that the idea of moral guilt has largely evaporated.

But when we look a bit closer, we see that this conclusion is not entirely correct. In the last few decades we have also seen a sharp increase in guilt, both in the subjective sense of guilt-feelings and in the objective sense of new "sins" that require atonement. Many things that in the past were not deemed sinful are now seen as serious offenses: causing environmental pollution; discriminating against people on the basis of race, gender, or sexual orientation; animal cruelty; and, more recently, male as well as female circumcision. Likewise, hypocrisy (in the sense of being inauthentic and merely playing a role) is now regarded as a serious shortcoming much more than it was in the past. These new sins, however, almost always turn out to be committed by others; we rarely meet people who regret that they have committed them themselves. Nonetheless, a greater sense of guilt has arisen, even if it tends no longer to be related to any concrete violation. We feel guilty about the Third World without exactly knowing what we are doing wrong. Moreover, many have a sense of guilt when they realize that they do not meet the ideals that the media constantly promote (e.g., in images of young, athletic men and thin, shapely women).

But do not these examples involve shame more than guilt? This distinction arose in the twentieth century at the hand of cultural anthropologists like Margaret Mead and Ruth Benedict. Supposedly, the West—traditionally a guilt culture—has for all kinds of reasons moved toward becoming a culture of shame. The idea has merit, but it is perhaps more a matter of accents and tendencies than of a radical change. Feelings of guilt and shame are both universal and often go together. Beneath the surface of Western culture we still undeniably find a widespread sense of failure, of not meeting the norms that we know we should reach. But the awareness of a common moral order has become diffuse, as people no longer know exactly what these norms are or why they are warranted. This uncertainty stems from the erosion of the Christian-theistic matrix of our culture and the failure of Enlightenment thinking, which replaced it, to create a new unequivocal morality. Much modern literature illustrates (see above, assignment 2) how dealing with guilt has become extremely complicated. Yet, this same literature shows that real guilt, and a sense of guilt, remain prominent themes in contemporary life.

Remarkably enough, current dogmatics pays scant attention to this issue. That the West is traditionally a guilt culture cannot be explained from its roots in classical antiquity or in the naturalistic Germanic world, but from the christening of Europe. We can cite, for example, Augustine's doctrine of original sin, the Penitential Books from Carolingian times (which overlooked no possible sin and stipulated exactly what penance was due for each), and the tympanums over cathedral doors, with their lively depictions of heaven and hell. The Christian message of grace could become relevant only in the context of a clear awareness of guilt. However faulty some of the attempts to foster this sense of guilt might have been, these measures undoubtedly contributed to the fact that Western people began to understand themselves as being responsible for their own actions, guilty before God, and needing his grace. This realization must be regarded as positive, for "nothing does more for the humanization of man than addressing him as one who is fully accountable before God and his neighbor" (Berkhof, CF 215).

The *Reformation* started with Luther's disturbing question about finding a gracious God; in that sense, it was born from an awareness of sin. The Reformation took a new step in christening the awareness of sin by turning it into an intensely personal matter of the heart; that is, sin is not just something outside of me and foreign to me, but it affects my entire being and can be removed only by God's gracious intervention. Sin and grace should have remained closely linked in Protestantism, but in practice an unhealthy fixation on the sense of guilt, detached from grace, often made people feel inferior. With the coming of the Enlightenment, good and evil were gradually relocated inside the individual; people were accordingly called to fight against their lower inclinations by enlisting their good potential. The nineteenth century had high hopes for this exercise, but in the twentieth century these hopes were shipwrecked by two world wars. MacIntyre (1985) has provided us with an impressive analysis of how and why this Enlightenment thinking (which was premised on the idea of human maturity) did not create a uniform account of morality. In our postmodern era we seem, at times, to be regressing to earlier phases of our civilization: elementary drives such as sex and vitality seem to be prominent, while moral guilt is no longer part of the discourse but has gone underground.

It is important for Christian proclamation, therefore, that we continue calling real guilt by its name. We should try to use the kind of clear language that avoids jargon. We must bring together as closely as possible the sense of guilt and actual guilt. The law of God remains the norm by which to "measure" good and evil. Because we urgently need such an objective norm, the law is also mentioned in the New Testament (Rom 7:12). But is this norm really so objective? Is it not subject to numerous problems of interpretation, for instance, about what has enduring value and what is culturally and situationally conditioned? Such difficulties may be true, but they cannot be used as an argument to ignore the law. For the core of the law is quite clear (Ps 19:8). We find it summarized in the two commandments of love, which, according to Jesus, are the axes on which the Torah and the Prophets turn (Matt 22:37-40 and pars.). Or in the words of the prophet Micah: "He has showed you, O man, what is good; and what does the LORD require of you but to do justice, and to love kindness, and to walk humbly with your God?" (Mic 6:8). This is the basis on which we can separate real guilt from all kinds of paralyzing feelings of guilt and inferiority. More than in the past we have to pay attention to the tragic aspects of life, for instance, to the damage people suffer because of traumatic experiences, whether as children or later in life. Yet, it is important always to focus on the possibility and reality of forgiveness. For it is precisely this message, which is so essential in the Bible, that is often badly ignored in our postmodern world.

The message of forgiveness is not exclusively Christian, but it does find its most fertile soil in the Christian message of God's pardoning love for guilty people (see the parable of the "wicked" servant, Matt 18:21-35). However, this is not just a feature of the New Testament; it is also fully documented in the Old (e.g., Pss 32; 51; 103; 130:4; Isa 38:17; Hos 2; Mic 7:19).

Along this line we should briefly mention the concept of *calling* (*vocatio*), which is part of the classic *ordo salutis*. Calling is the means by which we are brought out of the sphere of sin and meaninglessness so that we may, via repentance or conversion, share in God's salvation. To that end God sends along people who show us our real situation and how things could be different. This is his way of ensuring that things will indeed change. The concept of being called implies that language and communication play a major role in our relationship with God. Thus, if we want to comprehend how someone turns around so as to share in God's salvation, we have no need of metaphysical constructions, such as grace being "pumped" into us, or our being "infused" with an ability to believe. In biblical idiom we read that God calls things that do not exist as if they already do (Rom 4:17), which he accomplishes through his word (Gen 1:1; see also Luke 7:7b). God speaks to us, which makes it happen.

With regard to *vocatio*, a distinction is often made between an external and an internal calling, sometimes creating the impression that the latter is the genuine article, while the former is little more than a superficial maneuver. Those who follow along with Canons of Dort III/IV.8 ("Nevertheless, all who are called through the gospel are called earnestly") may use such a distinction to underline that God's calling is directed to our inner life, but they should not take this point too far. Scholasticism, both Roman Catholic and Protestant, made abundant use of such metaphysical concepts as *gratia infusa* (grace that has been "poured into" people), *habitus fidei* (the ability to have faith), and so on, in order to understand how people come to repentance and conversion. Some confessional documents also come very close to using such expressions. Canons of Dort III/IV.11, for instance, speaks of the "new qualities" that "God fuses into the will"), and they reemerge very prominently with A. Kuyper. Even though the Bible does refer to the Spirit and his work in terms of "pouring out" (Acts 2:33; Rom 5:5), we must be careful how we use such terminology (see Berkouwer 1952, 81-82). We consider such terms inadequate because they risk making salvation into a thing, reduced further to something inside us. From a Reformed and a Catholic perspective, God's salvation is not a substance but a matter of a relationship. And relationships are not created by causality but through community. God uses people of flesh and blood—a guy in the pulpit, a book, a movie, or a chance meeting with someone at the airport. Being externally called and inwardly touched go together. In Mark 2:14 the calling of the tax collector Levi provides a striking example. His "sitting" in his tax office symbolizes how he is caught in the tangle of extortion and exploitation, of being hated and despised because of his occupation. Jesus, when he passes by, does only two things. He sees Levi (where others presumably turned their head), and he says, "Follow me." These words penetrate so deeply that they give Levi the power to withstand the pull of sin, get up, and become a different person.

A profitable reflection on the way language functions to mediate a faith relationship is found particularly in Vanhoozer, DD. Note his emphasis on the Bible as a "divine communicative action" (65-68, 176-81); that is, God uses human words as a means to involve people in his salvation. Here, the so-called speech-act theory (see esp. John Searle and W. P. Alston) of analytic philosophy is of more use than Aristotelian metaphysics. See also Horton, CF 569-70, and the seminal study of Wolterstorff (1995) referenced in chapter 5.

Strangely enough, concepts like repentance and conversion are known as "heavy" words, often thought to be suitable only in the more conservative segments of Christianity. Yet, it is important to recognize how hopeful these words can be, for they point to the possibility of change. Even if you have chosen the wrong path, the direction of your life is still undetermined. You are not doomed to continue indefinitely in the track of evil. You can escape; the Bible tells us that things can change. Those on the right road have the choice to give up; in contrast, so-called hopeless cases can develop into beautiful human beings. Our history does not determine our future; traumatic childhood experiences do not have to be decisive for what we can become. It is possible to break the chain of intergenerational evil. Nobody has to accept the idea that what others have taught us or done to us will forever determine our life. When we read, in this context, the impressive chapter 16 of Ezekiel alongside Jesus's parable of the two sons (Matt. 21:28–32), which almost seems a midrash on that chapter, we are immersed in the inner world of the Bible, which in this regard differs sharply from Israel's *Umwelt* and Greek philosophy, with its tendency toward determinism and fatalism. Paganism is mainly interested in what remains unchanged and will always return (e.g., the seasons, the circle of fertility), while Jewish-Christian thought is particularly interested in contingency; that is, things are not totally fixed but can always change.

15.3. Justification

The New Testament highlights a crucial change, at the core of which lies *justification*. At first sight this seems a strange name for the process of salvation; terms like "forgiveness" and "atonement" are more accessible. Nonetheless, the reality that is expressed by the word "justification" is possibly even more fundamental. For justification refers not only to something being taken away from us or restored in us (as is the case with forgiveness and atonement), but it affirms that I am put back on my feet and have received a new identity. Being justified means that I may stand before God and my neighbor.

The theme of justification is found in the entire Bible, but especially Paul discusses its issues in theological terms. The Old Testament often mentions the innocent person who is justified (meaning that that one has received justice and is acquitted) or begs to be justified. We see this sense, for instance, in the so-called psalms of innocence (Pss 7, 17, 18, 26, and 44), where the writers plead their case with an appeal to God's justice. That is, *there is something like the justification of a righteous person.*

Although "there is none that does good" (Ps 14:3; Rom 3:12), it does not negate the fact that in some situations we may plead our innocence, hoping that God will judge in our favor. The universality of sin does not make all cats gray. When we have acted as we should in a particular situation but are treated unjustly, we may expect to find God on our side. We remember that Jesus himself (as the Righteous One without comparison, 1 John 2:1) was "vindicated" in the Spirit (1 Tim 3:16) in his resurrection from the grave.

However, the main reason why justification became a fundamental theological concept stems from the opposite possibility, namely, that someone not righteous is nevertheless treated by God as if he or she were. For Paul, justification is not something that happens to people who are just but to those who deserve judgment. With a paradoxical statement that has become famous, Paul ventures to speak of the "ungodly" who are justified (Rom 4:5). People who, when confronted with God, see that their case is hopeless because of the evil they have done are nevertheless not only acquitted but are even deemed to be righteous. This is possible, so Paul explains, because of redemption through the Messiah (Rom 3:24), who "was put to death for our trespasses and raised for our justification" (Rom 4:25). Even outside the epistles where he speaks most emphatically about justification—Romans and Galatians—Paul makes the same connection: "For our sake he made him [Jesus] to be sin who knew no sin, so that in him we might become the righteousness of God" (2 Cor 5:21). Some kind of exchange occurs: Jesus takes our sins upon himself, and we get his righteousness instead.

Paul's argument appeals to Old Testament texts about forgiveness (e.g., to Ps 32; Rom 4:6–8). These texts received a new meaning and reality in the ministry of Jesus, but Paul uses them for intense reflection on the meaning of Jesus's self-sacrifice in his death and resurrection. He sees how these acts benefit anyone who shares in the divine forgiveness of sin; Christ's death and resurrection form the real secret behind the event of justification. Because Christ sacrificed his life, God's righteousness can take the place of our guilt. If it were not so, it would be unthinkable for God to acquit a guilty person, for "shall not the Judge of all the earth do right?" (Gen 18:25).

We have noted in particular what Paul says in Rom 4, but we find this connection between Jesus's sacrifice and our forgiveness in the Gospels as well, for example, in the record of the institution of the Lord's Supper. See Matt 26:28 and other passages (about his body that was given to his followers and about his "blood

... which is poured out for many for the forgiveness of sins"). The doctrine of justification is not a Pauline invention but reaches back to the Christ-event. The offense, that people who deserve to be punished are acquitted and readmitted to the community, that people who have hardly lifted a finger now receive a major bonus, also becomes tangible in the Gospels. See, for example, Matt 20:11–16, Mark 2:16–17, Luke 18:9–14, and (the secondary, but ancient) John 8:1–11, just to mention a passage from each of the four gospels.

The way that we can share in God's righteousness because of Christ is, according to Rom 4, a matter of *attribution*. This is a key concept and brings up a difficult question. Does God actually give us a new righteousness that he then attributes to us, or does he attribute a righteousness that is not in any way found in us but is only from Christ? In other words, does God really *make* us righteous, or does he *declare* us righteous while, in reality, we are not? Church history is thick with debates on this question, especially after Martin Luther's crucial rediscovery of the Pauline doctrine of justification. People have repeatedly been inclined to interpret justification as a more or less observable change that occurs in a person's life. This is quite understandable, for then things fit together again: God declares a person righteous, provided that person is already a little on his or her way toward that state. However, this view undermines the shocking and liberating character of the doctrine of justification. God turns all moral logic on its head by fully accepting people who have nothing to offer him in exchange. That is, I do not have to accomplish anything—whatever it might be—to become acceptable to God, but I may believe that, in spite of my sins, I am immediately acceptable because of Jesus Christ. His perfect life and atoning death are reckoned as mine. I am merely a recipient of God's salvation, without having a part in its realization.

In technical terms we speak in this context of a forensic, imputative, declaratory, or synthetic justification, to differentiate it from an inherent, substantial, sanitary, or analytically understood justification.

The first two concepts are of particular importance. "Forensic" is derived from the Latin *forum*, or "marketplace." Traditionally, the marketplace was the venue for the court, where people were condemned or acquitted. The opinion of the judge was decisive, of course; my fate is determined, not by whether I really committed the murder, but by whether the judge will acquit me, whatever my accusers say. By analogy, we may say that my status before God is not determined by what is in me—my own sinfulness or piety—but only by God's judgment, which is

665

pronounced without any involvement on my part. If a judge acquits me, even though I actually did commit the murder, it is a miscarriage of justice; when God acquits me, though I have sinned and deserve to be punished, this is no error but results from Christ crediting his righteousness to my account. Strictly speaking, this is a dual imputation or attribution: the suffering and death of Christ come as a benefit to me in the form of forgiveness, while the perfect life that Jesus lived is attributed to me as righteousness. Something is taken away, but because the net result of that transaction would still be nil, something else is added. The seed of this twofold approach is found in the Heidelberg Catechism, Q/A 60; it was further developed in Reformed Scholasticism in terms of passive and active obedience. The former (*obedientia passiva*) was connected with Christ's suffering and death; the latter (*obedientia activa*), with his life. However, the attribution of Jesus's active obedience has been controversial in the tradition. In the seventeenth century the so-called neonomians ("believers in the new law") in England and in New England argued that God forgives our sins on the basis of Christ's sacrifice but accepts our own weak, yet persistent, obedience as a fulfillment of his law (see Allen, RT 82, 186). The New Testament does not provide us with any clear statements on this point, but the idea of a twofold attribution does appear to do justice to the Pauline texts about attribution, especially Rom 4:3-8, Phil 3:9, and 2 Cor 5:21.

Concerning the other terms mentioned above: I am righteous because God *declares* me so, not because I actually am. Therefore, my righteousness is not inherent in me as a kind of healing substance (*sanatio*, "making healthy") but is outside of me in Christ. In other words, my righteousness is not based on an *analysis* of my moral state, but—to use Kantian terms—on a synthetic judgment in which the predicate is not implied by the subject (as is the case in "the circle is round"); rather, it is applied from outside myself. See further the survey of McGrath, CT 385-87, and his important monograph (2005) on the history of the doctrine of justification in general.

As formulated, the doctrine of justification retains legal jargon while reversing the legal argumentation. All types of moralistic thinking emphasizing that everyone gets what he or she deserves are dissolved. The traditional patterns of reward and punishment do not have the final word but begin to shift and crack under the weight of God's passion. At the same time, it makes it difficult for us to understand its strictly forensic form. We are attached to the principle of fairness. When push comes to shove, we do not believe in grace as a free gift. Even Augustine—who keenly saw that for Paul justification does not happen because of our good works but rather precedes them—explains justification as a "sanitary" process: "What else could 'being justified' mean than 'being made upright'?" (*On the Spirit and the Letter* 45; NPNF¹ 5:362). In this way, quite subtly, there is something in us that corresponds to the divine acquittal. Medieval thinking about justification became much less subtle. In part this change happened because the Latin word *iustificatio* (lit. "making righteous") served as the common translation for Paul's word *dikaiōsis* ("putting into a right relationship"). The influence of the Roman (and, behind that, the Aristotelian) concept of justice proved strong as well. It was entirely distributive in nature; righteousness is distributed based on what a person deserves. The "godly" are rewarded, while the "ungodly" are punished.

In his fascinating personal development, Martin Luther made a radical break with this type of thinking. Having been educated in the ambit of Augustine and the Middle Ages, he step by step explored the way back to a forensic understanding of Paul's concept of justification. In the process he made the discovery of his life, which he would never give up and wanted to protect at all costs. When the first volume of his *Collected Latin Works* appeared, near the end of his life (1545), Luther wrote the following famous autobiographical reflection:

> I had certainly been seized with a wondrous eagerness to understand Paul in the Epistle to the Romans, but hitherto I had been held up—not by a "lack of heat in my heart's blood," but by one word only, in chapter 1: "The righteousness of God is revealed." For I hated this word "righteousness of God," which by the customary use of all the doctors I had been taught to understand philosophically as what they call the *formal* or *active righteousness* whereby God is just and punishes unjust sinners. For my case was this: however irreproachable my life as a monk, I felt myself in the presence of God to be a sinner with a most unquiet conscience, nor could I believe him to be appeased by the satisfaction I could offer. I did not love—nay, I hated—this just God who punishes sinners, and if not with silent blasphemy, at least with huge murmuring. I was indignant against God . . . yet I knocked importunely at Paul in this place, with a parched and burning desire to know what he could mean. At last, as I meditated day and night, God showed mercy and I turned my attention to the connection of the words, namely—"The righteousness of God is revealed, as it is written: the righteous shall live by faith"—and there I began to understand that

667

the righteousness of God is the righteousness in which a just man lives by the gift of God, in other words by faith, and that what Paul means is this: the righteousness of God, revealed in the Gospel, is *passive*, in other words that by which the merciful God justifies us through faith, as it is written, "The righteous shall live by faith." At this I felt myself straightway born afresh and to have entered through the open gates into paradise itself. There and then the whole face of scripture was changed. . . . And now, in the same degree as I had formerly hated the word "righteousness of God," even so did I begin to love and extol it as the sweetest word of all. Thus was this place in St. Paul to me the very gate of paradise. (WA 54:185-86)

Clearly, Luther's doctrine of justification was born from an exegetical discovery, namely, when Romans speaks of God's righteousness, it is not a distributive, punishing righteousness, but one that is given to us and enables us to stand before him without fear. This crucial insight stands at the center of Luther's entire Reformation theology. It enables us to understand all the so-called *sola*s of the Reformation as well: it is just because of faith (*sola fide*) and not our worthy conduct that we can stand before God. It is it only through grace (*sola gratia*) and not our good works, for justification is, as Paul affirms, totally free, without anything we can do (Rom 3:24). It is possible only through Christ (*solo Christo*), for his "strange" righteousness is attributed to us. Luther even approaches *sola Scriptura* (the Bible only) through the doctrine of justification, as he regards writings that do not reflect this doctrine, like the Epistle of James, as hardly belonging to the canon.

Luther did not regard Christian dogmatics as a series of topics to be dealt with one by one, as (following an old and proven method) we do in this book. He saw it instead as a circle with justification by faith at its center. From this point lines are drawn to the different themes, such as the doctrine of Scripture or anthropology. All these themes, however, must always be studied strictly from the perspective of justification. This approach to the content of the Christian teachings does not necessarily have consequences for the format of its presentation.

This is seen in the so-called loci method, which we use in this book and which was, remarkably enough, developed by Luther's colleague Melanchthon (see his *Loci communes* [1521]).

The main point is that, while in our own eyes we remain sinners, God views us as righteous. Luther does not deny that believers do indeed

668

grow in righteousness, but their status before God does not depend on their growth. It should not cause us any anxiety that sin continues to thwart us; rather, it should stimulate us even more to seek our salvation in Christ and not in our own moral progression, which will, after all, remain limited in scope. In that sense the believer is *simul iustus et peccator*, "at the same time righteous and beset by sin." Believers are righteous because of the promise of acquittal that they accept in faith, even though they remain a sinner. Only in this way can believers be assured of their salvation; they do not have to worry their whole life long whether they have reached the required level of righteousness. God's gracious acceptance because of Christ is unconditional!

The other Reformers and their followers eagerly accepted these new insights, but Roman Catholic theologians had grave objections. The Council of Trent (at its sixth session, in 1547) officially declared that it would stay with the traditional Catholic view, that justification is a process of our gradual renewal after the example of Christ. Admittedly, the process begins with a transition to a state of grace and must absolutely not be detached from it. But Rome feared that Luther's proposal would produce lazy, easygoing Christians who no longer tried to do good, since their status was already assured (the kind of suggestion that, remarkably enough, Paul also encountered; Rom 6:1). Luther, and Calvin too, replied that, as soon as a person is justified through faith, he or she will try to do what is good as a matter of course. In this connection Calvin (*Inst.* 3.11.1) spoke of a twofold grace (*duplex gratia*): we are justified by Christ and sanctified by the Spirit. To further clarify that "the faith by which alone, through the mercy of God, we obtain free justification, is not destitute of good works," he even let his treatment of sanctification—which he referred to as new birth (*regeneratio*)—precede that of justification. But as for justification, it happens by faith alone and not by performing good works as well. It is totally forensic in nature. Rome condemned this approach, denying that we are justified "by faith alone." Even though faith, indeed, constitutes the root of our justification (i.e., of our renewal), our good works must play a role. In sum, the notion of forensic justification became the issue that definitively divided Protestants and Roman Catholics.

In the meantime, the forensic character of justification was even more emphatically stressed by Philipp Melanchthon, Luther's disciple, friend, and successor as leader of the Reformation in Wittenberg. Even though it would be incorrect to distinguish his view of justification from that of Luther, it must be acknowledged that Luther saw justification

669

primarily as something that takes place in the context of the believer's communion with Christ, while Melanchthon defended a more extrinsic variant, that is, outside of the believer. In response, the more mystically inclined Lutheran Andreas Osiander (1498-1552) began to promote the idea that justification results from Christ's dwelling in the heart of the believer, who had to demonstrate this act of God as a reality before he or she could claim it personally. In this subtle manner the pressure to do good works, which had so troubled Luther, was reintroduced and the free character of justification was endangered. Calvin therefore attacked Osiander's views at length in the last edition of his *Institutes*—probably also because of Lutheran suspicions that, with his attention to a *duplex gratia* and emphasis on sanctification, Calvin actually was quite close to Osiander. Berkhof (CF 439-42) notes in this connection that living as a sinner while holding to the attribution of salvation only on the basis of faith is usually hard to sustain for long. Nonetheless, Paul's radical thoughts have reemerged time and again in history as "eruptions" of short duration: first with Augustine, then with Luther, then in the eighteenth century with John Wesley (1703-91, the father of Methodism), in the nineteenth century with H. F. Kohlbrugge (whose views were later dogmatically elaborated by his son-in-law E. Böhl, 1836-1903), and in the twentieth century with Barth, who ever after his *Römerbrief* (Letter to the Romans) would cling to his view of the centrality of the imputative aspect of justification.

15.4. The Nature and Role of Faith in Connection with Justification

If justification takes place outside of us, as in a courtroom where we are acquitted (perhaps even in absentia), how does it enter into our experience? How does it become part of us? How can we begin to actually live on the basis of the liberation it promises? The answer, which Luther found in Paul, is *by faith*. The motto *sola fide* may not literally occur in Paul's writings (and could therefore be rejected by Trent); it is nonetheless an intrinsic part of the Reformers' doctrine of justification. For them, however, "faith" did not have today's generic meaning of "religion" (as in, Are you religious?). It involved something much more specific, namely, submitting ourselves in complete trust to God and Christ (note the dual emphasis in John 14:1). This faith does not first of all entail statements about our various beliefs (the so-called *fides quae creditur*, the "faith that is believed") but the very act of faith—the *fides qua creditur*, the "faith that enables us to believe." Classic Protestant dogmatics distinguished three elements in this act: knowledge (*notitia*), assent (*assensus*), and trust (*fiducia*; e.g., see Heppe, RD, chap. 20). The first element was emphatically contrasted with the Roman Catholic teaching of *fides implicita* (implicit faith), according to which we need only to believe what the church believes, without necessarily knowing the object of that faith ourselves (Aquinas, STh II-II.1.7). For Protestants, however, faith requires, first, a knowledge of God as he encounters us in the Bible—hence the Protestant emphasis on catechesis. Assent proceeds forthwith: the affirmation that what God says is true, and, even more intimately, that we place our existential trust in it.

Luther liked to speak about this trust in graphic terms, like "grasping" Christ. Calvin described faith in a famous dictum as "a firm and sure knowledge of the divine favor toward us, founded on the truth of a free promise in Christ, and revealed to our minds, and sealed on our hearts, by the Holy Spirit" (*Inst.* 3.2.7). This wording seems to place a heavy emphasis on the aspect of knowledge, but taking the last few words seriously, and also taking into account what comes earlier in this paragraph in the *Institutes*, we see how this knowledge is completely infused with trust. The message changes somewhat when the Heidelberg Catechism says that genuine faith is not only "a sure knowledge" but also "a firm confidence" (21). This understanding in itself gives no cause for worry, but things became more dubious when, over time, the distance between the objective element of knowledge and the subjective element of trust grew ever wider. The problem lay not so much on the side of knowledge but rather with the element of trust. A *fides historica* (historical faith) is not automatically a *fides salvifica* (saving faith), pious folk worried; the latter requires a certain inner disposition. And this distinction easily led to a situation where spiritual introspection took command, instead of looking for our salvation outside ourselves as Luther had insisted. Thus the uncertainty that always tormented Catholics over whether they had done enough good works returned through the backdoor—do I have the right heart?

The Reformers had wanted to dispel this uncertainty via the insight that justification comes by accepting God's message of salvation through faith. The "through" in "through faith" (*dia* in Paul's Greek) must emphatically be understood in an instrumental and not a causal sense. Faith is not the cause of justification—the only cause is God's gracious intervention in Christ—but it is the means by which it is received. Of course, faith in the message of God's acquittal is essential; without such faith there is no justification. But it is not some kind of prerequisite that we must first fulfill, something we must first do. Faith is like the empty hand the beggar spontaneously extends when someone approaches him with a coin. The needy one has to extend a hand, but this is no big achievement, nothing to brag about. It is, in fact, a metaphor for our inability to accomplish anything ourselves and for simply committing ourselves to God in trust that he is someone who is true to his word. Knowing that we cannot ourselves ensure a right relationship with God, we simply get it handed to us on a silver platter by entrusting ourselves to God with all we are and have. This indeed is the kind of faith that the New Testament presents as essential, and to which the church calls and invites us.

For the nature and importance of Paul's references to Abraham's trust in God, see Gen 15:6 (Rom 4:3–5; Gal 3:6). There are also many stories in the Gospels that give the nature and results of faith a central place, particularly those of Jesus's encounters with others. Such narrative language is at least as evocative as Paul's conceptual approach. James presents essentially the same view of faith, even though he stresses the flip side, the danger that faith will be reduced to a mere intellectual acceptance of truths. Where Paul says that faith "is working through love" (Gal 5:6), James maintains that without works, faith is dead (Jas 2:17).

It is artificial to try to localize faith in one specific human faculty or ability, whether the intellect (as often in the Middle Ages, but also during the Enlightenment), conscience (Kant), or feeling (Schleiermacher). Faith involves our whole being. As the Reformers noticed, the Bible localizes faith in the *heart*, so we may justly say that the Reformation personalized the relationship with God. More recent Roman Catholic theology has also adopted this view (see NK, 340).

In post-Reformation Protestantism, however, the liberating character of justification was at risk of being lost in abstract discussions about the nature of ("true") faith and its exact relationship to the event of justification. The Heidelberg Catechism, Lord's Day 23, still defines this relationship in all its purity, but seventeenth-century Scholasticism was not satisfied. Some began to suggest that faith was some sort of act or process within us, with justification appended as a kind of bonus, so that it was no longer the "ungodly" person who was justified but the believer. Thus the *sola gratia* could easily be ignored. Others, fearing that this approach would place too much emphasis on the human act of faith, began to speak by contrast of a "justification from eternity," namely, that justification is already a fact but surfaces only at the moment when a person actually becomes a believer. This view marginalizes the human faith response, and with it the *sola fide*. The first tendency was found in W. à Brakel, while the second view was adopted by A. Comrie and later also by Kuyper. Bavinck (RD 4:209–23) tried to escape this dilemma by closely relating the objective and the subjective moments in justification ("He himself comes to us in the gospel with the universal offer of grace and gives to every human the right to accept the forgiveness of sins with a believing heart," 221). Berkouwer (1954, 171) continued in the same vein by referring to a "correlation" between faith and justification. Faith and justification had thus once again become ontological substances rather than relational concepts, which proved particularly confusing. The possibility and need to make the causal chain totally clear disappear when the encounter with God becomes the point of departure. We may compare this understanding with romantic love: the sparks fly, and something so special happens that it proves impossible to say where exactly it began and what caused it. But you don't care, for as lovers, you know you have found each other, and you can only open yourselves to each other. Likewise, faith is the road along which God's grace is received. For these various issues, see also Berkhof, CF 447–49.

15.5. A New Relevance

But is any of this history still relevant for faith and theology today? For quite some time it seemed that the doctrine of justification had become obsolete. Even Lutherans in the twentieth century could find it difficult to say why it mattered. In his arresting book *The Courage to Be* (1954), Paul Tillich tried to translate it into the psychological terms of our coming to a basic sense of acceptance, but too many important theological notions (like Christ's substitutionary role) fell by the wayside. The fourth assembly of the Lutheran World Federation, held at Helsinki in 1963, made a concerted attempt to render the doctrine of justification in a way plausible and convincing to contemporary ears. Tellingly, the delegates did not succeed and concluded that the doctrine of justification, however crucial it might have been in the past, simply no longer appealed to the modern person. Ten years later Berkhof remarked, "At the time that we are writing this book, justification no longer commands this central interest in theology (and to a large extent not in preaching either) but is again pushed to the periphery by other accents, particularly the emphasis on sanctification" (CF 442).

But recently the doctrine has made a remarkable comeback, not least among contemporary cosmopolitans. Redeemer Presbyterian church, led by Tim Keller (b. 1950), has grown rapidly in New York City in the heart of Manhattan by placing a new emphasis on justification—in this case reinterpreted in terms of finding one's true identity in Christ (e.g., see Keller 2008, 190-96, 244-47). But it has also revived unexpectedly within the theological guild, to which we here restrict ourselves. Since Berkhof wrote the remark quoted above, a flood of publications on the subject has appeared, putting justification—like the doctrines of the Trinity and pneumatology—once again at the center of attention. How is this turnabout to be explained? We suggest three reasons: because of ecumenical developments, biblical scholarship, and research in historical theology. We focus briefly on developments in each.

1. In the world of *ecumenism* a new era began with the significant doctoral thesis of Hans Küng (in 1957; see 2004) in which he compared the Reformers' doctrine of justification with the Roman Catholic position. Küng concluded that reading these with mutual good will would yield a high degree of consensus. The differences between Rome and the Reformation owed largely to the different use of various concepts; in addition, the two traditions each emphasize one pole of the process of renewal without, however, denying the other. This thesis led to a period of intense ecumenical dialogue between Roman Catholic and Lutheran theologians, resulting in a *Joint Declaration* on the subject in 1997. Eventually, with a few supplementary documents, this Declaration was officially signed at a solemn meeting in Augsburg by representatives of the Roman Catholic Church and the Lutheran World Federation (see Joint Declaration 2000). This achievement occurred after long hesitation on the Catholic side and despite fierce criticism from many, especially German Lutheran theologians (among them Eberhard Jüngel). Both churches had gone as far as they could to do optimum justice to the views of the other. In 2006 the Methodists also added their signature.

The Declaration consists of forty-four articles. It proceeds under a forensic understanding of justification—nowadays we find a considerable consensus among biblical scholars that the relevant Pauline passages must indeed be interpreted in that sense—but closely linked to a recognition of the sinner's actual renewal. A core statement in the document reads:

> Together we confess: By grace alone, in faith in Christ's saving work and not because of any merit on our part, we are accepted by God and receive the Holy Spirit, who renews our hearts while equipping and calling us to good works. (§15; Joint Declaration 2000, 580).

Faith is here understood as a gift from God (art. 16). We cannot in our own strength earn justification or reach salvation; it comes by faith alone (art. 19). Protestants can only affirm these statements. Lutheran critics worried about losing the so-called criteriological function of the doctrine in their tradition. Although that expression was not literally coined by Luther, he regarded the doctrine of justification "as the article [of faith] that makes or breaks the church" (*articulus stantis et cadentis ecclesiae*). All Christian teaching must be developed on this basis. Along that line, the Declaration refers to the doctrine of justification as "an indispensable criterion" needed to keep the church oriented to Christ, but it adds that Catholics want to emphasize other criteria as well (art. 18). This point, and the Declaration's speaking of "a" rather than of "the" criterion, created resistance on the part of some Lutherans. From a Reformed perspective, however, we can only agree: Calvin himself wanted to avoid overemphasizing the doctrine of justification by speaking of a dual grace: justification in Christ *and* true renewal of life through the Spirit. In accordance with our Trinitarian approach in this book, we consider this the most mature and balanced way of dealing with the issue.

The Declaration acknowledges a lack of agreement on some points. More important, the parties reached a consensus on the "fundamental truths" of justification and agreed that the remaining differences would no longer be reason for mutual condemnations of each other's teachings (§5). And the dialogue continues. The Declaration, therefore, is not the end of the road but an undeniable milestone. It succeeded in creating a new enthusiasm for a classic doctrine whose importance seemed to have long and largely disappeared from the collective memory of Protestants and Catholics alike. The gap between the different interpretations proved to be spanned, at least in part, by a thorough and careful return to the sources.

For discussions about and after the Declaration, see, for example, Jüngel 2001, Lane 2002, and Rusch 2003; to this short list others could easily be added. We have the impression that the Roman Catholics took the biggest step—in part, no doubt, because it had become clear that Paul's concept of justification indeed had to be understood forensically and that any human part in the realization of salvation had to be rejected. However, radical Lutherans like Jüngel and O. Bayer go very far (even further than Luther himself) in insisting that justification must be seen as the absolute criterion for all theological statements (Beilby and Eddy 2011, 50–51).

2. Likewise *biblical scholarship*, especially in New Testament studies, took a remarkable turn on the subject of justification. The trend orig-

inated in the last quarter of the twentieth century and is now usually referred to as the New Perspective on Paul (NPP). The movement might be traceable to Albert Schweitzer (1875-1965), but most scholars date it to E.P. Sanders's study *Paul and Palestinian Judaism* (1977). In this book Sanders (b. 1937) used emerging scholarly insights (stimulated by the famous Qumran discoveries, the Dead Sea Scrolls) into the character of Judaism around the time that Christianity was born. If the traditional Reformation perspective on Paul suggested, in reaction to late medieval abuses, that Judaism was a "religion of law," Sanders argued that the relevant religious literature from the time (ca. 200 BCE—ca. 200 CE) very clearly put God's grace first. This grace was the core of the covenant, and it was within the context of the covenant that Israel was supposed to honor certain laws and regulations—not as a way to *become* right with God but to *remain in communion* with him. Sanders speaks in this connection of a covenantal nomism: people must certainly obey God's commandments (hence "'nomism," from Gk. *nomos*, "law") but in response to God's covenant, not as a way to earn salvation. And if a person were to fail to in this effort, God in his righteousness—that is, in his faithfulness to the covenant—had graciously provided various atonement rituals for making amends.

But why would Paul so fiercely criticize the Judaism of his day if it were indeed a religion of grace? Because Paul believed, Sanders answered, that with the beginning of the messianic era, the road of adoption into God's covenant now ran through faith in Jesus as the Christ. This enormously broadened the bounds of the covenant; from now on salvation included not just Jews but also gentiles. However, this did not mean that Paul had a structurally different concept of how salvation was realized. So when Paul spoke, for instance, about "the righteousness of God" (Rom 1:17), he was referring to God's covenant faithfulness and not, as Luther thought, to a righteousness that allows someone to stand before God. Sanders's new perspective on Paul was soon picked up and developed by other New Testament scholars, particularly James D. G. Dunn (b. 1939) and N. T. Wright (b. 1948), who, together with Sanders, constitute the "big three" of recent Pauline research. Dunn concentrated especially on the formula "works of the law" (Rom 3:20, 27-28; Gal 2:16; 3:2, etc.), arguing that Paul was not thereby pointing to Jewish attempts to earn their own salvation; he could hardly have encountered such. Rather, Paul was faulting ethnic-Jewish *identity markers*—the Sabbath, circumcision, and dietary laws—that were used to keep gentiles away from God's covenant, or at the very least, to make them obligatory for all (e.g., Dunn

1983). Wright (1978, 2009) likewise thinks that Paul identifies Israel's crucial sin to be its exclusive claim on God's election, its attempt to create a direct link between *grace* and *race* (ethnicity). Against that, Wright argues, Paul stressed that justification comes through faith and thus applies to all those who share in this faith.

In more recent publications Dunn and Wright maintain that they never intended to deny the classic Reformation understanding of Paul's doctrine of justification but wanted to complement and correct it with these new accents. Nonetheless, we should not underestimate the consequences of the NPP for the nature and status of this doctrine. For in this view justification no longer functions primarily as the solution for a universal human dilemma (how, as a sinner, may I share in God's grace?); it refers to a specific social problem that played out then and there—people claiming an exclusive status on the basis of ethnic superiority. Therefore, what Paul teaches about justification should not be seen as the heart of his theology but as a concrete reaction to the refusal to take seriously the eschatological character of the salvation that has appeared in Jesus Christ. Since God has, in the resurrection of Christ, conclusively opened the way to salvation for Jews and non-Jews alike, a social exclusion of the gentiles is no longer possible. In this approach it is not primarily Rom 3 but Rom 5–8—chapters that deal with the consequences of justification for living a life in the service of righteousness—that constitute the heart of the epistle. Thus the doctrine of justification belongs not first of all to soteriology but to ecclesiology. It does not refer to the individual but to the social dimension of salvation. It answers the question, who belongs to the people of God?

This new approach to Pauline scholarship has aroused considerable criticism, along with approval. Not all New Testament scholars were convinced, let alone everyone else interested in this topic. First, was not Judaism during the Second Temple period more pluriform than Sanders would acknowledge? Were there no currents that we could consider legalistic? Are there not important similarities between the nomism (whether or not connected with the covenant) of ancient Judaism and the situation Luther protested against in his time? And should we not acknowledge that Paul's doctrine of justification does indeed also refer to individuals sharing in God's salvation (a point that, by the way, Dunn concedes)? In this connection Paul argues that those who want to keep the law will have to do so *perfectly* (Gal 3:10). That makes it impossible for us to deal with our mistakes by obeying the stipulations of the covenant (good works, atonement rituals, etc.). Our only avenue to salvation, therefore, is faith in Christ. In brief, is not Paul's soteriology structurally different from that of his Jewish contemporaries? If so, is not the entire NPP perhaps just another attempt to obfuscate his offensive antimoralistic doctrine of justification (as McGrath 2005, 418-20)?

Concise surveys of the NPP are found in the contribution of Dawn DeVries to Webster et al., OHST (199-201), and especially in Beilby and Eddy 2011, 53-82 (see here also for various other publications, including those by critics, 63-67). Piper 2007 offers a valuable example of criticism on the content of NPP. Below we follow Allen, RT 79-80, in our evaluation.

We contend that the truth lies in the middle. It is certainly true that the traditional image of ancient Judaism as purely legalistic is wrong. At the very least it must be treated with much more nuance, all the more so, given the ready connection between Luther's extremely negative picture of that religion and his intense anti-Semitism. Moreover, recent scholarship has shed new light on the real social dimension in Paul's doctrine of justification. Those who are convinced that our salvation originates completely from the outside (*extra nos*) and is therefore not linked to any moral or religious facet in us can no longer see the latter as precondition for being accepted into the community of faith. The doctrine of justification helps us to think inclusively and not exclusively—precisely what Paul's judaizing contemporaries were not prepared to do, and what presented a challenge even to Paul himself (Gal 2:11-14). However, all such factors entail qualifications or complements to the Reformers' doctrine of justification, not a correction or rejection of its basic principles. In the Pauline epistles justification by faith *is* closely connected with his struggle against Jewish ethnocentrism, and by extension with the relationship between Jews and gentiles in the Christian community. But Paul did not regard ethnocentrism as an isolated evil; it was a concrete form of the general human inclination to boast about one's own abilities and achievements instead of relying exclusively on the work of Christ. For that reason, the doctrine of justification has a much broader meaning, which we can properly appreciate if we do not only see it in the context of Jewish-Christian relationships.

3. New light on the doctrine of justification has also emerged in *historical theology* by way of the so-called new Finnish interpretation of Luther. Inspired by a long-running dialogue between Finnish Lutherans and representatives of Russian Orthodoxy, the leader of this school, Tuomo Mannermaa (b. 1937), began reading Luther anew. In the process he dis-

covered that Luther's forensic doctrine of justification is closely related to the idea of the mystical union of the believer with God in Christ. Even though our justification happens outside of us in the acquitting judgment of God, when this justification is attributed to us, so is Christ. He comes to dwell in our heart, carrying his righteousness along. Our faith unites us with Christ, who then renews our life from within. Forensic justification, therefore, is also *effective* justification; it—or rather, Christ in us—applies its various aspects to the life of the believer (see Mannermaa 2005).

The Finnish school suggests that this accent in Luther's oeuvre was lost in the later development of Lutheran orthodoxy, to be replaced by a sharp distinction between justification and sanctification that Luther himself never intended. If asked how this came about, the Finnish scholars often blame Melanchthon, who, much more than Luther, taught an exclusively forensic justification, with major effect on later doctrinal developments. If we focus on Luther instead, so the Finnish school insists, we will see an important link between the ontological categories in which Luther embedded his doctrine of justification and Eastern Orthodox concepts about human renewal as *theōsis*, often translated "deification." On this understanding, we are not united with God's unknowable being; rather, we share in the divine energies or properties, including God's righteousness. This understanding also helps bridge the rift with the Roman Catholic view of grace more readily, considering that Luther kept faith and works more closely together than had been traditionally thought.

According to classic Roman Catholic teachings, found already in Augustine and Aquinas, faith in itself is insufficient and needs to be complemented and perfected by love. To use the Latin jargon, the *fides informis* (faith without form, which is in fact the intellectual faith faulted in Jas 2:17) must get flesh on its bones via the human will so that it may become a *fides caritate formata* (faith shaped by love). Luther believed that this argument made our faith meritorious and therefore rejected this dichotomy. The faith that justifies is powerful enough in itself to ensure our renewal. According to the Finnish school, faith as understood by Luther is definitely "formed," though in the sense of being complemented and perfected, which results from the presence of Christ in the believer. See Mannermaa 2005, 26–30, and DeVries in Webster et al., OHST 202.

Finally, the Finns contend that Luther understood Paul much better than the devotees of the New Perspective at first suggested, for Luther did acknowledge that, for Paul, forensic and concrete justification were two sides of the same coin.

679

Prominent American Lutheran theologians, including Carl Braaten (b. 1929) and Robert Jenson (1998), accepted and promoted the Finnish interpretation of Luther. Others reacted critically. The ensuing discussion clarified the point that the ontological dimensions to which the Finnish scholars pointed in Luther's doctrine of justification were most evident in the younger Luther. Toward the end of his life Luther increasingly emphasized the forensic aspect of justification in a way not essentially different from Melanchthon. Critics also wondered whether the Finns' ecumenical interests were not the father of their historical findings. Was Luther's precious discovery being sacrificed on the ecumenical altar?

Though some major issues remain, we think this critique is too hasty. Justification must not be presented in such an extrinsic way that it becomes fully detached from our faith relationship with Christ and from the transforming influence that results from the work of the Spirit. To the extent that the Finnish school reminds us of this aspect, also in Luther's legacy, it is to be appreciated. But we need to remain alert and not allow justification to be seen as just "one of the many metaphors" in which the New Testament speaks of salvation, which would fail to do justice to its decisive significance, which is based on God's eschatological intervention in Christ. Justification—as the new, divinely initiated *creatio ex nihilo* (note the allusion to Ps 33:9 in Rom 4:17)—is not a theme we can quickly leave behind to move on to other (and more interesting) facets of salvation. It is the source from which everything else emerges and to which everything else must consistently be related. More organic metaphors, such as rebirth or growing in faith and sanctification, show us how God's righteous judgment enables us to adjust in a concrete and decisive way to the new orientation of life that we have been promised in that judgment.

15.6. Participation as a Bridge between Justification and Sanctification

In this section we discuss the process of renewal on the basis of justification. We will discover that it does not entail our being changed into something we are not yet, but into what we already are in Christ: righteous and pure before God (see Horton, CF 652–53). Earlier (e.g., in 12.3) we urged that, in our Trinitarian unfolding of the Christian faith, clear distinctions be maintained between the christological and the pneumatological perspectives. That same distinction now reappears in a modulated form. Justification carries the stamp of God's one-time, decisive, "eschatological" intervention in Jesus Christ. But salvation is realized in the life of individual believers in another way. It unfolds as a process and bears the particular stamp of the Spirit of God. Over the centuries this second form has been given various labels, depending on one's specific tradition. We saw that Roman Catholic theology employs *iustificatio* (justification) as an umbrella concept that includes the process of life-renewal. The Eastern tradition prefers to speak of *theōsis*, or deification—a term that nowadays also has an increasing appeal in the Western church (see Christensen and Wittung 2007). Lutherans like to speak of *renovatio*, and the Reformed of *santificatio*, while Methodists prefer *perfectio*.

Calvin came up with another proposal: *regeneratio*, or new birth (*Inst.* 3.3 title and 3.3.9; see also 3.11.1). Considering the pivotal role this concept would acquire later in his tradition, we will examine it in some detail. Calvin's definition of regeneration was very appropriate, since it kept the new birth closely connected with the Christian's everyday life. Unfortunately, the two were separated in later versions of a "born-again theology," in which the new birth not only came to be seen as a one-time experience but also nearly monopolized attention. For many "born-again" Christians in the United States, this term is usually taken as something positive, but in Europe, where particular groups of Christians chronically worry about their salvation, it has often brought a sense of dread and uncertainty: have I indeed been born again? In itself this is a valid question, as long as we do not seek to answer it by looking within. We do not find that mistake in Calvin's theology, with its deep reverence for God and profound sense of human sinfulness. For him, the new birth is the constant effect in our everyday life of God's gracious acquittal. Yet, it is understandable that Calvin's specific use of the concept of the new birth found few followers. The metaphor of a new birth—a unique, one-time event—is not suitable for portraying the more gradual process of renewal. For this reason, the tradition after Calvin used the concept in a different way, applying it more and more to the experience that gives a person the assurance of salvation.

The term "new birth" is less broadly anchored in the New Testament than is often supposed. In several verb conjugations, and with varying meanings, it is found in Matt 19:28 (which refers to a cosmic-eschatological event), in Titus 3:5 (in connection with baptism), and in 1 Pet 1:3 and 23 (roughly with the meaning of our word "reborn"). By far the best-known text is John 3:3, where Jesus, in a discussion with Nicodemus, insists that only those who have been born anew (or "from above") will see the kingdom of God. This is indeed a seminal statement, but it should not be detached from its context, which makes clear that this intended new birth results from the act of believing in Jesus as the Son of God, sent into this world to ensure its salvation (see 3:12, 15–18). Thus, we are not born again so that we may have faith; it happens *through* faith, and not by introspection but by looking outside of ourselves, to Christ. The place and meaning of the new birth coincide with what we discussed earlier under the heading of justification; here, the experiential aspect of this event is highlighted.

This accent on the new birth as a decisive experience is especially strong in John Wesley, the famous revival preacher and founder of Methodism. Even though he was a longtime believer and an Anglican missionary, he longed for an experience that would give him full assurance—which he at last received at a specific place and at a specific moment (Aldersgate, 1738). In *A Farther Appeal to Men of Reason and Religion* (1745), he writes: "Faith, in general, is a divine, supernatural *elenchos* [persuasion] of things not seen, not discoverable by our bodily senses, as being either past, future, or spiritual. Justifying faith implies, not only a divine *elenchos* that God was in Christ reconciling the world to himself, but a sure trust and confidence that Christ died for my sins, that he loved me and gave himself for me. And the moment the penitent sinner believes this, God pardons and absolves him. . . . This beginning of that vast, inward change is usually termed 'the new birth.'" The event of justification is here such an extraordinary experience that it is referred to as a new birth. This is a very significant change from the Reformation.

Along this line the Methodist tradition made a sharp distinction between formal religiosity and a religion of the heart. One of the characteristics of heart religion is looking back at this experience of justification, that is, the new birth. It forms the capstone of the first phase of the journey of faith. That journey was then to proceed via further inner experience: being filled by the Spirit or being baptized in the Spirit (see 12.5). The work of the Spirit was increasingly defined as a moment of being touched in a special way, of being filled or being sanctified. While Wesley still regarded the quest for perfect love as a lifelong process, later generations increasingly emphasized what a person had achieved on his or her way to perfection. This transition from a theology focused on the justification of the ungodly (as in Luther) to a "theology of regeneration" revolving around human experience can also be found in the Reformed tradition, for example, in the Canons of Dort III/IV (esp. 11–12).

We can readily pose some critical theological questions about this subjectivizing process. How does our own experience relate to the Bible as the revelation that has been given to us? Does our own experience become the pivot or even the top priority in our life of faith? And does not the strong separation between justification and sanctification lead us to see our justification as a specific biographical moment that we have left behind to further pursue our trajectory of perfection?

It is important to see that these tendencies resulted from too extrinsic a view of justification. This "outside of us" could be stressed to the point that justification seems little more than a business-like transaction: the merits of Christ were credited to the believer's account and his or her guilt was deducted without the person necessarily entering into any kind of relationship with Christ. Luther's passionate rejection of any contribution to our salvation from our side has left deep traces; yet, again, Luther was misunderstood so far as this further extrapolation is concerned. For the personal, even mystical, faith relationship with Christ is an essential aspect of our renewal—for Luther, as well as for the other Reformers.

For this reason, we link justification and sanctification together under the common category of *participation*, along the lines laid out in chapter 12. "Participation" forms, we might say, the ecoduct, the natural bridge, connecting the two aspects of our renewal—the forensic and the transformational. This participation is simply the biblical teaching that the Spirit unites believers with Christ, thereby enabling them to participate in communion with the triune God. This point represents a remarkable retrieval of classic Christian thinking, which for all kinds of reasons—for instance, the Enlightenment promotion of individualism—had disappeared from view. Its source is found in the Pauline notion of *koinōnia*—the fellowship of believers with Christ and with one another—and in the Johannine accent on remaining (Gk. *menein*) in Christ. A crucial text of Paul in this connection is 1 Cor 1:9: "God is faithful, by whom you were called into the fellowship of his Son, Jesus Christ our Lord." As to John, the parable of the vine and the branches is characteristic: "Abide in me, and I in you. As the branch cannot bear fruit by itself, unless it abides in the vine, neither can you, unless you abide in me" (John 15:4).

Paul uses the term *koinōnia* and the verb *koinōneō* (sharing in, participating in) in quite a distinctive way, compared with the everyday Greek of his time. He meant not a mere formal sharing but intimate fellowship (see Balz and Schneider, EDNT 2, s.v.). This nuance allows Paul to deploy the expression in various combinations with *syn* (together with) that usually have Christ as their object. Moreover, *koinōnia* is sometimes specifically related to the different phases of Christ's life and ministry, especially his suffering and death, resurrection and ascension (Rom 6:8; 8:17; Gal 2:20; Eph 2:6; Phil 3:10-11; Col 3:1; see also outside the Pauline writings 1 Pet 4:13; 5:1). Fellowship with Christ finds its most intimate form in the sacramental communion of baptism (Rom 6:4-5; Col 2:12) and Eucharist (1 Cor 10:16-17). The Spirit plays her own role in this communion with Christ (Phil 2:1; 2 Cor 13:13). In the final analysis this fellowship points to the communion with God (2 Pet 1:4). From the Johannine writings we can refer to the impressive so-called high priestly prayer: John 17, especially vv. 21-23, but also to the lesser known, yet very expressive, words of 1 John 1:3, in which *koinōnia* indicates the communion of believers with one another and with the Father and the Son.

This New Testament concept of participation must be clearly demarcated on two sides. First, it is more than a simple external meeting of two or more partners, as when people belong to the same club. Therefore, such Latin terms as *societas* and *consortium* proved to be inadequate to translate *koinōnia*. The more intimate word *communio* became the standard translation. The metaphor of adoption, which is also used in the New Testament, gets to the heart of the matter: when we participate in communion with Christ, the Spirit adopts us as brothers and sisters of Jesus and thereby as children of God. As a result, we can share in everything that Christ has and receives (Rom 8:14-17). Second, this communion does not imply an ontological unity, as Greek Platonic and Neoplatonic philosophy proposes. This fellowship respects the ontological differences between God and his creation. To be even more specific: Christ, the Spirit, and the Father each have their own personality within the divine communion. The New Testament concept of participation fully corresponds with the Trinitarian ontology as we unpacked it in chapter 3: the Spirit brings the believers into unity with Christ (*unio cum Christo*), and thereby into communion with the Father. This results in a communion of persons-in-relationship, not a monolithic unity that obliterates the ontological boundaries between God and humanity. In this relationally defined communion with the triune God, we find our true identity and reach our destiny.

The emphasis on participation has been recently revived in the Radical Orthodoxy movement around John Milbank and his supporters (see Milbank, Pickstock, and Ward 1999; see also Boersma 2011). This movement mounts a fierce resistance to modern individualism and its stress on autonomy in favor of a participation ontology that is traced back to Plato through Aquinas and Augustine. Humanity and its world do not exist in themselves but in relationship to a higher, divine transcendence. Admittedly, creaturely existence retains its own integrity here (and is, therefore, not absorbed in the divine), but the combination of Christian and Greek-philosophical categories provokes the question of whether this understanding is indeed tenable. In any case it seems that, with its openness to Platonic/Neoplatonic metaphysics, Radical Orthodoxy is less radically orthodox than it professes to be. It also has stimulated others, by reaction, to criticize any form of thinking in terms of participation (e.g., Wisse 2011). This response is unnecessary and indefensible from a New Testament point of view. Yet, it is important to make a careful distinction. Participation is a pneumatological and not an ontological category; it does not concern the essence of things but is produced by the Spirit. For Calvin's careful thinking on this point, see the recent studies of Billings (2007; see also 2011) and Canlis (2010), written independently of each other but overlapping in their conclusions; both develop observations also made by Kooi (2005, e.g., 41-49, 209-21). Burger 2008 provides a thorough and very balanced study of participation in the Bible and the tradition in relation to other soteriological moments.

The New Testament theme of participation was developed in the early church particularly by Irenaeus and Cyril of Alexandria. Remarkably enough, during the Reformation it received a new interpretative stimulus from Calvin, who was well read in both of these Fathers and whose soteriology showed Alexandrian characteristics: it is through communion with Christ that we are connected with the source of divine life. In a discussion with Joachim Westphal (1510-74), Calvin said about the Lord's Supper: "For I teach that there is no term that better explains how the Body of Christ is given to us than the term fellowship [*koinōnia*], which implies that we become one with him, and being implanted in him, enjoy real life. It is clear and certain that this does not happen in any natural way but through the hidden workings of the Spirit" (CO 9:192).

Recent research has shown the extent to which various elements in Calvin's theology come together under the theme of participation in Chirst, also the mystical bond (*unio mystica*, *Inst.* 3.11.10) with Christ, even though he does not treat it as a separate locus. The dual aspect of grace that Calvin distinguishes finds its *one* ground in the notion of communion with Christ. Likewise, the *unio*-concept is closely related to Calvin's Christology, in which Christ's human nature receives special attention; we want to be united with Christ's human nature, which is also *our* nature. Even though such communion thus is not a form of deification, Calvin shows a significant concurrence with the Eastern idea of *theōsis* in the sense that we participate in the "energies" of God, his emanating glory and very life.

McCormack (2008) denies that a bridge can be made from Calvin's notion of union with Christ and the Eastern Orthodox concept of deification. We may wonder, however, whether he sufficiently took into account that the latter (at least in the form that predated the Eastern theologian Gregory of Palamas, 1296-1359) did not mean fusion between God and humanity. As Athanasius stated, "God is in his essence outside of all things, but is inside everything through his own power" (*De incarnatione Verbi* 17). Note as well that the energies by which we share in the divine life come to us from the Father, in the Son, and through the Spirit. Therefore, in Reformed theology, being "deified" comes very close to what is referred to as glorification (see Heppe, RD, chap. 28). It is not without reason that the story of Christ's glorification—or transfiguration—on the mountain (Matt 17:1-9) plays such a major role in Eastern spirituality. For a balanced description of the differences and agreements between the two traditions on this issue, see Horton, CF 689ff.: "There are nevertheless surprising parallels between the Reformed understanding of glorification and *theōsis* that . . . should be rediscovered for the enrichment of our Christian hope" (692). For the central place of the *unio mystica* in Calvin, see Vlastuin 2014, 39-43 and the literature there referenced.

Determining more precisely the connection between participation and the dual grace of justification requires that we not think in terms of what comes first and what comes next. The faith that lays hold on the righteousness of Christ unites the believer with Christ himself. Being in communion with Christ, therefore, corresponds with justification through faith. But it also leads immediately to an actual renewal of life that becomes increasingly visible. "Immediately" means that the sequence of justification and sanctification (or participation and transformation) cannot simply be reversed, with sanctification being able to be labeled "first grace." Concrete renewal of life is induced by the gift of forgiveness and acquittal and proceeds, as it were, as our spontaneous reaction. Calvin and the Heidelberg Catechism define this reaction as gratitude. This is a great idea, for it keeps us from getting stuck back in a climate of legalism (as if we, from our side, should contribute to our salvation). At the same time, it creates the space to give real substance to the transformation we experience.

15.7. Transformation as the Concrete Renewal of Life

We need to say more about this transformation, which in classic theology is usually called sanctification. We differ from this tradition on terminology but not as to content. In fact, by using "transformation," we hope to inject the concept with new meaning.

We have two interconnected reasons for the word change. In the first place, "sanctification" has numerous unintended associations (and not only for Christians); it can suggest individualistic attempts at self-improvement, confirming the common prejudice that Christians see themselves as holier than others. It is true that terms like "holy," "being holy," and "becoming holy" have strong biblical credentials, but the verb from which they are derived usually means something else in the Bible than what we intuitively have in mind. It most often refers to being set apart from others, inwardly or ritually, for God and his service (e.g., see Exod 19:6; Lev 19; Num 15:40; Deut 7:6; 28:9; Isa 62:12; Dan 7:21. 27; and in the New Testament, John 17:17, 19, probably Rom 6:22; 1 Pet 1:2; 2:9; 3:15). In addition, the Bible uses the substantive term "holy one" with a general meaning comparable to our term "believer" (e.g., as in Ps 34:10; Rom 1:7; 8:27; 2 Cor 1:1; Rev 5:8); and it may, as Kohlbrugge and his followers are keen to emphasize, correspond to a washing or cleansing of the righteous (1 Cor 6:11; 7:14, probably also 1:30).

Second, while the Bible—particularly in passages of exhortation like Rom 6:19, 1 Thess 4:3-4, and Heb 12:14)—does bring the moral component, to which sanctification is often reduced, under the heading of "holiness," this usage does not suffice to warrant the term as a dogmatic keyword. Not every concept affirmed in the Bible must be used in such a way. Language changes, and when, for whatever reason, a particular concept becomes outmoded or gives rise to misunderstandings, it may be good to look at the same topic through another lens. In fact, it belongs to the task of dogmatics to make such suggestions (see chap. 1).

In sum, we believe that the term "transformation" (esp. when used in close connection with "participation") comprises what Bible and tradition refer to as sanctification, but without the undesirable overtones just mentioned.

As we further reflect on the nature of this transformation, we must start at its source: our participation in Christ. In our justification we are delivered from any pressure to do things—from all efforts to free ourselves from the burden and melancholy of our existence. We relinquish the endless, tiring attempts to prove ourselves so as to deserve our true identity in submission to Christ (see Matt 11:28). Christ appreciated and still appreciates our value; we therefore embody that value, even if that does not correspond with how we feel. He was even prepared to become a corpse for us, as we read literally in Rev 1:18. For his love was a love without end (John 3:16).

Therefore, when we believe what is unbelievable—namely, that this love is also for us; indeed, that there is no one who loves us more deeply than Jesus Christ (Belgic Confession, art. 26)—it will lead to a fundamental transformation in how we lead our lives. We become free from ourselves and from the need to ensure our own existential certainty, and we are able to develop, in the spirit/Spirit of Jesus, a new orientation outside of ourselves. By this Spirit we are transformed from within into his image. The energies we used to invest in satisfying our interminable efforts at self-assertion are now available to serve God and our neighbors. Since we now have peace with God (Rom 5:1), we are also at peace with ourselves and no longer feel the need to constantly prove ourselves. This orientation enables us to be there—for God and the other and for all that is good. The paradox of the gospel becomes operational: "Whoever seeks to gain his life will lose it, but whoever loses his life will preserve it" (Luke 17:33). In other words, those who doggedly continue with their efforts toward self-realization will never find the inner rest and existential certainty they are searching for. But anyone who gives up such attempts will find his or her true destiny and become the kind of person God intended that one to be. We cannot speak too highly about this transformation, and the New Testament therefore uses some big words for it. It is a transition from death to life (John 5:25). Or to quote Paul, "If anyone is in Christ, he is a new creation; the old has passed away, behold, the new has come" (2 Cor 5:17).

The term "transformation" indicates a process that is rooted in what the Bible calls the human heart: our inmost part, the center of our feelings, convictions, and decisions (Prov 4:23; cf. 23:26a). This process goes far beyond any external modification of conduct. If we want to chase the devil away from the home of our life by just polishing its facade, it will not be long before we find him back with several friends in tow—unless the key has been given to its new occupant (Matt. 12:43-45). Reform begins when another spirit—the Holy Spirit—rules the home of our life, and when another wind begins to inflate our sails. When this change of ownership happens, our concrete words and acts will somehow become oriented toward what is good. In practice, however, we have little control over this wind. It might consist of many diverse and confusing experiences that make sense to us only at a later time. The Spirit who connects us with Christ is free to do as she sees fit.

The relation between the Spirit and our life is insightfully described in the Letter to the Philippians: the example of Christ and the communion with his Spirit leads us to inner sensitivity and unity and also prompts us to renounce our own interests and pride so that we are no longer focused only on ourselves but also on the other. Paul summarizes his appeal in these words: "Have this mind among yourselves, which is yours in Christ Jesus (Phil 2:5, as a conclusion to vv. 1-4). See also the appeal that follows a little later (4:8), to strive for whatever is honorable, just, pure, lovely, and gracious—a series of virtues that modified the so-called *transcendentalia*, the categories of the true, the beautiful, and the good, which classical philosophy said supersede everything else and form the essence of all that is.

The Bible abounds with life stories that can serve as examples of a deep and thorough transformation. The biographies of Peter and Paul as recorded in the New Testament are paradigmatic. From there, lines may to drawn to others who experienced the remarkable workings of the Spirit in their lives. In the Roman Catholic and Eastern Orthodox traditions, such figures have been recognized as saints, who, in all their variety, serve as examples for the rest of us. Even though Protestantism officially rejects the veneration of saints, in actual practice it recognizes some names that stand as extraordinary witnesses by virtue of their example or martyrdom. (Dietrich Bonhoeffer is one such.) The acknowledgment of personal transformation became an important characteristic in Methodism, resulting in a wide range of hymns of great theological depth (e.g., by Charles Wesley, John Newton, and William Cowper). Here the hymn became the bearer of the proclamation of God's *amazing grace* (see Noll 2004, 195-98).

Does this transformation occur more or less spontaneously, as a kind of automatic reflex that follows the gift of acquittal and new identity in Christ? It is tempting to answer this question affirmatively, not least to prevent any relapse into "sanctification by works," a desperate attempt to yet again ensure our own salvation. However, that answer would be incorrect. There is good reason why the New Testament epistles constantly exhort us to make sure that this new state of affairs indeed comes to pass, that our life is concretely transformed by a fundamental reorientation toward Christ. Apparently, we need such exhortations. Although there is no doubt that justification changes us into a new creation, an ongoing struggle will ensue to realize that indeed we are justified and accepted by God so that we live on the basis of the inner peace that it offers.

Emphasizing the reality of our transformation, as we do here, of course may have some drawbacks. On the one hand, the "old man" can fight back so stubbornly that it may seem doubtful that we are making any real progress; if we are then told that we *should* make such progress, we can easily become desperate. On the other hand, if we do observe spiritual progress in our Christian life, would it not tempt us to become proud, to feel morally superior to others, and to think that we can live from now on without the grace of Christ? Moreover, do we not often see that the hunter becomes the prey? When a person ostentatiously chases sin away from the front door, it may come back in through the garage. Think of the televangelists and megachurch pastors who are discovered in financial scandals or extramarital affairs.

Thus we can understand why Christian dogmatics often has little enthusiasm about trying to describe our progress in becoming transformed into the image of Christ. All our "glittering images" (à la Susan Howatch) can easily blow up in our faces. We must indeed be very circumspect in translating this transformation directly into moral categories. For instance, it is wrong to suppose that believers gradually acquire a nobler character so as to need less and less forgiveness, justification, and communion with Christ. For the transformation they experience is primarily a matter of growing "in the grace and knowledge of our Lord and Savior Jesus Christ" (2 Pet 3:18). His grace will never be a phase that we have left behind but will remain the source to which we constantly return and draw upon ever more purposefully. For growing in Christ also implies at least some increase in self-knowledge. When we become aware that we see but little improvement in the passions and imaginations at the bottom of our heart, that nasty tendencies such as jealousy, hedonism, and superficiality seem to be more resilient than we thought, we can become more modest and realistic. If we acknowledge these things in ourselves rather than denying them, we will more consciously deal with them—for instance, by making a greater effort, based on our participation in Christ, to focus on what pleases God and is good for others. This pattern is what the gospel refers to as denying oneself: not disparaging feelings of always having to be submissive to others, but the conscious choice, at different moments in life, to go the way of Christ and to be there for others (Matt 16:24 and pars.).

We must recognize that all these cautions are integral to the Christian message. Yet, at this point we must push back and sound a critical note toward the kind of theology that refers only to what Christ did and refuses to reflect on the question of how he reaches and transforms us. Such "objectivism" runs the risk of trivializing or rendering suspect the question of how God's Spirit touches us to change us and our environment. Especially in much middle-of-the-road Protestantism, the work of the Spirit has been subjected to all kinds of qualifiers. One reason was the fear of putting too much pressure for spiritual achievements, as often found in Roman Catholic, Anabaptist, and evangelical circles.

Was there also the concern that, given a radical doctrine of sin, the Spirit would not be able to do much with the human material in its deplorable state?

We have noted how Luther's aversion toward sanctification by works was further extrapolated by his followers, sometimes to the extreme. The "gnesio-Lutheran" Nikolaus von Amsdorf (1483–1565), for instance, taught that performing good works is actually damaging to salvation! By contrast, Melanchthon defended the specific role of the renewal of life (which he called *renovatio*) next to justification by faith. Calvin also paid due attention to this process but defined the content of transformation mostly in terms of dying to sin (*mortificatio*) and coming back to life (*vivificatio*), that is, as freeing up of new forces that bring renewal of life. We find these tensions in the Reformation mainstream reflected in the Heidelberg Catechism. It says that we are "inclined toward all evil," but that phrase serves most of all as a preface to the brighter side: "unless we are born again by the Spirit of God" (Q/A 8). In its third section the catechism pays extensive and very detailed attention to sanctification, but in its polemic against the Anabaptist striving for holiness, it reaches a dubious conclusion. Are those who have been converted able to keep God's commandments? "No. In this life even the holiest have only a small beginning of this obedience. Nevertheless, with all seriousness of purpose, they do begin to live according to all, not only some, of God's commandments" (Q/A 114). This answer is too meager and falls far short of the level that Paul indicates.

In the nineteenth century H. F. Kohlbrugge came close to dissolving sanctification in justification. With an erroneous appeal to the Greek verb, he translates the New Testament exhortation "put to death therefore what is earthly in you" (i.e., put an end to your worldly practices, Col 3:5) as: "Have put to death therefore what is earthly in you"; that is, be convinced that this has occurred in Christ and has already been credited to you in your justification. With very strong words he urges his readers to throw away all "sanctification-crutches." In the twentieth century Karl Barth embraced Kohlbrugge. We need to understand the context of Barth's condemnation of all forms of so-called Christian belief in progress, the disastrous results of which he had seen in World War I. The young Barth castigated the idea that the Spirit would produce visible forms of renewal, which he called a form of idolatry and a relapse into paganism. His focus on the objectivity of the salvation that Christ provides totally absorbed sanctification. Only later would he allow some space for the believer's creative response, as an *Entsprechung* (analogy, similarity, correspondence) to what Christ had accomplished. At the turn of the century, the ambivalence toward the doctrine of sanctification made a comeback in the dogmatic studies of A. van de Beek. In his fight against a politicized theology and a superficial humanism, van de Beek wants to call the church back to the cross and comes close to the early Barth.

Theological reflection about the relationship between justification and transformation remains challenging. Must we really choose between putting all our money on the former or encouraging the latter? The first option carries the danger of what Bonhoeffer called cheap grace, which, in the opening sentence of his book *The Cost of Discipleship* (1937), he called the deadliest enemy of the church. The second option risks dissolving the unconditional character of God's gracious turn toward us into a new kind of moralism. Berkhof (CF 456-57) wanted to use both models: he compares justification to both a tree and a springboard and suggests that the two must interact with, and correct, each other. Given such dissimilar images, however, it is hard to see how this interaction could happen. We prefer to use the metaphor of a skater who continuously shifts his or her weight from one leg to the other and, by doing so, moves forward. This duality can be found in Paul. The same apostle to whom Western theology owes its doctrine of justification exhorts us to "put on the new man," doing so without any relativizing or reticence (Eph 4:24).

We strongly suggest letting this call for inner and outer transformation stand forth in all its clarity, and not qualifying beforehand that in actual practice it is unrealistic. Those who no longer try will also have little need for constantly returning to the message of justification. Moreover, the New Testament gives much practical advice about the goals of our Christian life. It is remarkable how often we find exhortations in the New Testament that are borrowed from the Torah, especially from the Ten Commandments. Such wording has often caused people to wonder about the precise role the law should have in the life of the Christian. It is instructive to see that Melanchthon and Calvin referred to the law having a third use (*tertius usus legis*), namely, to serve as a guide for the process of transformation. Christ fulfilled the law, which means that its deadly sting has been removed, that it can no longer result in our demise. But this fulfillment does not imply that it is no longer valid as an expression of God's will, for that would mean that God's will is subject to change.

For the metaphor of the skater, see the structure of the Epistle to the Hebrews, in which theological instruction is continuously interchanged with exhortation. The latter sort of statement usually begins, "Let us therefore . . ." (e.g., 4:11; 6:1; 10:22-25; 12:1, 28; 13:13, 15). In other exhortatory passages as well (e.g., in Paul's writings), the imperative is always based on the indicative, as the subjunctive of salvation. These passages tend to occur especially toward the end of the Pauline epistles. The structure is invariably the same: if such and such is the case, then do something about it! For the role of the commandments in this process, see especially the sensitive way in which John interprets them on the basis of love, without playing one off against the other (e.g., 1 John 2:3–5).

Besides the law's civil use (*usus civilis*), as a tool for ordering society, Luther identified a theological or spiritual use, which he felt to be more important. Here the law serves as a means of impressing us with our own sinfulness; it is first of all a *paidagōgos* who leads us to Christ (Gal 3:24), a "child minder" who, if need be, will use force to do so. Because of our failures to live according to its principles, the law makes us aware of our need for forgiveness, which can be found only with Christ. But once we are living on the basis of God's gracious acquittal, we will need only the gospel and have no more need of the law, for Christ has borne the curse of the law on our behalf (Gal 3:13). Besides the *usus civilis* or *politicus* and the *usus paedagogicus* or *elenchticus* (i.e., as a tool for unmasking our miserable situation as sinners before God), Melanchthon and Calvin distinguished a third function, the *usus normativus* or *didacticus*. Since this role as guide or norm has an enduring significance for the new life of the Christian, Calvin regards it as the most important function of the law. The Heidelberg Catechism follows this line of reasoning; it speaks briefly about the pedagogical function of the law (Q/A 2) but much more extensively about its didactic function (Q/A 34–44) in the context of our life of gratitude. On these issues, see Muller, DLGTT 320–21, who points out that the Reformed tradition placed the law, also in its paedagogical use, in the *foedus gratiae* (the covenant of grace). Thereby, from the very first, its threat was mitigated by God's gracious turning toward us—the God who reminds us that he has brought his people out of Egyptian bondage (Exod. 20:2; cf. out of the slavery of sin). This understanding prompted Barth to reverse the traditional Lutheran sequence and to speak not of law and gospel but of gospel and law.

By locating the law in "the life of gratitude," Reformed Protestantism has sometimes fallen into a tendency toward legalism and moralism. This turn has been a breaking point for many—if in doubt, read the novels of nineteenth-century American authors who were fed up with the Calvinism of their forebears: Emerson, Hawthorne, Oliver Wendell Holmes Sr., or erstwhile Methodist Harold Frederic. A finely meshed, suffocating network of dos and don'ts covered all aspects of life. In response to this complaint we can simply commend reading Paul's Epistle to the Galatians from beginning to end. It delivers a passionate protest against a kind of Christian life that surrenders its freedom and once again accepts the yoke of law.

But this possibility does not mean that the law has no proper function in establishing some criteria for the transformation process of believer and church. One might argue that it is all about love, and that this love can be demonstrated only in a situation of freedom. However, the New Testament clearly engages in a delicate interplay between love (sometimes referred to as the law of Christ, Gal 6:2) and the concrete commandments. Just as love is expressed by doing what we know will please the other person (and by expecting the one to clearly indicate what does not), and just as lovers are properly sensitive on this point, we will express our love for God by taking the law seriously as a tool for fashioning our life in a way that will please him. As soon as love leaves this equation, however, everything becomes stifled and the law becomes a collection of dry regulations for our conduct. Once again a narrow middle road must be found between legalism and libertinism.

In Protestant history legalism is also referred to as nomism or neonomianism, while the term "antinomianism" has been used as a synonym for libertinism. Invariably, these labels are found in polemical contexts. The conflict about the role of law in the life of faith erupted in sixteenth-century Lutheranism, and also agitated many Puritans from the seventeenth century on (first in New England and later in Great Britain). Both cases concerned "antinomian" disputes at one phase or another. Most often the issue involved the third use of the law, but sometimes it was also, or exclusively, about the second. Best known is the controversy in England between "neonomians," such as Richard Baxter (1615-91), and "antinomians," such as Tobias Crisp (1600-1643). As often was the case, this conflict was also mixed with political frictions, this time around the political ideas of Oliver Cromwell and, in the case of Anne Hutchinson, with the new Puritan establishment in Boston. In the next century Jonathan Edwards—the revivalist preacher and philosophical theologian whose thought has kindled much renewed interest during the last few decades—held a balanced intermediate position. Edwards accentuated serving God in the freedom of the Spirit; here love sets the tune. The Decalogue, however, has not been abrogated; all its commandments recur in the New Testament, only intensified by Jesus (Matt 5–7). That is, believers will attempt to keep the commandments and will often struggle to do so. Yet, it would be better in this connection not to speak of the law but of the guiding principles for our faith. The law applies to servants; we as children have been delivered from its curse and serve God with joy, out of love. On various aspects of this discussion, see Vlastuin 2014, 237–39, 266–74, who also indicates how these quarrels continued well into the nineteenth century.

In the context of the relationship between faith and transformation, we need to discuss a special figure of speech found in the history of Reformed Protestantism: the *syllogismus practicus*, the capstone of daily praxis. We find this thought in a preliminary form in the Heidelberg Catechism when, in reply to the question of why we should perform good works, it lists as a second reason "that every one may be assured in himself of his faith, by the fruits thereof" (Q/A 86). The underlying idea is that believers may conclude that their faith is genuine when they spontaneously begin to perform good deeds. To put it positively, it means that our "small beginning" (Q/A 114) is not *so* small that it cannot be empirically established! However, what here is a secondary motif (as it is with Calvin), a side note drawn in passing, came to occupy an ever more important place in later Reformed Protestantism. Under the scholastic approach to theology, a taut syllogism took shape; somewhat simplified, it runs:

Premise 1 (major): Those who do good works have faith.
Premise 2 (minor): I do good works.
Conclusion: I have faith.

Whereas with the Reformation of Luther and Calvin, faith found certainty in trusting the promises of the gospel, people were now enjoined to reflect on their own actions for an added, indirect confirmation—which gradually demanded more and more attention. This move risks a *regressio ad infinitum*, however, for how can I know that what I do is truly good and whether I do enough of it? The risk was indeed realized, so that over the seventeenth century the *syllogismus practicus* was overtaken by the *syllogismus mysticus*, where the certainty of faith depends on our own feelings. In a climate in which feelings demanded their rights, it was easy to drown in the quicksand of subjectivism and endless introspection, with the loss of almost any assurance of salvation and joy. In the background of all this uncertainty loomed the big issue of election or predestination. The $64,000 question was, am I among the elect? We will consider that theme in our final section. But first we must consider the prospects of our achieving progress, or at least persistence, in the process of renewal.

The Bible calls for self-examination in only a few places (1 Cor 11:28; 2 Cor 13:5), usually only in connection with our personal relationship to Christ. First Corinthians 3:10–15 is the only passage that directs our attention to our works but, in spite of their urgency, these verses do not deal with our ultimate salvation (v. 15). For Calvin's identification of faith and the assurance of salvation, see, for example, *Inst.* 3.2.14. However, Calvin was very aware of the psychological fluctuations in our feelings of assurance, and his statement about the empirical aspect of the process of transformation must be read in that light (see Allen, RT 87–88). Even Richard Muller (1986, 85), who with unrelenting passion attempts to highlight the continuity between the doctrinal content of Reformation and post-Reformation theology, concedes that there was already a significant shift from Calvin on this point in the thinking of T. Beza, in whose later works "the syllogism rears its head in unabated form." After Beza, this focus only intensi-fied. In a thoroughgoing analysis of this issue, Barth (CD II/2:333–40) shows how things could (and almost had to) go wrong after the good start of Calvin and the Heidelberg Catechism (but see, in Muller 2012, the overall criticism of the "Calvin against the Calvinists" thesis). The concept of the *syllogismus practicus* became even more pronounced in the so-called Weber thesis (after sociologist Max Weber), which postulated that Puritan-Calvinistic impulses came to regard a prosperous society, rather than the good works of individuals, as proof of divine election. Presumably, that attitude led to a causal relationship between Calvin-ism and capitalism as a macroeconomic system. Nowadays, however, Weber's thesis, certainly in its rigid form, is seen as obsolete.

15.8. Progress and Persistence

We concluded in the previous section that we should not denigrate the importance of moral transformation, despite all the problematic issues that come with it. Such disregard would underestimate the work of the Spirit; our sanctification is just as much a work of God as our justification. Furthermore, it would invite excuses for the ongoing influence of sin in our lives. Even though Christ's appeal "You, therefore, must be perfect as your heavenly Father is perfect" (Matt 5:48) does not point to moral perfection (the Aramaic word in the background means "of one piece," and the previous vv. 45–47 show that this is indeed the idea at hand), it does underline how essential it is to allow ourselves to be transformed into the image of God.

But is it realistic to expect much progress in this process, let alone complete success? C. S. Lewis (1952, 175) stated that it certainly is realis-tic, but that we should always remember that our death plays an import-ant role in this process. In other words: the Spirit does not easily run out of breath. In one of his most profound statements, Paul wrote that we are transformed by the Spirit "from one degree of glory to another," that is, in the direction of the image of God (2 Cor 3:18). We are thus dealing with a process that begins in the here and now but will be definitively achieved only in the eschaton. In the meantime, we face the question of whether at least something of this transformation can be observed in the present. Did Jesus not say that a tree will be known by its fruit (Matt 7:16-18)? That is, only by looking at a person's concrete conduct can we tell whether he or she truly is a believer. But this evaluation does not allow for the kind of quantitative empirical research that scientifically oriented Western-ers might like. Lewis rightly differentiated between *nice people* and *new people*. The former are lucky enough to have been born with a pleasant character. The latter may have all kinds of nasty and awkward character traits, but they are oriented toward Christ (mostly, perhaps, because they have experienced these unpleasant things themselves). We encounter quite a few disagreeable people around us (as in Mark 2:16). They may not become as nice as the "nice people"—but the latter camp does not need salvation, while people in the former may change considerably by being in the company of Christ (Mark 2:17)

We take the liberty to quote at some length from Lewis's elegant prose:

> But if you are a poor creature—poisoned by a wretched up-bringing in some house full of vulgar jealousies and senseless quarrels—saddled, by no choice of your own, with some loathsome sexual perversion—nagged day in and day out by an inferiority complex that makes you snap at your best friends—do not despair. He [Jesus] knows all about it. You are one of the poor whom He blessed [Matt 5:3, Luke 6:20]. He knows what a wretched machine you are trying to drive. Keep on. Do what you can. One day (perhaps in another world, but perhaps far sooner than that) he will fling it on the scrap-heap and give you a new one. And then you may astonish us all—not least yourself: for you have learned your driving in a hard school. (Lewis 1952, 4.10, 169)

But we need to face another question, as simple as it is distressing: Can the process of transformation run aground? At first sight the answer seems obvious; we might better ask whether there is any chance that it will not! There are so many pits we might fall into. The Heidelberg Cate-chism speaks of a "three-headed enemy: the devil, the world, and our own flesh" (Q/A 127). Moreover, Western consumerist societies are characterized by the pursuit of ever-changing emotions and experiences—we live in what has been called an *Erlebnisgesellschaft* (Schulze 1992). It gets more and more challenging to remain true to a *commitment* we made at some point in the past. Young people construct their worldview on the basis of what scholars call bricolage: assembling elements from very disparate traditions, picking out what seems appealing and useful, and discarding the rest. People who live by this attitude may be touched by Jesus today but be done with him tomorrow. Yet, it would be too easy to blame the spirit of the age. There has always been the risk, and a significant one, that the renewal of life will at some point peter out or disappear. Jesus himself differentiated between people who accepted his message for a time and another (smaller?) group that became truly engaged (Mark 4:1-20 and pars.). It is certainly possible to stay with Jesus, but it is never self-evident.

In fact, having faith and becoming a believer is not self-evident. Jesus says it is more like a person who, while working hard in a field, accidentally finds a treasure. This discovery opens up a whole new world, but one will have to make sacrifices to enter it (Matt 13:44; se also vv. 45-46). How much more sacrifice is required to stay fixed on the kingdom of God! The question is whether we are prepared to make those sacrifices, and this question poses itself even more urgently when we suffer discrimination, feel pressured to abandon the faith, or, in the ultimate case, confront martyrdom. It is not without reason that the New Testament—which was largely written in such situations—regularly reminds us of the risks of relapse and apostasy and calls us to be faithful and to persist.

The same is true for the apocalyptic passages in the Gospels (Matt 24:13 is especially pregnant with meaning), but also in the Epistles (Rom 11:20; 1 Cor 10:11-12; Gal 5:4; 2 Pet 2:18-22). The Letter to the Hebrews, in fact, is fully dedicated to this issue—for example, see Heb 4:11 and also the passionate words in 6:4-8 and 10:26-31, immediately followed by encouraging admonitions in 6:9-12 and 10:32-39. We find something similar in Revelation (e.g., 2:10, 17, 25-26). Sometimes the authors had in mind specific people who had turned their back on the faith (1 Tim 1:20; 2 Tim 4:10). On some occasions Paul himself seems to doubt his ability to persist (1 Cor 9:27; Phil 3:12)—or does he just intend to underline how essential it is to remain continuously directed toward Christ? Whatever the case, these passages retain their immense importance for Western Christians. If anything is essential amid all the forms of secularization, church leaving, and postmodern agnosticism, it is the need to persist, to remain loyal to Christ and to the catholic faith of the ages as it continues to be confessed, celebrated, and transmitted in today's Christian community. The smaller the matrix in which this tradition is carried along, the more intent we must be to remain involved instead of drifting along with the cultural mainstream.

When we take time to reflect on these passages, we may increasingly wonder whether we have been left to our own devices. Do we still have to prove ourselves after our acquittal and unconditional acceptance in justification? In any case, if our intentions are so important and we must be totally involved in this process of renewal, what does it mean when these efforts—inevitably—falter? Precisely at such moments, when we threaten to succumb to doubt, when we are in danger of relapsing in our struggle against temptation, when our efforts seem to weaken and we ask ourselves whether we can go on—at just such moments the Spirit comes to our assistance with words that speak of God's faithfulness: "I am sure that he who began a good work in you will bring it to completion at the day of Jesus Christ" (Phil 1:6). For God is not one to "forsake the works of his hands" (Ps 138:8). Those who think they are secure must take care not to fall (1 Cor 10:12), but they may also know that their temptations are not superhuman, for God "will not let you be tempted beyond your strength, but with the temptation [he] will also provide the way of escape, that you may be able to endure it" (1 Cor 10:13). All this means that a steadfast life of renewal is no impossible challenge, but that everything depends on holding on to God.

Here again we can mention a long series of New Testament texts: Luke 22:32; John 6:37-40; 10:27-30; Acts 13:48; Rom 9:11, 16; Phil 1:6; 2 Thess 3:3; 1 Pet 1:4-5, 23; Jude 24. A high point in the New Testament comes in the words of Paul in which, after a long reflection on struggle and growth (Rom 7-8), he confesses his confidence that he *will* be able to persist: Rom 8:30-39. Also noteworthy is 1 John 2:19, where it is concluded from the departure of some (former?) believers that, in actual fact, they never shared in genuine faith. If they had, they would have endured. Such a text has often been abused and requires careful reading; note the instructions provided, for example, by Berkouwer (1958, 113-16). Finally, there is the exciting early Christian hymn cited in 2 Tim 2:11-13 with its contrast between, on the one hand, "If we deny him, he will also deny us," and, on the other, "If we are faithless, he remains faithful." The first part of the statement apparently applies to a situation in which one consciously turns his back on Christ, while in the second we are aware of our failures in following Christ.

This insight has entered history under the label "the perseverance of the saints (*perseverantia sanctorum*), where the word "saints" may be read simply "believers." The first profound thoughts on the theme come from Augustine, who spoke (more aptly) of the gift of perseverance (*De dono perseverantiae* 429; Horton, CF 684, is mistaken about the title), with God as the giver. During their lifetime, he noted, believers may stray far away or fail completely; David with his adultery-cum-murder and Peter with his denial of Jesus are the best known biblical examples. Yet, because of God's faithfulness they will not ultimately be lost. At this point in his life Augustine had broken with all forms of synergism, that is, with thinking in terms of a divine-human cooperation in the realization of salvation. He now insists that we owe not only the beginning of our renewal completely to God but also its progress and completion. This understanding is implied in accepting God's grace: grace would no longer be grace if, at the end, it once more depended on our own accomplishments. We believe Augustine saw very clearly that, in faith, we are and always remain recipients.

The line that Augustine started lapsed, reemerging only with Calvin. In one of his most poignant statements, he said (*Inst*. 3.2.28), "When God is reconciled all danger is past, and everything good will befall us." Calvin sees a direct link between perseverance and the assurance of salvation. This certainty (Lat. *certitudo*) consists of the confidence that, "however poor we may be in regard to present comforts, God will never fail us." But once again, an idea of Calvin became controversial after him. This time the trouble arose not from later forms of orthodoxy but among followers of Jacobus Arminius (1559-1609). They worried that the doctrine of perseverance would not be taken seriously enough, which could lead to a dubious moral conduct, so they laid increasing emphasis upon the necessity of human cooperation with God's grace (initially rather hesitantly in the Remonstrance of 1610, but later more forcefully). From a structural perspective their approach corresponded with mainstream medieval thinking, which likewise had not been able to stay with the lofty view of Augustine. By way of contrast, the Canons of Dort agreed in their fifth and final canon with Augustine and Calvin. This document had been preceded by the Anglicans (in the Thirty-Nine Articles, 1571), and would be followed by the Congregationalists (Savoy Declaration, 1658) and the Calvinistic Baptists (Confession of Faith, 1689).

With Berkouwer (1958, 112-13), we hold that, so long as we remember that the concept of the *perseverantia sanctorum* is a confession of faith, it will not easily lead to moral sluggishness. Believers know full well from their own experience that they do not have their faith in their pocket, that they are fallible and must take biblical admonitions to persevere and remain loyal to heart. Therefore, they badly need to be reminded from time to time that they are already safe in God's hands—which might be a fitting ending for our whole discussion of the *ordo salutis*.

15.9. Election as the Capstone

Many who have been involved with theological reflection have been convinced that, besides justification and sanctification, one more keyword must be mentioned and discussed—and we agree with them. It is a foundational term, one more shocking and controversial than most others; at the same time, it involves the profound interconnections of the biblical witness and is profoundly comforting: *election*.

The conviction that we can persevere in faith is rooted in one thought, namely, that everything of faith began with and depends on God's choosing us. This idea is precisely what the church has stated of itself; it owes its very existence to God's election. From this perspective it is possible—to borrow an image from A. A. van Ruler (VW 4B:731)—to stretch a straight line from God's eternal counsel to God's kingdom. The connections and perspectives that follow from this beginning are so overwhelming that we might well place the doctrine of election at the heart of the doctrine of God, rather than at the end of the doctrine of renewal. Had we done so, we would have been following some notable examples in the history of Christian thought—most recently, Karl Barth and those inspired by him.

However, we have decided to take another course, just as we decided not to end this chapter on the topic of perseverance but with a discussion of God's act of election as the capstone of the *ordo salutis*. This choice is not original; we are following ample precedent. Moreover, upon due reflection, we feel that treating election here has the best credentials. If we had taken it up before dealing with the history and the order of salvation, it would have been extremely difficult not to see election as determining the entire process. History, with all its vicissitudes, would then seem to be fully defined by the eternal decrees of God and would be very difficult to take as seriously as the Bible does. This would be true whether we start from the classic "double" form of predestination—that is, with an eternal decree of election (*electio*) of some individuals and simultaneously an equally eternal rejection (*reprobatio*) of others—or from its christologically defined variant, in which Jesus Christ is the Rejected One and the human race is elect (Barth). In either case the human response to the drama of history would lose its real meaning. For if the actual decision has already been made in eternity, we can hardly insist that our attitude toward God and his salvation is of much importance.

For that reason we prefer to follow the noetic rather than the ontic road. From the ontic angle, God's election precedes all history, or rather, it comprises history, just as God's eternity comprises our time. Seen from a noetic perspective, "election" comes to mind only as the final word. That is, the doctrine of election is not the main element in our thinking but an important auxiliary that ensures that grace remains grace and that we always realize how we owe our salvation from beginning to end to the triune God. This summary is how election originally functioned in the sector of Christianity with which it continues to be mostly closely associated, Reformed Protestantism. Amid frequent religious persecutions, massive infant mortality, and great uncertainty about the conditions of life, it was hugely comforting to know that God has chosen us from the very first and that therefore nobody can snatch us from his hand (see Oberman 2003, 147, 156–65). In this way confessing God's election indeed undergirds our perseverance. However, the doctrine soon began to work differently, primarily because the temptation of giving it first place in theological reflection could not be resisted.

We need to start at the beginning, however, since it is important not to view things in too narrow a perspective. The beginning, it is generally conceded, lies in the later writings of Augustine; the earlier church fathers did not deal explicitly with these questions. Neither did Augustine at first, but he changed as the result of his in-depth reading of Paul (Rom 9!), and especially because of his confrontation with the British monk Pelagius. Pelagius's opinion that human beings were and are able to refrain from sin after the fall activated certain thoughts in Augustine that had been latent in him for some time. Augustine understood his own experience of conversion as God overcoming his resistance to change. We cannot so easily detach ourselves from evil's sphere of influence, he concluded; we can escape only when God in his grace breaks through our sinful condition and, with a kind of "soft violence," bends our will in his direction.

But what about people who do not find God? Do they somehow resist God's grace? No, at least not more than others, Augustine thought, for undoubtedly he had done so. Therefore, it must be that God visits some with his irresistible grace while withholding it from others. But Augustine refrains from much further speculation on this point. He is very reticent about any "doctrine of rejection."

He only incidentally remarks that, apparently, God also predestines some people to be lost—for instance, when commenting on Rom 9:11-13, one of the "harsh expressions" (*phrases duriores*) pertaining to the doctrine of election. (Only later was it understood that, in light of the full passage, these expressions do not refer to the order of salvation but to the history of salvation, i.e., to God's special election of Israel.) Rather than speaking of rejection (*reprobatio*), Augustine speaks of God's "passing by" (*praeteritio*). God is not unjust when he elects some from the multitude of lost humanity (*massa perditionis*) and passes by others. Nobody is entitled to his grace. We simply cannot understand why God elects as he does.

Augustine's doctrine of grace comes first. Original sin, a will that is "bound," and predestination—all are different points in "the logic of grace" (Zeindler 2009, 35).

Medieval theology was heavily influenced by Augustine, but the high tension that his doctrine of election had caused gradually decreased. The consensus instead was that we owe our salvation in all respects to God's grace (in that sense, there was no question of semi-Pelagianism, as has often been suggested) but that this grace was de facto available to all people through the sacraments. If people were lost, it was, in the final analysis, their fault and not God's. This was a kind of toned-down Augustine, so that today we usually speak of it as semi-Augustinianism. But repeatedly certain theologians rose to insist that all of Augustine be taken seriously; to mention just a few, Isidore of Sevilla in the seventh century (he coined the term *predestinatio gemina*, "double predestination"), Gottschalk of Orbais in the ninth century (he was almost obsessed by his view of predestination to eternal death), and Thomas Bradwardine in the fourteenth century. Thomas Aquinas (thirteenth century) also insisted on a strict Augustinian doctrine in which election does not originate in God's foreknowledge of a person's faith (or its lack) but in God's will. But others, like Gabriel Biel in the fourteenth century, maintained that election and rejection were completely based on God's knowing beforehand which people would do their best to acquire salvation. Thus, people must *facere quod in se est*, that is, do what they can and trust God to do the rest.

Luther, who had grown up with this kind of thinking, broke with it in his passionate book against Erasmus *On the Bondage of the Will* (1525). Our human capacities are weak in this matter, Luther declared; we are not the rider but the animal ridden—either by God or by the devil. In that light Calvin introduced absolutely nothing new when he taught predestination, so one can hardly label the doctrine the *unique selling point* of Calvinism, as has often been repeated since the nineteenth century.

Perhaps this reputation was due not to Calvin but to the famous Canons of Dort, composed at the synod that met at that city in 1618-19. These canons do indeed have the reputation of being extreme, but upon closer inspection they actually present a relatively moderate version of divine election.

In the first edition of his *Institutes* (1536) Calvin does not treat the concept of election as a separate topic. In his later writings he treats it much more explicitly, but its place in his theology shifts from time to time. In the final edition of his *Institutes* (1559) he detaches it from the doctrine of providence and positions it at the end of his soteriology (3.21-24). We believe this was a fortunate choice, which we (like Berkhof, CF 482-86) gladly follow. However, it remains difficult to get a solid grip on Calvin's thinking. We hear a warm pastoral tone but then a strongly aprioristic line ("if there is an election, there must also be a rejection," 3.23.1), and Calvin has a problem keeping the two elements together. It is telling that he once felt compelled to brand predestination a "horrible decree" (*decretum horribile*, 3.23.7). However, even that wording has a positive side: at least Calvin was shocked by its implications, while some of his followers would just shrug their shoulders.

The doctrine of election in the Canons of Dort represented a reaction to Arminius's so-called predestination of attributes (God elects those people who have the attribute of faith) and is *infralapsarian* in character. This means that God's decision to elect people comes after (below, further on, *infra*) his decision to allow the fall (*lapsus*). Not that these decisions were made at different points in time but that one depends on the other. For simplicity's sake, and using temporal terms, we might explain it like this: God first decides to create free human beings, who are therefore capable of sinning. Foreseeing that they will indeed sin, God decides to save some people from a certain eternal death. However, conforming to his righteous judgment, he "leaves" others in their error. This model conflicted with that of the *supralapsarians*, who insisted that the decision of election was prior (above, *supra*) to God's decision to create the world and allow the fall. Well-known supralapsarians in those days were T. Beza, W. Perkins, and F. Gomarus. As mentioned above, the first two even designed a table in which they placed the main elements of Christian doctrine (*summa totius Christianismi*) in a precise, schematic system, headed by God's "double" decision of predestination; all other events in the history of salvation (and condemnation) then followed from that initial decision. Along the line of election, God glorifies the virtue of his mercy, while along the line in which he effects rejection, he glorifies the virtue of his justice (Graafland 1987, 48-49, 73). In actual practice the supralapsarian system was mitigated by a more nuanced scholastic interpretation, while from the pulpit and in pastoral practice it was usually communicated in a milder form. Nonetheless, the inflexible version of predestination gradually worked its way into collective Reformed consciousness, resulting in much spiritual apathy, indifference, despair, and resistance (strikingly summarized by Graafland in the word "tragedy").

Augustine's doctrine of grace and predestination also resurfaced from time to time, notably in the huge response to Cornelis Jansen's posthumous *Augustine* (1640). In this book Jansen defended a radical view of penance and grace (along with Augustine's ideas of predestination), precipitating a deep conflict between the "Jansenists" on the one hand—among them Blaise Pascal in the French monastery of Port-Royal—and the Jesuits on the other. The controversy did not abate, despite repeated papal interventions, and eventually resulted in what is today the Old Catholic Church.

The Canons of Dort extend one of the two lines that we see in church history, that of the late, or "complete," Augustine; they contain, in fact, nothing new. Yet, the ensuing fierce polemic (between so-called Remonstrants and Contra-Remonstrants) gave the impression that predestination constituted the heart of Christian theology. This way of dealing with the doctrine of election—though understandable in view of the stalemated conflict between Arminius and Gomarus—has left tragic traces in the Reformed experience of faith. If election means that our salvation has been determined by God's decree, where can we find any assurance of salvation? Calvin pointed his hearers to Christ as the mirror in which God makes his gracious will visible. But later generations were not satisfied with that mirror and tried to find in election as a divine decree a hook in the ceiling from which to hang everything. But this was to grope in an unfathomable space; people need solid ground on which to stand and to walk.

Could such ground perhaps be found in the *covenant*? This is what happened in actual practice, and in theory the doctrines of election and covenant usually remained closely linked. God first instituted the covenant of life (*foedus naturae*) and the covenant of works (*foedus operum*) with Adam in paradise. After Adam had failed to live up to its terms, God in his mercy unilaterally established a covenant of grace (*foedus gratiae*), beginning with the "mother of all promises" in Gen 3:15, immediately after the fall. As time passed, God revealed this covenant ever more fully until it was fulfilled in Christ and thereby received its final validity. Since then, the believers from the gentile nations are also included in the covenant if they accept the grace that Christ offers in faith. Thus a golden thread was woven through the Bible, doing justice to the close link between the Old and the New Testaments. At the same time, many added a further complement to the eternal covenant of grace: the covenant of redemption, or *pactum salutis*, on the basis of Eph 1:4 and 1 Pet 1:20. This covenant, sometimes also referred to as the covenant or counsel of peace, was established between the Father and the Son with the aim of saving the elect. But since the covenant of grace necessarily has the same scope as redemption, this made the covenant of grace also limited to the elect. Thus, the covenant and election run parallel: both originate with God, both maintain human responsibility by demanding a response (i.e., they do not make us passive but active), and both ultimately target the same group.

In the Latin jargon, the covenant is unilateral in its design but bilateral in its effects. For a concise but clear survey of the Reformed doctrine of the covenants, see Allen, RT 39-46. In seventeenth-century covenant or federal theology, the Reformed doctrine of the covenants became very refined (and diverse in its details): in the Netherlands at the hand of, for example, Johannes Cocceius, Frans Burman, and Herman Witsius, and in the Anglo-Saxon world by important figures such as John Owen and (in the eighteenth century) Jonathan Edwards. Even in the twentieth century the three covenants referred to played a role in various schisms in Dutch Reformed churches owing to different interpretations of their interrelationships. The strong biblical-theological credentials of the covenant concept (*berit* in the Old Testament and *diathēkē* in the New) doubtless explain the many recurring attempts to give it a central place in theological reflection and to make it fruitful for faith, although this positioning is increasingly difficult in our individualistic era.

As the traditional doctrine of election became a dead-end street, Karl Barth—building on the nineteenth-century theologian Friedrich Schleiermacher—decided to try another tack in his rethinking of classic Reformed theology. To Barth the chronic uncertainty that plagued classic interpretations of the doctrine conflicted with the joyful message of the gospel. If the gospel is to be believed, we must conclude that God is a God who in Jesus Christ has turned toward us in order to save us. That being the heart of the gospel, we have to do justice to it at every point in our theology. That is, in reconstructing the eternal decrees, we must do everything possible to avoid speaking of any other god than the one who entered our history in Jesus Christ and assumed our flesh and blood. In other words, the dramatic course of this Jesus of Nazareth from cradle to cross is essential to who God is. We know of no other God than this one, for "if anyone is preaching to you a gospel contrary to that which you received, let him be accursed" (Gal 1:8 and 9).

For this reason, the God who elects can be none other than the God who in his free grace turns toward us. Barth places election at the heart of the doctrine of God, since it shows how God works. Just like Beza, Barth regarded the doctrine of election as the apex of the gospel (*Summe des Evangeliums*), because the best news that can be said or heard is that God chooses us and loves us in freedom (CD II/2:3). Barth develops this thought concretely by designating Jesus as both the subject and the object of the divine decree; he is not only the God who elects but also the one elected. This second piece was not new, for Reformed theologians had always underlined (esp. on the basis of Eph 1:3-4) that God has "chosen" us in Christ and thus chose Christ first of all. But the first piece was new. Barth wanted to stress that there never had been something like a *logos asarkos*, an abstract Second Person of the Trinity (the *Logos*), whose destiny was completely undecided. No, this Second Person was from the very first identical with the incarnate Jesus Christ. He who came to us is also the one who elected us. That Jesus came to save us, therefore, is not something that "also" happened, something "extra" to his identity, but precisely that which makes him who he is. Only when we accept this view need we have no fear.

These new lines drawn by Barth (who appealed in particular to the prologue of the Gospel of John and the close connection between John 1:1 and 1:4) continue to captivate his disciples today. The ongoing discussions about the precise nature and implications of Barth's view of election are among the fiercest and most fascinating debates in contemporary dogmatics. They were ignited especially when Bruce McCormack (2000) began to argue that Barth's dogmatics, for consistency's sake, should have placed the doctrine of election before that of the Trinity—and that we should do the same. McCormack believes that the triune God cannot be thought of as detached from and prior to God's decision to be for us but is, in fact, defined by that decision. Therefore, there is no "prior" (indefinable) triune being that makes a decision out of the blue. No, God's being consists in the self-determination implied in that decree. God exists, as it were, through (and because of) his decision to choose our side. McCormack's view fits very well with our current distaste for all forms of "ontotheology" (i.e., thinking about God in terms of being). However, attributing this actualistic ontotheology (i.e., thinking about God as being determined by a deed or act) to Barth, as well as wanting us to subscribe to it, has raised many objections. For this discussion, see the various contributions in Dempsey 2011. We believe that we may very well say that the triune God made this decision about election without implying that it was a totally arbitrary decree. Rather, it fit God's nature, his eternal being, to take precisely this glorious step, which became reality in the coming of Christ and of the Spirit on our behalf.

707

Our principal objection to Barth's doctrine of election, however, is to the old threat that our human response to God's offer of salvation will be absorbed into an all-determining choice by God for us. Many have pointed out that such a massive "triumph of grace" (Berkouwer) poses some serious questions, "especially those that relate to the weight of the human 'no'; does this do justice to this human resistance?" (Berkhof, CF 486). We appreciate that question and think that, in view of the ambiguous fate of both the classic and Barthian versions of supralapsarianism, it is inadvisable to make election the first word in dogmatics or in the doctrine of God. We have repeatedly underlined that we are only the recipients of salvation. We are not in the central control room; we cannot watch over God's shoulder from the perspective of eternity and make the entire history of humanity transparent, for this history is far too confusing. It is much better to let election be the final keyword, the capstone of the doctrine of renewal. While we are so often in doubt about everything (esp. about ourselves!), we can be assured in faith that our renewed future is indeed certain because God has wanted it from all eternity. When we use the word "God"—and here we fully agree with Barth—we are referring not to a dark capricious power but to the one who has made himself known in Christ as a God of grace. In Jesus Christ we are justified, and God wants us to share in this new reality.

References

Barth, Karl. 1976. *Das christliche Leben: Die Kirchliche Dogmatik*, IV/4; *Fragmente aus dem Nachlass; Vorlesungen 1959-1961*, edited by H.-A. Drewes and E. Jüngel. Zurich: Theologischer Verlag.

Beilby, James K., and Paul R. Eddy, eds. 2011. *Justification: Five Views*. Downers Grove, IL: IVP Academic.

Berkouwer, Gerrit C. 1952. *Faith and Sanctifcation*. Grand Rapids: Eerdmans.

———. 1954. *Faith and Justification*. Grand Rapids: Eerdmans.

———. 1958. *Faith and Perserverance*. Grand Rapids: Eerdmans.

Bierma, Lyle D. 2013. *The Theology of the Heidelberg Catechism: A Reformation Synthesis*. Louisville: Westminster John Knox.

Billings, J. Todd. 2007. *Calvin, Participation, and the Gift: The Activity of Believers in Union with Christ*. Oxford: Oxford University Press.

———. 2011. *Union with Christ: Reframing Theology and Ministry for the Church*. Grand Rapids: Baker Academic.

Boersma, Hans. 2011. *Heavenly Participation: The Weaving of a Sacramental Tapestry*. Grand Rapids: Eerdmans.

Braaten, Carl E., and Robert W. Jenson, eds. 1998. *Union with Christ: The New Finnish Interpretation of Luther.* Grand Rapids: Eerdmans.

Burger, Hans. 2008. *Being in Christ: A Biblical and Systematic Investigation in a Reformed Perspective.* Eugene, OR: Wipf & Stock.

Canlis, Julie. 2010. *Calvin's Ladder: A Spiritual Theology of Ascent and Ascension.* Grand Rapids: Eerdmans.

Christensenk, Michael J., and Jeffery A. Wittung, eds. 2007. *Partakers of the Divine Nature: The History and Development of Deification in the Christian Traditions.* Grand Rapids: Baker Academic.

Dempsey, Michael T., ed. 2011. *Trinity and Election in Contemporary Theology.* Grand Rapids: Eerdmans.

Dunn, James D. G. 1983. "The New Perspective on Paul." *Bulletin of the John Rylands Library* 65:95–122.

Graafland, Cornelis. 1984. "Hat Calvin einen Ordo salutis gelehrt?" In *Calvinus ecclesiae Genevensis custos*, edited by Wilhelm H. Neuser, 221–44. Frankfurt: Peter Lang.

———. 1987. *Van Calvijn tot Barth: Oorsprong en ontwikkeling van de leer der verkiezing in het gereformeerd protestantisme* [From Calvin to Barth: Origin and development of the doctrine of election in Reformed Protestantism]. The Hague: Boekencentrum.

Immink, Frederik G. 2005. *Faith: A Practical Theological Reconstruction.* Grand Rapids: Eerdmans.

"Joint Declaration on the Doctrine of Justification." 2000. In *Growth in Agreement II. Reports and Agreed Statements of Ecumenical Conversations on a World Level, 1982–1998*, edited by Jeffrey Gros, Harding Meyer, and William G. Rusch, 566–82. Geneva: WCC Publications; Grand Rapids: Eerdmans.

Jüngel, Eberhard. 2001. *Justification: The Heart of the Christian Faith; A Theological Study with an Ecumenical Purpose.* London: T&T Clark.

Keller, Tim 2008. *The Reason for God: Belief in an Age of Skepticism.* New York: Dutton.

Kooi, Cornelis van der. 2005. *As in a Mirror: John Calvin and Karl Barth on Knowing God; A Diptych.* Leiden: Brill.

Küng, Hans. 2004. *Justification: The Doctrine of Karl Barth and a Catholic Reflection.* Louisville: Westminster John Knox. Orig. English pub., 1964.

Lane, Anthony N. S. 2002. *Justification by Faith in Catholic-Protestant Dialogue: An Evangelical Assessment.* London: T&T Clark.

Lewis, C. S. 1952. *Mere Christianity.* London: Bles.

Lieburg, Fred van. 2014. "Dynamics of Dutch Calvinism: Early Modern Programs for Further Reformation." In *Calvinism and the Making of the European Mind*, edited by Gijsbert van den Brink and Harro M. Höpfl, 43–66. Leiden: Brill.

MacIntyre, Alasdair C. 1985. *After Virtue: A Study in Moral Theory.* 2nd ed. London: Duckworth. Orig. pub., 1981.

Mannermaa, Tuomo. 2005. *Christ Present in Faith: Luther's View of Justification.* Minneapolis: Fortress.

McCormack, Bruce. 2000. "Grace and Being: The Role of God's Gracious Election in Karl Barth's Theological Ontology." In *The Cambridge Companion to Karl Barth,* edited by John Webster, 92–110. Cambridge: Cambridge University Press. Also in McCormack, *Orthodox and Modern: Studies in the Theology of Karl Barth,* 183–200. Grand Rapids: Baker Academic, 2008.

———. 2008. "Participation in God, Yes, Deification, No: Two Modern Protestant Responses to an Ancient Question." In McCormack, *Orthodox and Modern: Studies in the Theology of Karl Barth,* 235–60. Grand Rapids: Baker Academic.

McGrath, Alister E. 2005. *Iustitia Dei: A History of the Christian Doctrine of Justification.* 3rd ed. Cambridge: Cambridge University Press. Orig. pub., 1986.

Milbank, John, Catherine Pickstock, and Graham Ward, eds. 1999. *Radical Orthodoxy.* London: Routledge.

Muller, Richard A. 1986. *Christ and the Decree: Christology and Predestination in Reformed Theology from Calvin to Perkins.* Durham, NC: Labyrinth Press. Repr., 2005.

———. 2012. *Calvin and the Reformed Tradition: On the Work of Christ and the Order of Salvation.* Grand Rapids: Baker Academic.

Noll, Mark A. 2004. *The Rise of Evangelicalism: The Age of Whitefield, Edwards, and the Wesleys.* Downers Grove, IL: InterVarsity Press.

Oberman, Heiko A. 2003. *The Two Reformations: The Journey from the Last Days to the New World.* New Haven: Yale University Press.

Piper, John. 2007. *The Future of Justification: A Response to N. T. Wright.* Wheaton, IL: Crossway Books.

Rusch, William G., ed. 2003. *Justification and the Future of the Ecumenical Movement.* Collegeville, MN: Fortress.

Schulze, Gerhard. 1992. *Die Erlebnisgesellschaft: Kultursoziologie der Gegenwart.* Frankfurt: Campus.

Sittser, Gerald L. 2007. *Water from a Deep Well: Christian Spirituality from Early Martyrs to Modern Missionaries.* Downers Grove, IL: IVP Books.

Vlastuin, Willem van. 2014. *Be Renewed: A Theology of Personal Renewal.* Göttingen: Vandenhoeck & Ruprecht.

Waaijman, Kees. 2002. *Spirituality: Forms, Foundations, Methods.* Leuven: Peeters.

Willard, Dallas. 1988. *The Spirit of the Disciplines: Understanding How God Changes Lives.* San Francisco: Harper & Row.

Wisse, Maarten. 2011. *Trinitarian Theology beyond Participation: Augustine's "De Trinitate" and Contemporary Theology.* London: T&T Clark.

Wright, N. T. 1978. "The Paul of History and the Apostle of Faith." *Tyndale Bulletin* 29:61–88.

———. 2009. *Justification: God's Plan and Paul's Vision.* London: SPCK.

Zeindler, Matthias. 2009. *Erwählung: Gottes Weg in der Welt.* Zurich: Theologischer Verlag.

16 Renewal of God's World

Eschatology

AIM

This chapter brings us to the end of our survey of Christian dogmatics. In line with tradition, it is devoted to the so-called doctrine of the last things, or eschatology (Gk. *eschaton* = the last, the ultimate). In the past this topic often became tedious on the premise that, even though just about everything had been said on the subject, tradition required that a few words be added about how history would end. Especially under the ideology of progress, this was often thought to be quite a strange subject. Whatever kinds of scenarios might be devised, they seldom seemed relevant for life in the here and now. In the twentieth century this sentiment drastically changed. Eschatology decided, as it were, to claim its rights, and the resulting reorientation highlighted the subject's great significance in more ways than one. Rather than being a mere formality at the end of dogmatics, eschatology has developed into a locus that influences the entire doctrinal system and gives it an existential spark.

In this chapter we want to:
- explain the theological importance of our own personal future, as well as of the future of the world (16.1)
- survey the development of eschatology in the twentieth century (16.2)
- argue that the Christian expectation of the future does much to determine the way we aim to live in the here and now (16.3)
- show how the apocalyptic passages in the Bible may be taken seriously without confusing them with the script of a thriller (16.4)
- make us aware of the significant influence eschatological expectations have exercised throughout history (16.5)
- give a succinct description of millennialism as a concrete model for this expectation (16.6)

- briefly discuss the "four last things": the resurrection of the dead, the last judgment, heaven, and hell (16.7)
- say something, tentatively, about eternal life (16.8).

MAKING CONNECTIONS
1. Stream or watch a DVD of the movie *Left Behind* (2000) and jot down the feelings that it evokes in you. How are we to explain the success, or at least the popularity, of this film? Or watch Lars von Trier's film *Melancholia* (2011). What does it tell you about his view of life and the future?
2. Ask a few people where they think the world is going. Are they hopeful or pessimistic, and why? Then ask them what they believe will happen to them when they die, and try to discover whether there is a link between these two answers.

16.1. The Future of the World and the Future of Humanity

When asked about the future, we instinctively relate the matter first of all to ourselves: what will *our* future be like? Even more personally, what will *my* future be? The question becomes even more intriguing when it involves our future after death. Is there life after death? If so, can we speak with any degree of certainty about the kind of life this will be? Down through the ages people have been fascinated by these questions and have searched for answers—Christians included. As we saw in the previous chapter, reflection on our own personal salvation is an essential part of the Christian life. There is nothing wrong with such thinking. It is only good to think about what it means to be a human being and about how we are to arrive at our final destination. Moreover, we have learned— perhaps better than at any time—that to a certain extent we already *have* arrived at our final destination and have found our new identity in Jesus Christ, with the result that we may be there for others.

Nonetheless, our focus on our own salvation and future may derail us and become an unhealthy, unchristian "salvation-egoism." This happens when we are so totally engrossed in ourselves and our own destiny that other people and the world are lost from sight. Eschatology, in particular, always carries that risk. At times all the attention on this theme went to questions about resurrection and judgment, heaven and hell—and, furthermore, as these topics related to the individual person. What counted was for the individual to be saved from this doomed world, and from there it was easy to think that this world is not so important at all. However, this is a skewed view of things. In the Bible the earth and history are at least as important as the individual person. This balance is most clearly illustrated in the prayer that Jesus invited us to pray, which has already served us several times in this book as a guide for reflecting on our faith. Without exaggeration, the Lord's Prayer may be called an eschatological prayer. From beginning to end it stretches into the future. More strongly yet, it draws that future into the present. We see how the request in the beginning ("*may* your kingdom come") goes over to the statement of the closing doxology ("for yours *is* the kingdom"). This plea is not specifically related to the praying person but to the entire world in its relation to God: "Let your kingdom come and let your will be done on earth as it is in heaven." Only then does the prayer focus on the individual life of the praying person(s), "Give us today our daily bread," before ending with a reference to God's world-encompassing reign. Thus we can speak of a dual horizon or a dual expectation, which Christian theology cannot separate. On the one hand, we must reckon with our own future and the horizon of our own life, but on the other hand, we also see the horizon of the reign of God.

Apparently, humanity and the world belong indissolubly together. God does not save individuals (and especially their souls) *from* the world; this Greek-philosophical idea may be traced back to Plato and Parmenides. The God of Israel wants to save humanity together *with* the world. In both cases this salvation involves judgment, because the evil that has poisoned this world does not deserve any future. However, the world as such is God's creation and thereby a gift, as we saw in chapter 6; we cannot live without this gift from our Creator, just as a fish cannot survive on dry land. For that reason the eschatological perspective that the Bible paints includes a "new earth" (Isa 65:17; 66:22; 2 Pet 3:13; Rev 21:1).

Few recent theologians have expressed this point as powerfully as A. A. van Ruler. He maintained that the Old Testament is about the kingdom of God, about the fact that this earth, in all its concreteness, must be redeemed and saved. That is, we can never think too earthily and too concretely about the kingdom. We must not allow the eschatological expectation to be "emaciated to become a skinny mannequin" (Ruler, VW 3:122). For the twofold horizon and the twofold expectation, see Berkouwer 1972, 32–64.

We cannot accuse Calvin or, for instance, the Belgic Confession of a one-sided approach or any individualistic reduction of the biblical testimony regarding the future (see the essays of, respectively, W. Balke and W. Verboom in Egmond and Keulen 2001, 1:30–64 and 65–85). But that tendency undeniably did mark the subsequent development of Reformed Protestantism. In the Netherlands this is evident from the end of the seventeenth century on, when people began to despair of realizing their ideal of a "second reformation" of society; as a consequence, the personal, inner aspects of faith were more and more emphasized.

Therefore, our eschatological reflection may never detach the contemplation of our own personal future from the global nature of God's Trinitarian acts. But neither can we practice the reverse. We do not suggest ignoring the personal aspect as being hardly, if at all, relevant to eschatology. This was a trend particularly in the 1960s and 1970s, when reflection on the future was so geared toward societal dimensions and political structures as to practically lose sight of the individual human being. Some scholars developed very appealing, utopian scenarios of freedom and equality for all people—but which people would be able to continue enjoying these things remained quite unclear.

A notable example is J. Moltmann's *Theology of Hope* (1967), which offers appealing vistas of the future that God has in store for history, though he refrains from painting them in any concrete detail. It remained unclear whether our life definitely ends with death; if so, we would not have much use of such a renewed world. Three decades later Moltmann corrected this shortcoming in a more balanced (but, regrettably, less well-known) study of eschatology, *The Coming of God* (1996).

We must ensure a solid integration between individual and universal eschatology. It is not enough, however, to pay equal attention to both aspects; that would not mean integration. The important thing is to do full justice to the universal dimensions, as well as to individual applications, in our treatment of such themes as the (second) coming of Christ, the resurrection of the dead, the final judgment, and related topics—which we intend to do.

16.2. Developments in the Twentieth Century

The history of eschatology has had its high and low points, which usually coincided with the degree to which Christians were looking with eager expectation for God's future as promised in the Bible. Both millennial transitions (1000 and 2000 CE) witnessed significant revivals of eschatological interest, apparently inspired by a fascination with round numbers. In other periods—and honesty demands to say that these were often the longest—Christians became so attached to the status quo of everyday life that they felt little need of a fundamentally new mode of existence. This was generally the case at the end of the nineteenth century. The words of Ernst Troeltsch (TCF 38) on this point have often been quoted: "Modern theology says, today the eschatological office is mostly closed" because "the thoughts on which it is based have lost their roots." Troeltsch stated that modern theologians and their followers had insurmountable difficulties in accepting the idea of a *Jenseits*, a life after death, because of their scientifically defined worldview. He added that things were not much better on the Orthodox side, if for other reasons—namely, a large measure of satisfaction with the status quo, combined with a strong focus on intrachurch issues.

Remarkably enough, less than half a century later, Hans Urs von Balthasar (1957, 403) could state that, since the time of Troeltsch, the "eschatological office" was once again working, overtime. In fact, when Troeltsch wrote his oft-quoted words (1912-13), German theology had already rediscovered eschatology. To begin with, the influential liberal theologian Albrecht Ritschl demanded attention for the central place of the kingdom of God in the New Testament. Ritschl still considered this concept as a category belonging to this world; namely, the kingdom of God is where our society, here and now, becomes permeated by a lofty Christian moral awareness. However, Ritschl's son-in-law Johannes Weiss (1892), as well as the famous doctor, musician, and theologian Albert Schweitzer, showed that, according to the New Testament, Jesus himself expected and proclaimed an imminent breakthrough of the kingdom, accompanied by a lot more turmoil than would be the case with a gradually spreading Christian morality.

The discovery of Weiss and Schweitzer ushered in the first stage of renewed interest in eschatology, but it remained rather unfruitful from a theological point of view, for they believed that Jesus's expectations had not come true. Nineteen centuries had passed since Jesus's announcement of the coming of his reign, so it was impossible, they thought, to live so many centuries later as if the kingdom might break through any day. Schweitzer retained, however, a total dedication to God's rule, to a kind of life in harmony with God's intentions. This ethically charged devotion to his fellow human beings colored Schweitzer's further career as a medical doctor in Lambaréné, Gabon. Thus, with Weiss and Schweitzer, the eschatological office still largely remained closed. For example, see Schweitzer 1910, Hjelde 1987 (217ff.), and Schwöbel, in Fergusson and Sarot 2000 (220-21).

The real comeback of eschatology occurred when dialectic theologians began to have second thoughts about the linear concept of time, which until then had been taken for granted in all discourse about eschatology. This development was particularly due to the work of Barth, Bultmann, and Tillich; theirs is now often referred to as the second phase in the revival of eschatological interest in the twentieth century (as in Holmström 1936, 179ff.). This second phase was prompted by the shocking events of the First World War. Suddenly it seemed as if judgment over our human life no longer lay in some distant future but was unfolding in real time. History confronts us with a God who brings our existence to a crisis, pronounces his judgment, and offers us his grace—not at the end of time, but in the here and now. So we must understand the New Testament statements about the eschaton, not as statements about a faraway future, but as words that place us before God in the present in such a radical way as to demand our choice now.

Eschatology, the early Barth and Tillich argued, does not relate to *chronos*, the horizontal timeline that has no end and disappears over our horizon, but to *kairos*, the other Greek word that the Bible employs for time. *Kairos* points to the decisive moment here and now, the "acceptable" time (2 Cor 6:2), in which God's salvation is on offer and in which we must decide how to respond. Eternal life was recast as a present category, not as something in the future; "he who believes in me *has* eternal life" (John 6:47) became a favorite text. However, this focus on the present did not translate into a kind of middle-class moral decency. The Spirit of God, his judgment, and his acquittal are not encapsulated in the ethical values of a so-called civilized society, but they hit us as a complete surprise—*senkrecht von oben* (straight from above), to use a well-known expression of the early Barth. Barth (R2 51) had, in fact, found this expression in F. Zündel's description of the outpouring of the Holy Spirit in Acts 2:1-13.

In like manner these theologians began to understand the biblical themes of the resurrection, the last judgment, the kingdom of God, and so forth as present realities. Bultmann pushed this approach the furthest. He stated that Jesus did not arise at Easter—for such a miracle was unthinkable—but came to life again in the proclamation of the apostles. In that proclamation Jesus demands our choice. Bultmann (like the older liberal theology) was constricted by our scientific understanding of the world, which makes it hard to imagine any sudden divine intervention in history or at the end of time. Moreover, had not the expectation of an imminent return of Christ, as people understood it from the New Testament, always proven false? For Bultmann, however, these were no reasons to simply push the New Testament aside; rather, its message had to be interpreted differently, that is, strictly with a view to our life in the present. Under the influence of the existential philosophy that was then in its heyday, Bultmann proposed an "existential interpretation" of the gospel. The important thing is to follow Christ in the here and now; indeed, the New Testament is about "the presence of eternity" (Bultmann 1957). One might say that Bultmann and his followers turned a virtue into a necessity and worked a striking reversal: the last things come first and have priority. We will not stand before God sometime in the future but are confronted with God right now. We must not long for a paradisiacal existence in the hereafter but live a life that is oriented toward God, here and now.

As a result, eschatology no longer dangled like a theological appendix but moved to its core. Where previously it had been difficult to credit it with any meaningful content, now everything revolved around it. Eschaton and eschatology became defining concepts for the kerygma, the heart of the gospel of Jesus Christ—for the radical decision to which the gospel calls us, for which it liberates us, and finally even for the supratemporal acts of God. The early Barth (R2 430) could say, "A Christianity that is not fully and exclusively eschatological has absolutely nothing to do with Christ." From the very first, our theology must be understood in the perspective of the eschatological coming, speaking, and acting of God, interpreted in present terms. God's eternity arrives not only at the end of time but scrutinizes, qualifies, and judges the things of today.

Barth, Bultmann, and Tillich each developed this dialectic of time and eternity further in his own way and with his own jargon. Barth, for instance, did not deny that eschatology has historical dimensions, but these should not supersede the full revelation of what has already now been given in Christ. This focus on the present found support from the English New Testament scholar C. H. Dodd, who argued that the parables of the kingdom do not speak of a near or distant future but of an experience in the present. Christ calls his hearers to repentance and to conversion, and thus to enter the kingdom as a child. That is, the kingdom must already be here, even though it has not yet arrived in its full glory. Dodd spoke of the "already" and the "not yet" of the kingdom, but his emphasis was solidly on the already. He maintained that in Jesus's preaching the proclamation of the future hardly had any significance. For this reason, Dodd's approach has often been called *realized* or (with more nuance and more correctly) *realizing eschatology*.

Despite the enthusiasm that attended this radical dehistoricizing of eschatology, in the long run it failed to have much impact on theological reflection. Too many voices in the New Testament did not comfortably fit into the mold of a realized eschatology. The stress on the individual and on the ahistorical aspect was seen with increasing clarity to be a serious reduction of the biblical testimony (e.g., see Gunton, CCCD 234). However important might be God's decisive encounter with the individual in the present, much more remains to be said. As we noted above, eschatology cannot be related only to the individual person in a one-sided manner while ignoring the world and its future. Eschatology also concerns God's history with humanity and the world, as well as its future apotheosis. An eschatology that refers to God's judgment and liberating intervention today but has no hope that God will pursue his judgment further and make it universal shortchanges that judgment. Something is wrong when Christian eschatology is about everything except the actual future.

The first theologian to become acutely aware of this deficiency and to propose a different interpretation of the biblical evidence was the Swiss New Testament scholar Oscar Cullmann (1902-99). To him we owe the well-known image (one adopted by many others) of D-Day and V-Day, which powerfully illustrated the temporal dimension in New Testament statements about the meaning of Christ's work. The all-important battle for the dominance of this world took place at Easter, just as the invasion of Normandy, in the early morning of June 6, 1944, proved decisive for the outcome of World War II. But the final victory of Christ still lies in the future; Victory Day has not yet come. Today we live in an interim in which we can proclaim Christ's victory, while, despite continued resistance, his rule further expands among the nations (Cullmann 1964, 84-85). Cullmann's approach to the meaning of eschatology primarily followed the lines of the history of salvation. This view also meant for him that we are still waiting for a new, future act of God that goes beyond a revelation of what has already been given to us in Christ. Cullmann was heavily criticized, in particular by Bultmann and his disciples, but many agreed with him as well. For instance, the prominent Dutch theologian H. N. Ridderbos (1909-2007), with his salvation-historical view of God's kingdom (1962), in many ways paralleled the ideas of Cullmann. Moreover, under the influence of Cullmann, the later Barth came to attribute more significance to the historical and future aspects of eschatology. Although Cullmann's popular image must not be overemphasized (in reality, D-Day was only one of the decisive moments in World War II), we believe that he pointed Christian theology in the right direction on this matter.

This route was pursued even more consistently by a new generation of theologians, of whom the best known and most productive were Berkhof, Pannenberg, and Moltmann. Berkhof (1966) saw how the pattern of Christ's cross and resurrection was continuously and in ever greater intensity repeated in the history after Easter, until the definitive victory of Christ arrives in the eschaton, after the suffering of the end time. Pannenberg (1969) sees the kingdom of God, which he agrees was the central feature in Christ's teachings, to be a future category that nonetheless already impacts the present; in that sense it is already present, and it is already possible to live now in communion with God. But only the future will fully reveal what this kingdom really means and who God is; it is from the future that God's rule approaches us. (Pannenberg can therefore refer to God as the "power toward the future.") From that perspective God draws *all* history toward himself, for God is at work not just in salvation history, à la Cullmann. Yet, the meaning of the past and the present will be definitively disclosed only in the future. In the resurrection of Christ we experience an important portent (or, to use Pannenberg's jargon, a "proleptic anticipation") of that future, which grounds and motivates our hope. Jürgen Moltmann had even earlier caused some sensation with his *Theology of Hope*, in which he spoke enthusiastically about the Christian hope that focuses on the acts in which God approaches us. The Christian word for the future is not *futurum* but *adventus*: it concerns the things, or even better the person, who comes toward us (Moltmann 1967). According to Rev 1:4 God is the one "who is, who was, and who is to come," as opposed to the divine being of Greek thought, which is timeless and unchanging. The movement expressed by "the one who is and was and will be" is typical of the Christian concept of God; Christian eschatology unfolds in the context of the coming of God (Moltmann 1996, 23).

Pannenberg and Moltmann differed from Berkhof especially with regard to the theory of time underlying their eschatology. For the first two, the core concept for theological method is anticipation: already now we may anticipate in full confidence a future of peace and justice that God is in the process of bringing about. Berkhof, in contrast, works primarily by extrapolation: starting from the here and now, he draws some dotted lines toward the future. For that reason

Moltmann (1974) accused him of overemphasizing the status quo and of being insufficiently radical, but the reader who studies the later editions of CF will see that the charge apparently did not impress Berkhof very much. The aspect of discontinuity between the present and the future is, in his opinion, sufficiently addressed by his speaking of a "forward leap" between the two. We must also see a clear continuity, he argues, in what God has already given us in Christ and what we have received in the Spirit. Failing that, eschatology becomes so abstract that we no longer have any concrete idea of what it entails.

The three theologians fully agree, however, on the great theological significance of history; we cannot speak about God's eschatological acts detached from history or abstracted from the concrete direction in which our world is developing.

It is clear that this third stream of eschatological reflection represents an important catching-up process. Notions that had been removed from eschatology, such as future, history, and cosmos are reclaiming their place. However different and, at times, willful the elaboration of some ideas was in the third wave, it basically showed good biblical grounding. We can cite, for instance, the clear (salvation-) historical pattern in the two New Testament books of Luke as they interacted with the historical background of the Old Testament.

We don't mean to say that the ahistorical approach to eschatology is now fully in the past. It received fresh impetus in the extensive eschatological proposal of Beek 2008, which argues that, in the final analysis, God's decisive intervention in Christ is one single event that stretches from the coming of Christ into the world until his "second coming." (We intentionally place this term in quotation marks, since the notion "second" is not found in the Greek keyword *parousia*, "appearance.") According to van de Beek, we may therefore not speak of a second coming but rather of an arrival or an appearance, indicating its unity with Jesus's "first" coming to the earth (164). At issue is the one *kairos* of the breakthrough of the kingdom of God. Of course, we can distinguish a number of important moments (Good Friday, Easter, the coming at the end of time), but these are moments of one single event, just as giving birth has a certain duration but is nonetheless one event (166-67, with reference to John 16:21 and Rom 8:22). "The *parousia*, therefore, is the closing scene of the one event of God's intervention as king to get things in this world in order, and is not a separate second coming in the sense of a new eschatological occurrence" (165).

Van de Beek's view is remarkable and merits careful consideration. Nevertheless, we feel it does not do enough justice to the significance of the interim between Pentecost and the parousia as a period with its own character, content, and aim—namely, the spreading of the message of God's rule over the nations of the world—or to the signs God gives that point to this rule. Just as the God of the Old Testament was the God of history, so he is in and after the New Testament (see also chap. 9). We discuss this theme in more detail in the next section.

16.3. From the Future to the Present

But do we not relapse into a rather superficial dream of a distant future if we once again interpret eschatology in terms of *futurum*? Did not eschatology fall back into its old error in the second half of the twentieth century? Of course, the risk remains that eschatology will no longer touch us existentially if we apply it primarily to the future. However, it is demonstrably possible to avoid this risk, or even to achieve the opposite; the future of God motivates us not to drive the pegs of our tents down too deeply, not to be satisfied with the world as it now functions. If we trust that in the future God will put an end to all evil and create a new world, we know already today that the existing structures will not have the final word. However boldly totalitarian rulers may declare that their order will forever endure, there is another and better reality than theirs. Those who believe in that other reality will not easily let themselves be intimidated (note Acts 16:25!) and will not bow to the suggestion that they are simply clinging to utopian ideas. Rather, they see themselves as precursors and heralds of the new reality that God will bring. Today's political and social realities are to be measured by the degree to which they are a prelude of this reality. We here return to what we said about the work of the Spirit in history in chapter 12, on pneumatology. As soon as we have become acquainted with Jesus Christ and partake in the communion he establishes around his table, we will live on the basis of the notions of forgiveness, reconciliation, renewal, and justice that were demonstrated in his life and resurrection. Faith in Jesus Christ does not prompt us to withdraw from this world; rather, it inspires us to an engagement in and involvement with it. Faith and hope go together. Faith nourishes our hope.

Hence, though the Christian hope is thoroughly future oriented, it is not world avertive. At this point we note an interesting difference between *hoping for* something and *wishing* or *wanting to have* it. When we hope for something, that hope marks the way we live. When we hope for the coming of God's kingdom and its righteousness, we will also "seek" it here and now (Matt 6:33) by behaving in accordance with that hope. But when we merely wish for something (without any real hope that it will come to be), we may not be so eager in our daily life to prepare for the situation in which it will be realized. See C. Mostert in Egmond and Keulen 2001, 1:232. Christian eschatology concerns the future *and* the present, and these two are closely linked. Therefore, eternal life does not just begin later but has already begun, as we read repeatedly in the Gospel of John (e.g., 3:36; 5:24; 6:47, 54; 17:3). Or to cite the original title of E. Brunner's (1954) eschatology, *Das Ewige als Zukunft und Gegenwart*, eternity is future and present. Things go wrong when we let the two aspects compete in one-sided proposals that center on either the present or the future; Bultmann, as well as Hal Lindsey (1970), therefore, puts us on the wrong track.

At the same time, we must understand that our caring for the world and our faith in the power of God's gospel will never succeed in realizing the kingdom. It is a good thing that we no longer share in the naïveté of nineteenth-century European theology about the achievability of the kingdom of God, which was replicated in the overly optimistic and activist undertone of the theology of the 1960s and 1970s. Reality is more unruly than we think. Christian expectations of the coming of God's reign and of the completion of his work, however, are not based on optimism about human capacities but on the expectation that God will finish his work for the world. What he once began with the creation, and what he has (as it were) realigned in sending Jesus Christ and the Spirit, will be brought to completion by God himself, at his time and in the manner he chooses. This perspective indeed makes the completion or fulfillment a new act of God.

We said that faith and hope belong together. Paul stresses the close connection between faith, hope, and the work of the Spirit in Rom 8. Our eyes cannot witness our faith in the full realization of our salvation. That rests in the work that the Spirit already began for Jesus in restoring him to life (v. 11), which he will also do for those in whom the Spirit dwells. Calvin wrote compellingly about this combination of faith and hope. Where there is faith, hope will be its inevitable companion. To put it even more strongly, faith produces hope because faith and hope are both anchored in God's promises as they have come to us in the history of Israel and of Jesus Christ. Faith trusts that God is trustworthy in his promise of compassion, and this faith produces the hope and expectation of its fulfillment (*Inst.* 3.2.42–43). It is also important to note that this fulfillment is a new—in the full meaning of that word—eschatological act; fulfillment and completion do not automatically spring from what already exists but depend on a far-reaching act of God that changes everything; this act resumes what God has begun in Christ and now applies to his entire world.

Apparently, this radical newness is characteristic of God. The prophets of Israel already announced that, after the judgment of the exile, God would undertake something fundamentally new, without any precedent in the past (see Isa 43:18-19; Jer 31:31-32; Ezek 11:19). A real *novum* is also promised for the future: a *novum ultimum* (Moltmann 1996, 27-28, resorts to the Latin because "new" has suffered major word-inflation): "Behold, I make all things new" (Rev 21:5; see also 2 Cor 5:17). *This* newness represents a radical break with everything that now exists. Anything less is insufficient because what exists is too heavily marked by corruptibility and evil. Any changes our efforts might achieve may be compared to "rearranging the deck chairs on the *Titanic*," since we are unable to melt "the iceberg of our finiteness" (thus Bauckham and Hart 1999, 68; see throughout the accent on eschatological newness in this remarkable and informative study, e.g., 68-71, 77-80).

We come now to a question that has bewildered Christians throughout the ages: our relationship with the world that surrounds us as it continues its course through history. As baptized believers, we know we belong to Christ, and we live in the expectation that Christ will make everything new. But if, from a theological perspective, that completion is not the product of our efforts, what does this mean for human action, for our ethics? Or is our Christian hope, in fact, the context and inspiration for our actions? The fundamental Christian answer is that all human actions are impacted by our new God-given freedom. The community around Christ makes itself known in the new freedom that comes with the Spirit (2 Cor 3:17). It teaches us to pray for the coming of the kingdom and the "hallowing" of God's name. That prayer and that hope are decisive for our life and our future. It is a life that must conform to our newly acquired status as children of God. Obedience and sanctification, both individual and collective, are thereby branded by something God has already given, namely, the ultimate sacrifice of Christ's life. In him God has given himself. As a result, our Christian life will reflect this sacrifice as we offer our gratitude.

See, for example, the Heidelberg Catechism, where ethics, or obedience to God's commandments, is treated under the heading of gratitude. This wording agrees with an ancient tradition, as we find in the *Didache*, where at the beginning of the communion service, a prayer of thanksgiving is pronounced over the gifts that have been collected. In these gifts, we bring ourselves along as a thank offering for the life we have been given—and, ultimately, for Jesus Christ as well, the sacrifice that has provided us eternal life.

In emphasizing that human beings cannot organize God's kingdom, we follow the thread that runs through this book: with respect to the coming kingdom, we are mere recipients, receivers. But precisely as recipients of God's grace, we are enlisted in God's work in the world. Without reservation Paul points to himself and Apollos as colaborers with God (1 Cor 3:9), without implying that they considered themselves to be building the kingdom. The relationship between God's work and our work must always be carefully delineated. God is the guarantor of the coming of the kingdom, but this does not reduce what we do or don't do to utter meaninglessness. Neither is the New Testament expectation of a final judgment any excuse to think this way and to withdraw from the world under a kind of doomsday scenario. It is true that the order in which we presently live will pass away and will be exchanged for the new order that first appeared in the resurrection of Jesus Christ. In Jesus's death on the cross God has already pronounced judgment over the order of our day and age. "For the form of this world is passing away," Paul says (1 Cor 7:31b). This world with its rules and structures operates under premonitions of the future world, which permits us significant latitude in relativizing its demands. At the same time, this perspective makes the relationships and condition of our present life critically important. Work, marriage, career, friendships, economy, nature, environment, and politics do not lose all value; rather, we look at their challenges and possibilities in the light of what has come, and is coming, into the world in Christ.

Therefore it is actually too superficial to call the time between Pentecost and the parousia simply an interim, which might create the impression that our existence is no more than a sort of waiting room for eternity. It captures too little of the active expectation to which Jesus himself pointed the disciples in his parables. The parable of the five wise and the five foolish maidens (Matt 25:1-13) and that of the talents (Matt 25:14-30) follow on the heels of Jesus's discourse about the last things (Matt 24); they tell us that the hearers of the gospel must cultivate watchfulness. Not a life that dozes off in sleepiness, boredom, or just passing time, but a life of active expectation and concrete obedience. The New Testament makes us aware that we now live in the period of the last things, close to their climax. This eschatological consciousness did not disappear after Easter; rather, it was intensified by the experience of the Spirit. The time in which we live is marked by God's having poured out his Holy Spirit on the assembled disciples (Acts 2:4), by which he empowered them to respond to their calling in the time ahead. As we saw in chapter 12, the gift of the Spirit was intended, among other things, to provide this affirmation, to equip Jesus's followers for a life of witnessing to him (Matt 28:18-20). With this calling, the disciples could go into the world. The present before us thus does not lie empty but is filled because God has come to us in the Spirit, equipping us for witness and service. Paul calls believers to wake up, for daybreak is approaching (Rom 13:11-14), and to be filled with the Spirit of Christ (Eph 5:18). This note of the nearness of daybreak is the persistent theme in many appeals, in the Gospels and Epistles alike, to live in line with the new life that has begun in Christ. In the Sermon on the Mount, Jesus called his disciples to be a city on the hill, a light on a candlestick (Matt 5:14-15). In the Epistles we find repeated calls to "clothe" ourselves with the new life, as if it were a garment (Rom 13:14).

So we note that our lives today are absolutely not without value. Paul emphatically refers in his letters to being judged according to our works (1 Cor 3:10-23; 2 Cor 5:10). The foundation of our salvation is found in Jesus, the one who was crucified and exalted by the Father. That basis is certain. But it does not imply that we can build on the foundation in any way we please:

> Now if any one builds on the foundation with gold, silver, precious stones, wood, hay, straw—each man's work will become manifest; for the Day will disclose it, because it will be revealed with fire, and the fire will test what sort of work each one has done. (1 Cor 3:12-13)

All that we do here and now is subject to an "eschatological proviso"; it stands in the critical light of the day when Christ comes. On that day the all-changing might and power of Christ will be manifested (Phil 3:21), which will include a final judgment. The quality of the work of each of us will be visible, and it will be clear what can withstand the test and what is without value. We ourselves may be saved, but we nonetheless will have to pay the price of the loss of our work. Wood and hay will be burned, but precious metals will withstand the fire. The apostle speaks of a reward for those who have built with these costly materials, and of loss for those who were content with inferior things. "He himself will be saved, but only as through fire" (1 Cor 3:15). This is what we would call a *narrow escape*.

The passages cited above show the high degree to which the life and development of the early Christian church were characterized by eschatological expectations.

In 1 Cor 7:29-31, Paul states, "The time is short," which is the basis for his following words: "Let those who have wives live as though they had none, and those who mourn as though they were not mourning, and those who rejoice as though they were not rejoicing, and those who buy as though they had no goods, and those who deal with the world as though they had no dealings with it. For the form of this world is passing away" (1 Cor 7:29-31). For Paul, the expectation of an imminent return of Christ puts his current life under enormous pressure and produces a radical detachment in order to become totally committed to the coming kingdom. It leads him, for instance, to an ambivalent attitude toward marriage and sexuality (1 Cor 7:32-38).

The question to which contemporary dogmatics must reply is, how do we experience life today, now that the second coming—in a chronological sense—did not arrive "soon" but seems to be delayed? We do not have to wonder about the fact of the *Parusieverzögerung* (delay of the parousia) as such (see 2 Pet 3:9), but we need to engage in hermeneutical and dogmatic reflection on what this delay implies for the meaning of "ordinary" existence. We believe that the words of Paul quoted above remain important, especially in times when the church becomes totally preoccupied with the existing order and risks absolutizing it (including marriage and family). However, as time goes by, the "deposit of the Old Testament" (in which Miskotte rightly included the eroticism of the Song of Songs) proves to be more and more of unanticipated significance for the Christian church on its journey through time.

In sum, the future we expect in faith serves as a motivation for the present. Compare this perspective with the secular alternative; if we allow modern cosmology to present us with expectations and with a meaning for life, we are in for a great disappointment. Our solar system is finite, and one day its end will come. Such a doom scenario can hardly be expected to motivate action in the present because evil, as we know, is not selective and destroys both the good and the bad.

Do we live in a never-ending, onward moving time that will run out only when our sun is extinguished? Or will time continue so that, with Aristotle, we must assume that it is eternal? Modern cosmology does not offer a very happy view of the future. Speculations vary from the idea of an ever-expanding universe in which the temperature will drop further and further (the big chill), to the idea of this expanded universe eventually imploding and shrinking like an elastic band to its original, infinitely small beginning (Peacocke 1993, 71). In all these scenarios life on earth faces extinction. We are like someone who is condemned to death and sees only two possibilities, the bullet or the noose. Christians, however, believe that time too was created (Augustine, *Conf.* 11.14; *De civ. Dei* 11.6). As part of the created order, time receives specific significance; it is a gift from God (also with regard to time, we are the receivers). That is, only God has authority over time. From a New Testament angle, time has content because in time God stretches his two hands toward us and encounters us in Christ and in the Spirit. Apart from this encounter time becomes empty, and whether time is finite or infinite is, in this perspective, a question of secondary importance. For penetrating recent examinations of the relationship between the natural sciences and eschatology, see Peters 2006 and Wilkinson 2010, with both putting the notion of bodily resurrection center stage as the key Christian-theological contribution to the dialogue about the future of the physical universe.

Christian theology gets its hope from elsewhere: from the discoveries of what occurred in God's history with Israel and with Jesus, and in the experience of the sending of the Holy Spirit. The Trinitarian background is thus of essential importance, including with respect to eschatology. God is confessed as Creator; in the Son we get to know God as the Redeemer, and the Spirit is confessed as the one who will complete the work that was begun in Jesus Christ. The Spirit re-creates. In other words, in the Christian faith we come to know God as the one who takes a salvific initiative; as the one who will not give up, not even if it costs him everything; and as the one who does not draw back when things need to be finished. It reminds us of a phrase within the Genevan liturgical tradition that is derived from Ps 138:8: "God does not forsake the works of his hands." This statement gives a different meaning to the expectation of the future, and it changes the way time is divided, as the Christian holidays illustrate. Our hope is colored by what is given to us at Christmas, Easter, Ascension, and Pentecost. On that basis the church looks for another advent, the definitive coming of Christ.

16.4. Parousia and Eschatological Imagery

Through the ages the parousia, or second coming of Christ, and all that precedes it have been the topic of much discussion and speculation. Should we look for a bodily return of Christ on the Mount of Olives (see Acts 1:11), or for something else? Similar questions are raised regarding such specifics as the final judgment "at the sounding of the trumpet," the resurrection of the dead, heaven, and hell. How shall we interpret the Bible's many apocalyptic (= mysteriously revealing the future) images depicting the last things? Are these literal descriptions of what will happen, bits of information that we can put together like a jigsaw puzzle? Over the centuries, and still today, many have tried to explain the Bible's apocalyptic passages this way, but very often they got stuck in the process. For this reason, throughout church history many other voices have preferred a more symbolic interpretation of those images and texts. This is true, for instance, of the way in which the numbers and images in the Revelation were explained, especially the image of the "thousand years" in Rev 20:1-6 (see section 16.6). The mainstream of the Christian church thought that this number should not be taken literally but has a symbolic meaning. But in following such a route, are we not at risk of bleeding eschatology of everything concrete? How much meaning will remain after such a symbolic approach? And how do we decide what is really important as we try to interpret these images and passages?

In this section we try to provide some direction by listing a few hermeneutical principles that are important for interpreting and understanding these apocalyptic materials (we follow in the footsteps of others; see Rahner 2004; Berkouwer 1972, 9-31; Migliore, FSU 340-42). It will not surprise the reader that in this exercise also we attach a crucial significance to God's acting in Christ and in the Spirit.

1. *We must take the imagery of all these eschatological representations with utter seriousness.* What we said in chapter 5 about the earthliness of revelation applies to the future as well. The Christian hope will always be expressed in words and images that are borrowed from our own world and imagination. This assumption seems to invite vulnerability, but we must accept that God's revelation always takes the route of "accommodation." The prophets (Isaiah, Ezekiel, Daniel, the intertestamental period) already offer an enormous array of images that were inspired by the religion and politics of their day and that were reinterpreted in the New Testament against the background of the appearance of Jesus Christ. The images of *gehenna*, of an eternal fire, of a final tribunal when the Son of Man comes, and also of a secret rapture of the church (1 Thess 4:17)—all these have functioned as attempts to make the Christian hope concrete. The Apocalypse too, the last book of the Bible, must be read in this way. Here liturgical, political, and cosmological images have been welded together to express hope for God's eternal kingdom in glory. The presence of all these images has often been used as an excuse to take the things depicted somewhat less seriously, while others have taken it as a reason to deny the special character of symbolic language. These are serious misunderstandings. Recognizing that we are dealing with images and

symbols does not mean that they are all the arbitrary product of human fantasies that can be dismissed. Rather, they are to be taken very seriously indeed as means of expressing the center, the breadth, and the meaning of God's revelation in Christ and the Spirit. The images and symbols do so very exactly and provide us with important knowledge.

For some probing discussions (in Dutch) on the plausibility of belief in Christ's second coming, but also on the backgrounds of the rich imagery that plays a role here in Jewish apocalyptic expectations, see Jonge and Ruyter 1995. With respect to the Apocalypse, note especially Bauckham 1993. The antisymbolic alternative consists in an attempt to take all the images (including their numerology) altogether literally. This approach has been fiercely promoted by Hal Lindsey (b. 1929). In his bestseller *The Late Great Planet Earth* (1970), this American evangelist connected Bible texts—which were fancifully detached from their contexts—with actual events.We find this biblicistic method of interpretation, which is saturated in terms of impending doom, highly incredible. But the huge sales of his books indicate that Lindsey dealt with Bible passages to which mainstream churches should give more attention than they have for a long time.

2. Apocalyptic and eschatological passages must be read in view of *their basis in what was revealed in the life, cross, and resurrection of Christ and as further expanded by the Spirit.* The New Testament confesses in the resurrection of Jesus Christ from the dead that God the Father affirms him and exalts and transforms his earthly-bodily existence beyond the boundary of death. God does not thereby annul the work that he began in creation and the covenant; rather, it is all fulfilled—that is, it fully comes into its own. In a single word, God reaches his *goal*. We have noted that the very image of the resurrection is borrowed from daily life. As we are awakened from our sleep and rise, likewise Jesus was raised from death by the Father. In this image we see how continuity and discontinuity go together in God's eschatological acts in Jesus. The Christian faith expects that things will not stop with this one, but that he bore a promise for the entire world. In Christ, God said Yes, and God will maintain and confirm this Yes with regard to his church (see 2 Cor 1:19–20). The continuity lies in the faithfulness of God, who keeps this man safe and exalts him right through death and judgment, and thereby also all who are "in him" (an expression that occurs 137 times in the New Testament).

For his part, the Spirit keeps the expectation alive and inspires the church to look for the complete revelation of Christ and his kingdom. "The Spirit"—here mentioned first—"and the Bride say: Come!" (Rev

22:17). That is, the Spirit works from Christ toward the future. Note Berkhof, CF 526, 529 ("In a combination of continuity and leap, Christ and the Spirit move toward the future").

3. *The Christian hope and expectation of the future cover the totality of our existence.* The concepts of exaltation and resurrection apply not only to the spiritual aspect of our existence but also to our total creaturely life; in other words, body and soul. This Christian hope is anchored in the faith that Jesus Christ is the firstfruit in whom Israel's hope received a preliminary fulfillment. This event thus forms the basis for our hope that God will complete the work that he began in Christ for his entire creation. Just like Christ's resurrection, the raising of the dead will encompass the entire creaturely structure of life. Paul, in speaking of a "pneumatic body" (Gk. *sōma pneumatikon*, 1 Cor 15:44), did not mean a phantom-like existence but a physical reality that is fully defined by the indwelling and renewing operation of the Holy Spirit. The eschatological images cannot be lined up in a kind of "news-reporting eschatology" (Berkouwer 1972, 247), but we likewise fail to do justice to them when we spiritualize them and remove all bodily concreteness.

While this present life is still conditioned by the earthly breath of life ("we currently have this physical body [*sōma psychikon*]"), the resurrected body (*sōma pneumatikon*, 1 Cor 15:44) is fully conditioned by the Holy Spirit. It is a much richer mode of existence, which (to use another term of Van Ruler) has become "fireproof" against corruption and sin. However, this mode of existence retains a material substrate. In this connection we may think of a well-known and often (and in various forms) cited comment of the German Pietistic theologian F. C. Oetinger (1702–82): *Leiblichkeit ist das Ende des Werkes Gottes, wie aus der Stadt Gottes klar erhellet* (Corporeality is the end of God's work, as is clearly shown by the city of God [with reference to Rev 20]; *Biblisches und emblematisches Wörterbuch* [1776], 407).

4. *Indissoluble communion with the exalted Christ in the Spirit is the core of Christian hope* and the key to understanding these biblical images. In Rom 8:31-39 Paul expands this hope in a way that supersedes all the images he employs. The experience of indissoluble love that was given in the death and resurrection of Christ is of paramount importance:

What then shall we say to this? If God is for us, who is against us? He who did not spare his own Son but gave him up for us all, will he not also give us all things with him? Who shall bring any charge against

God's elect? It is God who justifies; who is to condemn? Is it Christ Jesus, who died, yes, who was raised from the dead, who is at the right hand of God, who indeed intercedes for us? Who shall separate us from the love of Christ? . . . For I am sure that neither death, nor life, nor angels, nor principalities, nor things present, nor things to come, nor powers, nor height, nor depth, nor anything else in all creation, will be able to separate us from the love of God in Christ Jesus our Lord. (Rom 8:31-39)

The central figure behind this vision is the Spirit, just as he is in the resurrection of Christ: "If the Spirit of him who raised Jesus from the dead dwells in you, he who raised Christ Jesus from the dead will give life to your mortal bodies also through his Spirit which dwells in you" (Rom 8:11).

To summarize, in caring for his children, God will deal with any obstructions. In his freedom God acquits people; he has handed over his own Son to the powers of death in order to give us, with him, everything; and he gives us his Spirit to connect us with Christ. Because Christ suffered death and because love was demonstrated as victorious power, no other power is able to remove us from the reach of divine love. Paul's personal expectation of the future was therefore characterized by his desire to die and to "be with Christ, for that is far better" (Phil 1:23). This is also the consistent story line in the book of Revelation. However much the martyrs may have to suffer from oppression (even until after their death, Rev 6:10-11), they have been bought and paid for, and they are therefore the possession of Jesus Christ. No other power can steal them.

5. *The eschatological images tell of the final victory over evil*, and thus they concern things that impact all people. We know that death comes to everyone and that therefore all our names will sink away in the oblivion of history. When separated from God, time and space are powers that estrange and frighten people, even in our modern times. In a cosmic perspective, we live in a faraway corner of the universe, which comprises an innumerable number of other galaxies, each with countless numbers of suns and planets. In addition, we see the concrete powers of evil—of which every human being, even every little child, is aware: oppression by tyrants big and small, the threat of loneliness and rejection, of not being seen, of having no name, of dissolution into nothingness. The Christian expectation of the future provides an answer to these fears, an answer based on the death and resurrection of Jesus Christ, which is symbolized in baptism. In baptism the name of Jesus Christ is attached to the

name given to the one who is baptized. The history of the newly baptized person from then on moves in unison with the drama of salvation that received its decisive turn in Jesus Christ. The primary thing that the Christian church can say about eschatology has, in fact, already been said in our baptism; in Jesus's name the evil powers will bow and be destroyed, and everyone who is connected with Christ will, through it all, be saved and kept safe for God's eternal future. Parts of the apocalyptic of a book like Revelation (but also Dan 7-12) may be extremely threatening, but the general outlook is always encouraging. It goes through deep valleys, but everything that seeks to destroy God's work will come to an end.

The last book of the Bible makes this comprehensive promise abundantly clear. It calls Jesus the Alpha and the Omega (Rev 22:13; cf. 1:17), after the first and last letters of the Greek alphabet. He comprises all things! His significance is illustrated by the use of images that often overlap and influence each other. On the one hand, Christ is referred to thirty-five times as the Lamb, based on his suffering for the world and offering himself. On the other hand, he is the one who is resurrected and now lives eternally (Rev 1:18). The two images are so intimately connected that John sees the Lamb "standing, as though it had been slain" (Rev 5:6). We get stuck as soon as we take this image literally, for a lamb that is slain can no longer stand, and a standing lamb, obviously, is not slain. So we must search for the meaning, which becomes clear from the context: the exalted Christ is in heaven "as slain"—that is to say, the signs of his having been slain are still visible. The wound is still there, but at the same time he is the conquering Lion from Judah (Rev 5:5). Lamb and Lion no longer form a contrast.

The last book of the Bible shows us in this bounty of kaleidoscopic images—which are often borrowed from the Old Testament, but also use contemporary material—what eschatology is. It is not an orderly list of events that are the grand finale of some future program. *Eschatology is primarily concerned with the question of who is actually in charge of the present and the future.* Is it the ruling powers under which we live, or is it the Lamb, the living Christ, whom we serve as Lord? The Christian hope becomes concrete in our faith that the same Jesus who walked on this earth, who healed people in God's name and gave vision to those who had lost their way, is the one who determines God's future intervention. This Lord has not yet come to the end of his road.

6. *The revelation of God's love in Jesus Christ therefore also implies judgment.* This sentence is the first that directly addresses the work of Jesus against evil. Modern theology greatly resents these images of judgment, eternal punishment, and of God as a consuming fire: it therefore,

theologically speaking, leads a very secluded life. But this resentment is clearly at odds with the widespread fascination with the themes of judgment, darkness, and forsakenness in modern culture. We can find plenty of examples in film, literature, and the other arts. In biblical theology, however, these threats are not just linked to thugs and villains, but—and this really hits home—to all those who have ignored the salvation that Jesus offers and who have opted for a life apart from God and his dealings with this world (Heb 2:3; 12:25).

In Jesus's entire ministry and in the proclamation of the resurrection, we hear the warning that rejecting God's love has momentous consequences. The rejection of God's love, the decision to be a god ourselves, or indifference toward the expectation of the future will come up against the judgment of God. If the blessing is rejected, the curse has free rein. The biblical images of hellfire, ultimate darkness, lake of destruction, and eternal death point to a mode of existence from which God has withdrawn because it withdrew itself from God; rejection *by* God is the consequence of our rejection *of* God. The central meaning of all these images is that we should take rejection of Jesus Christ as the revelation of God with utmost seriousness.

The first audience of the Apocalypse consisted of believers who lived under the yoke of Roman imperial reign. During their life on earth they confessed Jesus as their Lord. As a consequence they suffered persecution as martyrs. In their distress they called upon God: "O Sovereign Lord, holy and true, how long before thou wilt judge and avenge our blood on those who dwell upon the earth?" (Rev 6:10). God is the one who must put an end to injustice.

16.5. The Meandering of the Eschatological Expectation

The first generations of Christians lived in the expectation that the parousia of Jesus Christ would happen soon. When it did not, the infant church had to come to terms with a delay. In the fourth century the situation changed dramatically as the result of the public recognition of the moral strength of the Christian faith. It had become more than a culture-shaping influence; it had official preference. In these changed circumstances Christians faced the challenge of occupying a new place in this world, with a resultant loss of eschatological awareness. The idea of the imminent realization of a future with God was more and more exchanged for a focus on life on this earth; attention increasingly shifted from the "things above" (Col 3:1) to making a home, and feeling at home, in this world. This demise of eschatological awareness and its ascetic attitude toward life was criticized quite often during the twentieth century. We think of the criticism of the early Barth and, in our time, of Beek (2008).

These voices make a strong point in warning the church and Christianity not to surrender themselves to their own time and culture. The New Testament reminds us that, also for us, our life is hidden in Christ (Col 3:3). The church must not lose its orientation toward Christ as the firstfruit of God's new creation. At the same time, we must remember that such an orientation does not, in a theological sense, make our ongoing history empty and meaningless. In the progress of history after Easter and in the sending of the Spirit, Christians are challenged—and this too is the result of a divine decision—to build their lives and accept responsibilities for the time being, here and now. The challenge is multiplied in our circumstances of increased prosperity and longer life expectancy. Theology may not ignore the task of interpreting these realities in the light of God's revelation. We are to regard the flow of time not as empty or indifferent but as the space where God encounters people and where he now wants to change them to conform to his image, so that they will find courage for their lives. The future, both in the time that we live on earth and beyond, is God's.

In contemporary Western theology we see great reluctance to countenance a positive relationship between the Christian faith and our own culture. Prophetic criticism predominates, together with a fear of losing eschatological awareness. We often refer to the time in which society and Christianity seemed to coincide as the Constantinian era, or as the *corpus Christianum*, the "Christian body" that Europe in some sense indeed was, well into the nineteenth century. During the heyday of the Middle Ages the earthly kingdom and the heavenly kingdom (*civitas terrena* and *civitas caelestis*), which for Augustine were opposites, coincided. Otto von Freising (twelfth century) thought that, with the conversion of the Roman emperors, God himself had invested the church with all earthly authority. The authority of Christ embraced the worldly authorities. This ideal unity soon fragmented with the Investiture Controversy, but the eschatological expectation of an imminent realization of the kingdom of God lived on. This continuation was, no doubt, also influenced by the acute awareness of human finitude with its intense focus on God and the hereafter so characteristic of the Middle Ages (concerning the eschatological expectations in the Middle Ages, see Hebblethwaite 2010, 58–74). Europeans and North Americans largely considered themselves to be Christian nations until fairly recently, and their respective societies to be a *societas Christiana*.

The Enlightenment that followed may be seen as a prologue to a secularized form of eschatology. It adopted a linear view of history that was characteristic of Judaism and Christianity, but it also reduced belief to the kind of progress that we ourselves can and must achieve. The Enlightenment project, therefore, does not stand on its own feet but rests on religious presuppositions, as some prescient religious thinkers with a Jewish-Christian background clearly saw and made a topic for debate, notably Karl Löwith (1949) and Eugen Rosenstock-Huessy (1966, 75-76). In fact, even the metaphor "enlightenment" is itself an example of a secularized concept. Whereas in the past (particularly in the Augustinian tradition), enlightenment was consistently expected from the "sun of righteousness" (a metaphor for Christ, borrowed from Mal 4:2), it was now commonly believed that humankind should employ the instrument of reason in order to become divinely enlightened. In the twentieth century this "enlightenment optimism" suffered an enormous setback. The superficiality of Euro-American so-called civilization became very clear. Already in the nineteenth century unbridled capitalism showed its inhumanity; then Europe was hit by two world wars, and dreams of progress and of a modern model state led only to absolutist dictatorial systems, such as National Socialism and Marxist Communism. Both ideologies wreaked immense havoc in the name of progress and brotherhood. More recently the ideology of the free market and its myth of constant growth have brought to the brink the welfare and stability we thought had been achieved.

As we said in chapter 12, on the Holy Spirit, there is no reason to identify Europe or North America with Christianity. But the opposite attitude of totally rejecting culture and history, or suggestions in that direction, is just as irresponsible, theologically speaking. In many ways the commandment of love has continued to have its influence, and even today at the very least ensures an uneasy conscience about injustice. In the light of the last judgment, the call for obedience and justice in the personal and public sphere only gains in intensity (Rev 22:11), for only what conforms to God's intentions will survive it. In Rev 21:26 we read that "the glory and the honor of the nations" will be brought into the new Jerusalem. That is, everything good and beautiful that people and nations produce worldwide, and all their works of compassion and humanity, will be borne into the kingdom of God and there have their place.

16.6. Millennialism

May the flow of time after Easter and Pentecost be regarded so positively that we can discern therein a prelude to the eschaton? Does Christ's reign and the righteousness he will bring already, in a preliminary way, throw some light on the path of history? We deal with these questions in this section, on millennialism.

To repeat, when the end did not immediately arrive, Christians began to adjust to the idea of a longer duration for history, but then they had to face the question of why they had been given this longer time. New Testament reflections on this issue regarded the longer period as a harvest time during which, through the Spirit, all people may be drawn toward Christ (Acts), but it was also deemed to be a short time of testing in which the genuineness of people's faith can be demonstrated (1 Peter). In 2 Peter we find the idea that the delay has been given as an expanded window for conversion:

> But do not ignore this one fact, beloved, that with the Lord one day is as a thousand years, and a thousand years as one day. The Lord is not slow about his promise as some count slowness, but is forbearing toward you, not wishing that any should perish, but that all should reach repentance. (3:8-9)

Besides these reasons we find, particularly in Jewish-Christian circles, a movement toward what we call millennialism or chiliasm (Lat. *mille* and Gk. *chilioi* = a thousand), the idea that Christ's rule will come to definitive completion and shape in earthly time. The relation between the present and the final fulfillment was not thought of as an absolute break; rather, there will be a period of transition in which the conquering power of Christ takes concrete form. This undersanding was, in particular, linked to Rev 20:1-6. We read in this passage that the serpent, or Satan, is "seized" and will remain "bound" for a period of one thousand years so that "he should deceive the nations no more, till the thousand years were ended." The purpose of this "binding" is that the saints may rule together with Christ. "Then I saw thrones, and seated on them were those to whom judgment was committed. Also I saw the souls of those who had been beheaded for their testimony to Jesus and for the word of God, and who had not worshiped the beast or its image and had not received its mark on their foreheads or their hands. They came to life, and reigned with Christ a thousand years" (v. 4). After the period of a thousand years, in this thinking, the devil will be released, followed by a short time of intense persecution. From the very beginning some have understood this thousand-year period to be a literal, future period that would precede Christ's final parousia.

The motif behind this chiliastic expectation is fully biblical. It resists letting the salvation that Christ brings evaporate in a spiritualized interpretation.

Certainly this is Irenaeus's motif when, against the gnostics, he emphasizes the concreteness of salvation; the redemption and restoration that Christ brings stand out in earthly colors (*Against Heresies* 5.35.2). Christ restores creation and thereby lifts it to a higher level. Irenaeus connects creation, salvation history, and eschatology in an ascending line so as to achieve not only a restoration but also an elevation of what exists. In Lactantius we see a reflex response to the time of persecution mixed with a Greco-Roman notion of a golden era.

Church history has witnessed intense discussions about the interpretation of the thousand years. Should the period be taken literally? Or does it represent a very long time in which church and faith can develop in tranquility and safety? As we said, millennialism in the early church occurred in the situation of Christians being a persecuted minority. This situation changed as violence against Christians gradually decreased until the fourth century, when Christianity was recognized as the state religion. The historian Eusebius, who himself experienced persecution under Diocletian, described the new political and cultural situation in eschatological colors, which he derived from Isa 40ff.: "Strengthen your weak knees, because God creates something new" (*Hist. Eccl.* 10.4). A century later the enthusiasm about the new Roman state had significantly cooled. In *The City of God* (books 20–23) Augustine became one of the most prominent critics of the interpretation that applies these texts to the end of time. He connected this passage to the entire history of the church and thereby became the father of the spiritualized interpretation. On this reading the first resurrection stands for the new birth; already now those who are born again no longer fall under the power of Satan but under the rule of Christ. The second resurrection is the second coming, and in between these resurrections comes an interim period in which the devil may indeed wage war but in reality can no longer inflict damage on the believer.

This spiritualized interpretation has been dominant in Reformed and Lutheran Protestantism, for which the thousand years represent the period in which the church expands ever further in this world. This view has been called *amillennialism* (e.g., Hoekema 1979, 173). This view of a thousand years at the end of time is condemned in Augsburg Confession 17 as "Jewish opinions," and this characterization was subsequently adopted as well in article 11 of the Second Helvetic Confession.

Indeed, millennialism has traditionally been associated with Judaism, since in many of its scenarios the converted Jews (see Rom 11:25) would rule with Christ during the thousand years. Admittedly, anti-Judaic sentiments have played a role in the rejection of millennialism, but such criticisms could not always keep the historicized interpretation of the thousand-year period from exerting its influence. It has sympathizers even today among groups of Christians. We must distinguish between two main forms: *premillennialism* and *postmillennialism*. The premillennialists maintain that the first parousia of Christ occurs at the beginning of the thousand years, after the period of the "great tribulation"; postmillennialists situate the parousia of Christ at the end of a period of relative prosperity and growth in which the gospel has "leavened" the world. Postmillennialism resembles amillennialism with the added proviso that, because of the worldwide impact of the gospel, history will end in the millennium: a long period (perhaps not a literal one thousand years) of relative rest and prosperity before Christ returns.

For an overview of these various models (including clear diagrams), with arguments that lean toward premillennialism, see Grudem, ST 1109-31. In church history a temporal historical approach to the millennium often coincided with the expectation of an imminent second coming and a division of history into distinct periods. In this connection we may think of Joachim of Fiore (1135-1202), who divided history into three periods—the eras of the Father, the Son and the Spirit. The Old Testament covered the period of the Father, and the first thousand years of church history were the era of the Son. Joachim lived in the expectation that the next one thousand years would be the period of the Spirit, during which the contemplative spirit of monasticism would rule and reform the church. Joachim exerted great influence on end-time expectations during the Middle Ages.

At the time of the Reformation the expectation of an imminent end of the world reemerged in Anabaptist circles. The experiment in Münster (1534-35), which was an attempt to establish an Anabaptist regime and ended in bloodshed, was the most dramatic episode. Some regarded this event as the inauguration of the thousand years in which believers were to rule the earth and establish God's kingdom. In the Anglophone world the division of history into periods became known as *dispensationalism* (Lat. *dispensatio*; see Boyer 1992, 86-100, and

Hoekema 1979, 188–93). Its leading proponents were John Darby (1800–1882) and Cyrus Scofield (1843–1921) with his *Scofield Reference Bible* (1909). Scofield distinguished seven dispensations (innocence, conscience, human government, promise, law, grace, and the thousand years). According to this theory, seven years before Christ's second coming the church will be taken into heaven in the so-called rapture. Israel has a specific role in the final days of history as well. During the millennium Jesus will rule with the Jewish people from Jerusalem. Dispensationalism is one version of premillennialism, which places the return of Christ before the beginning of the thousand years. The twentieth century saw an enormous amount of speculations and calculations along this line, especially in nontraditional or free church groups. We point once more to the popular work of Hal Lindsey (1970), who applied the apocalyptic symbols of Gog and Magog (Ezek 38) directly to the cold war between the Communist Eastern bloc and the capitalist West under the leadership of the United States.

Like Rahner (2004, 324–43), Berkouwer (1972, 238) rejects attempts to devise an exact scenario of the events that will supposedly take place at the end of time. Such precision would mean a systematizing of the apocalyptic images into some sort of *antizipierte Reportage* (anticipatory journalism). We regard this way of treating the Bible and of dealing with the biblical expectation of the future as inadequate for both hermeneutical and theological reasons. Such an approach fails to respect the christological and pneumatological aspects of what the Bible expects of the future. In chiliastic accounts the future is not only fully fixed, like the plot of a thriller, but is supposedly also totally transparent. In fact, however, such fascination with future events often leads to a "de-eschatologizing" of the biblical text and thus to escapism. Our obedience *in* the world and *for* the world ceases to be important, since the world is going to its doom anyway. A concrete example: for many American Christians, this mode of thinking has resulted in gross indifference with regard to environmental issues.

This result is evident especially the case in *premillennialism*. Characteristic here is that some premillennialists developed the theory of a rapture of the church just before the great tribulation. The idea (which is not supported by all premillennialists) is built on a dubious exegesis of 1 Thess 4:17 and reinforces the de-eschatologizing tendency. It turns believers into a group of people who will get away scot-free at the very moment all hell breaks loose on earth. Bearing witness to the nations is left to the Jews, and even more important, the judgment over sin and death that is borne by Christ becomes of little significance; it no longer impacts believers' thoughts and hopes (Migliore, FSU 336–37). The drama of humanity and the world is treated as a performance that believers watch from their heavenly balcony seats, as mere spectators to this terrible end-time struggle. The notion of God's counsel becomes a blueprint to be passively watched from some distance on the human side. The eschatological passages in the Prophets and the Gospels, however, are distinguished by holding that the future always impacts our present encounter with God. The present, in which we are the objects of God's grace in Christ, forms a real moment in the realization of a still-hidden fulfillment (Rahner 2004, 331).

Postmillennialism is set to another tune. In this view the second coming will occur after the thousand-year period. Its central text is Matt 24:14: "And this gospel of the kingdom will be preached throughout the whole world, as a testimony to all nations; and then the end will come." Postmillennialism counts on the power of the gospel to permeate and transform peoples and cultures like a leaven. Matthew 28:18-20 is read not just as a command but also as a promise. The parables that speak of the growth of the kingdom and the passages in the Epistles that speak of surrender to Christ and the disarming of the powers (Col 2:15) arouse expectations of real change (Hoekema 1979, 175–80). Berkhof shows some sympathy for postmillennialism, particularly in his book about Christ as the one who gives meaning to history. These authors are attracted to the idea of an earthly reign of peace, since postmillennialism retains the belief that the glorious resurrection of Christ reveals itself in history over the full breadth of the cosmic front (see Berkhof 1966, chap. 7). God's salvation has to do with this—with our—reality. Berkhof is more prudent in his CF and emphasizes the ambiguity of cultural developments, but here too he maintains that there is "on the one hand, a general and voluntary acceptance of the gospel-inspired structural rules as the only means to preserve the viability of our existence, a 'Millennium,'" while on the other hand, there is an anti-Christian world dictatorship (CF 518-19). There is little doubt that Berkhof (as a person of his time) was affected at this point by a certain measure of optimism about the development of culture that we no longer share today; this change should not blind us, however, to the fact that his argumentation is fully theological. Beginning with God's liberating acts in Christ and the Spirit, he tries to draw lines toward the future so as to do justice to the many apocalyptic passages in the Scriptures.

If God is the Creator of heaven and earth and if Christ is the Judge of our history, the Yes that God has spoken in Christ also affects time, history, and the cosmos as we know it. These too will be brought to fulfillment, will be sanctified and thereby completed. In this respect, millennialism is correct. But how it all happens is not visible to us; it is truly hidden. The real core of Christian eschatology is that Christ will come and that his rule over time and history, over work and culture, will be revealed. Salvation will be just as real, physical, and tangible as our present life, but in a transformed, exalted way without the restrictions that were inherent in the initial creation. The work that God began as the Creator, which was saved from sin and death by the Son, will be completed by the Spirit. In this re-creation, creation returns *and* achieves its purpose.

A few remarks are in order about the role of the ascension, especially in the Reformed tradition. The ascension is presented as an important theme mainly in the book of Acts. It is in line with the faith of the early church that Christ will appear as the Judge (1 Cor 4:5; 6:14; 2 Cor 4:14; 5:10; Matt 25:31-46). The glorified Christ has been taken into heaven and thereafter was invisible (Acts 1:9). This same Jesus Christ will come again and appear as the Judge over the living and the dead (Acts 3:21). Jesus is the living Lord who determines our history and sends us his Spirit in the time before his second coming. The theme of the ascension accentuates both the hiddenness and absence of Jesus as a visible person, as well as the preliminary nature of this time in which the Spirit has been made available as the first gift (see Zwiep 1997).

In Barth's work the parousia, the presence or coming of Christ, takes different forms. The first manner of his coming or presence is the resurrection, while in the second form of the parousia, Christ testifies of himself in the power of the Spirit. The third, definitive coming will disclose the height, depth, and breadth of the new reality in Christ. While Barth initially suggested that the new reality was fully realized in Christ's death on the cross, he provides a much more dramatic picture in CD IV/3:325-33. The preliminary nature of our situation is grounded in the fact that Jesus Christ himself is "still engaged in conflict . . . and therefore is still a Pilgrim on the way to that goal" (329). Our present time offers "the great opportunity which He has given creation to freely enter His service" (333).

We have now treated the predominant models of eschatology during the twentieth century. This review was necessary to get better insight, at some distance, into the specific character of this domain of Christian doctrine and into the different ways of approaching eschatology. But we also discovered how important it is for eschatology not to get lost in second-order issues, since in our dogmatic reflection we must retain, and neither avoid nor go beyond, the concreteness of the biblical witness about the future. For that reason we began this section with a discussion of the concrete biblical data that deal with the future. In the following section we will continue on this track by focusing our attention on the *eschata*, which in the literature are usually referred to as the "four last things." Then we will zero in on the significance of our belief in eternal life—the final theme in both the Nicene and the Apostles' Creed.

16.7. The "Four Last Things": The Resurrection of the Dead, Final Judgment, Heaven, and Hell

The resurrection of the dead. If we want to reflect meaningfully on the resurrection of the dead, we must return to what we said earlier (11.1) about the resurrection of Jesus Christ. We noted that the confession of the second coming and the resurrection of the dead was significantly influenced by apocalyptic expectations as set forth, for instance, in Isa 25, Ezek 37, and Dan 7:13–14. Israel expected that God would establish his reign visibly before all peoples; he will execute justice, and in the process the powers of evil will be judged and destroyed. Belief in a general resurrection of the dead was thus nothing new for Paul. He could interpret the resurrection of Christ as an affirmation of an expectation he shared with his Jewish compatriots (1 Cor 15:12–19).

The New Testament tells us that this corrective action of God began in the ministry of Jesus Christ. That is, the kingdom of God has already become a reality in that ministry, and Christ is the beginning. For this reason, Christ himself could become the object of the proclamation, and his resurrection anchors the expectation that this Christ will one day soon appear in glory. Recall that, strictly speaking, this appearance is not just a return but a (royal) arrival, a definitive coming in glory (see Matt 24:3; 1 Cor 15:23; 1 Thess 3:13; 4:15; 2 Pet 1:16). According to the New Testament this parousia will signal the resurrection of the dead (1 Cor 15:22–23). This wording implies that all who belong to Christ will be given a new life in glory when God "calls." Just as God once began creation by speaking, so his "speaking" also marks the beginning of the full experience of eternal life. The entire human being, in his or her earthly, psychosomatic identity, is the object of God's call. God calls each of us by name. In this connection we are reminded of what happens at baptism: the person's name is called, and his or her whole existence is brought into communion with the triune God. This participation in God's life affects—we say it again—the entire human being.

How exactly this resurrection will happen we cannot say. Here again we are faced with the limitations of human language. We run into all sorts of problems as soon as we try to give literal descriptions of the resurrection and all its physical, biological, and geographic consequences. Those who try to do so deny the unique nature of the biblical language in these portions of Scripture. We must in all respects fall back on God's faithfulness; he will create something new in which the former things will find their fulfillment and completion.

The last judgment. The Apostles' Creed says that Christ is seated at the right hand of God, the almighty Father, from where he will come to judge the living and the dead. We have referred to the last judgment, or the trial, in the context of the coming of the exalted Christ. There is a direct link between parousia and judgment. In Matt 25 the coming of the Son of Man coincides with the judgment over the actions of the people. This is not a popular notion. It evokes the thought of a final settlement in which a large part of humanity will find itself doomed, forever relegated to godforsakenness and a terrible punishment in hell. Should we therefore put aside the concepts of a tribunal or trial, judgment, and punishment as pieces of an inhumane kind of theology? In the twentieth century, with its history of genocide, mass exploitation, and child abuse, it was often pointed out that the idea of judgment is, in fact, quite inadequate. Judgment involves doing justice—justice to the victims. We might, however, argue that the idea of a judgment is needed as a postulate. Without a final judgment criminals would get away with their acts, and victims would not get recognition and restoration. But this line of reasoning (based on Kant) is not biblical and theological enough. It would be better theologically to return to what we said earlier about reconciliation. God maintains his claim on humanity and the world and restores them. This restoration comes via the route of judgment and verdict.

What is the actual content of the final judgment? The final judgment has three functions: discovery of the truth, cleansing/purification, and verdict. First comes discovery of truth. In Matt 25 Jesus depicts the coming of the Son of Man as a king assembling the people before him and officiating as judge. He separates those who have lived according to the rules of God's kingdom from those who have ignored them. We see how the Son of Man identifies himself with those who have hungered, the sick, the prisoners, and the strangers; in them he is present in a hidden way. Both groups—those who are invited to enter the kingdom and those who are rejected—never noticed that hidden presence. The judgment brings to light how things really were. In fact, the very same thing took place during Jesus's ministry on earth; in his confrontation with people, Jesus reveals the truth of their lives. Consider a few examples: Zacchaeus sees his true state and shows sincere remorse (Luke 19:1-10); the Samaritan woman in John 4 recognizes the condition of her current life, and Peter is not spared by Jesus when they meet after the resurrection (John 21:15-19). In these passages judgment consists, first of all, in the discovery of truth, in recognizing one's true situation. Life is what it is in the eyes of God. But this discovery is not just negative, for judgment also implies that God takes us seriously and does not let us go. The fact that the Bible speaks of a judgment also discloses the dimension of hope.

Second, the Bible shows that the judgment of Christ involves cleansing and purification. We do not hear a quick and immediate word of forgiveness in Jesus's conversation with Peter. Their conversation initiates a process of reconciliation in which Peter senses the reality of his denial and shows genuine regret. The repeated questions of Jesus make him so desperate that his only way out is a direct appeal to Jesus: "Lord, you know everything; you know that I love you" (John 21:17). That is the situation of us all before God. Peter can only surrender to God and place his hope in him, and he is purified by the way Christ looks at him (see also Luke 22:61). In the Pauline epistles we also explicitly meet this function, but there it is linked to the judgment at the end of time. The final judgment is a fire that consumes everything that has no substance or is inferior and half-hearted—it all is burned and disappears (see 1 Cor. 3:10-15, a passage we discussed earlier).

The third element of judgment is that of verdict and punishment. These are unpopular words. They remind us that God appeals to us, and they point to the consequence of rejecting this offer of life and love. It implies a threat (1 Cor 4:5; 2 Cor 5:9-10). But it also, and primarily, includes a final cosmic settlement with the powers of evil and all their allies. In recent years exegetes have stressed the discontinuity that the New Testament posits at this point between the present and the future. A clear example occurs in the Second Epistle of Peter, which speaks of the current world order in terms of passing away, burning, dissolution, and melting (3:7, 10, 12). Some have tried to read into this description a kind of cleansing or purification that will leave the current world order intact. But that does not do sufficient justice to the radical language employed. We should rather speak of *recreatio* (re-creation) or even *nova creatio* (new creation) than of *renovatio*—a thorough makeover is not enough for our present world order. What we just said about the resurrection of the dead applies here as well; the continuity of present and future is not anchored in the things themselves but only in God's faithfulness. Whatever continuity there is, comes from God.

Therefore, the coming judgment has both cosmic and individual aspects. As to the latter, we may wonder when the judgment actually takes place: immediately after our death or when Christ comes with his day of judgment. This question is inextricably connected with the issue of the so-called interim state: where are we between our death and the eschaton? Or does the eschaton for each individual perhaps begin at his or her time of death, since that moment marks the transition between time and eternity? We leave this question for now, since we already discussed it above in 7.5.

Heaven and hell. The christological and soteriological pivot points that we have mentioned are also important when we ask about heaven and hell. Heaven and hell describe the two possibilities that the Bible mentions with regard to the last judgment. When Jesus speaks about the final judgment of the Son of Man, the hearers are confronted with them. Those who have lived according to the rules of the kingdom are invited into the kingdom and enter eternal life (Matt 25:46); those who have ignored that kingdom are excluded from it and face eternal punishment. In the parable of the talents we hear of an "outer darkness" where there is "weeping and gnashing of teeth" (Matt 25:30). In the last book of the Bible, Revelation, we read about a "lake of fire" into which death and Hades (the realm of the dead) are thrown. These verses express a terrible threat: "If any one's name was not found written in the book of life, he was thrown into the lake of fire" (Rev 20:15). We could multiply these texts manyfold; through the ages they have stirred the imagination of many people and caused great anxiety. Michelangelo's paintings of the final judgment in the Sistine Chapel in Rome show the condemned being sent away by the resurrected Son of Man. The biblical material refers to a separation, an undeniable duality of judgment, which, at the very least, confronts the early and later readers with the gravity and threat of God's judgment.

We repeat what we hinted at earlier: whatever may be said about these representations from the angle of religious history is no reason to ignore them. We need to take them seriously, with the history of Jesus Christ as the key. Around the earthly Jesus we already see a judgment and a separation between people. Not everybody was prepared to accept the offer of salvation.

However, some critical distinctions are needed regarding the questions we may ask. One frequently heard question asks about the future expectations of those who never, or hardly ever, heard the gospel message. (Moltmann 1996, 237, even refers to this issue as "the most controversial question in Christian eschatology.") From the angle of biblical theology it is remarkable and doctrinally important to note that the Bible hardly shows any interest in this question. In the Old Testament the judgment day, the day of the Lord, refers to the judgment over Israel's enemies. God separates Israel from the nations. When God comes with his righteousness, he brings judgment over the nations (e.g., see the book of the prophet Amos in its entirety, particularly 5:18-20). Only a "remnant" (Isa 11:11) will escape the judgment, even if that remnant includes Egypt and Assyria, the countries that have oppressed Israel (Isa 19:19-25).

In the New Testament, too, the question about what will happen to unbelievers is not of the same character as we take it in modern times. The New Testament does not reflect theoretically on the dual destinations; rather, it addresses those first readers or hearers in a rhetorical fashion. In his ministry and in his parables of the wise and the foolish maidens, the talents, and the stewards in the vineyard, Jesus sought to warn his listeners and call them to watchfulness. Likewise, in the Epistles and in the book of Revelation, the writers address an immediate public of readers with comfort and admonition. Undeniably, however, these warnings imply the possibility of being rejected. Berkhof (CF 534-35) argues that the concept "unbelievers" is an insufficiently differentiated label. Some unbelievers are so simply because they are ignorant and have never been reached with the gospel. But other unbelievers deserve the name: they know of the covenant and the love of God but have pushed them away (Matt 7:21-23; 25:1-30; perhaps today this parallels people who want to have their baptism annulled, or be "de-baptized"). And then there are those who oppose the gospel and consciously want to destroy God's work (2 Thess 1:6-10). In brief, there are differences, and the Bible does not present judgment in terms of one size fits all. In Jesus's words we discern gradations of judgment (Luke 10:10-15; 11:29-32). In this respect we agree with Berkhof but question how he subsequently explains the ways in which this judgment applies to different situations (see CF 533-34).

It is significant that the Apostles' and the Nicene Creed do not present heaven and hell as articles of faith but refer to them only in connection with the work of Christ ("he descended into hell and ascended into heaven"). It is indeed theologically inadequate to pose the question about the existence of heaven and hell as independent spatial realities. Heaven and hell are spinoffs of the judgment of Jesus Christ as the Judge of the people. They do not primarily denote places or spaces; they are terms that describe lasting relationships to God that come in consequence of the judgment. Heaven happens where God is present in his life-giving and saving nearness. Hell is the opposite; it becomes a reality where there is total separation from God or—to put it even more strongly—where one turns away from God and intentionally tries to break or destroy his life-giving love. The "outer darkness" that the Bible refers to is indeed a vivid expression of death and corruption in the biblical sense. Death means separation from the life-giving God, a complete rupture of the tie with the source of life.

What more can we say about the future of God's opponents? We will briefly enumerate the most discussed alternatives (but will skip less common options, such as so-called second-chance theology—the idea that people will, after their death, have another opportunity to decide for or against Christ).

1. *Hell as eternal punishment.* According to the classic view (which was not shared by all even in the early church), hell is an eternal state of separation from God, and thus of pain and remorse. A number of Bible texts point in this direction, such as Matt 25:41, 46; 2 Pet 2:4; Rev 20:10). Those who refuse salvation and are disobedient look on with "weeping and gnashing of teeth," images of regret about things that cannot be undone. Since the Second Council of Constantinople (553), the teaching of an eternal hell has been regarded to be official church doctrine. Some have suggested that God's authority and majesty are highlighted especially in this eternal punishment; God's grace becomes even more radiant against the background of sin. But is this conclusion true? One can also argue that an eternal hell indicates that God, in fact, fails to make his grace fully triumphant over sin. Speculation in both directions easily becomes excessive. Yet, subsequent to the doctrinal decision of Constantinople, our earthly life and personal response to the proclamation of the gospel greatly increased in importance. In our lifetime a decision of eternal weight is made—no second chance is possible. The tree lies where it falls.

Despite this being official church doctrine, many Christians do not act as if it is; that is, on this point in particular, we often witness a substantial difference between what is confessed in theory and how it works out in practice. Berkhof did not mince words when he said that many Christians would immediately warn their neighbors if their house is on fire, while they seem to quite easily accept that the same neighbors (so they believe) will be eternally damned. No doubt the disparity is one of the reasons that the discussion about the nature and duration of hell is reignited in the church at regular intervals. Note the recent debate that Rob Bell (2011) unleashed in the United States.

2. *Universalism*. Origen has become known in church history as the one who spoke about a "restoration of all things," the so-called *apoka-tastasis pantōn* (on the basis of Acts 3:21a). By a process of purification all souls, including those of God's opponents, ultimately return to God as the source of salvation and life; even the devil will eventually be reconciled. This view is usually labeled *universalism*. Origen had some theological basis for his opinion, since God does not let go of his creation. God's honor is best served if his entire creation—all things visible and invisible—reaches a state of glory. This view was rejected by the church, however, as not being congruent with the Bible's serious words about God's judgment over every human life.

We can make a subtle distinction between a universalism that includes the demons and one that applies only to people. The English term "universalism" often leaves unclear which of the two variants is under discussion. However, universalism always stresses the comprehensive character of God's salvation in the eschaton. It has always found support at the margins in church history, and an internet search with keywords "universalism" or "universal salvation" will quickly show the many, intense discussions of the matter going on in the Anglophone world today—also among Christians with an evangelical background. For a historical survey (with special attention to Gregory of Nyssa and Karl Rahner), see Ludlow 2009.

3. *Eternal nothingness*. Some Christian groups have difficulty harmonizing the idea that God's opponents will eternally suffer with a God who is loving as well as just. Moreover, cynics might say that Christ actually won a Pyrrhic victory in view of perhaps billions of people eventually suffering eternal pain in hell. For this reason, the theory of annihilationism has recently received broader support. It says that God will eventually annihilate all those who have deliberately refused the offer of grace and love. The lake of fire mentioned in Revelation then becomes (e.g., as the well-known evangelical theologian John Stott [1921–2011] insists) the transition to absolute disappearance, for nothing remains of what has been consumed by fire.

Stott, however, rightly pointed out that emotional considerations should not be decisive in this discussion, but rather theological (i.e., what is in harmony with

God's righteousness?) and exegetical arguments. From time to time annihilation is linked to a defense of human free will; that is, those who say No to God's love and friendship are exercising their freedom in so doing. See, for example, the report *The Mystery of Our Salvation* of the Anglican Church (1995) and Bell 2011, 72. But one may wonder what kind of freedom this is. In the track of the Reformation we should speak rather of the "bondage" of the will. For a more extensive discussion, with reference to Moltmann's universalist solution, see Ansell 2013. The Achilles' heel of annihilationism often lies in the somewhat narrow and artificial exegetical argumentation on which it is based.

4. *Hell as a stage of transition.* A fourth possibility is that judgment and hell are a kind of transitional stage. Quite a few texts profess that in the end "all" (e.g., Phil 2:10; sometimes "many," Rom 5:15) will bow down before Christ as Lord. We may think of the rather universalist tone of statements in Rom 5:12-21; 11:25, 30-32; 1 Cor 15:22; Eph 1:10; Phil 2:11; 1 Tim 2:4; 1 John 2:2. Others point out that, when Paul says that he has "delivered" Hymenaeus and Alexander to Satan (1 Tim 1:20), it seems that this delivery is temporary and is aimed at their salvation. This view actually comes close to that of Origen. It is also often connected with the concept of purgatory (*purgatorium*), frequently with reference to the text cited above: 1 Cor 3:9-15 (e.g., see Kelly 2006, 116; for the contemporary Roman Catholic return to the doctrine of purgatory, 114-32).

What path must dogmatics choose in this matter? The biblical material seems to allow us to compile different lists of texts that point in opposite directions. Theologians who want to be faithful to the Bible and avoid speculation arrive at opposite conclusions (e.g., see Bonda 1998 and Wentsel, D 3B:658-95). At this point dogmatics can remind us that the awareness that someone may actually lose his life has always been part of the Christian message. This grave thought does not only, or even in the first place, concern others, however; it applies to ourselves (see 1 Cor 9:27). One does not need to have arrived at a final doctrine of eternal damnation to recognize "that we (and, in second place, also others) are in real danger of actually being lost" (Beißer 1993, 293). The Bible's many images and words about judgment and defeat (some from Jesus himself) speak too loudly not to at least be taken seriously. At the same time, we must always remember that they are not intended as a form of objective information but as an encouragement to seek our salvation in Christ.

The gravity of the question of the two roads or two different destinations is not diminishing. Modern Christianity runs the risk of appealing too quickly and easily to the doctrine of the justification of the godless, or to God's compassion. From Schleiermacher and Ritschl to Barth and Moltmann, the idea of universal atonement has dominated the church and greatly influenced preaching in mainstream churches.

It was not always this way. In the early church the cosmological victory of God over the powers of evil stood in the forefront. After the sixth century the thought that the human race would be separated into two groups—the rejected and the elect—became the most accepted view. In modern times, under the influence of a shift toward the subject, many rejected the concept of an eternal, never-ending punishment. Such a thought is too gruesome and does not fit with the norms of what we today consider as humane. Yet, we also live with the paradox that genocide, new forms of slavery, despair, emptiness, poverty, exploitation of the environment, and general inhumanity are the order of the day, and that people simply ignore this state of affairs. Hell—as a reversal of God's intentions—is too much a present reality. Where do we stand when these things are examined and evaluated in the light of the divine judgment?

It is difficult to give a final answer to questions of eternal punishment on the basis of the biblical material. The data that the Scriptures provide us cannot be neatly fit together like the pieces of a jigsaw puzzle. To repeat once more, the Bible has not been given for that purpose. We cannot look over God's shoulders; we are the recipients, the hearers and readers, of these texts. They mean to urge us to believe in Jesus Christ and in the salvation he makes possible for us; we are admonished to get involved in this new history through the multifaceted work of the Spirit. What dogmatics has to say about the last judgment can never replace the words of Christ himself. Dogmatics must always retain its serving and referential function. It *points* to Jesus Christ and *to our relationship* with him. It is only in this "relationship between promise and expectation" (Berkouwer 1972, 10) that these realities can be understood and come into their own. Only within our relationship with God and his church— that is, in the circle where we find the praxis of reading, prayer, and the communion celebration—is this question answered and may the words of promise sound: "He who has the Son has life" (1 John 5:12a) in response to the question "who shall separate us from the love of Christ?" (Rom 8:35). Here people find that life is unthinkable apart from Christ. Anyone who attempts to understand these things without this faith experience will run into a brick wall.

Christian dogmatics must therefore remind us that justification and reconciliation are not principles that can be applied in a casual manner or executed like a business plan. In the daily round of ordinary life and work, such management styles usually lead to disaster; this conclusion applies even more to the realm of faith. These concepts refer to the reality of the living Christ as the Judge of the living and the dead. By implication, the living Christ is always involved in the present, in what people decide and do now. Therefore, when we speak of hell and heaven, eternal damnation and eternal salvation, we must always remember that Christ is the one who pronounces the verdict and that our speaking about these things can never be set in concrete. Church and theology must always point to Christ; they want to find a way into the future by exploring what they know about the history of Jesus Christ. That is the real puzzle. In the gospel we see how the death and resurrection of Christ is the event that radically changes the human situation. God himself decided that the verdict of death over Christ would become the definitive judgment over the sins of humankind. We must fall back on what we said earlier about Christ's death on the cross as the reconciliation for sin. God has let the judgment over our estrangement from God, over our godlessness, rest on his own Son. This turn in God's actions is the basis on which the church can point to the promises of life, to the good news!

At the same time, our dogmatics must always use three words: God not only acts in the Son, but also acts on our behalf *in the Spirit*. If Jesus Christ is the Redeemer, this title implies that we are not saved by anything we have ourselves, but that we will be saved only through him. Acceptance becomes a reality only through the work of the Spirit, which is how we can share in that salvation. Even though the Christ-event is the axis of what God does, there is more. The final goal is achieved only through our personal bond with Jesus Christ, which we discussed in chapter 15 under the heading of faith.

16.8. Eternal Life

Christian dogmatics encounters topics that seem to defeat any explanation and yet cannot be ignored. In the Lord's Prayer, Jesus wanted to lead his disciples to a life oriented toward the kingdom of God. In the threefold doxology at the end of the Lord's Prayer—which is not found in the most important manuscripts (cf. Matt 6:9-13) but was part of the practice of prayer in the early church (*Didache* 8.2)—we see this vista of God's glory reflected. But what can we say about the realization of God's kingdom, about his glory? Once again we find many images in the Bible that in earthly language, drawing off the context of the day, try to say something about God's glory. We must take into account the discontinuity that is present in many of those images, as, for instance, when the kingdom is compared with a seed that dies in the soil and then brings forth fruit (John 12:24; 1 Cor 15:35-37). First John 3:2 explicitly formulates the radical nature of the unknown: "Beloved, we are God's children now; it does not yet appear what we shall be, but we know that when he appears we shall be like him, for we shall see him as he is." These verses tell us that God's glory or majesty accompanies the coming of Jesus Christ. He has been taken into, and is fully determined by, the glory of the Father.

This glory is so unspeakable and incomparable with all that exists that the church has often tended to remain silent on the subject. Moreover, doubt and unbelief and the low interest in eschatology in mainstream churches have often prompted them to leave any concrete explanation of the new heaven and the new earth to evangelical churches and groups. However, we need not remain silent, for we have already noted that, besides much discontinuity, we may also expect continuity between our present life and that to come. Eberhard Jüngel (2000, 125) emphasizes that, already now, in the midst of our earthly existence, we are, "as it were, *beginners* of eternal life." If so, he continues, then we can speak in the language of this earthly life about its completion in eternal life, for Christ himself has done so in his parables. We must use our imagination in exercising our hope, but always in strict accordance with the images and parables that the Bible provides when it speaks about eternal life; going any further entails the risk of losing ourselves in speculation and fantasy. The eschatological expectation is fanned by taking biblical images seriously rather than by ignoring them.

In any case, God's glory will include a few aspects that we briefly touch upon below. But with regard to all these elements, it must be stressed again that they do not deal only with the future but also have impact on our lives here and now.

1. *Sin and evil have been eradicated.* Jesus implies in the prayer that he taught his disciples that the ultimate realization of the kingdom includes deliverance from all evil. This means that even the possibility of evil will then have been eliminated. We read in Rev 21:4 that God will wipe all our tears from our eyes and that "death shall be no more, neither shall there be mourning or crying." Evildoers will not be allowed into the kingdom. This prayer and expectation clearly have ethical implications, which leads us to a second characteristic.

2. *The preliminary nature of the first creation will have ended* because

God's creation is renewed and perfected. Total newness means that all vulnerability and fragility are done away with. This state is hard to imagine, since the materiality of the creation as we know it is always accompanied by risks and limitations. However, in eyewitness accounts from after Jesus's resurrection, we detect hints of an order in which the glorified Christ still somehow relates to materiality (the eating in John 21:10–13) but is not confined to it (John 20:19). This category of newness is especially typical for Christian hope and prophecy: "Behold, I make all things new" (Rev 21:5). The renewal and perfecting are a "forward leap" (Berkhof)—in other words, an event that cannot be explained on the basis of what now exists.

In line with Aristotelian philosophy, which maintained that nature does not "jump" (*natura non saltat*) and thus always wished to explain later phenomena from what already exists, contemporary natural science also aims to understand all existing things and all new variants as phenomena that we can understand on the basis of a complex of current conditions. However, this is not sufficient for Christian reflection about creation and re-creation. Paul refers to re-creation in parallel with the existing creation. Abraham had faith in God, "who gives life to the dead and calls into existence the things that do not exist" (Rom 4:17). That is, the new things cannot be explained or derived from what now already exists. The "not yet" must, in fact, be considered as what God in his freedom and sovereignty brings forth from himself. Therefore, criteria of conceivability and imagination with respect to the eschaton have only limited applicability. God's act in Christ's coming is decisive. For the ontological implications of this point, see Jüngel 1989, 95–123.

3. *Participation.* God's glory implies that God is all in all (1 Cor 15:28). That is, God's majesty and glory will be the determining element in all of his creation, and his Spirit dwells in all things. We might here perhaps use the term *theōsis*, or deification, but it can easily cause misunderstandings. Second Peter 1:4 says that we will become "partakers of the divine nature." Particularly in Eastern Orthodoxy, Lutheranism, and Radical Orthodoxy, this concept of participation has been strongly asserted as something that applies already in this life. We fully agree that, in baptism and in the Lord's Supper, the moment of communion with Christ is fundamental; we are already members of his body. Yet, the brokenness of this participation will be removed only in God's glory. Not until Christ appears in his glory and brings along the kingdom in its full splendor will this participation be unfolded and developed without any hurdles.

In the book of Revelation this "all in all" is expressed in images of a new creation in which the sun and the moon are no longer needed as luminaries because God's glory provides the light for the new Jerusalem; the Lamb himself is the lamp (Rev 21:23).

This participation in God's eternal life does not mean that the otherness of creation has been eliminated. Humanity remains humanity with its history but is now placed in the light of God's glory and completely transformed. This continuity of humanity as other, as neighbor, implies that interpersonality, relationality, and identity will not disappear. The ever-recurring question about mutual recognition and reunion in heaven can be approached only from this angle. According to John 20:16 Mary recognizes the risen Lord when he calls her by name. This experience corresponds with the Old Testament: "I have called you by name, you are mine" (Isa 43:1). The Good Shepherd also knows his sheep by name, and they recognize his voice (John 10:3-4). Again, this recognition refers to baptism, when the individual's name is connected with the name of the triune God. This is the acceptance into a community not of nameless people but of those who are known to God, who have received a name and call each other by that name. Therefore, yes, there will be recognition and reunion in glory. This point brings us to the covenant.

4. *The bond between God and humanity*. In the new life the covenant between God and humanity will be fully restored. The covenant implies that we will not live in God's glory as separate individuals but will experience togetherness in a perfect community in which people can experience true intimacy and help each other to fully develop. For that reason, the picture of heaven is not one of an idyllic pastoral landscape but of a city, the new Jerusalem, where the gates are always open to all the corners of the world (Rev 21:10-27). God's glory (*kabod*) will grace and permeate all human relationships. In other words, the things that are part of our nature (see 7.8)—love and relationships, friendship and company, giving and receiving—will then reach their full potential without fear or limitation.

5. *Reaching our full potential*. The new life constitutes a restoration of the first creation and a perfecting of the covenant between God and humanity. What has already become reality in Christ is now true for all creation. We read that the new Jerusalem is built with the most precious materials that were known in Bible times, and right down the middle of this city flows the river of the water of life. On the banks of this river grow trees that yield their fruits twelve times a year, and their leaves will

be for the healing of the nations (Rev 22:1–2). This image speaks of an incredible transformation of creation. In the radiance of God's love and glory, all possibilities reach their full potential, which will be outgoing and life-giving. The continuity between creation and re-creation is well captured in an adage often used in the Roman Catholic and the Reformed traditions: *gratia non tollit, sed perficit naturam* (grace does not eliminate nature but makes it perfect). This also means that the good and praiseworthy things that have been developed in culture and history and that people have enjoyed will not be lost; rather, as we learn from the image in Rev 21:24–26, they will be brought into the New Jerusalem.

We need to stress the perspective of healing and of reaching our potential for situations in which a person's life may be prematurely restricted or destroyed by circumstances, or through foolishness or guilt. In the radiance of God's love, things that were foreclosed or never realized in this life will flourish. However, we must not interpret this change to mean that in eternity our present life will be annulled, nor may we allow our contemporary ideals of health and success to govern our expectations. This life, even when it is marked by a severe handicap, will be transformed and glorified. Glorification does not mean that all the diversity and unique features that characterize life as lived on this earth will suddenly be erased; these rather are the materials that will be used in re-creation and that will share in the riches and majesty of God. The focus will no longer fall on limitations as limitations but on superseding them and on the possibilities that will obtain in the radiance of God's love and friendship. See Yong 2007, 281–88, and Reinders 2008.

6. *Christ and the Spirit as guarantors.* Christ occupies the central place in this new life. In the book of Revelation he calls himself the Alpha and the Omega. The image of the throne of God and of the Lamb tells us that the Lamb, seen objectively, guarantees the definitive nature of the new creation. It will be impenetrable by sin; it will have become "fireproof" by God's renewal. There is a progression in God's acts that must dismiss speculations about a reincarnation of "souls" or about a new cycle of world history. Seen from a subjective perspective, this guarantee is given as a "deposit" of the Spirit (2 Cor 1:22; 5:5, Eph 1:14; cf. Rom 8:16, 23), who has been given to the church as a foretaste of the future life.

In classic theology glorification was tied to theodicy. God's rule can never be justified by human beings (as was argued in the modern theodicy project that began with Leibniz); rather, God will justify himself with regard to history. At the end of time it will become clear that all God's acts are glorious and just. Here Rom 11:33 puts us on the right path: "O the depth of the riches and wisdom and knowledge of God! How unsearchable are his judgments and how inscrutable his ways!" After having explored God's journey with Israel, Paul comes to this exclamation and praise. Even though these concepts remain beyond Paul's intellectual capacities, he has no doubt that God will always be faithful to his covenant with Israel. He has discovered this faithfulness in God's revelation in Jesus Christ. In Christ and his death for human sin, God has demonstrated his justice, and this gift is enough for our faith. For that reason we cannot really answer the question about the meaning of history from creation to redemption (and, of course, especially about the meaning, or lack thereof, of evil in that process). We are not in a position where we can check what God does. In fact, we can only retell the story of salvation. We are participants, active recipients in a history that is marked by sin and evil. But even more, in all this story we are the objects of God's compassion, of the care of him who bore our sins and who has destined us as his creatures for glorification. For this reason, Paul ends, despite the opacity of many things, with a doxology: "For from him and through him and to him are all things. To him be glory forever" (Rom 11:33).

7. *The eternally rich God*. Should we then imagine eternal life as an unchanging, infinite state? As soon as heaven is portrayed as a place where nothing ever changes, misconceptions about endless singing and waving of palm branches become nearly unavoidable. Static infinity seems to augur infinite boredom, for we associate situations in which nothing ever changes with tediousness. In contrast, if we exchange these images for those of dynamism and change, we might once more be projecting contemporary ideals on the screen of eternity. Therefore, we do much better not to think of eternal life in terms of time but rather in categories of quality, in terms of the depth and richness of God's being. God, as Father, Son, and Spirit, is the eternally rich God whom we have come to know in history as the God of love. In all his acts he is propelled by love. We read in 1 Cor 13:12-13:

> For now we see in a mirror dimly, but then face to face. Now I know in part; then I shall understand fully, even as I have been fully understood. So faith, hope, love abide, these three; but the greatest of these is love.

Why is love the highest of the three Christian virtues? In eternal life we will no longer have to live by faith, and hope will have been overtaken by the fulfillment of our expectations. Love is the "greatest" because it will always remain. In short, eternal life will be characterized by the creativity and inexhaustibility of God's love.

References

Ansell, Nicholas J. 2013. *The Annihilation of Hell: Universal Salvation and the Redemption of Time in the Eschatology of Jürgen Moltmann.* Milton Keynes: Paternoster.

Balthasar, Hans Urs von. 1957. "Eschatologie." In *Fragen der Theologie heute,* edited by J. Feiner, J. Trütsch, and F. Böckle, 403–21. Einsiedeln: Benziger.

Bauckham, Richard. 1993. *The Theology of the Book of Revelation.* Cambridge: Cambridge University Press.

Bauckham, Richard, and Trevor Hart. 1999. *Hope against Hope: Christian Eschatology in Contemporary Context.* London: Darton, Longman & Todd.

Beek, A. van de. 2008. *God doet recht: Eschatologie als Christologie.* Zoetermeer: Meinema.

Beißer, Friedrich. 1993, *Hoffnung und Vollendung.* Gütersloh: Mohn.

Bell, Rob. 2011. *Love Wins: A Book about Heaven, Hell, and the Fate of Every Person Who Ever Lived.* New York: HarperOne.

Berkhof, Hendrikus. 1966. *Christ the Meaning of History.* London: SCM.

Berkouwer, Gerrit C. 1972. *The Return of Christ.* Grand Rapids: Eerdmans.

Bonda, Jan. 1998. *The One Purpose of God: An Answer to the Doctrine of Eternal Punishment.* Grand Rapids: Eerdmans.

Boyer, Paul. 1992. *When Time Shall Be No More: Prophecy Belief in Modern American Culture.* Cambridge, MA: Harvard University Press.

Brunner, Emil. 1954. *Eternal Hope.* Philadelphia: Fortress. Orig. German ed., *Das Ewige als Zukunft und Gegenwart.* Zurich: Zwingli-Verlag, 1953.

Bultmann, Rudolf. 1957. *The Presence of Eternity: History and Eschatology.* New York: Harper.

Cullmann, Oscar. 1964. *Christ and Time: The Primitive Christian Conception of Time and History.* Philadelphia: Fortress.

Egmond, A. van, and D. van Keulen, eds. 2001. *Christian Hope in Context.* 2 vols. Zoetermeer: Meinema.

Fergusson, David, and Marcel Sarot, eds. 2000. *The Future as God's Gift: Explorations in Christian Eschatology.* Edinburgh: T&T Clark.

Hebblethwaite, Brian. 2010. *The Christian Hope.* Oxford: Oxford University Press. Orig. pub., Basingstoke: Marshall, Morgan & Scott, 1984.

Hjelde, Sigurd. 1987. *Das Eschaton und die Eschata: Eine Studie über Sprachgebrauch und Sprachverwirrung in protestantischer Theologie von der Orthodoxie bis zur Gegenwart.* Munich: Kaiser.

Hoekema, Anthony A. 1979. *The Bible and the Future.* Grand Rapids: Eerdmans.

Holmström, Folke. 1936. *Das eschatologische Denken der Gegenwart*. Gütersloh: C. Bertelsmann. Orig. Swedish ed., Stockholm, 1933.

Jonge, H. J. de, and B. W. J. de Ruyter, eds. 1995. *Totdat Hij komt: Een discussie over de wederkomst van Jezus Christus* [Until he comes: A debate on the return of Jesus Christ]. Baarn: Ten Have.

Jüngel, Eberhard. 1989. "The World as Possibility and Actuality: The Ontology of the Doctrine of Justification." In *Theological Essays*, translated by John Webster, 1:95–123. Edinburgh: T&T Clark.

———. 2000. "Evangelischer Glaube und die Frage nach Tod und ewigem Leben" [Protestant faith and the question of death and eternal life]." In *Das Wesen des Christentums in seiner evangelischen Gestalt*, edited by Christine Axt-Piscalar et al., 112–32. Neukirchen: Neukirchener Verlag.

Kelly, Anthony. 2006. *Eschatology and Hope*. Maryknoll, NY: Orbis Books.

Lindsey, Hal. 1970. *The Late Great Planet Earth*. Grand Rapids: Zondervan.

Löwith, Karl. 1949. *Meaning in History: The Theological Implications of the Philosophy of History*. Chicago: University of Chicago Press.

Ludlow, Morwenna. 2009. *Universal Salvation: Eschatology in the Thought of Gregory of Nyssa and Karl Rahner*. Oxford: Oxford University Press.

Moltmann, Jürgen. 1967. *Theology of Hope*. London: SCM. Orig. German ed., Munich, 1964.

———. 1974. "Extrapolation und Antizipation: Zur Methode in der Eschatologie." In *Weerwoord: Reacties op Dr. H. Berkhofs "Christelijk geloof,"* edited by James Barr et al., 201–8. Nijkerk: Callenbach.

———. 1996. *The Coming of God: Christian Eschatology*. Minneapolis: Fortress. Orig. German ed., Gütersloh, 1995.

Pannenberg, Wolfhart. 1969. *Theology and the Kingdom of God*. Philadelphia: Westminster.

Peacocke, Arthur. 1993. *Theology for a Scientific Age*. Enlarged ed. London: SCM.

Peters, Ted. 2006. *Anticipating Omega: Science, Faith, and Our Ultimate Future*. Göttingen: Vandenhoeck & Ruprecht.

Rahner, Karl. 2004. "The Hermeneutics of Eschatological Assertions." In *Theological Investigations*, 4:323–46. Limerick, Ireland: Mary Immaculate College. Orig. German ed. of the volume, 1962.

Reinders, Hans S. 2008. *Receiving the Gift of Friendship: Profound Disability, Theological Anthropology, and Ethics*. Grand Rapids: Eerdmans.

Ridderbos, Herman N. 1962. *The Coming of the Kingdom*. Philadelphia: P&R Publishing.

Rosenstock-Huessy, Eugen. 1966. *The Christian Future; or, The Modern Mind Outrun*. New York: Harper & Row. Repr., Eugene, OR: Wipf & Stock, 2013.

Schweitzer, Albert. 1910. *The Quest of the Historical Jesus*. London: Black.

Weiss, Johannes. 1892. *Die Predigt Jesu vom Reich Gottes*. Göttingen: Vandenhoeck & Ruprecht.

Wilkinson, David. 2010. *Christian Eschatology and the Physical Universe*. London: T&T Clark.

Yong, Amos. 2007. *Theology and Down Syndrome: Reimaging Disability in Late Modernity*. Waco, TX: Baylor University Press.

Zwiep, Arie W. 1997. *The Ascension of the Messiah in Lucan Christology*. Leyden: Brill.

Bibliography

Allen, RT
Allen, R. Michael. *Reformed Theology*. London: T&T Clark, 2010.

Alston & Welker, RT
Alston, Wallace M., and Michael Welker, eds. *Reformed Theology: Identity and Ec-umenicity*. Grand Rapids: Eerdmans, 2003.

Aquinas, STh
Thomas Aquinas. *Summa theologiae*.

Augustine, *Conf.*
Augustine. *Confessiones*.

Augustine, *De civ. Dei*
Augustine. *De civitate Dei*.

Balz & G. Schneider, EDNT
Balz, Horst, and Gerhard Schneider, eds. *Exegetical Dictionary of the New Testament*. 3 vols. Grand Rapids: Eerdmans, 1990-93.

Barth, CD
Barth, Karl. *Church Dogmatics*. Edited and translated by G. W. Bromiley and T. F. Torrance. 5 vols. in 14. Edinburgh: T&T Clark, 1936-69.

Barth, ER
Barth, Karl. *The Epistle to the Romans*. Translated by Edwin C. Hoskyns. London: Oxford University Press, 1933. Repr., 1968.

Barth, GA
Barth, Karl. *Gesamtausgabe*. Commissioned by Karl Barth Stiftung, published by Hinrich Stoevesandt, Hans Anton Drewes, and Peter Zocher. Zürich, 1973-.

Barth, R2
Barth, Karl. *Der Römerbrief.* 2nd ed. Munich: Kaiser, 1922. Repr., ed. C. van der Kooi and K. Tolstaya. Zürich: TVZ, Theologischer Verlag, 2010.

Bavinck, RD
Bavinck, Herman. *Reformed Dogmatics.* Edited by John Bolt, translated by John Vriend. 4 vols. Grand Rapids: Baker Academic, 2003-8.

BC
The Book of Confessions. Part 1 of *The Constitution of the Presbyterian Church (U.S.A.).* Louisville: Office of the General Assemby, 2007.

BEM
Baptism, Eucharist, Ministry. Faith and Order Paper 111. Geneva: WCC Publications.

Berkhof, CF
Berkhof, Hendrikus. *Christian Faith: An Introduction to the Study of the Faith.* Translated by Sierd Woudstra. Grand Rapids: Eerdmans, 1985.

Berkhof, 200YT
Berkhof, Hendrikus. *Two Hundred Years of Theology: Report of a Personal Journey.* Grand Rapids: Eerdmans, 1989.

Berkouwer, SD
Berkouwer, Gerrit C. *Studies in Dogmatics.* 14 vols. Grand Rapids: Eerdmans, 1952-76.

Bonhoeffer, WDB
Bonhoffer, Dietrich. *Works of Dietrich Bonhoeffer.* Edited by Clifford J. Green et al. 16 vols. Minneapolis: Fortress, 1996-2013.

Brakel, CRS
Brakel, Wilhelmus à. *The Christian's Reasonable Service.* Edited by Joel R. Beeke, translated by Bartel Elshout. 4 vols. Grand Rapids: Reformation Heritage Books, 2015. Orig. pub., 1700.

Brink, PST
Brink, Gijsbert van den. 2004. *Philosophy of Science for Theologians: An Introduction.* Frankfurt: Peter Lang.

Brunner, D
Brunner, Emil. *Dogmatics.* 3 vols. Cambridge: J. Clark, 2002. Orig. pub., 1946-60.

Bultmann, ThNT
Bultmann, Rudolf. *Theology of the New Testament.* Translated by Kendrick Grobel. 2 vols. Waco, TX: Baylor University Press, 2007. Orig. pub., 1948-53.

Calvin, CO
Ioannis Calvini opera quae supersunt omnia. Edited by G. Baum, E. Cunitz, and

E. Reuss. 59 vols. Corpus Reformatorum 29–87. Brunswick: Schwetschke, 1863–1900.

Calvin, *Inst.*
Calvin, John. *Institutes of the Christian Religion*. Translated by Henry Beveridge. Peabody, MA: Hendrickson, 2007.

CCSL
Corpus Christianorum: Series Latina

Denzinger, ES
Denzinger, Heinrich, ed. *Enchiridion symbolorum definitionum et declarationum de rebus fidei et morum / Compendium of Creeds, Definitions, and Declarations on Matters of Faith and Morals*. Edited by Peter Hünermann. 43rd ed. San Francisco: Ignatius, 2012.

Dorner, SCD
Dorner, Isaac A. *A System of Christian Doctrine*. Translated by Alfred Cave and J. S. Banks. 4 vols. Edinburgh: T&T Clark, 1888–90. Repr., Eugene, OR: Wipf & Stock, 2005.

Faulenbach et al., RB
Faulenbach, Heiner, Eberhard Busch, and Emidio Campi, eds. *Reformierte Bekenntnisschriften*. Neukirchen: Neukirchener Verlag, 2002–.

Feiner & Löhrer, MS
Feiner, Johannes, and Magnus Löhrer, eds. *Mysterium Salutis: Grundriß heilsgeschichtlicher Dogmatik*. 5 vols. in 7. Zürich: Benziger, 1965–81.

Fiorenza/Galvin, STRCP
Fiorenza, Francis Schüssler, and John P. Galvin, eds. *Systematic Theology: Roman Catholic Perspectives*. 2nd ed. Theology and the Sciences. Minneapolis: Fortress, 2011.

Genderen & Velema, CRD
Genderen, J. van, and W. H. Velema. *Concise Reformed Dogmatics*. Translated by Gerrit Bilkes. Phillipsburg, NJ: P&R Publications, 2008.

Gerrish, CF
Gerrish, Brian A. *Christian Faith: Dogmatics in Outline*. Louisville: Westminster John Knox, 2015.

Goppelt, ThNT
Goppelt, Leonhard. *Theology of the New Testament*. Edited by Jürgen Roloff, translated by John Alsup. 2 vols. Grand Rapids: Eerdmans, 1981–82.

Grudem, ST
Grudem, Wayne. *Systematic Theology: An Introduction to Biblical Doctrine*. Leicester: Inter-Varsity, 1994.

GS
Gaudium et spes. Pastoral Constitution on the Church in the Modern World. Vatican II, 1965.

Gunning, BidO
Gunning, J. H., Jr. 1929-30. *Blikken in de openbaring* [Glances into revelation]. 4 vols. Rotterdam: J. M. Bredée's.

Gunton, CCCD
Gunton, Colin, ed. *The Cambridge Companion to Christian Doctrine.* Cambridge: Cambridge University Press, 1997.

Gunton, CF
Gunton, Colin. *The Christian Faith: An Introduction to Christian Doctrine.* Oxford: Blackwell, 2002.

Gunton et al., PT
Gunton, Colin, Stephen R. Holmes, and Murray A. Rae, eds. *The Practice of Theology. A Reader.* London: SCM, 2001.

Harnack, HoD
Harnack, Adolf von. *History of Dogma.* Translated by Neil Buchanan. 7 vols. in 4. New York: Dover Publications, 1961. 3rd German ed., pub. 1894-98.

Hebblethwaite, PTCD
Hebblethwaite, Brian. *Philosophical Theology and Christian Doctrine.* Oxford: Blackwell, 2005.

Henning & Lehmkühler, STGS
Henning, Christian, and Karsten Lehmkühler, eds. *Systematische Theologie der Gegenwart in Selbstdarstellungen.* Tübingen: Mohr Siebeck, 1998.

Heppe, RD
Heppe, Heinrich. *Reformed Dogmatics.* Translated by G. T. Thomson, edited by E. Bizer. Eugene, OR: Wipf & Stock, 2008. Orig. pub., 1861.

Heyns, D
Heyns, Johan A. *Dogmatiek.* Pretoria: Kerkboekhandel Transvaal, 1978.

Higton, CD
Higton, Mike. *Christian Doctrine.* London: SCM, 2008.

H.-M. Barth, D
Barth, Hans-Martin. *Dogmatik: Evangelischer Glaube im Kontext der Weltreligionen.* Gütersloh: Gütersloher Verlagshaus, 2001.

Hodge, ST
Hodge, Charles. *Systematic Theology.* 3 vols. New York: Scribner, 1871-73. Repr., London, 1960.

Honig, HGD

Honig, Anthonie G. *Handboek van de gereformeerde dogmatiek.* Kampen: Kok, 1938.

Horton, CF

Horton, Michael. *The Christian Faith: A Systematic Theology for Pilgrims on the Way.* Grand Rapids: Zndervan, 2011.

Jenni & Westermann, TLOT

Jenni, Ernst, and Claus Westermann, eds. *Theological Lexicon of the Old Testament.* Translated by Mark E. Biddle. 3 vols. Peabody: Hendrickson, 1997.

Jenson, ST

Jenson, Robert W. *Systematic Theology.* 2 vols. New York: Oxford University Press, 1997–99.

Jüngel, GMW

Jüngel, Eberhard. *God as the Mystery of the World: On the Foundation of the Theology of the Crucified One in the Dispute between Theism and Atheism.* Translated by Darrell L. Guder. Grand Rapids: Eerdmans, 1983.

Kelly, ECC

Kelly, J. N. D. *Early Christian Creeds.* 3rd ed. London: Longman, 1972.

Kraus, ST

Kraus, Hans-Joachim. *Systematische Theologie im Kontext biblischer Geschichte und Eschatologie.* Neukirchen: Neukirchener Verlag, 1983.

Kreck, GD

Kreck, Walter. *Grundfragen der Dogmatik.* Munich: Kaiser, 1970.

LG

Lumen gentium. Dogmatic Constitution on the Church. Vatican II, 1964.

Luther, SC

Luther, Martin. *Small Catechism.* Milwaukee: Northwestern, 1998. Orig. pub., 1529.

Luther, WA (DB / TR)

Luther, Martin. *Werke: Kritische Gesamtausgabe* (Weimarer Ausgabe [Deutsche Bible / Tischreden]). Weimar: Böhlau et al., 1883–2009.

McClendon, ST

McClendon, James W. *Systematic Theology.* 3 vols. Nashville: Abingdon, 1986–2000.

McGrath, CT

McGrath, Alister E. *Christian Theology: An Introduction.* Oxford: Blackwell, 1994.

Melanchthon, LC

Melanchthon, Philipp. *Commonplaces: Loci Communes 1521.* Translated by Christian Preus. St. Louis: Concordia, 2014.

Migliore, FSU
Migliore, Daniel L. *Faith Seeking Understanding: An Introduction to Christian Theology*. 2nd ed. Grand Rapids: Eerdmans, 2004.

Miskotte, VW
Miskotte, K. H. *Verzameld werk*. Kampen: Kok, 1982–.

Muller, DLGTT
Muller, Richard A. *Dictionary of Latin and Greek Theological Terms: Drawn Principally from Protestant Scholastic Theology*. Grand Rapids: Baker Book House, 1985.

Muller, PRRD
Muller, Richard A. *Post-Reformation Reformed Dogmatics*. 4 vols. Grand Rapids: Baker Book House, 2003.

NK
De Nieuwe Katechismus: Geloofsverkondiging voor volwassenen. Edited by P. Schoonenberg et al. Hilversum, 1996.

Noordmans, H
Noordmans, Oepke. *Herschepping: Beknopte dogmatische handleiding voor godsdienstige toespraken en besprekingen*. Zeist, 1934.

Noordmans, VW
Noordmans, Oepke. *Verzamelde werken*. Edited by J. M. Hasselaar et al. 10 vols. Kampen: Kok, 1978–2004.

NPNF
The Nicene and Post-Nicene Fathers. 2 series, with 14 vols. each. Edited by Philip Schaff. Repr., Grand Rapids: Eerdmans, 1988–91.

OF
Our Faith: Ecumenical Creeds, Reformed Confessions, and Other Sources. Grand Rapids: Faith Alive Christian Resources, 2013.

Ott, AG
Ott, Heinrich. *Die Antwort des Glaubens: Systematische Theologie in 50 Artikeln*. Berlin: Kreuz Verlag, 1972.

Pannenberg, ST
Pannenberg, Wolfhart. *Systematic Theology*. Translated by Geoffrey W. Bromiley. 3 vols. Grand Rapids: Eerdmans, 1991–97.

PG
Patrologia graeca. Edited by J.-P. Migne. 162 vols. Paris, 1857–86.

PL
Patrologia latina. Edited by J.-P. Migne. 217 vols. Paris, 1844–64.

Rad, TOT
Rad, Gerhard von. *Theology of the Old Testament*. Translated by D. M. G. Stalker. 2 vols. Louisville: Westminster John Knox, 2001.

Rahner, FCF
Rahner, Karl. *Foundations of Christian Faith: An Introduction to the Idea of Christianity*. Translated by William V. Dych. New York: Seabury, 1978.

Rahner, TI
Rahner, Karl. *Theological Investigations*. 23 vols. Limerick, 2004.

Rohls, RC
Rohls, Jan. *Reformed Confessions: Theology from Zürich to Barmen*. Translated by John F. Hoffmeyer. Louisville: John Knox, 1998.

Ruler, IB
Ruler, A. A. van. *I Believe*. Translated by Garth Hodnett. Bloomington, 2015.

Ruler, VW
Ruler, A. A. van. *Verzameld Werk*. 4 vols. Zoetermeer: Boekencentrum, 2008-11.

Schleiermacher, CF
Schleiermacher, Friedrich D. E. *The Christian Faith*. Translated by H. R. Machintosh and J. S. Stewart. Edinburgh: Clark, 1928. Orig. pub., 1830-31.

Schneider, HdD
Schneider, Theodor, ed. *Handbuch der Dogmatik*. 2 vols. Düsseldorf: Patmos, 1992.

Tillich, ST
Tillich, Paul. *Systematic Theology*. 3 vols. Chicago: University of Chicago Press, 1951-63.

Troeltsch, TCF
Troeltsch, Ernst. *The Christian Faith: Based on Lectures Delivered at the University of Heidelberg in 1912 and 1913*. Translated by Garrett E. Paul. Minneapolis: Fortress, 1991.

Vanhoozer, DD
Vanhoozer, Kevin J. *The Drama of Doctrine: A Canonical-Linguistic Approach to Christian Theology*. Louisville: Westminster John Knox, 2005.

Warfield, W
Warfield, Benjamin B. *The Works of Benjamin Warfield*. 10 vols. Grand Rapids: Baker Book House, 1978.

Weber, FD
Weber, Otto. *Foundations of Dogmatics*. 2 vols. Grand Rapids: Eerdmans, 1981-83.

Webster et al., OHST
Webster, John, Kathryn Tanner, and Allan Torrance, eds. *The Oxford Handbook of Systematic Theology*. Oxford: Oxford University Press, 2007.

Wentsel, D
Wentsel, B. *Dogmatiek*. 4 vols. Kampen: Kok, 1981-98.

WS
The Worship Sourcebook. 2004. Grand Rapids: Baker Books.

Index of Names

Balthasar, Hans Urs von, 448, 480, 715
Barnard, M., 612, 614
Barnard, W., 16
Barr, James, 189, 568
Barth, H.-M., 66, 196
Barth, Karl, 14, 20, 68, 285, 315, 348, 609; analogy, theory of, 137–38; anthropology, theological, 253–54, 257, 258, 518; apologetics, 21; atonement, doctrine of, 318, 451–52, 652–53, 750; Bible/Word of God, 173–74, 543, 560; Christology, 25, 388, 400, 402, 480; church, 591, 622, 634, 636–37; conservative approach, 27, 29, 192; creation, 203, 206, 224, 225; culture, 330, 519, 521–22, 523; dogmatics, 12, 13; election, 701, 706–8; eschatology, 440, 716–17, 718–19, 734, 741; finiteness, 326–27, 331; free will, 276, 280; God, doctrine of, 36, 42, 43, 123–24, 147, 148, 264; Holy Spirit, 492, 499; natural theology, 56, 58–59, 186–88; revelation, 161, 164, 175, 179, 182–83, 594; salvation, 448, 478, 670, 696; sanctification, 691–92; sin, 310, 313, 317; theological mode of existence, 29–30; Trinity, doctrine of, 76, 78, 79, 89, 146
Barton, John, 568
Basil of Caesarea, 93
Bauckham, Richard, 86, 391, 723, 729
Baumert, Norbert, 509, 510, 528
Baur, Ferdinand C., 130
Bavinck, J. Herman, 17, 36, 196, 361, 520; Bible, 537, 544–45, 565; church, 626, 631; revelation, 161, 182, 186, 191; salvation, 320, 445, 510, 648
Baxter, Richard, 694
Bayer, O., 675
Beauvoir, Simone de, 284
Becker, Matthew L., 36
Becking, Bob, 124
Beek, Abraham van de, 58, 203, 329, 330, 361; Christology, 406, 408, 412, 427, 480, 614; church, 617, 622, 623, 628, 640; eschatology, 720–21,

734; Israel, 350, 352, 353; Mariology, 575; salvation, 444–45, 447; sanctification, 691–92; supersessionism, 346
Beerling, R. F., 62
Beilby, James K., 270, 675, 678
Beißer, Friedrich, 749
Bell, Rob, 748, 749
Ben-Chorin, Schalom, 374, 389
Benedict, Ruth, 659
Ben-Gurion, David, 341
Berengarius of Tours, 613
Bergmann, Sigurd, 203, 526
Berkhof, Hendrikus, 62–63, 360; anthropology, theological, 249–50, 256–57, 259; Bible, 70, 181, 563, 567; Christology, 391, 401, 406, 410, 411, 430; church, 580, 592; creation, 210, 221, 228, 230; culture, 519, 520; dogmatics, 3, 11, 36; eschatology, 441, 719–20, 730, 740, 746, 747, 753; God, doctrine of, 79, 124, 144, 147–48, 152, 153, 261–62; Holy Spirit, 499–500, 501, 525–26; Israel, 351, 352; justification, 673, 692; Old Testament, 343, 354, 358, 370; pre-existence of Christ, 423, 427, 435; prolegomena, 36, 49, 553; providence, 236–37, 244; renewal, 650, 652; repentance/guilt, 656, 660; revelation, of God, 41–42, 71, 125, 161, 168, 170, 176, 190; sacraments, 598, 603–4; salvation, 194, 393, 466, 480, 670, 673, 704, 708; sin, doctrine of, 302, 318, 320
Berkouwer, Gerrit C., 187, 269, 299; Bible, 536, 569; church, 574, 578; eschatology, 713, 728, 730, 739, 750; faith and revelation, 117, 169, 189–90; salvation, 609, 662, 673, 708; transformation, 699, 700; work of Christ, 434, 442, 480
Berlin, Isaiah, 279
Besser-Jones, Lorraine, 508
Beuer, Walter, 384
Beza, Theodore, 648, 696, 704, 707
Biel, Gabriel, 703

Index of Subjects

Christian Reformed Church (CRC), 102, 455

Christians, individual, 8, 170, 192; Trinity and, 107-10

Christology, 71; Bible, 394-96, 399-400; context, historical, 389-91, 393-94; definition, 382-84; early church, 384-85, 391-93, 396-97, 401, 410; Eastern Orthodox, 411, 412, 455; Enlightenment, the, 386-87; experience, 398-99; historical Jesus, 387-89, 391-93; Holy Spirit and, 108, 395, 398, 410-11; John, Gospel of, 387, 395, 403; Lutheran, 400, 414; models/perspectives, 399-403; parousia/second coming of Christ, 720, 721-22, 726, 727, 729, 742; Reformed, 396, 400, 414; soteriology and, 403, 405-6, 407, 415, 442-47, 657-68; tradition, 396-98; Trinity, 401-3, 429-30; two natures (hypostatic union), 384, 386-87, 391-92, 398, 406-12, 413-15. *See also* Jesus Christ

Church, the: apostolicity, 631-32; authority, 551-52; baptism and, 575, 584-85; Bible and, 552-53, 556-58, 561-64, 565-66; body of Christ, 513-14; catechesis/education, 615-16; catholic/episcopal model, 584, 589-91, 623; congregationalist/free model, 584-85, 591-92, 600-601, 622, 627, 631, 641; culture and, 637-38, 734-35; deacons/diaconate, 618-19; definition, 580-83, 626; eschatology, 575-76; holiness, 628-30; Holy Spirit and, 496-97, 506-7, 512-16, 574-75, 593-97; institutional, 36-37, 574, 581, 583, 588; Jesus Christ and, 512, 574-75, 578-79, 587; journey of, 585, 592, 609, 612; kingdom of God and, 588-92; kingdoms, two, doctrine of, 517-18, 619, 632-33, 635-36, 638; Lord's Supper/Eucharist, 506, 578, 580, 584, 627-28, 685, 753; metaphors for, 581-82; mission, 579-80,

582, 617-18, 631-32; monasticism, 589-90; offices, 579, 585-86, 617-23, 625; origin of, 576-77, 593; pastoral care, 615-16; proclamation, 593-97, 617, 660-61; prophetic role, 636-38; Reformed/presbyterian model, 585-87, 592, 621-23, 640-41; sacraments, 592, 597-602; states/nations and, 517-20, 521-22, 633-35, 639-41; synagogue (Judaism) and, 358-59, 367, 373-74, 376-78; Trinity and, 574-76; unity, 514-15, 626-28, 630; visible and invisible, 577-78, 590-91; Word, 592, 593-97; worldwide, 512-15, 587-88, 630-31

Communion/Lord's Supper. *See* Lord's Supper/communion/Eucharist

Compatibilism, 275-76, 277-78, 279

Condescension, of God, 115, 118, 124-25, 127

Confessions of faith, 24. *See also* Apostles' Creed; Augsburg Confession; Belgic Confession; Heidelberg Catechism; Nicene Creed

Congregationalists, 578, 627, 628, 641, 700; church model, 584-85, 591-92, 600-601, 622, 631, 641; free churches, 527, 574, 578, 585, 600, 622, 631

Constantinople, Councils of, 93; first (381 CE), 91, 127, 407, 413, 500, 548; second (553 CE), 412, 413, 747; third (680/81 CE), 413

Contemporary philosophy, 16, 19-20, 27-29, 56-57

Covenants of God, 124, 224, 304, 327-28, 359-66; Abrahamic, 314, 315-16, 340-42, 355-56, 359-62, 365-66; with animals, 230-31; characteristics of, 359-62; eschatological perspective, 365-66; of grace (new), 314-15, 611-12, 676-77, 705-6, 754-55; Jesus Christ and, 367-68, 473-74; of life, 310-11; nations and, 365-67; Noahic, 314-15, 359-60, 362; Sabbath, 362-63; signs

names of God, 125–28; Old Testament and, 357–58, 370; Trinity in, 83–86, 87–88, 103

Nicaea, Councils of, 391, 413; first (325 CE), 91–92, 93, 397, 405–6, 411, 413, 425, 548; second (787 CE), 413

Nicene Creed, 240, 530; Christology, 92, 401, 405, 442, 447, 746; church, 574, 576, 626; creation, 200, 205–6; Trinity, 95, 99, 127

Nihilism, 52, 65–66, 254, 519

Noah, 314–15; covenant, 359–60, 362

Nomism, covenantal, 676–77, 694

Nonnecessity of God, 56–57

Old Testament, 746; creation, theology of, 218–22; God, doctrine of, 127, 132–33, 183–84, 262–63; Jesus Christ and, 354–56, 357–58, 369–72; names of God, 121–25; New Testament and, 357–58, 370; Sheol, 455–57; structure, 354–55, 357–58; Tanak/ Torah, 133, 339–40, 341–42, 357–58; Trinity in, 81–83; value of, 350–51

Omnipotence, of God, 77, 145, 146–47

Orthodox/orthodoxy, 129; Radical, 575–76, 684–85, 753

Orthodox theology, 67, 80; Christology, 396, 411; eschatology, 715; Russian, 678–79; Trinity, 100–102. *See also* Eastern Orthodox theology

Ousia, 90–91, 93–94

Panentheism, 215–16

Pantheism, 214–15

Paul, apostle, 191–92, 428; body and soul, 269–70; church and, 513–15; justification, 664–65, 667–68, 670, 674–75, 677–78; New Perspective on, 676–78, 679; participation, 683–84; sin and grace, 316, 320–21, 483

Pentecost, 510, 530, 577

Pentecostal movement/churches, 509–11, 526–29, 584; Azusa Street Revival, 527–28

Perfect-being theology, 45, 47, 77, 117, 135–36, 138, 140

Persecution, 513, 737

Personhood, 333–34, 398; Holy Spirit, 499–500

Philosophy, 44; contemporary, 16, 19–20, 27–29, 56–57; postmodern, 118–19, 254, 287, 519. *See also* Greek philosophy

Physicalism, 270–73

Pietism, 177, 178, 491, 586, 648

Pilgrimage/faith journey, 115–16, 160, 509–10, 600, 651–53; of church, 585, 592, 609, 612; with God, 118, 241, 340, 356–58, 369, 390

Platonism, 58, 65, 78, 105, 249; creation demiurge, 212, 213, 214; Neoplatonism, 96–97, 131, 207, 214; ultimate Being, 78, 131

Pluralism, 124, 192–93, 194, 546, 628

Pneumatology. *See* Holy Spirit/ pneumatology

Postmillennialism, 738, 740

Postmodernism, 11, 40, 163, 504; Bible, 538–39, 544–47; hermeneutics, 538–39, 544–47, 554–55; moral guilt, 660–61; philosophy, 118–19, 254, 287, 519; theology, 170, 177, 178; transcendence, 524–25

Power, 242; creative, 219–20; liberating, 494–96; sin and, 298, 306–7, 308, 323

Practical theology, 16, 80, 560, 580, 650

Prayer, 167, 529, 624, 640; encounter with God, 158–60; Holy Spirit, 500, 596, 618; of Jesus Christ, 72, 101, 426, 484–85. *See also* Lord's Prayer

Premillennialism, 738, 739–40

Presbyterian churches, 585–87, 592; Redeemer Presbyterian, New York, 22, 673–74; Reformed model, 585–87, 592, 621–23, 640–41

Proclamation/preaching, 593–97, 617, 660–61

Procreation, 284–85

Index of Scripture References